LITERACY

SIXTH EDITION

LITERACY

Helping Children Construct Meaning

J. David Cooper
Ball State University

with **Nancy D. Kiger**

with an introduction by
Kathryn H. Au

Houghton Mifflin Company   *Boston   New York*

To the memory of my mother Isabelle who continues to give me the strength to succeed, and to Michael, Melissa, David, Molly, and Cooper, the most important people in my life.
—J. David Cooper

To the people in my life who share my love of the written word and provide steadfast support for my work—my daughters Katherine and Laura, my dear friend, colleague, and co-author J. David Cooper, members of my book group, and members of my writing group—and to the memory of my mother Ruth, a gifted writer, and my son Michael, a gifted reader.
—Nancy D. Kiger

Publisher: Patricia Coryell
Senior Sponsoring Editor: Sue Pulvermacher-Alt
Senior Development Editor: Lisa A. Mafrici
Editorial Assistant: Dayna Pell
Project Editor: Reba Libby
Senior Composition Buyer: Sarah Ambrose
Senior Art and Design Coordinator: Jill Haber Atkins
Senior Photo Editor: Jennifer Meyer Dare
Manufacturing Coordinator: Chuck Dutton
Marketing Manager: Jane Potter
Marketing Assistant: Erin Lane

Printed in the U.S.A.

Library of Congress Control Number: 2004115567

ISBN 0-618-47393-9

123456789-VH-09 08 07 06 05

Brief Contents

Contents

Focus on Literacy Learning   1

A Comprehensive Literacy Program   23

Prior Knowledge: Activating and Developing Concepts and Vocabulary   75

4 How To Teach Strategies for Constructing Meaning 133

5 Beginning Literacy: Decoding, Vocabulary, and Meaning 177

6
Beyond Beginning Literacy: Decoding, Vocabulary, and Meaning — 237

7
Responding and the Construction of Meaning — 295

10 Developing a Management System for a Comprehensive Literacy Classroom

Preface

The world of literacy instruction continues to change. *"No Child Left Behind,"* *"Adequate Yearly Progress,"* and *standards* are only a few of the phrases and terms that the literacy teacher hears and is directed to think about today. Now in its Sixth Edition, *Literacy: Helping Children Construct Meaning,* continues to provide preservice and in-service teachers a resource that will help them do the most effective job possible in helping children become literate.

Focus of This Revision

In this revision, my colleague Nancy Kiger and I placed emphasis on continuing to make the text more supportive of the needs of preservice and in-service teachers. To accomplish this goal, we concentrate on the following:

- **Greater focus on standards.** Standards influence every aspect of literacy– teachers' skills, instruction, diagnosis, and assessment. To meet this growing challenge, we have placed a focus on standards for the students who are developing literacy and a focus on standards for the teachers who will teach them. The NCTE/IRA standards are listed on the inside front cover of this text. On the inside back cover are the IRA Standards for reading professionals. Each chapter begins with a chart that shows which standards are covered in that chapter.

- **Revised comprehensive literacy model.** After working with many schools in developing literacy programs, we have revised the two models presented in previous editions for a balanced literacy program and combined them into one model for a comprehensive literacy program K–8. This simplified model will help teachers better understand how to develop a comprehensive literacy program in their classrooms and school.

- **Classroom application of strategies and research.** Through a new feature, Educators Speak, practitioners throughout the country describe how they use a particular technique or procedure in their program. They focus on accommodating individual needs, technology, and diversity.

- **Marginal callouts.** Notes in the margin let you know where to find more information on a given topic without interrupting the flow of your reading.

- **Support for struggling readers.** A new Chapter 9, "Helping Struggling Readers," provides a framework to guide teachers in helping struggling readers in the classroom. In this chapter, we outline a plan that will help teachers bring all the information in other chapters to bear on the special needs of struggling readers.

- **Reordered chapters to increase ease of use.** The sequence of chapters has been changed to provide a more logical flow of information. The chapter on teaching strategies follows the chapter on prior knowledge because it relates to all of the chapters that come after it.

- **Retitled chapters.** Chapter titles have been reworded to more accurately reflect the content and changes that were made in the chapters. For example, Chapter 3, on prior knowledge, is now titled "Prior Knowledge: Activating and Developing Concepts and Vocabulary." This change shows that vocabulary is an integral part of prior knowledge development. Chapters 5 and 6 have also been retitled.

- **Greater emphasis on decoding, vocabulary, and meaning.** Throughout the text, greater emphasis is placed on the importance of decoding, vocabulary, and meaning. More focus is given as to how these areas should be taught at every level.

- **Greater emphasis on upper grades and middle school.** A new Chapter 6 provides teachers more direction in how to teach literacy to upper elementary and middle school students.

- **More user-friendly standards-based literacy lessons.** All Standards-Based Literacy Lessons now reflect the specific NCTE/IRA standards that they cover. Lesson language was simplified and made more teacher-friendly.

- **Updated references and research.** To maintain the strong research base, references and research have been updated where appropriate.

- **Updated literature examples.** Where appropriate, references to new pieces of literature are given.

Chapter-by-Chapter Organization

The eleven chapters and the Handbook Resource provide complete coverage of the topics needed to help all teachers develop a comprehensive literacy program that will lead all students to make adequate yearly progress.

"To the Student Reading This Text" is a brief introduction that provides guidance to the reader, focusing on what to do before reading, during reading, and after reading each chapter.

Chapter 1, "Focus on Literacy Learning," provides background on how literacy develops. Emphasis is placed on stages of literacy development, the role of standards, the impact of diversity on literacy learning, and the place of technology in literacy development. A brief history of literacy is provided. The **new** Educators Speak feature focuses on how to use computers to enhance scheduling.

Chapter 2, "A Comprehensive Literacy Program," presents a **revised and updated** model for developing a literacy program for grades K–8. The importance of standards in the comprehensive literacy program is stressed. Basic skills that teachers need are developed. These include the Standards-Based Literacy Lesson, the Minilesson, and the listening lesson. Guidelines for selecting texts for the literacy program are provided. A complete discussion about the components of basal reading systems is provided. A sample listening lesson is included. The **new** Educators Speak feature focuses on using different modes of reading to accommodate diversity in the classroom.

Chapter 3, "Prior Knowledge: Activating and Developing Concepts and Vocabulary," presents a **revised and updated** chapter that stresses the importance of connecting prior knowledge and vocabulary development. This chapter presents strategies that lead students to become independent in developing their own prior knowledge and vocabulary. A **new** Standards-Based Literacy Lesson focusing on prior knowledge is provided. It uses a **new** book, *Gladiator.* A **new** Educator Speaks feature focuses on using projects that cut across the curriculum.

Chapter 4, "How to Teach Strategies for Constructing Meaning," was formerly Chapter 7. It was moved to this earlier position in the book because it provides information that is important at the beginning literacy level and beyond. This chapter shows teachers how to model strategies for students systematically and explicitly. Seven strategies supported by the research are presented: visualizing, monitoring, inferencing, identifying important information, generating and answering questions, synthesizing, and summarizing. Sample lessons are provided. Two **new** Educators Speak features show how an elementary school teacher and a middle school teacher use strategies to meet the needs of students.

Chapter 5, "Beginning Literacy: Decoding, Vocabulary, and Meaning," presents instructional routines for beginning literacy instruction. A Standards-Based Literacy Lesson using the book, *No, No, Titus!* is provided. Two **new** Educators Speak features show how teachers are using various routines to meet the diverse needs of learners.

Chapter 6, "Beyond Beginning Literacy: Decoding, Vocabulary, and Meaning," focuses on reading instruction in the upper elementary grades and the middle school. A Standards-Based Literacy Lesson using *Ananse's Feast* is provided. A **new** Educators Speak feature provides an example of how a classroom teacher meets the needs of diverse learners.

Chapter 7, "Responding and the Construction of Meaning," presents ideas for making responding an integral part of comprehension development. A variety of techniques are presented. Two **new** Educators Speak features show how classroom teachers incorporate responding into their literacy programs.

Chapter 8, "Writing and the Construction of Meaning," illustrates the role of writing in the comprehensive literacy program. Ideas are presented for connecting reading and writing, teaching spelling, and teaching grammar. A **new** Educators Speak feature focuses on using technology to improve writing instruction.

Chapter 9, "Helping Struggling Readers," a **new chapter,** provides teachers a framework and guidelines for helping struggling readers in the classroom. The **new** Educators Speak feature shows how one teacher provides intervention help for struggling beginning readers.

Chapter 10, "Developing a Management System for a Comprehensive Literacy Classroom," identifies the steps required for developing a management system for a comprehensive literacy classroom. The chapter presents guidelines for creating a literate environment, organizing the classroom, and keeping needed records. Procedures for developing student routines are included. A **new** Educators Speak feature shows how one teacher approaches organization and management in her classroom.

Chapter 11, "Assessment and Evaluation in the Comprehensive Literacy Classroom," focuses on how to provide assessment and evaluation in a classroom guided by standards. A **new** Educators Speak feature shows how a curriculum specialist helps teachers use assessment in diverse classrooms.

The Handbook Resource, "Word Skills: Phonics and Structural Analysis for Teachers," is designed to help teachers develop the content of phonics and structural analysis. A **new** section has been added to show teachers how to deal with the scope and sequence of decoding instruction. This section can serve as a useful reference handbook for teachers.

Materials to Support Preservice and In-service Instruction

The complete package accompanying *Literacy: Helping Children Construct Meaning*, Sixth Edition, provides resources to assist the college instructor and the staff development leader in providing effective training for teachers.

Instructor's Resource Manual

The Instructor's Resource Manual (IRM) contains many suggestions for using this text in preservice courses as well as in-service training. For each chapter of the text, the manual provides organizing tools such as chapter outlines and summaries, questions and activities to encourage discussion and active learning, and pedagogical aids such as transparency masters to reinforce key concepts in the text. The IRM can also be viewed on the Web site in Word format.

The Web Site

This edition is accompanied by a rich Web site resource for both students and instructors. Highlights of the Web site include: student study materials such as ACE self-test quizzes and interactive glossary flashcards, additional Standards-Based Literacy Lessons, videos, weblinks, and an enhanced version of the "Educators Speak" features from the text. The site can be accessed at http://college.hmco.com/education.

Houghton Mifflin Video Cases

Available online and organized by topic each "case" is a 3- to 5-minute module consisting of video and audio files presenting actual classroom scenarios that depict the complex problems and opportunities teachers face every day. The video and audio clips are accompanied by "artifacts" to provide background information and allow preservice teachers to experience true classroom dilemmas in their multiple dimensions.

Eduspace Online Course

For instructors who teach the course online, Houghton Mifflin's new ***Eduspace course*** offers a convenient format. Eduspace is Houghton Mifflin's proprietary version of Blackboard. In addition to its handy gradebook and other course management tools, Eduspace includes special interactive components such as videos, a discussion board, reflective journal questions, test items, and additional materials to aid students in studying and reflecting on what they have learned.

Acknowledgments

This sixth edition of *Literacy: Helping Children Construct Meaning* is a reflection of the ideas from many preservice and in-service teachers across the country. My colleague Nancy Kiger and I are very appreciative of the suggestions and ideas we received from them. Many individuals have provided support that helped to make this book a reality.

Dr. P. James B. Dyck at the Mayo Clinic in Rochester, Minnesota, developed and guided the treatment that has led me to a near full recovery from Chronic Inflammatory Demyelinating Polyneuropathy (CIDP).

Nancy D. Kiger, a special friend and colleague, collaborated with me on making this revision even better than the previous one.

Michael D. Robinson for his wonderful support both personally and professionally.

Melissa Cooper Bingham, my outstanding daughter, and her wonderful husband, David G. Bingham, for their continued love, support, and encouragement.

Kathy Au, University of Hawaii, gave excellent suggestions regarding second language learners and diverse populations.

David C. Chard, University of Oregon, provided helpful ideas about the new chapter on struggling readers.

Gregory W. Brooks (Nazareth College of Rochester), Elaine Pierce Chakonas (Northeastern Illinois University), Deborah Doty (Northern Kentucky University), and Margaret L. Janz (Jacksonville University), college and university professors who gave valuable suggestions for improving this text.

Kristen LeFevre, Development Editor, guided us through a new electronic revision process that was both challenging and productive.

Reba Libby, Production Editor, shepherded the manuscript through the stages of production.

Sue Pulvermacher-Alt, Senior Sponsoring Editor, supported this project with
    excitement and enthusiasm.

Lisa Mafrici, Senior Development Editor, provided helpful advice throughout
    the publishing process.

John T. Ridley, friend and former Vice President and Publisher in the Houghton
    Mifflin School Division, was the first person in 1985 to believe in this book
    and support its publication.

To each of these individuals I extend a very special THANK YOU!

We are immensely proud of this sixth edition, as we have been of each previous
edition. Each edition brings new challenges and opportunities for us as teachers and
authors. The success of this book has continued to grow through tumultuous and
exciting times in literacy instruction. It is good to know that we have been able to
provide college instructors and in-service trainers a resource that has only improved
in its effectiveness over eighteen years. Working together, we will continue to ensure
that WE LEAVE NO CHILD BEHIND and that WE LEAVE NO TEACHER
BEHIND.

J. David Cooper

Introduction

It's a beautiful, sunny August day as I write this introduction. However, a cloud of uncertainty is hanging over the public schools here in my home state of Hawaii. Student achievement is the name of the game these days. Schools in Hawaii have just received their overall test scores from this past spring, and are awaiting the breakdown of results by subgroups. As designated by the federal government, these subgroups include students with limited English proficiency and economically disadvantaged students. Schools must show improvement in the results for each of these subgroups in order to show adequate yearly progress.

This concern for test scores is certainly not limited to Hawaii. The situation I've described is being duplicated in every state in this great nation of ours. High expectations for students' literacy achievement are reflected in the rigorous standards for reading and writing in place in many states. These standards at the state level follow the lead of the National Assessment of Educational Progress (NAEP), popularly known as the Nation's Report Card. NAEP sets the tone for higher performance with its declaration that America's students will become proficient readers who can analyze and apply ideas in challenging subject-area texts. Accurate word identification and decoding are a starting point, but students must go far beyond these lower-level skills to meet the new, higher expectations for their achievement. And there is more to come. Hard on the heels of tough tests for reading, writing, and math are equally tough tests for science and social studies.

What is the impetus for these higher expectations? The answer is none other than globalization, the worldwide economic movement resulting in a decreased need for workers in manufacturing and agriculture and an increased need for workers in the knowledge and service industries. In Hawaii, this shift is evident in the decline of the sugar and pineapple industries, with their neat green fields, mills, and canneries that once employed thousands. Today Hawaii's economy depends on the visitor industry. Other states have seen the closing of factories, as manufacturing jobs have been lost to overseas competitors. To maintain its economic position, the United States must have an educational system that produces workers who can out-think workers in other parts of the world. These developments serve to remind us that a good education has never been more important than it is today. We must prepare our students to be thinkers and not just workers, because it is the thinkers who will have the best chances for advancement in the era of globalization.

I still encounter a few educators who bemoan the fact of higher standards and accountability pressures. I share this nostalgia for the past, when the field of education was a kinder, gentler place. However, I believe that we must get on with the job and embrace the challenge of higher standards for all students. Schools have been successful in bringing some students to high levels of literacy, often students of mainstream backgrounds living in affluent communities. Historically, schools have not been successful in bringing students of diverse cultural and linguistic backgrounds, from low-income communities, to high levels of literacy. Students of diverse backgrounds represent a steadily increasing percentage of school enrollments, and they already account for the majority of students served by all of the nation's large urban districts. The need to take steps to close the gap between the literacy achievement of students of diverse backgrounds and mainstream students has never been more urgent.

Still, despite the strength of its ideals, the path towards standards-based education has been fraught with peril. Chief among these perils is the fallacy of equating standards-based education with high-stakes testing. First, just raising the bar higher does little good. Higher standards, as reflected in rigorous tests, must be accompanied with professional development that empowers teachers with knowledge of the latest developments in instruction and assessment. This knowledge enables teachers to teach more effectively and to bring their students to higher levels of literacy. Second, relying on a score on a single test to determine a student's academic future seems foolhardy at best. Multiple measures of a student's performance, including assignments completed in the classroom, form a far more reliable basis for making decisions.

In short, this increased pressure to improve students' reading achievement is pushing us to make sure that each and every child is receiving the best instruction we can offer—and that is certainly a good thing. But expectations for students' literacy achievement today are higher than they have ever been in the past. This means that teachers must be prepared to teach in more purposeful and powerful ways than ever before—and that is no small task.

Where should teachers turn? This new edition of *Literacy: Helping Children Construct Meaning* by J. David Cooper and Nancy D. Kiger is certainly an excellent starting point. It introduces the necessary components of sound curriculum, instruction, and assessment, and it shows teachers how to put the components together to develop a strong school and classroom literacy program. The reason that this book is now in its sixth edition is that it continues to provide current, reliable information.

David and Nancy have taken a great deal of trouble to keep abreast of new trends and to incorporate the needs and concerns of teachers. Earlier editions of this book focused on reading comprehension, a topic that had fallen into neglect. That emphasis on comprehension is maintained in this book, along with a strong new emphasis on vocabulary development, which is the foundation for effective reading in content areas such as science and social studies. A new chapter on helping struggling readers is an especially welcome addition, as these are the students most in need of effective instruction. David and Nancy have ensured that teachers will actually be able to apply all of these wonderful ideas for instruction in their classrooms, by presenting actual units based on readily available literature and by sharing the experiences of real teachers in real schools.

David and Nancy know that all students need to get the message that reading is always about constructing meaning. This is as true at the very earliest levels, kindergarten and first grade, as it is at grade 8. Although beginning readers must devote large amounts of attention to word identification and decoding, they must be taught that the purpose of reading is to construct meaning. Skills of word identification are tools to this larger end. It does not work to assume that comprehension can wait until later. Such an approach does a disservice to students by leading them to believe that the only purpose for reading is to call words accurately. In keeping with the consensus emerging in the field, David and Nancy believe that children are best served when we provide them not only with skill instruction but with a focus on higher-level thinking and motivating contexts for real reading.

Hold on, I've just received a piece of good news with which to close this introduction. Here is an email message from the principal of a Title I school where I've worked for the past eight years. The proportion of low-income students served by this school has steadily grown to 50% and is expected to rise in the years ahead. Ten percent of the students now qualify for special education. Hawaii has a rigorous reading test, tied to state standards. For the past two years, scores in reading at this school remained flat. The good news? The principal is writing to let me know that his school's latest reading test scores show significant gains. In comparison to the previous year, 13% more of the third graders and 20% more of the fifth graders attained scores showing that they met or exceeded the state standards.

Now you are probably wondering how this school raised its test scores. This school has reading curriculum that the teachers developed themselves, including grade level benchmarks and rubrics tied to the state standards. Teachers at each grade level wrote their own curriculum guides in reading. It took them several years to do so, and they continue to refine their reading curriculum, even as they moved into creating their own curriculum guides for writing and math. The teachers have focused their instruction on developing students' reading comprehension and written responses to literature. All teachers collect evidence on their students' progress in reading at the beginning, middle, and end of the school year. Following each of the three periods for collecting evidence, the whole school gathers for a meeting at which each grade level gives a presentation. These presentations focus on bar graphs of the evidence, indicating the number of students who are working on, meeting, or exceeding standards. Along with the bar graphs, the teachers share their ideas for improving instruction, in order to help more students meet or exceed standards.

These teachers do much of what David and Nancy recommend in this book, and they have worked hard to create standards-based classrooms and a standards-based school. The administrators at this school—over time, I have worked with two different principals and three different curriculum coordinators—set a course and stayed the course. There are no shortcuts and there is no quick fix, but teachers and schools with access to sound ideas about the teaching of reading, such as those provided in this book by David and Nancy, can and will be successful in bringing their students to high levels of literacy.

Kathryn H. Au
University of Hawaii
August 2004

To the Student

Reading This Text

Literacy: Helping Children Construct Meaning, Sixth Edition, was written for preservice and in-service teachers. How you use this text will depend on your purpose for using it. The following ideas will help you gain the most knowledge and skills possible from each chapter:

Before Reading

- Preview the chapter by reading over the graphic organizer presented at the beginning of each chapter.
- Review the list of "Terms You Need to Know" found at the conclusion of each graphic organizer.

During Reading

- As you read, think back to the chapter preview and terminology.
- Highlight key points or make notes as you read.
- List questions that you have.

After Reading

- Return to the chapter preview. Make notes about key points you learned.
- Review the "Terms You Need to Know."
- Seek answers to questions you still have by using some of the sources in the "For Additional Reading" sections or some of the suggestions in the sections entitled "For Exploration: Electronic Products and Resources."

Focus on Literacy Learning

1

✓ **STANDARDS FOCUS**

NCTE/IRA Standards: Develops foundation for all standards.
Standards for Reading Professionals: 1, 2, 3

Educators Speak   p. 14

Sixth-Grade Literacy Block Enhanced with Computers
—*Jill Baker, Citrus Heights, California*

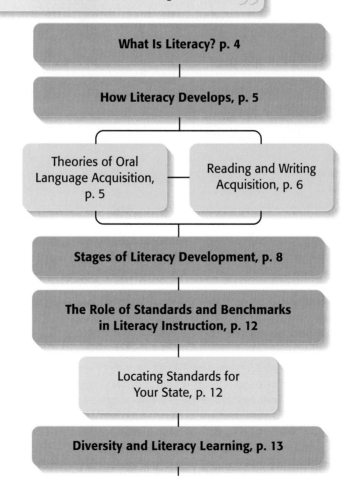

What Is Literacy? p. 4

How Literacy Develops, p. 5

Theories of Oral Language Acquisition, p. 5

Reading and Writing Acquisition, p. 6

Stages of Literacy Development, p. 8

The Role of Standards and Benchmarks in Literacy Instruction, p. 12

Locating Standards for Your State, p. 12

Diversity and Literacy Learning, p. 13

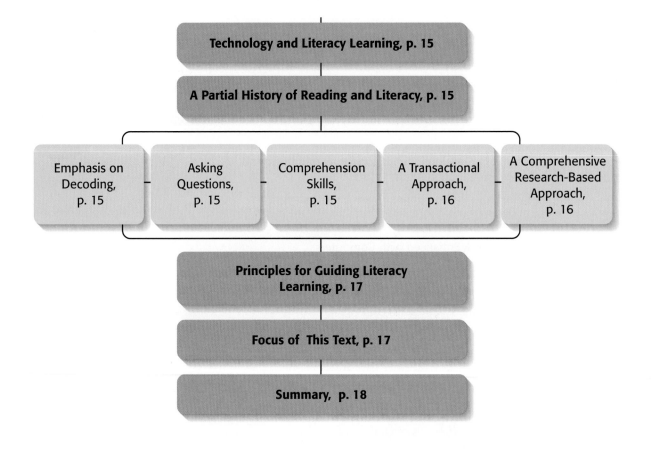

Technology and Literacy Learning, p. 15

A Partial History of Reading and Literacy, p. 15

| Emphasis on Decoding, p. 15 | Asking Questions, p. 15 | Comprehension Skills, p. 15 | A Transactional Approach, p. 16 | A Comprehensive Research-Based Approach, p. 16 |

Principles for Guiding Literacy Learning, p. 17

Focus of This Text, p. 17

Summary, p. 18

Terms
You Need to Know

- benchmarks
- differentiated instruction
- diversity
- explicit instruction
- fluency
- literacy
- stages of literacy development
- standards

*T*oday, we are visiting Mrs. Miller's fourth-grade class of twenty-six students—twelve boys and fourteen girls. As we enter the classroom, Mrs. Miller hands us a copy of her lesson plan for the day. We notice immediately that she has indicated to the side of each activity which standard she is focusing on.

Three of the students are second-language learners who have already made the transition to English. The children who are working independently are using listening centers and completing computer activities. Seven students—Eddie, Andrew, Lisa, Christina, José, Terri, and Gil—huddle together in a special spot to read *Tomás and the Library Lady (Mora, 1997)*, which is about a young Mexican boy whose family migrates from state to state picking crops. As each finishes reading, he or she begins writing a personal response in a journal. Lisa writes that she thinks Tomás was very brave. Gil draws a picture of his favorite part and writes, "Tomás is so-o-o smart."

Soon Mrs. Miller asks those who are reading *Tomás* to meet in a discussion group. A chart listing predictions students have made about *Tomás*, like the one shown, is displayed. First, students share their personal responses from their journals. They are so eager to share that Mrs. Miller has to remind them to take turns.

> ## Our Predictions About Tomás
>
> 1. Tomás is going to be afraid to go to the library.
> 2. Tomás is going to find a good friend in the library.
> 3. Tomás is going to learn new things in the library.

Next, Mrs. Miller asks, "How did we do with our predictions?" Students discuss which predictions were confirmed in their reading and which were not. For example, Terri said she found out right away that the first prediction was not right.

Mrs. Miller then asks the other children whether the first prediction on the chart was confirmed. Three students said it was not, but the others were not sure. Terri suggests, "We could look back in our books to see if it was true." After several students respond, Mrs. Miller directs the group to their books. She asks them to think about the first prediction as she reads the page aloud. Then she models her thinking involved in using the skill of evaluating predictions by saying, "Tomás is looking through the door of the library. When the librarian invites him in, he goes. He doesn't seem to be afraid after he meets the librarian. Our first prediction is not true. Tomás really likes to go to the library."

The children discuss how predictions change as one gathers information during reading. After discussing each prediction, Mrs. Miller leads the children to discuss how making predictions helps them understand books. Finally, the students decide if they want to do anything further with the book. Some want to rewrite it as a play and act it out. Others want to go on the Internet and learn more about migrant workers.

Standards are discussed later in this chapter.

These fourth graders were developing **literacy** with the help of their teacher. Today's lesson focused on several standards that need to be covered repeatedly.

They read and responded to an original piece of literature, one that had not been adapted or rewritten. The group had previewed the book and predicted that certain events would happen; with their teacher, they revisited the story to think about how their predictions had been confirmed or changed. When Mrs. Miller realized that students were having difficulty with this, she used the think-aloud process to model her own thinking about changing a prediction. After a discussion about each prediction, students reflected about how predicting leads to a better understanding of a story.

Mrs. Miller encouraged the students to respond to the book in personal ways. Their responses included writing, drawing, talking with others, making a play, and exploring the subject further; all of these activities help to improve each student's comprehension.

This classroom and its activities are typical of classrooms throughout the country:

- The class is composed of native English speakers and second-language learners.
- Lessons are designed to cover multiple strategies each day.
- Students read original works of literature.
- Reading and writing activities are developed and used together.
- Personal and creative responses are encouraged and respected.
- Students and teacher work together to formulate an understanding of the book.
- The teacher teaches skills and strategies directly as needed.
- Technology is an integral part of the classroom program.
- The teacher strives to foster positive attitudes and maintain a high degree of motivation.

Teachers, reading specialists, and researchers have learned a great deal about how children and young adults learn to read and write, or become literate. Recent research on literacy clearly supports the idea of providing a comprehensive literacy program that is designed to help all children succeed (Snow, Burns, & Griffin, 1998). This balanced program incorporates the best elements of both authentic reading and writing experiences and **explicit instruction.**

Technology is a major part of a comprehensive literacy classroom. New ways of using computers, exciting software, and the use of the Internet make it possible for you to meet a greater range of students' needs (Valmont, 2003). Children of all abilities from a variety of backgrounds will have the best opportunities to become literate, and a large majority of students will succeed in this effort.

🦋 What Is Literacy?

There are many definitions of *literacy* (Harris & Hodges, 1995). Over the years, most definitions have focused on just reading and writing (Venezky, 1995). However, discussions of literacy have broadened the term to include listening and speaking and other types of literacy, such as mathematics literacy and technology literacy. This broadened concept of literacy makes it a term that includes all of the communication and calculation skills needed in today's society.

This text focuses on the communication aspects of literacy, which include listening and speaking (oral language), reading, and writing. An integral part of each of these elements is the process of thinking. Another aspect of communication literacy that is often discussed is viewing: using the various strategies and skills involved in listening, speaking, reading, writing, and thinking when watching television, viewing a movie or video, and so forth. The goal of communication literacy is twofold: to construct meaning from what is heard and read and to convey meaning through

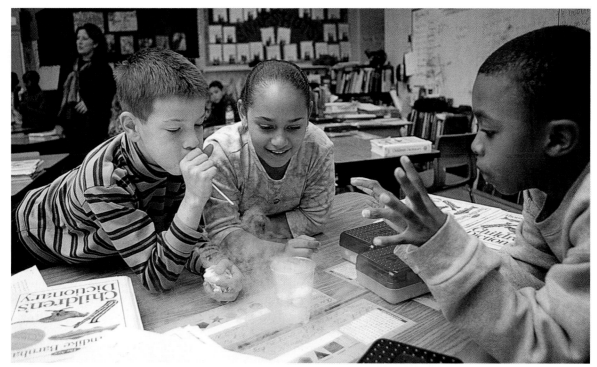

Literacy develops when students are actively involved. © Elizabeth Crews

speaking and writing (National Reading Panel, 2000a). To reach this goal, we must answer the question, How do individuals develop literacy?

How Literacy Develops

Children and young adults develop literacy by participating in a variety of real literacy experiences and a considerable amount of direct or explicit instruction. They begin by developing oral language (listening and speaking) and then later learn to read and write. All of the elements of literacy-speaking, listening, reading, writing, and thinking-continuously develop together (Wilkinson & Silliman, 2000). Understanding how these components develop helps us create an effective literacy program for our students.

Theories of Oral Language Acquisition

The process of acquiring language is unending; each of us continues to acquire new aspects of language through our interactions and experiences. Therefore, language acquisition is first and foremost a social process (Cook-Gumprez, 1986; Wells,

1990). Taylor and Dorsey-Gaines (1988) report that inner-city families "use literacy for a wide variety of purposes (social, technical, and *aesthetic* purposes), for a wide variety of audiences, and in a wide variety of situations" (p. 202). Thus, *all children come to school with a language base*, and this base may or may not match the base on which the school is trying to build. Since a strong connection between oral language and reading has been clearly established for all learners (Cazden, 1972; Garcia, 2000; Loban, 1963; Menyuk, 1984; Ruddell, 1963; Snow et al., 1998; Wilkinson & Silliman, 2000), it is important that schools build literacy experiences around whatever language a child has developed.

There are many theories of language acquisition. *Nativists* believe that children acquire language innately, without practice or reinforcement (Chomsky, 1965; Lenneberg, 1967; McNeil, 1970). Those who hold the *cognitive development* point of view stress that children acquire language through their various activities (Piaget & Inhelder, 1969). Vygotsky proposes a concept known as the *zone of proximal development*, a range in which a child can perform a task only with the help of a more experienced individual (Vygotsky, 1978).

Halliday (1975) views language acquisition as an active process in which children try out their language and make approximations of real language. According to Halliday, we should therefore accept errors during literacy development, because it is through these approximations that children gradually develop their perfected forms of language.

All of these theories contribute to our understanding of how children acquire language. Basically, we know that children acquire language:

- when they have a need that is meaningful and real.
- through interactions with peers and adults.
- by making approximations of real language.
- at varying rates and in various stages, even though they all go through similar phases of development.
- by having language modeled for them both directly and indirectly.

This understanding provides a solid basis on which to develop a literacy program that fosters students' abilities to construct meaning.

Reading and Writing Acquisition

Oral language development serves as the foundation for learning to read and write. Reading and writing are complex processes that grow from oral language and are built on listening and speaking. For example, the child who develops a good listening and speaking vocabulary has formed many concepts and ideas. This is known as *prior knowledge*, and it is critical for effective reading and writing (Anderson & Pearson, 1984; Pressley, 2000).

Reading involves two basic processes—decoding and comprehension. Decoding is the ability of the individual to figure out the pronunciation of printed words and ultimately determine the word's meaning (Harris & Hodges, 1995). The only way a child knows that a word has been pronounced correctly is by checking it against his or her oral language. For example, when a child hears the sentence, "We had eggs and *bacon* for breakfast," he or she encounters the word *bacon*. A child who does not immediately recognize the word *bacon* tries to sound it out. First, she says *băcun* but that does not sound like a real word. Next, she says *bācun* which sounds like a word she knows. The child mentally compares the word to his or her oral language to determine if it has been pronounced correctly and makes sense—that is, it is something that goes with eggs. A child with limited oral language or limited English may not be able to determine the accuracy of the word's pronunciation. In other words, the word must be in the child's head before pronunciation can be verified. However, even without the word *bacon* in the child's head, thinking can verify that—based on the context of the sentence—the word probably names a food that people eat for breakfast.

Oral language is also critical to comprehension, which is the ability to construct meaning by interacting with a text. Think back to the sentence read above: "We had eggs and bacon for breakfast." As the child decodes the word *bacon*, he or she uses the meanings developed in oral language to associate meaning with the written word. A child who does not have these meanings in his or her oral language cannot associate meaning with the word or text. For example, read the following sentence to yourself:

> *The Gayzorniplatz was noving his tonk.*

Since you have good reading skills, you obviously recognize the words *The*, *was*, and *his*. You may recognize the inflected ending *-ing* in the word *noving* and decide it must be a verb. Because of the noun markers *"The"* and *"his,"* you also know that *Gayzorniplatz* and *tonk* are probably nouns, and that *Gayzorniplatz* is probably a proper noun, since it is capitalized. You are also able to come up with some semblance of pronunciation for the words. However, since these words are not in your oral language, you cannot be absolutely sure of their pronunciation or construct their meaning. If, on the other hand, I show you a picture of a Gayzorniplatz (see Figure 1.1) and give you the meanings of *noving* and *tonk*, you begin to be able to construct meaning.

Decoding and comprehension are the two big jobs in the process of learning to read. Refer to Figure 1.2. Notice that as an individual moves from beginning reading to mature reading, the emphasis in learning shifts from more focus on decoding to more focus on comprehension. Both comprehension and decoding are *always* a part of the process. However, as students become adept at decoding, they are free to pay more attention to constructing meaning. This process is not as smooth and linear as the diagram shows; it is a "jerky continuum" (Cooper & Kiger, 2005).

Writing is the process of conveying meaning or ideas by using graphic symbols. For very beginning writers, this may be drawing or scribbling, as shown in Figure 1.3. This type of writing occurs long before the child can form letters. Once the child begins to form letters, he or she uses invented or temporary spelling (see Figure 1.4).

Writing involves the reverse of decoding, the process that is used in reading; writing involves encoding or spelling. Again, by using the concepts and ideas you have developed through your own prior knowledge and oral language, you convey your

FIGURE 1.1

A Gayzorniplatz

ideas for others to read. You use the knowledge of language you have gained to express your ideas. You must be able to spell words and formulate sentences and paragraphs.

Throughout the processes of speaking, listening, reading, and writing, children learn to think. As they learn language, they become more adept at expressing themselves, solving problems, and making judgments. The process of thinking (often referred to as critical thinking or higher-order thinking skills) develops along with all of the other aspects of literacy. Exactly what happens as children develop literacy?

Stages of Literacy Development

There is general agreement among researchers and literacy specialists that children and young adults go through various stages as they develop literacy (Adams, 1990; Chall, 1983; Cooper & Kiger, 2005; Ehri, 1991, 1997; Juel, 1991; Rupley, Wilson, & Nichols, 1998). Although detailed study of these stages is beyond the scope of this text, it is important that we be aware of these stages and know the role that they play

FIGURE 1.2

Changing Emphasis in Learning to Read

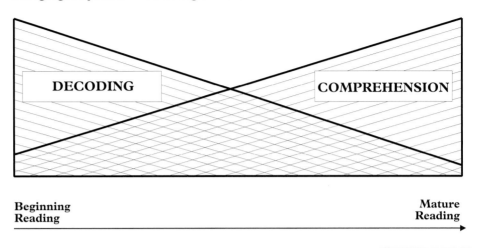

| DECODING | COMPREHENSION |

Beginning Reading

Mature Reading

in literacy instruction. For detailed discussions about the **stages of literacy development,** see Cooper and Kiger (2005), listed in "For Additional Reading."

A stage is a point in time during the development of an overall process. There are five stages or phases in literacy development:

1. **Early Emergent Literacy.** This is the stage during which children develop the foundations of literacy. It usually occurs before the child enters kindergarten, and includes such aspects of literacy as developing oral language, writing by drawing or scribbling, and being curious about print. Second-language learners have usually done these things in their first language.

2. **Emergent Literacy.** During this stage, the child becomes more interested in literacy. He or she uses more standard oral language patterns, and forms and names letters. Concepts about print, such as recognizing a letter or word, also develop during this stage. Most children complete most of this stage by the end of kindergarten or at the beginning of grade 1.

3. **Beginning Reading and Writing.** In this stage, oral language expands and students begin to actually read and write in conventional ways. They figure out the pronunciation of words and also develop **fluency** (the ability to recognize words automatically, accurately, and rapidly) in reading. They understand the meanings of more and more words. This stage continues through first grade for most students and into second or third grade for some.

4. **Almost Fluent Reading and Writing.** During this stage, the child is growing more sophisticated with all aspects of literacy. He or she reads silently more than in the previous stage, does more writing, and has a larger oral language vocabulary. For most students, this stage may begin toward the end of second grade, and may continue into the beginning of fourth or fifth grade.

FIGURE 1.3

A Beginning Writer's Scribbles

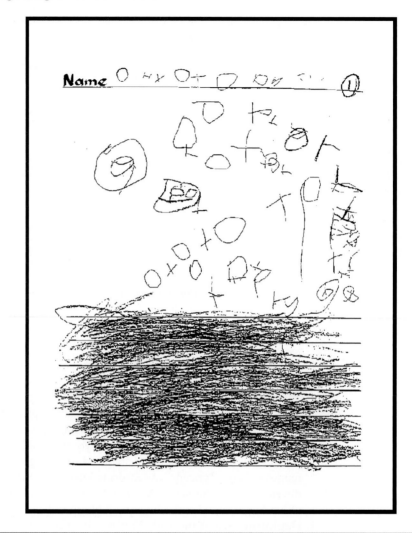

5. **Fluent Reading and Writing.** By this stage, the student is using reading, writing, and oral language for a variety of purposes. He or she has attained most of the skills of reading and writing. This stage may begin for some students in fourth grade; it continues through the upper elementary grades and into middle school and high school. In fact, fluent reading and writing development continues throughout one's life.

There is much overlap between the stages. No student ever completely finishes one stage and then moves into another. Some students reach a plateau and remain at a particular stage for a period of time.

FIGURE 1.4

Sample of a Kindergartner's Writing

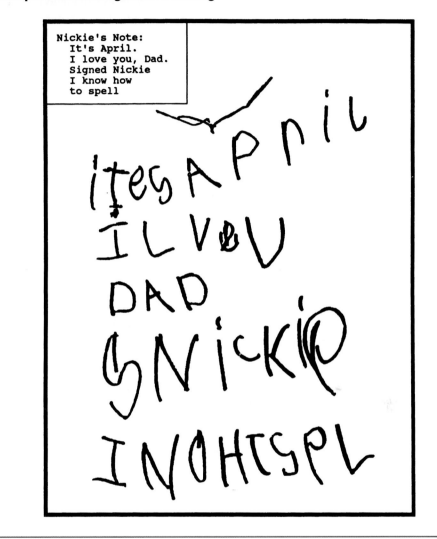

For many years, literacy development was viewed as having a period of "readiness," a time when children developed a discrete set of "prerequisite" skills. At some magical moment, they were supposedly ready to learn to read. Research evidence indicates that this is not true (Durkin, 1966). In the past, educators also tended to rigidly associate levels of achievement with specific grades; they did not allow for variation in individual development.

In the light of all that has been learned through research over the past several decades, thinking about literacy development in stages is the most reasonable way to approach literacy instruction. Consider the following findings:

- All of the language arts—speaking, listening, reading, writing, viewing, and thinking—are interrelated. Essentially, what happens to a student's development in one area affects the other areas (Shanahan, 1990).

- Researchers (Yaden, Rowe, & MacGillivray, 2000) have been able to document and describe the earliest stages of literacy as an emergent literacy stage. Students do not develop or learn one part or piece of literacy at a time. Rather, they gradually develop all the parts. They grow into literacy with the appropriate support and instruction.

- Stages of development are clearly evident in beginning readers as they develop decoding and word identification skills (Ehri, 1991, 1997; Juel, 1991).

- When students' reading comprehension abilities have been studied in the elementary grades, evidence shows that they go through stages or phases as they develop their reading abilities (Rupley et al., 1998). As their comprehension builds, students use a consistent set of strategies repeatedly, gradually becoming more sophisticated in their use.

Within each stage of literacy development, students exhibit certain behaviors, strategies, and skills that are identified through the use of **standards** and **benchmarks.** Let's define these terms and examine their role in literacy instruction.

🦋 The Role of Standards and Benchmarks in Literacy Instruction

Standards are statements that express what is valued or expected in a given field or area at certain times. Look at the inside front cover of this text: you will find the *Standards for the English Language Arts* (NCTE/IRA, 1996). These are the standards schools should meet with their students in their reading≠language arts programs. Notice that these standards are very general.

Benchmarks, however, are descriptions of behaviors that indicate whether students have achieved a given standard or reached a certain stage of development. For example, a benchmark in relation to the first standard might read as follows:

The child reads ten fiction and nonfiction books during the semester.

This benchmark gives you as the teacher something to look for and allows you to evaluate student performances against the standard about wide reading. Educators sometimes use the terms *standards* and *benchmarks* interchangeably. Generally, however, standards are broader statements about what students are expected to accomplish, and benchmarks are more precise, measurable behaviors that let the teacher determine whether students have accomplished a given standard.

Standards and benchmarks are important for both assessment (testing and evaluating) and instruction. They let you know what you are to assess and what you are to teach. There are national standards, such as the Standards for the English Language Arts (National Council of Teachers of English/International Reading

Association, 1996), state standards, and many times even local standards. Usually, local standards are based on state standards. At the present time, the U.S. government has not recommended or required any national standards for literacy. However, this situation could change during the next decade (Education Commission of the States, 2001).

The use of standards and benchmarks for literacy instruction (and other subject areas) is becoming an increasingly significant issue for schools. In many instances, standards and benchmarks are designated for each stage of literacy development (Cooper & Kiger, 2005). These serve as the guidelines for both assessment and instruction.

Now open this book to the inside back cover. These are the *Revised Standards for Reading Professionals* published by the International Reading Association (Revised 2003). These standards identify the knowledge and skills that you should have in order to become a reading-language arts teacher.

Turn to the beginning of this chapter. At the top of the graphic organizer on page 1 you can see the standards that we address in this chapter. This information appears at the beginning of every chapter to alert you to which standards are given attention in the chapter.

Locating Standards for Your State

As we have noted, each state usually has its own set of standards. If you do not have a copy of the standards for your state, use the Internet to locate them. For example, if you want the standards for Iowa, go to your favorite Internet search engine and type in: "Iowa Department of Education" in the search box, and then click on Search or Go. Once you have located and accessed the appropriate state site, look for a link to information on the standards for that state.

🦋 Diversity and Literacy Learning

Classrooms throughout the United States are diverse; that is, they include students who are English Language Learners (ELLs) or second-language learners, as well as students with a variety of special needs, such as learning disabilities, giftedness, reading problems, and the wide cultural and familial differences that exist in any community. Some educators see **diversity** as a problem. However, from the perspective of this text, diversity is considered a strength. The diverse classroom allows us to create more "real-world" classrooms where students learn in a context that more realistically represents the world in which we live.

Diversity in the classroom also means that we as teachers must always adjust instruction to the needs of students. Think back to Mrs. Miller's classroom, which we read about at the beginning of this chapter. She had three ELL students. Her students had made the transition to English. However, as she taught, she always made sure that all students, including the ELL students, had the needed background and concepts to understand the texts they were going to read. This is just one example of how Mrs. Miller was providing **differentiated instruction.** Regardless of the types of diversities we have in our classrooms, we must always adjust our instruction to meet the needs of our students.

We must keep in mind that good teaching is good teaching. "Considerable evidence supports the conclusion that the differences in achievement between students of mainstream and non-mainstream backgrounds are not the result of differences in their ability to learn, but rather of differences in the quality of instruction they have received in school" (Association for Supervision and Curriculum Development, 1995, p. x). There are not specific procedures that are designed just for learning-disabled students or ELL students. We must tailor our instruction to meet the needs of *all* students, because instruction has a great impact on how *all* students learn. Throughout this text, we will continually focus on how to meet the needs of students by differentiating instruction.

🦋 Technology and Literacy Learning

Technology is a significant part of nearly everyone's life (Valmont, 2003). Certainly it is an important part of literacy learning as well. The computer, CD-ROMs, audio and video resources, and DVDs offer real possibilities for improving literacy instruction and thereby improving literacy learning.

Research in literacy learning and technology offers many interesting possibilities for enhancing literacy instruction, but it offers few clear guidelines as to the *best* use of technology (National Reading Panel, 2000a). We must continue to explore and research ways to use technology to enhance literacy learning.

Throughout this text, we focus on many possibilities for using technology to enhance the quality of literacy learning and for differentiating literacy instruction. Each chapter concludes with a section entitled "For Exploration: Electronic Products and Resources." These sections should help you expand your ideas for using technology in literacy instruction.

🦋 A Partial History of Reading and Literacy

Literacy learning and reading instruction have a long history (Smith, 1965). Understanding what has happened in the past often helps us to understand things we do now.

Throughout the history of reading and literacy instruction, many changes have occurred. The past forty to fifty years have seen some of the most aggressive changes in reading and literacy instruction. Let's examine some of these.

Sixth-Grade Literacy Block Enhanced with Computers

"Meeting the individual needs of thirty-four sixth-grade students can prove to be a daunting task for anyone. One thing that I have established in my classroom to help with this task is a 45-minute block of time each day when every student is reading at his or her level. It is during this time that I am able to work in a small group with my most critical students. Technology is extremely beneficial during this time. I present my students with extensive research projects. These projects often relate to our social studies curriculum. The students delve deeper into a certain aspect of an ancient civilization that we are in the midst of studying. They are able to use the computers to conduct in-depth research, practice their word processing skills, and turn their research into slide show presentations to share with the rest of the class.

The use of computers allows them access to a wealth of information that otherwise would not be available. They are developing critical thinking skills by being able to locate the necessary information. In order to pull out the important, relevant facts they need, they must sift through the extraneous information. The reading strategies of summarizing, clarifying, and questioning that have been ingrained in these students now must be used at a much higher level. The students enjoy these challenges, and it is a great way for them to extend their learning through the use of technology.

At first glance, word processing skills may not seem to tie into literacy at all. However, if students are quick and accurate with their typing skills, it is going to help them in many different aspects of their education as they progress through the grades. The less they have to concentrate on where the keys are, the more attention they can pay to the content of what they are writing. Allowing students access to the computers during this research time gives them the hands-on application and practice they need to become proficient in these skills.

After the students have completed their research and typed a paper, they then make a presentation in the form of a slide show on the computer. This allows them to share what they have learned with the rest of the class. For this, they need to again gauge the importance of the information they have found and whittle it down to the main details. They also must think about the sequencing of events and how this will affect their presentations.

In essence, having students complete these projects independently while I am working with a small group allows them to apply several different reading and writing strategies that they have been taught thus far in elementary school. It also allows them to improve on a variety of technology skills that are a necessity in today's world."

Jill Baker, Sixth-Grade Teacher
Grand Oaks Elementary School
Citrus Heights, California

Emphasis on Decoding

During the 1960s and 1970s, a number of reading specialists believed that reading was an end product of decoding (Fries, 1962); if students could name the words, comprehension would occur automatically. However, as teachers placed greater emphasis on decoding, they found that many students did not understand what they read. Comprehension was *not* taking place automatically.

Asking Questions

Educators then began to speculate that perhaps teachers were asking the wrong types of questions. The emphasis in reading instruction shifted, and teachers began asking students a greater variety of questions based on a taxonomy, such as the Barrett Taxonomy of Reading Comprehension (Clymer, 1968). Research on the use of questions in classroom practices and in basal readers supported the view that questions were generally asked to *check* comprehension, not to *teach* it (Durkin, 1978, 1981). They were mostly used for checking student recall of facts. Research supports teachers' using questions as prompts to focus students' attention on the important aspects of a text (Beck & McKeown, 1981; Shake & Allington, 1985). Comprehension improves further if students question the author by posing questions that the author could answer if he or she were present (Beck et al., 1996).

Comprehension Skills

During the late 1960s, 1970s, and early 1980s, educators began to believe that the best way to develop reading comprehension was to identify a set of discrete skills called "comprehension skills" (Otto et al., 1977). The focus of reading instruction in many classrooms then became teaching and practicing individual skills, even though previous researchers and educators had questioned the efficacy of these practices (Goodman, 1965).

Research does not clearly identify any one set of comprehension skills (Rosenshine, 1980). However, it does support the idea that readers need to learn key comprehension strategies, or systematic plans for helping them construct meaning (National Reading Panel, 2000a). Multiple skills are involved in each strategy.

A Transactional Approach

During the 1970s and 1980s, researchers in education, psychology, and linguistics began to theorize about how a reader comprehends, and then attempted to verify certain aspects of their theories through research (Anderson & Pearson, 1984; Smith, 1988; Spiro, 1979). Rosenblatt was the first to propose that reading is a transaction between the reader and the text; she believed that readers have the right to, and do, establish or construct their own meanings (Rosenblatt, 1938/ 1976, 1978).

The research and theories of the 1970s and 1980s broadened the thinking of many educators and led them to focus on a literacy perspective rather than on the isolated elements of reading, writing, speaking, listening, viewing, and thinking. The Russian psychologist Lev Vygotsky (1978) has provided a basis for the concept that children learn through support from adults and peers. At the same time, researchers established the idea that children learn language holistically rather than in bits and pieces (Halliday, 1975). The work of these researchers and others had led educators to focus on reading in the broad perspective of *literacy learning* (Clay, 1979, 1982, 1985, 1991; Teale & Sulzby, 1986). The resulting methodology of this period came to be known as the *whole-language* approach, an integration of all aspects of literacy, largely using authentic literature.

A Comprehensive, Research-Based Approach

The work with whole-language programs during the 1980s and 1990s again revealed that there is no one way to think about literacy learning. Researchers found that it was important to teach certain prerequisite skills at the beginning stages of reading (Adams, 1990). It became clear that a more comprehensive approach that combined direct instruction with authentic reading and writing experiences was needed (Snow et al., 1998). Many educators called for a research-based approach that provided systematic explicit instruction in phonemic awareness, decoding, fluency, vocabulary, and key comprehension strategies (Armbruster & Osborn, 2001; National Reading Panel, 2000a). Writing and the other aspects of literacy should also be systematically taught (Learning First Alliance, 2000). Some individuals raised questions as to which research educators should consider (Allington, 2004; Krashen, 2004; Lyon & Chhabra, 2004).

We still believe that we must focus on the full body of research available to us and draw the best conclusions possible at the time. We realize that new research may lead us to new understandings that change what we believe and do for our students. As of the writing of the Sixth Edition of this text, we believe more strongly than ever before that we should provide all students a comprehensive literacy program based on the best conclusions we can draw from the current research. We don't think that we should follow fads or one-sided points of view. Therefore, the remainder of this text focuses on our best interpretation of the current research combined with our many years of successful experiences of teaching children and young adults to read and write. We use the following principles in developing a comprehensive, research-based literacy program.

🦋 Principles for Guiding Literacy Learning

Constructing meaning, or comprehension, is the ultimate goal of all literacy instruction (National Reading Panel, 2000a). To achieve this goal, we must plan instruction to meet the range of diverse needs in our classrooms. This chapter has developed a basic point of view about literacy learning that is based on four principles:

1. *Reading, writing, speaking, listening, viewing, and thinking develop simultaneously as learners develop literacy.* This principle is clearly supported by the research on liter-

acy learning and language acquisition. Therefore, the major focus of instruction should be providing direct instruction and activities that promote the authentic use of reading, writing, speaking, listening, viewing, and thinking.

2. *The foundations of literacy learning are oral language, prior knowledge, and background experiences.* All aspects of the literacy program must account for these elements in all students' learning. Native English speakers and ELL students must be given the needed support and instruction to develop oral language, build on the background and experiences they bring with them, and expand their knowledge.

3. *Effective literacy instruction must include a combination of systematic, explicit, direct instruction and other types of activities that support literacy learning.* From the history presented and the research reviewed, it is clear that literacy learning does not occur with just one type of instruction. A well-designed, comprehensive literacy program must include a variety of types of instruction.

4. *Literacy instruction should be differentiated to meet the diverse needs of every student.* This differentiation should be based on the use of standards and benchmarks. To meet the needs of diverse classrooms, we should use technology in a variety of ways to accommodate individual differences.

These four principles form the basis for all of the ideas for developing literacy presented in this book. Teachers who use these ideas to guide their thinking about literacy development will be effective in schools of the future.

🦋 Focus of This Text

Literacy: Helping Children Construct Meaning, Sixth Edition, is written for preservice and inservice teachers. Its primary focus is to help teachers develop and expand their knowledge and skills in applying the three principles discussed above. The remaining chapters support this overall goal in the following ways:

- Chapter 2 develops the concept of a comprehensive literacy program that provides appropriate blocks for successful literacy learning.

- Chapter 3 discusses the important concepts of prior knowledge and background in relation to literacy learning.

- Chapter 4 presents a detailed discussion about how to model strategies for effective comprehension for all students.

- Chapter 5 focuses on helping children in beginning literacy stages develop decoding, vocabulary, and meaning.

- Chapter 6 develops important concepts related to decoding, vocabulary, and meaning beyond the beginning literacy stage.

- Chapter 7 discusses helping students construct meaning by responding in a variety of ways to a variety of text types.

- Chapter 8 emphasizes the role of writing in helping children construct meaning; it also addresses teaching spelling and grammar.

- Chapter 9 focuses on helping struggling readers of all ages.
- Chapter 10 focuses on developing a management system for making classrooms run smoothly.
- Chapter 11 presents ideas for using standards and benchmarks for effective assessment in the literacy program.
- The "Handbook Resource" provides detailed information on word skills, including phonics and structural analysis. Suggestions for a teaching sequence are given.

Each of these chapters emphasizes dealing with diversity, using technology appropriately, and using standards to guide instruction and assessment.

🦋 Summary

Standards are serving as the basis for schools throughout the country to develop comprehensive literacy programs. The emphasis is on differentiated instruction that focuses on the needs of individual learners.

Literacy involves all of the communication and calculation skills needed to survive in today's world. This text focuses on the communication aspects of literacy—listening, speaking, reading, writing, and thinking. Viewing is a form of literacy in which the individual applies communication skills to watching a movie or a television program.

Oral language (listening and speaking) is the foundation of all literacy learning. Reading and writing build on listening and speaking. Thinking is an integral part of all of these processes.

As students develop literacy, they go through several stages or phases: Early Emergent Literacy, Emergent Literacy, Beginning Reading and Writing, Almost Fluent Reading and Writing, and Fluent Reading and Writing. Students do not progress through these stages smoothly, and there is much overlap between the stages.

Standards are statements of what is expected or valued in an area. Benchmarks are statements of behaviors that indicate whether a student has achieved a given standard. Standards and benchmarks are becoming increasingly more important in education at the national, state, and local levels. They form the foundation for all instruction and assessment.

All classrooms are diverse classrooms, containing English Language Learners, learning-disabled students, gifted students, and many others. There is strength in this diversity. Technology plays an increasingly more important role in helping us meet the needs of all learners.

Over the past forty to fifty years, literacy learning has gone through many phases. Knowing about these phases helps us better understand what we do currently and see how and why we have arrived at a more balanced approach to instruction. Four principles should guide all literacy instruction:

1. Reading, writing, speaking, listening, viewing, and thinking develop simultaneously as learners develop literacy.
2. The foundations of all literacy learning are oral language, prior knowledge, and background experiences.
3. Effective literacy instruction must include a combination of systematic, explicit, direct instruction and other types of activities that support literacy learning.
4. Literacy instruction should be differentiated to meet the diverse needs of every student.

For Additional Reading

Armbruster, B. B., & Osborn, J. (2001). *Put reading first: The research building blocks for teaching children to read (K–3)*. Ann Arbor: Center for the Improvement of Early Reading Achievement, University of Michigan.

Cooper, J. D., & Kiger, N. D. (2005). *Literacy assessment: Helping teachers plan instruction* (2nd ed.). Boston: Houghton Mifflin.

National Council of Teachers of English and International Reading Association. (1996). *Standards for the English language arts*. Urbana, IL: Newark, DE: NCTE/IRA.

National Reading Panel. (2000). *Teaching children to read: An evidence-based assessment of the scientific research literature on reading and its implications for reading instruction*. Washington, DC: National Institute of Child Health and Human Development.

Peregoy, S. F., & Boyle, O. F. (1997). *Reading, writing, and learning in ESL* (2nd ed.). New York: Longman.

Wepner, S., Valmont, W., & Thurlow, R. (2000). *Linking literacy and technology: A guide for K–8 classrooms*. Newark, DE: International Reading Association.

For Exploration: Electronic Products and Resources

Helping all children become literate has always required that teachers keep up with new materials, new practices, and new research. The following Web sites will help you learn about changes in a variety of areas of educational interest, especially technology.

AskERIC

AskERIC is a personalized Internet-based service providing education information to teachers, librarians, counselors, administrators, parents, and anyone else interested in education throughout the United States and the rest of the world. Need to know the latest information on special education, curriculum development or other education topics? Just AskERIC! When you submit your education question to AskERIC Q&A, you'll receive a personal e-mail response within two business days from one of the network information specialists in the ERIC system. You will receive a list of ERIC database citations that deal with the topic and refer you to other Internet resources for more information. Additionally, The AskERIC Lesson Plan Col-

lection contains more than 2,000 unique lesson plans that have been written and submitted to AskERIC by teachers from all over the United States.
http://ericir.sunsite.syr.edu/

Discovery School: Kathy Schrock's Guide for Educators to Literature and Language Arts

Kathy Schrock's Guide for Educators is a categorized list of sites useful for enhancing curriculum and professional growth. It is updated often to include the best sites for teaching and learning.
http://school.discovery.com/schrockguide/arts/artlit.html

Educational Resources Information Center

The Educational Resources Information Center (ERIC) is a national information network of education information from all sources. Search the ERIC Database to find education-related journal articles, research reports, curriculum and teaching guides, conference papers, books, and more. Or, visit the ERIC Clearinghouses' content-rich Web sites for brief and in-depth publications, virtual libraries, directories, and links to other resources in their areas of subject expertise. Browse ERIC Resources to explore more than 2,400 ERIC Digests on current topics, and link to resources for parents, a conference calendar, an online question-answering service, and other resources.
http://www.eric.ed.gov/

Houghton Mifflin's Education Place for Reading and Language Arts

Graphic organizers, resources, lesson plans, and links for K–8.
http://www.eduplace.com/rdg/index.html

International Reading Association

The International Reading Association (IRA) provides resources for teachers, reading specialists, tutors, and others concerned about literacy. Topics range from performance-based assessment to classroom discussion strategies, integrated instruction, motivation for reading, and teaching English as a Second Language. Visit the IRA's Web site to learn about books, journals, videos, and multimedia products about reading comprehension and literacy. You may be particularly interested in the IRA's five professional journals:

- *The Reading Teacher*—for preschool, primary, and elementary teachers
- *Journal of Adolescent and Adult Literacy*—for teachers of middle school, high school, and adult learners
- *Reading Research Quarterly*—a journal of reading research
- *Lectura y vida*—a Spanish-language journal for all teaching levels
- *Reading Online*—an electronic journal using the Web to explore research, instruction, and communication

http://www.reading.org

International Society for Technology in Education

The International Society for Technology in Education (ISTE) helps K–12 teachers and administrators share effective methods for enhancing student learning through the use of new classroom technologies. The Web site offers information about publications as well as conferences and workshops.
http://www.iste.org

National Council of Teachers of English

The National Council of Teachers of English (NCTE) is devoted to improving the teaching of English and the language arts at all levels. NCTE publishes a member newspaper, three monthly journals, and ten quarterlies. It also publishes position papers, teaching ideas, and other documents on professional concerns such as professional standards. Explore the Web site to learn more. The following journals may be of particular interest to you.

- *Language Arts*—for elementary teachers and teacher educators
- *Primary Voices K–6*—a journal written by different teams of elementary educators
- *School Talk*—a newsletter for classroom teachers
- *Voices from the Middle*—for middle-school teachers

http://www.ncte.org

U.S. Department of Education's Just for Teachers Site

The U.S. Department of Education's mission is to ensure equal access to education and to promote educational excellence throughout the nation. At its Just for Teachers Site, check out the Toolkit for Teachers, and the Reading Resources compendium.
http://www.ed.gov/teachers/landing.jhtml

A Comprehensive Literacy Program

2

✓ **STANDARDS FOCUS**
NCTE/IRA Standards: 1, 2, 3, 5, 7, 9, 10, 11, 12
Standards for Reading Professionals: 1, 2, 4, 5

Educators Speak   pp. 42, 54

Using a Classroom Speaker System and the Read-Aloud Mode to Meet the Needs of Diverse Listeners
        —*Joy Nelson, Allentown, Wisconsin*

Using Listening Across the Curriculum
        —*Diane Alsager, Cedar Rapids, Iowa*

Comprehensive Literacy Instruction, p. 26

Comprehensive Literacy Instruction Defined, p. 26

A Model for Comprehensive Literacy Instruction, p. 27

Standards and Instruction in a Comprehensive Literacy Program, p. 31

The Role of Standards, p. 31

The Role of the Teacher, p. 31

Modes of Reading as Forms of Instruction, p. 33

Modes of Writing as Forms of Instruction, p. 40

Formats for Developing Standards-Based Literacy Lessons, p. 45

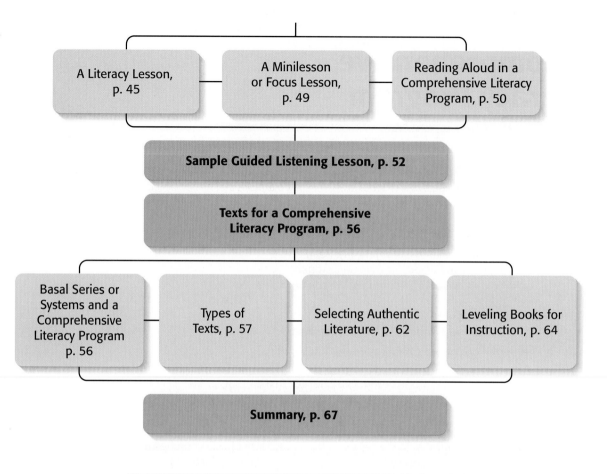

*L*et's begin by visiting two different second-grade teachers, Ms. Marks and Mr. Anzo. As you look at their classrooms, think about how they are alike and how they are different..

Ms. Marks has twenty-three second graders: twelve boys and eleven girls. Three of her students speak mainly Spanish, and the child from Bosnia speaks a little English. Four of her students are having difficulty learning to read; they attend a special reading program for 30 minutes a day, three days a week, for extra instruction.

Ms. Marks uses a published reading and language arts program. She divides her class into three groups for language arts and reading instruction, and she is using the second-grade book for all groups. She follows the manual and uses all of the practice pages that are provided with the program. One group contains three English Language Learner (ELL) students and four native English speakers who all need English-language development work. Ms. Marks often reads the stories aloud to the students, because they are unable to read them on their own. Her second group contains twelve students who are making good progress in language arts and reading; this group includes one ELL student. Her last group consists of four students who are her best readers.

Ms. Marks explained that the school is currently focusing on standards for language arts. She says that she doesn't have time for any additional instruction, and can't see how she will ever have time to meet the standards.

Mr. Anzo teaches across the hall from Ms. Marks and uses the same published reading and language arts program. He is also supposed to be focusing on the new language arts standards. Mr. Anzo has twenty-four students: thirteen boys and eleven girls. He has five ELLs: three speak primarily Spanish and can read in Spanish; the two children from Bosnia speak only their native language.

Three days each week, Mr. Anzo has his entire class working from the grade-level book from the published program. He varies the instruction by having students work with the same text differently. For example, today one group is being directed by Mr. Anzo, while other students are reading aloud with partners. Later in the morning, another group of students meets with Mr. Anzo for a lesson on a phonics skill, while other students are doing phonics practice activities at centers and on the computer. Mr. Anzo said that on the other two days of the week, he has all students placed in books appropriate to their reading level. Mr. Anzo explains that he has looked at the standards for second grade and compared them to what the teacher's manual provides to support the standards. He has literacy instruction planned in blocks. He starts each morning with a 15-minute block for independent reading. During this time, he always has conferences with a few students. His ELLs sometimes read books in their native language or listen to English books on tape.

Just as we are getting ready to leave, Mr. Anzo says that it is time for the class to start the writing block. He explains that this takes place every day. He adds that his ELLs also go to English Language Development class each afternoon, and his struggling readers attend the special reading program for 30 minutes, three days per week.

Although our visits to these two classrooms were brief, we can begin to see the differences in the approaches of these two teachers. Ask yourself several questions:

- Which teacher tried to focus on the standards?
- Which teacher provided a balance of reading and writing instruction?
- Which teacher provided direct instruction in skills?
- Which teacher appeared to do more to differentiate instruction to meet students' needs?
- Which teacher was trying to provide a more **comprehensive literacy program?**

If you answered *Mr. Anzo* to all of these questions, you are correct. Certainly Ms. Marks was attempting to meet the needs of her students in the ways that she knew best. However, there are areas where she needs to change her instruction. For example, the group with the students who need English Language Development also needs books that these students can read. Just reading aloud to them is not going to teach them to read.

Mr. Anzo was coming much closer to having a comprehensive program. He was looking at how to differentiate instruction using the published program to meet the new language arts standards. He organized daily independent reading time, he provided instruction using the grade-level text as well as texts appropriate to the students' abilities, and he provided direct instruction in the skills his students needed. Mr. Anzo also had a block for daily writing instruction. Within his program, we can see that Mr. Anzo was incorporating technology. Overall, Mr. Anzo was providing **comprehensive literacy instruction** for his class.

In this chapter, we focus on developing a framework for comprehensive literacy instruction. We concentrate on key concepts that are needed to provide differentiated instruction within a comprehensive literacy classroom.

🦋 Comprehensive Literacy Instruction

Over the years, considerable research has been conducted in the field of reading and literacy. Given the current state of our knowledge, some type of a balanced, comprehensive approach to literacy instruction is recommended to ensure that all children and young adults achieve success in literacy (Armbruster & Osborn, 2001; Lyon & Chhabra, 2004; Snow, Burns, & Griffin, 1998). First, let us answer the question: *What is comprehensive literacy?*

Comprehensive Literacy Instruction Defined

A *comprehensive literacy program* combines teacher-directed instruction and student-centered activities, and is based on the best research evidence available now. There are many educators and researchers who discuss comprehensive literacy instruction (Au, Carroll, & Scheu, 1997; Freppon & Dahl, 1998; Pressley, 1998; Snow, Burns, & Griffin, 1998; Strickland, 1994). Today, the term *comprehensive literacy program* is often used instead of the term *balanced literacy program*. Although there are various models and points of view, there is a great deal of overlap and similarity among them. When the many points of view are examined, it can be seen that comprehensive or balanced literacy always combines teacher-directed instruction and student-centered activities. Some individuals feel that research supports more teacher-directed instruction (Chall, 2000), and some think that research supports more student-centered activities (Weaver, 1994). However, in the big picture, a comprehensive or balanced approach appears to be the most effective for all students (Pressley, 1998; Snow, Burns, & Griffin, 1998). Note that we use the term *comprehensive literacy program* throughout this text, because we feel it more aptly reflects all the elements that should be included in a well-designed literacy program that promotes success for all students.

Teacher-directed instruction involves systematically and explicitly modeling or showing students how to use a skill, strategy, or process. For example, in writing, we model the process of writing a good sentence. Then students write their own sentences.

In student-centered instruction, students perform a given task, from which they are expected to learn certain things. For example, in reading, we have students read a short story that includes two or three words they do not know, expecting that they will learn the meanings of the words by using the context in which the word occurs; this might be a sentence, a paragraph, or the entire story. If we had used teacher-directed instruction, we would have taught the word meanings prior to reading.

Some students may learn one task better with more direct instruction, whereas others might learn better with more student-centered instruction. An effective literacy teacher differentiates instruction for students in accordance with their strengths, their needs, and the tasks they are performing. All students need both teacher-directed instruction and student-centered instruction, depending on what they are learning. Thus, comprehensive literacy instruction is a combination of teacher-directed instruction and student-centered activities.

A Model for Comprehensive Literacy Instruction

In order to develop an effective comprehensive literacy program, you need a model or framework to guide you. The basic framework presented in Figure 2.1 is the same for kindergarten through grade 8.

Modifications are made across the grades as needed.

The Comprehensive Literacy Program has six blocks for the **core instruction,** which is the part of the program that all students need.

- Daily Independent Reading
- Daily Independent Writing
- READING: Learning Skills and Strategies
- READING: Application of Skills and Strategies
- WRITING: Learning to Write
- WRITING: Developmentally Appropriate Writing

FIGURE 2.1

A Model for a Comprehensive Literacy Program

Intervention		
Writing: Learning to Write		Writing: Developmentally Appropriate Writing
Reading: Learning Skills and Strategies		Reading: Application of Skills and Strategies
Daily Independent Reading		Daily Independent Writing

The seventh block, intervention, provides for additional instruction for struggling readers who are not making **adequate yearly progress.**

Let's examine each block to discover what takes place in each.

Daily Independent Reading

Two activities—*self-selected reading* and *reading for fluency practice*—take place during this block. For self-selected reading, children read books of their own choosing. Beginning in preschool, children usually look at the pictures and often pretend to read the text by running their fingers along the lines of print. This time in the program establishes the habit of independent reading. As children develop their skills through instruction in reading, they begin to read a greater variety of texts.

See Chapter 10 for a discussion of creating learning areas in the classroom.

To support self-selected reading, you need many different books, a variety of children's and young adult periodicals, and perhaps some newspapers. These can be displayed attractively in the library area.

Starting in preschool, children usually select books by looking at the covers and illustrations. As they progress in learning to read, you help them learn to select books they can read. Teach a procedure that many teachers use called "Thumbs Up." Tell children to read a page in the book. Each time they come to a word they don't know, they fold a finger down on one hand. If the child's thumb is still up at the end of the page, the text is probably appropriate for the child to read. You will need to model this procedure for your students.

See Chapter 5 for routines for fluency practice.

A second part of daily independent reading is allowing time for fluency practice. For fluency building, you will need books that are at the children's independent and instructional reading levels. Books used in previous instruction can be used for practice through repeated reading (Rasinski, 2003). Table 2.1 presents a number of activities that can be used for fluency practice at all grade levels.

Self-selected reading at the beginning of kindergarten will usually last about 5 minutes each day. As the year progresses, this time is usually extended to 10 minutes. In first and second grades, independent reading is usually 10 to 15 minutes per day. In grades 3 through 8, independent reading increases to 15 to 20 minutes per day. Approximately 5 minutes per day should be allotted for fluency practice. Fluency practice may also occur at other times in the two reading blocks.

Daily Independent Writing

During this time, children write what they want to write. In preschool, kindergarten, and the beginning of first grade, this "writing" may actually be drawing a picture with a few scribbles under it. Independent writing, like independent reading, provides students with the needed practice time to become proficient and establishes the habit of writing daily. As students progress through the grades, they will write a greater variety of products on varying topics.

The amount of time for independent writing will range from 5 minutes per day at the beginning of kindergarten to 10 minutes or more by the end of the year. In first and second grades, the amount of time for independent writing is usually 10 to 15 minutes per day. For grades 3 through 8, the amount of time should be 15 to 20 minutes per day.

| TABLE 2.1 | **Daily Fluency-Building Activities** |

Activity	Description
All students read	Students read aloud a book at their independent reading level. Everyone reads at once.
Partner reading	Two students read aloud to each other from the same text. Both students must be reading at the same reading level.
One-minute reads	Same as ALL STUDENTS READ except teacher times for 1 minute. Teacher directs students to start and stop at designated times. Students mark their stopping places and then count the number of words they read.
Tape-recorded readings	Students read on to a tape recorder and then listen to their reading and check for accuracy.
Teacher coaching	Teacher listens and provides corrective feedback as student reads.
Teacher read aloud	Teacher models fluent oral reading. Have a copy of the text on a transparency or in a big book to show students where to pause, change expression, and stop.
Repeated reading	Teacher and students read aloud the same text several times. This can be done in groups by level or individually.
Readers theater	Students act out stories they have read by taking parts and reading a script.

See Chapter 5 for information on corrective feedback.

See Chapter 5 for more information on repeated reading.

Reading: Learning Skills and Strategies

For more discussion on basal readers and core texts, see pages 56–57.

For more discussion on decodable text in anthology and little book form, see the section later in this chapter.

Authentic literature is defined later in this chapter.

In this block, students receive instruction centered around the anthology of the basal series being used or a core book selected for the grade level. Explicit, direct instruction and student-centered instruction are used to teach the skills and strategies involved in decoding, comprehension, and study skills as needed. For example, in this block, beginning readers are systematically and explicitly taught to decode words through phonics and other skills and strategies. As they develop their ability to figure out words, they immediately begin to read **decodable texts** that allow them to practice and apply the skills they are learning. These texts may be in little book form and/or in the anthology of the basal program.

As children become more skilled at reading words, they should then move beyond these decodable texts to authentic literature that has been selected to help them continue to practice and apply the skills they have learned. As children gain power in decoding and as they develop independence, they will read more and more authentic literature. Independence in decoding for most children usually occurs by the end of second grade; for others, this might take a bit longer.

During this block, children are also taught a number of **high-frequency** words, ones that occur often in English. They practice reading these words in the decodable texts being used for practice and application of phonics and other decoding skills and strategies.

See Chapters 5 and 6 for instructional routines to use during this block.

Constructing meaning, or comprehension, and research and study skills and strategies are also taught during this block. A variety of teaching routines are used throughout this block.

In summary, the *Reading: Learning Skills and Strategies* block is where students at all grade levels are taught the skills and strategies of reading. The anthology or core book is used for this instruction, which may be given to the whole class or to small groups. The anthology or core book may be too difficult for some students. In this case, you will adjust your instruction to meet the needs of individual students. All chapters that follow will help you learn to adjust instruction to the needs of your students.

Reading: Application of Skills and Strategies

This is the block of the core instruction where students apply the skills and strategies they have been learning in texts appropriate to their reading levels. This block requires the teacher to operate several reading groups in the classroom. The texts used here may include created, or specially written, texts, as well as authentic literature.

Writing: Learning to Write

See Chapter 8 for writing, spelling, and grammar instructional routines.

In this block, children are taught how to write, either in groups or as a whole class. In preschool, kindergarten, and first grade, you begin by modeling how to form letters, words, and sentences. As students develop their ability to write, you model different types of writing; spelling and grammar are taught as appropriate.

Writing: Developmentally Appropriate Writing

In this block, students write their own pieces. In the beginning, they may draw pictures and write a few letters or single words as captions for their pictures; gradually they begin to write stories, reports, and other pieces. The children do the same type of writing taught in the previous block, *but they select their own topics.* Through this block, teachers provide time for the practice and application of grammar and spelling.

Intervention

For a detailed discussion of intervention, see Chapter 9.

This block is *provided in addition to the six blocks of core instruction for students experiencing difficulty learning.* It is designed to stop or prevent failure for those students. This intervention block is supported by the six blocks of the classroom program, showing that students who need intervention also need strong, quality classroom instruction.

The amount of time required for the six blocks varies from grade level to grade level. In kindergarten, you need a minimum of 3 hours per day. In grades 1 and 2, approximately 2 1/2 to 3 hours per day are needed. In grades 3 through 5, approximately 2 hours per day is needed, and in grades 6 through 8, approximately 90 minutes per day is needed to provide the core instruction of a comprehensive literacy program. Any intervention instruction is *in addition to these times.*

In summary, the model we have presented for comprehensive literacy instruction provides a framework for planning instruction in line with *all students' needs* as they progress through the stages of literacy development. Although this program model stops at grade 8, literacy development continues throughout life.

Standards and Instruction in a Comprehensive Literacy Program

As we have already discussed, a comprehensive literacy program includes a combination of teacher-directed instruction and student-centered instruction. Instruction within the program may be delivered in many forms. The teacher is key to planning this instruction, which is based on the standards to be covered and the individual students needs.

The Role of Standards

For further reading on assessment-based or diagnostic literacy instruction, see "For Additional Reading."

The standards for your state or district guide the content that should be taught in your classroom's comprehensive literacy program. Just as we are using the NCTE/IRA Standards to guide the lesson examples presented in this text, you will use your state standards to help you determine what you teach in your program. You will always look at individual student needs to determine exactly where each student is in relationship to the standards for your grade. This is called *assessment-based* or *diagnostic literacy instruction* (Cooper & Kiger, 2005).

The Role of the Teacher

The teacher creates the circumstances and conditions within the classroom that support learning. **Focus lessons,** or **mini-lessons,** are concise lessons that teach a specific skill, strategy, or process. These lessons may use *modeling*; that is, they may show or demonstrate for students how to use the processes of reading or writing or how to use particular strategies that might help in decoding words or constructing meaning. For example, when teachers read a story to the class, they are modeling fluent reading; when they write a group story with the class, they are modeling writing. Many times, modeling involves the use of "think-alouds," sessions in which teachers share the thought processes they have gone through in constructing the meaning of a text (Clark, 1984; Meichenbaum, 1985).

For a detailed discussion of modeling and sample lessons using think-alouds, see Chapter 4.

For further reading on cooperative learning, see the "For Additional Reading" section.

In other instances, the teacher may set up an activity in which students work together on a task. This is known as *cooperative learning*. The teacher observes the activity while students are working, and provides directive support or coaching through questions and suggestions.

Instruction also gives students the opportunity to respond to their reading and writing. *Responding* is the essence of literacy: it is the construction of personal meanings (Rosenblatt, 1938/1976, 1978). Students may react to, talk about, or do something appropriate with a piece of literature they have read or listened to, or a story they have written. For example, after writing a mystery, a student might want to read it aloud to some classmates or have it read and reacted to by others. Students who have read a piece such as *Bridge to Terabithia* (Paterson, 1977) might respond to it by getting together in a group for a discussion. Such responding must be authentic in that it must be the type of activity one naturally does with reading and writing. It may take place before, during, or after students read or write. See Table 2.2 for examples of responding.

TABLE 2.2   Examples of Responding

- *Before reading:* Students might look at a book and predict what will happen based on their knowledge of the topic or the author. This is the beginning of responding.
- *During reading:* As students are reading, they might have a reaction to a particular character and write a note about it in their journal or change a prediction in the light of new information.
- *After reading:* Because students loved the book they read, they may select another book by the same author, or may choose to retell the story to someone else.

For more discussion of responding, see Chapter 7.

    The teacher plans and supports the activities and experiences that encourage responding. Teachers should include lessons that involve reading many kinds of books, all the time prompting students to respond in ways of their own choosing or directing them by offering suggestions for the type of response they might make.

    Reading the literature in a variety of ways is an important part of instruction. The support the teacher provides while students are involved in any aspect of reading or writing is called **scaffolding** (Collins, Brown, & Newman, 1987). This might be questioning that helps students understand what they have read or modeling to show students how to think through a particular piece of text or to learn a strategy. As students become increasingly competent, the teacher begins to remove the scaffolding, and provides less and less support. This is what Pearson (1985) calls the "gradual release of responsibility." In other words, the teacher gradually gives more responsibility to the students. This process can be observed in any learning situation. For example, young children who learned to read before going to school learned in this way: first someone read to them, and then gradually that person read less and less and the children read more and more.

    Instruction may be planned or unplanned (Durkin, 1990), and both types are necessary. However, once you have learned how to provide quality planned instruction, you are more likely to be comfortable seizing the teachable moment, or responding spontaneously to a situation that arises unexpectedly during a lesson or activity. For example, suppose the children have read *Today Was a Terrible Day* (Giff, 1980). In the discussion that follows, you realize that several children do not understand why Ronald Morgan is feeling so unhappy in school. Therefore, you begin by directing them to the first unhappy incident: when Ronald Morgan drops his pencil. By questioning and discussing, you help the children see how dropping the pencil and Miss Tyler's response make Ronald unhappy. You continue through the story in this way, looking at all events that take place. You are providing the support, or scaffold, when it is needed, to help the children construct meaning.

Another important part of the instruction in a comprehensive literacy program is using different types of reading and writing to scaffold the support that students need. In the following section, we look at different modes of reading and writing. Knowing how to use different modes of reading and writing along with explicit, direct instruction provides you with a powerful combination of teaching tools that will ensure that *all* students succeed in reading and writing.

Modes of Reading as Forms of Instruction

Students may read a piece of literature in a variety of ways, depending on their stage of literacy development, as well as the complexity of the literature. No one mode is exclusively for reading at one stage or another. Rather, decisions as to which mode to use in a given lesson or instructional situation should be made by the teacher and/or students on the basis of the literature, the students' reading abilities, and the particular lesson or situation. The primary concern for you as the teacher is to be aware of each of the possible ways to approach reading and when, why, and how to use them. We will discuss five **modes of reading:**

- independent reading
- cooperative reading
- guided reading
- shared reading
- read aloud

Independent Reading

During independent reading, students read an entire selection or part of a selection by themselves. As a mode of instruction, independent reading should not be confused with the independent, self-selected (voluntary) reading portion of the literacy program discussed earlier in this chapter. Since independent reading involves the least support possible, it is used when students have sufficient ability to read a piece of literature without any support from the teacher or peers. It can also be used for rereading after students have received sufficient support through other modes of reading. Unfortunately, we know that struggling readers may get few, if any, opportunities to read whole pieces of quality literature independently (Allington, 1977, 1983; Allington & Walmsley, 1995). *All students at all levels need to have instructional experiences in independent reading.*

Cooperative Reading

Cooperative reading uses the principles of cooperative learning (Slavin, 1990). Pairs of students take turns reading portions of a piece of literature aloud to each other, or they read silently to a designated spot and then stop to discuss what they have

| TABLE 2.3 | Guidelines for Cooperative Reading |

1. *Preview and predict.* Have the students look through the text and examine the illustrations or pictures; ask them to read the beginning portion of the text and predict what they think will happen or what they will learn.
2. *Read orally or silently.*

Oral Version	**Silent Version**
Skim silently. Each student skims the text silently before beginning oral reading.	*Read.* Each student reads the same portion of text silently, keeping in mind the predictions made.
Read orally. One student reads aloud the first part of the text while the other(s) follow along.	*Discuss, respond, and check predictions.* The students stop and retell or summarize what they have read. They tell how they feel about what they have read or what they have learned, and they talk about whether their overall predictions were verified or need to be changed.
Discuss, respond, and check predictions. The students stop and retell and/or discuss how they feel about what was read. They talk about whether they have verified or need to change their overall predictions.	
Predict and read. The students predict what they think will happen or what they will learn in the next section. The second student then reads aloud the next section. This pattern continues until the selection is completed.	*Predict and read.* The students predict what they think will happen next or what they will learn. They continue reading the next section silently. This pattern is followed until the entire piece has been completed.

3. *Summarize and respond.* After completing the entire selection, the students summarize what they have read. They respond by discussing how they feel about what they have read and deciding what they might do with it (tell someone about it, write their own summaries, use art to share what they read, and so forth).

read. The students predict what they think will happen next and continue reading the next portion of the text, either aloud or silently, and stop again for discussion. This pattern continues until they have finished the book or selection.

Cooperative reading is sometimes called *buddy reading, partner reading,* or *paired reading* (Tierney, Readence, & Dishner, 1990). It should be used when students need *some support* and are not quite able to handle an entire selection independently. The guidelines in Table 2.3, based in part on the successful reciprocal teaching model (Palincsar & Brown, 1986), should be helpful for using cooperative reading in your classroom. You may want to model this process for your students.

Students may take turns reading a sentence, paragraph, or page. Be sure that they are allowed to pass when their turn comes if they do not feel prepared to read the text.

Guided Reading

Detailed use of observational guided reading is discussed in Chapter 5.

Guided reading or *leveled reading* is an important part of helping readers develop fluency (National Reading Panel, 2000a). There are two basic types of guided reading: *observational* and *interactive*. Observational guided reading (our term) is the type discussed by Fountas and Pinnell (1996). Students read a text that has a minimal number of new concepts and skills. The teacher introduces the text, and students make some predictions. As they read, the teacher observes and coaches them in their use of strategies. The text is usually a short book or text that is read in its entirety.

With *interactive guided reading*, the teacher carefully guides, directs, or coaches students through the silent reading of a meaningful chunk of text by asking them a question, giving prompts, or helping them formulate a question that they then try to answer as they read the designated section of text. Sometimes the teacher helps students make predictions. At the conclusion of each section, the students stop and discuss with the teacher the answer to the question or their predictions, as well as other points. The teacher also encourages students to reflect on the strategies they have used and to discuss how those strategies have helped them construct meaning. At each stopping point, the teacher encourages students to respond to what they have read.

Interactive guided reading, as the name implies, is interactive, with students and teacher each participating in the process. It is used when students need a great deal of support in constructing meaning from the text because of the complexity of the text or their limited abilities. This approach also allows the teacher to adjust the support, or scaffolding, according to students' needs. For example, suppose your students are reading *Matilda* (Dahl, 1988) and you are guiding them through the first chapter, "The Reader of Books." As students are reading the first portion of the chapter, you realize they do not have the appropriate or sufficient background needed to construct meaning from it. For example, students cannot relate to a child who can begin school already reading as well as Matilda does. Therefore, you introduce into the discussion the background points they need. This is the type of unplanned instruction that uses the "teachable moment." *The lesson scenario using interactive guided reading might go as follows. The annotations in parentheses should help you see what is happening.*

(Relate prior knowledge to first chapter.)

> *Teacher:* We have previewed the book *Matilda* and know that it is about a little girl who is gifted. We are now ready to read the first chapter. Who can find it in the book and read the title?

> *Sammy:* "The Reader of Books."

(Get students to think about what might happen.)

> *Teacher:* What do you think that title tells you about Matilda?

> *Megan:* She might read books.

> *Beth Ann:* I think the teacher reads books.

> *Teacher:* Let's turn through the chapter and look at the illustrations that Quentin Blake, the illustrator, drew. What does Matilda seem to be doing?

> *Tara:* She's reading lots of books.

> *Sammy:* It looks like she is in the library.

Juro: Maybe she just looks at the pictures. She's so young to read.

(Guides students to predict. Helps students set purpose for reading.)

Teacher: What would you predict is going to happen in this chapter?

Sammy: Matilda is going to read a lot of books.

Juro: Matilda is a little girl, but she reads a bunch of books.

Teacher: [Records predictions on chalkboard.] Let's read pages 7, 8, and 9 silently to see if either of these predictions is correct. (Students read.)

(Follow up by having students check predictions. This is all a part of the scaffolding.)

Teacher: Were either of our predictions confirmed?

Larry: No. The author just told us that some parents think their kids are geniuses.

(Support students in clarifying.)

Teacher: Did he mean the kids really are geniuses?

Juro: No. Parents just think they are.

Teacher: How can you tell that Roald Dahl is making fun of these types of parents?

Analise: Because of the funny things he would write about the kids.

Teacher: Like what?

Beth Ann: He said he would write that Maximillian is a total washout and that he hopes there is a family business for him.

Sammy: That's funny.

Teacher: Why?

Sammy: Because it just is. Maximillian must be lazy or dumb.

Megan: No, he isn't. Roald Dahl is just being funny.

(Coach students to notice how authors motivate readers.)

Teacher: Do you think he is trying to get us interested in his book?

Most students: Yes.

(Encourage personal response.)

Teacher: How did these pages make you feel?

Larry: They were kind of funny.

Beth Ann: Sad. I hope a teacher wouldn't really write those things.

(Support students in thinking about their predictions.)

Teacher: Do you think we should change our predictions?

Juro: No, we haven't read enough yet.

(Support students in having a purpose for reading.)

Teacher: Let's read pages 10 and 11 silently and think about our predictions.

(Follow up on purpose for reading.)

Larry: She's smart.

Juro: She's a little kid.

> *Analise:* Her mother and dad don't like her.
>
> *Juro:* That's sad.
>
> *Teacher:* It is sad. Why do you think they feel that way?
>
> *Sammy:* I don't think they understand her.
>
> *Teacher:* Are there books for her to read?
>
> *Beth Ann:* No. Just one on cooking.

(The lesson would continue in this manner.)

Interactive guided reading is a very flexible tool; you can provide more support for students at the beginning of the reading, and gradually release the responsibility to them as the reading progresses. In this process, you control the amount of support through:

1. the types of questions you ask or the prompts you give before reading and during discussion,
2. the amount of text you have students read, and
3. the type of discussion held between reading sessions.

When students need more support, you can direct the discussion; then, as you give students more responsibility, they may carry out and direct the discussion with a partner.

Throughout interactive guided reading, be aware of the role of questions and prompts. Simply asking children about what they have read is not going to teach them how to construct meaning (Durkin, 1978, 1981). However, we do know that the questions asked and the prompts given during interactive guided reading can help if they are of the appropriate types (National Reading Panel, 2000b). Effective questions or prompts meet the following criteria:

- Questions or prompts given before reading should lead students to the important ideas in the text. In narrative text, they should focus on the setting of the story (time and place), the major characters, the story problem, the action, the resolution, and the overall moral or theme. In expository text, they should focus on the main ideas. For example:

  Narrative text: Who are the two important characters introduced in the story, and what do they do?

  Expository text: Think about the important things we know about plants.

- Questions and prompts used during discussion *between* the reading of sections should pull together ideas brought out in reading and should help build relationships among ideas. For example:

  Narrative text: Who were the two characters? What did you learn about them and how they usually work together?

  Expository text: What was the first important thing you found out about plants? How is this likely to help people?

- Questions and prompts should follow the order of the text.

By using these guidelines, you will help students develop what Beck calls an overall mental picture of the text being read (Beck, 1984).

A *monitoring guide* can be used independently by students who still need structured support during reading. Sometimes called a *study guide* by content-area teachers, this is a sheet that poses questions and gives activities that carefully guide students through the reading of the text. Although often used in content classes, it can be used in reading any text. Figure 2.2 shows a portion of a monitoring guide that students could use while reading the first chapter of *Matilda* (Dahl, 1988).

FIGURE 2.2

Monitoring Guide for *Matilda*

by Roald Dahl, illustrated by Quentin Blake
Chapter 1, "The Reader of Books," pages 7–21
Previewing and Predicting
- Try to get an idea about this chapter
  —Look at the illustrations
  —Read page 7
- Write your prediction about what you think will happen in this chapter:

  _____

  _____

Reading Pages 7–11
- Now read pages 7–11 to see if your prediction was verified. Maybe you will want to change your prediction. As you read, make notes about any thoughts you have about the chapter.

- Notes: _____

  _____

  _____

After Reading Pages 7-11
- What did you learn about your prediction?

  _____

  _____

- Complete this chart showing what you learned about Matilda. Add other ovals if you need them.

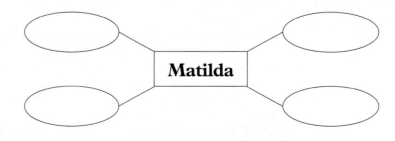

Shared Reading

Holdaway (1979) developed a procedure known as the *shared book experience* for introducing beginners to reading by using favorite stories, rhymes, and poems. In this procedure, the teacher reads aloud a story and invites children to join in the reading or rereading when they feel comfortable. Stories are read several times, and children receive many opportunities to respond through writing, art, drama, discussion, and in other ways. In Holdaway's early description of this procedure, some of the children's favorite books were enlarged for group study; this is the basis for the "big book" concept that many teachers use. The shared book experience has come to be known as *shared reading*.

For a detailed discussion of how to use shared reading, see Chapter 5.

Shared reading provides very strong support for learners. It allows for the modeling of real reading and mimics the ways "natural readers" have learned to read by being read to, reading along with an adult or older child, and ultimately reading on their own. Although shared reading can be used for beginning reading, it can also be used with students at other levels.

Read Aloud

Sometimes the best way to help children understand a particular piece of literature is to read it aloud and discuss it with them. This type of reading helps to activate knowledge that the students have already acquired and to develop their background vocabulary and concepts. It also is a way for the teacher to model real reading.

Reading literature aloud for instructional purposes provides very strong teacher support for students. It is used when a particular piece of literature has many difficult concepts or words, would be hard for students to decode, or is difficult to follow. After the teacher has read a piece aloud, students may then read it under the teacher's guidance, cooperatively, or independently.

Combinations of Reading Modes

Table 2.4 summarizes the five modes of reading we have discussed. Figure 2.3 shows how these modes of reading provide different amounts of scaffolding. Frequently it is appropriate to combine several modes of reading at once. For example, if students are reading a short story or a chapter in a book, you might begin by reading aloud the first portion of the piece and discussing it with them. Next, you might put students into pairs and have them do the oral version of cooperative reading. Finally, you might complete the chapter by having each student read a small portion of the text independently. In this way, each child would also have the opportunity to read alone. This combined instructional reading strategy can be called *read aloud, read along, read alone*. By combining these forms of reading, you provide a scaffold for learning that gradually releases some responsibility to the students. At the same time, you activate prior knowledge, develop background, and model real reading.

Remember that you can create different combinations as you work to meet the differing needs of your students. You should also give students the opportunity to select their own mode of reading. Finally, you may vary the mode of reading to add fun and variety to your instruction.

TABLE 2.4 **Modes of Reading**

Mode	Description	When to Use
Independent reading	Students read text alone without support, usually silently.	When students are likely to have no difficulty with the text or are highly motivated about the text or text topic.
Cooperative reading	Students read with a partner or partners, either orally or silently.	When students' abilities show need for some support. May also be done just for fun.
Guided reading	Teacher talks, coaches, and walks students through sections of text with questions and student predictions.	When text or students' abilities show need for much support. May be used for variety.
Shared reading	Teacher reads aloud as students view the text. Students chime in when they are ready to do so.	When students need a great deal of support for reading. Often used with beginning readers.
Read aloud	Teacher reads text aloud. Students usually do not have a copy of the text.	Used when text is too difficult, when background needs to be developed, or for fun or variety.

Modes of Writing as Forms of Instruction

Chapter 8 discusses the writing process along with spelling and grammar.

Throughout the literacy program, students will also be writing in response to literature and for other purposes. When they write, they will frequently do *process writing*; that is, they will follow the same steps that effective writers use (Graves, 1983; Hillocks, 1987a, 1987b): selecting the topic, drafting, revising, proofreading, and publishing.

Five basic modes of writing may be used as part of instruction and learning:

- independent writing
- collaborative/cooperative writing
- guided writing
- shared writing
- write aloud

Independent Writing

Independent writing is what students do when they write alone. It assumes that they are able to develop their product with little or no support. Independent writing builds power and fluency.

FIGURE 2.3

Varying Modes of Reading Provide Differing Amounts of Instructional Support

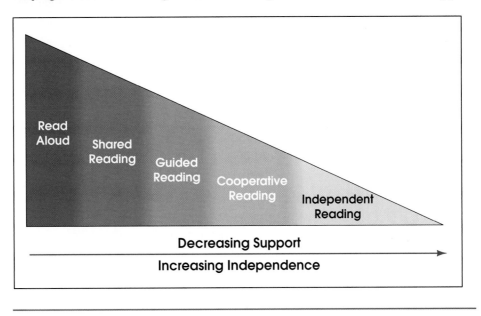

Collaborative/Cooperative Writing

When students write collaboratively/cooperatively, they work with one or more partners on a single product, often taking turns doing the actual writing. This mode of writing (comparable to the cooperative reading mode) gives students support by letting them work together and share ideas. It is often a good way to support writers who are unmotivated.

Guided Writing

This type of writing is comparable to guided reading. The students work on their own products, and the teacher is available to guide them through prompting and questioning. Routman (1991) suggests that this is the heart of the writing program.

Shared Writing

Just as there is shared reading, so there can be shared writing (McKenzie, 1985), sometimes called *interactive writing*. In this type of writing, teacher and students work together to write a group story on the chalkboard, a chart, or the overhead projector following the steps of process writing. In the beginning, the teacher might do the actual writing, but as the class progresses, different students take turns writing parts of the story. You may also choose to address problems that you know students

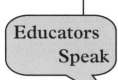

Educators Speak

Using a Classroom Speaker System and the Read-Aloud Mode to Meet the Needs of Diverse Learners

"I have been blessed this year with a microphone speaker system in my fifth-grade classroom. It has proven to benefit students at all levels. The speaker amplifies my softest voice, grabbing attention immediately. For the student who tunes out or cannot attend as well as others, the system has worked nicely. ESL students can benefit by hearing proper slow diction of the new language. Anything I say into the microphone is definitely heard by all. My daily read alouds are more effective. I do not, however, use it exclusively, thus ensuring its effectiveness when I do use it.

The students also love to use the microphone. They eagerly volunteer to read aloud when they can use the mike. I have seen improvement in oral reading, decoding, and pronunciation skills with the system. A teacher without a classroom speaker system could purchase a version of it, such as Mr. Microphone or even a karaoke machine.

There are various activities that can be done with the system to help students with diverse needs to become better readers. I show old filmstrips with text at the bottom of each frame, and the students take turns handing the microphone around to read the story. PowerPoint presentations can be developed and read aloud in class. The students can find a poem and read it aloud using the microphone. I have children go to the board with the microphone and explain how to do a math problem. Vocabulary guessing games can be played, with one student reading a definition and others guessing the word. Anything spoken in class can be done with the speaker system. It improves all oral language activities, because all students can hear what is spoken."

Joy Nelson, Fifth-Grade Teacher
Allenton Elementary School
Allenton, Wisconsin

are having in their own writing. In this way, you can model a particular aspect of grammar or spelling for a group of students without pointing out those problems in their writing. At the same time, you model the full process of writing and can share the thinking processes involved in the construction of meaning.

Write Aloud

This mode of writing allows the teacher to model the thinking process that occurs during writing. As the teacher writes at a chart or overhead, he or she thinks aloud to share with students his or her thought process. Students listen and read what is being written. This modeling process may be used at any grade level to teach writing.

Figure 2.4 shows a sample of shared descriptive writing that the teacher and students have revised. You can use shared writing when you think students need a great deal of support to help them expand their writing abilities. It is a powerful vehicle for developing minilessons to help students overcome problems in writing at all grade levels.

FIGURE 2.4

Sample of a Shared Writing Experience

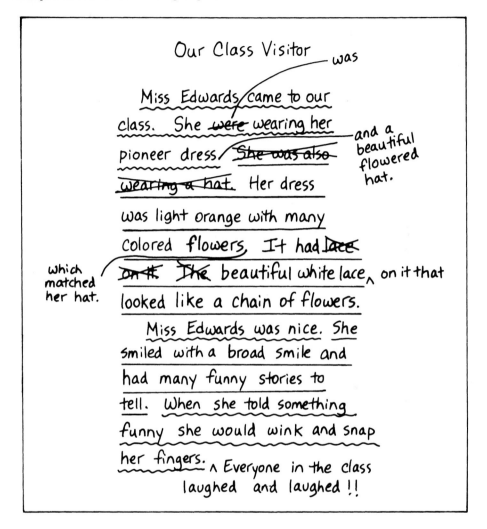

Combinations of Writing Modes

Table 2.5 summarizes the five modes of writing. You may use these modes with any students at any grade level, and you may also find you want to combine them. For example, you might begin a product with shared writing and move to collaborative/cooperative writing and then independent writing, depending on the amount of support you believe students need. *All students at all levels* need to have the experience of independent writing. You will need to vary the modes of writing you use in the light of students' needs and growth stage. Figure 2.5 shows that by changing the mode of writing you use with students, you change the amount of support you give

TABLE 2.5   **Modes of Writing**

Mode	Description	When to Use
Independent writing	Students write alone.	Students need little or no support.
Collaborative/cooperative writing	Students write with one or more partners on a single product.	Students need limited support in their writing.
Guided writing	Students write their own product; teacher prompts and guides.	Students have had models of writing but need support in learning how to write their own product.
Shared writing	The group or class writes together, working with the teacher.	Students need a large amount of support in their writing, or teacher sees the need to focus on a particular writing convention.
Write aloud	Teacher writes at a chart or overhead, sharing the thinking process being used.	Students need to have the process of writing modeled for a particular type of writing.

FIGURE 2.5

Varying Modes of Writing Provide Differing Amounts of Instructional Support

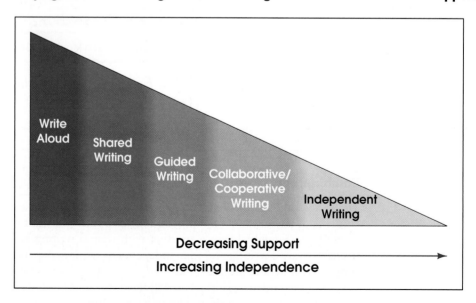

them. As when they read, you should encourage students to select the mode of writing that most appropriately meets their stage of development.

Formats for Developing Standards-Based Literacy Lessons

To plan effective literacy instruction based on standards, you need lesson plans to organize what you do. In this section, we discuss two frameworks that help you achieve this goal: a literacy lesson and a minilesson or focus lesson.

A Literacy Lesson

Various formats have been suggested for reading lesson plans. These include the DRTA, or Directed Reading Thinking Activity (Stauffer, 1969); the DRA, or Directed Reading Activity (Harris & Sipay, 1985; Burns, Roe, & Ross, 1988); and the DRL, or Directed Reading Lesson (Cooper, 1986; Cooper, Warncke, Ramstad, & Shipman, 1979), among others. Although these plans differ somewhat, they are similar in that they focus primarily on reading. The following **literacy lesson** format focuses on both reading and writing and helps the teacher and students relate both activities as integrated literacy learning processes. It has three simple parts: Introducing the Text, Reading and Responding to the Text, and Extending the Text.

First, you must know the standards you want to develop in your lesson. List these standards. Remember that a given standard will be addressed many times. Next, you read the text that is to be used for the lesson. If the text is a story, identify the parts, such as setting, characters, and problem. If the text is informational (expository), identify the main ideas and supporting details.

Introducing the Text

When you introduce each piece of text, two things must happen:

See Chapter 3 for information on vocabulary and concept development.

1. Students' prior knowledge must be activated and assessed, and pertinent additional background and concepts must be developed. This should include the recognition of key concept vocabulary.
2. Students must develop their purpose(s) for reading.

These two things are accomplished in a variety of ways and with differing levels of teacher support, depending on the text and the students' needs. Sometimes you teach words that are keys to understanding the text, or you might use the illustrations in the text. For example, if students in a second-grade class are going to read *The Art Lesson* (de Paola, 1989), you might have them preview the story by looking at the pictures and discussing what they think the book will be about. Their purpose for reading then becomes seeing whether their predictions are verified. Throughout, you provide support according to their needs. Many times you may incorporate writing into this phase of the lesson; for example, you may have students do a "quick write" (an activity in which students are given a topic and a short time to write on it) to activate prior knowledge or to write predictions that will be checked during and after reading.

Reading and Responding to the Text

Reading and responding to the text take place concurrently; that is, students respond while they are reading as well as after they have read.

Different pieces of text need to be read using different modes of reading, depending on the text and students' abilities. Beginning readers and writers and those having difficulty learning need more teacher support or scaffolding than those who are making effective progress. Moreover, some pieces of text are more complex than others and require more teacher support even for students who are progressing well.

The primary focus of this part of the lesson is reading and getting to know the text. As students read, remind them to monitor their reading by asking themselves whether what they are reading makes sense. This process is **metacognition,** knowledge of one's own thinking process. If the text does not make sense, the students should know and use appropriate strategies to help overcome the problem and construct meaning. Metacognitive development is a vital part of constructing meaning and comprehension (Paris, Wasik, & Turner, 1991).

You do not always have to select the mode of reading that students use. This decision can and should be made in part by the students. When you give students the opportunity to choose their own modes of reading, they select those that are most appropriate for their own needs and take greater ownership of their learning.

When responding to the text, students need to do something: *think about it, talk about it, write about it, or do something creative with it involving art, music, or drama.* Responses may be personal and creative. An important part of responding is summarizing or retelling what was read. Again, some students and some pieces of text will require more teacher support than others. By observing carefully how students respond, you can determine whether they need additional support or lessons to develop needed skills and strategies further.

Let's suppose your class is now ready to read *The Art Lesson* (de Paola, 1989). This book seems easy enough for all students in your class to read independently. However, you offer them the option of reading it independently or cooperatively. You remind students to check whether their predictions were verified or changed as they read and encourage them to make running notes about their feelings or reactions in their journals. After reading, the students could form small groups to retell the story and share their favorite parts. From the responses, you may discover that some students do not understand why Tomie was upset about the art lessons. You then go back to the book and model how Tomie's expectations for art lessons had been built up and how he became disappointed in school. You can do this by developing a graphic organizer like the one shown in Figure 2.6. Throughout the reading-and-responding component, students should be encouraged to reflect on both the meanings they have constructed and how various strategies they have used helped them construct meaning.

See Chapter 7 for more information on responding.

FIGURE 2.6

Chart Modeling Tomie's Disappointment in *The Art Lesson* (de Paola, 1989)

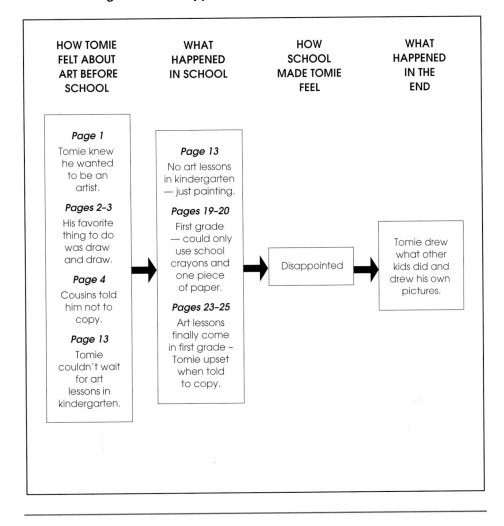

Extending the Text

Extending the text involves further instruction as well as integration of other language arts and other curricular areas. Students are encouraged to use what they have learned in various appropriate ways or in different curricular areas such as science, social studies, art, music, and writing. Minilessons or focus lessons may be taught at this point, as well as at other places in the lesson.

Writing may also be tied directly to reading by using the text as a model for a certain type of writing. For example, a natural writing extension for *The Art Lesson* is writing a story. Of course, you would vary the mode of writing according to students' needs.

This simple, easy-to-use literacy lesson is flexible and can be used throughout all grades. Make adjustments and variations in accordance with the students' stages of development, the text being read, and the needs of the individual students. Table 2.6 summarizes the parts of the literacy lesson.

TABLE 2.6 **Summary of the Standards-Based Literacy Lesson Format**

Lesson Part	Purposes	Remarks
Introducing	Activate and assess prior knowledge and develop background. Help students set purposes for reading.	The amount of teacher support provided will depend on both the text and the students' needs. Sometimes the support will include development of key concepts and vocabulary. Activities used will incorporate reading, writing, speaking, listening, and thinking.
Reading and responding	Read and have access to the entire selection. Do something creative and personal during and/or after reading the selection.	The mode for reading the selection is determined by students' needs and the text. This portion of the lesson focuses on the personal construction of meaning.
	Summarize what has been read.	By observing students' responses, you will be able to determine the need for additional support or mini-lessons.
	Reflect on the text and how various strategies helped in constructing meaning.	This part of the lesson helps students develop their metacognitive abilities, which leads to more effective comprehension.
Extending	Use the understandings and ideas gained from the literature. Use the literature as a model for writing.	Extension of the text will use the knowledge gained in many creative ways or in other curricular areas. Writing may be taught using the text as a model for the type of writing being developed.

A Minilesson or Focus Lesson

Throughout all literacy lessons, you need to provide different levels of support to help students continue their process of learning to read and write. Sometimes you provide this support when *introducing* the text, sometimes while students are *reading* and *responding*, and sometimes as they are *extending* the text. *You provide this support in many forms and ways. Minilessons* or *focus lessons*, introduced earlier in this chapter, are one effective way to provide the systematic direct instruction that is an important part of a comprehensive literacy program. The minilesson concept makes instruction more effective by breaking down instruction into smaller units, or chunks.

You can use minilessons based on the text that students have just read or on the students' own writing. These lessons model the construction of meaning, a skill, or a strategy and may take place before, during, or after reading or writing. You determine the need for a focus lesson by observing how students read and respond to the literature or how they write and respond to their writing. Figure 2.7 shows how all of these elements fit together.

Minilessons may be informal or formal. For example, suppose your students are reading *Mufaro's Beautiful Daughters: An African Tale* (Steptoe, 1987), which tells a version of the Cinderella story. As students are responding and discussing the fairy tale, you realize they have not understood that the snake, the hungry little boy, and the old woman are all the same person—the king, Nyoka. You immediately go back to the story and have them locate the places where each character appeared and show them that these are all the king, who has changed himself into these characters. This is a minilesson that takes place immediately when the "teachable moment" arises.

Most minilessons are more formal and more carefully and thoroughly planned. First, the standard or standards for the lesson must be identified. Then, a typical planned minilesson incorporates the following steps:

1. *Introduction:* Let the students know what they will learn and relate it to the text or their writing.
2. *Teacher modeling:* Model the element being taught using the text or writing to show examples. Incorporate think-alouds as needed.

See Chapter 4 for a discussion of think-alouds.

3. *Student modeling and guided practice:* Guide students in modeling and using what is being taught by finding other examples of what they have learned in the text or in their writing. If a skill, strategy, or process is being taught, provide **corrective feedback** as needed. Corrective feedback is the process of helping a student overcome a mistake or error by asking leading questions or guiding him or her to achieve the correct response.
4. *Summarizing and reflecting:* Help students summarize what they have learned, and talk about how and when they might use this knowledge.
5. *Independent practice:* Have students read or write using what has been taught.
6. *Application:* Give students repeated opportunities to immediately use or apply what they have learned in other reading and writing experiences.
7. *Reflecting about use:* After students have had several opportunities to apply what was taught, encourage them to talk about how they have used what they have learned and what they might do to improve it. Again, this promotes metacognitive development, which leads to better construction of meaning.

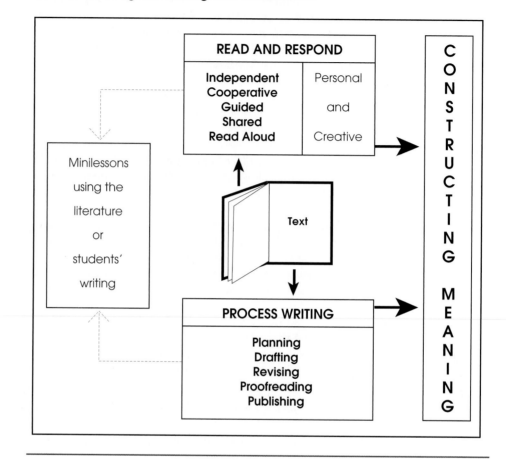

FIGURE 2.7

Model of Reading and Writing with Minilessons

Research shows that directed lessons such as the type being suggested here do help some students learn to read and write (Pearson & Dole, 1987). These lessons should be short, focused, and directed toward students' needs and the standards being developed. Most minilessons should last only 5 to 15 minutes.

Reading Aloud in a Comprehensive Literacy Program

Reading aloud to students is an important part of instruction throughout a comprehensive literacy program. When teachers read aloud a favorite book such as *The Best Town in the World* (Baylor, 1982), they convey their love and excitement for both reading and learning. Some consider such reading to be "the single most important activity for building the knowledge required for eventual success in reading"

(Anderson et al., 1985, p. 23). Indeed, research shows that preschool children who learn to read on their own generally have had an adult read to them repeatedly (Clark, 1976; Durkin, 1966). The overall value of reading aloud to children at home has been clearly documented (Cain, 1996; Strickland & Taylor, 1989). As teachers, we should encourage all parents to read to their children as much as possible.

Research also verifies the value of reading aloud to children as part of the classroom program (McCormick, 1977). It not only helps to motivate students but also provides a basis for expanding oral language and prior knowledge (Feitelson, Kita, & Goldstein, 1986), especially for children who have not had these experiences at home. Reading aloud also influences children's writings (Dressel, 1990). When children hear a great variety of stories, they reflect many story features in their own writing. Certainly there is no substitute for reading to children at home; however, classroom read-aloud periods can provide some of the same benefits (Strickland & Taylor, 1989; Taylor & Strickland, 1986), especially for those children who have not been read aloud to at home. There are three important purposes for reading aloud in a comprehensive literacy program:

1. *Provide motivation and enjoyment.* When we read aloud a good book such as *Snowflake Bentley* (Martin, 1998), we encourage students to read this book as well as others and allow them to enjoy the book.
2. *Build background and develop vocabulary.* Reading aloud exposes students to many new ideas and provides chances for them to hear and learn more vocabulary. This is important for all students but is especially important when teaching ELLs and other students who do not have a well-developed oral language. Reading aloud the exciting book *The Little Painter of Sabana Grande* (Markun, 1993) exposes students to many forms of expression, as well as a great variety of vocabulary.
3. *Teach specific strategies and skills for comprehension.* Learning to construct meaning or to comprehend begins at the oral language level. Strategies for effective comprehension should first be taught through listening and then taught through reading.

See Chapter 4 for a full discussion of this process.

There are two kinds of read aloud: *general* and *instructional*. General read aloud primarily provides motivation and enjoyment. Instructional read aloud builds background, introduces vocabulary and concepts, models fluency, or teaches a particular comprehension strategy or skill. Read aloud may take place during any of the blocks of a comprehensive literary program. Each occasion is likely to have more than one purpose. The following guidelines will help you plan read-aloud sessions in your program:

- ● ***Provide instructional read alouds.*** For instructional purposes, a **guided listening lesson** format should be used that includes the same basic parts as the literacy lesson presented earlier, except that the mode of operation is listening. The parts of this lesson are:
  1. Introduce the text.
  2. Listen and respond to the text.
  3. Extend the text.
- ● The parts of this lesson are described in Table 2.7. In most schools, one or more reading/language arts standards focus on listening (National Council of Teach-

ers of English and International Reading Association, 1996). A sample guided listening lesson is presented in the next section of this chapter.

- ***Read aloud every day.*** Select a consistent time so that children will look forward to the reading session. Many teachers prefer to read aloud first thing in the morning because it gets the day off to a positive start. If you have a few unexpected extra minutes throughout the day, use them for additional read-aloud time.

- ***Have a comfortable, inviting place in the classroom for reading aloud.*** Use the library area if it is large enough; sit in a favorite or special chair such as a rocker as you read to the children.

- ***Select books that both you and the children will enjoy.*** Some books may relate to specific themes or topics of study, but they do not have to. If you find you have selected a book the class is not enjoying, stop reading it and take some time to discuss why you have stopped. You should also vary the types of books you read, and be sure to include some poetry, since children of all ages enjoy poetry that rhymes and has humor (Thomas, 1989). Two favorite poets of most children are Shel Silverstein and Jack Prelutsky.

- ***Read with expression and feeling.*** Make the book come alive for children. Trelease (1989) suggests adding a real-life dimension to your read-aloud session; for example, if you are reading *Blueberries for Sal* (McCloskey, 1948), have a bowl of fresh blueberries for children to taste.

- ***Allow time for discussion during and after each read-aloud period.*** If students have questions during the reading, take time to discuss them, and use the discussion to talk about favorite parts, feelings, or reactions. Also, be sure to share your own thoughts about a book or story.

- ***Don't allow the discussion to become a time to "test" children on the book.*** When you simply ask students a series of questions that require 'right' answers, this is not a discussion. Instead, encourage students to share their thoughts, being careful to curb digressions.

- ***Allow students to write or draw as they listen.*** Some may find it easier to pay attention if they are allowed to write or draw while listening. Of course, they should not be completing work assignments at this time.

A list of Shel Silverstein and Jack Prelutsky's better-known works and a list of poetry anthologies appear at the end of this chapter.

The *New Read-Aloud Handbook* by Trelease listed in "For Additional Reading" will be helpful in planning general read-aloud periods.

🦋 Sample Guided Listening Lesson

The following sample guided listening lesson illustrates how to use the listening lesson format summarized in Table 2.7 (page 53). The lesson also illustrates how to incorporate standards into your lessons. When we discuss classroom organization

TABLE 2.7 **Guided Listening Lesson Format**

Component	Description	Comments
1. Introduce the text.	• Show the book or other text. • Read aloud the title and give the author's name. • Ask students to predict what the text is about or what they will learn. Record these for later use.	• Builds background, vocabulary, and concepts and develops a purpose for listening.
2. Listen and respond to the text.	• Remind students to keep their predictions in mind as they listen. • Read aloud part or all of the text, depending on the length of text and time available. • After listening, return to students' predictions. • Discuss and revise as needed. • Model any strategies or skills you want students to learn.	• Keeps students focused on their purpose for listening. • Helps students learn that predictions change as they get more information. • Provides a place to teach strategies for constructing meaning at the listening level.
3. Extend the text.	• Do one or more of the following: complete a graphic organizer, focus on words, or discuss the strategy or skill taught.	Provides a time to pull the parts of the lesson together.

and management in Chapter 10, you will see how to work listening lessons into the daily schedule of your balanced literacy program.

Before Reading the Lesson

1. Review the parts of a guided listening lesson.
2. Locate and read the book used as a basis for this lesson: *Raising Yoder's Barn* by Jane Yolen, paintings by Bernie Fuchs (Boston: Little, Brown, 1998). The Yoders are an Amish family who encounter a devastating fire that engulfs the windmill and barn on their farm. Their neighbors and friends come to help fight the fire. Once the ashes are raked away, Samuel Stulzfoot is summoned with plans for a new barn. Teams of men haul in beams and boards, and wagons of women and children arrive with hampers of food. The community, family, and friends work to raise Yoder's barn in one day.

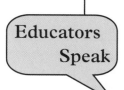

Educators Speak

Using Listening Across the Curriculum

Listening is a skill that I assumed my students had conquered. I was puzzled when they didn't follow directions after I had told them exactly what to do. They would ask me questions that I had just answered. I realized after directly teaching listening skills, that, like other literacy skills, the ability to listen can be improved. Due to time limitations, I decided to integrate the teaching of listening skills into one content area, science.

Initially I taught listening by using a nonfiction text for a science read aloud. I selected *A River Ran Wild: An Environmental History* by Lynne Cherry (1992) for the read aloud to accompany the environmental unit. I discovered that just like other literacy behaviors, there are things listeners do before listening, during listening, and after listening.

Before listening to the read aloud, students were given guidance and instruction on listening skills and strategies. I prepared a graphic organizer listening guide to assist students in focusing on key pieces of information as they listened to the book. Together we generated a list of questions we had about the book: What is the author's purpose? Do I know something about this topic? What is my purpose for listening? Should I take notes on subject matter? We filled in the listening guide together and displayed it on the overhead.

Next, we discussed what we would do during listening. This list of questions included: Am I learning what I need to know about pollution? Am I putting information about pollution into categories? Am I thinking about the story?

I then read *A River Ran Wild* aloud, twice. Once was for the experience of hearing the story, and the second reading was to focus on the important information about pollution. I stopped at key points during the second reading. I did this to show students how to respond to the questions on the listening guide. We filled in the graphic organizer together on the overhead.

Finally, we considered what good listeners do. The questions generated were: Do I have questions for the author, Lynne Cherry? Was any part unclear? What was the most interesting thing I learned? Is the listening guide complete? Students selected one of the above questions to respond to in writing. The completed listening guide was posted in the classroom.

We completed two more listening guides over the course of the week. One listening guide was filled out when directions were read for a recycling experiment. A video on litter was the source for our next completed listening guide. Students were then ready to fill out their own listening guides in table groups. Eventually students were able to create their own listening guides. The guides were extended to a variety of listening events (guest speakers, intercom announcements, assemblies). This taught students how to listen and shifted the responsibility for listening to them.

Diane Alsager, Reading Facilitator
Cedar Rapids Community School District
Cedar Rapids, Iowa

Reading the Lesson

1. Note the standard focus for the lesson (see below). This focus is on the standards list for several states.
2. Make notes about questions you want to discuss.

After Reading the Lesson

1. Meet with a colleague to discuss the lesson.
2. Identify ways you might change the lesson.

Lesson Format

Approximate grade level: second or third grade
Standard focus: Students listen to material and retell it in their own words; NCTE/IRA Standard 3, 4, 12.
Support for English Language Learners: Since this is a listening lesson, all ELLs can participate. Lesson notes indicate activities that might be needed to support these learners.

Introduce the Text

- Show students the cover of the book and read aloud the title, author, and artist. Point out that *Yoder* is the family's last name.
- Ask students to describe what they see on the cover. (Ask ELLs to describe what they can; if students are just becoming fluent in English, have them work with an English-speaking partner to describe what they see.)
- Ask students what they think the word *raising* means. Discuss the multiple meanings: *lifting*, *building*.

```
┌─────────────────────────────────┐
│           STORY MAP             │
│  ┌───────────────────────────┐  │
│  │ Setting: Time      Place  │  │
│  └───────────────────────────┘  │
│       ↓                         │
│  ┌───────────────────────────┐  │
│  │ Characters:               │  │
│  └───────────────────────────┘  │
│       ↓                         │
│  ┌───────────────────────────┐  │
│  │ Problem:                  │  │
│  └───────────────────────────┘  │
│       │    ┌──────────────────┐ │
│       │    │ Action:          │ │
│       ↔    │                  │ │
│       │    └──────────────────┘ │
│       ↓                         │
│  ┌───────────────────────────┐  │
│  │ Outcome:                  │  │
│  └───────────────────────────┘  │
└─────────────────────────────────┘
```

- Modeling prediction: Tell students that you are going to show them how to think about what is likely to be in the story by using the prediction strategy. For example:

  Teacher models: "I see a man and woman in a wagon in front of the barn. I predict that this is Mr. and Mrs. Yoder going to visit their neighbors."

- Ask several students to make predictions. Record predictions for later use.
- Tell students that after listening to the story, you will help them learn to retell it in their own words.
- Present the story map. Review the parts.
- Tell students as they listen to think about these parts of the story. Remind students to keep their predictions in mind as they listen.

Listen and Respond to the Text

- Read aloud the text in its entirety or in parts, as time permits.
- As you read, show each illustration.
- After listening, review all predictions. Discuss whether they were verified.
- Summarize the story using the story map. As students provide information, record their thoughts on the story map.

Extend the Text

- Using the completed story map as a prompt, demonstrate how you would retell the story in your own words.
- Have students work with partners to retell the story. Depending on the level of your ELLs, have them retell in their native language or in English.

Texts for a Comprehensive Literacy Program

An effective comprehensive literacy program uses a variety of types of texts. The goal is to have students reading real, or authentic, literature. However, as students develop through the various stages of literacy, different texts may be needed to serve different purposes of instruction and learning. As students develop the ability to read, they need texts that are sequenced from simple to complex until they can decode independently (Clay, 1991). Many schools use a published set of materials referred to as a **basal series or system** for their literacy program.

Basal Series or Systems and a Comprehensive Literacy Program

A basal series or system is a set of published materials that schools adopt and purchase for use as the core instructional materials for their literacy program. These series, which are usually for grades K–6 or K–8, come with a variety of texts and support materials, which usually include the following:

- **Anthologies.** These are collections of text that usually include specially written texts and excerpts from original literature. Anthologies typically include both narrative and expository material, as well as poetry. At the kindergarten level, a variety of big books and little books are provided. Anthologies usually begin with the first grade.
- **Practice books.** Often referred to as workbooks, these are pages that provide support for instruction, guided practice, and independent practice. Many often include work on spelling, grammar, and writing.
- **Teacher's manual.** The manual contains directions and lesson plans for the teacher. It is often correlated to the standards of each individual state.

- **Paperback books**. These are usually authentic works of literature, both narrative and expository.
- **Decodable texts**. For beginning readers, there are usually little books that have been written to provide practice and application of the phonics and decoding skills being taught. These are usually available through second grade.
- **Other support materials**. These include a variety of things, such as transparencies, CD-ROMs and other technology, books on tape, posters, and charts.

No basal series provides all the materials you will need to meet the needs of all students. Therefore, the remainder of this section addresses three issues:

1. What are the different types of texts needed?
2. How do you select appropriate texts and literature?
3. How can texts be leveled and placed in a continuum of difficulty for appropriate instruction?

Let's examine each of these issues.

Types of Texts

There are four major categories of text in an effective literacy program:

- wordless books
- predictable texts
- created texts
- authentic literature

Table 2.8 summarizes the major uses of each type of text.

Wordless Books

Wordless books are children's *picture books* that tell their story or present their information through illustrations or photographs without printed words. Wordless books have varying degrees of detail and complexity. Therefore, they can be used for a variety of purposes at a variety of levels.

Wordless books have been recommended for developing oral language and self-expression for all students (Strickland, 1977). They are especially useful for working with ELLs (Peregoy & Boyle, 1997). Examples of well-known wordless books are *Bobo's Dream* (Alexander, 1970), *Do You Want to Be My Friend?* (Carle, 1971), *The Mysteries of Harris Burdick* (Van Allsburg, 1984), *Tuesday* (Wiesner, 1991), and *Sector 7* (Wiesner, 1999).

Wordless books are useful for introducing concepts such as the parts of a book and the idea that a book presents a story or information. Because there is no threat from print on the page, these books are fun. Use them at the early stages of literacy development to develop vocabulary, oral language, and self-expression. Tiedt (2000) recommends using wordless books even in middle school. For ELLs, wordless books help build connections between first languages and English. For all learners, they can motivate students to write.

TABLE 2.8	Types of Texts for a Comprehensive Literacy Program

Type	Description	Major Use
Wordless books	Text composed of only illustrations or photographs. No print is given.	Used to help children develop a concept of themselves as readers, develop oral language, and develop self-expression.
Predictable texts	Texts that use a repeated pattern of some type. May be authentic literature or created text.	Used to introduce children to literature through shared reading and to provide practice through repeated readings.
Created texts	Published texts that may be decodable or written to control high-frequency words, concepts, skills, strategies, and overall difficulty.	Used for practice and application of decoding skills for beginning readers. Also used for practice and application of skills for students who may be experiencing difficulty in certain aspects of learning to read.
Authentic literature	Stories and informational texts in which no attempts have been made to control the words, patterns, or decoding elements used in the text. The unedited and unabridged text is in the original form as written by the author.	Used for practice and application of reading once students have developed beginning decoding skills. Also used for shared reading and read aloud at any point in the literacy program.

Predictable Texts

Predictable texts have a repeated pattern of some type. Bridge, Winograd, & Haley (1983) identified seven patterns of predictability in texts:

1. Phrase or sentence repeated. Examples: *Mary Wore Her Red Dress and Henry Wore His Green Sneakers* (Peek, 1985) and *"Slowly, Slowly, Slowly," said the Sloth* (Carle, 1999).
2. Repetitive-cumulative pattern in which a phrase or sentence is built. Examples: *Nobody Listens to Andrew* (Guilfoile, 1957) and *This is the House That Jack Built* (Taback, 2002).
3. Rhyming patterns. Example: *Mrs. McNosh Hangs Up the Wash* (Weeks, 1998).
4. Familiar cultural sequences, such as cardinal and ordinal numbers. Examples: *Feast for Ten* (Falwell, 1993) and *Ten Little Ladybugs* (Gerth, 2000).
5. Familiar cultural sequences, such as the alphabet. Examples: *Dr. Seuss's ABC* (Seuss, 1963), *Old Black Fly* (Aylesworth, 1992), and *Girls A to Z* (Bunting, 2002).

6. Familiar cultural sequences, such as days, months, and colors. Examples: *Chicken Soup with Rice* (Sendak, 1962) and *One Lighthouse, One Moon* (Lobel, 2000).
7. Predictable plots. Examples: *Mr. Gumpy's Outing* (Burningham, 1970) and *We're Going on a Picnic* (Hutchins, 2002).

Predictable texts help children very quickly come to think of themselves as readers (Holdaway, 1979). For example, hearing or reading aloud a book such as *Brown Bear, Brown Bear* (Martin, 1967) in a shared fashion several times allows children to very quickly be able to recite the text. Often the children memorize the text and can repeat it without even looking at it. In this way, they think of themselves as readers and have fun reading.

However, *too great a reliance on predictable text can cause beginning readers to over-rely on the illustrations rather than focus on the print.* Brown (2000) has developed a strong case for limited use of predictable texts to get children who need oral language development started in the process of reading. After students experience success with *some* predictable text, Brown recommends moving them into what she calls transitional and *decodable texts* (defined below) to help students develop sequential decoding.

Created Texts

Created texts are written for students at all stages of literacy development so that they can apply various skills and strategies in a text that is usually easy for them to read. Within this category of texts, there are two basic types, **decodable texts** and other created easy-to-read texts.

Decodable texts contain a high percentage of words that use the sound-letter relationships that children are currently being taught, as well as a limited number of high-frequency words (Chard & Osborne, 1999). These texts *may* also include a limited number of "special words" or "story words." For example, if students know the letter-sound relationships for *m* /m/, *s* /s/, *t* /t/, *p* /p/, *e* /e/, and *a* /a/ and the high-frequency and special words *the, elephant, said, no,* and *thank you,* they can read the following story:

Pat and the elephant.

> Pat met the elephant.
> The elephant met Pat.
> Pat sat.
> The elephant sat.
> The elephant sat on the mats.
> The elephant sat and sat.
> Pat sat and sat.
> Pat said, "Elephant, pat the pets."
> The pets said, "No, thank you, Elephant."
> (Chard & Osborne, 1999, p. 113)

The benefit of this type of text is that it allows students to practice sequential decoding and develop fluency and **automaticity,** the ability to read words quickly and accurately. These are critical parts of beginning reading instruction (National

Reading Panel, 2000a). Students are able to experience immediate success since the text is based on the instruction they have received.

The first major use of text *similar* to this type occurred in the 1960s (Bloomfield & Barnhart, 1961). It was referred to as *linguistically controlled text*. As long ago as 1967, Chall raised the issue that some of the control in beginning reading materials needed to result from a consideration of the phonic elements previously taught. In the example presented above, *beginning* readers are given an opportunity to apply their decoding skills in a real reading situation.

One of the major issues related to decodable text is the percentage of decodability (number of words that students can decode based on phonic elements taught thus far) that should be required in the text. Although there is limited research suggesting that some decodable texts should be used for beginning reading instruction (Juel & Roper/Schneider, 1985), there is little research to guide the decision about the percentage of decodability a text should have. The best rule of thumb we can follow is to use decodable text until students become independent in sequential decoding. Recently, some researchers have recommended that, especially for potentially low beginning readers, decoding should be systematically taught quickly up through about February of the school year (Juel & Minden-Cupp, 2000). Decodable texts are used to apply the skills and strategies being taught in a text. Some students will become independent in decoding by the end of grade 1, and others may become independent at a later grade. Although decodable texts are most important in the beginning reading program, they may be needed in later grades for students who have not achieved independence in decoding. In all instances, *decodable texts must be used along with other types of texts to help students continue to broaden their oral language base, develop vocabulary, and develop the use of comprehension strategies and skills.*

Easy-to-read texts, the other type of created text, are written for students beyond the beginning level of reading. With them, students can apply both decoding and comprehension skills and strategies. These texts give students the opportunity to practice and apply skills and strategies they are being taught in texts that they can read.

For students who are progressing normally, easy-to-read texts provide a chance for practice and application of strategies and skills using text that is easy to decode. Students can then return to grade-level material and apply the strategies and skills in more challenging texts. Easy-to-read texts are also appropriate to help students build fluency. However, created, or specially written, easy-to-read texts should not comprise a student's entire reading experience. Rather, they, like decodable texts, serve as a stepping stone to authentic literature.

Authentic Literature

Authentic literature (often referred to as trade book literature) consists of narrative and expository texts in the original form as written by the author. Narratives tell a story and have a structure known as a story grammar that is represented by a story map (see Figure 2.8). Expository texts present information and are organized around various structures. They are usually more challenging for readers because they incorporate several structures rather than having a single structure like a narrative text. They come in the form of books, anthology selections, magazine articles, newspaper articles, and others.

FIGURE 2.8

A Story Map

STORY MAP

Setting: *Time*   *Place*

Characters:

Problem:

Action:

Outcome:

Authentic literature is motivating for students; it captivates their attention and engages them in learning (Huck, 1989; Sanders, 1987). It provides students with natural language texts that continually help them develop and expand their own language structures (Sawyer, 1987). Real (authentic) literature is generally easy for most students to understand (Simons & Ammon, 1989).

Sometimes authentic literature is too difficult for beginning readers to read on their own. Students may lack the skills to sequentially decode the words and often do not know many of the high-frequency words because they have not yet been taught them. For this reason, authentic literature needs to be used concurrently with other types of texts.

Having students read authentic literature is the goal of the literacy program. In beginning reading, this literature should be used in read alouds to develop and expand students' oral language, vocabulary, background, and prior knowledge. The listening experiences at these levels should serve as the basis for directly and systematically teaching critical comprehension strategies (National Reading Panel, 2000a).

As soon as students develop some degree of independence in decoding, they should have repeated instructional and independent opportunities to read authentic literature. This literature should then continue as the core of the literacy program. It should be carefully selected so that it is appropriate for the students' reading abilities.

Selecting Authentic Literature

Selecting the appropriate texts and authentic literature for the literacy program is both a critical and a challenging process. What constitutes "good literature" is a much-debated topic (Goodman & Goodman, 1991). Although this judgment is generally a personal matter, it is possible to select a variety of quality literature for your students. Since thousands of new books are published annually, literature selection is an ongoing process that should involve you, other readers, the librarian or media specialist, students, parents, and other interested persons. There are four basic criteria to consider in selecting literature: developmental appropriateness, student appeal, literary quality, and cultural and social authenticity.

The developmental appropriateness of a book is determined by looking at the concepts and general complexity of the text. Are the concepts ones your students will know? Have they had experience with them? Is the text written in a clear style that your students will find easy to understand? These are the types of questions that can guide your selection.

The general nature of the guidelines just described may prompt you to think that determining developmental appropriateness is an arbitrary process. However, keep in mind that literature has no grade level; a book is not appropriate solely for one grade level. Rather, a book may be used in different ways at different grade levels. For example, *Ira Says Goodbye* (Waber, 1988) may be read aloud to children in kindergarten but may be read independently by second or third graders.

Student appeal may well be one of the most important aspects to consider. The books selected need to appeal to students, capture their imaginations, and entice them to want to read more and more. Appeal may best be determined by the students themselves. However, when you cannot consult with each student, you should consider such sources as "Children's Choices" and "Young Adults' Choices," published annually each fall in *The Reading Teacher* and the *Journal of Reading*, both publications of the International Reading Association. These listings present favorite books voted on by children and young adults. *The Reading Teacher* also publishes an annual list of teachers' choices. You may want to consult editions from previous years for those listings.

Literary quality is determined by looking at elements of plot, characterization, setting, theme, style, and point of view that create memorable texts. Determining the literary quality of books is a large task for a busy teacher. A major reason that many schools use a basal series is that groups of professionals have selected quality literature for their program. Even so, you need to know how to select additional appropriate books for your class. The following sources can help you evaluate new books as they become available:

- *The WEB* describes how books on specific topics may be used in the classroom. Published four times a year by Martha L. King Center for Language and Literacy, The Ohio State University, 29 Woodruff Avenue, Columbus, OH 43210-1177.

- *The Horn Book Magazine* reviews books from many perspectives. Write to The Horn Book Magazine, Park Square Building, 31 St. James Avenue, Boston, MA 02116.

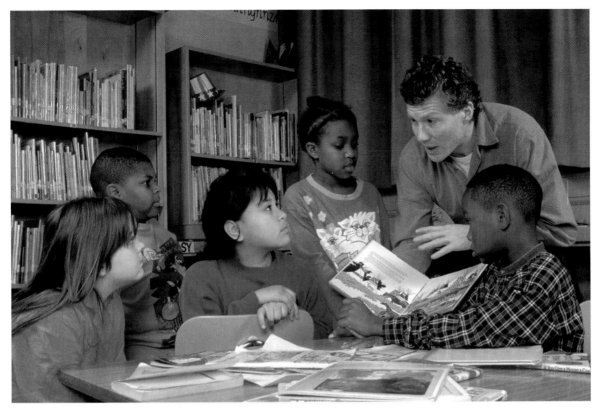

The librarian helps students select new books. © Will Hart/PhotoEdit

- *The New Advocate* provides articles and book reviews. Published four times a year by Christopher-Gordon Publishers, 480 Washington Street, Norwood, MA 02062.
- *Book Links* presents reviews of books that have been grouped by thematic areas. Published bimonthly by the American Library Association, 50 East Huron Street, Chicago, IL 60611.

In addition, the following professional journals review literature in each edition:

- *The Reading Teacher* (elementary), published by the International Reading Association
- *Journal of Adolescent and Adult Literacy* (middle school, junior high school, high school), published by the International Reading Association
- *Language Arts* (elementary), published by the National Council of Teachers of English

You can keep up with reviews of new books or books about children's literature by contacting the National Council of Teachers of English (NCTE) Web site at www.ncte.org and the International Reading Association (IRA) Web site at www.ira.org.

Cultural and social authenticity must also be considered when you are selecting literature. "Through multicultural literature, children of the majority culture learn to respect values and contributions of minority groups in the United States and the values and contributions of people in other parts of the world. . . . The wide range of multicultural themes also helps children develop an understanding of social change" (Norton, 1999, p. 581). Reading and responding to books about a variety of cultural and social situations helps students develop an appreciation and understanding of how others live and work together. Books such as *The Patchwork Quilt* (Flournoy, 1985), *Hawk, I'm Your Brother* (Baylor, 1976), *Felita* (Mohr, 1979), and *The Rainbow People* (Yep, 1989) are examples of the types of literature that should be a part of every literacy program. You may also want to read Norton's (1999) chapter on multicultural literature.

TABLE 2.9	Criteria for Leveling Books for Beginning Reading
Levels 1–4	Consistent placement of print Repetition of 1–2 sentence patterns (1–2 word changes) Oral language structures Familiar objects and actions Illustrations provide high support
Levels 5–8	Repetition of 2–3 sentence patterns (phrases may change) Opening, closing sentences vary Or, varied simple sentence patterns Predominantly oral language structures Many familiar objects and actions Illustrations provide moderate to high support
Levels 9–12	Repetition of 3 or more sentence patterns Or, varied sentence patterns (repeated phrases or refrains) Blend of oral and written language structures Illustrations provide moderate support
Levels 13–15	Varied sentence patterns (may have repeated phrases or refrains) Or, repeated patterns in cumulative form Written language structures Oral structures appear in dialogue Conventional story, literary language Specialized vocabulary for some topics Illustrations provide low–moderate support
Levels 15–20	Elaborated episodes and events Extended descriptions Links to familiar stories Literary language Unusual, challenging vocabulary Illustrations provide low support

Source: Reprinted by permission from *Bridges to Literacy: Learning from Reading Recovery* by Diane DeFord, Carol Lyons, and Gay Su Pinnell. Published by Heinemann, a division of Reed Elsevier, Inc., Portsmouth, NH. All rights reserved. Copyright © 1998 by Barbara Peterson. Originally appeared in *Characteristics of Texts That Support Beginning Readers* by Barbara Peterson and published by The Ohio State University.

TABLE 2.10	Criteria for Leveling Books for Grades 3–8

Category I	Small amount of print per page. (The majority of pages have 1–3 sentences.)
	Pictures/illustrations are clear and uncluttered and directly support the text.
	Text for both fiction and nonfiction is narrative, with a clear, easy-to-follow story line.
Category II	Still a small amount of print per page, but text can increase to 1–2 paragraphs on the majority of pages.
	Short lines of dialogue may increase the amount of text per page.
	Pictures/illustrations still give direct text support; 2–3 spot vignettes on a page are appropriate.
	Expository nonfiction on highly focused topics with simply stated main ideas and few supporting details. (Often a picture or photograph illustrates each main idea.)
	Short captions (a word, a phrase, or one sentence) may accompany pictures. Simple diagrams with clear labels are appropriate.
	Narrative story lines remain simple.
Category III	Increasing print with several paragraphs per page. Books themselves become longer.
	Pictures/illustrations are less supportive of text. Captions may increase in length.
	Clear story line, but now multiple characters are appropriate (narrative texts).
	Topics may broaden; main ideas increase in complexity with more supporting details (expository texts).
	Text may contain a secondary element, such as sidebars or speech balloons.
	More inferencing is required by the nature of the text.
Category IV	Text increases to fill the page.
	Story lines become more complex: there may be subplots, mysteries, or multiple problems (narrative texts) that require critical thinking.
	Topics expand to include subtopics, which may be organized by chapter; main ideas increase in complexity and contain more details, requiring readers to organize and analyze information.
	Picture support is less direct; pages may be designed more for visual effect than to help readers with the text. Chapter books may contain spot art or none at all.
Category V	Number of chapters increases.
	Size of print decreases as amount of text per page increases.
	Picture support is minimal or nonexistent. Book length may increase to 80–100 pages.

(continued)

TABLE 2.10	**Criteria for Leveling Books for Grades 3–8** (continued)
	Greater inferencing skills are required to follow complex story lines containing multiple characters. Problems, which are multiple, are more sophisticated (narrative texts).
	Increasing amount of new information is presented with more complex text organization. Readers may be required to sift through information and make decisions about how relevant each detail is to the topic at hand.
Category VI	Book may increase in length past 100 pages.
	Size of print may decrease, reflecting the style of on-level literature.
	Pictures as support tools are nonexistent. Photos or illustrations may appear as resources in expository texts.
	Complex story lines require retention of details and application of inferences based on cumulative reading of text. Text may require readers to make judgments about characters and events.
	Expository text organization is increasingly complex and specific. Text may explore issues that arise within certain historical, social, or scientific topics. Readers will need to evaluate information to distinguish fact from opinion.

Source: From *Soar to Success!: The Reading Intervention Program* Teacher's Manual, Level 7 in *Houghton Mifflin Reading: Invitations to Literacy* by J. David Cooper, and John J. Pikulski, et al. Copyright © 2001 by Houghton Mifflin Company. All rights reserved. Reprinted by permission of the publisher.

Leveling Books for Instruction

Texts and literature for the literary program need to be placed in a sequence of difficulty, especially at the beginning levels of reading instruction. This is essential until students become independent in decoding, which occurs by the end of grade 2 for most students. Even beyond the beginning reading levels, however, there are times when books need to be placed in an order of difficulty for instructional purposes. For many years, this was done by using some type of a readability formula; however, many problems are associated with the various readability procedures (Weaver & Kintsch, 1991). It is best to use criteria other than some score derived from a formula to place texts in a sequence or gradient of difficulty. Table 2.9 presents criteria for leveling texts for beginning reading, and Table 2.10 presents criteria for leveling books in grades 3–8. There are several variations of these criteria (Fountas & Pinnell, 1996, 2001).

The leveling procedure is usually carried out by a committee of teachers. Each teacher reads the text under consideration and compares the text to the criteria to determine the level of placement; a consensus is then reached. This procedure involves judgment; it takes into consideration more factors than a score derived from a mathematical formula. Many publishing companies now use similar criteria for their books.

🦋 Summary

A balanced or comprehensive literacy program combines teacher-directed instruction and student-centered activities. The model for the comprehensive literacy program includes these components: Daily Independent Reading, Daily Independent Writing, Reading: Learning Skills and Strategies, Reading: Applying Skills and Strategies, Teacher Modeled Writing, and Developmentally Appropriate Writing. For struggling readers, there is a block of additional instruction called Intervention.

Within the classroom, the teacher creates the circumstances and conditions that support instruction. Scaffolding is a significant aspect of all instruction as students move toward independence. The five modes of reading are: independent reading, cooperative reading, guided reading, shared reading, and read aloud. The five modes of writing are: independent writing, collaborative/cooperative writing, guided writing, shared writing, and write aloud. By using various modes of reading and writing, you scaffold instruction to meet the individual needs of students.

The three important frameworks for developing standards-based lessons are: the literacy lesson, minilessons or focus lessons, and guided listening lessons. Components of each framework have been described and illustrated in this chapter.

Different types of texts are used in a comprehensive literacy program: wordless books, predictable texts, created texts, and authentic literature. The first three types are particularly appropriate as students acquire strategies and skills. However, the goal of all literacy instruction is to have students read authentic literature.

Guidelines are needed for selecting quality authentic literature. These include: focusing on developmental appropriateness, student appeal, literary quality, and cultural and social authenticity. Another important part of selecting books is leveling them for appropriate instructional use. Two sets of criteria were presented for leveling texts.

For Additional Reading

Au, K. H., Carroll, J. H., & Scheu, J. A. (1997). *Balanced literacy instruction: A teacher's resource book* (pp. 1–26). Norword, MA: Christopher-Gordon Publishers.

Dorn, L., Frenc, C., & Jones, T. (1998). *Apprenticeship in literacy.* York, ME: Stenhouse.

Drucker, M. J. (2003). What reading teachers should know about ESL learners. *The Reading Teacher, 57*(1), 22–29.

Educational Leadership. (1990). Vol. 47, No. 4. Entire issue on cooperative learning.

Falk, B. (2000). *The heart of the matter: Using standards and assessment to learn.* Portsmouth, NH: Heinemann.

Ivey, G. (2003). "The teacher makes it more explainable" and other reasons to read aloud in the intermediate grades. *The Reading Teacher, 56*(8), 812–814.

Jenkins, J. R. et. al. (2003). Decodable text—Where to find it. *The Reading Teacher, 57*(20), 185–189.

Leu, Jr., D. J., Castek, J., Henry, L. A., Ciro, J., & McMullan, M. (2004). The lessons that children teach us: Integrating children's literature and the new literacies of the Internet. *The Reading Teacher, 57*(5), 497–503.

Peterson, B. (2001). *Literacy pathways: Selecting books to support new readers.* Portsmouth, NH: Heinemann.

Risko, V. J., & Bromley, K. (Eds.). (2001). *Collaboration for diverse learners.* Newark, DE: International Reading Association.

Trelease, J. (1989). *The new read-aloud handbook.* New York: Penguin Books.

Zemelman, S., Daniels, H., & Hyde, A. (1998). *Best practice: New standards for teaching and learning in America's schools* (pp. 24–82). Portsmouth, NH: Heinemann.

Poetry by Shel Silverstein and Jack Prelutsky

Where the Sidewalk Ends (Silverstein, 1974)
A Light in the Attic (Silverstein, 1981)
Falling Up (Silverstein, 1996)
The Baby Uggs Are Hatching (Prelutsky, 1982)
The New Kid on the Block (Prelutsky, 1984)
Ride a Purple Pelican (Prelutsky, 1986)
Tyrannosaurus Was a Beast (Prelutsky, 1988)
Poems of a Nonny Mouse (Prelutsky, 1989)
Beneath a Blue Umbrella (Prelutsky, 1990)
Something Big Has Been Here (Prelutsky, 1990)
A Pizza the Size of the Sun (Prelutsky, 1996)
It's Raining Pigs and Noodles (Prelutsky, 2000)
Awful Ogre's Awful Day (Prelutsky, 2001)
Dog Days: Rhymes Around the Year (Prelutsky, 2001)
The Frog Wore Red Suspenders (Prelutsky, 2002)

Anthologies of Poetry

A Child's Garden of Verses (Stevenson, 1885/1981)
Cool Melons—Turn to Frogs (Gollub, 1998)
Insectlopedia (Florian, 1998)
Joyful Noises: Poems for Two Voices (Fleischman, 1988)
Neighborhood Odes (Soto, 1992)
A New Treasury of Children's Poetry: Old Favorites and New Discoveries (Cole, 1984)
The Poetry of Black America: Anthology of the 20th Century (Adoff, 1973)
Random House Book of Poetry for Children (Prelutsky, 1983)
This Same Sky (Nye, 2001)

🖳 For Exploration: Electronic Products and Resources

Online Children's Literature Journals

ALAN: The Assembly of Literature for Adolescents

The Assembly on Literature for Adolescents is one of the NCTE's special-interest groups. Founded in November 1973, ALAN is made up of teachers, authors, librarians, publishers, teacher-educators and their students, and others who are particularly interested in the area of young adult (YA) literature. ALAN also publishes *The ALAN Review*, which contains articles on YA literature and its teaching, interviews with authors, reports on publishing trends, current research on YA literature, and reviews of new books.
http://www.alan-ya.org/

Book Links

An online magazine designed for teachers, librarians, library media specialists, booksellers, parents, and other adults interested in connecting children with high-quality books. *Book Links* provides comprehensive information for using books in the classroom, including thematic bibliographies with related discussion questions and activities, author and illustrator interviews and essays, and articles by educators on practical ways to turn children onto reading. Reviews are from quality children's journals such as *Horn Book, Library School Journal, Book Links,* and *Kirkus*. Each issue of *Book Links* focuses on a core curriculum area (science, social studies, language arts, history, geography, or multicultural literature). On this site you will find highlights of the current issue, a searchable index, information about subscribing, and submissions guidelines.
http://www.ala.org/BookLinks/

The Bulletin of the Center for Children's Books

One of the nation's leading children's book review journals for school and public librarians, this *Bulletin* is devoted entirely to the review of current books for children. For each book, it provides concise summaries and critical evaluations; information on content, reading level, strengths and weaknesses, and quality of format; and suggestions for curricular use.
http://alexia.lis.uiuc.edu/puboff/bccb/

Carol Hurst's Children's Literature Site

This comprehensive Web site provides information on featured and reviewed children's literature, curriculum and thematic topics, and professional resources, including a free online newsletter. This is a collection of reviews of great books for kids, ideas of ways to use them in the classroom, and collections of books and activities about particular subjects, curriculum areas, themes, and professional topics.
http://www.carolhurst.com

The Children's Corner of the *Boston Book Review*

The Children's Corner of the *Boston Book Review* seeks out and promotes the highest achievements in contemporary writing. Bringing readers into the ongoing project of literary life, the *BBR* features independent comment from preeminent writers, scholars, and intellectuals on today's most important children's books. Together with fiction, poetry, interviews, and essays, provocative reviews assess works in a wide variety of topics. The *BBR* provides high-quality book reviews.
http://www.bookwire.com/bookwire/bbr/children/children.html

The Horn Book Guide Online

Instant access to more than thirty-five thousand reviews can be found at *The Horn Book Guide Online*. All reviews are searchable by author, illustrator, title, subject, bibliographic information, as well as by rating. This site is available by subscription.
http://www.hornbookguide.com/

The Lion and the Unicorn

A theme- and genre-centered journal of international scope committed to serious, ongoing discussions of children's literature.
http://muse.jhu.edu/journals/lion_and_the_unicorn/index.html

The Looking Glass

An electronic journal about children's literature that combines an interest in the traditional with an eye for the modern. Includes scholarly articles of interest to both specialists and nonspecialists.
http://www.the-looking-glass.net/

School Library Journal Online

Provides librarians who work with young people in school and public libraries with indispensable information needed to manage libraries—from creating high-quality collections to understanding how technology can assist (or hinder) learning.
http:// www.slj.com/

Electronic Products and Resources: Web Sites on Children's Literature

Andy Holt's Virtual Library KIDStack

This page targets *Collections of Children's Literature*. Collections are divided into "English," "French," and "Spanish" sections.
http://www.utm.edu/vlibrary/docust5.shtml

Barahona Center for the Study of Books in Spanish for Children and Adolescents

The Barahona Center at California State University, San Marcos, provides information about recommended books in Spanish for children and adolescents. More than six thousand books are in the center's database, selected because of their quality of art and writing, presentation of material, and appeal to the intended audience.
http://www.csusm.edu/csbs/english/

The Center for Children's Books

The Center for Children's Books (CCB) houses a noncirculating collection of more

than fourteen thousand recent and historically significant trade books for youth, birth through high school, plus review copies of nearly all trade books published in the United States in the current year. There are over one thousand professional and reference books on the history and criticism of literature for youth, literature-based library and classroom programming, and storytelling. Although the collection is noncirculating, it is available for examination by scholars, teachers, librarians, students, and other educators.
http://www.lis.uiuc.edu/~ccb/

Children's Book Council

The Children's Book Council (CBC) is a nonprofit trade organization. Its members are U.S. publishers and packagers of children's and young adult trade books. The CBC "is dedicated to encouraging literacy and the use and enjoyment of children's books." Check out the CBC *Showcase*, which features a thematic bibliography of books published by members. A new list is featured every other month. Each bibliography features over forty poetry books for children, with a link to cover art and a detailed summary for each book. The *Showcase Archives* contains about thirty bibliographies. The topics include multicultural books, nature and science, folk and fairy tales, historical fiction, and biographies. Other topics include holidays, mysteries, and the African-American experience.
http://www.cbcbooks.org

Children's Literature: Beyond Basals

This site provides hundreds of in-depth guides for using children's literature in K–12 classrooms, curriculum ideas, picture books for older and reluctant readers, and links to other Web sources on children's literature.
http://www.srv.net/~gale/

Children's Literature Web Guide

This site is a wonderful resource on authors and stories on the Web; readers theater; resources for teachers, parents, storytellers, writers, and illustrators; book awards; recommended book lists; journals; reviews; indexes; research on children's books; and much more. It gathers together and categorizes the growing number of Internet resources related to books for children and young adults. Much of the information provided in these pages comes from fans, schools, libraries, and commercial enterprises involved in the book world.
http://www.acs.ucalgary.ca/~dkbrown/index.html

Database of Award-Winning Children's Literature

Search this database to create a tailored reading list of quality children's literature or to find out if a book has won one of the indexed awards. Designed primarily for use by librarians or teachers intervening for a child-reader, but anyone can use it to find the best in children's literature, including parents, book store personnel, and children and young adults themselves. *DAWCL* has over four thousand records from *fifty awards* across five English-speaking countries (United States, Canada, Australia, New Zealand, and the United Kingdom).
http://www.dawcl.com/

Jim Trelease on Reading

This site offers a complete guide to Jim Trelease's work and is aimed at parents, teachers, librarians, and college students—anyone interested in children's reading and education. Stresses the importance of reading aloud to children of all ages.
http://www.trelease-on-reading.com/

Kathy Schrock's Guide for Educators: Literature and Language Arts

This comprehensive site lists numerous Web sites on children's literature, including poetry, fables and multicultural stories, lesson plans, and writing and grammar.
http://school.discovery.com/schrockguide/arts/artlit.html

Kay E. Vandergrift's Special Interest Page

Created by Dr. Kay E. Vandergrift of Rutgers University, this comprehensive Web site on children's literature is an outstanding resource for educators of all levels. The site consists of information on gender and culture in picture books, young adult literature, research, literature and technology, the history of children's literature, censorship, intellectual freedom and the Internet, and copyright laws and the World Wide Web.
http://www.scils.rutgers.edu/~kvander/

Once upon a Time

This site, created by Dr. Mary Ellen Van Camp of Ball State University, contains many resources on children's literature. Includes information on professional associations, children's literature around the world, children's literature awards, poetry, authors and illustrators, and professional resources.
http://www.bsu.edu/classes/vancamp/ouat.html

Random House's Teachers' Resource Center

This site, sponsored by Random House, has teacher's guides on books for reluctant readers, thematic instruction, authors and illustrators, books by grade level, and Newbery Award winners.
http://www.randomhouse.com/teachers/

Read Aloud Books Too Good to Miss

The Read-Aloud Books Too Good to Miss program is a project of the Association for Indiana Media Educators. Each year, a committee of media specialists, classroom teachers, reading teachers, principals, bookstore operators, and university faculty members is formed to develop five read-aloud lists–one each for primary school, intermediate school, middle school, high school, and ageless.
http://www.ilfonline.org/Programs/ReadAloud%2001-02/readaloud.htm

For Further Online Reading

Balanced Reading Instruction: A Review of the Literature

Children's learning within the social context of interactive writing depends on many different dynamics. A sociocultural perspective provides an opportunity to view and interpret writing instruction as socially constructed, dynamic, and situated in multiple interdependent cultural and historical contexts.
http://www.ncrel.org/sdrs/timely/briiss.htm

Electronic Collaboration: Children's Literature in the Classroom

This article is based on a project that explored whether electronic discussion can increase students' breadth and depth of thinking about issues in complex children's literature. Another goal was for teachers to extend their experience into the classroom by engaging their own students in similar projects.

http://www.readingonline.org/electronic/elec_index.asp?HREF=/electronic/RT/9-99RT.html

"A Horizon of Possibilities": A Critical Framework for Transforming Multiethnic Literature Instruction

http://www.readingonline.org/articles/art_index.asp?HREF=willis/index.html

Inclusion Literature

This article from the *ALAN Review* includes children's and adolescent literature written by parents and teachers related to inclusion issues such as self-esteem and individuality.

http://scholar.lib.vt.edu/ejournals/ALAN/spring98/andrews.html

Reading Aloud—Are Students Ever Too Old?

This article on the *Education World* site discusses why children are never too old to be read to. Includes a list of resources on reading aloud.

http://www.education-world.com/a_curr/curr081.shtml

Using the Internet and Children's Literature to Support Interdisciplinary Instruction

This article describes several types of resources on the Internet for children's literature that may be used to support interdisciplinary instruction: central sites, project sites, author Web sites, lesson plans, and electronic mailing lists to support others as they seek to integrate the Internet and children's literature with classroom instruction.

http://www.readingonline.org/electronic/elec_index.asp?HREF=/electronic/RT/9-00_column.html

Electronic Communication Resources

Mailing lists, or listservs, can provide support for people interested in children's literature. To subscribe to a list, send a subscription message to the administrative address listed beside each list name below. Type the administrative address in the "To:" box of your e-mail window. Leave the "Subject" box blank. Then type a subscription message in the first line of the "Message" box. The subscription message should contain the following information:

> *Subscribe [listname] [your first name] [your last name]*

Example for subscribing to KIDLIT-L:
To: listserv@bingvmb.cc.binghamton.edu
Subject:
Message: subscribe KIDLIT-L Jane Doe

Mailing Lists

CHILDLIT (listserv@email.rutgers.edu)

This is a list for people interested in the criticism and theory of children's literature. Subscribers include librarians, K–12 teachers, teacher educators, publishers, authors, illustrators, and parents who are very supportive.

KIDLIT-L (listserve@bingvmb.cc.binghamton.edu)

This is a list for people interested in children's literature. Many librarians, teachers, and teacher educators subscribe. It is also a very supportive list.

Prior Knowledge: Activating and Developing Concepts and Vocabulary

3

✓ **STANDARDS FOCUS**
NCTE/IRA Standards: 1, 2, 3, 7, 10, 11, 12
Standards for Reading Professionals: 1, 2, 3, 4, 5

"Educators Speak p. 110

Using a Project That Cuts Across the Curriculum
—*Lynne Pistochini, Folsum, California*"

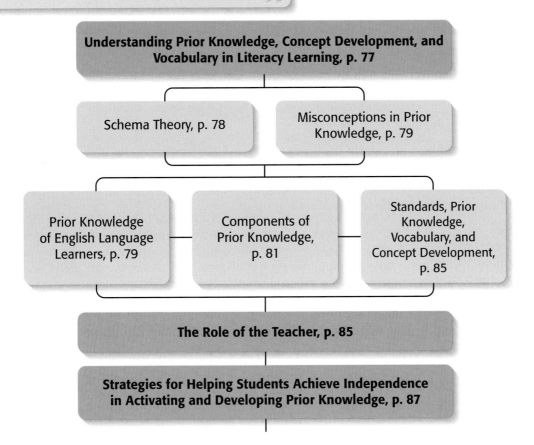

Understanding Prior Knowledge, Concept Development, and Vocabulary in Literacy Learning, p. 77

Schema Theory, p. 78

Misconceptions in Prior Knowledge, p. 79

Prior Knowledge of English Language Learners, p. 79

Components of Prior Knowledge, p. 81

Standards, Prior Knowledge, Vocabulary, and Concept Development, p. 85

The Role of the Teacher, p. 85

Strategies for Helping Students Achieve Independence in Activating and Developing Prior Knowledge, p. 87

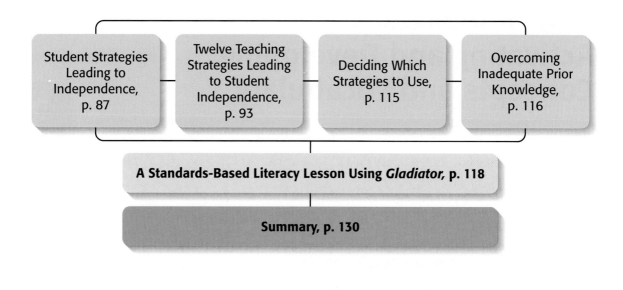

Terms
You Need to Know

- anticipation guide
- background knowledge (or prior knowledge)
- concept development
- expository text
- graphic organizer
- K-W-L
- narrative text
- picture walk
- prediction
- preview and predict
- prior knowledge
- project
- quick writing
- role playing
- schema theory (pl. schemata)

L et's visit a fourth-grade classroom where the teacher and students are beginning a unit about Abraham Lincoln.

Mr. Willett uses several strategies to engage students right from the beginning. Mr. Willett wants to know what his students already know about Abraham Lincoln and about the historical period in which Lincoln lived. These include concepts related to trouble between the North and South, as well as vocabulary terms used to discuss those concepts, such as the word emancipation.

First, Mr. Willett had given his students five minutes to write what they knew about Abraham Lincoln. He then had students work in small groups. They were to pool what they, as a group, already knew about the topic. They were also to brainstorm about what they would like to learn about Lincoln during the unit of study. One student in each group served as a recorder, writing the information to be shared with the class later. After the small-group discussion, Mr. Willett brought the groups together.

Mr. Willett then displayed a chart (the K-W-L chart will be discussed in detail later in this chapter). Each group reported what it had discussed and recorded, and Mr. Willett summarized this group information on the chart. Now Mr. Willett had a picture of the collective background knowledge and interests of his students.

The chart showed that the students already knew a great deal about Lincoln, though some of that knowledge was erroneous and there were some gaps in their background knowledge. During the unit, Mr. Willett would be sure to lead students to correct mistaken ideas as well as increase their background knowledge. The chart also showed that the students were very interested in learning more about Lincoln.

Terms
You Need to Know

- semantic mapping
- story map
- strategy
- structured preview
- text structure
- text walk
- vocabulary

In this example, Mr. Willett was activating his class's prior knowledge before starting the theme on Abraham Lincoln. Through his observations, he was able to assess how much the students knew, and to determine what additional background he needed to develop before introducing the first book they would read: the Newbery Award winner *Lincoln: A Photobiography* (Freedman, 1987). Mr. Willett used four techniques for activating prior knowledge: a quick-writing exercise, brainstorming, the K-W-L strategy (Ogle, 1986), and small- and large-group discussion. Through these techniques, Mr. Willett determined the level of prior knowledge students already had in terms of vocabulary likely to be met in reading about this historical period and something about their understanding of the concepts such as the issues confronting Lincoln.

In Chapter 1 of this text, we established the importance of prior knowledge to successful literacy learning for students of all ages. In this chapter, we examine this area in more detail and focus on techniques and strategies that help students activate and develop their prior knowledge of concepts and vocabulary in thematic units and literacy lessons. Throughout this chapter, two major points are stressed:

- *Purpose:* Students must have a purpose for reading and writing; in part, this purpose is created by activating and developing prior knowledge, vocabulary, and concepts.
- *Independence:* Students must become independent in activating and developing their own prior knowledge and developing vocabulary if they are to construct meaning effectively.

All of the strategies presented in this chapter lead to these two goals.

Understanding Prior Knowledge, Concept Development, and Vocabulary in Literacy Learning

The concept of prior knowledge is not new to educators. For many years, educators have recommended that teachers make sure that their readers have the appropriate background for reading a given selection, because such background was believed to enhance learning (Smith, 1965). Essentially, *prior knowledge* is the sum of a person's previous learning and experience (Harris & Hodges, 1995) including **concept development** and **vocabulary.** The information Mr. Willett gained from his students through quick writing, discussion, and the use of K-W-L constituted their collective prior knowledge about Abraham Lincoln.

Research has clearly established that the process of constructing meaning through reading, writing, speaking, and listening is based on the **background knowledge,** or **prior knowledge** that individuals bring to the situation (Alexander & Jetton, 2000; Snow, Burns, & Griffin, 1998). The term *prior knowledge* always includes both understanding of concepts contained in the text to be read and the vocabulary, or language, used to talk about those concepts. After reviewing extensive research, Tierney and Cunningham (1984) concluded that "intervention research has supported the existence of a causal relationship between background knowledge and comprehension" (p. 612). More recent researchers have drawn similar conclusions. Researchers and educators use the terms *prior knowledge, background, background knowledge or information,* and *world knowledge* interchangeably; in this text, we will use the term *prior knowledge* when referring to all of these areas.

Prior knowledge affects construction of meaning for everyone, young and old, emergent reader and competent reader. A three-year-old child without some personal experience will not understand a story he or she hears. The most sophisticated reader will not understand a text when the concepts and language included in it are completely new. We are able to learn from texts only when we can, in effect, hook them onto something that is already in our background of experience. Prior knowledge and background development include the development of concepts and vocabulary.

Schema Theory

Our understanding of the importance of prior knowledge in literacy learning has developed through research based on **schema theory** (plural *schemata*), which assumes that individuals develop a cognitive structure of knowledge in their minds (Bartlett, 1932; Rumelhart, 1980). As individuals experience the world, they add new information to their schemata, which are divided into various interrelated categories. One way to picture this concept more concretely is to think of the mind as a large system of file folders. As one gains new knowledge and information, the mind creates a new file folder, or schema, or adds the information to an existing schema (Anderson & Pearson, 1984; Rumelhart, 1980). Then, as individuals develop and expand their schemata, they construct meaning by drawing from various schemata and building connections among them; that is, they make inferences. This process goes on continuously while a person engages in literacy tasks. Example 3.1 illustrates how the experience of reading expands one's schemata.

Example 3.1

You are going to read a magazine article about the pleasures of sailboat racing. As you begin to read, you think about what you know about sailboat racing; in the process you activate your schemata, which probably formed over many years of experience. If your schemata include positive, pleasant ideas, you will read the article differently than if they included negative, unpleasant ideas. If you have no schema or very limited schemata for sailboat racing, you will begin to form a schema as you read the article, and you will relate the information you gain to any other schemata you have about boats. For example, you may have a schema that relates sailboat racing to danger; if you read about how training reduces the dangers, you may form a new, broadened schema. Throughout the process of reading, you take the information from the text and either relate it to an existing schema or form a new schema.

Schema theory contends that individuals understand what they read only as it relates to what they already know. Anderson, Reynolds, Schallert, and Goetz (1977) demonstrated this very clearly through their research. They asked students in an educational psychology class and students in a weightlifting class to read the following passage and tell what they thought it was about. Read this passage for yourself and see what you think:

Rocky slowly got up from the mat and planned his escape. He hesitated a moment and thought. Things were not going well. What bothered him the most was being held, especially since the charge against him had been weak. He considered his present situation. The lock that held him was strong but he thought he could break it. He knew, however, that his timing had to be perfect. Rocky was aware that it was because of his early roughness that he had been penalized so severely—much too severely from his point of view. The situation was becoming frustrating; the pressure had been grinding on him far too long. He was being ridden unmercifully. Rocky was getting angry now. He felt he was ready to make his move. He knew that his success or failure depended on what he did in the next few seconds. (p. 372)

What was the focus of this paragraph? What topic came to your mind as you read? Most psychology students interpreted the passage as a prison escape, whereas the weightlifting students related it to a wrestling match. Thus, research supports the idea that individuals construct meaning in light of their prior knowledge and interests. Construction of meaning is an individual and personal matter (Rosenblatt, 1938/1976). Research in emergent literacy further supports this conclusion (Sulzby, 1989).

Misconceptions in Prior Knowledge

Although research has documented the significance of prior knowledge in students' ability to construct meaning, there is also evidence that some students bring incomplete or erroneous ideas to certain learning tasks. Such misconceptions can interfere with meaning construction (Driver & Erickson, 1983; Lipson, 1982, 1983), and numerous researchers have attempted to look at how this happens (Alvermann, Smith, & Readence, 1985; Dole & Smith, 1989; Hynd & Alvermann, 1986; Pace, Marshall, Horowitz, Lipson, & Lucido, 1989). In all instances, they have found that an individual's interpretation of the text was clearly influenced by erroneous or incomplete prior knowledge. Strategies for overcoming misconceptions are discussed later in this chapter.

Prior Knowledge of English Language Learners

In classrooms throughout the country, many children are learning English as a second language; such children may be referred to as multilingual, ESL (English as a Second Language) students, LEP (Limited English Proficiency) students, Students Acquiring English, or English Language Learners (ELLs).

Regardless of the term used, these are all students whose native language is not English. Some may have learned to read in their native language. Research has been shown that second-language learners are able to learn to read in their native language and in English at the same time (Barrera, 1983). They develop literacy and the ability to construct meaning through essentially the same process first-language learners use, the only differences being language structure, knowledge of the language, and cultural prior knowledge (Weber, 1991). Since second-language learners have an extensive base of prior knowledge that has not been developed around English and the cultural traditions of English, their prior knowledge needs to receive special attention. What children know in one language, they can access in a new language; they just need the English words for known concepts (Cummins, 1981).

Rigg and Allen (1989) have proposed five principles regarding the literacy development of second-language learners:

1. *People who are learning another language are, first of all, people.*
2. *Learning a language means learning to do the things you want to do with people who speak that language.*
3. *A person's second language, like the first, develops globally, not linearly.*
4. *Language develops best in a variety of rich contexts.*
5. *Literacy is part of language, so writing and reading develop alongside speaking and listening.* (p. viii)

You will notice that these principles do not differ significantly from what we already have said about helping all students learn to construct meaning. Second-language learners bring their own language and prior knowledge to the classroom, which we must build on and expand. As Rigg and Allen (1989) conclude, "We should offer our second-language students a rich bath of language, not a string of language beads, one bead at a time" (p. xi).

For further reading on this topic, see Au (1993), listed in the "For Additional Reading" section at the end of this chapter.

One way to access prior knowledge for English learners is through the technique called "preview, view, review" (Freeman & Freeman, 2000). A teacher, aide, or bilingual student previews the lesson in the student's first language, which activates background knowledge. If possible, students can discuss the topic with others who speak the same language. The lesson itself is the "view" portion and is taught in English. Then the "review" covers the key concepts in the student's first language; this can be done in pairs or small groups of students who speak the same language. After the review, students report to the teacher in English.

What does this mean for you as a teacher? Given the vast quantity of research related to schema theory and prior knowledge, you need to remember these points as you develop and conduct your literacy program:

* Prior knowledge is crucial to the successful construction of meaning for *all* learners.

* Some students will have incomplete or erroneous prior knowledge related to a topic. It is therefore important to assess a student's state of knowledge, if possible, before any learning experience.

* When students have erroneous or incomplete prior knowledge, it is possible to alter it and help them construct meaning more successfully.

In the remainder of this chapter, we focus on how to help students achieve independence in activating their own prior knowledge and how to build necessary prior knowledge when it does not already exist.

Components of Prior Knowledge

We know that an individual's prior knowledge includes concept development as well as the vocabulary, or language, to talk about concepts. We can also think about prior knowledge in these two ways: as overall prior knowledge and as text-specific or topic-specific prior knowledge.

Overall prior knowledge is the entire base of knowledge that students possess as a result of their accumulated experiences both in and out of school, such as being read to, taking trips, watching television, or seeing movies. The *independent reading and writing* component of the literacy program is critical for expanding this knowledge base (Center for the Study of Reading, n.d.). The more students read and write, the more extensive prior knowledge they build, which in turn improves their ability to construct meaning.

Two kinds of prior knowledge are important for a particular topic or theme. The first is called *text-specific knowledge;* it refers to knowledge about the structure of the text. Students need to know that informational text isn't organized the same way stories are and that not all informational texts are organized alike. The second kind of prior knowledge is called *topic-specific knowledge;* it refers to information related to the topic about which students are going to read. For example, suppose students are going to read *The Boys' War* (Murphy, 1990), a book about the experiences of the young boys who fought in the Civil War. You will want to be sure students have both kinds of background necessary: text-specific knowledge about how this book is organized and topic-specific knowledge about the Civil War.

Knowledge About the Text

Recall from Chapter 1 the two basic types of text: narrative and expository. Since students need some knowledge about both types of text, it is important that you have some basic understanding of them.

Narrative Texts. **Narrative texts** tell a story and are usually organized into a sequential pattern that includes a beginning, a middle, and an end. Within this pattern, any given narrative may be composed of several episodes, each consisting of characters, a setting, a problem, action, and a resolution of the problem (the outcome). These elements are the story's grammar, or basic plan. A graphic representation of these elements is called a **story map,** which can take many different forms. The exact map for a story depends on the story's structure.

The *theme* of a story is the basic idea, stated or unstated, around which the whole story is written. Often the theme is unstated, requiring the reader to infer it. The *plot* is the way in which the story is organized; it is made up of episodes. The *setting* is the place and time at which the story occurs. The *characters* are the people or animals who carry out the action in the story. The *problem* is the situation or situations that initiate, or lead to, other events in the story. Finally, the *action* is what happens as a result of the problem; it is composed of events that lead to the solution of the problem, which is called the *resolution,* or outcome.

Expository Texts. **Expository texts** present information organized around main ideas. These are the types of materials commonly found in informational books, textbooks, the World Wide Web, CD-ROMs, newspapers, and magazines. Students may have more difficulty reading expository texts than narrative texts because they have had less experience with them and because these texts may not follow a clear-cut pattern; instead, the organization depends on the type of information and purpose of the text. There are five commonly used organizational patterns of expository writing (Meyer, 1975; Meyer & Freedle, 1984):

- description,
- collection
- causation or cause-effect
- response, problem-solution, question-answer, or remark-reply
- comparison.

Let's take a look at each of these patterns in detail:

- *Description* presents information about a particular topic or gives characteristics of the topic. Unlike the other types of expository text structure, descriptive passages may not provide readers with clue words to aid in comprehension; therefore, readers must use the basic strategies they have learned for noting details and selecting the important information from the passage. However, the structure of descriptive passages can help the reader anticipate the type of content that is likely to follow.

- *Collection* presents a number of ideas or descriptions in a related group. Since the writer is presenting lists of related points, this structure is often called a *listing* or *sequence*, and the author frequently uses clue words such as *first, second, next,* and *finally* to introduce the points. Readers must infer the relationship between the listed points and the overall topic, noting details and identifying the sequence of ideas.

- The *causation,* or *cause-effect,* type of expository structure presents ideas so that a causal relationship is either stated or implied. This structure is frequently used in content-area textbooks and in newspaper and magazine articles. The author often uses clue words: *therefore, consequently, because, as a result of, since,* or *the reasons for.* The reader must identify the elements being related and either recognize or infer the cause-effect relationships.

- The *response* structure presents a problem, question, or remark followed by a solution, answer, or reply. This type of structure is often used in mathematics, science, and social studies. Sometimes (as in mathematics) the reader is expected to provide the solution. The author may use clue words such as *the problem is, the question is, one reason for the problem is, a solution is,* or *one answer is.*

- *Comparison* requires the reader to note the likenesses and differences between two or more objects or ideas. This type of structure is frequently found in social studies and science texts. The author uses clue words and phrases such as *like, unlike, resemble, different from, same as, alike,* or *similar to* to make comparisons. The reader must recognize the objects or ideas being compared and the points of similarity or difference among them. Often these points are not directly stated.

Table 3.1 presents an example of each of the five types of expository **text structure.** Remember, however, that one paragraph is not sufficient to determine the overall structure of a particular text, and within a given expository text, several of these structures may be present.

Students need to know enough about text structure to understand the basic differences between narrative and expository texts and to realize how this will help them construct meaning. This knowledge is gained through reading and writing and through mini-lessons, if needed. Knowledge of text structure will assist you in helping students activate the appropriate type of prior knowledge; it will also help you identify which words are key to understanding a selection and the types of questions to ask when using interactive guided reading.

See Chapter 5 for more about key vocabulary.

See Chapter 2 for more about interactive guided reading.

TABLE 3.1   **Examples of Expository Text Structures**

Expository Structure	Example
Description	The tiger is the master of the Indian jungle. It stalks its prey in deadly silence. For half an hour or more, it carefully watches and then slowly, placing one foot softly in front of the other, closes in.
Collection	As master of the Indian jungle, the male tiger plays many roles. First, he is the hunter of prey who stalks in deadly silence. He is the beauty of the jungle, an expert at doing nothing so that he can rest to be ready for his hunt. Finally, the lord of the jungle is the active seeker of mates, who begins his mating with a nuzzle but ends with a roar.
Causation or cause-effect	We observed the tiger from our vehicle as it stalked the herd of deer. As a result of the slight noise from our running camera, the tiger turned and knew we were there. This didn't stop it from returning to its intended prey. Slowly and carefully it moved forward, not making a sound. The deer were initially unaware of its presence, but because of the shifting winds they caught the tiger's scent. This was enough to scare them away.
Response, problem-solution, question-answer, or remark-reply	One problem to be resolved in tiger watching is transportation. How is it possible for observers to get close enough to a tiger without scaring it away or being attacked? Nature has helped solve this problem by making the tiger and the elephant friends. It is possible for an elephant carrying several people to get very near a tiger without even being noticed. If it weren't for this natural friendship, tiger watching would be virtually impossible.
Comparison	The power of the great tiger is like that of no other animal in the jungle. With one steady lunge, it can destroy its prey, seemingly without any effort at all. Unlike other predators, the tiger basks in the sun after an attack to prepare for its next kill. The actions of the tiger resemble those of no other animal in the Indian jungle.

Knowledge About the Topic

The second component of prior knowledge has to do with the topic of the materials to be read, which includes the key concepts and key terminology. This knowledge must be activated along with knowledge of text structure.

If your students were reading *Ronald Morgan Goes to Bat* (Giff, 1988), you might think you needed to activate prior knowledge of baseball, but this book is narrative. The problem is that Ronald really wanted to play baseball, but he couldn't catch or hit. The prior knowledge that is most likely to improve students' ability to construct meaning from this text is understanding what it is like to really want to do something even though one is not very good at it. This is what Beck (1984) refers to as *schema-directed prior knowledge development*. If the students had been preparing to read an expository text about baseball, the focus of the prior knowledge activation and development would have been the main ideas about baseball. However, strictly topical prior knowledge activation and development without consideration of the actual structure of the text does not improve students' ability to construct meaning (Beck, Omanson, & McKeown, 1982).

The prior knowledge needs for narrative text are determined by the story line. The needs for expository text are determined by the topic, main ideas, and structure of the text.

Suppose your students are about to read an article entitled "Birds in Winter," which describes the survival of birds during a blizzard. To construct meaning from this article, students must understand both the words and the concepts of *survival* and *blizzard*. Study Examples 3.2 and 3.3 to see the incorrect and correct ways to activate prior knowledge.

Example 3.2

Incorrect Method of Activating Prior Knowledge

Today we are going to read the article "Birds in Winter." Have you ever seen birds during the winter? What kinds of birds do you usually see in winter? How do birds get food in winter?

Notice that while the discussion in Example 3.2 is topical, it is too general. It does not include background development related to the main point or key concepts of the article. The discussion in Example 3.3, in contrast, clearly requires students to use whatever past experiences or schemata they have developed about birds and winter to make predictions. The teacher develops what students already know by relating that information to the concepts of *survival* and *blizzard*. Key-concept vocabulary is developed within the context of the background development. Finally, the teacher guides the students in summarizing the key points to make sure they have a schema for reading that relates directly to the article's main point.

Example 3.3

Correct Method of Activating Prior Knowledge (Schema Directed)

Today we are going to read the article "Birds in Winter." Before we read it, I want you to think about some important ideas that will help you understand what you read. From the title, what would you say this article is going to be about? (Record student responses, and discuss them.) This article is about how birds survive during a blizzard. (Relate the students' predictions to surviving in a blizzard.) What is a blizzard? (Students respond. Write a sentence on the chalkboard that contains the word *blizzard*, and discuss its meaning.) What does it mean to survive in a blizzard? What kinds of problems might birds have surviving during a blizzard? (Discuss these questions; list students' responses on the board, and discuss them. Add your own points to the discussion.)

Example:

1. A blizzard is a bad snowstorm with high winds.
2. Birds could have many problems surviving in a blizzard. These could include:
   getting food.
   not freezing to death.
   having water to drink.
   having a place to sleep that is protected from the wind.

Standards, Prior Knowledge, Vocabulary, and Concept Development

Students will be more likely to meet standards for reading with the teacher's thoughtful attention to helping them activate and develop the vocabulary and concepts that make up prior knowledge. All students have been acquiring concepts and vocabulary since the day they were born. However, not all students know how to bring that knowledge to the task of dealing with text. Through the kinds of interaction and guidance suggested throughout this book, you can help students draw on the prior knowledge they bring with them, as well as develop new concepts and vocabulary that result in expanded prior knowledge.

The Role of the Teacher

Whether planning literacy lessons within thematic units or for individual pieces of text, it is important to think about two things in relation to prior knowledge:

1. What prior knowledge probably needs to be activated and/or developed for the overall theme, for each book to be read during the theme, and for writing to be done? Or, what is needed for this particular piece of literature?
2. How independent are your students in using strategies to activate their own prior knowledge?

To make the first decision effectively, you must consider three elements: (1) the theme goals, (2) the theme topic, and (3) the literature.

You begin by considering what you want your students to accomplish in relation to the theme, in terms of their attitudes and habits and their ability to construct meaning.

Next, you think about the theme topic. What are the big ideas or concepts that students need to understand? For example, for a science fiction theme, do students know what science fiction is? Have they had prior experiences with it?

Then you think about each book to be read. Are the books narrative or expository? What are the story lines for the narratives? What are the main ideas of the expository texts? Knowing this will help you determine the prior knowledge that is most likely to help students construct meaning.

To judge students' independence, think about your students in relation to the theme goals, the topic, the literature to be read, and their ability to use various strategies. You can make this assessment by observing your students and using the strategies and techniques suggested in the next section of this chapter. *Good instruction incorporates assessment, and every instructional activity can also be used for assessment.* Therefore, the assessment of prior knowledge becomes a natural part of instruction.

Holmes and Roser (1987) have identified and compared five techniques for assessing prior knowledge during instruction:

- *Free recall:* "Tell me what you know about _____."

- *Word association:* "When you hear the words *thief, stolen,* and *detective,* what do you think of?"

- *Recognition:* Display the following key terms (phrases or sentences may be used), and ask students to tell which ones they think may be related to the book they are about to read, *The Polar Express* (Van Allsburg, 1985): *train, North Pole, wagon, conductor, sand, snow.*

- *Structured question:* In preparation for reading the book *Martin Luther King, Jr.: Free at Last* (Adler, 1986), ask students a set of prepared questions that will help you assess their prior knowledge: "Who was Martin Luther King, Jr.?" "What was Martin Luther King's concern in life?" "How did Martin Luther King try to reach his goal in life?"

- *Unstructured discussion:* "We are going to read about outer space. What do you know about it?"

Assessment is discussed in detail in Chapter 11.

Holmes and Roser (1987) found the last procedure, unstructured discussion, to be *least* effective and useful for assessing prior knowledge. Note that each of these techniques is designed to activate, or access, as well as *assess* prior knowledge.

One issue that concerns most teachers is how to assess and develop each student's prior knowledge when working with many students at the same time. It may not be possible to know everything about every student's prior knowledge of a particular theme, but you can get a good sense of what the group knows and the group's level of independence by using the types of teaching strategies suggested in the next section and by helping students develop independence in activating their own prior knowledge. The sample lesson presented at the conclusion of this chapter illustrates the process of selecting prior knowledge for a theme and for one book. You might want to look at that lesson now before reading the remainder of the chapter to get an overview of how the lesson functions (see page 118).

🦋 Strategies for Helping Students Achieve Independence in Activating and Developing Prior Knowledge

There are many ways to help learners become more strategic and independent readers (Paris et al., 1991), and prior knowledge activation and development may occur at three points:

1. When introducing a unit theme, at which time the focus is on the broad concepts and ideas needed to understand the theme
2. When each piece of literature is introduced within the lessons
3. Throughout the unit when you observe that certain students need more prior knowledge to better understand what they are reading or writing

A **strategy** is a plan selected deliberately to accomplish a particular goal (Paris, Lipson, & Wixson, 1983; Paris et al., 1991). When students reach the point where they can use a strategy automatically, they have achieved independence in its use. A *student strategy* is one that students can use on their own to construct meaning. A *teaching strategy* is a plan or an activity that the teacher can use to accomplish a desired outcome.

This section of the chapter presents student and teaching strategies you can use to activate and develop the necessary concepts and vocabulary, or terminology, that constitute prior knowledge in various places throughout a thematic unit or for a specific piece of text. For each, we provide a description, procedures, advice on when to use, assessment value, and sometimes comments related to how the use might vary at various grade levels.

Student Strategies Leading to Independence

Two basic strategies students can use to activate their prior knowledge and set their own purposes for reading are **preview and predict** and **K-W-L.** Table 3.2 presents an overview of these strategies and indicates when they should be used.

TABLE 3.2 **Student Strategies for Activating and Developing Prior Knowledge**

Strategy	Type of Text	Comments
Preview and predict	Narrative or expository	For all students; variations may
• Story map prediction	Narrative	be used to increase motivation
• Preview and self-question	Expository	and interest in using the strategy.
K-W-L	Expository	For all students; good for introducing a thematic unit.

Preview and Predict

Description. This strategy combines the processes of previewing and **prediction,** both of which have been shown to be effective in helping students construct meaning (Fielding, Anderson, & Pearson, 1990; Graves & Cooke, 1980; Graves, Cooke, & LaBerge, 1983; Hansen, 1981). Students look over the material to be read and then predict what they think will happen (narrative text) or what they will learn (expository text). This is the first step in inferencing, which is ongoing in the process of constructing meaning. As they read or after completing the reading, students decide whether their predictions have been confirmed, verified, or changed.

Procedures. Students begin by reading the title. Then they look at the pictures or illustrations to get a sense of what will be covered. They decide whether this is a story or informational text. Using their prior knowledge, or background of experiences, and the information gained from their preview, students then predict what will happen or what they will learn. For beginning readers and primary children, the preview should be very simple, focusing on the title and illustrations. Older students can read the first few paragraphs of the text and/or captions under the illustrations.

See Chapter 7 for a discussion of monitoring strategies.

Chapter 4 discusses modeling in detail.

After completing the preview, students read to verify predictions. They will be monitoring their reading (thinking about their predictions and changing them as they read). One effective way to help students learn and remember to use this and other strategies is to display a strategy poster such as is shown in Figure 3.1. Adjust the wording on the poster for different grade levels. Remember that all strategies must be modeled to be learned effectively (Pressley et al., 1990).

When to Use. The preview and predict strategy is effective with both narrative and expository text and is most effective when students have some knowledge of the topic. With second-language learners or students having difficulty constructing meaning, this strategy works best under the teacher's direction and/or in combination with another strategy. When students are just beginning to learn any strategy, teacher guidance is recommended.

Assessment Value. By observing responses during the preview and predict process, you should be able to assess the status of students' prior knowledge in terms of type of text, concepts, and vocabulary. From this information, you can decide on the need for additional prior knowledge development activities.

Comments. The preview and predict strategy will help students activate their prior knowledge and set their own purposes for reading. The real power of this strategy will become evident when students use it on their own. If students do not see its importance or refuse to use it, it is critical that you discuss and model its importance. This is most likely to succeed when students have repeated successful opportunities to use the strategy.

One variation of preview and predict is story map prediction, which is specifically for narrative texts. Training in the use of story maps has proven to be effective in helping students improve their comprehension (Pressley et al., 1990). Beginning readers should predict about one or two elements of the story. For example, the title and pictures may be sufficient to predict setting and characters. Of course, you won't ask students to predict all the action in a story, because this is usually not possible; furthermore, even if it could be done, there would be little point to reading the story.

FIGURE 3.1

Strategy Poster for Preview and Predict

PREVIEW AND PREDICT

BEFORE READING

(1) What is this about?

(2) I think this story/ informational text is going to…

DURING READING

(3) Am I confirming my predictions? Do I need to change my predictions?

AFTER READING

(4) Were my predictions confirmed or changed?

A variation, preview and self-question, is used with expository texts. Students preview the text and then pose questions they think they can answer from their reading.

K-W-L Strategy

Description. K-W-L is another strategy for activating students' prior knowledge and helping them determine their purpose for reading expository texts. This strategy requires students to focus on three questions, two before they read and one after they read: what I *know* (K), what I *want* to learn (W), and what I *learned* and still need to learn (L). This strategy, developed by Ogle (1986), is the one Mr. Willett was using at the beginning of this chapter. The two before-reading questions help students activate their prior knowledge and set their purposes for reading by raising questions they want to answer. The driving force behind this strategy is the students and their ideas and questions.

Procedures. Each student has a worksheet such as the one in Figure 3.2. For the first two steps, the teacher leads students in a discussion of the topic for the selection they are going to read. During the last step, students write down their answers to the questions posed before reading.

1. *Step K—what I know* begins with students brainstorming what they know about the topic. In keeping with the need to have schema-directed prior knowledge activation and development, the teacher selects a topic specific to the main ideas and key concepts of the material students will read. Ogle (1986) states the following:

FIGURE 3.2

K-W-L Strategy Sheet

K-W-L STRATEGY

1. K—What we *know*	W—What we *want* to find out	L—What we *learned* and still need to learn

2. Categories of information we expect to use
   - A.
   - B.
   - C.
   - D.
   - E.
   - F.
   - G.

When the class will read about sea turtles, use the words sea turtles *as the stimulus, not "What do you know about animals in the sea?" or "Have you ever been to the ocean?" A general discussion of enjoyable experiences on the beach may never elicit the pertinent schemata. . . . If there appears to be little knowledge of sea turtles in your students' experiences, then ask the next more general question, "What do you know about turtles?"* (p. 565)

Students record what they know on their worksheets and add to it as they share their ideas. At the same time, you should record these ideas on a larger version of the worksheet on the chalkboard, chart, or overhead projector. To broaden and deepen students' thinking during the discussion, Ogle suggests that the teacher ask students such questions as, "Where did you learn that?" or "How might you prove it?" When disagreement occurs, students must look for answers in the reading. If they seem to have little knowledge about the topic, you should ask more specific questions to draw out what information they do have.

The second part of the brainstorming involves identifying *categories of information* students might find in the material they will read. You might ask students to look over their list of what they know to see if any of the items fit into categories of information that might be found in their reading: for example, "foods turtles eat" or "use of sea turtles by humans."

2. *Step W—what I want to learn* is a natural outgrowth of step K. As students continue to share ideas, areas of uncertainty or lack of knowledge will arise, and you can help them turn these into questions they may answer by reading the text. As the discussion continues, students may think of other questions about sea turtles. Record all questions on the group chart. Just before the students are ready to read, ask them to write several questions on their worksheets that *they* want answered. This step helps students set their own purposes for reading. If the text is long or complex, you may preview it with them before they read. Sometimes you will want to have students read the text in parts.

3. *Step L—what I learned* requires students to write the answers to their questions after reading. This helps them determine which questions they still need to answer or whether they have additional questions. It can lead students to further reading.

When to Use. K-W-L is used with expository texts and with students of any age. Primary children and older students experiencing difficulty constructing meaning may need a more simplified version that focuses just on the K-W-L without thinking about additional sources of information. This strategy is a good way to initiate a thematic unit, because it sets students up to continue to read several selections on a given topic. It is also useful when reading chapters in textbooks in areas such as science, social studies, or health.

Students of all ages and levels of reading competency will benefit from using this strategy. Because it is so interactive, it gives students many opportunities to learn from one another. K-W-L is especially strong for second-language learners and students experiencing difficulty constructing meaning, because it immerses them into a natural discussion and offers a strong scaffold provided by teacher support and student interaction. Sometimes it will be necessary to combine K-W-L with other teaching strategies, such as previewing and the use of concrete materials, to further develop prior knowledge.

Assessment Value. K-W-L affords many opportunities to assess students' prior knowledge during all three steps. During the K and W steps, you can tell whether students have prior knowledge relative to the topic and how accurate it is. During the L step, you can tell whether students have gained new knowledge and how well they have integrated that knowledge with what they already know.

Comments. K-W-L has a sound theoretical research base (Ogle, 1986). However, additional research evaluating its effectiveness is still needed.

See Chapter 4 for a discussion of modeling.

Initially, the teacher should model the use of the strategy. Repeated opportunities to use the strategy under teacher direction are important.

Although K-W-L was designed as a teaching strategy, students can learn to use it as an independent study strategy in working alone or cooperatively. A poster such as the one shown in Figure 3.3 may be helpful.

FIGURE 3.3

K-W-L Strategy Poster

Twelve Teaching Strategies Leading to Student Independence

This section discusses twelve teaching strategies for supporting students in *becoming independent* in activating their prior knowledge and setting their purpose(s) for reading. Each strategy will help students bring to mind what they already know about the topic, including the vocabulary associated with the topic, as well as develop new concepts and vocabulary. These are the twelve strategies: discussion, brainstorming, quick writing, picture walk/text walk, semantic mapping, prequestioning and purpose setting, anticipation guides, structured previews, reading aloud to students, role playing, projects, concrete materials and real experiences.

Table 3.3 describes when to use these strategies. Remember that your goal should always be to move students toward independence as quickly as possible. Each of these strategies will benefit ELL students, and each can be used successfully for all students, from beginning readers to fluent.

1. Discussion

Description. Discussion is one of the most widely used strategies for activating students' prior knowledge before reading or writing. However, much of what is done in the name of discussion is nothing more than teacher assessment of students' comprehension (Durkin, 1978, 1981) or conducting of a recitation period (Dillon, 1984). Such unstructured discussions have been found to be ineffective in activating appropriate prior knowledge (Holmes & Roser, 1987).

A discussion is an interactive procedure whereby the teacher and students talk about a given topic; it is not simply the teacher telling students a body of information. According to Alvermann, Dillon, and O'Brien (1987), discussions must meet three criteria:

- *Discussants should put forth multiple points of view and stand ready to change their minds about the matter under discussion;*
- *students should interact with one another as well as with the teacher;*
- *and the interaction should exceed the typical two or three word phrase units common to recitation lessons.* (p. 7)

Procedures. Conducting an effective discussion requires careful planning on the part of the teacher, as well as on-the-spot decisions during the discussion. The following guidelines should be helpful in carrying out this process:

1. *Review the text to be read.* Determine the story line or main ideas to help you decide what key background concepts and vocabulary are needed to comprehend the text. For example, if your class is going to read the expository text *Monarch Butterfly* (Gibbons, 1989), focus your discussion on what students know about monarch butterflies (or, if nothing is known about monarchs, then butterflies in general) and their life cycle. If your students are reading the story (narrative) *Imogene's Antlers* (Small, 1985), the discussion should focus on how they might react if a strange or unusual circumstance occurred in their lives.

TABLE 3.3 **Teaching Strategies for Activating and Developing Prior Knowledge**

Strategy	Type of Text	Comments
1. Discussion	Narrative or expository	For all students.
2. Brainstorming	Narrative or expository	Use when students have some knowledge of topic; for all students.
3. Quick writing	Narrative or expository	For all students; often needs to be combined with other strategies.
4. Picture walk/text walk	Narrative or expository	For students requiring a very structured framework for what they are going to read.
5. Semantic mapping	Most effective with expository; can be used with narrative	For all students; gives a visual picture of concepts.
6. Prequestioning and purpose setting	Narrative and expository	For beginning learners or those having difficulty constructing meaning; usually combined with other strategies.
7. Anticipation guides	Best with expository; may be used with narrative	Useful for overcoming misconceptions in prior knowledge; for all students.
8. Structured previews	Narrative or expository	Especially for second-language learners or students experiencing difficulty constructing meaning.
9. Reading aloud to students	Narrative or expository	Good to use when students have limited or erroneous knowledge; for all students, especially second-language learners.
10. Role playing	Narrative; sometimes expository, especially in social studies	For students needing more concrete prior knowledge development.
11. Projects	Narrative or expository	For all students; develops long-term prior knowledge throughout a theme.
12. Concrete materials and real experiences	Narrative or expository	For students with limited prior knowledge and second-language learners.

2. *Ask questions that require students to respond with more than yes or no.* Questions should require students to elaborate on and explain their answers. Teachers who are just learning to lead a discussion should plan such questions in advance. The suggested guidelines that accompany basal readers, content texts, or some trade books can be helpful.

3. *Encourage students to raise their own questions about the topic or about other students' answers.* It is a good idea to model such behavior and tell students that they can ask similar questions of you or other students.

4. *Call on individual students to answer questions; don't always wait for volunteers to answer.* You want to encourage maximum participation by all students, even those who are sometimes reluctant to respond.

5. *When calling on individual students to answer questions, ask the question before calling on the student.* This practice encourages everyone to listen.

6. *After asking a question, give students sufficient time to answer.* Students need varying amounts of time to think.

7. *Participate in the discussion and model good questioning and question-responding behavior.* Encourage students to ask questions in a discussion in the same manner you do.

8. *Keep the discussion focused on the topic.* A short, lively discussion is better and more motivating than a lengthy one.

9. *Conclude the discussion by having students summarize the points that were made.* For the discussion to be of value to them, students must be able to internalize and verbalize the points that were developed.

Discussions may be planned for the whole class or small groups. Sometimes it is useful to begin with small-group discussions and then use the whole-class format to pull together the ideas discussed in each group. This is a natural way to lead to a summary and to involve all students in a more interactive lesson. In either instance, the preceding nine guidelines apply. It is also a good idea to develop with students a set of guidelines or suggestions to follow during discussions. Table 3.4 presents a sample set of guidelines developed by a group of fifth graders and their teacher.

TABLE 3.4 **Sample Discussion Guidelines Developed by One Fifth-Grade Class**

Our Discussion Guidelines

1. Stick to the topic.
2. Pay attention to the person talking.
3. Ask questions about ideas given.
4. Give everyone a chance to participate.
5. Think about what is being said.
6. Try not to interrupt others.

When to Use. Discussion is a teaching strategy you can use with any group at any time to activate and develop prior knowledge. When students have limited or incorrect knowledge or difficulty constructing meaning, combine discussion with other strategies to make prior knowledge activation and development more concrete. For example, a group that has limited prior knowledge about frogs will profit from a discussion combined with photographs, a film, or a filmstrip on frogs. To help students move toward independence, encourage them to take the lead in small-group discussions.

Assessment Value. Discussion is an excellent way to assess students' prior knowledge; however, it must not be unstructured (Holmes & Roser, 1987). Students' responses and interactions will reveal their knowledge and their misconceptions.

See Chapters 7 and 8 for additional uses.

Comments. Discussion is a powerful technique. Knowledge of the different cultural rules that guide the process of asking and answering questions affects the effectiveness of discussions. Mason and Au (1990) found that Hawaiian children responded best when the teacher asked a question and all children were allowed to respond if they had something to say. Several children spoke at once, and the teacher then repeated the highest-quality response for the group. Mason and Au point out that this pattern reflects the Hawaiian emphasis on the group rather than the individual.

Your job is to try to match your teaching strategies and procedures to fit not only the students' language base but also their cultural values. This is true, of course, for all teaching strategies.

2. Brainstorming

Description. Brainstorming requires students to tell all they know about a particular topic or idea, which begins to activate their prior knowledge.

Procedures. Students can work individually or in pairs, first generating all of the ideas they have for a particular topic and then sharing their ideas with the group. The teacher lists the ideas on the chalkboard, and then they are discussed. By hearing others' ideas, students may activate additional information in their memories or learn new information. The following steps offer one way to carry out a brainstorming activity:

1. Provide cards on which students can record information.
2. Tell students they are to write any words, ideas, or phrases they know about the given topic. Provide a time limit.
3. Have students read their lists aloud to the group as you record all of their ideas on the chalkboard or overhead projector.
4. Discuss the information recorded, pointing out ideas that directly relate to the selection students are going to read. If incorrect information is on the list, you may leave it until after reading. Through discussion and responding, students may correct themselves. However, if the error is significant and is likely to interfere with meaning construction, discuss it at this point.
5. Direct the discussion of the ideas generated by the students to the story line or main ideas of the selection. Conclude the discussion by helping the students set a purpose for reading or giving them a purpose for reading.

When to Use. Use brainstorming when students have some knowledge of the topic. It is useful as an opening activity for a thematic unit, or for reading a story or informational text. For example, if your sixth graders are going to read *Cousins* (Hamilton, 1990), brainstorming will help them think about what might happen when conflicts between cousins arise.

The following script shows how a teacher used brainstorming to introduce an article about whales:

(Teacher focuses the brainstorming.)

Teacher: Today we are going to read an article about whales and why they are in trouble. I want you to write on this card all the things you can think of about whales. Don't worry about spelling. [The ideas of two students are shown on the accompanying cards. After a few minutes, the teacher asked the students to stop writing.]

Ted

Whales are mammals.
Whales live in the ocean.
These are killer whales.
Whales can talk.

Elsie

fish
big
eat people

Teacher: I want each of you to read what you have written on your card, and I will write your ideas on the board. [The teacher accepted all responses from each student, unless it was a duplicate.]

(Students are looking for incorrect information.)

Teacher: Let's look at our list of ideas to see if there is anything that is incorrect.

Whales are mammals

Whales live in the ocean

There are killer whales

Whales can talk

Fish

Big

Eat people

Can be made into oil

Can be eaten

Are hunted by fishermen

Student: Whales aren't fish.

Teacher: Whales live in the ocean; they look like fish, but they are much bigger. We will learn why they are not fish in our reading. [The teacher removed *fish* from the list.]

Teacher: You know that dinosaurs once lived on the earth, but for many reasons they disappeared. The same thing is happening to whales. Look at this list to see if you can identify any reasons that whales might be in danger of disappearing. [The students responded. The teacher discussed their answers and identified items the students missed.]

Teacher: We are going to read the article entitled "Disappearing Whales." Based on the information we have just discussed about whales and why they might be in danger of disappearing, what do you think would be a good thing for us to think about or look for as we read?

Student: Maybe we could look to see if our reasons about why whales disappear are right, and maybe we can find some others.

(Setting a purpose for reading.)

Teacher: That's a good idea. [The teacher wrote the student's response on the board and had students read the article silently, telling them they would later discuss the article based on that purpose.]

Assessment Value. Through student brainstorming, the teacher is able to identify and *begin* to correct errors in students' prior knowledge, as shown in the above dialogue about whales.

Comments. It is important to keep the brainstorming focused without controlling it. If students have a limited amount of knowledge about the subject, the small-group activity may be more effective because it will enable them to learn from one another.

Like the other strategies presented in this chapter, brainstorming is often more effective if used in conjunction with another strategy, such as preview and predict or purpose setting. Not only will you more effectively meet individual needs; you will also keep interest high by varying your teaching strategies.

3. Quick Writing

Description. Writing has been shown to be an effective way to activate prior knowledge before students read (Marino, Gould, & Haas, 1985; Moore, Readence, & Rickleman, 1989). **Quick writing** is structured by the teacher and is done in a brief amount of time.

Procedures. The procedures are general because they depend on the selection being read and what is to be written. The following guidelines should be helpful:

1. *Select what you want students to write about.* This should relate directly to the story line or main ideas in the text. For example, if students are going to read *The Stupids Have a Ball* (Allard & Marshall, 1978), you might ask them to pretend they are a person who does everything the opposite of normal, telling funny things

that might happen to them. (The characters in this story do just that.) Quick writing can focus on a character, on the story problem, or on the major topic developed in an expository text.

2. *Have students write.* Allow students 3 to 5 minutes to complete the writing. Remind them that these papers will not be evaluated and graded.

3. *Invite students to share what they have written.* Direct students in a discussion of the ideas shared.

4. *Help students formulate a purpose for reading.* For example, they can now read *The Stupids Have a Ball* to see how the Stupids are like the characters they have written about.

When to Use. Writing can be used as soon as students begin to be able to write and express their ideas. If you know students have limited prior knowledge relative to the topic, it will be best to use some other technique that will more concretely develop the concepts and ideas needed. Second-language learners should, in most instances, have an activity that introduces key words and phrases prior to writing; discussion combined with more concrete materials such as pictures would accomplish this goal.

Assessment Value. Although writing is a valuable way to assess students' prior knowledge, you must be cautious about drawing conclusions from a response to a written task, since students may be hampered by limited writing skills or a dislike for writing rather than by limited prior knowledge. A good rule is to make no firm conclusion about a student's prior knowledge on the basis of a single sample *from any source*. It is always wise to look at two or more samples from different sources.

For more discussion of writing, see Chapter 8.

Comments. Quick writing is an important element in the overall process of constructing meaning and helps students build the connections between reading and writing, but it does not replace other kinds of writing.

4. Picture Walk/Text Walk

Description. A **picture walk** or **text walk** is a technique whereby the teacher guides students through a piece of literature to be read, using the pictures, illustrations, or other graphics to develop the big picture of what the text is about. The advantage of this technique is that it sets the reader up to succeed with the text by developing key concepts, vocabulary, and a general picture of the text before it is read. This technique has been used in New Zealand (Goldenberg, 1991) in regular classrooms and in special support programs such as Reading Recovery in both New Zealand (Clay, 1985) and the United States (DeFord, Lyons, & Pinnell, 1991; Hiebert & Taylor, 1994). Clay (1985) says that carrying out this type of procedure before reading ensures that "the child has in his head the ideas and the language he needs to produce when prompted in sequence by printed cues" (p. 68). The term *picture walk* is usually used when referring to a picture book, and *text walk* is used when referring to an informational text.

Procedures. You may adapt the following procedures to any level, including middle school or high school content classes:

1. Before working with students, read the text to get a picture of important ideas developed, the story line, key terms, and so forth.
2. If appropriate, show students the cover, and have them predict what the text is likely to be about or what is likely to happen.
3. Turning through the pages and using the pictures, illustrations, or graphics as prompts, tell key things that will happen in the text, or have students predict what is likely to happen. As you tell the major elements of the text, use some of the key vocabulary students will encounter in the text.
4. In most instances, tell the entire text that is to be read. In some cases, however, you may tell only enough to develop a framework without giving away a surprise or exciting ending.

When to Use. Picture walk or text walk is especially helpful when working with students who need a great deal of extra support to construct meaning. However, you can use it any time students are going to read a text when you think they need very structured scaffolding to help them understand the material. For example, students reading a social studies chapter in grade 6 may need the structured support of text walk to help them understand the chapter.

For more information on using observation, see Chapter 11.

Assessment Value. As students respond during the picture walk or text walk, you can get a sense of their prior knowledge, their ability to make predictions, their familiarity with key vocabulary, and their general ability to express themselves orally. Throughout the use of this teaching strategy and others, observe and listen to students' responses.

Comments. By sharing with students what they are going to read before they read it, you set them up for success when they read.

5. Semantic Mapping

Description. **Semantic mapping** can help students develop prior knowledge by seeing the relationships in a given topic. A semantic map is a visual representation of a particular concept. Ovals represent the concepts, and lines with arrows and words written above them represent the relationships. The relationships depicted on a map can be *class* (pine trees), *example* (white pine), or *property* (needles). Figure 3.4 shows a semantic map created with a group of third graders who were preparing to read an article about the uses of pine trees.

Procedures. There are many ways to use semantic mapping. The first set of guidelines that follows is structured and directed by the teacher; the second set is also teacher directed, but it incorporates brainstorming followed by grouping and labeling of concepts. The second set uses many of the ideas suggested by Taba (1967) many years ago, as described by McNeil (1987); the Taba lesson was known as List-Group-Label and was suggested for social studies, but it can be used in many more situations.

Guidelines 1

1. Write the major concept being discussed on the chalkboard or overhead, and draw an oval around it. (In Figure 3.4, the concept is pine trees.)

2. Ask students to think of words to describe the topic. Write those words in boxes, and link them with arrows to the main concept oval. Above the arrows, write words and phrases such as *have* or *are used for* to indicate the relationship between the main concept and the boxed words.
3. Ask students to give some examples of the topic, and write these in ovals with arrows indicating examples.

Guidelines 2

1. Present the concept to be discussed by placing it in an oval on the chalkboard or overhead.
2. Ask students to brainstorm words or ideas related to the concept. If necessary, probe for additional information.
3. Guide students in grouping the words or ideas to create the semantic map for the concept. Use different shapes to depict the different categories of information: rectangles for uses or descriptions, circles for examples, and squares for other types of information. Figure 3.5 shows how this process worked in one class.

There is no one right way to develop a semantic map. The words written on the arrows to show relationships will vary according to the topic being discussed.

When to Use. Semantic mapping is most effective when used with expository texts. It can also be used with narratives, but you must be certain that the concept used for activating prior knowledge is central to the story line.

You can use semantic mapping with students, from kindergarten through adulthood, to help them visualize the relationships among ideas. Second-language learners and students with limited prior knowledge may respond best when the second set of guidelines is used, because they start out on a more global basis and move to specifics. You should always keep the activity focused on the central ideas in the text.

Semantic mapping is a particularly good procedure to use when students will read several sources related to the same topic. The teacher and students can start the map before students begin the reading, and add to it as they gain new information while they read. After they have completed their reading, they can return to the map to make additions or changes.

Assessment Value. As you use semantic mapping with students, you are able to assess their understandings of various concepts and relationships, as well as deal with key vocabulary.

Semantic mapping is discussed in more detail in Chapter 6.

Comments. Semantic mapping has been suggested for many other uses in helping students construct meaning. These include summarizing the text, expanding their vocabulary, and writing (Noyce & Christie, 1989; Stahl & Vancil, 1986; Weisberg & Balajthy, 1985).

6. Prequestioning and Purpose Setting

Description. Asking a question or giving students a topic to think about that will continue to focus their attention as they read has been shown to be effective in activating prior knowledge and in improving meaning construction (Tierney & Cunningham, 1984).

Procedures. Following are some simple guidelines that should be used flexibly with various reading tasks:

1. Examine the text to determine the story line or main ideas.
2. Decide what prior knowledge students are likely to need.
3. Formulate a question(s) or a statement of purpose for students to think about before reading. These should focus students on the big ideas.

Recall the article "Birds in Winter" discussed earlier. The focus of that article was on the survival of birds during a blizzard, and the main point was that birds often have to depend on humans to survive under extreme winter conditions. The following prequestions would be useful for this article:

* How do the problems the birds in this article face compare to the problems you have seen birds experience during bad winter storms?
* On the basis of "Birds in Winter" and of your own experience, why do you think it is important for people to help birds during winter storms?

The following is an appropriate purpose-setting statement:

FIGURE 3.4

Semantic Map for Pine Trees Using Guidelines 1

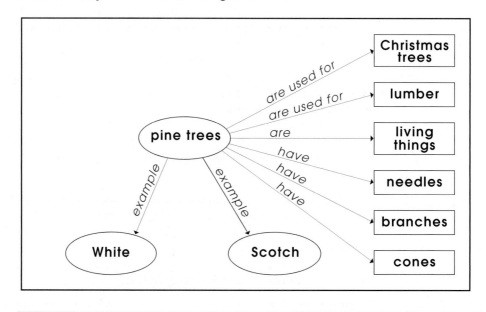

⚬ You have discussed some of the problems that birds can have surviving in winter. Read this article to find out if there are other reasons that birds have difficulty surviving in blizzards.

Notice that the only real difference between this purpose statement and the questions is the form in which the purpose is stated.

The following prequestions would *not* be appropriate because they focus on specific points rather than the overall text: "What two birds have the greatest difficulty surviving during blizzard conditions?" and "What three reasons does the author give to justify why people should help birds during blizzards?" Furthermore, these questions do not require readers to draw from their prior knowledge.

4. Have students read the text to answer the question or to accomplish the purpose given.
5. After reading, return to the question or purpose statement to see if students have achieved their goals and to discuss what they found. Returning to check the purpose for reading helps students construct meaning.

FIGURE 3.5

Semantic Map for Pine Trees Using Guidelines 2

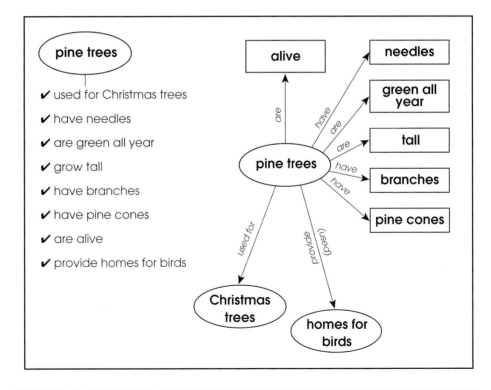

When to Use. This strategy should be used when students are not yet able to formulate their own purposes or prequestions or when the text is extremely difficult. Your real goal, however, should be to get students to use the independent strategies discussed in the first portion of this chapter. Usually you should combine prequestions and purpose statements with other strategies, such as discussion or brainstorming, to activate prior knowledge.

Assessment Value. Prequestions and purpose statements are not as helpful as other strategies in assessing students' immediate prior knowledge relative to a topic or an idea. Their assessment value comes after reading, when students respond and show how well they have constructed meaning.

Comments. Prequestions and purpose statements provide the scaffold for learning that some students need, and you will find you frequently use them when you employ the teacher-guided reading mode discussed in Chapter 2.

7. Anticipation Guides

Description. An **anticipation guide** is a series of statements about a particular text that students are going to read. Students indicate whether they agree or disagree with the statements before reading and return to them after reading to do the same. This strategy is designed to activate prior knowledge and to give students a purpose for reading.

Procedures. Readence, Bean, and Baldwin (1981, 1985, 1989) suggest eight steps in constructing and using anticipation guides:

1. *Identify major concepts.* Review the text to identify the major concepts or main ideas to be learned.
2. *Determine students' prior knowledge of these concepts.* Drawing on your experiences with your students, think about what they know about these concepts or ideas.
3. *Create statements.* Using the information gained from steps 1 and 2, write out four to eight statements for students to react to that relate to the concepts to be learned and the students' prior knowledge. The exact number of statements will depend on the amount of text to be read, the number of concepts in the text, and the age of the students. The statements should reflect information about which students have some knowledge but not complete knowledge. They should not be just a true-false type of check. Some good statements for a chapter on food and nutrition might be the following:

   > *An apple a day keeps the doctor away.*
   > *If you wish to live a long life, be a vegetarian.*
   > *Three square meals a day will satisfy all your body's nutritional needs.*
   > *Calories make you fat. (Tierney, Readence, & Dishner, 1990, p. 48)*

4. *Decide on the statement order and presentation mode.* Sequence the statements to follow the text, inserting spaces for responses. Create a set of directions. Finally, decide whether the guide is to be presented individually or in a group mode, such as on the chalkboard or overhead.

5. *Present the guide.* Tell students they are to react to each statement by indicating whether they agree or disagree with it. Tell them they will share their responses with the group.
6. *Discuss each statement briefly.* Encourage students to share their opinions and tell why they feel as they do. You can tally the responses to each item.
7. *Direct students to read the text.* Have students read the text, keeping their opinions in mind. As they read, they should think about how the text relates to the statements on the guide.
8. *Conduct a follow-up discussion.* First ask students to respond to each statement in the light of what they have read. Then have them discuss the statements, focusing on what they have learned and how their opinions and ideas have changed. Figure 3.6 presents a sample anticipation guide for a social studies chapter on transportation.

When to Use. Anticipation guides may be used for any students at any level. They are generally more useful for expository texts. This strategy is effective when students have misconceptions in prior knowledge. By interacting with the text and comparing prior opinions with what was learned from reading, students are likely to correct their misconceptions.

Assessment Value. The anticipation guide is an excellent diagnostic tool. By looking at and listening to students' responses, you can tell the state of their prior knowledge and easily recognize their misconceptions. Then, by looking at the after-reading responses, you can tell whether those misconceptions have changed.

Comments. Construction of an anticipation guide is sometimes challenging. The statements must require students to think.

FIGURE 3.6

Anticipation Guide for Social Studies

Chapter 6, Transportation

Directions: Read each statement. Mark *A* for agree or *D* for disagree. Do the same after reading the chapter.

Before Reading		After Reading
_____	1. Travel has not changed much in the last 25 years.	_____
_____	2. The car is still considered the safest way to travel.	_____
_____	3. The safest way to travel is by air.	_____
_____	4. Large cities need to have more parking garages for increased populations.	_____
_____	5. Cars should be banned from the central business district of large cities.	_____

8. Structured Previews

Description. We discussed the value of previewing a text before reading earlier, but some students may need to have the previewing process structured more carefully. A **structured preview** is carefully guided by the teacher and often involves some type of graphic display of information to help students see the ideas that are forthcoming in the text and how they are organized. The concept is based on research showing that students' prior knowledge needs to be directed toward the story line (Beck, 1984; Beck, Omanson, & McKeown, 1982). To be helpful to students, this process needs teacher guidance (Neuman, 1988).

Procedures. The procedures for conducting a structured preview are different for narrative texts and for expository texts, though there are similarities.

Narrative Structured Preview

1. Look through the book to get a sense of the story line. Identify the setting, characters, problem, action, and outcome.
2. Formulate questions or statements that will direct students to read the title and the opening paragraph or two (depending on the level), and look at the first few illustrations. Have students share what they learn.
3. Display the story map (see Figure 3.7) and discuss with students the elements in the story. For beginning learners and those having difficulty constructing meaning, focus on only one or two elements. Include other elements later.
4. Ask students to predict what they can about the story elements from their preview, keeping students focused on the story line.
5. Have students read the story silently in its entirety or in sections. Then return to the story map to help them see whether their predictions were verified or changed. Together, complete the story map.

The steps involved in the structured preview must always be adjusted to fit the story content, illustrations, and level. The primary focus of the preview should always be to get students to begin to think about the particular story problem and relate what they already know to it. If your third-grade students are going to read *Wilfrid Gordon McDonald Partridge* (Fox, 1985), a book about how a young boy helps an elderly woman in an old people's home get her memory back, you begin the structured preview by having the children look at the cover and tell who they think this book is going to be about. Next, while looking through the first three or four pages, you ask children to talk about old people's homes and the types of things that might be problems for people living in them, focusing on the idea that some people become forgetful as they get older. You then complete the preview by presenting the story map and asking the children to predict the characters and the possible problem in the story.

Expository Structured Preview

The narrative structured previews are similar because most narrative texts have the same basic structure. The expository structured preview will vary more because such text has varying text structures. Therefore, you will need to adapt the following guidelines to fit the structure of the text:

Story Map for Structured Preview

STORY MAP

Setting: *Time* *Place*

↓

Characters:

↓

Problem:

Action:

←→

Outcome:

---

1. Review the text to determine the main ideas. Try to identify a **graphic organizer** that will help students see how the information fits together. For example, if the text has three main ideas, the graphic organizer might be like the one shown in Figure 3.8. However, many texts do not lend themselves to such a neat outline.

2. Formulate questions and statements to help students preview the text by reading the title, looking at the illustrations and captions, and reading subheads.

3. Guide students through a preview of the text, having them begin to predict the type of information they will learn.

4. Present the graphic organizer, and tell students that the ideas in this text are organized in the pattern shown.
5. Have students read the text to look for the main ideas depicted in your organizer. As they become more sophisticated readers, they can also identify the information that supports the main ideas.

In conducting a structured preview for an expository text, you must pay close attention to how the main ideas are presented in the text. For example, if your second graders are going to read *Fiesta!* (Behrens, 1978), you should note that this work has only one main idea with many facts given about it. Figure 3.9 shows how this idea with its supporting facts might be depicted. When conducting your preview, you should present only the basic outline of the graphic organizer, telling students they will learn one big idea about fiesta and six areas of information about what happens during fiesta. This type of structured preview activates prior knowledge about the topic and also gives students a framework to use in thinking about how the information is organized.

FIGURE 3.8

Graphic Organizer Showing Three Main Ideas in an Expository Text

Main Idea One
- 1. Supporting detail
- 2.
- 3.

Main Idea Two
- 1. Supporting detail
- 2.

Main Idea Three
- 1. Supporting detail
- 2.

FIGURE 3.9

Graphic Organizer for Structural Preview of *Fiesta!*

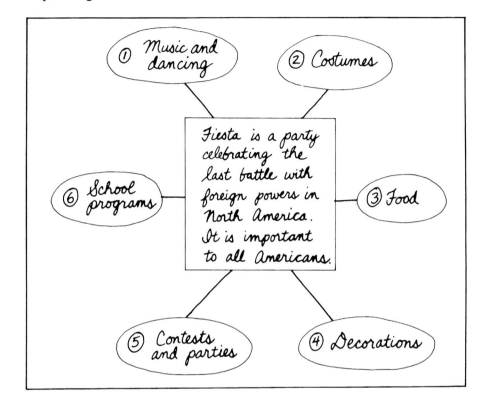

When to Use. Structured previews are useful on a number of occasions:

- When the text is particularly difficult
- When students are second-language learners
- When students are having difficulty constructing meaning
- When you know students have limited prior knowledge about either the topic or the type of text

Assessment Value. Students' responses during the preview session may help you determine the status of their prior knowledge and what they are gaining from the preview, but because the preview is so teacher directed, what you learn may be limited. Select this strategy only if you are sure your students need this type of scaffold.

Comments. Structured previews and graphic or semantic organizers can be very helpful to students, but they can also be unnecessarily complicated. Therefore, you should keep your structured previews as simple as possible, making certain that any graphic organizers used actually *do* help students see how the text is organized. The structured preview may be combined with many of the other strategies discussed in this chapter.

Using a Project That Cuts Across the Curriculum

Cross-curricular projects as a culminating activity have been used successfully by many of the teachers in our schools to meet the needs of our diverse population. Students are provided "structured choice" and are to select a number of items from a menu of activities that require reading, writing, and knowledge of content. The menu must include something for everyone in order to allow all students to participate. The depth and complexity of the items, as well as the reading and writing skill level required to complete the task, is an important feature of the project design. Some teachers assign a point value to each of the activities and require that each student select items that total a particular number. These are in addition to the group tasks. The point value allows the teacher to include a variety of assignments that range in level of difficulty, complexity, and time required to complete, with the expectation that all students will take responsibility for demonstrating their knowledge of the content through reading and writing.

Teachers determine in advance the components of the project that are to be completed by each individual and those that are to be completed as a group. The students are then assigned to predetermined heterogeneous working groups. Each group is responsible for completing all of the menu items and is encouraged to take into account each member's strengths when dividing the responsibilities among the group. Each group is given a pre-planning sheet on which they must establish a time line for completion of each group activity, with check points along the way. They must also list the possible sources from which information may be obtained, materials they may need, as well as any other issues essential to the completion of the project. In order to ensure the equal and appropriate distribution of tasks, the teacher conferences with each group and guides and supports their decision making as the project components are distributed among the members.

Here are examples of some activities teachers have found to be meaningful and of interest to their students as a culmination of a social studies unit on a particular time period:

- Develop a time line that includes pictures or phrases that depict the major events of the period.
- Draw a cartoon and write a caption that illustrates a key point or main idea from the period.
- List ten quotes, paraphrase the quotes, and describe their significance to the causes, effects, or events related to the period.
- Select ten of the most significant events from this period, and support their importance with factual information as well as personal commentary as to why you selected these particular events.
- Select a song with lyrics that support some of the ideas brought forward during this time period. Explain the connections.
- Write two letters to the editor. One letter must be pro (select a key player in this time period) and the other must be con.

It is important to keep in mind that the purpose of the cross-curricular project is to provide an opportunity for students to apply their reading and writing skills across the curriculum as they demonstrate their knowledge of content through project-based activities that

(continued)
range in level of difficulty and amount of reading and writing required. As teachers continue to come together to brainstorm and share ideas, the menu of project activities continues to grow. We must continue to self-check in order to ensure the activities do not become so elaborate that they overshadow the intent and we lose sight of their purpose.

–Lynne Pistochini, Curriculum Resource Specialist
San Juan Unified School District
Folsum, California

9. Reading Aloud to Students

Description. The importance of reading aloud to students was well established in Chapter 2. In this strategy, the reading is specific to a thematic topic or selection.

Procedures.

Reading Aloud Background Material

Use the following guidelines to carry out this strategy:

1. Select a book, article, or other background material that relates to the topic or selection.
2. Tell students what it is about and why you are reading it.
3. Give students a purpose for listening. For example, have them listen to identify some important idea or concept to retell an important part of the story. As an alternative, you can also ask them to make predictions about what they expect to learn as they listen.
4. After the read aloud, discuss the material by checking the purpose for which students were to listen, or discuss whether predictions were confirmed.

Reading Aloud a Portion of a Selection

Guidelines for using this strategy are as follows:

1. Decide on the story or article students will read.
2. Identify how much of the initial part of the selection you are going to read aloud.
3. Introduce the selection, and give students a purpose for listening.
4. Read aloud the selected section.
5. Discuss the portion read aloud, checking the purpose given for listening.
6. Have students predict what they think will happen or what they will learn in the remainder of the text.
7. Have students read silently to check their predictions.
8. Discuss the entire selection, focusing on students' predictions.
9. Have students respond to the selection in their own way.

You may vary this second read-aloud strategy by reading aloud part of the text and alternating these sessions with students reading cooperatively or independently. The amount of reading aloud you do will depend on the students' needs and the text. This is a variation of the read aloud, read along, read alone strategy discussed in Chapter 2.

When to Use. The read-aloud strategy is excellent to use when you know students have limited or erroneous prior knowledge. It is also good for second-language learners because it helps to develop oral language.

Assessment Value. By reading aloud to students, you can generally tell how they comprehend through listening. You can tell how well they remember and organize ideas, and understand key vocabulary, without being concerned about decoding or their ability to figure out words. It is more difficult to use the read-aloud strategy as a way to assess students' specific prior knowledge.

Comments. Reading aloud is an excellent way to build students' background and increase motivation. It should not be overlooked for helping all students. Reading aloud is also useful in building prior knowledge for writing.

10. Role Playing

Description. In **role playing,** students take parts and act out a situation. The purpose of this strategy is to get students to think about a problem or circumstance and bring their prior knowledge to bear on it.

Procedures. Role playing can be fun, but it requires careful planning to make it a valuable experience for prior knowledge activation:

1. Select the book you want students to read. Determine the story line.
2. Select a situation that would be easy and fun for children to role-play. Make sure it relates to the story line but does not give away the story.
3. Describe the situation to the children. Divide them into small groups to decide on parts and determine how they will act out their situations.
4. Have each group perform. Then discuss the situations, focusing the discussion on the book to be read, not on an evaluation of their performances.
5. Have students read the book to compare their experience with that described in the book.

Suppose your sixth graders are going to read *Wayside School Is Falling Down* (Sachar, 1989), a hilarious book about the adventures of children in Louis Sachar's imaginary school. You could ask children to role-play the strangest and funniest thing they could imagine happening in school. As each group performs, you then discuss the incident, leading the children to focus on the book by directing them to see how their experiences compare with those of the Erics and other children in Wayside School.

When to Use. Role playing is a good strategy to use for students who need concrete experiences. Often second-language learners who are reluctant to speak out individually in an open discussion will relate to and interact with their peers in a role-playing situation. Although role playing is often used with narrative texts, it may also be useful with expository texts, especially social studies.

For more discussion about observations, see Chapter 11.

Assessment Value. Observing students in a role-playing situation can give you a sense of their prior knowledge as well as the ways they think and solve problems.

Comments. Too often prior knowledge activation is handled only through discussion. Remember that many children enjoy role playing and are more likely to be themselves and use what they actually know in this activity. At the same time, some students may be too shy to participate, in which case you may consider using simple puppetry to accomplish the same purpose.

11. Projects

Description. A **project** is a task undertaken to achieve a particular goal; it is usually long term, and because of its goal, you can tell when it is completed. Though often a culminating activity, projects can be an ongoing part of a thematic unit. Thus, a project may summarize what has been learned, activate prior knowledge, and develop new knowledge. A brief explanation of projects is given here; they are discussed in more detail in Chapter 6.

Procedures. The following guidelines are useful with projects:

1. *Identify the project.* This can be done by you or your students.
2. *Select resources.* Assign the use of certain resources, or let students select them.
3. *Make a plan.* Decide what will be done and when.
4. *Decide how projects will be shared.* Will there be a display? An oral report? Something else?

When to Use. Ongoing projects are not the most efficient way to activate prior knowledge for reading a particular text. However, as students use resources for such a project, they are developing prior knowledge for future reading of upcoming texts within the unit of study. Projects are also very effective in helping ELLs develop prior knowledge.

Assessment Value. As you observe your students while they work, you can assess various work habits, independence, ability to use resources, and so forth, as well as their developing knowledge about the topic. Projects also lend themselves to student self-evaluation.

Comments. Projects do much more than activate prior knowledge. They also help students learn new strategies and skills and gain new information. Projects often create the need for students to read and do research. They help students integrate new knowledge with old knowledge, learn to work cooperatively and independently, develop critical thinking, and learn new skills and strategies. Students may do projects independently or in groups, depending on their purposes. They should be encouraged to select and plan their own projects.

Be cautious when using this strategy. Sometimes students get so caught up in completing a project that it replaces most, if not all, of the reading and writing they should be doing.

12. Concrete Materials and Real Experiences

Description. Often the best way to activate and develop students' prior knowledge is to use concrete materials and real experiences. These could include the Internet,

Fifth graders model Xian soldiers during an ancient civilization unit. © David Young-Wolf/PhotoEdit

CD-ROMs, pictures, films, filmstrips, videos, field trips, or classroom planned experiences. For example, a classroom science experiment involving treating three plants differently—one gets water and no light, one gets light and no water, and one gets water and light—would be a good way to develop prior knowledge before starting a theme on plants or on air and water.

Procedures. The only procedure to follow is to ensure that the materials or experiences actually help to activate and develop prior knowledge that is relevant to the theme, the text to be read, or the writing experience. Always be sure that what you are using really helps students to construct meaning more effectively.

When to Use. Concrete materials and real experiences are most important when students lack prior knowledge on a particular topic. Second-language learners and children who have limited background often need this type of support because it makes the input comprehensible (Krashen, 1982). This strategy is also useful for introducing a new topic to all students.

Assessment Value. Since concrete materials and real experiences are used to develop prior knowledge, they will have limited assessment value. However, as in all other learning experiences, students' responses will give you an indication of what they know and what they are learning.

Comments. Real experiences may seem to lack a clear connection to the instruction, so you should always introduce such experiences by letting children know their purpose. After the experience, you and the students should talk about what was learned and how it relates to the topic or theme being covered. For example, in preparation for a thematic unit on wild animals, students should make predictions about certain animals before going to the zoo on a field trip. Then they can discuss which predictions were confirmed and summarize what they learned about the animals. This knowledge will help them as they work in this unit.

Deciding Which Strategies to Use

Each of the fourteen strategies—two student strategies and twelve teaching strategies with variations just discussed—has as its primary focus activation and/or development of prior knowledge of concepts and vocabulary, leading students to set their purpose for reading. As the teacher, you must continuously make decisions about which strategies to use. Some lessons will call for combining several strategies, and others will require only one strategy. Some will require heavy teacher support, others almost none. The following guidelines should help you decide which strategies to use and when to use them.

Motivation and Interest

Student motivation and interest for a topic or book will directly influence the amount of prior knowledge activation and development needed. Usually students who select their own topics or books are either very highly motivated or have good prior knowledge about the topic. If they are highly motivated to read or write about a certain topic but have little prior knowledge about it, they will need support in developing this knowledge. Those who know a great deal about the topic will need little or no support.

The Text

You must also know the type of text (narrative or expository) and its difficulty when deciding which strategies to use. With narrative text, focus on the story line; for expository text, focus on the main ideas.

When topics or texts have complex concepts, ideas, or structures, more prior knowledge activation will be needed, and some strategies will be more useful than others. Refer to Tables 3.2 and 3.3 for a summary of when to use the strategies presented in this chapter.

Student Needs and Level of Independence

As you become familiar with your students, you will know which ones need the most prior knowledge support. Students who have achieved independence may need no support, but this need will change from situation to situation. Students with limited English proficiency may benefit from pictures, objects, and gestures.

Lesson Variety

A final factor to consider is lesson variety. Using the same strategies over and over again becomes boring to both you and the students. Vary your strategies to keep interest and motivation for learning high.

Overcoming Inadequate Prior Knowledge

Students who experience difficulties in constructing meaning often have limited or erroneous prior knowledge (Lipson, 1984). These students often need more prior knowledge development that is *directed specifically to the reading or writing task* they are expected to perform. You can use all of the strategies presented in this chapter to help in these circumstances, but you may need to approach them more systematically and somewhat differently than for other students.

Limited Prior Knowledge

All students come to school with prior knowledge. *It is our goal to help students take whatever prior knowledge they bring to school and expand and build on it.*

Sometimes students' background experiences don't match what the school requires. Within the framework of the literacy program, there are many opportunities to expand students' world knowledge and knowledge and experience with literacy events. You must do this systematically, always emphasizing the value of each individual and what he or she brings to school. The following suggestions should be helpful in planning classroom experiences that will help expand students' prior knowledge.

Sharing and Talking. Create many opportunities for students to share and talk about their own experiences and backgrounds. You are in effect saying, "What you know is good and of value." Opportunities for these experiences can be provided in opening morning exercises, sharing times, or throughout the day. Sharing should also give students time to talk about books they have read or writing they have done.

See Chapter 2 for guidelines on reading aloud to students.

Read-Aloud Time. Reading aloud to children is one of the best ways to broaden their prior knowledge and language experiences. If children have not been read to at home, this activity is even more significant in school.

See Chapter 2 for suggestions.

Independent Reading and Writing Time. Students who have limited prior knowledge need *more time to read and write independently*.

Use of Technology. Some students with inadequate prior knowledge will be motivated to seek information on the Web and to share that information in meaningful ways with peers.

Plan Lessons and Experiences to Develop Prior Knowledge. Use the strategies suggested in this chapter and those you learn from other sources to systematically develop prior knowledge when you start a new theme, when students read a selection, or when they begin a writing experience. Use the literacy lesson format presented in Chapter 2 with the strategies that lend themselves to more concretely developing prior knowledge for students.

Students who have limited prior knowledge often need continued support throughout their reading lessons to develop and relate this knowledge to what they read.

Erroneous Prior Knowledge

Correcting misconceptions or erroneous prior knowledge is difficult, but research indicates it is possible to make these corrections and improve students' ability to construct meaning (Alvermann & Hynd, 1987; Alvermann et al., 1985; Dole & Smith, 1989; Hynd & Alvermann, 1986; Maria, 1988). The following guidelines may be helpful.

Activate and Assess Prior Knowledge. Find out what students know and/or think about the topic by using some of the strategies discussed in this chapter. As students respond, note misconceptions or errors.

Decide on the Best Time for Correcting the Error or Misconception. This is not an easy decision to make. Research suggests that changing students' misconceptions is a long-term process that takes place through reading and writing over a period of time. Minor errors or misconceptions may be corrected before reading, but more serious ones will need to be viewed in the long-term process of instruction. Brainstorming and discussion may be natural strategies for correcting minor misconceptions before reading (Flood & Lapp, 1988). However, Maria (1990) cautions that too heavy a focus on correcting errors or misconceptions before reading may deter students from wanting to read.

Select the Strategies to Be Used. Whereas all the strategies discussed in this chapter might be useful in correcting minor misconceptions, those that involve longer-term thinking processes are more likely to be effective in overcoming more deeply rooted misconceptions. One such strategy is the anticipation guide presented on pages 104–105.

Research on the role of misconceptions in prior knowledge and the construction of meaning is continuing. Although the guidelines presented here are certainly supported by the limited amount of research that exists, you should be on the lookout for new information in this area.

✓ **NCTE/IRA Standards developed in this lesson: 1, 2, 3, 7, 8, 9, 10, 11, 12**

Standards-Based
**Literacy
Lesson**

A Standards-Based Lesson Using *Gladiator*

This lesson focuses on introducing a theme and introducing one of the books to be read during the theme. You will see how global prior knowledge is activated and developed when introducing the theme and how text-specific and topic-specific prior knowledge are activated and developed for the first chapter.

This portion of the sample unit is based on a thematic unit plan on "Ancient Civilizations" designed for middle school in which one of the books to be read is *Gladiator* (Watkins, 1997).

Before Reading the Plan

1. Think about what you have learned about prior knowledge activation and development.
2. Read the excerpt from *Gladiator,* which includes the cover, the Table of Contents, the Introduction, and the first chapter, "Ancient Rome."
3. Read the teacher preparation section that follows this section to see how we decided which prior knowledge to activate for the theme and for the literacy lesson. Read the plan that follows the excerpt from *Gladiator.*

While Reading the Plan

1. Notice how prior knowledge was activated and developed for this theme and lesson.
2. Think about why each strategy was used. Note any questions.
3. Think of other ways you could have activated and developed prior knowledge for this theme and lesson.

🦋 Teacher Preparation

The unit "Ancient Civilizations" with the literacy lesson using *Gladiator* (Watkins, 1997) was planned for a middle-school class. The school is in a small southern town and draws from both the town and the surrounding rural area. A few students have computers with Internet access in their homes, but there are limited technological resources in the school and no computers in classrooms. The following outlines the steps used to plan the lesson and gives a rationale for each step.

Unit Activities Prior to Reading the Book *Gladiator*

1. Several resources were gathered with the help of the school librarian. Some will be available only in the library (e.g., CD-ROMs), but many books will remain in the classroom for the duration of the unit. Because the topic will have wide appeal, all students will read *Gladiator;* therefore, we have multiple copies of the book. As students select other aspects of ancient civilizations to study, individuals and groups will read other materials and share what they learn with the class.

Standards-Based
Literacy
Lesson

continued

2. We decided what text-specific and topic-specific background students would need in order to read the first chapter of the book with understanding.
   a. Text-specific background: Students will recall that historical information is often organized chronologically. (The class has been learning organizational patterns of informational text.) The content of the first chapter, "Ancient Rome," gives an overview of Roman history, from the traditional explanation of its founding in 753 B.C. by Romulus and Remus to its fall.
   b. Topic-specific background: Students may have some knowledge (whether correct or not) about Roman history in general and gladiators in particular. To activate prior knowledge about Roman history, we will use a map or globe and focused discussion. We will return to the map many times during reading. Prior knowledge about gladiators will be dealt with as we begin the book.

Specific Outcomes to be Developed in This Lesson

1. Vocabulary: understands topic-specific words for the selection
2. Vocabulary: uses context to determine meaning of unfamiliar words
3. Comprehension: confirms predictions after reading a given text
4. Comprehension: determines main ideas and important supporting details
5. Study skills: locates places on maps and globes
6. Literary response: increases knowledge about an ancient civilization and relates to current civilizations; shares ideas with peers; demonstrates understanding through discussion and a project

About This Lesson

See Chapter 2 for discussion of modes of reading.

1. Prior knowledge of concepts and vocabulary will be activated and developed using semantic mapping, focused discussion, prequestioning, and concrete materials.
2. Because of the dense text and because of the students' scant, and probably inaccurate, prior knowledge, the lesson uses three modes of reading: read aloud of the Introduction and the beginning of the chapter, then interactive guided reading, and finally cooperative or independent reading. Until we begin reading, we cannot determine at what point the final mode will occur.
3. We will not preteach additional vocabulary beyond that developed during the prior knowledge activity for the first chapter. Instead, students will draw on their ability to use context to determine the meaning of unfamiliar terms.
4. The lesson includes initial planning for independent or group activities that will result in a unit project.

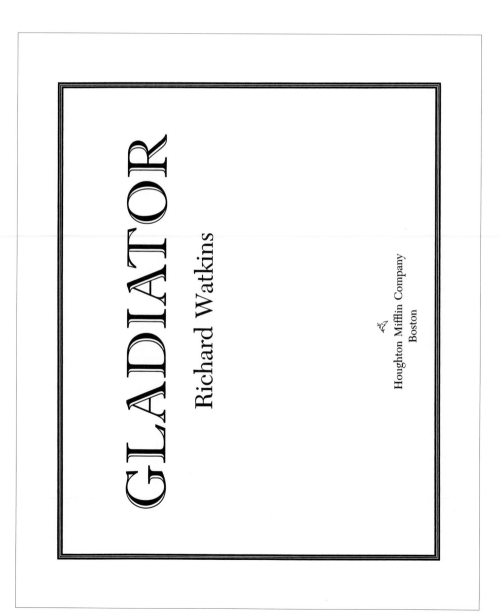

GLADIATOR

Richard Watkins

Houghton Mifflin Company
Boston

CONTENTS

Standards-Based
Literacy
Lesson

continued

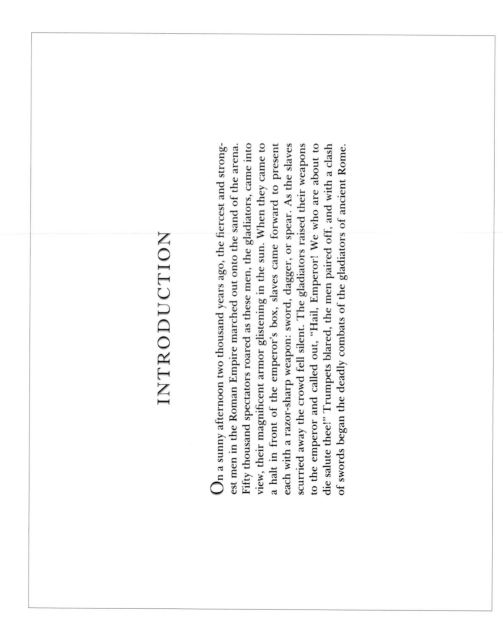

INTRODUCTION

On a sunny afternoon two thousand years ago, the fiercest and strongest men in the Roman Empire marched out onto the sand of the arena. Fifty thousand spectators roared as these men, the gladiators, came into view, their magnificent armor glistening in the sun. When they came to a halt in front of the emperor's box, slaves came forward to present each with a razor-sharp weapon: sword, dagger, or spear. As the slaves scurried away the crowd fell silent. The gladiators raised their weapons to the emperor and called out, "Hail, Emperor! We who are about to die salute thee!" Trumpets blared, the men paired off, and with a clash of swords began the deadly combats of the gladiators of ancient Rome.

I

ANCIENT ROME

The gladiator's world was a Roman world. The civilization that developed and exploited them was the most powerful empire of its time. At its height, it governed the lives of 60 million people, one-fifth of the world's population, all of whom obeyed its laws, paid taxes to its emperor, and were familiar with its language, religions, and customs.

According to tradition, Rome was founded on April 21, 753 B.C. The legend says that Romulus and Remus were the twin sons of the war god, Mars. As infants, they were abandoned in a basket by the River Tiber. There they were found by a she-wolf, who carried them back to her den and protected and nurtured them until they were old enough to survive on their own. It was as a young man that Romulus established the city that bears his name by carving its borders with a plow. Watching his brother hard at work and doing nothing to help, Remus teased Romulus mercilessly, making fun of his hard labor. When he could take it no

2

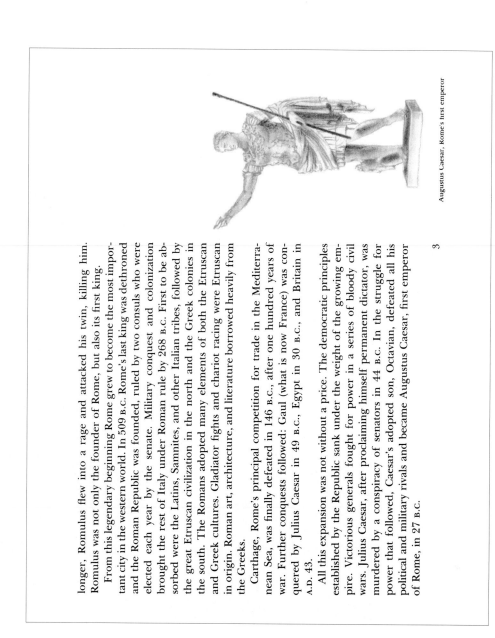

Augustus Caesar, Rome's first emperor

longer, Romulus flew into a rage and attacked his twin, killing him. Romulus was not only the founder of Rome, but also its first king.

From this legendary beginning Rome grew to become the most important city in the western world. In 509 B.C. Rome's last king was dethroned and the Roman Republic was founded, ruled by two consuls who were elected each year by the senate. Military conquest and colonization brought the rest of Italy under Roman rule by 268 B.C. First to be absorbed were the Latins, Samnites, and other Italian tribes, followed by the great Etruscan civilization in the north and the Greek colonies in the south. The Romans adopted many elements of both the Etruscan and Greek cultures. Gladiator fights and chariot racing were Etruscan in origin. Roman art, architecture, and literature borrowed heavily from the Greeks.

Carthage, Rome's principal competition for trade in the Mediterranean Sea, was finally defeated in 146 B.C., after one hundred years of war. Further conquests followed: Gaul (what is now France) was conquered by Julius Caesar in 49 B.C., Egypt in 30 B.C., and Britain in A.D. 43.

All this expansion was not without a price. The democratic principles established by the Republic sank under the weight of the growing empire. Victorious generals fought for power in a series of bloody civil wars. Julius Caesar, after proclaiming himself permanent dictator, was murdered by a conspiracy of senators in 44 B.C. In the struggle for power that followed, Caesar's adopted son, Octavian, defeated all his political and military rivals and became Augustus Caesar, first emperor of Rome, in 27 B.C.

3

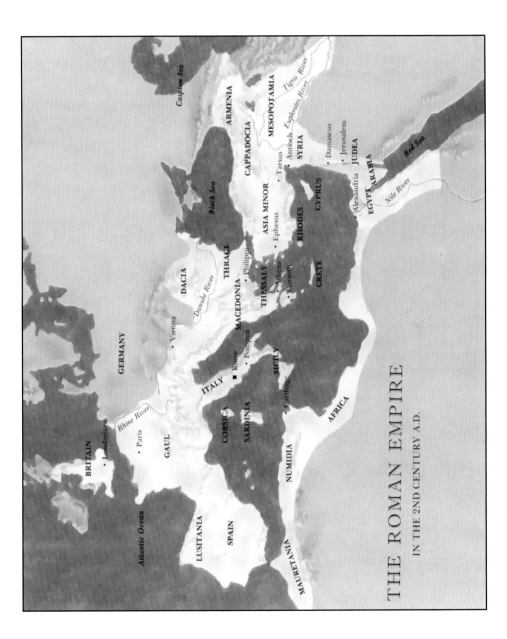

THE ROMAN EMPIRE
IN THE 2ND CENTURY A.D.

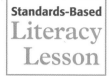

Until its fall four hundred years later, Rome was ruled by eighty-six emperors, some wise and just, others insane and corrupt. At its height, the Roman Empire controlled all of southern Europe, Britain, Asia Minor, Syria, Egypt, and North Africa. Cities were established, trade was regulated, taxes were collected. Rome built 53,000 miles of roads, bridges, aqueducts, and sewers, some of which are still in use. Its laws, manners, and customs were adopted all over the empire.

But for all its glory, it's difficult to ignore the fact that the Roman Empire was won by military force and built by the labor of millions of slaves. To the average Roman citizen, life was hard, war was a constant threat, and slaves were just another piece of property. And in spite of their sophistication in government, business, and the arts, Romans had a crude taste for violence and cruelty. For almost a thousand years Roman society represented both the best and the worst of human civilization.

5

Standards-Based
Literacy
Lesson

continued

🦋 Introducing Ancient Civilizations Unit

Activity	Procedures and Comments
Thematic opening activities; map/globe; brainstorm	Display a world map and/or a globe. Tell students they are going to begin their study of ancient civilizations with a study of one part of what is now known as Europe. Be sure students understand the meaning of the terms *ancient* in the historical sense and *civilization*. Brainstorm about the value of such study.
Focused discussion	Ask questions such as the following, keeping the discussion focused and brief: Where is Rome? What do we know about the role Rome played in history?
Word wall	Begin a word wall related to Rome by writing the name of the country and any topic-specific words or place names that arise during the discussion. Continue to add to the word wall as the unit progresses.
Introduce unit activities	Tell students to begin jotting down ideas for possible unit projects related to ancient civilizations and ancient Rome in particular. Explain what project resources will be made available during the unit of study: the library for reference books, CD-ROMs, and Web sites; additional books and maps within the classroom.
	Note: *These activities activate global prior knowledge for future reading, motivate, and provide additional topic-specific vocabulary.*

🦋 Introducing *Gladiator*

Activity	Procedures and Comments
Picture; independent semantic mapping	1. Display the cover of the book. 2. Have students work in pairs or small groups to make semantic maps of the term *gladiator*, with one student as the recorder. 3. Tell students they will add to and/or revise these later.
Word wall	Call students together in a large group, and ask for terms from independent activities to add to the word wall.
Preview the book and the first chapter; note text structure	1. Have students preview the entire book by looking at the title and the table of contents and leafing through pages. 2. Discuss the cover art and the chapter titles, and record predictions about the content.

Activity	Procedures and Comments (continued)
	3. Have students locate the first chapter, and lead them to examine and discuss the pictures and the captions under them.
	4. Recall with students what they know about how informational text might be organized. Ask them to predict how they think a chapter on this topic might be organized. Record these ideas and tell students you will return to them later.
	Note: *These activities help students know that informational text is approached differently from story; it is a good idea to get a general idea about the entire text before beginning. Also, the chapter they will read has no organizational markers such as headings and subheadings. As they read, the organization will become clearer.*
Read aloud; predict	**1.** Read aloud the Introduction. Discuss how this introduction is unlike others in that it is designed to motivate one to want to read rather than provide an overview of the book.
	2. Have students predict what they think they will learn from the first chapter based on the title.
	3. Record the predictions, and tell students they will return to these predictions after completing the chapter.
	4. Remind students they will return to their semantic webs to add (or change) information.
	Note: *Reading aloud to students models fluent reading and motivates interest.*

🦋 Reading and Responding to *Gladiator*

Activity	Procedures and Comments
Guided reading of the chapter	**1.** Read aloud the first paragraph or two. Lead students to compare the general information about the Roman civilization with their knowledge of current civilizations. Then have students read the next paragraph silently.
	2. Ask a volunteer to summarize the main idea of the paragraph.
	3. Ask students to suggest words to add to the word wall.
	4. Verify understanding of key terms such as *legendary* and *colonization*.

Activity	Procedures and Comments (continued)
	5. Have students predict what they will learn in the following paragraph(s).
	6. Continue guiding the reading until you think students will be able to carry on by reading with a partner or independently. You may want to discuss the content in great detail to be sure students understand the information and the terminology, and are able to place the information in time and place.
	Note: *Guided reading models the value of summarizing, predicting, and dealing with concept vocabulary while reading informational text. You will vary the depth of your guidance according to the needs of your group and of individual students.*
Cooperative or independent reading (when students are ready)	**1.** Have students continue reading the chapter.
	2. Remind students to summarize main ideas, details, and vocabulary as they read. If they are reading with a partner, they may discuss the reading.
	3. Have students list concept words as they read to add to the word wall later.
	Note: *Students should be thinking about how they deal with unfamiliar words in context and be ready to talk about their strategies later.*
Discussion	**1.** After all students have read the chapter, have students recall the main idea(s) and important details of this chapter.
	2. You may want to have students independently devise a graphic way of showing the important information in the chapter and then share this with the class.
	3. Display a current map of the same area as is shown in the map of the Roman Empire in the first chapter. Lead students to note what seems basically the same and what is different. Lead a focused discussion about possible causes of such change.
	Note: *During the chapter discussion, students may want to return to the text to support their ideas.*
Return to predictions	Have students review the predictions they made before reading and confirm or revise them.
	Note: *Returning to predictions helps students understand that ideas change as one reads.*

🦋 Extending "Ancient Rome" to the Remainder of the Book

1. Observation during the read-aloud, guided reading, and cooperative or independent reading of Chapter 1 will dictate how to have students read the remainder of the book. Some students may be able to read the rest of the book independently, with group discussions every chapter or two. Others may do better with continued guided reading and/or cooperative reading. It is not necessary that all students read the book in the same mode.
2. As students get ideas for projects, they will present them to me, and I will give whatever support individuals need to carry out their projects independently or with a partner.
3. Throughout the unit, we will add to the word wall and to our group background knowledge about Rome and other ancient civilizations.
4. Throughout the reading of the book, I will hold individual conferences with students to assess their ability to deal with new vocabulary in context, summarize main ideas and supporting details, and predict. Based on these conferences, I will plan any needed direct skill instruction.

After Reading the Plan

1. Review the plan and discuss it with your peers. Focus on how prior knowledge was activated and developed before and throughout the lesson.
2. Plan a different lesson for the first chapter of *Gladiator* using two or three other strategies for activating prior knowledge.

🦋 Summary

This chapter focused on the importance of activating and developing the concepts and vocabulary that constitute prior knowledge. Second-language learners, students with limited prior knowledge, and students with misconceptions need special support. Fourteen strategies—two student strategies and twelve teaching strategies—were described, with emphasis on how and when to use them. *The ultimate goal of the literacy program is to get students to use strategies independently and to call up their own prior knowledge to determine their purpose for reading.* The chapter concluded with a sample lesson illustrating the process of planning a lesson that focuses on prior knowledge.

For Additional Reading

Alvermann, D. E., Dillon, D. R., & O'Brien, D. G. (1987). *Using discussion to promote reading comprehension*. Newark, DE: International Reading Association.

Au, K. H. (1993). *Literacy instruction in multicultural settings*. Fort Worth, TX: Harcourt Brace.

Buehl, D. (2001). *Classroom strategies for interactive learning* (2nd ed.). Newark, DE: International Reading Association.

Duke, N. K., & Purcell-Gates, V (2003). Genres at home and at school: Bridging the known to the new. *The Reading Teacher. 57*(1), 30–37.

Leu, D. J. Jr. (Ed.). (1998). Exploring literacy on the Internet. *The Reading Teacher*, *51*(8), 694–700.

Nilsen, A. P., & Nilsen, D. L. J. (2003). A new spin on teaching vocabulary: A source-based approach. *The Reading Teacher*, *56*(5), 436-439.

Simpson, A. (1996). Critical questions: Whose questions? *The Reading Teacher*, *50*(2), 118–127.

For Exploration: Electronic Products and Resources

Use the following Web sites to gain additional ideas for developing prior knowledge with your students:

INSPIRATION or Kidspiration is a powerful visual learning tool that inspires students to develop ideas and organize their thinking. Teachers can download a free trial from the Web site.
http://www.inspiration.com

This Web site, sponsored by the University of West Georgia, provides over one hundred online anticipation guides, complete with comprehension questions for grades K–12.
http://www.westga.edu/~kidreach/antguide2.html

This site offers a variety of teaching resources relating to the role of prior knowledge and schema in literacy development.
http://reading.indiana.edu/

This is a fabulous online encyclopedia that offers information, pictures, and additional Web resources on thousands of topics. This could be helpful in developing background and prior knowledge for students.
http://encarta.msn.com

This online article discusses what teachers and parents can do to shorten the length of the assimilation process and help children process new information by encouraging the child to build a network of prior knowledge.
http://www.thelibrarylady.net/Childhood%20%20From%20the%20Inside %20Out/building_a_network_of_prior_know.htm

Lesson plans and information on Ancient Rome from proteacher.com!
http://www.proteacher.com/090084.shtml

History of Rome for Kids
http://www.historyforkids.org/learn/romans/

The Roman Empire for Children
http://www.roman-empire.net/children

How to Teach Strategies for Constructing Meaning

4

✓ **STANDARDS FOCUS**

NCTE/IRA Standards: 3, 5
Standards for Reading Professionals: 1, 2, 4, 5

Educators Speak   pp. 139, 158

Using Monitoring to Help the Diverse Learner
                        —*Monte Slaven, Maize, Kansas*

Can You Relate? Graphic Organizers, Strategies, and
Literature in the Middle School
                        —*David Burgess, New Castle, Indiana*

Strategies and Standards, p. 135

Strategies for Constructing Meaning, p. 135

Visualizing, p. 136

Monitoring, p. 137

Inferencing, p. 142

Identifying Important Information, p. 142

Generating and Answering Questions, p. 142

Synthesizing, p. 147

Summarizing, p. 148

Planning Effective Strategy Instruction, p. 152

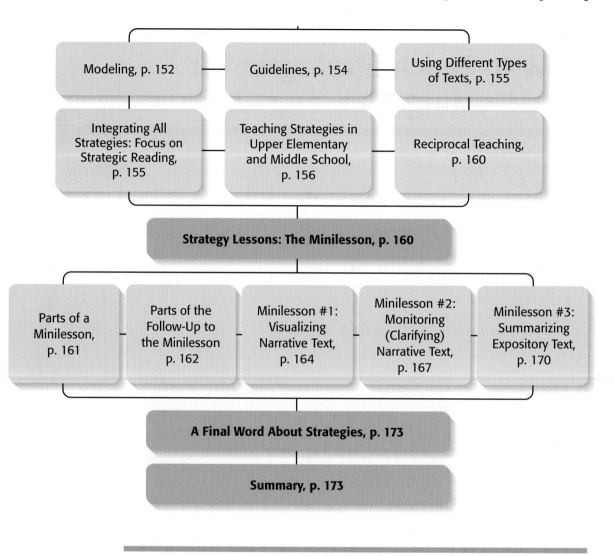

Let's walk through Brownsville Elementary School to see what is happening in three different classrooms.

Mr. Robinson is reading the big book Pretend You're a Cat (Marzollo, 1990) with his first graders. As he reads aloud each page, he reminds the children to make pictures in their heads. After reading the entire book aloud once, he briefly discusses with the children what they liked in the story. Then he talks about what they visualized while listening to the story.

Down the hall, Ms. Garza's third-grade class is finishing story time. She has just read aloud Princess Furball (Huck, 1989), after which all the students returned to their seats and immediately started independent reading time. Ms. Garza has several strategy posters displayed to remind students to apply what they learned.

Upstairs, Mr. Lee shows his fifth graders a strategy poster for previewing and self-questioning. The class is looking at the book Lurkers of the Deep: Life Within the Ocean Depths (Robison, 1978). Mr. Lee says, "As I look through this book, I can see from the section headings and pho-

tographs that it is going to give me a lot of information about light in the ocean. One question I would like to answer as I read this book is: How does the light in the ocean affect life there? What question might you want to answer?" Terri volunteers that she would like to know how plants and animals grow in the dark.

In each of these Brownsville Elementary School classrooms, a different activity was taking place, but one thing was common to all of them: the students were learning to use strategies to construct meaning:

- Mr. Robinson guided students to use the strategy of visualizing to help enhance the construction of meaning.
- Ms. Garza used posters to remind students of the steps for various strategies.
- Mr. Lee modeled a particular strategy, preview and self-question, to help students do what expert readers do: determine their purpose for reading. By sharing his thinking as he used this strategy, Mr. Lee made his mental processes public to help the students think about this strategy.

These three scenes show how the use of strategies for constructing meaning is a part of every classroom's day-to-day activities. Mr. Robinson used the time when he read aloud to encourage his first graders to "make pictures in their heads," or visualize as they listened. Listening is a perfect time for visualizing, because children can close their eyes. Later, Mr. Robinson's students will visualize as they read for themselves. Ms. Garza has taught a number of minilessons on strategy use to her third graders. Whenever they are reading independently, she is sure to display posters to remind her students to use strategies. Mr. Lee modeled a strategy he found useful in his own reading.

Strategies and Standards

Part of being a strategic reader is recognizing which strategy is appropriate and when to use it. A good reader often uses several strategies simultaneously.

Look back at the NCTE/IRA Standards listed on the inside front cover of this book. Notice that strategies 3 and 5 focus on having students learn to use strategies in reading and writing to help them construct and convey meaning. In some way, all state standards focus on helping students learn to use strategies. As you develop your skills as a teacher of literacy, you should pay close attention to the strategies students need to learn. These strategies should be taught to students from kindergarten through eighth grade. In preschool, groundwork can be developed for the strategies through read alouds. Let's examine the strategies for constructing meaning.

Strategies for Constructing Meaning

Research has clearly shown that reading comprehension is a process in which individuals construct meaning by interacting with the text (Pearson et al., 1990). This constructive interaction involves the individual's prior knowledge, the text, and the reading situation or context (Lipson & Wixson, 1986).

Expert readers have strategies or plans to help them solve problems and construct meaning before, during, and after reading (Paris et al., 1991). Although the number of these strategies is small, they should be thoroughly developed (Pearson et al., 1990). Many unanswered questions remain and much research needs to be done in this area (Dole et al., 1991); nevertheless, you must address two major questions:

1. What strategies do my students need as they become expert constructors of meaning?
2. How are these strategies best taught in the literacy program?

We will examine both of these questions in this chapter.

Volumes of research have attempted to identify the strategies that expert constructors of meaning use (Baker & Brown, 1984a, 1984b; Dole et al., 1991; Harvey & Goudvis, 2000; Keene & Zimmermann, 1997; Paris et al., 1991; Pearson, Roehler, Dole, & Duffy, 1992; Pressley, 2000; Pressley, Johnson, Symons, McGoldrick, & Kurita, 1989; National Reading Panel, 2000). When these studies and others are examined as a group, seven important strategies emerge:

1. Visualizing
2. Monitoring
3. Inferencing, including prediction
4. Identifying important information (story line in narrative texts and main ideas in expository texts)
5. Generating and answering questions
6. Synthesizing
7. Summarizing

Although the research discusses many other strategies, these appear to have the greatest support for inclusion in the literacy program. These strategies should be taught to students from kindergarten through eighth grade. In preschool, groundwork can be developed for the strategies through read alouds. Let's examine each of the seven strategies.

Visualizing

Strategic readers make pictures in their heads as they read. This process of **visualizing,** sometimes called *mental imaging,* enhances understanding. The mental picture we form while we read is a kind of inferential thinking that connects with the questions we have mentally generated. Consider your own experience as you read a book such as a murder mystery. The author describes the discovery of a body, and you make a picture in your head of that scene. Perhaps you add some details that are not even in the text, drawing on your own prior knowledge about the setting, about dead bodies, and about the genre, and from your own past experiences. This mental

FIGURE 4.1

Strategy Poster for Visualizing Narrative Text

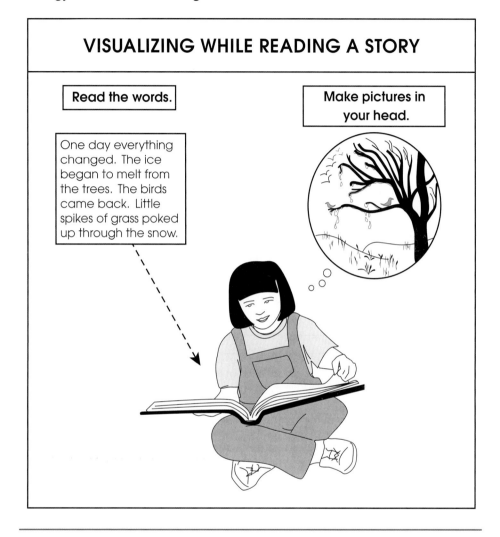

VISUALIZING WHILE READING A STORY

Read the words.

One day everything changed. The ice began to melt from the trees. The birds came back. Little spikes of grass poked up through the snow.

Make pictures in your head.

picture enhances your construction of meaning. You read on, adjusting your mental picture as you receive new information. Figures 4.1 and 4.2 show possible strategy posters that can remind students to make pictures in their heads as they read. A sample lesson on visualizing is presented on pages 164–167.

Monitoring

Monitoring, sometimes called *clarifying,* is the process of knowing that what you are reading is not making sense, and then having some plans for overcoming this

FIGURE 4.2

Strategy Poster for Visualizing Expository Text

VISUALIZING WHILE READING INFORMATIONAL TEXT

✔ The words on the page can put pictures in your head. Pictures in your head help the words mean more.

✔ As you read, change the pictures in your head.

Sale $1.49 per pound

"Chickens are an important part of our economy."

"For one thing, eggs are a staple in the diet of many people."

Educators Speak

Using Monitoring to Help the Diverse Learner

❝ I teach in a predominantly white middle-class suburban school district. Diversity is not immediately recognizable in my sixth-grade classroom, but it does exist. The variety of diversity I face as a teacher is primarily that of learning styles and academic abilities. Seven students in my classroom are identified as gifted, and four are performing well below grade level in reading. The other thirteen students are reading on grade level.

We are currently enjoying Mark Twain's *The Prince and the Pauper* as an extension of the theme "Growing Up" from our reading series. Although this classic novel is identified as an early adolescent piece of literature, it is difficult for my students to comprehend. Monitoring has therefore become an extremely valuable tool in meeting my students' individual needs.

The monitoring strategy I am using during this portion of my reading class actually employs a variety of reading strategies, including summarization, visualization, prior knowledge, rereading, questioning, inference, and predicting. As we are reading, we frequently pause so that a passage may be summarized. A student voluntarily explains a passage while his peers listen actively by visualizing this scene. Many of my students have prior knowledge of historical events of this time period and readily share their insight, assisting others in their comprehension. This insight provides clarity to difficult cultural differences presented by this novel. The complicated sentence structure, dialogue, and word choice of this work of historical fiction often requires that a passage be reread. After rereading, the class collectively asks questions, discusses, and interprets text meaning. Students often take an additional step and make inferences and predictions within the framework of this discussion. As the teacher, my role almost becomes secondary and that of a facilitator in this situation. I try to allow the students to take the lead with their discussion and interaction like that of a book discussion or literature circle.

Through monitoring and use of these various reading strategies, I am able to determine understanding and encourage students to look beyond the mechanics of simply reading the words from the page. Monitoring works well with the diversity in my classroom. I am able to assist my low readers with their needs and encourage growth with my students who are at a higher reading level. This strategy has also proven to be effective in previous years when the diversity has been more widely varied. ❞

Monte Slaven, Sixth-Grade Teacher
Maize East Elementary
Maize, Kansas

problem. This is an important part of students' metacognitive development (Baker & Brown, 1984a, 1984b; Brown, 1980) and is a developmental process that improves with age (Paris et al., 1991). Expert constructors of meaning are able to anticipate problems in reading and correct them as they occur. This "fix-up" process may involve these processes: rereading, reading ahead, raising new questions, changing predictions or making new ones, evaluating what is read, using strategies for identifying words, looking up words, seeking help from an outside source.

Figure 4.3 presents a strategy poster you can use in teaching students how to use a monitoring strategy known as **stop and think** and is useful for both narrative and expository texts. A sample lesson for modeling this strategy appears on pages 167–169.

FIGURE 4.3

Strategy Poster for Stop and Think (Monitoring Narrative or Expository Text)

FIGURE 4.4

Strategy Poster for Inferencing

Inferencing

Inferencing, the process of judging, concluding, or reasoning from some given information, is the heart of meaning construction for learners of all ages (Anderson & Pearson, 1984). Even very young readers and readers performing a simple task such as reading a sentence use inferencing to supply information that is not given (Kail, Chi, Ingram, & Danner, 1977). When students make predictions before or during reading, they are *inferencing*: using available information and prior knowledge to construct meaning (recall the preview and predict strategy). A strategy poster such as the one in Figure 4.4 on page 141 can be used to help students think about this process as they read both narrative and expository texts.

Identifying Important Information

Strategic readers identify the important information in what they read. In narrative texts or stories, they identify or infer the story line or story grammar (see Mandler, 1984); in expository texts, they identify or infer the main ideas (Baumann, 1986). Although identification is similar in both types of texts, the task differs because the structures of the texts are different. Text structures differ across languages; therefore, English Language Learners may not be familiar with the structures of texts in English. Teachers can help students by making explicit the typical structures of various genres of English writing (Kaplan, 1966).

Whatever terminology is used to describe this process, we know that construction of meaning can be improved when students learn a strategy for identifying important information in each type of text (Baumann, 1984; Short & Ryan, 1984; Winograd & Bridge, 1986). Figures 4.5 and 4.6 present strategy posters you can use to help students learn this important strategy for narrative and expository texts.

Generating and Answering Questions

Another strategy readers can use to improve their meaning construction is **generating and answering their own questions** (self-questioning) (Davey & McBride, 1986; Singer & Donlan, 1982). This process involves teaching students how to generate questions that require them to integrate information and think as they read. For example, a good "think" question might be, "Why did the dinosaurs become extinct?" This question helps focus the reader's thinking on more than just facts. Figure 4.7 presents a poster for this using this strategy with expository text. Figure 4.8 is a poster for using this strategy with narrative text. Generating questions may have little value unless it is taught thoroughly (Denner & Rickards, 1987; Pressley et al., 1990).

FIGURE 4.5

Strategy Poster for Identifying Important Information in Narrative Text

IDENTIFYING IMPORTANT INFORMATION IN STORIES

As I read stories, I will look for:

Setting:
               Time   *Place*

Characters:

Problem:

Action:

Outcome:

In addition to generating and answering questions of their own, readers often benefit from answering questions generated by others, such as the teacher or other students (National Reading Panel, 2000a and 2000b). This process is an integral part of reciprocal teaching. See page 160 for a more detailed discussion of the reciprocal teaching process.

FIGURE 4.6

Strategy Poster for Identifying Important Information in Expository Text

FIGURE 4.7

Strategy Poster for Question Generating and Answering (Expository Text)

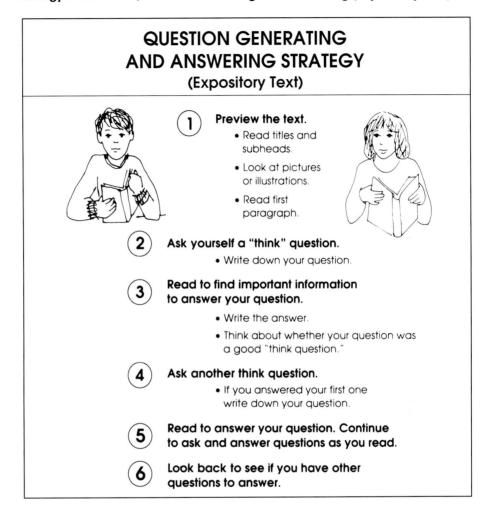

QUESTION GENERATING AND ANSWERING STRATEGY
(Expository Text)

1. **Preview the text.**
   - Read titles and subheads.
   - Look at pictures or illustrations.
   - Read first paragraph.

2. **Ask yourself a "think" question.**
   - Write down your question.

3. **Read to find important information to answer your question.**
   - Write the answer.
   - Think about whether your question was a good "think question."

4. **Ask another think question.**
   - If you answered your first one write down your question.

5. **Read to answer your question. Continue to ask and answer questions as you read.**

6. **Look back to see if you have other questions to answer.**

Synthesizing

Synthesizing is combining elements and integrating them into a new whole. When a reader synthesizes, he or she begins with the knowledge in his or her head, and then continually adds new information and recombines the old and the new. The new merges with the known and forms a new pattern—gives a new perspective—until in the end, the reader has constructed a meaning that is greater than

FIGURE 4.8

Strategy Poster for Question Generating and Answering (Narrative Text)

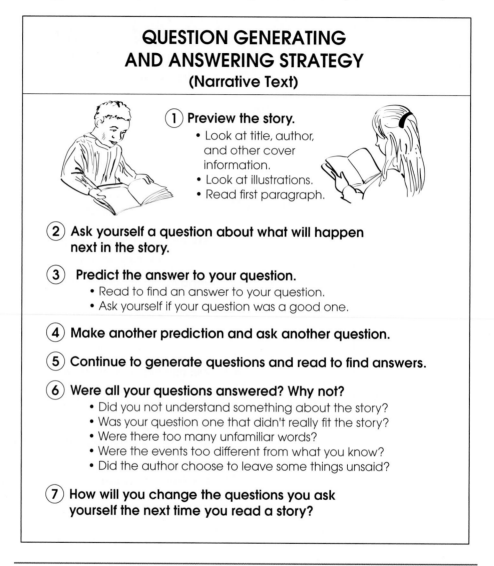

QUESTION GENERATING AND ANSWERING STRATEGY
(Narrative Text)

(1) **Preview the story.**
   - Look at title, author, and other cover information.
   - Look at illustrations.
   - Read first paragraph.

(2) **Ask yourself a question about what will happen next in the story.**

(3) **Predict the answer to your question.**
   - Read to find an answer to your question.
   - Ask yourself if your question was a good one.

(4) **Make another prediction and ask another question.**

(5) **Continue to generate questions and read to find answers.**

(6) **Were all your questions answered? Why not?**
   - Did you not understand something about the story?
   - Was your question one that didn't really fit the story?
   - Were there too many unfamiliar words?
   - Were the events too different from what you know?
   - Did the author choose to leave some things unsaid?

(7) **How will you change the questions you ask yourself the next time you read a story?**

Fifth graders generate questions about social studies.

© Michael Zide

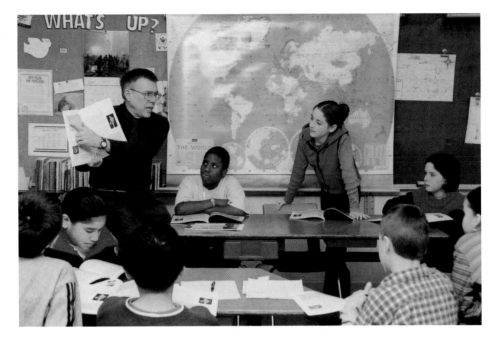

what was individually either in his or her head and/or in the text. The strategy of synthesizing can be applied to a single piece of text or across various texts.

While reading a narrative, the reader may begin with visualizing and calling on prior knowledge about the setting or perhaps the problem. While reading expository text, the process is similar, but the synthesis is more likely to be an accrual and integration of factual information, though inference will also contribute to the new perspective.

Synthesizing also extends across texts. Thus, when one reads in a social studies text about the westward expansion, one must draw on and combine information one might already hold based on other texts about that period in history, biographies, films, CD-ROMs, informational programs on television, or even family journals. The reader's understanding of genre and story elements deepens with each narrative through the process of synthesis.

Figures 4.9 and 4.10 show possible strategy posters to help students remember to synthesize as they read.

Summarizing

Summarizing is the process of pulling together the essential elements in a longer passage of text. Effective constructors of meaning are able to use this strategy, and research has shown that certain guidelines can help students develop this skill

FIGURE 4.9

Strategy Poster for Synthesizing Narrative Text

> # READING STORIES: ON THE PAGE AND IN MY HEAD
>
> **Before reading, ask yourself:**
> - What do I know about this kind of story?
> - Have I read other stories by this author? Do I recognize the illustrator?
> - Do I know already what the story is about?
> - Did someone recommend the story to me? Why?
>
> **While you read, think:**
> - Do I understand the setting of this story?
> - Do I understand the characters and the problem?
> - Are the story events unfolding the way I thought they would?
> - How are my ideas changing as I learn more about the story?
>
> **After you read, think:**
> - What were the important parts of the story? Could I retell them to someone?
> - Would I recommend this to a friend? What would I say it is about?
> - What have I learned about this kind of story? About how stories are told?

(Brown & Day, 1983). Although much of this training research has focused on expository texts, the same types of guidelines can be applied to narrative texts using the story grammar concept already discussed. Figures 4.11 and 4.12 present strategy posters to use in teaching summarizing. A sample lesson using informational text is presented on pages 170–172.

Ongoing research should add to our understanding of how the literacy learner uses various strategies. However, the current level of our knowledge supports helping readers learn to use the seven strategies just discussed. Table 4.1 shows when each strategy would fit into an individual's reading.

For information on story grammar, see Chapter 2.

FIGURE 4.10

Strategy Poster for Synthesizing Expository Text

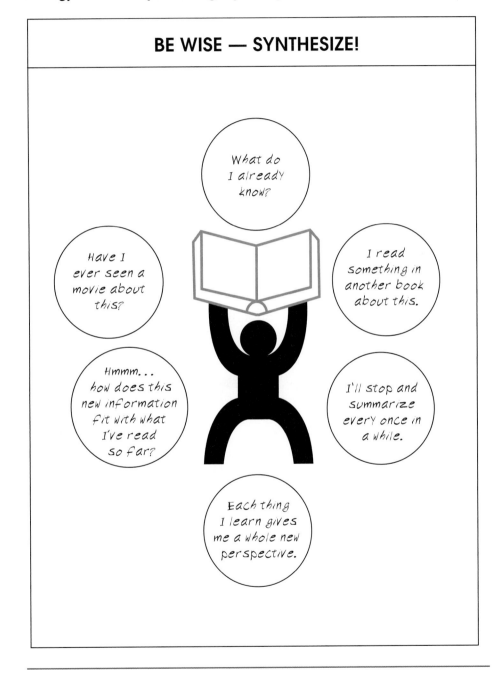

FIGURE 4.11

Strategy Poster for Summarizing Narrative Text

SUMMARIZING STORIES
(Narrative Text)

1. Read your story to find the important parts:
   • Setting
   • Characters
   • Problem
   • Action
   • Outcome
   Make notes.

2. Look over your notes and decide what can be left out.

3. First I will tell the title and author. Then I'll tell...

   Think about how you will tell or write your summary to make it clear.

4. Tell or write your summary.

FIGURE 4.12

Strategy Poster for Summarizing Expository Text

| TABLE 4.1 | Points Where Strategies May Help Students Construct Meaning |

	READING		
Strategy	**Before**	**During**	**After**
Visualizing	✓	✓	
Monitoring		✓	
Inferencing (includes predictions)	✓	✓	
Identifying important information	✓	✓	✓
Generating and answering questions	✓	✓	✓
Synthesizing	✓	✓	✓
Summarizing		✓	✓

🦋 Planning Effective Strategy Instruction

Carefully planned instruction is the key to successful strategy learning. In this section we examine the factors that teachers need to consider in helping students use strategies to become effective constructors of meaning.

Modeling

Literacy learning is an interactive, constructive process. In essence, children develop literacy (writing, reading, speaking, listening, viewing, and thinking) by having real literacy experiences. However, as they have these experiences, they need carefully scaffolded instruction (Dole et al., 1991). Modeling is an important form of such support.

Modeling Defined

Modeling is the process of showing or demonstrating for someone how to use or do something she or he does not know how to do; most human behaviors are acquired in this way (Bandura, 1986). Modeling can also be described as the process by which an expert shows students (nonexperts) how to perform a task, so that they can build their own understanding of how to complete that task (Collins et al., 1987). With literacy learning, this expert may be an adult outside of school, an adult in school (usually the teacher), or a peer. When a child sees a parent writing a letter or reading a book, modeling is taking place. When Mr. Lee talked aloud using previewing and self-questioning, he was modeling. When a child sees a friend successfully complete a piece of writing and share it, modeling has occurred.

Modeling can be implicit or explicit (Roehler & Duffy, 1991). **Implicit modeling** takes place when the processes or ideas being modeled occur as a part of an experience and are *not directly* identified or stated. Reading aloud to students and letting students see you write a letter are examples. Implicit modeling always occurs within the context of the complete process of reading and writing. **Explicit modeling** involves directly showing and talking with students about what is being modeled, using a **think-aloud** process (Roehler & Duffy ,1991).

In this approach, teachers actually share with students the cognitive processes, or thinking, that they go through:

> *As I read through this paragraph, I can immediately tell that the topic of it is space travel because it mentions outer space, rockets, and planets. Even though mention is made of early pioneers, I can see that this is only a point of comparison. I notice that all of the points compared show me how early pioneer travel and space travel have been similar.*

Notice that the teacher is sharing his thinking to reveal the process one goes through in formulating or inferring a main idea.

An inherent danger in explicit modeling is that the activities will become nothing more than the modeling of an isolated skill, which is not effective in helping students construct meaning (Pearson et al., 1990). *Explicit modeling must be done within the context of a specific text* (Duffy et al., 1987; Roehler & Duffy, 1991). All examples of modeling presented in this chapter and throughout the rest of the text adhere to this important guideline.

Where Modeling Takes Place

Modeling can occur at numerous points throughout the literacy program:

- *During daily activities:* Although the daily activities of the literacy program will afford many opportunities for both implicit and explicit modeling, most of the modeling will be *implicit*. Read-aloud times, shared writing experiences, periods for independent, self-initiated reading and writing, and cooperative reading are just a few examples. Because the literacy-centered classroom operates on the premise that children learn to read and write by reading and writing, all of the activities associated with real reading and writing play a significant role in the modeling of these processes.

See Chapter 8 for information on writing.

- *Process writing:* This is another important point where modeling occurs. The process of writing, shared writing, and writing conferences present many opportunities for both implicit and explicit modeling.

- *Literacy lessons:* The literacy lesson consists of three parts: introducing, reading and responding, and extending. Within introducing and reading and responding, there will be opportunities for explicit modeling of prior knowledge, vocabulary, and particular strategies that students need to construct meaning. Implicit modeling by the teacher and peers will occur in all three parts of the lesson.

See Chapter 10 for information on reading and writing workshop.

- *Minilessons:* Minilessons, developed on the basis of students' needs, include explicit modeling of strategies for both reading and writing. These lessons can be developed around the framework presented in Chapter 2. They may also take place during your reading workshop or writing workshop.

Modeling helps students become more expert readers and writers and gives them better control over their metacognitive processes (Paris et al., 1991). However, the teacher must effectively balance implicit and explicit modeling.

Guidelines

A great deal is known about effective strategy instruction (Duffy, 1993; Pressley & Harris, 1990). The following guidelines should be helpful in developing this instruction within your classroom:

- *Determine the need for strategy instruction on the basis of student performance.* Students will learn some strategies through their reading and writing experiences. When you observe that their construction of meaning would be enhanced by a minilesson involving modeling, provide it. *Students' needs should be the primary determining factor in using explicit modeling.*

- *Introduce all the major strategies you want students to learn early in the school year.* This allows you to present the strategies you want students to learn, and then have them use their time focusing on using the strategies while reading. At first, students may seem uncomfortable or uncertain with a given strategy, but this uncertainty will fade. More time should be spent on using the strategy than on modeling and practicing the strategy in isolation.

- *Model and practice the strategy in the meaningful context of a reading experience.* An inherent danger in strategy instruction is that the strategies will remain isolated. When strategies fail, it is often because they have been taught and practiced as isolated elements. A meaningful reading experience means students will (1) work with a text where the strategy is useful, (2) use that text as the basis for having the strategy modeled by the teacher, and (3) use additional texts for practicing the strategy. No fill-in-the-blank, mark, circle, or underline types of exercises should be used, because such activities isolate the strategy.

- *Model each strategy at the point where it is most useful.* Make the modeling of a strategy as authentic as possible by doing it when students are most likely to use it in reading. For example, model the preview and predict strategy before reading a text, and then follow it up after reading.

- *Be sure that modeling and practicing are interactive and collaborative activities.* Strategy learning and use is most effective when students are active participants and work alongside their peers. For example, students learning to summarize may first work together to help the teacher construct a summary and later work with a partner to write a collaborative summary chart of a story they have read.

- *Gradually transfer modeling from yourself to the students.* This is the scaffolding of instruction. Once you have modeled a strategy enough times for students to begin using it comfortably, have students model it for one another and use it independently. If you see that more modeling is needed, provide it and then begin to release responsibility to the students again.

- *Help students experience immediate success with each strategy.* Nothing encourages students more than success. Have them explain how the strategy helped them, and point out successes you have seen. If you find a particular strategy is not working for a student, discontinue using it and move on to another one.

- *Encourage the use of a strategy across the curriculum.* Once students have started to use a strategy, model its use in curricular areas such as science and social studies. As students use strategies in these areas, have them reflect on and discuss how the various strategies helped them understand more of what they read. This will help them see the value of the strategy and will interest them in learning additional strategies.

- *Guide students to become strategic readers.* Once they are familiar with each strategy, model and encourage the use of all strategies together. (See below for a discussion of how to do this.)

These guidelines are applied in the sample minilessons beginning on page 164.

Using Different Types of Texts

See Chapter 3 for a discussion of text structures.

When planning effective strategy instruction, you must consider the types of texts students will be reading. You have learned about the differences between narrative texts and expository texts; narrative texts contain the elements of a story grammar (characters, setting, problem, action, and outcome), and expository texts are organized around main ideas and supporting details using different text structures. Sometimes authors combine narrative and expository structures in the same text. For example, *The Popcorn Book* (de Paola, 1978) tells a story and at the same time presents information. This type of book is sometimes known as an informational story.

Content texts used in such classes as health, science, and history are usually expository texts. These books often combine several text structures; for example, a U.S. history chapter may have passages presenting information in sequence, combined with passages showing cause-effect; these passages may be combined with some narration that explains how things fit together.

Navigating texts on CD-ROMs and the World Wide Web presents some challenges that are beyond the scope of this chapter. However, no matter where one reads text—whether the print is on paper or on a computer monitor—all of the strategies presented in this chapter are both applicable and necessary.

In planning strategy lessons, you should consider how to adjust the strategies for the type of text to be read. Table 4.2 shows the type of text and circumstances under which the seven strategies discussed earlier work best. Remember that all strategies work with any type of text; however, some modifications are needed to adjust to the different types of texts.

Integrating All Strategies: Focus on Strategic Reading

When people read a text, they use several strategies simultaneously. Therefore, as strategies are taught, it is important at some point to pull all the strategies together

| TABLE 4.2 | Strategy Use in Different Types of Texts | | |

Strategy	Narrative Texts	Expository Texts	Comment
Visualizing	Yes	Yes	Adjust based on presence of pictures or other graphic information in text.
Monitoring	Yes	Yes	Adjust the monitoring strategies to the type of text.
Inferencing	Yes	Sometimes	Since expository texts present factual information, too much inferencing in a text reduces the text's quality.
Identifying important information	Yes; focus on story elements	Yes; focus on main ideas and supporting details	Must adjust strategy to structure of text.
Generating and answering questions	Yes; focus questions on story elements	Yes; focus questions on main ideas and key concepts	Must adjust strategy to structure of text.
Synthesizing	Yes	Yes	Integrates new knowledge with prior knowledge.
Summarizing	Yes; focus summary on story elements	Yes; focus summary on main ideas and details	Must adjust strategy to structure of text.

and focus students' attention on being strategic readers by learning to select the strategy or strategies that will best help them construct meaning.

A good way to accomplish this focus on strategic reading is to first teach all of the strategies quickly, using suggestions and guidelines presented in this text. Then use the posters for the various strategies along with a poster such as that in Figure 4.13 to remind students about all of the strategies. Before students read any text, discuss with them which strategies they might use as they read. If you are guiding or coaching the reading, periodically model and discuss the use of various strategies during reading. After reading, have students reflect on how the use of various strategies helped them construct meaning. At any point before, during, or after reading, you may need to model the concept of strategic reading by modeling the use of one or more of the strategies.

Teaching Strategies in Upper Elementary and Middle School

A goal for upper elementary and middle school is to help all students be strategic readers every time they read, no matter what kind of text. Each teacher, in each subject area, must focus on helping students learn how to read the texts that are particular to that content area. Since reading in each content area presents unique challenges for readers, one must teach each of the strategies anew with each subject area.

Poster Promoting the Use of All Strategies Together

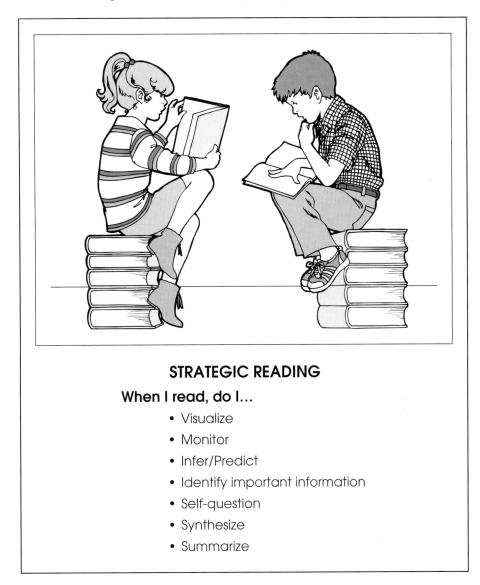

STRATEGIC READING

When I read, do I...

- Visualize
- Monitor
- Infer/Predict
- Identify important information
- Self-question
- Synthesize
- Summarize

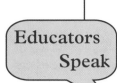

Educators Speak

Can You Relate? Graphic Organizers, Strategies, and Literature in the Middle School

"Helping middle-school students relate to literature and therefore to life is one of the challenges that middle-school language arts teachers face every day. The use of graphic organizers and story maps has been most helpful in getting students to be able to use these strategies.

Students enjoy predicting by trying to match wits with authors as they read. When I teach the poem "Barbara Frietchie" by John Greenleaf Whittier, we begin by brainstorming what it means to be a hero. Then students chart the names, beliefs, and actions taken of contemporary, historical, and fictional characters that they consider heroes. After reading the poem, they see if any of their predictions about heroes are true of Barbara.

Before reading the short story "The Landlady" by Roald Dahl, students have fun jotting down questions and predictions of what might happen based on the many clues offered in the story. The fun comes when Dahl outwits them, and their predictions turn out to be incorrect.

There are computer programs with ready-made graphic organizers I use to help with visualizing and summarizing. Before students read the short story "The Treasure of Lemon Brown" by Walter Dean Myers, I have them create a Venn diagram that investigates the topics: I value . . . Adults value . . . We all value . . . After reading, the task is to compare the diagram to one they create based on the characters in the story.

Summarizing really helps the middle-school reader relate to the literature being read. We read "Broken Chain" by Gary Soto. I use a graphic organizer by Inspiration to help students organize a brief summary. Using the organizer, each student then relates orally what happened, who the main characters are, the sequence of events, and how the main problem is finally solved. For students who struggle getting started, try first thoughts to help get them started. "Alfonso wanted . . . but . . . so . . . "

One of the easiest and least time-consuming methods of using any of these strategies is to simply have students keep a journal handy. (I store each class set in a plastic shoebox.) Readers relate by an ongoing dialogue with the text. They do this by writing down questions, predictions, main points for summarization, and even visualizations of what is going through their minds. By learning to use these strategies, readers can relate to literature."

—David Burgess, Seventh- and Eighth-Grade Language Arts Teacher
New Castle Middle School
New Castle, Indiana

It is impossible to master the ability to construct meaning. Although strategy lessons were taught in earlier grades, they must be retaught as reading material becomes more complex. As students face more difficult material, they need continuing strategy lessons. Some students, of course, may have greater need than others; they may need to be retaught with several minilessons. Other students may need only to be shown how the strategies they already know should be applied to a particular text.

Furthermore, as students develop in their literacy and face increasing textual demands, they must not only use each strategy, but they must integrate the use of all strategies into the seamless process called "constructing meaning." Teachers must model and guide students in this integration. A checklist such as that shown in Figure 4.14 may help students remember to use the strategies they have been learning. Subject-area teachers may adapt such a checklist to suit their content areas.

FIGURE 4.14

Checklist to Help Students Focus on Using All Strategies in All Subject Areas

My Strategic Reading Guide

As I read, do I . . .

1. *Visualize*
   - Make pictures in my head?
   - Use mental images to answer my questions?

2. *Monitor*
   - Ask: Does this make sense to me?
     Does it help me meet my purposes?
   - Try fix-ups?
     - Reread
     - Read ahead
     - Look at illustrations
     - Ask for help
     - Think about words
   - Evaluate what I read?

3. *Infer/predict*
   - Look for important information?
   - Look at illustrations?
   - Think about what I know?
   - Think about what may happen or what I want to learn?

4. *Identify important information*
   - Look for story elements?
   - Look for main ideas and important details?

5. *Self-question*
   - Ask questions and look for answers?

6. *Synthesize*
   - Combine what I know with what I read?
   - Change my predictions as I read?
   - Integrate new knowledge with known?

7. *Summarize*
   - Summarize after I read?
     - Stories—think about story parts
     - Informational texts—think about main ideas and important details

Reciprocal Teaching

An excellent way to develop the use of strategies in upper elementary and middle-school students is through the use of **reciprocal teaching** (Palincsar & Brown, 1986). Reciprocal teaching is an interactive process in which the teacher and students take turns modeling four strategies after reading a meaningful chunk of text—*predict, question, clarify,* and *summarize.* Though the labels differ somewhat, the strategies parallel those discussed in this chapter; in fact, the procedure works with any strategy. This reciprocal modeling process takes the place of the typical discussion that follows reading.

Reciprocal teaching begins with heavy teacher modeling, which helps students see how a competent reader deals with text by using different strategies, depending on the demands of the text (Oczkus, 2003). Teacher modeling also helps students see how a competent reader recognizes when text is challenging and knows which strategies to use in each situation. Gradually, as with all other modeling, the teacher's need to lead the process diminishes and students are able to model strategic reading themselves. The goal is for students to activate strategy use as they read independently. Reciprocal teaching helps them reach that goal.

Research has demonstrated that reciprocal teaching is effective in helping all students increase their comprehension ability. However, it is most effective in helping below-level readers accelerate their reading in a short amount of time (Rosenshine & Meister, 1994).

🦋 Strategy Lessons: The Minilesson

As noted earlier in this chapter, explicit modeling may take place within the literacy lesson or through minilessons. For example, if, as part of a literacy lesson, you see the need to help students summarize stories, the most logical place to do this is at the conclusion of the lesson, after a story has been read. Students will then practice using the strategy in reading the next selection.

This section presents three sample strategy lessons organized around the minilesson concept. These lessons may be taught before or after the literacy lesson or as part of it, depending on the particular strategy and where it needs to be placed.

The minilesson is a very flexible plan for developing strategy lessons based on the principles of effective instruction using explicit, or direct, teaching and effective strategy learning. The parts of the plan should flow into an interactive dialogue that makes up the entire lesson. As the name *minilesson* implies, the lesson is short and focused, lasting from 5 to 10 minutes and rarely longer than 15 minutes. Some lessons may need to be taught several times, depending on the students' stage of literacy development and how they respond, and some lessons may not work for certain students and should be discontinued as you move on to more effective experiences. The four parts of the minilesson are:

1. introduction
2. teacher modeling

3. student modeling and guided practice
4. summarizing and reflecting

The three parts of the follow-up to the minilesson are:

1. independent practice
2. application
3. reflection

These follow-ups occur over several days or more following the minilesson.

Parts of a Minilesson

Four parts constitute the minilesson:

1. *Introduction:* During this portion of the lesson, you tell students what they are going to learn and relate it to reading or writing and their prior knowledge. You may talk directly with them and point out relationships, or you may draw information from them through an interactive discussion. For example, when teaching a lesson on inferencing, you might say:

   > *Tell me some examples in the last book we read where the author gave clues about something but didn't tell you directly what was intended.* [Students respond.] *This happens many times in books. When you figured out information from the clues, you were using a strategy called* inferencing. *Today we are going to think more about inferencing.*

   This very focused introduction should take just a few minutes.

2. *Teacher modeling:* During this part of the lesson, you show students how to use and how to think about the strategy being taught by "thinking aloud" with them. As you do this, you want to make certain that you incorporate three elements in your modeling:

   • Concept
   • Listening
   • Reading

   For example, with the strategy of inferencing, you develop the *concept* by starting with something concrete, such as a text illustration, and talk about what it shows and what you can infer from clues such as facial expressions or objects pictured. For *listening,* read aloud a piece of text and show students how to make inferences as they listen. Finally for *reading,* use a piece of text as the basis for your modeling; have students read the text, making this part of the lesson interactive by drawing students into the modeling. Think aloud, showing students how to make inferences as you read. After you have modeled for students, gradually transfer the modeling to them and help them "think aloud" about how they are using the strategy as they read the text. This process flows naturally into the next part of the lesson.

3. *Student modeling and guided practice:* Students are now using the strategy under your guidance, usually within the same text where the strategy was originally

modeled. They are reading sections silently, and you call on individuals to share their thinking aloud. For example, if you are using a short story to model inferencing, you might have students continue through the story to find other places to use inferencing, all the while encouraging them to share their thinking aloud as they work. In some cases, you will need to prompt students with questions, examples, or additional modeling. Throughout, give students feedback about how they are doing in using the strategy. The teacher modeling, student modeling, and guided practice flow together so closely that it is often difficult to tell where one begins and the other ends. The purpose of this portion of the lesson is to ensure that students are able to use the strategy before releasing them to practice it independently.

4. *Summarizing and reflecting:* Finally, prompt students to summarize what they have learned and get them to reflect on how and where they might use the strategy. Use prompts such as the following:

   - How did we make inferences in this story?
   - What did we use besides story information?
   - Where do you think you will use this strategy?

Remember that *students* need to verbalize what they have learned and where and how they might use it.

Parts of the Follow-Up to the Minilesson

The follow-up to the minilesson consists of opportunities to practice, apply, and think about how the strategy has been useful to the student. This consists of independent practice, **application,** and **reflection:**

1. *Independent practice:* This is the time when students use the strategy in authentic reading or writing situations that are very similar to those in which the strategy was developed and taught. For example, if you have modeled inferencing while reading a mystery, you can have students read other mysteries and ask them to write solutions to the mysteries in their journals to show how they have used this strategy. Since each strategy must be thoroughly taught, many students will need repeated practice before they are comfortable applying it on their own. Keep in mind, however, that students have been using inferencing throughout their lives. They are merely transferring to reading something they already know how to do.

2. *Application:* Now students will use their newly learned strategy in a situation totally different from the one in which they have learned it. For example, for the inferencing strategy, they might self-select mysteries to read or write a mystery in which they provide clues, leaving the solution up to their readers. You may check application during conferences or group discussions. The application phase creates conditions that encourage transfer of the strategy to other areas and to different kinds of narrative.

3. *Reflection:* As students are practicing and applying the strategy, encourage them to look back and think about how they have used it. Encourage them to talk about ways to improve and other times and places where they might use the strategy. This activity helps students make the strategy their own and also helps them see how they have succeeded.

The minilesson with follow-up affords a flexible plan for helping students learn to use strategies to construct meaning. These procedures must be viewed as basic; that is, they may need to be adapted and adjusted to fit the strategy being taught. Table 4.3 summarizes the parts of the minilesson and follow-up.

TABLE 4.3 **Summary of Minilesson and Follow-up Plan for Developing Meaning Construction Strategies**

	Purpose	Possible Activities
Minilesson		
Introduction	Let students know what they will learn. Relate it to prior knowledge and reading and writing.	Interactive discussion led by teacher
Teacher modeling	Show students how to use and think about the strategy. Incorporate Concept, Listening, & Reading into your modeling.	Teacher-led "think-alouds" Student "think-alouds"
Student modeling and guided practice	Students gradually take charge of the strategy. Students try the strategy under teacher direction.	Student "think-alouds" Cooperative groups
Summarizing and reflecting	Pull together what has been learned. Think about when it might be useful.	Teacher-prompted discussion Cooperative groups
Follow-up		
Independent practice	Try the strategy.	Reading in text similar to type used in modeling Writing
Application	Use the strategy in a new situation.	Self-selected books Writing Content-area work
Reflection	Think about how the strategy has been useful.	Student-teacher discussion

Sample Strategy Lessons

Mini-
lessons

The following sections present minilessons dealing with three of the strategies suggested for helping students construct meaning: visualizing narrative text, monitoring narrative text, and summarizing expository text. Each lesson should be viewed as a *generic model* to help you plan lessons of your own. Although parts of the lessons are scripted to show you the types of things you might say, they are *only examples* to help you plan. The lessons may be read as a group or used selectively to meet your needs. The follow-up portions merely suggest the direction you might take and are not presented in their entirety.

Before Reading the Lessons

1. Review this chapter to clarify any questions you have on modeling or minilessons.
2. Read the introduction and text on which each lesson is based. *Gladiator* was featured in Chapter 3. *No, No, Titus!* begins on page 217 and *Ananse's Feast* begins on page 276.

While Reading the Lessons

1. Think about how each element of the minilesson was developed.
2. Think about how you might change the lesson.

✿ Minilesson #1

Visualizing Narrative Text

> ### Introduction
>
> **Purpose:** To visualize while reading narrative text
>
> **NCTE/IRA Standard:** 3
>
> **Reading level:** Primary (K–1)
>
> **Text:** *No, No, Titus!* (Masurel, 1997; text shown beginning on page 217.)
>
> In this sample lesson, assume that children will not have read the story or looked at the pictures, but they have been involved in a unit about farms. This story will be used to model and teach visualizing. At the same time, students will activate prior knowledge and use prediction. Here, this book is being used for a strategy lesson. At a later time, the teacher will use the same book for a literacy lesson (see Chapter 5). *No, No, Titus!* is a picture book, but for purposes of this strategy lesson, the children will not see any picture except the one on the cover of the book. Their mental images may not match the art in the book, and that's just fine. In fact, when the children do see what the illustrator did, they can talk about how an artist illustrates a book using pictures in his or her head.

Mini-lessons

continued

Activity	Procedures and Comments
Introduction	**1.** Ask children to discuss how they know what people and things in stories look like when there are no pictures.
	Note: *Relates strategy to children's experience.*
	2. Tell children they will learn to make pictures in their head to go with words in a story.
	Note: *Lets children know what they will learn.*
	3. Tell children they will listen to a story about a farm.
	Note: *Relates lesson to a familiar unit of study.*
Teacher Modeling *Develop the concept of visualizing*	**1.** Show the cover of the book *No, No, Titus!* Point to and talk about each of the items shown. Read the title. Tell the children you can already make pictures in your head that include more than what shows on the cover.
	Note: *Tells children you know how to use the strategy.*
	2. Model visualizing using the think-aloud below.
	Teacher Think-Aloud "When I look at the cover of *No, No, Titus!* I see a cow, a chicken, a cat, a dog in a doghouse, a girl, and a man. The cow and the chicken are big clues that this story probably takes place on a farm. In my mind, I have pictures of what farms look like. There is a barn, a farmhouse, more cows and chickens, and maybe a horse or goat or sheep. There might be fields of corn in the distance. I think it's a nice day. In my picture I see the sun shining and fluffy clouds in the sky."
Student modeling and guided practice	Have children make pictures in their heads and share them.
	Note: *Gives children a chance to think aloud and practice visualizing.*
Teacher Modeling *Listening to visualize*	**1.** Tell students to listen as you read the words on the first page of the story and then listen as you think aloud about the pictures in your head that go with the words.
	Note: *Models for children how to make pictures to go with words and also models how their prior knowledge contributes to visualizing.*

Mini-lessons

continued

Activity	Procedures and Comments *(continued)*

Reading to visualize

Student modeling and guided practice

> *Teacher Think-Aloud*
>
> "When I listen to the first page of the story, I learn that Titus (from the title, *No, No, Titus!*) is the dog, and I have a picture in my head from the cover. I now know that the man is a farmer and he is talking to the dog. I can see the dog wagging his tail. The farmer is patting the dog on the head. I think the girl may be there . . . and maybe other people in the family."

2. Have students read the text on the next page as you read it aloud: The farm was big and everyone was busy.

> *Teacher Think-Aloud*
>
> "At first, I was picturing a snug little farm with just a few animals. Now I learn that the farm is big and busy, so I've changed and added to my picture. Now I think there is a huge barn and maybe other buildings besides the house, like a silo. And if it's busy, maybe there are trucks, and tractors, and people doing work."

Note: *Lets children see that visualizing changes as new information is revealed.*

Continue by having students read as you read aloud, one page of text at a time. First, have children make and revise the pictures in their heads. Then ask volunteers to share their mental images by describing them.

Note: *Students try what has been learned. Some children may need prompting, and some may need continued teacher modeling with think-alouds. The teacher assesses the level of need as the lesson progresses. Very young children may need help understanding that though visualizing takes place in their heads, it must be based on a combination of their own knowledge and what the words say. Continue to emphasize how mental pictures change as one reads.*

Summarizing and reflecting

1. Ask children to explain what they can do when they hear or read stories to help them picture what is happening.

Note: *With continued minilessons, children will learn that even when there is art on the page of a story, they will still make pictures in their heads to enhance their understanding.*

2. Ask children to talk about when they might use this strategy.

3. Show Strategy Poster (Figure 4.1) and discuss it.

Mini-
lessons

continued

Discussion

Visualizing not only enhances comprehension; it enhances enjoyment. After this lesson, children should be reminded to visualize as they listen to and read many stories and poems, either those read aloud by you or those on audiocassettes. Most students will need repeated teacher modeling and guided practice; this can be done informally throughout the day. Separate minilessons should be planned to teach visualizing expository text. As you continue to encourage children to visualize, help them understand that visualizing requires the use of other strategies, such as inferencing, identifying important information, monitoring, synthesizing, or summarizing. Strategies are not used in isolation, and should not be.

Minilesson #2

Monitoring (Clarifying) Narrative Text

Introduction

Purpose: To monitor meaning construction while reading narrative text

NCTE/IRA Standard: 3

Reading level: Third or fourth grade

Text: *Ananse's Feast* (Mollel, 1997; text shown beginning on page 276.)

Good readers monitor their reading automatically. No longer needing to pay conscious attention, they continually ask: "Does this make sense? Do I understand what I'm reading?" And if the answer to such a question is, "No," then good readers use "fix-up" techniques to clarify meaning. These include rereading, reading ahead, looking up unfamiliar words, and seeking help. It is unlikely that children will read strategically without direct instruction. Therefore, minilessons on monitoring need to be taught. Use of the strategy can be modeled by the teacher before reading and then continued during teacher-directed reading with teacher and students taking turns modeling. Children can be introduced to this strategy at the earliest literacy stage, when they are listening to stories read aloud to them. Minilessons will need to be taught and retaught as children advance through the literacy stages and through the grades. Even fluent readers may need occasional minilessons to remind them to make this strategy a part of every reading experience.

Activity	*Procedures and Comments*
Introduction	**1.** Tell students that good readers monitor their understanding as they read, which means they "stop and think" while reading to be sure what they are reading makes sense to them. Display the strategy poster in Figure 4.3. Explain each step on the poster. Note: *Lets students know what they are going to learn.*

Mini-lessons

continued

Activity	Procedures and Comments (continued)
	2. Introduce the book *Ananse's Feast*. Have students examine the cover art and predict what will happen in the story.
Teacher modeling *Develop the concept of monitoring*	**1.** Ask students if they have ever watched a video and missed something . What did they do? They ran the tape back and watched it again. Tell them that when they realized that they didn't understand something, they were monitoring what they were watching.
Modeling monitoring through listening	**2.** Read aloud the first page of the story, stumbling on the word *drought*. Then stop and use the think-aloud shown below. Write the word *drought* on the chalkboard. Note: *Creates a "problem" situation. Though artificial, it is necessary in order to demonstrate monitoring.*

> *Teacher Think-Aloud*
>
> "I'm not sure of this word [mispronounce *drought*]. I don't know how to pronounce it and I don't know what it means. I haven't read far enough in the story to know if I need to know what it means . . . and since I'm reading to myself, it's okay if I don't know exactly how to pronounce it. I guess it has something to do with the earth being hot, and no one having much to eat. I think I'll just read on without stopping to look up the word for now."

Activity	Procedures and Comments
Student modeling and guided practice	**1.** Direct students to listen as you read aloud the next four pages. Tell them to decide if what they are listening to makes sense. Tell them you will call on volunteers to model their thinking during "stop and think." Note: *Puts modeling at the listening level in the hands of students. Students may need prompting at first, but with repeated practice, they will become comfortable modeling.*
	2. Prompt students who model thinking aloud: Were there any words you didn't know? What did you do about it? Was there anything you would reread? Why? Did you have to adjust your predictions as you read? Why?
Teacher modeling *Modeling monitoring through reading*	**1.** Have students read the next four pages silently (beginning with "Akye stared at the mountain of food . . .") and stop. Then model the monitoring strategy using the think-aloud shown. Note: *Shows students how to use another fix-up technique.*

Activity	Procedures and Comments (continued)
	Teacher Think-Aloud "I understand most of what I'm reading just fine. I wasn't sure what all the foods were, but I decided it didn't matter if I didn't know what each one was—I knew they were foods the turtle wanted to eat. When Ananse told the turtle to wash his hands, I didn't quite "get it." I knew Ananse doesn't want to share his food, but I didn't see what sending the turtle off to wash his hands would accomplish. I read on and learned that Ananse is going to make the turtle go to the river. Then I figured out what was happening: the river was dry, so how could the turtle wash his hands? And when I read that the river was dry, I figured out what that word *drought* on the first page probably means. It probably means there hasn't been much rain; that's why the river is dry."
Student Modeling/ Guided Practice	**2.** Continue having students read chunks of text, alternating between teacher modeling and student modeling, for the remainder of the story. Note: *Releases more and more responsibility to students. Your decisions about how much teacher modeling is needed will be assessed as you teach.*
Discussing the story	Encourage students to talk about the story and how it compares to other folk tales. Note: *Pulls the story together.*
Summarizing and reflecting	Ask students to tell what they learned about the strategy of monitoring, or "stop and think." Encourage them to talk about when they plan to use this strategy. Note: *Helps students verbalize the strategy and internalize it.*

Discussion

Students will practice and apply this strategy with everything they read, both narrative and expository text. Most students need not only direct instruction, but also continued reteaching to activate use of the strategy. Younger children, or struggling readers, will learn best if only one fix-up technique is introduced and practiced at a time. Early in the school year, after your first minilesson on this strategy, you will want to focus on it over several days to try to instill the habit in your students. When students have become adept at student modeling alternating with teacher modeling, you might have them read in a group or with a partner, with each student taking a turn modeling. During these activities, you can observe and assess how well students are verbalizing their monitoring; if any students are struggling, you can join in briefly for a session of teacher modeling.

Mini-lessons

continued

🦋 **Minilesson #3**

Summarizing Expository Text

Introduction

Purpose: To summarize informational (expository) text

NCTE/IRA Standard: 3

Reading level: Upper elementary and higher

Text: "Ancient Rome," from *Gladiator* (Watkins 1997; text shown beginning on page [120].)

Summarizing informational or expository text requires the student to focus on a particular kind of element. The lesson here is based on rules developed by Brown and Day (1983) and successfully researched by others (Bean & Steenwyk, 1984). These steps are included in the strategy presented on the poster presented in Figure 4.12. It is best to teach this strategy after students have learned to identify important information in expository text. The first lessons would focus on summarizing paragraphs; later lessons would be extended to longer text. The lesson below would be taught after students had read the chapter "Ancient Rome" and already knew how to summarize paragraphs.

Activity	*Procedures and Comments*
Introduction	Ask students to recall the strategy they have learned for summarizing paragraphs. Tell them they are going to learn how to apply this strategy to longer texts. Note: *This relates what students will learn to what they already know.*
Teacher modeling *Develop the concept of summarizing longer texts*	1. Display the strategy poster shown in Figure 4.12 (page [151]). Review each step with students. 2. Ask students to talk about times when they have had to write reports using information from several books. Point out that they needed to summarize from longer amounts of text. Note: *Focuses students' attention on what they will learn.*
Modeling summarizing at the listening level	1. Ask students to recall "Ancient Rome" and briefly discuss it. 2. Tell students you are going to show them how to apply the summarizing informational text strategy to more than one paragraph as they listen to text. Read aloud the first three paragraphs. Use the following think-aloud,

Mini-lessons

Activity	Procedures and Comments (continued)
	along with a transparency of the first three paragraphs of the text. As you use the think-aloud, mark out the text and make notes in the margin.

Note: *Shows students how to think through the steps of the strategy.*

Teacher Think-Aloud

"As I listened to the first three paragraphs on pages 2 and 3, I could tell that ancient Rome was the main topic. Much of the other information presented was just interesting details. Even Romulus, the founder of Rome, liked fighting. As Romans conquered other countries or areas, they borrowed ideas from them—fighting and chariot racing were Etruscan; Roman art and architecture came from the Greeks. There isn't a main topic sentence in these three paragraphs. Therefore, I create one of my own: 'Ancient Rome was created by taking ideas from other countries through fights and conquests.'"

Note: *Pulls together ideas modeled.*

Modeling summarizing at the reading level

1. Direct students to silently read the remainder of the chapter. Tell students that you will model the use of this strategy at the reading level.

2. Use a transparency of the pages and the following Think-Aloud to model the strategy.

Teacher Think-Aloud

"As I read these paragraphs, I see that the topic is how the Roman Empire came into existence. Each paragraph tells how Rome won a different war or took over someone or something else. The last paragraph on page 5 summarizes the entire chapter."

Note: *Models using the strategy in reading.*

3. Have a student read aloud the last paragraph on page 5. Discuss additional items that need to be included.

4. Assist students in writing a summary for these paragraphs.

Mini-lessons

continued

Activity	Procedures and Comments (continued)
Student modeling and guided practice	**1.** Using a transparency of chapter 2 ("The First Gladiators"–not shown), guide students in writing a summary. Note: *Lets students try the strategy with teacher support if needed.* **2.** Have students work with a partner to develop the summary for Chapter 3, "Who Were the Gladiators?"
Summarizing and reflecting	Prompt students to summarize the parts of the strategy and talk about its uses: What steps do you follow when summarizing longer text? How is summarizing longer text different from summarizing paragraphs? How and when do you think you might use this strategy? Note: *Helps students verbalize what they have learned and why it is important.*

Discussion

After this lesson, students would read and summarize Chapter 4, "The Schools." Students could begin by working in cooperative pairs while you observe how well they are using the strategy. Most students will need repeated teacher modeling and guided practice. Since summarizing is difficult for students to learn, lessons are more effective if they are short and very focused. The poster shown in Figure 4.12 on page [151] will help students stay aware of the steps to use in summarizing. Encourage students to help each other improve in their use of the strategy, and periodically invite students to reflect about their strategy use.

After Reading the Plans

1. Select any strategy lesson plan presented in this chapter. Working with a partner, develop several more "think-alouds" that you would use to model the strategy.
2. Working with a partner, select any strategy you would like to teach, and prepare two lessons on it—one for expository text and one for narrative text. Teach the lessons to a small group, and discuss the results.
3. Select a grade level of your choice and observe for an hour or two, looking for evidence of students using the strategies mentioned in this chapter. Talk with the teacher to see how the children learned them. Were they taught? Did the students learn them through their literacy experiences?

🦋 A Final Word About Strategies

The strategy lessons just described should serve as models to help you develop your own lessons. Although research supports the inclusion of the strategies discussed here in the literacy program, remember that just teaching the separate strategy lessons is not enough. In order for strategies to help students read more effectively, the students must be engaged in reading and using the strategies (Taylor, Pearson, Peeterson, & Rodriguez, 2003). You should introduce all the strategies you want students to learn during a given year and then provide repeated opportunities to use them in reading and writing throughout the year. *Many students may do very well by reading, writing, and interacting with their peers and you about their reading and writing.* Teaching strategies may be a helpful form of support for some students, but not necessary for others. Only the wise, informed, observant teacher can decide whether students are profiting from strategy instruction. You must be that teacher!

🦋 Summary

This chapter focused on strategies that help readers construct meaning. Seven strategies were discussed: visualizing, monitoring, inferencing, identifying important information, generating and answering questions, synthesizing, and summarizing.

Guidelines were presented for planning and implementing strategy instruction in the classroom. The chapter discussed both implicit and explicit modeling incorporating "think-alouds." A detailed explanation for minilessons was presented, including what should occur before, during, and after reading.

Three sample minilessons were presented, based on literature that appears in this book. As always teachers must base their teaching decisions on the students, teaching lessons when there is a need, but encouraging independence whenever possible.

For Additional Reading

Barton, J., & Sawyer, D. M. (2003–2004). Our students are reading for this: Comprehension instruction in the elementary school. *The Reading Teacher, 57*(4), 334-347.

Cortese, E. E. (2003–2004). The application of Question-Answer Relationship strategies to pictures. *The Reading Teacher, 57*(4), 374-380.

Fisk, C., & Hurst, B. (2003). Paraphrasing for comprehension. *The Reading Teacher, 57*(2), 182-185.

Harvey, S., & Goudvis, A. (2000). *Strategies that work: Teaching comprehension to enhance understanding.* York, ME: Stenhouse Publishers.

Hashey, J. M., & Connors, D. J. (2003) Learn from our journey: Reciprocal teaching action research. *The Reading Teacher, 57*(3), 224-232.

Massey, D. D. (2003). A comprehension checklist: What if it doesn't make sense? *The Reading Teacher, 57*(1), 81-84.

McLaughlin, M., & Allen, M. B. (2002). *Guided comprehension: A teaching model for grades 3–8*. Newark, DE: International Reading Association.

Oczkus, L. D. (2003) *Reciprocal teaching at work: Strategies for improving reading comprehension*. Newark, DE: International Reading Association.

▣ For Exploration: Electronic Products and Resources

Use the following Web sites to gain additional ideas for developing prior knowledge with your students:

Stay abreast of new research on strategy instruction by checking with Web sites such as *Reading Online*, a journal of K–12 practice and research, published by the International Reading Association. Here you can find articles, discussions, ideas, and communities dedicated to serving teachers as the leading online source of information for the worldwide literacy-education community. **http://www.readingonline.org**

International Reading Association

The International Reading Association (IRA) provides resources for teachers, reading specialists, tutors, and others concerned about literacy. Topics range from performance-based assessment to classroom discussion strategies, integrated instruction, motivation for reading, and teaching English as a Second Language. Visit the IRA's Web site to learn about books, journals, videos, and multimedia products about reading comprehension and literacy. You may be particularly interested in the IRA's five professional journals:

* *The Reading Teacher*—for preschool, primary, and elementary teachers
* *Journal of Adolescent and Adult Literacy*—for teachers of middle school, high school, and adult learners
* *Reading Research Quarterly*—a journal of reading research
* *Lectura y vida*—Spanish-language journal for all teaching levels
* *Reading Online*—an electronic journal using the Web to explore research, instruction, and communication

www.reading.org

National Council of Teachers of English

The National Council of Teachers of English (NCTE) is devoted to improving the teaching of English and the language arts at all levels. NCTE publishes a member newspaper, three monthly journals, and ten quarterlies. It also publishes position papers, teaching ideas, and other documents on professional concerns such as professional standards. Explore the Web site to learn more. The following journals may be of particular interest to you.

- *Language Arts*—for elementary teachers and teacher educators
- *Primary Voices K–6*—a journal written by different teams of elementary educators
- *School Talk*—a newsletter for classroom teachers
- *Voices from the Middle*—for middle-school teachers

http://www.ncte.org

Visit Vocabulary University to access Learning Activities that are separated into three levels of difficulty: High Elementary, Junior High—Middle School, and High School. These interactive vocabulary puzzle and activity sessions use Latin and Greek "roots and cells" to help decode words, and include Fill-in-the-Blanks, Definition Match, Synonym & Antonym Encounters, Crosswords, Word Finds, True/False, and Word Stories.

http://www.vocabulary.com

At EdHelper.com, you can build over forty customized worksheets using the words you are using in your classroom, or check out the preformed Spelling and Vocabulary Worksheet Lessons for Grades 1–12.

http://www.edhelper.com/vocabulary.htm

Beginning Literacy: Decoding, Vocabulary, and Meaning

5

✓ **STANDARDS FOCUS**

NCTE/IRA Standards: 1, 2, 3, 5, 7, 9, 10, 11, 12
Standards for Reading Professionals: 1, 2, 4, 5

"Educators Speak   pp. 193, 206

Decoding Routines and Diverse Learners
—*Greg O'Connell, Cedar Rapids, Iowa*

Using Technology to Build Fluency
—*Shari LaMunyon, Maize, Kansas* **"**

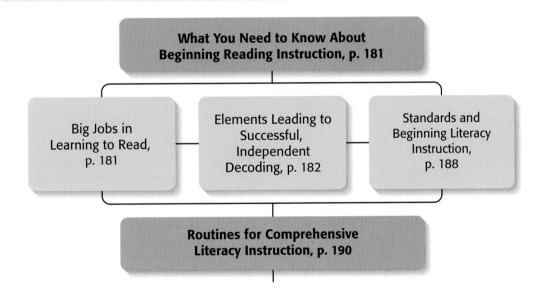

**What You Need to Know About
Beginning Reading Instruction, p. 181**

**Big Jobs in
Learning to Read,
p. 181**

**Elements Leading to
Successful,
Independent
Decoding, p. 182**

**Standards and
Beginning Literacy
Instruction,
p. 188**

**Routines for Comprehensive
Literacy Instruction, p. 190**

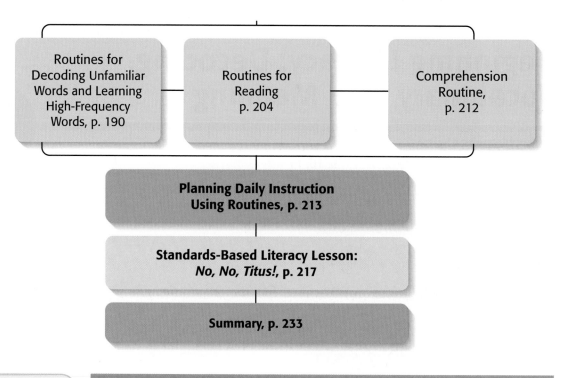

Routines for Decoding Unfamiliar Words and Learning High-Frequency Words, p. 190

Routines for Reading p. 204

Comprehension Routine, p. 212

Planning Daily Instruction Using Routines, p. 213

Standards-Based Literacy Lesson: *No, No, Titus!*, p. 217

Summary, p. 233

Terms
You Need to Know

- analogy
- concepts of print
- cueing systems
- grapheme
- phoneme
- phonemic awareness
- phonics
- routine
- structural analysis

*B*eginning readers must learn to read words quickly, accurately, and automatically; this ability is critical to the process of constructing meaning, or comprehension (Adams, 1990). A look at how two different first-grade teachers approach reading will help you begin to understand this process.

Mr. Paredes and his students were rereading aloud the book The Lady with the Alligator Purse (Westcott, 1988). As Mr. Paredes read, the children chimed in: "Miss Lucy had a baby, / His name was Tiny Tim." After rereading the whole book, the children talked about their favorite parts and found pages to show examples. Luanda said, "I like the pizza page" and showed the page where the characters are eating pizza in the bed. Mr. Paredes encouraged every child to respond.

After the discussion, Mr. Paredes returned to the first page and said, "Let's reread this page together: 'Miss Lucy had a baby, / His name was Tiny Tim.'" All the children joined in. Mr. Paredes said, "What was the baby's name?" The children responded, "Tiny Tim." Mr. Paredes wrote the name on the chalkboard and asked, "What is the beginning letter of the baby's name?" Several children responded, "t." Mr. Paredes underlined the T and said, "This letter stands for /t/."* Then he said, "We are going to talk about the /t/ sound today."

"Does anyone in our class have a name that begins with the /t/ sound?" he asked. As the children called out names, Mr. Paredes listed them under Tiny Tim. He then asked different children to come up and underline the t and give the sound it stood for:

---

* When a letter is set off in slash marks, /t/, you are to give the sound for the letter. It is difficult to give the sound of a consonant without adding a schwa sound. Be aware of this difficulty and try to keep the sound as pure as possible. For example, the sound for *t* is not /*tuh*/; it is /t/ with quick, breathy sound.

```
Tiny Tim
Terry
Tom
Tanisha
teacher
```

One child said, "Lisa." Instead of telling the child she was wrong, Mr. Paredes listed the name to the side of Tiny Tim *and said, "Let's compare these two beginning sounds. Which one begins with /t/?" "Tiny Tim." "Which one begins with /l/?" "Lisa." "Are these the same sound?" asked Mr. Paredes. "No," the children chorused. Then he said, "Let's look at our lists on the wall to see if we have one where Lisa's name will fit."*

The children did not find a list for the letter L, *because it had not been taught yet. Mr. Paredes tore off a long strip of paper, wrote* Lisa *at the top, and underlined the* L. *He said, "We will talk about this letter another day."*

Mr. Paredes returned to the list of t *words, reread it with the children, and said, "Now we are going to play our game, EVERYONE SHOW. When I say a word, if it begins with the* t *sound /t/, everyone show the t-card. If it doesn't begin with /t/, show your* No *card. Mr. Paredes read* teacher, top, dog, say, tiger, tap, run, toss. *He had a checklist of names for noting any child having difficulty for reteaching later. He then directed children back to the big book,* The Lady with the Alligator Purse, *and had the group reread it with him. He then asked the children to read several pages and locate and read aloud words that began with /t/. He gave each child a little book he had written and duplicated called* Tip at the Top. *This book contained many t-words and used only CVC (consonant-vowel-consonant) words that children could decode and sight words they already knew. He said, "Here is a book that will let you apply what we have learned about the letter* t. *It uses only skills and words you have learned. Read it to yourself to tell the others in the group what happened to the bird in the story."*

Compare Mr. Paredes's class to Ms. Anderson's class.

"Boys and girls, we are going to meet a new phonics character today," said Ms. Anderson. She printed the letter B *on the board. "His name begins with this letter. What is this letter?" The group called out "B." "Yes," said Ms. Anderson, who then showed a picture of a bear. "Here is a picture of our character. What is he?" "A bear," responded the children. "Our character's name is Boris Bear. You say it." The children all replied "Boris Bear." "Boris Bear is our character for the* b *sound. Listen to the /b/ sound at the beginning of his name /B/-/B/-Boris /B/-/B/-Bear. You say it." The children responded /B/-/B/-Boris /B/-/B/-Bear.*

"Now we are going to learn to read words that begin with /b/." Ms. Anderson printed the word book *on the board. She modeled for the children how to read the word aloud. She placed*

her hand under the b and said: "This letter stands for /b/ and I remember /ook/; /b/-/ook/. I blend it faster /b/-/ook/—book. I can read the word. Now you will practice reading words together. I will point to the letter or letters and say SOUND. You say the sound; then I will say BLEND. You will blend the sounds to say the word. Let's try it again with book."

Ms. Anderson repeated the SOUND/BLEND process using bag, bug, boy, bump.

"Boys and girls, now take out your magic slates. We are going to learn to spell words that begin with /b/. Number 1 to 5 down the side. I will say five words. Write b beside the number if the word I say begins with /b/ as in Boris Bear."

Ms. Anderson read "1. cap, 2. box, 3. baby, 4. sing, 5. bunny." She walked around looking to see who was having problems so she could give them help later.

"Now we are going to read a story using what you already know and what you have learned about the sound for b." Ms. Anderson passed out copies of a little book titled Bing, which is part of her published reading program. "Read this story silently to find out who the main character is and what he does. Remember, use the sound at the beginning of Boris Bear and what you already know to figure out the words." After silent reading, children discussed the story and read it aloud as a group.

Mr. Paredes and Ms. Anderson were each teaching students to read words. Look back over the examples and think about how these two teachers were alike and different. Compare your ideas to the following:

- Mr. Paredes started with a big book, and returned to that big book after students had been taught the sound. Ms. Anderson started by teaching the individual sound.
- Both Mr. Paredes and Ms. Anderson explicitly modeled the sound being taught by isolating it for students.
- Ms. Anderson modeled for children how to read words sequentially.
- Ms. Anderson had the children learn to spell words using the sound being taught.
- Both teachers had children immediately practice reading a book that was controlled by containing only the sounds and words that had been previously taught.
- Both teachers were using procedures and practices that could be defended from current research.

In Chapter 2, we presented a model for a comprehensive literacy program. As you will recall, the model includes:

- blocks for daily independent reading and writing.
- learning reading skills and strategies.
- applying reading skills and strategies.
- learning to write.
- developmentally appropriate writing.
- a block of intervention for students who are having difficulty learning to read.

Adjustments are made in individual blocks to suit student literacy development.

In this chapter, you will learn how to teach readers at the beginning stages of literacy development learn to identify words by using phonics and other cueing systems, to increase their vocabulary, and to construct meaning. Then you will have a better understanding of why Mr. Paredes and Ms. Anderson taught the lessons as they did. Although the opening scenario showed first-grade classrooms, acquiring literacy is much the same whatever the age of the individual. If you are teaching an older beginning reader, you use material that matches the maturity of the student in terms of interest and experience, but the process is essentially the same as what is described in this chapter.

🦋 What You Need to Know About Beginning Reading Instruction

Effective beginning reading instruction is critical for the success of all children. All teachers need to understand the process in order to teach students of any age. Research from the past several decades has led us to some very clear conclusions about beginning reading.

Big Jobs in Learning to Read

Learning to read is not a simple process. Many factors and elements interact as a child learns to read (Juel, 1991). However, within the process, two big jobs work together: *decoding* and *comprehension*. Figure 5.1 shows how these jobs change in emphasis from beginning reading to mature reading.

Decoding is the process of translating written language into verbal speech (oral reading) or inner speech (thinking the words in one's head) (Eldredge, 1995). Many people equate decoding with reading, but they are not equal. Decoding is necessary, but not sufficient, for reading. Reading does not occur unless an individual comprehends. Comprehension is the process whereby the reader constructs meaning by interacting with the text (Anderson & Pearson, 1984; Cooper, 1986).

See more about comprehension in Chapters 1, 3, and 4.

FIGURE 5.1

Changing Emphasis in Learning to Read

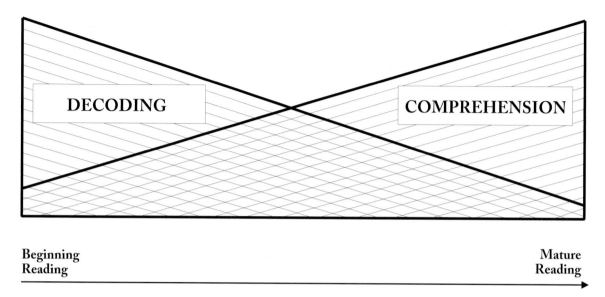

Decoding and comprehension interact as individuals learn to read. At first, most words children meet in print are already in their oral vocabulary; they understand them when listening and they use them when speaking. The task at the beginning stages of learning to read is how to recognize those words when they meet them in print. As readers gain skills and fluency, and learn to decode and comprehend words that may not yet be in their oral language, their vocabulary continues to grow. The element of vocabulary, then, is implicit in all decoding and comprehension instruction.

We discussed in Chapter 1 how both decoding and comprehension are always part of the process of reading. Figure 5.1 shows that the instructional emphasis on the "big jobs" of reading needs to shift from the beginning to the mature stages. In other words, the two jobs of decoding and comprehension are not equal at the various stages; the amount of instructional emphasis shifts from one component to another, with *both always being included.* Let's focus on the "big job" of beginning reading—decoding.

Elements Leading to Successful, Independent Decoding

The ultimate goal of reading words is fluency. *Fluency is the process of automatically, accurately, and rapidly recognizing words* (LaBerge & Samuels, 1976; Perfetti, 1985; Stanovich, 1980, 1986). Developing fluency leads to comprehension. As students become fluent readers, they build a stockpile of *sight words,* or words that they recognize instantly. If readers come to words they do not recognize as sight words, they must use decoding to hypothesize the pronunciation of the word (orally or silently). In other words, children must be *independent decoders* and have the skills and strategies to figure out words on their own.

In the beginning stages of learning to read, a learner must depend heavily on his or her decoding abilities to pronounce words. As the learner has repeated practice in reading, he or she learns to recognize more words automatically, accurately, and rapidly (learns more sight words) and becomes a more fluent reader. Researchers have found that good comprehenders (constructors of meaning) are also fluent decoders (Carnine, Carnine, & Gersten, 1984; Chall, 1967; Lesgold & Curtis, 1981).

Teaching decoding systematically is a critical part of beginning literacy instruction. As readers become more fluent, they use decoding skills and strategies only when they come to words they do not recognize instantly.

Students must develop six critical elements as they learn to independently decode words:

- oral language,
- phonemic awareness,
- concepts of print,
- letter-sound associations (phonics/structure),
- analogy, and
- learning a way to think about words.

In addition, readers develop a stockpile of sight words, including a number of high-frequency words (words that occur most often in language). This combination of independent decoding and sight words helps individuals become efficient, independent readers.

Oral Language

Children begin to develop oral language the day they are born:

- They develop the sounds of language (phonology).
- They learn how words are formed and related to each other (morphology).
- They learn how language conveys meaning (semantics).
- They develop a stockpile of word meanings and pronunciations (vocabulary or lexicon).
- They learn how individuals use language to achieve certain goals (pragmatics).

These aspects of language development form the foundation for reading, including both decoding and comprehension. For example, if a child decodes the word *horse*, his language base serves as the checking system to tell whether the word has been decoded properly. The child's language base also serves as the basis for assigning meaning to the word *horse*.

Most children develop their use of language with ease (Snow, Burns, & Griffin, 1998). For these children, the school must provide activities that support continued language development. However, some children come from an environment with limited adult language models, or they have a neurological problem; they may not have a good language base. For these children, the school must provide specific instruction and activities that develop oral language. For all learners, school-provided language development activities should include such things as the following:

- Good language modeling provided by teachers' reading aloud to students and discussing what was read.
- Language lessons that model uses of various types of language. For example, use of a photograph as the basis for a discussion. Model expansion of language by taking children's comments and adding more description.

    Child: It's a dog.

  Teacher: Yes, it is a big, brown dog. What else do you notice about this dog's face?

    Child: A white spot.

  Teacher: Yes, the big, brown dog has a white patch or spot on its face.

- Experiences such as field trips, class visitors, movies, videos, and CD-ROM stories that expand students' background and knowledge followed by good discussions.
- Opportunities for children to use language in a variety of ways. This may occur through various centers in the kindergarten and first-grade classroom.

Continued language development forms and expands the foundation for children to effectively develop their abilities to decode and comprehend. Weak or limited oral language may interfere with a child's ability to learn to read (Chard & Osborne, n.d.).

English Language Learners (ELLs) may have developed oral proficiency in their first language, but they may not yet have developed English oral language. These students need extra support to develop English oral language as they are learning to read English.

Phonemic Awareness

Directly related to oral language development is another important element that is a part of helping children develop independence in decoding: **phonemic awareness.** Phonemic awareness is the knowledge that spoken words are composed of a sequence of sounds, or **phonemes.** Phonemic awareness is a part of the broader category known as *phonological awareness*, which includes all the aspects of the sounds of language separate and apart from meaning.

Research has supported the importance of phonemic awareness in relation to learning to read (Ball & Blachman, 1991) and learning to spell (Juel, Griffith, & Gough, 1986). English is an alphabetic language. This means that the sounds of the language (phonemes) are represented by symbols or the alphabet (**graphemes**). For example, the word *cat* has three phonemes (/c/-/ă/-/t/) and three graphemes *c-a-t*. The word *goat* also has three phonemes /g/-/ō/-/t/ and three graphemes *g-oa-t*, but one of the phonemes, /ō/, is represented by a two-letter grapheme.

Most children do not naturally learn this alphabetic principle—that is, the idea that each sound of the language is represented by a graphic symbol (Eldredge, 1995). It must be explicitly taught (Adams, 1990). Phonemic awareness is a part of learning the alphabetic principle. If children have not yet acquired phonemic awareness, instruction in letter-sound associations will not be effective in helping them decode words. Researchers have identified several aspects of phonemic awareness. (Adams, 1990; Eldredge, 1995). Although there is some disagreement, researchers commonly identify the following elements of phonemic awareness:

- *Rhyming words.* Being able to tell that two words rhyme (*hot-not; mat-fat*).
- *Counting words in sentences.* Being able to tell that the following is a four-word sentence: *This is my mother.*
- *Counting syllables in words.* Being able to tell that *horse* has one syllable, *listen* has two syllables, and so forth.
- *Counting phonemes in words.* Knowing that *hat* has three sounds /h/-/ă/-/t/.
- *Segmenting and blending syllables.* Hearing the word *happy* and giving the two syllables /hăp/-/ē/ is segmenting; hearing /rŭn/-/ing/ and giving the word *running* is blending.
- *Segmenting and blending onset and rime.* Hearing the word *brook* and identifying the onset /br/ and the rime /ook/ is segmenting; and hearing the onset /c/ and the rime /ard/ and being able to make the word *card* is blending.
- *Segmenting and blending phonemes.* Hearing the word *hot* and giving the three phonemes /h/-/ŏ/-/t/ is segmenting; hearing the phonemes /p/-/ă/-/t/ and saying the word *pat* is blending.
- *Substitution of sounds.* Taking the word *hot* and substituting the sound /c/ for /h/ and saying the word *cot.*

The two most important processes for students to learn as a part of phonemic awareness training are segmentation of sounds and blending of sounds. Activities for teaching and developing phonemic awareness are discussed later in this chapter.

Assessing phonemic awareness for ELLs is difficult because these students are still acquiring the English phonological system. Tests of phonemic awareness given in a student's second language are not good indicators of their ability to use this process (Freeman & Freeman, 2000).

Concepts of Print

As children learn to identify words as an aid to constructing meaning, they must develop some **concepts of print.** Clay (1985) divides these concepts into four categories: *books, sentences, words,* and *letters* (see Table 5.1).

Beginning readers and writers must learn that books convey meaning through print. In this process, they also need to know the left-right, top-bottom orientation on a page, as well as facts about the book, such as the cover, title, author, illustrator, beginning, and ending.

Students must develop some understanding of the sentences on the page. They need to recognize a sentence, know that it represents a spoken message, and be able to tell the beginning and ending by recognizing the capital letters and the end punctuation. They also need some understanding of other forms of punctuation, such as quotation marks.

TABLE-5.1	Concepts of Print

BOOKS

Knows:
- Cover
- Title, author, illustrator
- Beginning, ending
- Left-right orientation
- Top-bottom orientation
- Print tells story, not pictures

SENTENCES

Identifies:
- Sentence
- Beginning, ending of sentence
- Capital letter at beginning
- Punctuation: period, comma, question mark, quotation mark, exclamation point

WORDS
- Identifies words (knows that day is a word)

LETTERS

Knows:
- Letter order
- Capital and lower case

Source: Based on Clay (1985).

See "Routines for Reading," page 204.

It is important that students develop the concept of a word, and know that each word is composed of letters and that these letters appear in a certain order. Part of that learning includes knowing the difference between capital and lowercase letters. Although many children come to school understanding these concepts about print, some do not; so it may be necessary for you to help those children understand.

Letter-Sound Associations (Phonics and Structural Analysis)

A strong, consistent body of research has accumulated over several decades showing that beginning readers get their best start by being *explicitly* taught letter-sound associations (Adams, 1990; Anderson, Hiebert, Scott, & Wilkinson, 1985; Armbruster & Osborn, 2001: Chall, 1967, 1983; National Reading Panel, 2000; Snow, Burns, & Griffin, 1998). This instruction must include **phonics** and **structural analysis.** Phonics is the study of letter-sound (grapheme-phoneme) relationships. Structural analysis is the study of meaningful word parts. The instruction in and acquisition of phonemic awareness leads directly to teaching letter-sound associations.

For a detailed discussion of phonics and structural analysis, see the Handbook Resource, page 501.

Over the years, phonics has been a controversial issue for teachers (National Reading Panel, 2000a, 2000b; Allington, 1997; Garan, 2001; Flesch, 1955). Some educators and laypersons feel that phonics is the only and best way to teach children to read. Others strongly disagree. Sometimes these controversies have also involved parents, other educators, or the community at large. As a teacher, the best way to be prepared to deal with phonics issues (or any other issues) is to:

You may want to read this section now (page 501).

- **Be knowledgeable.** Make sure that you know what phonics is and understand the role it plays in learning to read and spell. "Word Skills: Phonics and Structural Analysis for Teachers," a special section presented in the Handbook Resource at the end of this text, is designed to help you learn the basic elements about phonics and structural analysis.

- **Know the research.** While not all teaching decisions grow out of research, there is much good research that can guide many decisions about phonics and other areas. Look for patterns in such research rather than depend on one isolated study to provide an answer. Throughout this text, we give patterns that are clearly documented in the research. This is important in all areas of teaching, but is perhaps most important when it comes to phonics because of the often controversial and emotional nature of statements made or positions taken regarding phonics instruction.

Later in this chapter, we will look at how to teach phonics and structural analysis in ways that lead to effective reading and spelling.

Analogy

Analogy (when used in relation to decoding) is the process of noting similarities or patterns in words and using this to figure out an unfamiliar word. As beginning readers learn to read and spell words, they often use analogy to figure out the words (Gaskins et al., 1988). For example, if a child comes to the unknown word *ring*, she might recognize that the word looks like *sing*, a word she knows. Using letter-sound correspondences for the *r* and knowledge of the word *sing*, the child can make the analogy and decode the word *ring*. Analogy is *not* the process of looking for little words in big words—for example, *fat-her* in *father*. Such misinterpretation of analogy can lead beginning readers astray (Pinnell & Fountas, 1998).

Most readers don't use analogy immediately; they must learn some letter-sound correspondences (Ehri & Robbins, 1992) before they begin to use the process on their own. Analogy, however, becomes an important part of a reader's strategy for independently decoding words.

A Way to Think About Words

As students learn the elements of effective, independent decoding, they must develop a strategy to apply what they have learned in order to decode words by themselves. Independent decoders use multiple **cueing systems,** or clues to figure out unknown words:

- phonics,
- structural analysis,
- context or meaning, and
- their sense of language (syntax).

At the very beginning stages of reading, children are learning to "read through the word" or "sequentially decode" words. As they come to words they don't instantly recognize—for example, *horse*—they must learn to use their letter-sound correspondence knowledge to read through the word starting at the beginning—/h/-/or/-/s/—and proceeding in order.

The need for students to independently decode unknown words becomes increasingly important as they read more and read better; therefore, students need a strategy for approaching unknown words (see Figure 5.2). Students can use this strategy well beyond beginning reading; it is based on research showing that readers do indeed look at all the letters in words to decode them (Adams, 1990; Just & Carpenter, 1987). The following explanation will help you understand how students use the strategy presented in Figure 5.2:

1. Students begin by looking for the largest sound chunks they recognize. This may involve an ending (*-ing* or *-ed*); it may be making an analogy from a known word to the unknown word (known word: *base;* unknown word: *case*); or it may be recognizing a word pattern such as *-op*. The student tries to decode the word and checks it by reading to the end of the sentence or paragraph. If this doesn't work, the student moves on to the next step.

2. The student tries to use the individual letter-sound associations (phonics and structural analysis). The student then sequentially decodes or sounds out the word and checks it by reading to the end of the sentence or paragraph. This places context in a checking or confirming position and focuses the student initially on the letter-sound correspondences that will lead to more accurate decoding (Adams, 1990; Stanovich, 1980).

3. Finally, if the student is unable to decode the word, he or she asks someone or refers to a dictionary as appropriate skills are learned.

The six elements we discussed in this section are critical to helping students become independent decoders. Keep in mind that while students are developing this independence in decoding, they are also learning high-frequency words and building a stockpile of sight words.

Standards and Beginning Literacy Instruction

Standards shape instruction in most schools today. State standards for each area of education, such as language arts, are available on the Internet. As you read the standards for your state or school, you will note that they are consistent with the instructional practices presented in this text. The wording may vary slightly, but the intent is the same. There are certain abilities that all students must acquire in order to be literate. This text teaches you how to help students acquire those abilities.

Standards are usually stated in behavioral terms. For example, here is the third standard from the IRA/NCTE Standards for the English Language Arts: "Students apply a wide range of strategies to comprehend, interpret, evaluate, and appreciate texts. They draw on their prior experience, their interactions with other readers and writers, their knowledge of word meaning and of other texts, their word identifica-

FIGURE 5.2

A Way to Think About Words

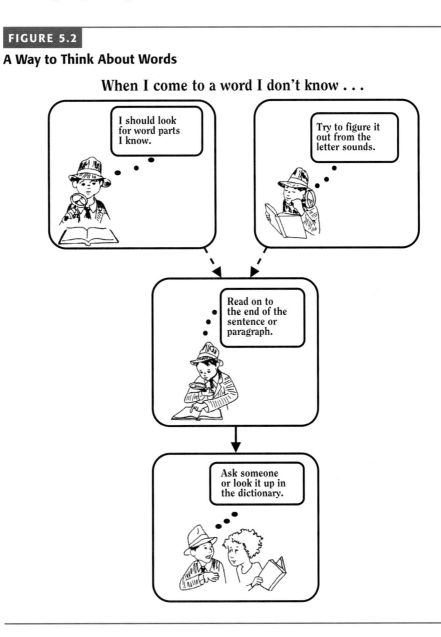

tion strategies, and their understanding of textual features (e.g., sound-letter correspondence, sentence structure, context, graphics)." This standard is quite broad, and therefore many lists break down each broad standard into specific behaviors. For example, there may be several specific standards related to each aspect of word recognition, stating specific abilities students are expected to demonstrate at each grade level. Now let's focus on how to teach beginning reading by looking at routines for instruction.

🦋 Routines for Comprehensive Literacy Instruction

See Chapters 2 and 3 for teaching a literacy lesson, developing skills and vocabulary, and developing prior knowledge.

A **routine** is a set of procedures that can be used repeatedly. Within your classroom, you will use and develop many routines for instruction. You have already learned those for teaching a literacy lesson, developing skills and vocabulary, and developing prior knowledge.

This section presents fifteen routines that are particularly effective for beginning literacy instruction. These, along with the others you have already learned, provide a resource from which to choose to meet the needs of your students.

Table 5.2 lists the fifteen routines and indicates their specific functions. You will note that some routines are for teaching, practicing, or applying some aspect of literacy. Others are for developing oral language or concepts of print. The remainder of this section will describe each of the routines by following a consistent format: purpose, when to use, description/procedures, and discussion/comments. The sample literacy lesson found on page 217 illustrates the use of some of the routines. As you study each routine, look for overlap. For example, when you are using a decoding routine, you are also developing vocabulary.

Routines for Decoding Unfamiliar Words and Learning High-Frequency Words

🦋 Phonemic Awareness Routine

PURPOSE   Routines for phonemic awareness help children develop the awareness of sounds in words and the ability to blend sounds to make words. Since phonemic awareness involves several related components, there are different routines involving each component.

WHEN TO USE   Phonemic Awareness Routines are used in the Reading: Learning Skills and Strategies block of the comprehensive literacy program. These routines can be used in kindergarten through second grade or beyond if needed.

For other activities for developing phonemic awareness, see the "For Additional Reading" section.

DESCRIPTION/ PROCEDURES   Three sample routines are presented for phonemic awareness. When you use one of the routines, it should be used for short periods of time (5–10 minutes) repeatedly over several days or weeks until children have developed the component being taught.

Rhyming Routine

Teach:

1. Read aloud a book that contains many words that rhyme. (Use books such as *Sheep in a Jeep* [Shaw, 1986], *There's a Wocket in My Pocket* [Seuss, 1974], and *Hop on Pop* [Seuss, 1963].)

2. After reading the book, have children chant some of the lines with you:
"Beep, Beep
Sheep in a Jeep."

TABLE 5.2	**Routines for Comprehensive Literacy Instruction**

			FUNCTIONS		
Routines	**Teach**	**Practice**	**Apply**	**Develop Oral Language**	**Develop Concept of Print**
Routines for Decoding					
• Phonemic Awareness Routine					
• Explicit Phonics Routine	X				
• Analogy Routine	X				
• Making Words Routine		X	X		
• Word Wall Routine*		X			
• Decodable High-Frequency Words Routine	X	X			
• Irregular and Phonetically Unpredictable High-Frequency or other Words Routine	X	X			
• Word Wall Routine*		X			
Routines for Reading					
• Decodable Text Reading Routine		X	X		
• Fluency Reading Routine		X	X		
• Read-Aloud Routine	X			X	X
• Shared Reading Routine	X			X	X
• Observational Guided Reading Routine		X	X		
• Cooperative Reading Routine		X	X		
Routine for Comprehension					
• Explicit Comprehension Strategy Routine	X				

*A word wall (a place on the wall to display words) may be used as a decoding routine and a high-frequency word routine. In this chapter it is described as a decoding routine with comments about how to use it as a high-frequency word routine.

3. Identify several words from the text that rhyme (Example: *hop-pop*). Say the words slowly, noting that they rhyme. Give several other examples (*top-hop; pop-top*). Begin to ask children to tell whether the words rhyme.

Practice:

- Play the game STAND UP/SIT DOWN. This game is like SIMON SAYS.
- Say pairs of words that rhyme and pairs that don't rhyme. Children go from one position to the next only if the words rhyme (Sample words: *cat-hat; big-pig; cat-pig; big-jig; hat-sat; sat-rat; sat-big*). Note how children respond to tell whether they are getting the concept.
- Model and practice daily until children master the skill. Then drop the modeling, but continue to provide repeated practice.

Counting Sounds and Syllables Routine

Teach:

1. After reading aloud a favorite book to children, select a two- or three-sound word to model the number of sounds (Example: *top*).
2. Say the word slowly by stretching it out; tell children that this word has three sounds. Use several other examples (*red, cat, pig*). Model the number of sounds by slowly saying the word and clapping once for each sound. Ask children to clap with you.

Practice:

- Play the CLAPPING GAME. Use only words that have three phonemes. As you say words, have children clap for each sound heard. At first, stretch the words out; as children develop their ability to do this, say the words at a more normal speed.
- Repeat this process over several days or weeks. Drop the modeling when it is no longer needed, and provide short daily practices until students develop the ability to hear sounds.

This same procedure may be used for counting syllables.

Segmenting and Blending Routines

Teach:

(Segmenting)

1. Select words of two syllables from a book that has been read aloud (Examples: *baby, table*).
2. Say each word, slowly stretching it out /bā→//bē→ /. Tell children that this word has two syllables (parts): *bāā* and *bēē*.
3. Repeat with several other words.

Practice:

- Play the MATCH GAME. Give each child a stack of colored tiles or colored squares of paper.
- Use five to seven two-syllable words. Say each word slowly. Direct children to place a tile or colored square on their desks for each syllable they hear in the word. In the beginning, stretch the words by saying them slowly. As children become adept at using this skill, say the words normally.

Teach:

(Blending)

1. Select several two-syllable words from a book that has been read aloud.
2. Say the words in their parts /hăp//ē/. Tell children that you can blend these syllables together to make the word *happy*. Repeat the modeling using several more examples. Gradually ask children to take over the responsibility to blend the words.

Educators
Speak

Decoding Routines and Diverse Learners

"Teaching phonemic awareness is key for students who learn to read phonetically, but not all students learn to read this way. In my primary classroom, I use a number of different strategies to teach students about phonics.

Each week we have five new word wall words up on the board that we work with. One day a week, we work on rhyming words that we can think of for the word wall words in our Grant Wood book. I start off another day with the students telling me the sounds they hear in the words. During this activity, we are able to divide the word into sounds that they hear, blends, diagraphs, vowels working together, and ending sounds. Then different groups in my room make the sound, and we blend them together to make the whole word. I believe that this really helps with "blending" words together. I try to use this phrase instead of "sounding" out words with both students and parents. When "training" my parents for our Wise Owl Book Club, I discuss with them how to blend sounds and to look for chunks inside words. Parents know which "chunk" we are working on by reading my weekly newsletter.

During our Guided Reading block of time, the students are usually working with making words by manipulating the letters given to make new words. The words they make are important to the context of the book they have been reading, or a vowel or consonant blend that is noticeably a problem. This is also done on marker boards that are easy to write on and erase.

During a shared reading time, I have a chunk wall where we discuss a chunk, for example, "ell," that we can make many words from. This helps the students to use what they know when blending letters together to make an unknown word. They love coming up with rhyming words to go on the various shapes on our chunk wall. It is something that I can refer them to when they are writing on their own. It is a great tool that we leave up all year. This really helps my lower-level spellers when writing.

During the poetry time of the day, I use the *Fun Phonics* CDs that give us various spellings for the sounds of the short and long vowels. These CDs are very interactive, and the students are able to highlight which words make that vowel sound. We have had many times when the students have referred to their poetry folders when trying to figure out the spelling of a word. They can see the different patterns that exist to make the various sounds. There are also CDs for the blends and diagraphs; these give the children opportunities to hear and see the sound in a variety of words."

Greg O'Connell, First-Grade Teacher
Grant Wood Elementary, Cedar Rapids Community School District
Cedar Rapids, Iowa

Practice:

- Play the game THREE CHEERS!
- Identify five to seven words that you will say in parts. Say each word by giving the two syllables. Ask children to say the word three times as a cheer (Example: Teacher: /bŏt•əl/ Children: *bottle, bottle, bottle*).

This same procedure can be used for blending onset and rime.

For more activities for teaching and practicing phonemic awareness, see the "For Additional Reading" section.

DISCUSSION/ COMMENTS

The elements on page 185 present a possible sequence for teaching phonemic awareness; you may find others suggested elsewhere. It is important that you have a sequence to follow so that you can help children *systematically* develop phonemic awareness. All lessons for phonemic awareness should be *short, fun,* and *exciting* for children. They are much more meaningful if they are connected to books that are being read aloud.

🦋 Explicit Phonics Routine

PURPOSE

This routine provides two patterns that can be used repeatedly for explicitly teaching phonic skills (letter-sound associations) and structural analysis. Two options are presented: *Option A,* Starting with Sounds, and *Option B,* Starting with Known Words. (Research supports explicitly and systematically teaching letter-sound associations, but it does not indicate whether it is better to start with sounds or with known words.) You may have some children who learn phonics and structural analysis better one way than the other. Therefore, you need to know both routines.

WHEN TO USE

The Explicit Phonics Routine (Option A and/or Option B) is used in the Reading: Learning Skills and Strategies block of the comprehensive literacy program. Many teachers use Option B following the reading of text that contains some examples of the sound element to be taught (as Mr. Paredes did in the example at the beginning of this chapter). Others teach Option A, teaching the sounds before reading the text containing examples of the elements (as Ms. Anderson did at the beginning of this chapter).

DESCRIPTION/ PROCEDURES

This routine builds on the best research that we have to date on explicitly teaching phonics (Adams, 1990; Eldredge, 1995). It incorporates five steps: (1) *awareness,* (2) *segmentation,* (3) *association,* (4) *reading,* and (5) *spelling.*

Use the procedures that follow to explicitly teach phonics and structural analysis. Each of the five steps is incorporated within every phonics lesson, with adjustments being made to meet individual needs of students.

The following guidelines will help you plan explicit letter-sound association instruction using Option A and Option B:

Option A—Sounds First Illustration Using Short *a*

1. Awareness

a. Today you will learn to read and spell words with the short *a* sound—/ă/. Listen to each word I say; raise your hand when you hear /ă/ (/c/•/ă/•/t/ *cat;* /ă/•/p/•/əl/ *apple;* /t/•/ă/•/p/ *tap*).

b. If students respond correctly, move on to the next step. If students do not respond correctly, provide more instruction in phonemic awareness. (See earlier discussion.)

2. Segmentation

a. Say, "You can hear /ă/ in the middle of *cap.* Sometimes /ă/ will be in the beginning of a word, as in *at.*" Model using several other words (*apple, act, pat, pass*).

b. Say, "Listen to each of these words and tell me if you hear /ă/ and whether it is the middle or beginning of the word" (*at, cap, mat, dog, ask, cast*).

If students respond correctly, move on to the next step; if they do not, provide more teaching and practice in segmentation.

3. Association

A ă

Abby Astronaut

a. Tell children that they are now going to look at the letter that stands for /ă/. Write *a* on the board. Ask children to tell what letter this is.

b. Next tell children they are going to meet a special character who will help them remember the sound for short *a*. Her name is Abby Astronaut. Ask children to repeat her name, say /ă/, and hold up the *a* letter card. Repeat two or three times.

4. Reading

a. Say, "Now let's read some words using /ă/." Print the word *mat* on the board. Remind children that they know the /m/ and /t/ sounds. Model sequential decoding saying the sounds together and showing the direction of reading by quickly moving your hand under the word:

/m//ă//t/

b. Print the following words on the board. Call on different children to come to the board and model sequential decoding, moving their hand under the word to show the direction of their reading. Remind children that they know all the sounds in the words (*at, lap, sat, Pam, man, rap, rat*).

c. Print a sentence or two on the board containing only words with sounds and high-frequency words children know. Guide individual children to read the sentences.

Tom is a man.
Tom sat on a mat.
Pam sat on a mat.
Pam has a cap.
Tom has a cap.
Cap! Cap!
Rap! Rap!

5. Spelling

a. Say, "Now we will learn to spell words with /ă/. Say the word *sap* slowly. Write the letters for each sound as you say the word slowly—*sap*. Remind children that they have already learned the *s* and *p* sounds. Model spelling two or three more words with short *a*.

b. Ask children to write (using paper or magic slates) the letters for each word you say (*sat, man, tap, tan, map*).

c. Note children's performance.

Option B—Starting with Known Words
Illustration Using Initial Sound /b/

1. Awareness

a. Say, "Today you will learn to use the sound for the letter *b* to help you read and spell words."

b. "Listen to this word: /b/•/ō/•/t/." (Say it again slowly.) "How many sounds do you hear in this word?" (Students respond—three.) "What is the first sound you hear?" Repeat using words *big, boy, box.*

c. If students respond correctly, move on to the next step. If students do not respond correctly, provide more instruction in phonemic awareness (see page 190).

2. Segmentation

a. Say, "The first sound in *box* is /b/. What is the first sound in *barn*?" (Students respond—/b/.) Repeat using words *bet, bang, bake.*

b. If students respond correctly, move on to the next step; if they do not, provide more teaching and practice in segmentation.

3. Association

Bb

Boris Bear

a. Write the words *box, boy, bear* (these words come from a book the students have listened to or read using shared reading) on the chalkboard. Underline the *b*. Say, "Each of these words begins with the same letter and the same sound. The letter is *b*; the sound is /b/." Say each word slowly, emphasizing the /b/ sound. Have children repeat with you.

b. Have a picture card with a bear. Show the card. Say, "This bear's name is Boris—Boris Bear. He will help us remember the sound for *b*—/b/."

c. Write groups of words on the chalkboard. Have students read the words with you and decide which ones begin with the same letter and sound as Boris Bear.

- *band, car, bell*
- *hat, beg, big*
- *top, Bob, cap.*

4. Reading

a. On the chalkboard write a word that students know—*pig.*

b. Say, "This word is *pig*. If we change the beginning letter to *b*, what sound will be at the beginning of this word?" (/b/) "What is the new word?" (Students respond.) Repeat using other words.

c. Say, "Now let's use what we have learned about the *b* sound to read some more words." Use only letter-sound associations students have been taught. Print each word and model sequential decoding:

bat - /b/•/ă/•/t/

ban - /b/•/ă/•/n/

bug - /b/•/ŭ/•/g/

Bab is a bug.

Bab is a big bug.

d. Write a sentence or sentences on the chalkboard using only letter-sound associations and high-frequency words students have been taught. Ask students to read, emphasizing the sound for *b*.

5. Spelling

a. Tell children that they are going to learn to spell words with /b/. Use words starting with *b* that have ending patterns that children know. Say, "I want to spell the word *bat.* I write *b* for /b/ and *at* for /at/. b-a-t." Model another word—*bit.*

b. Using small chalkboards, magic slates, or sheets of paper, ask students to write the following:

- the letter you hear at the beginning of *bake*
- the letter that stands for the /b/ sound

c. Dictate several words, mixing in words that begin with other sounds students know (*bank, best, cup, zoo, box*). Have students write the words. Look for accuracy in using the *b* and any other previously taught sounds.

Follow the instruction with practice by having students read and reread decodable texts. Gradually move students to authentic literature, encouraging them to apply what they have been learning and practicing in decodable texts.

See the Handbook for ideas of sequencing phonics instruction.

DISCUSSION/ COMMENTS

The use of routines for teaching phonics is not new (Cooper et al., 1979). Many teachers have found them effective for years. Placing a routine within the framework of a comprehensive literacy program helps to make the program more effective. You should follow a sequence for teaching phonics. Use the one suggested in the published program your school uses, or identify one from some of the sources listed in the "For Additional Reading" section.

🦋 Analogy Routine

PURPOSE

The Analogy Routine is designed to be used after children have learned quite a few sight words and have learned to use most letter-sound associations (Ehri & Robbins, 1992). The purpose of this routine is to teach children to look at an unknown word such as *reach* and think about it in terms of a known word *(peach)* that will help them figure out the unknown word.

WHEN TO USE

This routine is used in the Reading: Learning Skills and Strategies block of the comprehensive literacy program. It may be used with students at any stage of literacy development if students are not effectively using analogy to decode words.

DESCRIPTION/ PROCEDURES

With this routine, children learn how to approach an unknown word by relating it to a word they know. This becomes a part of the strategy A Way to Think About Words (see page 187).

Teach:

1. Print a sentence on the chalkboard and underline a word that is unknown.

The <u>goat</u> drank milk.

2. "Let's say I'm reading along and I come to this sentence. I read *The*; the next word I don't know." (Point to *goat*.) "It looks like a word I know—*coat*. I see the *g* at the beginning of *g-o-a-t*. I know the *g* sound is /g/. I put the /g/ at the beginning of *oat*. I say the word *goat*. I then read the sentence and it seems to make sense."

3. Print several more words in sentences on the board, and have children help you decode them and explain how they made the analogy (*lame/same; make/cake; willow/pillow*).

Practice:

• Write several sentences on the board containing one unknown word where children could make an analogy. Underline the unknown word.

Unknown	Known
lark	mark
cable	able
spot	hot

Ask children to read the sentence and explain how they thought of a known word to help them with the underlined word.

• When children are reading aloud and come to a word they cannot pronounce, prompt them to make analogies:
 – Say, "Does some part of this word look like a word you already know?"
 – "If so, say that word; then cover up the part you don't know. Say what you know. Then uncover the part you don't know. Give the sound for this part. Then blend the sound with the familiar part to pronounce the word."

• Relate the use of analogy to A Way to Think About Words strategy presented on page [187]. Help children internalize this process by prompting them to use it again and again.

DISCUSSION/ COMMENTS

After children have learned to use the basic concept of analogy, teach other lessons focusing on word parts such as suffixes and prefixes. Always help students see how this skill fits into their overall strategy for independently decoding words (see page [187]).

🦋 Making Words Routine

PURPOSE

Making Words (Cunningham & Cunningham, 1992) is a hands-on manipulative activity for practicing the use of letter-sound associations and word patterns to decode and spell words. Students at any level can use this routine to help them learn to decode words more effectively. The activity can be done as a whole class or as a small-group activity.

WHEN TO USE

This routine fits into the Reading: Learning Skills and Strategies block of the comprehensive literacy program.

**DESCRIPTION/
PROCEDURES**

This routine may be done with the whole class using a pocket chart and large letter cards, or it may be done with small groups using individual trays (like Scrabble™ letter holders) and letters. The following guidelines are for using this routine with a small group:

1. Select a target word such as *bathtub* from a book students have read. List the words you want students to make leading to the target word, progressing from two-letter words to the target word:

   – at
   – bat
   – bath
   – hub
   – tub
   – bathtub

   | bathtub | (target word)

   Print each word to be made during the lesson on a card to use for word sorting at the end of the lesson.

2. Give each student a set of letters for the target word and a tray. (The tray can be made by folding tagboard.) Make the vowels one color and the consonants another color.

3. Before students begin, ask if anyone can guess the target word. Respond only by saying, "We'll check at the end." Ask students to make a word: *at.* Use in a sentence—"We are *at* school."

4. You make the word in your tray; show students. Say, "Does your word look like mine? If it doesn't, fix it." Have students show you their words.
5. Next, ask, "What one letter would you add to *at* to make *bat*?"
6. You make your word. Show students; have them check and show you.

7. Continue the lesson building the words you want to have made: *bath, tub, bathtub.*
8. Throughout the lesson and at the end, help students see various patterns in the word building:

   at → *bat* (Add one letter; make a new word; could do more rhyming here, if needed)

   bat → *bath* (Add one letter; make a new word; if *th* has been taught, note the digraph *th*)

   hub → *tub* (Change one letter; make a new word)

   bath + *tub* → *bathtub* (Compound word)

9. Using the word cards for each word made, have children sort the words into various patterns:

    at   h*ub*   b*ath*

    b*at*   t*ub*   b*ath*tub

10. Add any or all of the words to the word wall.

11. Finally, locate the target word in the book from which it was taken to help children build the connection between what they are learning and reading.

For more information on Making Words, see the "For Additional Reading" section.

DISCUSSION/ COMMENTS

Although this routine is designated as a practice routine, it also teaches children about letter-sound associations and letter patterns. By regularly using this procedure, children develop their abilities to decode words independently.

🦋 Word Wall Routine

PURPOSE

Over the years, teachers have often placed words on the wall in their classrooms in groups or categories to help children learn them. In recent years, this concept has been given more formal attention (Cunningham, 1995). When using the Word Wall Routine for decoding practice, the purpose is to help children see patterns in letter-sound associations. (When using the routine for high-frequency words, the purpose is to help children learn the high-frequency word by alphabetizing it by the initial letter.) The Word Wall Routine helps students remember the sounds and words that they are learning and use them as they read and spell.

WHEN TO USE

The Word Wall Routine is used in the Reading: Learning Skills and Strategies block of the comprehensive literacy program. It is especially useful at the beginning literacy levels but may also be used at other levels for other purposes, such as to display an ongoing collection of words related to a particular topic.

DESCRIPTION/ PROCEDURES

The Word Wall Routine for decoding is used to place words on the wall that have the same sound patterns. A picture of a key word helps children remember the sound. The following guidelines will help you use the Word Wall Routine to reinforce the learning of letter-sound associations for both reading and writing:

1. As new letter-sound associations are taught, identify a key word that can be pictured to use as an exemplar of the sound:

Example:

2. Display this on a bulletin board or on the wall.

3. As children learn to read words that contain the sound, add *some* of them to the wall. These words may be selected from any texts children are reading or from their writing. When a word is added to the wall, underline the common sound element.

4. At least once a week or more, play short games or do activities using the words on the wall:

Examples:

- READ AND THINK—Call on different children to *read* all the words under a particular sound and *think* of one or more to add.
- FIND AND READ—Say, "I'm thinking of words that start with /b/. Find the key word on the wall, read it, and read the list below."

DISCUSSION/ COMMENTS

When using the Word Wall Routine for letter-sound association instruction, group words by their common sound patterns even though the spellings are different. For example, words with the hard *c* or *k* sound, as in *cat,* should be grouped together or side by side to note that the same sound is represented by different letters. Print the letters representing the common sound in a bright color. Figure 5.3 shows sections of a partial word wall.

Word walls are often used for high-frequency word practice (Cunningham, 1995). These words are also put up alphabetically but not by sound patterns. When using word walls for either letter-sound associations or high-frequency words, do follow-up activities such as "Read and Think" or "Find and Read."

FIGURE 5.3

Partial Word Wall for Practicing Letter-Sound Associations

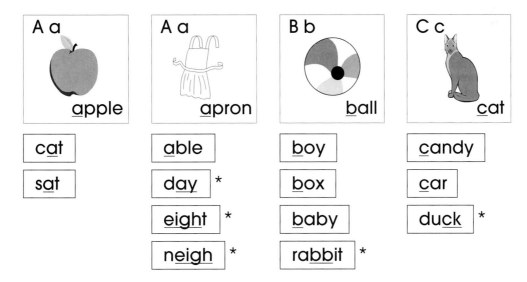

*These words are added as elements are taught. The most common elements are taught first. The variant spellings are not taught at the same time as the common spelling.

🦋 High-Frequency Word Routines

High-frequency words are those that occur many more times than other words in spoken or written language. These words must be given special attention in instruction because they occur in reading and writing so frequently (Hiebert, Pearson, Taylor, Richardson, & Paris, 1998). There are many lists of high-frequency words; one of the most common is the Dolch List of 220 Basic Sight Words (Dolch, 1936).

Decodable High-Frequency Words Routine

PURPOSE	This routine is used to teach high-frequency words that are completely decodable (examples: *at, it*) as soon as children have learned the decoding elements involved in the word.
WHEN TO USE	This routine can be used in both the Reading: Learning Skills and Strategies block and in the Reading: Application of Skills and Strategies block comprehensive literacy program. It is used to introduce new high-frequency words before children read a text.
DESCRIPTION/ PROCEDURES	The following procedures should be used (Example—teaching *an*):

1. *Review the Sounds*

- Show the key pictures for *a* and *n*.

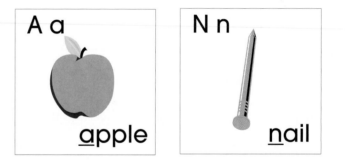

- Ask children to give the sounds /ă/ and /n/. If they are unable to do so, use the Phonetically Unpredictable Words routine that follows and reteach the sounds later.
- Say, "We are going to use these two sounds to read a new word."

2. *Sound and Blend*

- Print the new word on the board:

$$an$$

(Do not say the word.)

- Point to each letter. Ask students to give the sound. Model or coach as needed.

- Say, "Now let's blend the sounds to read the word [or "let's read the word"]."

  Sweep your hand under the word as children blend. Model or coach as needed.

3. *Read the Word*

- Print the word in a sentence:

I see <u>an</u> apple.

(All words except *an* are known words or are decodable.)

- Ask children to read the sentence.

See Chapter 6 for discussion of word banks.

DISCUSSION/ COMMENTS

Following the reading of the word in the sentence, give each child a 3" × 5" card. Tell the child to copy the word on one side and the sentence on the other side. Place the word in alphabetical order in a word bank. Two or three times each week, have children play games with words in their banks, such as having them draw words from another person's bank and reading it or play a game like FISH.

Mark's Word Bank

Irregular and Phonetically Unpredictable High-Frequency Words Routine

PURPOSE

Use this high-frequency word routine with phonetically irregular and unpredictable words (ones that cannot be decoded, such as *the*) or with words for which children have not yet learned the necessary decoding skills.

WHEN TO USE

This routine can be used in the Reading: Learning Skills and Strategies and the Reading: Application of Skills and Strategies blocks of the comprehensive literacy program.

DESCRIPTION/ PROCEDURES

Use the following procedures for this routine:

1. *Read the Word*

- Write a sentence on the board with the word:

<u>The</u> car is red.

- Read the sentence aloud to the group. Ask children to read the sentence with you.

2. *Match the Word*

- Distribute several 3" × 5" cards containing the word. Ask each child to find the word, match it by holding the card under it, and read the sentence aloud. Have the other children watching clap their hands softly if the child with the card is correct.

3. *Write the Word*

- Hold up a word card containing the word or point to the word in the sentence. Say, "This word is *the, t-h-e.*"
- "Now you say and spell it."
- Ask children to write the word on their papers or slate boards, saying and spelling the word as they write.

**DISCUSSION/
COMMENTS**

Follow the instruction with many opportunities to read text containing the words taught. Provide repeated practice like that described in the Decodable Words Routine.

Routines for Reading

See Chapter 2 for a description of modes of reading.

Reading routines require students to read different types of texts in different ways. Many of the ideas related to the modes of reading concept also apply for these routines.

🦋 Decodable Text Reading Routine

PURPOSE

As discussed earlier in this chapter, decodable texts provide beginning readers immediate opportunities to practice and apply in text what they are learning about decoding words and high-frequency words. Even though these texts are limited by the small number of words that can be used, they will give children a chance to experience the enjoyment and pleasure of being able to read. Remember, children will find both humor and fun in little books that may seem silly to an adult.

WHEN TO USE

This reading routine is used in the Reading: Learning Skills and Strategies block of the comprehensive literacy program.

**DESCRIPTION/
PROCEDURES**

Decodable text reading is provided after each two or three skills are taught, in order to provide immediate practice and application. There is minimal focus on comprehension. You can use the literacy lesson to carry out this routine.

1. *Introduce the Text*

- Show the cover of the text. Tell children that they are going to read this text to practice and apply the skills they have been learning.
- Ask children to read the title.
- Introduce any high-frequency words needed, using one of the two routines presented earlier in this chapter.

2. *Read and Respond*

- Direct children to read the text silently. Remind them to use the skill that has been taught. As they read, observe their behaviors and/or move from child to child asking each to read orally to you. Note their ability to apply skills.
- After reading, discuss the story. Call on individuals to read aloud favorite parts, sentences that match illustrations, or places to prove or support their ideas.

- Ask children to tell how they used the decoding skill being practiced or applied to figure out words.

3. *Extend the Text*

- Provide opportunities for children to reread the text alone or use the Cooperative Reading Routine.
- Reteach any decoding skills that seem to be causing difficulty.

DISCUSSION/ COMMENTS

The reading of decodable texts is a very short routine. In fact, at the very beginning stages of reading, you may use a new decodable text each day. Keep in mind that this reading is only one part of the literacy program. Your goal is to get children to the point of independent decoding and move them quickly to reading on their own using authentic literature.

🦋 Fluency Reading Routine

PURPOSE

A major need for all children, but especially beginning readers, is to develop fluency (the ability to read texts quickly and accurately). The Fluency Reading Routine provides a procedure to help meet this goal.

WHEN TO USE

The Fluency Reading Routine is used in both the Reading: Learning Skills and Strategies block and the Reading: Application of Skills and Strategies block of the comprehensive literacy program. Of course, fluency is also building during the Daily Independent Reading block when students read a book they choose. Here we discuss a planned routine for building fluency.

DESCRIPTION/ PROCEDURES

The texts used for the Fluency Reading Routine may be *any* of the texts used in your program after they have been read by the students. These texts are *always* easy for children to read. Use the following guidelines to carry out this routine:

See Chapter 11 for a description of the criteria used for a formal evaluation of oral reading fluency, including measures of both accuracy and speed.

1. Select a book each child can read, or have children select their own from choices you provide. Often selections are made from baskets of books that children have read previously. Usually you will have a small group all reading the same book.

2. Have children read their books silently.

3. As children read, move from child to child, asking him or her to read sections aloud to you. Note the child's fluency (i.e., speed of reading and accuracy). These observations will help you determine other skills that need to be taught. Students reading in a second language often read more slowly, and it is good to encourage them to increase their speed. An ELL mispronouncing some words does not reflect a lack of accuracy.

Note: Some educators recommend timing a child's oral reading to determine fluency. We prefer to simply note whether the child is reading the words quickly, smoothly, and accurately without worrying about the exact time.

4. After reading, have children share and discuss their books with each other for just a few minutes.

See Chapter 2 for a complete description of several fluency building activities.

DISCUSSION/ COMMENTS

The Fluency Reading Routine should be done regularly in your program. In the beginning, it should be a daily routine. Often you may also use the Cooperative Reading Routine for building fluency.

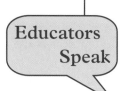

Educators Speak

Using Technology to Build Fluency

The students in my class are in their second year with me. This looping class has really bonded with each other and knows each other and their personalities. This group is made up of some very creative individuals, along with some very organized students. I have some very high achievers and students who struggle with learning at different degrees. I have used lots of peer tutoring and projects over the past year and a half to help build literacy learning. Here is one example of how I use technology to build fluency.

This project took us about three weeks to complete. After finishing theme two, Surprises, we started to work on a class book that would cover our number words and high-frequency words. My goal was to have the students take some ownership in the story, which would in turn make them want to reread their story over and over again for fluency.

Week 1: Students were asked to use the computers with the Kidspiration software program to develop their prewrite for a story about monsters. The students were asked to include some labeling with pictures in their webs. These were printed at the end of their session and kept for the next step. During this week, the students were making lists of descriptive words for monsters. They were gathering information from library books, their anthologies, and some gathered information at home from the Internet. I assigned each student a partner to work with to develop a page for the class book. By the end of this week, the pairs of students had been together to discuss their word lists, make some notes, and compare their graphic organizers.

Week 2: Students were assigned a number word. Their page would involve that number of monsters, and that number word would have to be used in their paragraph about their monster or monsters. They also knew that I would be looking for some of the descriptive words we had compiled in our word lists the week before. Students were assigned times to work on the computers in my room while others developed their picture for their page after they had their thoughts organized. Then we'd rotate. Each group had to print off what they produced during their computer time, as well as save to a disk for future use. I worked with each group to help revise and edit their work.

Week 3: Students took final copies of their work and illustrations and glued them to a page in our big book. I scanned each page and put it into a PowerPoint slide show and recorded myself reading the story. I burned the finished project to compact disks and placed one at each computer. The students were able to listen while reading and follow along with their story. They listened repeatedly to the story through the next week and still ask for it today.

This project truly helped my students develop fluency with vocabulary recognition and meaning.

Shari LaMunyon, First-Grade Teacher
Vermillion Primary
Maize, Kansas

🦋 Read-Aloud Routine

PURPOSE

The Read-Aloud Routine is designed to help children develop vocabulary, oral language, and comprehension strategies. It is a critical part of helping children develop literacy. This routine uses wonderful, rich narrative and expository literature such as *Lucky Song* (Williams, 1997) or *Goldilocks and the Three Bears* (Marshall, 1988). The read-aloud routine can be used with students at all grade levels.

WHEN TO USE

The Read-Aloud Routine is used during the Reading: Application of Skills and Strategies block of the comprehensive literacy program.

DESCRIPTION/ PROCEDURES

The format for the literacy lesson introduced in Chapter 2 can be adapted and used for the Read-Aloud Routine. You present and read aloud a wonderful book. However, the primary focus of the routine here is instructional. This routine does not replace the many times that you read aloud to children solely for pleasure. The following suggested procedures will help you use this routine.

1. *Introduce the Text*

- Show the cover of the text. and read the title; talk about other book parts. Discuss briefly content related to build background and concepts.
- Ask children to *predict* what they think will happen or what they will learn or pose *questions* they think will be answered. During this time, you can begin to model comprehension, or construction of meaning, strategies. Record children's predictions or questions on the chalkboard or on a chart for later use.

2. *Read the Text*

- Remind the children to think about their predictions or questions as you read the text aloud.
- Read aloud all or part of the text following the guidelines given in Chapter 2. Stop to discuss points or to clarify the meaning of words as needed.
- After reading, discuss children's predictions or questions. If you are reading a story, orally model summarizing by following the story map framework. If you are reading an informational book, summarize by listing the key points presented.
- From time to time, ask children to respond individually by drawing or by having brief discussions about favorite parts, characters, or what they learned.

3. *Extend the Text*

- Following the read aloud, use the text to develop oral language, vocabulary, concepts, and additional background through discussion, role playing, puppets, or other oral activities.

DISCUSSION/ COMMENTS

The Read-Aloud Routine is used for instructional purposes. Every step teaches vital comprehension strategies. Keep in mind, however, that there should also be times when reading aloud is done just for pleasure and enjoyment.

See Chapter 4 for a thorough discussion of comprehension strategies.

🦋 Shared Reading Routine

See Chapter 9 on struggling readers.

PURPOSE

Shared reading, or the shared book experience, was developed by Holdaway (1979) as a means of introducing beginners (in kindergarten and first, second, and third grades) to reading using favorite books, rhymes, and poems. Shared reading may also be adapted and used with older students. With this procedure, the teacher models reading for students by reading aloud a book or other text and ultimately inviting students to join in.

Shared reading builds on children's natural desire to read and reread favorite books. The repeated reading of texts over several days, weeks, or months deepens children's understanding of them (Yaden, 1988). Au (1991) suggests that such reading is not just random rereading. Rather, each time a child rereads a book with the teacher, the reading should be for a different purpose to extend, refine, and deepen the child's abilities to read and construct meaning.

Shared reading is especially good for ELLs because this technique helps make the written language comprehensible or understandable. Research has shown that shared reading improves English proficiency for ELL students (Elley, 1998).

WHEN TO USE

The Shared Reading Routine is used in the Reading: Application of Skills and Strategies block of the comprehensive literacy program.

DESCRIPTION/ PROCEDURES

1. *Materials Needed*
   - One copy of the book to be read in big-book form.
   - Multiple copies of the book in little-book form for individual rereading after the big book has been read.

2. *Introduce the Book*

   - Gather the children where they can all see the big book.
   - Show and discuss the book cover; read the title, author, illustrator, and other appropriate book features.
   - Motivate children by discussing the cover and some of the pages in the book, but don't give away the entire story. This activity also encourages children to activate and develop their prior knowledge.
   - Invite children to predict what they think will happen in the book. If they have difficulty, model predicting by "thinking aloud" to show them how you would do it. Record predictions on the chalkboard or a chart for later reference. As the children gain experience, you can formally introduce the preview and predict strategy using the poster presented in Chapter 3 (page 88). The entire process for introducing the book should take no longer than 3 to 6 minutes.

3. *Read and Respond to the Book*

   - Read the book aloud to the children, holding it so they can see each page. Many teachers use an easel for this purpose. As you read, run your hand or a pointer under each line of print to help children develop a sense of left-to-right orientation, speech-to-print match, and other concepts of print. If some children wish to join in, encourage them to do so, though for a first reading, many children will just listen.

- As you read, you may stop briefly to discuss the story or respond to reactions, but you should progress through the entire book rather quickly to give children a complete sense of the story.
- At the conclusion of the reading, encourage children to respond, using questions such as the following prompts:

> Were your predictions right?
> What did you like in this story?
> What was your favorite part?
> What made you happy (or sad)?
> Who was your favorite character? Why?

- Return to the book, rereading the story and inviting children to read along. Many will feel comfortable doing this right away, but others may not join in until another day. After the second reading, many children will say, "Let's read it again." This is especially true for books, songs, or rhymes that are lots of fun. Under most circumstances, when children are excited and want to reread, you *should* reread.
- After you have read the book again, have children respond, using activities such as the following:

  - Talking with a friend about a favorite part
  - Retelling the story to a partner
  - Drawing a picture about the story and writing a word or a sentence about it
  - Drawing and writing about a favorite character
  - Writing a list of favorite characters

For more ideas for responding, see Chapter 7.

Help children become comfortable with making decisions about responding by giving them only a couple of choices initially. The amount of time devoted to reading and responding will be from 10 to 20 minutes, depending on the book and the children.

4. *Extend the Book*

You may want to wait until children have read a book several times before extending it or wait until they have read several books within a thematic unit and combine them for extension activities.

Each time you carry out a repeated reading, you continue to model for the children. At the same time, you scaffold your instruction by transferring more and more responsibility to them. Although each repeated reading may seem to be just fun for the children, it carries very important responsibilities for learning. The following suggestions should be helpful:

- Invite children to recall the title and what the book was about. Prompt and support them if needed.
- Tell children why they are rereading the book with statements such as the following:

"As we reread this book, let's think about who the important characters are." (comprehension)

"In our story today, notice how the author repeats lines over and over." (exploring language)

"Today, as we reread one of our favorite stories, look for places to use the phonic skills we have been learning." (decoding)

• After completing the rereading of the book, have children complete a response activity that again draws their attention to the purpose–for example:

Purpose: Comprehension

Prompt: Dramatize your favorite character.

Purpose: Explore language

Prompt: Write a group story using the story pattern. For example, after reading *Brown Bear, Brown Bear* (Martin, 1967), have children help write a story using the following pattern:

Brown Bear, Brown Bear, what do you see?

I see a redbird looking at me.

Red Bird, Red Bird, what do you see?

I see a _____ _____ looking at me.

_____ _____ , _____ _____, what do you see?

I see a _____ _____ looking at me.

This response may also be done individually.

Purpose: Decoding

Prompt: List the words that have the sounds we have been learning. (Encourage children to use these words in stories they write.)

See "For Additional Reading" for more on shared reading.	**DISCUSSION/ COMMENTS**	Shared reading is powerful, versatile, and flexible. The activities of shared reading will allow children to apply what they are learning in the Reading: Learning Skills and Strategies block of the comprehensive literacy program.

🦋 Observational Guided Reading Routine

	PURPOSE	We refer to this routine as Observational Guided Reading to differentiate it from Interactive Guided Reading discussed in Chapter 2. Most literacy authorities just use the term *guided reading* and don't make the distinction given here. The Observational Guided Reading Routine is designed to help children use and develop the strategies of independent reading (Fountas & Pinnell, 1996). It provides children a time to apply what they are learning in the Reading: Learning Skills and Strategies block of the comprehensive literacy program.
	WHEN TO USE	The Observational Guided Reading Routine is used during the Reading: Application of Skills and Strategies block of the comprehensive literacy program.
See the discussion on leveling texts in Chapter 2.	**DESCRIPTION/ PROCEDURES**	During Observational Guided Reading, children read texts that have a minimum of new words or skills to learn (Fountas & Pinnell, 1996). These texts are leveled and are at the students' developmentally appropriate reading level.

The children read in small groups (usually 5–8) with their teacher. The following guidelines, organized around the literacy lesson concept presented in Chapter 2, should be helpful to you in learning to use Observational Guided Reading.

1. *Introduce the Book*

- Materials: Multiple copies of the book
- Show the book cover. Read the title. Discuss information on the cover. Ask students to *predict* what is going to happen in the text. Record the predictions. Do not give away the ending.
- Conduct a picture walk using the book.

See Chapter 3 for an explanation of a text or picture walk.

2. *Read and Respond to the Book*

- Direct students to read the book silently to see if their predictions are accurate. At the very beginning stages of reading, however, students may read aloud softly to themselves.
- As the children read, observe their behaviors. Are some having difficulty with certain words or types of words? Are some tracking with their fingers while others are not?
- Are children applying the decoding skills they have been taught? You can tell this when they read sections orally.
- As you observe, look for one or two things you might help children with. For example, if several children seem to have trouble with the word *day,* print it on the board and help them sequentially decode or read through the word by identifying each sound in order if they have the skills.
- After reading, discuss students' predictions and what actually happened in the text.
- Teach any decoding or comprehension skill or strategy needed.

3. *Extend the Book*

- Have children reread the book alone or with a partner.
- Children may also choose to act out or role-play the story with partners.

See Chapter 11 on running records.

For books on guided reading, see the "For Additional Reading" section.

DISCUSSION/ COMMENTS

Observational Guided Reading should be a daily routine in the comprehensive literacy program. It allows you to see children's progress and immediately help correct problems. When using this routine, you should take a running record on each child once every couple of weeks using books they have read.

🦋 Cooperative Reading Routine

PURPOSE

The concept of cooperative reading was introduced in Chapter 2. As a routine for beginning reading instruction, cooperative reading involves partners' rereading texts that have been previously read. The primary function of this rereading is to build fluency and comprehension.

WHEN TO USE

This routine may be used in either the Reading: Learning Skills and Strategies block or the Reading: Application of Skills and Strategies block of the comprehensive literacy program.

DESCRIPTION/ PROCEDURES

After the initial reading of decodable text or authentic literature, the Cooperative Reading Routine can be used to provide students practice in reading. It is best that this reading be done with partners as opposed to triads (groups of three) because with the latter, there is always an odd person out. Use the following procedures with this routine:

1. Assign or have students select partners for cooperative reading.
2. Explain and model the process of cooperative reading with students:
   - Briefly discuss the book that has been previously read, drawing as much as possible from the children.
   - Have children take turns reading aloud sentences, paragraphs, or pages.
3. Observe the children to note their use of decoding skills and their fluency. Coaching or supporting some children may be needed during this time.
4. Direct students to briefly discuss what they have read with their partners.

DISCUSSION/ COMMENTS

The Cooperative Reading Routine is an effective way for children to practice reading of previously read text.

Comprehension Routine

🦋 Explicit Comprehension Strategy Routine

See Chapter 4 for a detailed discussion of each strategy and procedures for teaching.

PURPOSE

The Explicit Comprehension Strategy Routine provides a pattern for explicitly teaching and modeling comprehension strategies. The strategies that should be taught include visualizing, monitoring, identifying important information, inferencing/predicting, monitoring/clarifying, generating and answering questions, synthesizing, and summarizing.

WHEN TO USE

This routine can be used in the Reading: Learning Skills and Strategies block or the Reading: Application of Skills and Strategies block of the comprehensive literacy program.

DESCRIPTION/ PROCEDURES

This routine has three parts, with the teacher modeling the strategy at the *concept, listening,* and *reading* levels as described in the chapter on strategies. This description is based on teaching the strategy of inferencing to beginning readers or struggling readers of any age.

1. Concept

    a. Begin by developing the concept of inferencing. Use concrete materials and examples:

        Say, "Look outside. Is the sun shining? Is it cloudy?" (Students respond.) "What do these things indicate the weather is likely to be later in the day?" (Students respond depending on the conditions.)

    b. Discuss with students how they arrived at their answer (important information they gained by looking outside, prior knowledge they had, logic). Tell students that this process is called *inferencing.*

2. Listening

    a. Read aloud a short paragrap h that requires students to infer.

        Say, "Listen to this paragraph and tell what you think happened when Sara and Lisa went to the beach."

Sara and her friend Lisa went to the beach. They took their beach ball, a blanket, and a picnic lunch. They wanted to play in the water and lie in the sun. As soon as they put out their blanket, the sun went behind a cloud. They heard a loud clapping sound.

b. Discuss students' responses. If they have difficulty with this process, model for them using a think-aloud and repeat the process using several additional examples.

c. Talk with students about how they arrived at their conclusion.

3. Reading

a. Select a piece of text students have read that requires inferencing.

b. Model the use of inferencing with a think-aloud.

Provide repeated practice and application through reading until students are comfortable using the strategy.

DISCUSSION/ COMMENTS

Routines for teaching comprehension have been recommended for many years and have been refined as our knowledge about comprehension has increased. In kindergarten, comprehension strategies can be modeled within the various reading routines. As texts become more challenging for readers and readers become independent decoders, a more formal approach to modeling strategies should be used.

See Chapter 4 on strategies.

We have looked at a variety of beginning literacy routines. You will learn many others in your classroom. The ones presented in this section give you good resources to begin to plan a comprehensive literacy program. Let's take a closer look to see how this can be done.

🦋 Planning Daily Instruction Using Routines

As you plan daily instruction for the children, you will use some routines every day and others only occasionally. The following four guidelines will help you as you plan:

1. Keep in mind the model for the comprehensive literacy program presented in Chapter 2. The six major blocks (Daily Independent Reading, Daily Independent Writing, Reading: Learning Skills and Strategies, Reading: Application of Skills and Strategies, Writing: Learning to Write, and Writing: Developmentally Appropriate Writing) should be included in each day's plan. There may be rare occasions when this is not true, but for the most part, this is your goal.

2. Lay out your daily schedule in blocks following the comprehensive literacy model. You will find that there is often overlap in your blocks. (See the following example of Ms. Barbizon's schedule.)

First and second graders work together in learning centers.
© Elizabeth Crews/The Image Works

3. Vary the routines you use. Although children like repetition and learn effectively when it is used, they also need some variety in their routines.

4. Select the routines based on students' needs. Teaching is assessment; therefore, as children respond in all teaching-related activities, note their responses, and use this information to plan your instruction. For example, if during a Shared Reading Routine several children's responses show that they are not applying certain phonic elements that you have taught, you should return to the Explicit Phonics Routine and the Decodable Text Reading Routine for reteaching and more practice.

For a detailed discussion about how to organize and manage your class-room, see Chapter 10.

The following lesson plan from Ms. Barbizon, a first-grade teacher, shows how she uses a variety of routines each day. We reformatted her schedule and added comments to help you see the different routines she uses.

🦋 As You Read Ms. Barbizon's Plan

- Look for the variety of routines she uses.
- Note how she manages small groups by using independent reading and learning centers.
- Note how she works in the blocks of a balanced beginning literacy program.

Ms. Barbizon's Schedule
(19 first graders)
November 12

• Literacy block—8:45 to 11:45 daily
• Independent work—Five learning centers for writing, vocabulary, and spelling practice

TIME	ACTIVITY	ROUTINES	COMMENTS
8:45	READING: Application of Skills and Strategies – Reread the big book *The Lady with the Alligator Purse* (Wescott, 1988). – Discussion.	• Shared Reading Routine	• This previously read book provides application of previously taught letter-sound associations and high-frequency words. This also serves as a warm-up or opening activity.
9:00	Daily Independent Reading – Conference with Jeff, Lisa, Elaine, and Martha.		• During this time students are practicing reading. Conferences help Ms. Barbizon check for decoding and other skill application to self-selected books.
9:10	READING: Learning Skills and Strategies – Teach digraphs *sh, ch, th*. – Practice and apply digraphs. • Read *Charlie's Shoes*.	• Explicit Phonics Routine • Decodable Text Reading Routine • Observational Guided Reading Routine • Irregular and Phonetically Unpredictable Words Routine	• Ms. Barbizon is continuing to teach the decoding skills students need. • Ms. Barbizon combines three routines. She meets with three small groups. While she meets with one group, the other children go to an assigned learning center.
10:10	Daily Independent Writing – Children add to journals.		• Ms. Barbizon moves from child to child to check to see how they are spelling using the letter-sound associations taught so far this year.

TIME	ACTIVITY	ROUTINES	COMMENTS
10:20	**WRITING: Learning to Write** – Writing a group story. – Spelling words with *sh, ch, th.* *Spelling List* • chair • show • think • much • shop	• Shared Writing Routine	• Ms. Barbizon is connecting the explicit phonics instruction with spelling. The children help her write a group story. She works the spelling words into the story.
10:40	**READING: Learning Skills and Strategies** –Practice spelling words with digraphs *sh, ch, th.* –Add spelling words to word wall. –Review words on word wall.	• Making Words Routine • Word Wall Routine	• Ms. Barbizon returns to this block to provide more practice and connections for students.
11:00	**WRITING: Developmentally Appropriate Writing** – Children write own stories. – Encourage use of words from word wall.		• This is a follow-up to the teacher-modeled writing. Ms. Barbizon moves from student to student to provide coaching. She is looking for application of skills previously taught and evidence of students' writing abilities.
11:15	**READING: Application of Skills and Strategies** –Read aloud *The 500 Hats of Bartholomew Cubbins* (Seuss, 1938) to teach noting important details using a simplified story map.	• Read-Aloud Routine	• Ms. Barbizon is teaching listening comprehension.

TIME	ACTIVITY	ROUTINES	COMMENTS
11:15 *continued*	–Partner practice reading (select any book read).	• Cooperative Reading Routine • Fluency Reading Routine	• Children select any books they have read today or on another day. They read with a partner. Ms. Barbizon moves from pair to pair to note fluency and application of skills.
11:35	– Discuss what was learned today. Make a list on the board.		• Ms. Barbizon concludes her day by having children talk about what they learned. For example, children might say, "I learned a new word" or "I learned to read better." This helps to keep children focused and see the value of their day.

You have focused on the important components of a beginning literacy program. You have learned a variety of routines to use within this program. Now let's focus on a specific literacy lesson that can be used in the program.

☑ **IRA/NCTE Standards to be developed in this unit and lesson: 1, 2, 3, 4, 9, 10, 11, 12**

Standards-Based
Literacy
Lesson

No, No Titus!

1. Recall what you already know about the Shared Reading Routine. Discuss the chapter with a peer to clarify concepts.
2. Read the text and study the art of *No, No, Titus!* beginning on page 218.
3. Read the Teacher Preparation section beginning on this page, which explains the decision-making process of planning this lesson.

While Reading the Plan

1. Notice how the Shared Reading Routine is carried out.
2. Consider any changes you might have made had you written the lesson. Be ready to explain your thinking.

🦋 Teacher Preparation

This plan was developed for a first-grade class of twenty-two students in an urban setting. English is the second language for thirteen of these children, in whose homes several different languages

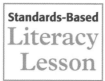

continued

are spoken. Two children have not yet begun speaking English at all, though they are beginning to understand some. The other eleven are at varying stages of acquiring oral English. The following outlines the steps used to plan the lesson and gives a rationale for each.

Unit Activities Prior to Reading The Book *No, No, Titus!*

1. The class is learning about farms and farm life as part of a larger unit about "work." The children have shared what they know about what foods are produced on farms, how the work is done, the animals, and how life on a farm differs from what they know in their urban setting.
2. The librarian has provided picture books, pictures, poems, and computer programs for children to share.
3. I have identified a number of high-frequency words in the book: the words *said, the, a, to, be, what, was,* and *do* are on the first page.
4. Children have seen pictures of each animal, person, and vehicle in the book. They have learned the associated "noise" for each: bus, HONK-HONK; tractor, VROOM-VROOM; cow, MOO-MOO . . . and so forth. We have played a rhythm game that involved children taking turns wearing a mask indicating what vehicle or animal they are. As each is named, the child stands and all clap and say the appropriate "noise" words.

Major Outcomes and Standards Developed in This Lesson

1. Decoding and word recognition: reads common sight words (words that are often seen and heard).
2. Decoding and word recognition: uses initial consonant sounds (*t, s, b*) to read words.
3. Comprehension: confirms predictions after reading a given text.
4. Comprehension: uses details of a pattern story to understand farm life.
5. Literary response: increases knowledge about farm life; shares knowledge with peers and others; demonstrates understanding of story through discussion and writing of new text.

About This Lesson

1. The sample lesson that follows for *No, No, Titus!* uses the Shared Reading Routine.
2. The lesson includes ways to reread the book to practice known skills.
3. The first (and possibly second) reading of *No, No, Titus!* will be completed in one day. As long as the group is interested, further rereadings can be carried out on several subsequent days to build fluency, reinforce known skills, and deepen understanding.

Claire Masurel

No, No, Titus!

Illustrated by Shari Halpern

NORTH-SOUTH BOOKS / NEW YORK / LONDON

Standards-Based
Literacy
Lesson

continued

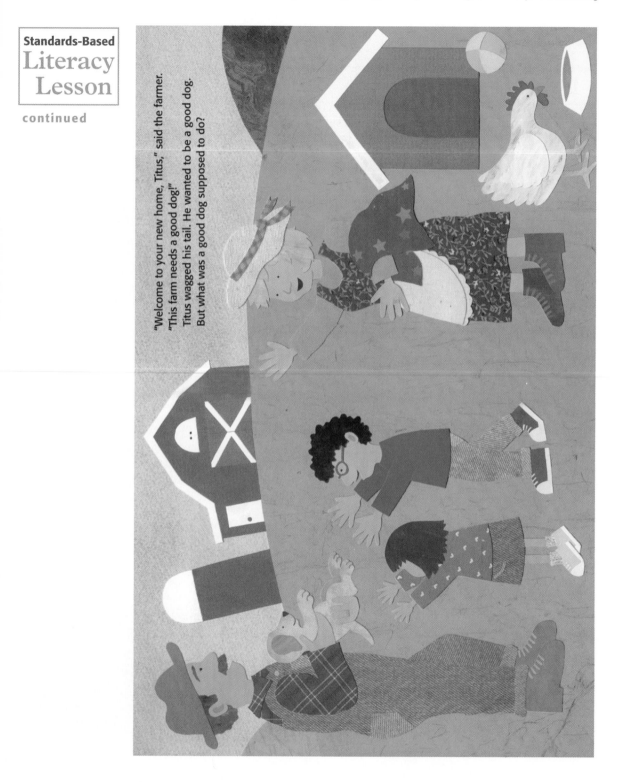

"Welcome to your new home, Titus," said the farmer.
"This farm needs a good dog!"
Titus wagged his tail. He wanted to be a good dog.
But what was a good dog supposed to do?

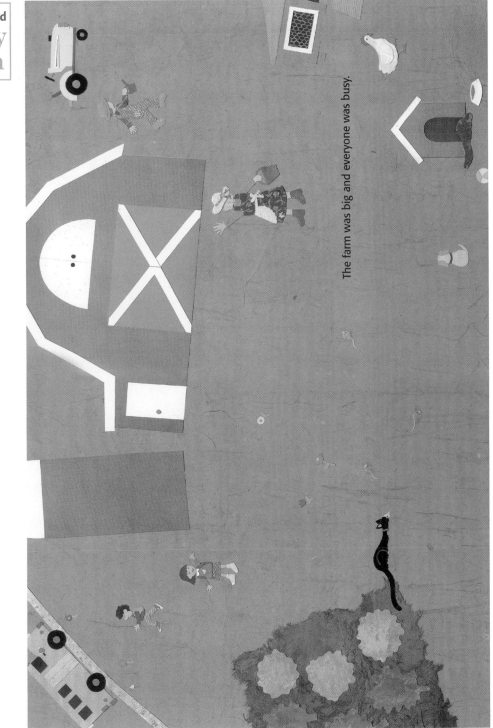

The farm was big and everyone was busy.

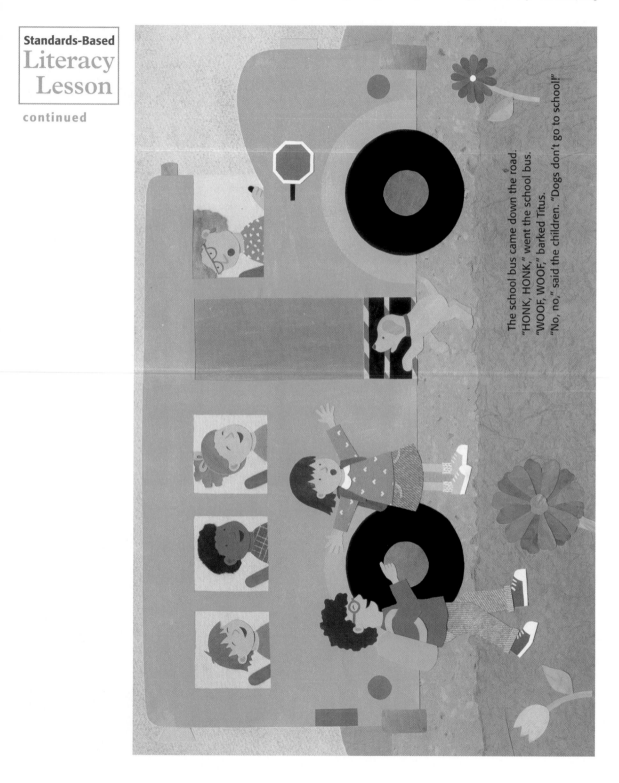

The school bus came down the road.
"HONK, HONK," went the school bus.
"WOOF, WOOF," barked Titus.
"No, no," said the children. "Dogs don't go to school!"

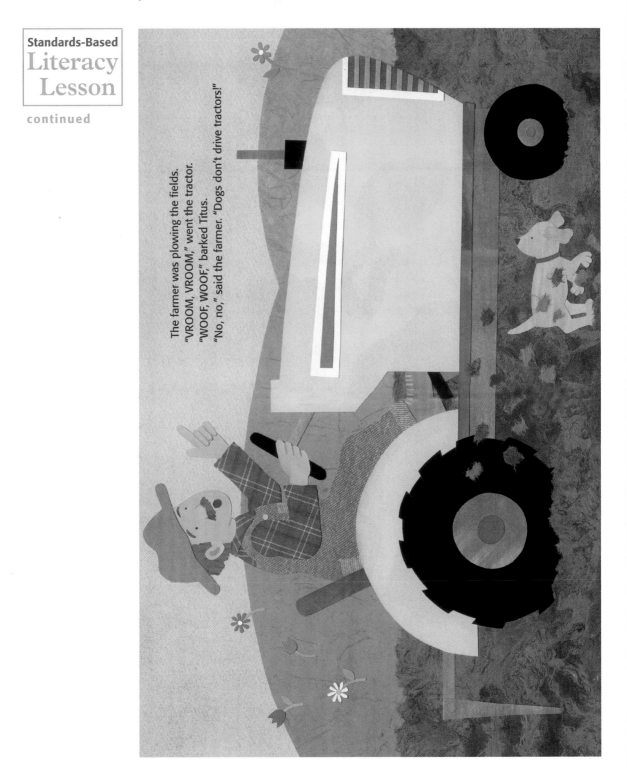

The farmer was plowing the fields.
"VROOM, VROOM," went the tractor.
"WOOF, WOOF," barked Titus.
"No, no," said the farmer. "Dogs don't drive tractors!"

Standards-Based
Literacy
Lesson

continued

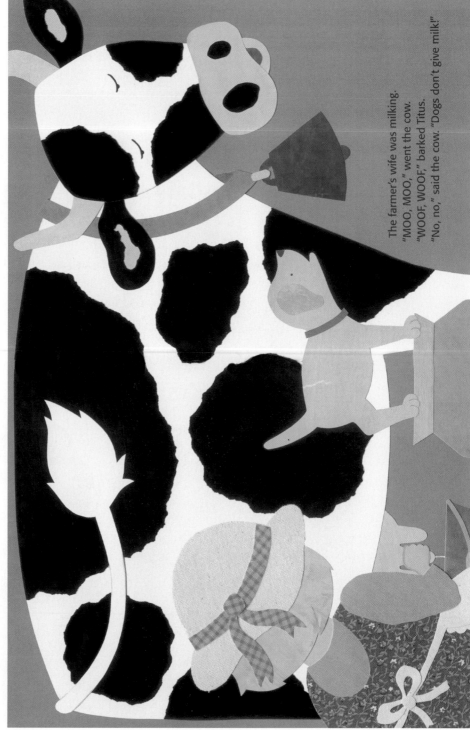

The farmer's wife was milking.
"MOO, MOO," went the cow.
"WOOF, WOOF," barked Titus.
"No, no," said the cow. "Dogs don't give milk!"

The cat was chasing mice.
"MEOW, MEOW," went the cat.
"WOOF, WOOF," barked Titus.
"No, no," said the cat. "Dogs don't chase mice."

Standards-Based Literacy Lesson

continued

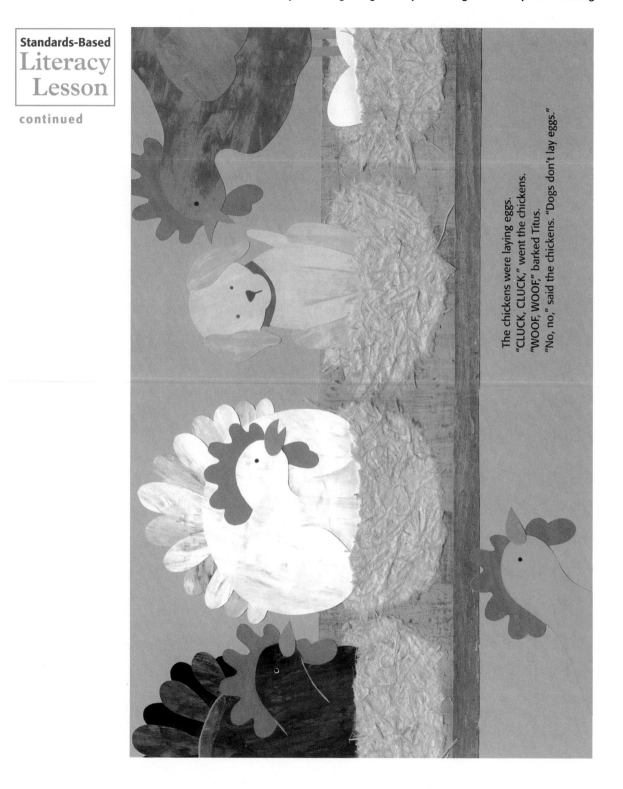

The chickens were laying eggs.
"CLUCK, CLUCK," went the chickens.
"WOOF, WOOF," barked Titus.
"No, no," said the chickens. "Dogs don't lay eggs."

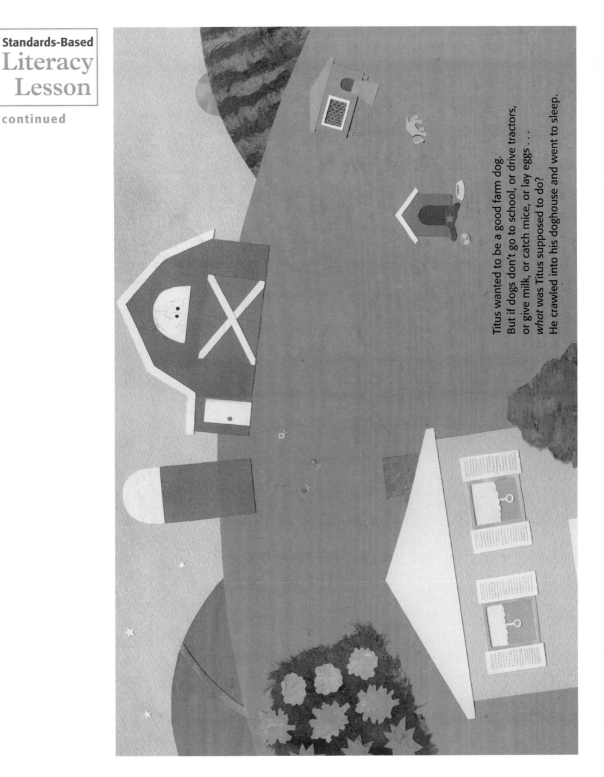

Titus wanted to be a good farm dog.
But if dogs don't go to school, or drive tractors,
or give milk, or catch mice, or lay eggs . . .
what was Titus supposed to do?
He crawled into his doghouse and went to sleep.

Standards-Based Literacy Lesson

continued

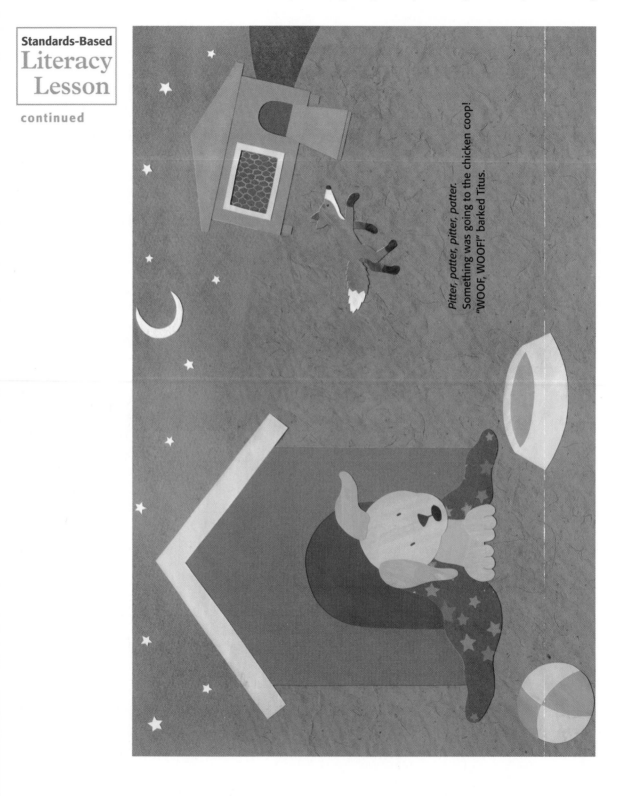

Pitter, patter, pitter, patter.
Something was going to the chicken coop!
"WOOF, WOOF!" barked Titus.

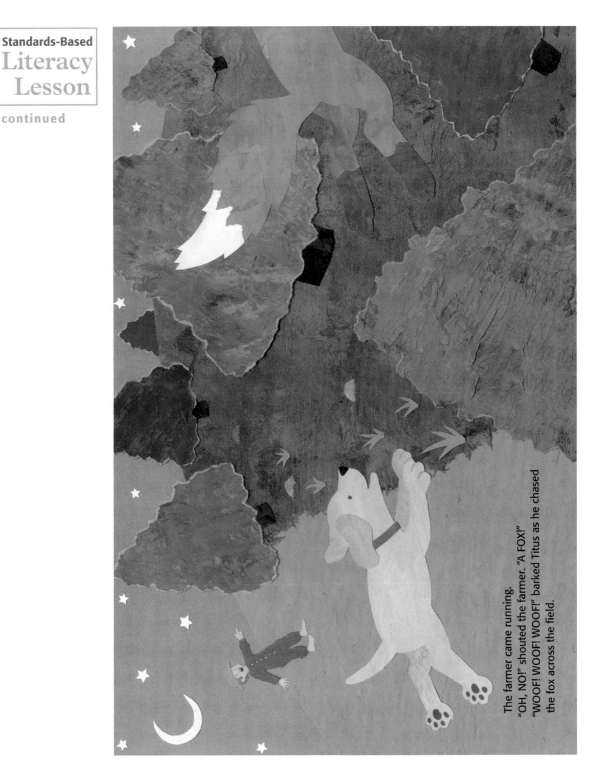

The farmer came running.
"OH, NO!" shouted the farmer. "A FOX!"
"WOOF! WOOF! WOOF!" barked Titus as he chased the fox across the field.

Standards-Based
Literacy
Lesson

continued

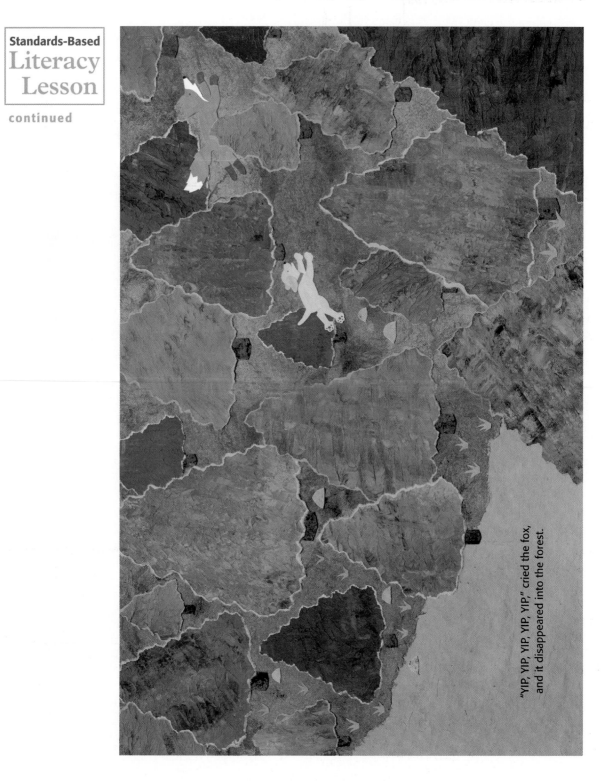

"YIP, YIP, YIP, YIP," cried the fox, and it disappeared into the forest.

Standards-Based
Literacy
Lesson

continued

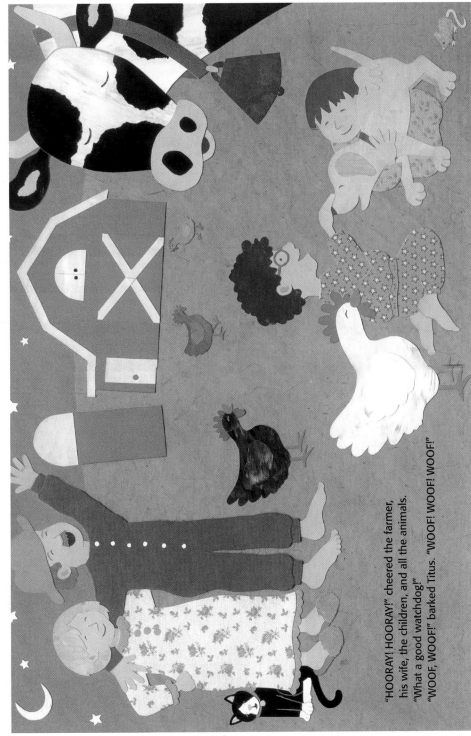

"HOORAY! HOORAY!" cheered the farmer, his wife, the children, and all the animals.

"What a good watchdog!"

"WOOF, WOOF!" barked Titus. "WOOF! WOOF! WOOF!"

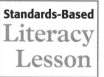

Standards-Based
Literacy Lesson
continued

🦋 Introducing *No, No, Titus!*

Activity	Procedures and Comments
Song; opening activity	1. Teach children the song "Old MacDonald Had a Farm" to use as a framework.
	2. Display and teach the following words and sounds from the book. Sounds should be shown in capital letters as in the book, but you might also show them in lowercase letters: *tractor* (VROOM-VROOM), *bus* (HONK-HONK), *dog/Titus* (WOOF-WOOF), *cow* (MOO-MOO), *cat* (MEOW-MEOW), *fox* (YIP-YIP-YIP), *farmer, wife, and children* (HOORAY-HOORAY). Sing the song together, pointing to words in random order.
	3. Review what the children remember from what they know about farms and the role of each of the people and animals on a farm.
	Note: *Motivates, activates prior knowledge, stimulates oral language.*
Present the book and make predictions	1. Show the big book; read the title, author, and illustrator. Discuss the role of the author and the illustrator.
	2. Focus attention on the cover art, and ask volunteers for comments related to the pictures or the print.
	Note: *Accept all comments; these could relate to the people or animals, colors, facial expressions, or the print. Some children may note familiar letters and say the sounds. Children who speak other languages may name the people, animals, and colors in their languages.*
	3. Reread the title and ask for predictions. Record the predictions, and tell students they will think about these predictions again later.
	Note: *When children make predictions, they give themselves a purpose for reading.*
	4. Show the first two-page "spread." Have children tell what they think is happening. Read aloud the page ending with, "But what was a good dog supposed to do?" Invite children to change their predictions based on what they now know about the story.
	Note: *Revising predictions with new information is a valuable thinking skill. You may want to lead children to "think like an author" at this point. Ask them to consider what story they would write with this title and this beginning.*

🦋 Reading and Responding to *No, No, Titus!*

Activity	Procedures and Comments
Read the story aloud to children	**1.** Position the big book so everyone can see. Read each page aloud, sweeping your hand or a pointer under the words. Watch the childrenís faces for signs that they want to stop and talk about something. Otherwise, read straight through for pleasure.
	Note: This method of reading aloud to children models fluent reading.
	2. Reread the story, inviting children to join you. Hesitate before reading the ìnoisesî so children can chime in.
	3. Return to the predictions and compare them to the story.
	4. Return to the text and ask differentiated questions of individual children to focus them on oral language, phonic skills, vocabulary, or comprehension.
	Note: Such questions allow you to include children at all literacy stages. Following are some examples of such questions: Find a word on this page that begins with the same sound as your name. Come up and point to a word that begins with the sound /d/. What parts of this story could be real? What couldn't? Which jobs on the farm have to be learned? Which are done naturally? Give a word that rhymes with dog.
Respond to the story; collaborate on a new story	**1.** Use *No, No, Titus!* as a framework, and help children dictate a new story. Make copies of the collaboration for each student.
Subsequent rereadings	*Note: The following are some possible ways to use subsequent rereadings to build fluency, construct meaning, reinforce skills, build oral language, and relate to literature.*
	1. Help children summarize or retell the story. Record the events as they recall them, and then compare to the book as you reread.
	2. Distribute copies of the book to partners, and have pairs of children reread the story together.
	Note: Circulate as partners read to assess, coach, and guide children to use their skills.
	3. Encourage children to reread the version the class wrote independently or with a partner.
	4. If children keep individual journals, encourage a written or picture response to the book.

After Reading the Plan

1. With a partner, talk about other ways you could have planned this lesson.
2. Use one or more routines to plan a lesson for a different book.
3. Observe a primary teacher (K–2) who uses the Shared Reading Routine. Make notes about the teacher and the children. Make an appointment with the teacher to discuss your observations. Be prepared to share your observations with your peers.

🦋 Summary

This chapter discussed the beginning stages of learning to read. The two big jobs are decoding and constructing meaning (comprehension). At the beginning stages, greater emphasis is placed on decoding, where most words met in print are already part of a child's oral language, though comprehension is always included. Six elements necessary to gaining independence in decoding are oral language, phonemic awareness, concepts of print, letter-sound associations (phonics/structure), analogy, and learning a way to think about words. Each of these elements was discussed, along with ways to promote their development. Fifteen routines for comprehensive literacy instruction were presented. The following was provided for each: purpose, when to use, description and procedures for teaching, and comments. The fifteen routines were grouped into decoding (phonemic awareness, explicit phonics, analogy, making words, word wall, and high-frequency words, both decodable and irregular or phonetically unpredictable words); reading (decodable text, fluency reading, read aloud, shared reading, observational guided reading, cooperative reading); and comprehension (explicit comprehension). A sample first-grade literacy lesson showed how routines can be used in effective comprehensive literacy instruction.

For Additional Reading

Barton, J., & Sawyer, D. M. (2003/2004). Our students *are* reading for this: Comprehension instruction in the elementary school. *The Reading Teacher, 57*(4), 334–347.

Bear, D. R., Invernizzi, M., Templeton, S., & Templeton, F. (1999). *Words their way: Word study for phonics, vocabulary, and spelling instruction* (2nd ed.). Englewood Cliffs, NJ: Prentice Hall.

Brown, K. J. (2003). What do I say when they get stuck on a word? Aligning teachers' prompts with students' development. *The Reading Teacher, 56*(8), 720-733.

Clark, K. F. (2004). What can I say besides "sound it out"? Coaching word recognition in beginning reading. *The Reading Teacher, 57*(5), 440–449.

Cunningham, P. M. (1999). *Phonics they use: Words for reading and writing* (3rd ed.). Boston: Allyn & Bacon.

Eldredge, J. L. (1995). *Teaching decoding in holistic classrooms.* Englewood Cliffs, NJ: Merrill.

Ericson, L., & Juliebö, M. F. (1998). *The phonologic awareness handbook for kindergarten and primary teachers.* Newark, NJ: IRA.

Fountas, I. C., & Pinnell, G. S. (1996). *Guided reading: Good first teaching for all children.* Portsmouth, NH: Heinemann.

Gambrell, L. B. (2004). Exploring the connection between oral language and early reading. *The Reading Teacher, 57*(5), 490–492.

Gonzalez-Bueno, M. (2003). Literacy activities for Spanish-English bilingual children. *The Reading Teacher, 57*(2), 189–192.

Meier, T. (2003). "What can't she remember that?" The importance of storybook reading in multilingual, multicultural classrooms. *The Reading Teacher, 57*(3), 242–252.

Neuman, S., & Roskos, K. (1998). *Children achieving: Best practices in early literacy.* Newark, DE: International Reading Association.

Palmer, R. G., & Stewart, R. A. (2003). Nonfiction trade book use in primary grades. *The Reading Teacher, 57*(1), 38–48.

Richards, J. C., & Anderson, N. A. (2003). How do you know? A strategy to help emergent readers make inferences. *The Reading Teacher, 57*(3), 290–293.

Villaume, S. K., & Brabham, E. G. (2003). Phonics instruction: Beyond the debate. *The Reading Teacher, 56*(5), 478–482.

Wright, G., Sherman, R., & Jones, T. B. (2004). Are silent reading behaviors of first graders really silent? *The Reading Teacher, 57*(5), 546–553.

For Exploration: Electronic Products and Resources

Visit the following Web sites to gain more information about beginning reading instruction:

Teaching Word-Identification Skills and Strategies: A Balanced Approach
http://www.eduplace.com/rdg/res/teach/

The National Association for the Education of Young Children (NAEYC) is the nation's largest and most influential organization of early childhood educators and others dedicated to improving the quality of programs for children from birth through third grade.
http://www.naeyc.org/

The following software is useful for helping children during beginning reading instruction:

• *Arthur's Reading Race, Dr. Seuss's ABC, Just Grandma and Me, Stellaluna, Sheila Rae, The Brave and the Berenstain Bears,* CD-ROMs available for purchase from the Learning Company.
http://www.learningco.com/Category.asp?CID=208

• *Bailey's Book House* and *Let's Go Read! An Island Adventure* by Edmark, a leader in the development of children's educational software.
http://www.edmark.com

• *Curious George Learns Phonics,* by Houghton Mifflin.
http://www.hmco.com

• *Pair-It Books CD-ROMs: Exploring Fiction and Nonfiction,* by Lioncrest,
http://www.lioncrest.com.au/early.htm

• *Wiggleworks* by Scholastic.
http://teacher.scholastic.com/wiggleworks/index.htm

Beyond Beginning Literacy: Decoding, Vocabulary, and Meaning

6

✓ **STANDARDS FOCUS**

NCTE/IRA Standards: 1, 2, 3, 4, 5, 6, 7, 8, 9, 10, 11, 12
Standards for Reading Professionals: 1, 2, 3, 4, 5

❝**Educators Speak**   **p. 255**

Vocabulary Instruction Across the Curriculum
—*Barbara "Bobbie" Lee, Sterling, Virginia*❞

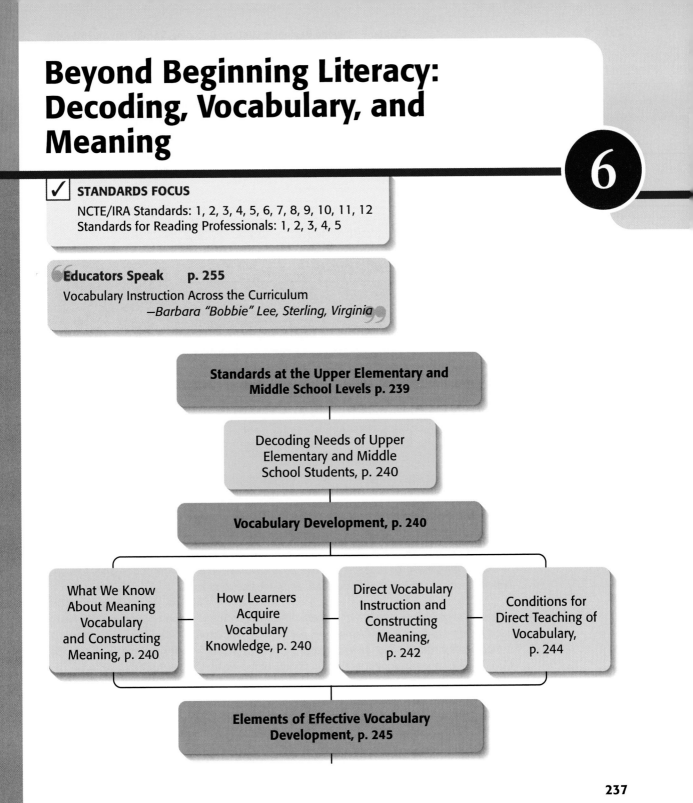

Standards at the Upper Elementary and Middle School Levels p. 239

Decoding Needs of Upper Elementary and Middle School Students, p. 240

Vocabulary Development, p. 240

What We Know About Meaning Vocabulary and Constructing Meaning, p. 240

How Learners Acquire Vocabulary Knowledge, p. 240

Direct Vocabulary Instruction and Constructing Meaning, p. 242

Conditions for Direct Teaching of Vocabulary, p. 244

Elements of Effective Vocabulary Development, p. 245

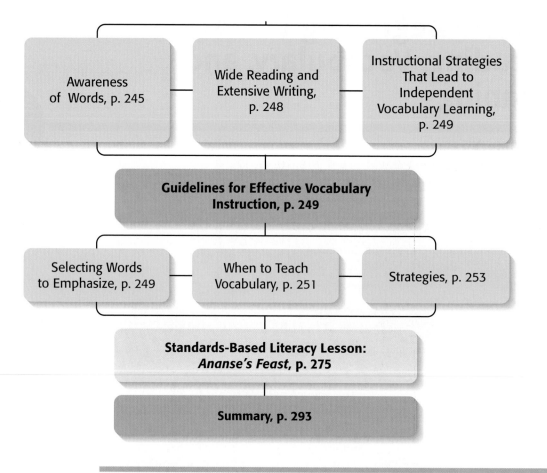

Let's sit in the back of the room and enjoy an interlude in Ms. Li's sixth-grade class. Students have just returned from lunch.

Ms. Li grins and pulls out several books that the students obviously recognize. They turn and high-five each other. They clearly expect to enjoy themselves.

Ms. Li asks if anyone has a favorite poem he or she would like her to read. Several call out together, "Never Mince Words with a Shark." Ms. Li opens The New Kid on the Block (Prelutsky, 1984) and reads the poem with pleasure, her class chiming in on the last line of each verse. Ms. Li then reads a couple of her own favorites: "What Is the Matter with 'P'?" (Words, Words, Words, O'Neill, 1966) and "Apology" (If I Were in Charge of the World, Viorst, 1981).

Finally, she pulls out The Annotated Alice (Carroll, 1960) and reads the first stanza of "Jabberwocky." Ms. Li displays the first stanza, tells students to focus on just the sounds, and has them read it aloud with her. Students then identify words they didn't understand (brillig, slithy, mimsy), and Ms. Li reads aloud the annotations about each made-up word in the first stanza. Afterward, they reread the stanza together.

Most students enjoy "Jabberwocky," but some have puzzled looks on their faces, and one says, "That's silly!" Ms. Li allows a free discussion about word play, including making up words. One student comments about the made-up language of the Klingons on Star Trek: The Next Generation.

Ms. Li tells the students to get into their discussion groups. She directs them to select, read aloud, and discuss pieces of poetry from several different anthologies that she has available. As the groups work, she calls a small group of students to the reading area for a lesson on the strategy of decoding longer words. She has determined from her observations that these students need this instruction.

After she completes her lesson, Ms. Li closes the reading period with a promise to read more poetry the next day. Several students want to know about the rest of the words in "Jabberwocky," and Ms. Li gives them the annotated book for independent perusal.

Terms
You Need to Know

- base words
- context
- direct teaching
- hierarchical array
- inflectional endings
- linear array
- prefixes
- root words
- semantic feature analysis
- suffixes
- vocabulary
- word bank (word file, word book)
- word wall

This short visit to Ms. Li's classroom reflects the varying needs of upper elementary and middle school students beyond the beginning literacy level. This was not a **vocabulary** lesson, but it served a valuable purpose: to share pleasure in language—to increase awareness of words. The student who found "Jabberwocky" silly may relish the language in a different poem on another day. Ms. Li shares a wide variety of poems and clearly appreciates and values all kinds of poetry. She encourages students to share poems they have found and to compile personal anthologies of favorites. Ms. Li also includes the direct instruction students need to continue their growth in decoding.

In Chapter 3, we dealt with the importance of activating and developing prior knowledge. In Chapter 4, we focused on strategies for constructing meaning that students need at all levels of literacy learning. In Chapter 5, we concentrated on how beginning readers and writers learn to identify words and construct meaning; these were mostly words that were already familiar in the child's oral language but not yet recognized in print. In this chapter, we look at strategies and techniques for developing decoding, vocabulary, and meaning for upper elementary and middle school students. We will focus most heavily on vocabulary strategies, because the strategies and routines suggested for decoding at the beginning literacy levels (Chapter 5) and the strategies and routines suggested for constructing meaning (Chapter 4) will continue to be used at the upper elementary and middle school levels.

Standards at the Upper Elementary and Middle School Levels

Look at the inside cover of your text; review all of the NCTE/IRA Standards. Each of these standards continues to be important in guiding the instruction that you plan for your students at these levels. Look at a copy of your own state standards. Note that at the upper elementary and middle school levels, the decoding, vocabulary, and meaning standards continue as at the beginning literacy levels but become more sophisticated.

See Chapter 5, "Routines for Decoding Words."

Decoding Needs of Upper Elementary and Middle School Students

See Chapter 9, "Helping Struggling Readers."

Most students will have mastered the basic decoding strategies and skills by the end of second or third grade. As they move into the upper elementary and middle school levels, they will need to apply these decoding skills and continue to use them with an increasing number of words that are not in their oral vocabularies. Ms. Li in our opening scenario taught a small group of students the strategy for decoding longer words. For students who have not mastered the basic decoding skills, it is necessary to continue with the basic instruction for beginning readers.

The major focus of decoding instruction at these levels should be on teaching students to gain more independence. This includes applying the decoding skills and strategies they have learned, learning structural analysis, and learning to use the dictionary more effectively. Teaching structural analysis and using the dictionary will be discussed later in this chapter.

❧ Vocabulary Development

The goal of vocabulary development is to help students become independent learners with strategies for inferring or learning the meaning of unknown words when they encounter them in reading. This process helps students increase the number of words that are familiar as they read and the number of words that they can use when they speak and write.

As readers develop vocabulary, they learn two aspects about words: recognition and meaning (Chall, 1987). These two aspects, however, *are not* separate from each other. Children's *recognition vocabulary* consists of that body of words they are able to pronounce or read orally. Beginning literacy learners focus much of their attention on recognizing words (Chall, 1987), even though their primary focus is on meaning. Children's *meaning vocabulary* is that body of words whose meanings they understand and can use. *Recognition and meaning vocabularies develop simultaneously as students learn to read and write.*

Students' recognition vocabulary ultimately becomes sight vocabulary, or words they are able to read instantly and use in constructing meaning. Beginning readers and writers rapidly build such vocabularies through reading and writing experiences.

What We Know About Meaning Vocabulary and Constructing Meaning

Vocabulary reflects an individual's prior knowledge and concepts in a particular area. For example, a person who is knowledgeable about music will understand and use the words *meter, clef,* and *timbre* in ways that reflect musical knowledge, and an avid gardener will know and use terms such as *perennial, deciduous,* and *Gaillardia.*

The study of vocabulary has interested researchers and educators for many years (Beck & McKeown, 1991). Research clearly has established a strong relationship between the knowledge of word meanings (vocabulary) and reading comprehension (Anderson & Freebody, 1981; Davis, 1971; Johnston, 1981). In the past, the strength of this relationship led educators to recommend that students be taught crucial word meanings before reading selections (Tierney & Cunningham, 1984). Later researchers challenged the wisdom of this procedure and others related to teaching vocabulary to improve comprehension (Nagy, 1988).

Improving an individual's ability to construct meaning involves a great deal more than just teaching a few words before a selection is read. We will address two significant issues to help you more fully understand the strong relationship between vocabulary knowledge and comprehension. First, how do learners acquire vocabulary knowledge? Second, does direct instruction in vocabulary lead to improved comprehension?

How Learners Acquire Vocabulary Knowledge

Studies of the size of children's vocabularies have given varying estimates for various grade levels (Loban, 1963; Lorge & Chall, 1963; Nagy & Anderson, 1984; Seashore, 1947). The discrepancies may have arisen because researchers used different definitions for what constituted a word, different concepts of what it means to know a word, and different bodies of words to represent English (Beck & McKeown, 1991). In light of these problems, researchers have concluded that the early estimates of vocabulary size are much too low (Nagy & Anderson, 1984). A reasonable estimate based on research places the *average* high school senior's vocabulary at approximately forty thousand words (Nagy & Herman, 1987). When the figures on vocabulary size are compared from year to year, it appears that students must learn twenty-seven hundred to three thousand new words per year (Beck & McKeown, 1991; Nagy & Herman, 1987), or approximately seven new words per day, to achieve this forty thousand average by the time they are seniors in high school.

The question, then, is: How do students acquire this astounding vocabulary? There are several plausible answers: through reading and/or listening to a wide variety of texts and other media and/or through direct instruction in word meanings. Extensive research on both of these points of view (Beck & McKeown, 1991; Blachowicz & Fisher, 2000; McKeown & Curtis, 1987; Nagy, 1988) has led to four major positions on how students acquire vocabulary (Beck & McKeown, 1991):

1. Students develop vocabulary knowledge through wide reading (Fielding, Wilson, & Anderson, 1986; Nagy & Herman, 1987).
2. Students learn vocabulary from context but need instruction about context to use it effectively (Jenkins, Stein, & Wysocki, 1984; Sternberg, 1987).
3. Students are often hindered as much as they are helped by context. Therefore, they should be encouraged to use the dictionary as an aid in acquiring word meanings (Schatz & Baldwin, 1986).
4. Students can profit from direct instruction in vocabulary (Beck, McKeown, & Omanson, 1987; Graves, 1986, 1987; Stahl & Fairbanks, 1986).

Given the strength of the research supporting these four positions and our own experiences with children, we must consider all of these proposals as viable ways for students to acquire vocabulary. The research supporting wide reading as a means of

The components of the literacy program are described in Chapter 2.

improving both vocabulary and overall reading is very powerful and must be taken seriously. This is part of the rationale for having an independent reading and writing component in the literacy program. But while students are reading widely, they need to become independent in inferring word meanings; therefore, helping them develop an independent strategy for doing this through the use of context, the dictionary, and structural analysis will serve them well. Finally, *some students under some circumstances* may profit from the direct teaching of vocabulary; however, direct teaching is not as powerful in achieving overall growth in vocabulary and comprehension as is wide reading (Nagy & Herman, 1987). We need to carefully examine what we know about direct teaching of vocabulary to determine how and when we should do it.

Direct Vocabulary Instruction and Constructing Meaning

As noted earlier, it has been a long-standing practice to preteach words that are perceived to be crucial for understanding a selection. This practice has been justified on the basis of the extensive body of research that shows a strong correlation between the knowledge of word meanings and comprehension. There are two important questions to consider when thinking about the **direct teaching** of vocabulary: (1) Does it improve comprehension? and (2) If direct teaching is used, how and when should it be done?

Direct Vocabulary Teaching and Improved Comprehension

The goal of teaching students vocabulary is to improve their overall comprehension. Early studies in this area had mixed results: some found that direct teaching did improve overall comprehension, whereas others found that it improved knowledge only of the specific words taught and had little or no effect on overall comprehension (Jenkins & Pany, 1981; Mezynski, 1983). Still other studies have found that the direct teaching of selected words results in small but significant improvements in comprehension (Beck, McKeown, & Kucan, 2002; McKeown, Beck, Omanson, & Pople, 1985; Stahl, 1983; Stahl & Fairbanks, 1986; Weiss, Mangrum, & Liabre, 1986; Wixson, 1986). The determining factors seem to have been how the words were taught.

How and When Direct Teaching Is Effective

Direct teaching of vocabulary refers to activities in which information about the meanings of words is made directly available to students. This may range from very strong, teacher-led lessons to weaker forms of instruction, such as having students look up words in a dictionary (Beck & McKeown, 1991). In several studies, effective instruction appears to have had several important qualities:

1. *Only a few words central to the content of the story or informational text were taught* (Beck, Perfetti, & McKeown, 1982; Wixson, 1986). In other words, the random teaching of any unknown word does not help students improve their comprehension. The words must be key-concept words.

2. *Words were taught in meaningful contexts that conveyed the particular meanings relevant to the text* (Gipe, 1978/1979; Nagy & Herman, 1987). Because words have multiple meanings, teaching a meaning that does not fit the material to be read is fruitless for students and may even hinder overall comprehension.

3. *The teaching of vocabulary was integrated with the activation and development of prior knowledge.* Vocabulary is a specialized version of prior knowledge (Nagy & Herman, 1987). In all studies that succeeded in improving comprehension by teaching vocabulary, the words taught were in some way related to the students' prior knowledge.

4. *Teachers taught words thoroughly by offering students rich and varied information about them* (Beck et al., 1987; Nagy & Herman, 1987; Stahle & Fairbanks, 1986). Simply presenting definitions is not sufficient to teach students words; the words must be related to one another and to students' experiences. When possible, they were grouped into topical or semantic categories (Stevens, 1982).

5. *Students were exposed to a word many times* (Nagy & Herman, 1987). Knowledge of word meanings is gained in increments through many experiences. Therefore, words must be used in a variety of situations, such as writing and reading, to help students achieve ownership of them.

6. *Students were actively involved in the process of learning the words* (Beck et al., 1987; Nagy & Herman, 1987). Students were not passive learners who were simply being told information or definitions. They verbalized what they had learned and related it to their own lives.

A middle school teacher teaches vocabulary.
© Bill Aron/Photo Edit

Although research reveals these consistent characteristics of effective teaching, *it does not show that there is any one best method for achieving these qualities* (Beck & McKeown, 1991). Rather, a variety of techniques should be used for such instruction.

Another question about direct vocabulary teaching is when to provide it: before reading, during reading, or after reading. Researchers recommend that teachers teach vocabulary before, during, and/or after reading depending on the text to be read and the students involved (Beck, McKeown, McCaslin, & Burkes, 1979).

Many researchers have looked at the effects of preteaching vocabulary on students' overall comprehension (McKeown et al., 1985; Stahl, 1983; Weiss et al., 1986; Wixson, 1986). Although they all obtained positive results, they did not compare their preteaching with the effects of vocabulary instruction provided during or after reading instruction. As Tierney and Cunningham (1984) state, "These conclusions lead us to question the practice of cursorily introducing new word meanings before having students read. This practice is probably only justified when just one or two crucial words are taught at some depth" (p. 612).

Conditions for Direct Teaching of Vocabulary

Given the mixed results of the research on direct teaching of vocabulary, it is not reasonable to consider direct teaching the major source for vocabulary learning for students. It is not possible to teach the extensive number of words one by one. Furthermore, vocabulary research shows that while direct teaching of vocabulary often helps students learn the words, it does not improve comprehension.

Despite the strong research evidence that the direct preteaching of vocabulary is of little value in helping students improve their meaning construction, many teachers have persisted in following this practice. But why? A number of reasons exist, *but these reasons are no longer valid.*

First, educators did not thoroughly understand the process of comprehension. They believed that meaning in a text resides in individual words. Therefore, they erroneously assumed that the direct teaching of words would improve comprehension. Now we know that comprehension is a process of constructing meaning by using one's prior knowledge and interacting with the text; learning the meanings of separate, individual words has a very small relationship to this overall process.

Second, educators (and publishers of basal readers) believed that teaching words before a selection is read improves comprehension for students, even though no strong research base for this practice existed. Now that we have a strong research base showing that this practice is of limited value in improving comprehension (and then only under certain circumstances), educators are beginning to let go of it.

Finally, teachers did not know what to do in place of direct vocabulary teaching. Now, however, we know of many teaching strategies that help students become independent vocabulary learners and develop an extensive meaning vocabulary. These strategies include independent reading and writing and the use of word maps and vocabulary self-collection, discussed later in this chapter.

Direct teaching of vocabulary may lead to improved comprehension *only* when the following conditions are met (Stahl & Fairbanks, 1986; Snow, Burns, & Griffin, 1998):

* A *few* key words are thoroughly taught in meaningful context.
* Words are related to students' prior knowledge in ways that actively involve them in learning.
* Students are given multiple exposures to the words.

The teacher can use the few words that are taught to model the process of learning word meanings. Direct teaching of vocabulary-related skills, such as the use of context clues, prefixes, suffixes, base words, and the dictionary, should occupy a *very* small proportion (if any) of instructional time; incidental teaching at point of use or need may be of more value. Again, *it is more advantageous for students to spend their time reading and writing*.

🦋 Elements of Effective Vocabulary Development

Vocabulary knowledge may be considered part of prior knowledge. Students who have prior knowledge about a topic usually have the vocabulary to talk about that knowledge. They know the words for the concepts, although some, such as second-language learners, may have the prior knowledge but lack the words to express that knowledge. Vocabulary development as described in this chapter will stimulate growth in the vocabulary of all students. You will decide which students need which kind of support.

As a teacher, you are responsible for implementing the literacy program in your classroom. Effective vocabulary development takes place within that same program. It includes three important elements: awareness of words, wide reading and extensive writing, and independent strategies that lead to vocabulary learning (Blachowicz & Fisher, 2000). In the following pages, you will learn about each of these three elements of vocabulary development:

* *Awareness of words*. This refers to students' self-awareness and motivation to learn words. This section presents activities that develop awareness of words.
* *Wide reading and extensive writing*. This refers to reading and writing that students choose to do; that is, it is self-selected. This section suggests ways to support this in and out of the classroom.
* *Independent strategies that lead to vocabulary learning*. This section contains strategies that initially may be taught but eventually become part of students' ability to independently determine word meaning and increase vocabulary.

Awareness of Words

Considering the large number of words students encounter and the need to learn them, it is obvious that all of these words cannot be taught. Therefore, we must make students aware of learning words and create an intrinsic motivation and interest, so that they will learn words independently. Teachers, peers, books, magazines, and electronic books are excellent catalysts for this motivation and interest.

Being aware of and interested in words helps students develop ownership of them. This happens when students see how a word relates to their overall backgrounds (Beck, 1984). Students develop networks of words and their relationships through repeated experiences with the words in their reading and writing and through activities specifically designed to help them build relationships among words. Thus, first encounters with a word may help students learn its meaning, but it is repeated use that develops ownership. As readers develop ownership of words, they relate them to their existing schemata and develop new schemata, thus cementing the ownership.

By making students aware of and interested in learning words, you will provide the support that helps them expand their schemata and create new ones. Many different types of activities help to promote this awareness. Notice how all of the following suggestions are integral parts of reading and writing or extensions of reading and writing.

Noting Words in Journals

For more information on the use of journals, see Chapter 7.

As students keep journals, have them make personal lists of words that interest them or that they would like to discuss with a group, a peer, or you. Direct students to choose words that interest or puzzle them rather than having them simply identify all the words they do not know. This places the focus of such activities on what students can do, and makes it a positive learning experience. A related strategy, self-collection, is discussed later in this chapter.

Reading Aloud to Students

Listening to someone read aloud is an excellent way for students to become aware of words and expand their oral vocabulary, which is the foundation for all other vocabulary learning. As you are reading aloud a book such as *Anastasia Krupnik* (Lowry, 1979), stop periodically and discuss words such as *Hubbard Squash, ostentatious,* and other words that might be interesting, unusual, or fun for children to think about. Books that are especially written to focus on certain types of words can be read aloud before students read them independently. Some examples are *Delivery Van: Words for Town and Country* (Maestro & Maestro, 1990), *Taxi: A Book of City Words* (Maestro & Maestro, 1989), *The Weighty Word Book* (Levitt, Burger, & Guralnick, 1985), and *Murfles and Wink-a-Peeps* (Sperling, 1985). For your own reference, you might want to have available a book about word histories, such as *Word Mysteries and Histories* (Editors of the American Heritage Dictionary, 1986) or other books about words such as *Miss Alainious* (Frasier, 2000) and *Word Wizard* (Falwell, 1998).

Discussion Groups

See Chapter 7 for a discussion of literature discussions.

After students have finished reading a book, encourage them to get together in discussions to respond to the book and talk about words of interest. Even when all students have not read the same book, they enjoy sharing funny or unusual words from what they have read. This motivates other children to want to read the book and to become more interested in learning about words.

Word Banks, Word Files, and Word Books

These devices are the students' personal files of words they have learned or are interested in learning. The words can be taken from books they have already read, from areas of study such as science, from interest areas, from writing, and from other sources, such as newspapers or the Internet. The student writes each word on a card or in a word book with a sentence he or she has written using it and relating it to prior knowledge. Today, **word banks** or **word files** can be created in a word-processing program and saved on students' personal floppy discs or CDs. For example, a student might write the following sentence for the word *periodic:* "In my class, we have *periodic* tests in math two or three times a month." At the primary levels, the word bank idea is motivational because words and sentences can be written on cards shaped like coins and dropped into banks made of plastic bottles, boxes, or other containers. Students can then "withdraw" words from the bank and review them frequently. Always encourage students to use the banked words in their writing.

Writing

One of the best ways to make students aware of words and to promote ownership is to encourage them to write. By using shared writing and minilessons, you can help children be conscious of using a variety of words and more descriptive words. Whenever students use new words in their writing, you can be sure they have started to take ownership of them.

Word Expansion Activities

After several students have read the same book or worked together in a unit on the same topic, they can use such activities as word maps, semantic maps, or **semantic feature analysis** to play with the words that interest them. These activities are discussed later in this chapter.

Bulletin Boards or Word Walls

Bulletin boards that students develop to display words of interest or words on a particular topic, or **word walls** with lists of these words, also promote awareness and ownership. Students can then be encouraged to use the words from the bulletin board or word wall in their writing.

Electronic Books and Software

At this time, more and more classrooms can support current technology. If you have access to writing programs on CD-ROMs and software for student writing, take advantage of the exciting ways they support literacy development. Do not, however, feel defeated if your students do not have access to these materials.

See Chapter 8 on writing.

All of these activities are based on the students' listening, reading, and writing. Words are not studied in isolation from meaningful contexts. The constant focus of these experiences is relating new knowledge to old, constantly expanding students' schemata. The benefits of awareness and ownership activities are far-reaching. They promote independence in word learning and motivate students to want to learn more about words.

Wide Reading and Extensive Writing

"Increasing the volume of students' reading is the single most important thing a teacher can do to promote large-scale vocabulary growth" (Nagy, 1988, p. 32). Writing in conjunction with reading and writing alone both engages students in much more thoughtful learning and improves their ability to construct meaning (Tierney & Shanahan, 1991). Therefore, it is critical to promote wide, independent reading and self-initiated writing. Reading provides models of rich language that help students learn many new words, and writing provides an authentic reason for students to use those words and develop ownership of them. Because these two processes are so closely related and interrelated, they are mutually supportive.

Children *must* be encouraged to read self-selected books and do self-initiated writing every day. This should be a significant component of the literacy program, and not something done during "extra time" or outside class. Some researchers suggest that *in-school independent reading time may be even more important to improving students' ability to construct meaning than out-of-school reading time* (Taylor, Frye, & Maruyama, 1990).

In-school reading and writing are not sufficient, however; teachers must support and encourage wide reading and writing at home as well. Students can keep book journals, chart books read at home, share writing done at home, and have informal book chats with each other. Teachers should share some of their own reading and writing that they do outside school. As awareness of words increases, the potential for developing vocabulary through independent reading and writing also increases.

In addition to the ideas suggested in Chapter 2, try the following activities.

Book Displays

Have exciting and colorful displays of your favorite books and new books. Take a few minutes to read or tell a little about the book, just enough to get students hooked on reading it. Encourage students to place books they have read in the display and give a very brief comment about them. This transfers much of the ownership for learning to the students and makes them active participants.

Discussions of Interesting Words

Periodically invite children (or parents, other adults from students' homes, school staff, and so forth) to talk about interesting or humorous words from books they have read or things they have written. By sharing the sentence in which a word appears and telling others what they think it means, children learn to apply all aspects of vocabulary learning to independent reading and writing. Such words can be placed on a class word wall for all students to use.

Instructional Strategies That Lead to Independent Vocabulary Learning

Although wide reading and extensive writing are the primary ways through which students develop their vocabulary knowledge, certain strategies and techniques will help students become independent in their vocabulary learning and their ability to construct meaning.

Carr and Wixson (1986) give four guidelines for evaluating vocabulary instruction, all of which are based on the research conclusions discussed earlier:

1. *Instruction should help students relate new vocabulary to their background knowledge.* Because vocabulary is a specialized part of prior knowledge, students are more likely to improve their meaning construction when they do this.
2. *Instruction should help students develop extensive word knowledge.* Merely learning a definition is not learning a word (Nagy & Herman, 1987). To really learn a word and develop ownership, students must relate it to other concepts and words they know (Beck, 1984).
3. *Instruction should provide for active student involvement in learning new vocabulary.* Student-centered activities are most effective in helping students understand a word. For example, the teacher should have students take the lead in crafting their own sentences rather than simply giving them sentences.
4. *Instruction should develop students' strategies for acquiring new vocabulary independently.* Because of the large number of words in our language, students must be able to learn many words on their own. The strategies and techniques the teacher uses should lead to this independence.

🦋 Guidelines for Effective Vocabulary Instruction

All of the strategies for vocabulary instruction suggested here meet the criteria given above. As the teacher, you must constantly decide which words to teach, when to teach them, and which strategies to use for teaching.

Selecting Words to Emphasize

When selecting the words you will focus on during a literacy lesson, you must consider both the text and your students. The process for selecting vocabulary is similar to that suggested in Chapter 3 for identifying prior knowledge. Figure 6.1 summarizes the decisions involved in vocabulary teaching. The first five decisions are discussed next; the remaining two decisions are discussed in the following two sections of the chapter:

1. *Review the text to identify the story line(s) or main ideas.* This will be your basis for selecting the words for direct teaching. As we discussed in Chapters 2 and 3, this knowledge can also help you select the prior knowledge that needs to be activated or developed and decide what questions to ask if you use guided reading.

FIGURE 6.1

Decisions to Make About Teaching Selection Vocabulary

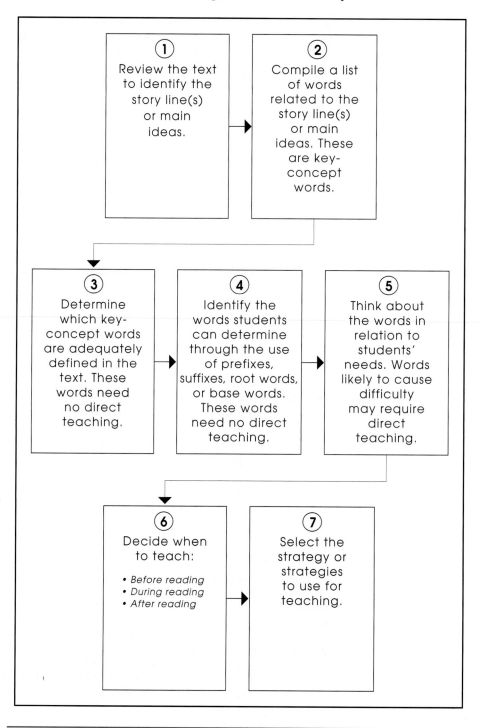

Creating a story map for a narrative text or a graphic organizer for an expository text will be very helpful as you work throughout a thematic unit.

2. *Compile a list of words related to the story line(s) or main ideas.* By looking at your story map or graphic organizer, you can see the important ideas in the story or informational text and can then select words that are crucial to understanding the selection; these are your key-concept words.

    Sometimes it is easier to carry out this process with expository text such as *Gladiator* than with narrative text. However, it can also be done using narrative text as long as the story line is used and the terms selected focus on the problem and action within the story (Wixson, 1986). The sample lesson at the end of this chapter illustrates the process using a narrative text.

3. *Determine which key-concept words are adequately defined in the text.* Some of these words will be defined through context and some by direct definition. Furthermore, pronunciation guides and footnotes may be given for words that are not likely to be in the students' oral vocabularies and prior knowledge. A word usually does not have to be directly taught if the text contains adequate clues to its meaning and pronunciation, but sometimes you may want to focus on such words after reading as a way to expand vocabulary.

4. *Identify the words students can determine through the use of prefixes, suffixes, root words, or base words.* Some of the key-concept words remaining on the list may include structural elements that students can use to determine pronunciation and meaning. Such words will not need to be taught directly.

5. *Think about words in relation to students' needs.* Finally, think about the words remaining on the list. If any of them are likely to be in students' prior knowledge, they need not be taught directly, though you might want to focus on these words after reading as a means of expanding students' vocabularies.

The words remaining on the list are those that may require direct teaching. They are unknown from students' prior knowledge, and are unlikely to be learned independently through the use of context and/or structural analysis. Only two or three words should remain on the list. If the number is larger, you may want to use guided reading and divide the reading of the selection into sections so that you teach only two or three words before reading each section. Keep in mind that research supports teaching only a *few*, if any, key words before reading as a means of improving comprehension (Beck et al., 1982; Tierney & Cunningham, 1984; Wixson, 1986).

Now that you have identified the words that need direct teaching, you must decide when and how to teach them. A lesson illustrating this process for a narrative text appears at the conclusion of this chapter.

When to Teach Vocabulary

Vocabulary may be developed before, during, or after reading, depending on a number of factors. You must make decisions in relation to each instructional situation. Some students may need vocabulary support throughout their reading, and others may need no support. Let's look at the conditions under which vocabulary should be taught before, during, and after reading.

Before Reading

Provide vocabulary instruction before reading in the following situations:

* Students are experiencing difficulty in constructing meaning and seem to have limited prior knowledge of any kind, including vocabulary. They might be second-language learners, students with learning disabilities, or students who are generally experiencing difficulty with comprehension.

* The text to be read contains words that are *clearly* a part of the prior knowledge students need to understand the text and you are confident students do not know these terms.

* The text has unusually difficult concepts. Even though your students do not normally need vocabulary support before reading, they may benefit from it in these situations. For example, suppose your third graders really want to read *The Mouse Rap* (Myers, 1990), which is developmentally somewhat above their age level. Before reading the book, you introduce some of the words and concepts that you think are beyond their knowledge and experience.

* Students have previewed the text they are going to read and have identified words they believe they need to know to understand the text. Sometimes this is a good way to identify words that students really do need to know. A word that is giving them difficulty, even one that is unimportant to understanding the text, may interfere with students' overall meaning construction. Through direct teaching before reading, you can help them see that knowing this word (or every word) is not important to their overall understanding of a text. However, you have to exercise caution when teaching vocabulary before reading based on student self-selection, because you could end up devoting too much time to words that really are not important to understanding the material.

During Reading

Vocabulary instruction during reading is usually recommended only for students who need overall teacher support through guided reading. These students are likely to be experiencing difficulty in constructing meaning, or to be reading a text that has particularly difficult concepts. When you use guided reading, it may be more appropriate to deal with words and concepts at the beginning or end of each segment of reading. Vocabulary support during reading has the advantage of giving students immediate opportunities to use the words.

In addition, during reading many teachers in grades 4 and above have students note interesting or unknown words in their journals. Students bring these words to discussion groups, and the teacher uses them as the basis for vocabulary instruction.

After Reading

Vocabulary instruction after reading has two primary purposes: (1) to help students clarify the meanings of any words that were of interest to them during reading or that caused them difficulty and (2) to expand students' vocabularies by having them focus on interesting words that are related to the text they have read. For example, you might use *Johnny Tremain* (Forbes, 1971) to help upper elementary students see how an author uses rich, descriptive language. Focusing on some of these passages would be a good way to expand vocabulary and relate the importance of descriptive language to writing.

Base decisions about when to provide vocabulary instruction and support on students' needs and the nature of the text; *sometimes no instruction will be necessary.* Table 6.1 summarizes these considerations in relation to the appropriate times to teach vocabulary.

Strategies

The final decision you must make is *how* to teach vocabulary directly (see Figure 6.1). You can use many different strategies in this process; there is no one best method. However, the procedures must help students improve their ability to construct meaning, and not just learn isolated words. Therefore, the strategies and techniques for supporting vocabulary development presented here are ones that help students relate new knowledge to old knowledge, actively involve students in the process of learning, help students thoroughly learn words, and support students in the process of learning to use their own strategies for independently inferring word meanings. *The ultimate goal of all vocabulary development is to help students become independent learners who have strategies for inferring the meanings of unknown words when they encounter them in reading;* furthermore, these students will have extensive vocabulary knowledge that they are able to use in constructing meaning through reading and writing.

TABLE 6.1 When to Provide Direct Vocabulary Instruction

FACTORS TO CONSIDER	VOCABULARY INSTRUCTION		
	Before Reading	**During Reading**	**After Reading**
Student considerations	*Any* students are experiencing difficulty constructing meaning.	Students are receiving guided reading support.	Students have identified words of interest or that cause difficulty.
	Students have previewed text and identified words they want to know.		Students need to expand their vocabularies.
Text considerations	Text has words that are definitely keys to understanding. Text has unusually difficult concepts.	Text has words that are keys to understanding the text and are likely to cause students difficulty in constructing meaning.	Text has good opportunities for expanding vocabularies.

Table 6.2 presents an overview of strategies you can use in your literacy lessons to help students gain independence in vocabulary learning. They should *not* be used to develop isolated vocabulary lessons apart from reading and writing.

Independently Inferring Word Meanings from Context

A necessary part of effective vocabulary development is teaching students a strategy for independently inferring word meanings (Calfee & Drum, 1986; Graves, 1987; Paris et al., 1983). If students are reading extensively and come to an unknown word, they need a plan for trying to determine its meaning. Getting students to use such a strategy is well worth the time and effort.

The student strategy presented here is based on the suggestions of Calfee and Drum (1986) and Graves (1987) and on our own experiences with students. You

---

TABLE 6.2 **Overview of Vocabulary Strategies That Promote Student Independence**

Strategy	Purpose	When to Use	Comments
Inferring meaning from context	Help students learn independent strategy	During reading All texts	Must be taught before it can be used independently
Concept of definition (word maps)	Help students become independent word learners by teaching elements of a good definition	Before or after reading expository texts	Good support strategy for independently inferring word meanings
Semantic mapping	Integrate prior knowledge and vocabulary learning	Before or after reading All texts	Develops in-depth word knowledge
Semantic feature analysis	Develop word knowledge by comparing words	Before or after reading Expository text and some narratives	Often more effective after reading
Hierarchical and linear arrays	Develop word relationships	After reading All texts	Encourages students to compare and contrast words
Preview in context	Use text context to develop word meanings	Before reading All texts	Must have text with good context clues
Contextual redefinition	Use context to determine word meaning	Before reading All texts	Useful when texts do not provide strong context clues
Vocabulary self-collection	Help students learn self-selected words	After reading All texts	Makes students responsible for own vocabulary learning
Structural analysis	Help students infer meaning independently	During reading All texts	Needs specific lessons before independent use
Dictionary/Thesaurus	Help students infer meaning independently	During and after reading All texts	A lifelong skill; needs to be taught

Educators Speak

Vocabulary Instruction Across the Curriculum

"Vocabulary instruction in the content areas can be taught in a variety of ways. It is usually taught with a particular unit of study where many concepts are also being presented and developed. Most vocabulary words are teacher selected, while others are taught as the need arises.

One way to teach vocabulary is with a direct example of the word. For example, when studying the parts of a flower in science, one can actually see the item represented by the vocabulary word. Students are given opportunities to label samples. After some experience with the words, students can also be asked to role-play as the teacher and teach the words to someone in their group or another group.

To provide more practice with vocabulary words, students can be asked to sort the words into categories. The categories are meaning based and can vary by student. Students must be able to rationalize why the words are grouped in a particular way.

Having students look at the affixes and base/root words can help children assign meaning to words and to see the relationships between words. For example the root *chron*, meaning time, can be used with the teaching of *chronology, synchronize*, and *chronicle*. This often allows students to build on prior knowledge and connect known information to new.

Many children benefit from adding kinesthetic activities to learning, as it stimulates different parts of the brain and can enhance learning. Asking students to play charades or in some other way dramatize vocabulary words creates a learning opportunity for the actor as well as the viewer.

It is beneficial to have the vocabulary words available and accessible for ready use. One way is to use word walls. The use of word walls keeps the words visible and allows for a quick review. "Find a word that means . . . Find two words that relate to . . . " Word walls allow daily instant reviews of the words allowing multiple exposures so often needed by students to ensure learning.

The teaching of vocabulary requires repeated exposures in different settings. Direct telling/teaching, modeling, restating, dramatizing, categorizing, and seeing relationships to other words can enhance vocabulary instruction."

Barbara "Bobbie" Lee, Reading Specialist
Horizon Elementary School
Sterling, Virginia

will need to adjust the steps to meet the varying grade levels of your students. Teach the following steps to students:

1. When you come to a word you do not know, read to the end of the sentence or paragraph to decide if the word is important to your understanding. If it is unimportant, continuing reading the book..
2. If the word is important, look for **base words, prefixes,** or **suffixes** you recognize.
3. English learners: look to see if there is a word in your language that looks like the word you don't know.
4. Use what you know about phonics to try to pronounce the word. Is it a word you have heard before?

5. Reread the sentence or paragraphs containing the word. Try using **context** to infer the meaning.
6. If you still don't know the word, use the dictionary or ask someone for help.
7. Once you think you know the meaning, reread the text to be sure it makes sense.

See Chapter 4 for a strategy poster you might use with primary-grade children.

Teach these steps in accordance with your students' level of maturity in reading. For example, a beginning reader may be mature enough to focus on only a simplified version of the strategy. Figure 6.2 shows a strategy poster that you could use with intermediate or higher grades. Students may need guidance in learning to determine which words are "unimportant." When students are learning this strategy, they should help in verbalizing the statements that go on the strategy poster; in this way, the strategy becomes theirs. They should then be reminded to refer to the poster and use the strategy as they read.

Concept of Definition Procedure (Word Maps)

Description. Schwartz and Raphael (1985) describe a strategy known as the *concept of definition procedure,* more commonly called a *word map* strategy. The purpose of the procedure is to help students in the middle grades and above gain control of the vocabulary acquisition process by teaching them the type of information that makes up a definition and teaching them how to use context clues and background knowledge to increase their understanding of words. This is done by using a word map, which helps students visually depict the elements of a given concept. Each concept is composed of three types of information:

1. Class: *What is it?*
2. Properties that distinguish the concept from others: *What is it like?*
3. Examples of the concept: *What are some examples?*

Figure 6.3 shows a completed word map for the concept *ice cream.*

Procedures. Schwartz and Raphael (1985) suggest that this strategy can be taught in four lessons. The following procedures are adapted from their guidelines.

Lesson 1

1. Select three or more concepts children already know, and develop a list of information about each; include class, at least three properties, and at least three examples. Here is a sample list for *ice cream:*

ice cream	
chocolate	frozen
cold	sweet
dessert	peach
strawberry	smooth

FIGURE 6.2

Intermediate and Middle-School Strategy Poster for Inferring Word Meanings

FIGURE 6.3

Completed Word Map for *Ice Cream*

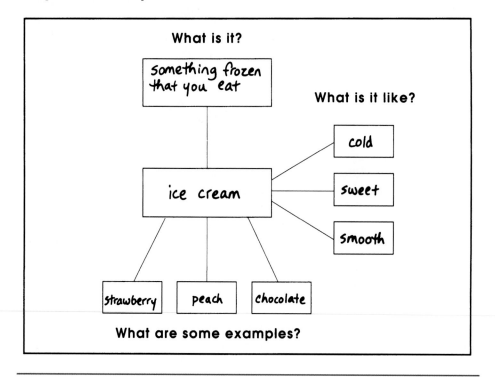

2. Discuss the importance of being able to accurately determine word meanings to better comprehend texts. Tell students that the strategy they will be learning during the next four lessons will help them determine whether they really know the meaning of a word.

3. Present students with the structure of a word map. Tell them that this map is a picture of the three things that let us know when we really understand a word: class (what it is), properties (what it is like), and examples. Go over each part with them.

4. Have students help you complete a word map for two of the concepts you prepared.

5. After students have completed the two word maps with you, have them work with a partner to complete the third. Have students share their work and discuss it.

6. Have students select a concept to map, independently or with a partner.

7. Have students write a definition for one of the concepts developed during the lesson. The definition for *ice cream* might be as follows:

A dessert that is a frozen, sweet food that you eat. It is cold. Some examples of ice cream are chocolate, strawberry, and peach.

Lesson 2

1. Locate or write several sample passages that give complete information about the concepts to be discussed (class, at least three properties, at least three examples). Content textbooks are often a good source for these passages. A sample passage for the concept *flowers* might read as follows:

    ### Flowers

    Have you ever thought about plants and how they reproduce? Flowers are the parts of seed-bearing plants that help to make this happen. You may think that flowers are just pretty to look at or nice to smell. But they are important to making more plants. Each flower has special parts. You probably have noticed only the petals. Look more closely. Flowers have other important parts, such as the pistil and the stamen. Look at some of your favorite flowers such as a tulip, rose, or daisy to see if you can find these parts.

2. Present the passages along with the blank word map. Tell students to read each passage and complete the word map.
3. Have students give oral or written definitions for the concepts presented.
4. Once students seem to understand the concept of the word map, tell them it is not necessary to limit properties and examples to three items.

Lesson 3

1. Write or locate several passages that are less complete in their definitions than those used in lesson 2.
2. Direct students to read the passages and complete the word maps as they did in lesson 2. If they do not see that the information provided in the passages is incomplete, help them see this by asking such questions as, "Does the passage tell you what _____ is like?" or "Does the passage give any examples of _____?"
3. Have students use other sources and their own prior knowledge to complete the word maps.
4. Guide students to the conclusion that texts do not always give complete definitions.

Lesson 4

1. Write or locate several more passages with incomplete contextual information for several concepts. For each concept, write incomplete definitions, leaving out one or more parts of the definition developed through the use of the word map. An incomplete definition might read as follows:

    A musician is a person who plays an instrument. A musician is very talented.

2. Tell students that the purpose of this lesson is for them to use what they have learned from developing word maps to decide whether some definitions are complete or incomplete.
3. Have students read the passages and evaluate the definitions for their completeness. Tell them to write the information that is missing from the definitions.

4. Conclude the lesson by discussing with students how they were able to tell the definitions were incomplete. Discuss how they should use this type of thinking any time they are reading and come to words they don't know.

It may be necessary to repeat one or more of these lessons several times for review purposes before students can use this procedure independently.

When to Use. Research on the concept of definition procedure has been conducted using fourth and eighth graders. It appears to work best with students in the intermediate and higher grades and with expository texts. Maria (1990) also reports that it is effective with at-risk (hard-to-teach) students in the upper elementary grades. This strategy can be used in four lessons throughout a thematic unit to help students develop the understanding needed to apply the concepts in later units. The four lessons are likely to be more meaningful if they are placed after the reading of selections.

You may also use the word map portion of the lessons as a way to thoroughly develop the meanings of several related words before or after the reading of a selection or at the beginning of a particular theme. For example, if you are beginning a thematic unit on space travel, you might use the word map activity to develop concepts such as *astronaut, space shuttle, rocket,* and *pilot.* When developing closely related terms, include questioning such as that used in the rich vocabulary instruction program reported by Beck and her colleagues (Beck, McCaslin, & McKeown, 1980; Beck, McKeown, & Omanson, 1987; Beck, Omanson, & McKeown, 1982). Probe relationships by asking such questions as, "Is an astronaut the same as a *pilot?*" and *"Do pilots fly rockets?"*

Assessment Value. You can learn two things about your students as they learn and use this strategy: their ability to determine unknown word meanings, and their prior knowledge of the concepts being developed. Schwartz and Raphael (1985) report that students who have been taught this strategy are more aware of what to do to figure out the meaning of a new word. When asked how to do this, students "indicated they would ask themselves questions and think about what they already knew. In contrast, the students without this instruction tended to answer, 'I would look it up'" (pp. 162–163).

You can determine students' knowledge and understanding of the particular concepts being developed through their responses to the structured portions of the lessons, and through their answers when they generate their own words for word maps and definitions. If you are using the word map concept to develop related terms, you can tell by the responses students give to your probing questions whether they really understand the terms.

Comments. The concept of definition procedure is excellent for preparing students to use the strategy for independently inferring word meanings. This procedure helps students develop a concept of what they must know to understand a word and begin to think about the sources within the text that might help them define a word; that is, this strategy promotes the integration of existing prior knowledge with new knowledge. However, it requires heavy initial teacher support and guidance, and it does not work with all words; for example, it works with nouns but not with verbs.

Since many words have similar properties, Schwartz (1988) has expanded the word map concept to include the idea of comparisons. In one such revised version, the teacher and students place a word similar to the main concept in a comparison box and discuss how this word and the main word have common properties. This procedure helps students become more precise in thinking about the properties they identify for the main concept and also helps them to further integrate knowledge within their schemata.

Be careful, however, that making word maps does not become the goal of the activity, which *must always remain the development of vocabulary knowledge to improve the construction of meaning* and independence in word learning.

Semantic Mapping

See Chapter 8 on writing. For a detailed look at ideas for using semantic mapping, see Heimlich and Pittelman (1986), listed in the

Semantic mapping, discussed in detail in Chapter 3 as an excellent strategy for activating and developing prior knowledge, uses a mapping strategy similar to the word map used in the concept of definition procedure. It can be used before reading and then expanded after reading to integrate students' new knowledge into their prior knowledge.

"For Additional Reading" section at the conclusion of this chapter.

Semantic mapping is a time-consuming procedure. Therefore, when you use it before reading, you must be certain you have selected key-concept words for the text to be read. It is often better to use it after reading to expand vocabulary and pull together concepts students already possess. Semantic mapping has many variations and uses; it is a good way to brainstorm for writing.

Semantic Feature Analysis

Description. With semantic feature analysis, students develop vocabulary and learn important concepts by looking at how related words differ and how they are alike (Johnson & Pearson, 1984). Figure 6.4 shows how some fourth-grade students set up a semantic feature analysis grid to compare vegetables after completing observations made during a plant unit. They then discussed each word, indicating what they knew about the word in relation to each characteristic. This strategy has been very effective in helping students develop vocabulary and learn to construct meaning (Anders & Bos, 1986).

Procedures. Use the following procedures to develop semantic feature grids:

1. Select a category or class of words (such as vegetables).
2. List items that fall into this category down the left side of the grid.
3. List features that some of the items have in common across the top of the grid. Sometimes you can ask students to do this.
4. Have students put pluses (+), minuses (−), and question marks (?) in the squares of the grid to indicate whether the items in the category have the feature under

consideration. Discuss each item, making sure students understand that some items are sometimes characterized by a feature and sometimes are not. For example, for the grid in Figure 6.4, be sure students understand that the tomato can be both green and red but is usually cooked when green.

5. Add additional words and features to the grid.
6. Complete the grid and discuss each word.

Repeat the process several times, using different categories and moving from the concrete to the abstract. Encourage students to look regularly for new words to add to the grids. Students can keep grid sheets in folders or notebooks, and add to them throughout the year.

After completing a semantic feature grid, students should examine the pattern of pluses and minuses to determine how the words are alike and how they differ. Question marks should serve as a basis for further research to clarify their understanding of the words. This strategy will help students expand their vocabularies as well as refine the meanings of words they already know.

When to Use. Semantic feature analysis may be used before or after reading to develop vocabulary, but it is often more effectively used after reading as a means of expanding vocabulary. It is helpful as a way to chart new knowledge during a unit of study. It is usually most helpful with expository texts but may also be used with some narrative texts. Finally, it is an excellent way for students to develop understanding in various content areas.

FIGURE 6.4

Semantic Feature Analysis Grid

VEGETABLES	GREEN	HAVE PEELINGS	EAT RAW	SEEDS
Potatoes	−	−	+	?
Carrots	−	+	+	−
Tomatoes	− +	+	− +	+
Broccoli	+	?	+	−
Squash	+ −	+	+	+
Cabbage	+	−	+	−

In addition to developing vocabulary, semantic feature analysis is very effective for reinforcing vocabulary and related concepts in content textbooks (Stieglitz & Stieglitz, 1981). Students at all levels can use it to review chapters before tests or pull together concepts in concluding a thematic unit. For younger students, semantic feature grids using very simple categories and features can serve as oral language activities.

Assessment Value. As students develop semantic feature grids, you will be able to assess their prior knowledge in relation to the categories and words being discussed. Students' responses will help you assess their understandings of word relationships, as well as their thinking abilities.

For in-depth reading on semantic feature analysis, see Pittelman, Heimlich, Berglund, and French (1991) in the "For Additional Reading" section.

Comments. Semantic feature analysis is one of the strategies that concentrates on helping students build relationships among concepts. Although both the concept of definition procedure and semantic mapping also do this, they are not as effective. The strength of semantic feature analysis comes when students are actively involved in constructing the grids and discussing them. This, along with cooperative learning, is an excellent way to foster active participation in the process of learning.

Nagy (1988) suggests that the Venn diagram is another way to apply semantic feature analysis in the classroom. Figure 6.5 presents a blank Venn diagram. In these diagrams, two things are compared: the properties of each item, listed along the sides of the circles, and the properties common to both, listed in the intersection.

FIGURE 6.5

Blank Venn Diagram

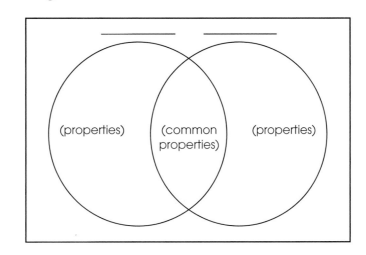

Hierarchical and Linear Arrays

Description. Words sometimes have hierarchical relationships, for example, the names of scientific organisms (Nagy, 1988). A **hierarchical array** such as that in Figure 6.6 can help students understand these relationships. The exact structure of the array will depend on the concepts being analyzed.

At other times, words have a linear relationship, for example, *good, better, best; tepid, hot, scalding*. A **linear array** such as the one in Figure 6.7 shows this relationship.

The use of hierarchical and linear arrays helps students learn to think independently about word relationships and develop concepts.

FIGURE 6.6

Hierarchical Array

Linear Array

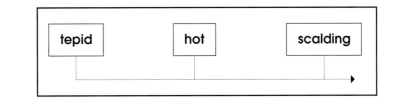

Procedures. Use the following procedures to develop hierarchical or linear arrays with students:

1. Select a concept or group of words from literature or from students' writing for study.
2. Begin by showing students the type of array they will construct.
3. Guide students in constructing the array. Discuss the relationship among the words as the array is developed.

After students have had considerable experience with arrays, they can select the words for study and decide on the type of array they will use.

When to Use. Arrays are best used after reading to help students expand their vocabularies. The visual aspect of arrays can help at-risk learners or second-language learners see the relationships among words more concretely. You can also use arrays to activate students' prior knowledge; for example, if students are going to study the places where people live, you can begin with the basic framework of the array presented in Figure 6.6 and ask students to generate the information. As the unit progresses, students can add to or change the array.

Assessment Value. Students' responses during the development of arrays will help you assess their prior knowledge and their ability to develop word relationships.

For a detailed discussion of arrays, see Nagy (1988) in the "For Additional Reading" section.

Comments. The value of arrays is that they encourage students to compare and contrast words. Blachowicz (1986) suggests several variations, called *semantic gradients* and *concept ladders*. Another variation of the hierarchical array is the *thinking tree*.

Preview in Context

Description. The preview-in-context strategy, developed by Readence, Bean, and Baldwin (1981, 1985, 1989), does just what the term says: it previews words in context. With this strategy, the teacher guides students to use the context and their prior knowledge to determine the meanings of a selected set of words.

Procedures. Use the following four steps for this strategy:

1. *Prepare.* Select the words to be taught following the procedures suggested earlier in this chapter (refer back to Figure 6.l). These must be key-concept words, and *you should teach no more than two or three.* Identify passages within the text that contain strong context clues for the word. For example, we will focus on teaching *decay* and use the following passage from *Mummies, Tombs, and Treasure* (Perl, 1987):

   > *Without preservation, dead animal matter usually decays very quickly. This is true of plant matter, too. A dead bird or cat, a piece of rotting fruit, can show the stages of decay. Decay is caused by bacteria. (p. 2)*

2. *Establish the context.* Present the word and the context to students; read aloud the passage as students follow along. Then have students reread it silently.

3. *Specify the word meaning.* Now lead students toward a definition of the word under study. By asking them questions, you encourage them to use their prior knowledge and clues in the text to arrive at a meaning for the word. An example of this type of questioning follows:

   Teacher: What does this text tell you about the word *decay*?

   Student: That dead animals decay.

   Teacher: What happens to them when they decay?

   Student: They rot.

   Teacher: How could you tell from this text that *decay* means "to rot"?

   Student: By what it says about rotting fruit.

4. *Expand the word meaning.* After students have a basic understanding of the word, try to deepen their understanding by discussing synonyms, antonyms, other contexts, or other examples where the word might be used. The purpose of these activities is to expand students' knowledge of the word. If students have access to a dictionary or a thesaurus, they can use it. The discussion might go as follows:

   Teacher: Can you think of other things that decay?

   Student: Teeth. I get cavities sometimes.

   Teacher: How do we prevent decay?

   Student: Put something on things that keep them from decaying.

   Teacher: Like what?

   Student: Fluoride keeps your teeth from decaying.

   Teacher: What about dead things? How do we keep them from decaying?

   Student: You embalm dead people.

   Teacher: So the fluid used for embalming preserves things or keeps them from decaying. Can you think of words that mean the same thing as *decay*?

   Student 1: Rot.

   Student 2: Spoil.

After you teach the words, encourage students to place them in their word banks or notebooks.

When to Use. Use preview in context before reading, but *only* when the context for the word is strong. It is appropriate for all students at all grade levels but not for students who have limited prior knowledge.

Assessment Value. As students respond in the discussions, you will be able to assess the extent of their prior knowledge and their ability to use context clues.

Comments. The preview-in-context strategy is simple and easy to use. However, it is often difficult to identify contexts that contain enough clues to help students infer word meanings. Nagy (1988) points out that "context may look quite helpful if one already knows what the word means, but it seldom supplies adequate information for the person who has no other knowledge about the meaning of the word" (p. 7).

The strength of this strategy comes through the intensive discussion between the teacher and students, which deepens students' understanding. Therefore, it is important to skillfully direct the discussion.

Contextual Redefinition

Description. Since texts frequently do not provide sufficient context for students to determine the meaning of an unknown word (Schatz & Baldwin, 1986), contextual redefinition helps students use context more effectively by presenting them with *sufficient context* before reading and showing them how to use the clues to *make informed guesses* about a word's meaning (Cunningham, Cunningham, & Arthur, 1981).

Procedures. The following five-step procedure for using contextual redefinition is adapted from Tierney, Readence, and Dishner (1990):

1. *Select unfamiliar words.* Using the procedures suggested earlier in this chapter, select two or three words to preteach. This example will use *hippophagy* and *carapace.*

2. *Write a sample.* Write one or more sentences that provide sufficient clues to teach the meaning of the word. Try to use different types of context clues, such as direct definition, synonyms, and comparison and contrast. If the text has sufficient context clues for the word in question, use it. Here are two samples:

   The drought had been so long and severe that the cattle had died. Only the horses survived. Yet the natives were so hungry that they had to resort to hippophagy *to avoid starvation.*

   Without its carapace, *a turtle has no protection and is subject to certain death from its enemies or the elements.*

3. *Present the words in isolation.* Using the chalkboard or overhead projector, present the words in isolation and ask students to pronounce them, or pronounce the words for them. Then encourage students to provide a definition for each word. Wild guesses may occur; this is part of the learning process. Encourage students to come to a consensus about the meaning of each word.

4. *Present the words in context.* Using the contexts prepared for the lesson, present each word and have students read the contexts aloud, or read the contexts for them. As students discuss each word, have them come to a consensus about its meaning. Encourage guessing from the clues; in this way, at-risk students are able to participate. To help students become more attuned to the value of context, ask them to discuss the differences between trying to define the words in context and in isolation.

5. *Use a dictionary for verification.* Discuss the dictionary definition, and compare it to the one developed by the students.

When to Use. Use the contextual redefinition strategy to teach totally *new* words before reading. It is appropriate for all students who possess some skill in using the dictionary and is especially useful when the text does not provide context that will help students infer the meanings of the words selected for preteaching. Students who are having difficulty learning to construct meaning and second-language learners may benefit from this strategy.

Assessment Value. You can assess students' prior knowledge from their responses in guessing definitions in isolation and in context. The use of the context samples will let you know how well students are able to use context. Finally, dictionary verification will give you opportunities to see how effectively students use the dictionary.

Comments. Many questions have been raised about the value of using context sentences to teach vocabulary, as we noted in the discussion of the preview in context strategy (Nagy, 1988). However, when the words to be pretaught are *carefully selected, kept to a minimum of two or three,* and *thoroughly taught,* preteaching to improve comprehension may have value (Tierney & Cunningham, 1984; Wixson, 1986). The keys to effectively using preview in context and contextual redefinition are careful word selection and thorough discussion of the words. Also, remember that students need repeated encounters with the words through reading and writing to develop ownership of them.

Vocabulary Self-Collection

Description. Vocabulary self-collection places the responsibility for learning words on the students (Haggard, 1982, 1986). After a reading experience, students select a word they think the entire class should study. They are also encouraged to select additional words for their own personal study. This strategy has the advantages of being interactive and being based on authentic reading experiences.

Procedures. The following procedures are based on Haggard's suggestions (1986):

1. *Select words for study.* After students have read a story or an informational text, ask them to review it and select one word for class study. They may do this as individuals, partners, or teams. You should also select one word for study so that you are an active learning partner and gain some influence in the process. Encourage students to select words that seem important or interesting.

2. *Compile and define the words.* Ask each student or group to provide the word selected for study and the definition (determined from context) of the word. List each word and the definition on the chalkboard or overhead; include your own word as well. Use the dictionary to verify or complete definitions as needed, and encourage all students to participate in this process. With the students, agree on a final list of words and definitions.

3. *Finalize the list.* With the students, review the list to eliminate duplications, words that seem unrelated to the story or topic of study, and words that students simply do not want to study. Agree on a reasonable number (three to five) for the final list, and have students put the words and definitions in their vocabulary notebooks or journals. Some may choose to record words eliminated from the class list in their personal lists. When they write the words in their journals, ask them to write a sentence demonstrating the use of the word in their own lives or showing their understanding of it.

4. *Use and extend the words.* Encourage students to use the words in their writing and to look for them in other books they read. Plan activities that reinforce the words, such as semantic maps, semantic feature analysis, and arrays.

These procedures are based on the concept of vocabulary development after reading, but you can adapt them for use before reading by having students preview the text and select for study words that they think will be important.

When to Use. You may use this strategy with both narrative and expository texts and with all students at any grade level. If students do not have sufficient skill to use the dictionary, you will need to provide the definitions.

Assessment Value. This strategy gives you many opportunities to assess students' word knowledge. When students select words for study and give definitions from context, you can assess their use of context clues. As they participate in expanding definitions given by other students, you can determine the extent of their prior knowledge.

Comments. Vocabulary self-collection has many appealing features: it is easy to implement, interactive, based on authentic reading experiences, and very versatile.

Vocabulary self-collection lends itself to the concept that children learn to read and write by reading and writing. By selecting their own words, students become active participants in their own process of learning, and also learn to see the classroom as a community of learners. Some teachers may worry that students will not select important words, but when the teacher participates in the process, students and teacher become partners in learning. Moreover, there is no guarantee that students will learn words the teacher selects any more readily than they will learn self-selected words. This strategy respects the students as learners and incorporates all of the ideas about authentic learning that are stressed throughout this text.

Structural Analysis as an Aid to Decoding and Independence

Recall that the goal of vocabulary development is for students to achieve independence in word learning because the number of words to be learned is too large for each one to be taught individually. The way to achieve this independence is to be aware of words and develop a strategy for independently inferring word meanings. Structural elements within the word may help students determine a word's meaning. However, direct teaching of structural elements is of limited value and should be done only under certain circumstances.

Students may learn skills, such as the use of structural elements, through reading and writing, but sometimes they require the teacher's support. You may provide this support through direct vocabulary teaching strategies or through minilessons that focus on a particular skill, such as structural analysis.

Structural analysis is the study of meaningful word parts. It may help students as they learn to recognize words (pronunciation) and as they determine the meanings of words. The following elements are usually considered part of structural analysis:

- *Base words:* Meaningful linguistic units that can stand alone and contain no smaller meaningful parts; also called *free morphemes* (re*sell*: *sell* is the base word).

- *Root words:* Words from which other words are derived. Usually the derivational word is from another language and is a bound morpheme; that is, it cannot stand alone (*scribble* comes from the Latin root *scribere,* meaning "to write"). Teachers frequently use the terms *base word* and **root word** synonymously, but they are not the same.

- *Prefixes:* Units of meaning that can be added to the beginnings of base words or root words to change their meanings. These are bound morphemes and cannot stand alone (*un*happy: *un-* is the prefix meaning "not").

- *Suffixes:* Units of meaning that can be added to the ends of base or root words to change their meanings. These are bound morphemes (tear*ful*: *-ful* is the suffix meaning "full of").

- *Inflectional endings:* Word parts that can be added to the ends of root or base words to change their case, gender, number, tense, or form; these are bound morphemes (boy*'s*: possessive case; steward*ess*: gender; tree*s*: number; walk*ed*: tense; funni*est*: form). Sometimes **inflectional endings** are called *suffixes.*

- *Compound words:* Two or more base words that have been combined to form a new word with a meaning that is related to each base word (*run* + way = *runway*).

- *Contractions:* Shortened forms of two words in which a letter or letters have been replaced by an apostrophe (*do* + *not* = *don't*; *there* + *is* = *there's*).

Students will become familiar with compound words and contractions through their reading and writing experiences, and for most students simply showing them what these are as reading and writing take place is usually sufficient. Some students, such as ELLs, may need more directed support using the minilesson, as discussed in Chapter 2; but even when this is required, the lesson *always goes back to the literature* to help students see how the compound or contraction was used in context. For example, if your students have just completed reading *Aunt Flossie's Hats (and Crab Cakes Later)* (Howard, 1991) and you noticed they were having trouble figuring out compound words or contractions, you can use this story as the basis for a minilesson involving the following simple steps:

1. Go back to the story (revisit it) to identify a compound word or contraction. Read the section containing it aloud to students as they follow along. Ask them if they notice anything special about the compound word or contraction.
2. Define *compound* or *contraction*. Point out another example; then point out words that are not examples.
3. Direct students to read a page containing another example. Ask them to find the compound word or contraction.
4. Make a chart of other examples that students find.
5. Conclude the lesson by discussing with students how they should use this new knowledge in reading and writing.
6. As students read and write, you may need to do periodic reviews.

Aunt Flossie's Hats (and Crab Cakes Later) is particularly good for this experience, because it contains numerous examples of both compounds and contractions such as *afternoons, hatboxes, here's,* and *she's.* Reading material for students in intermediate and higher grades will contain increasing examples of compound words and contractions frequently used in dialogue.

Knowledge of the remaining elements of structural analysis also develops through reading and writing. The addition of prefixes and suffixes to words accounts for a large number of words for students in grade 4 and above (Nagy & Anderson, 1984). However, the prefixes and suffixes encountered have variant meanings, which makes it difficult for students to see a pattern (Graves, 1987). If you have to provide a minilesson, it is important to know which prefixes and suffixes to focus on and how to construct your lesson (for guidelines, see Graves, 1987; Nagy & Anderson, 1984; White, Sowell, & Yanagihara, 1989).

White, Sowell, and Yanagihara (1989) determined, on the basis of frequency of occurrence, that there are nine prefixes and ten suffixes of sufficient use to students to merit instruction (see table on page XXX in the Handbook). They also determined that knowing the prefixes listed would account for 76 percent of prefixed words, and knowing the suffixes would account for 85 percent of suffixed words. Graves (1987) reported that knowing just four prefixes (*un-, in-*[not], *dis-,* and *non-*) would account for nearly 50 percent of all prefixed words. Therefore, in planning minilesson support focusing on word parts, you should give greatest attention to the nine prefixes and ten suffixes listed in the table on page xx in the Handbook.

In addition to knowing which prefixes and suffixes are the most beneficial for students, you must be aware of some of the pitfalls of using prefixes as an aid to word meaning (White et al., 1989):

- Prefixes are not consistent in their meanings; for example, *un-, dis-, re-,* and *in-* each have two meanings.

- False analysis with prefixes often occurs. For example, removing *in* from *intrigue* leaves no recognizable base word. The prefixes *re-, in-,* and *dis-* have a particularly high risk of false analysis.

- Looking only at word parts may mislead the reader in determining the word's true meaning. For example, *unassuming* means "modest" instead of "not supposing."

If you are aware of these possible pitfalls and know how often the affixes occur, you can plan minilessons that will help students who demonstrate the need for such support. The suggestions that follow are adapted from White et al. (1989) and are for suffixes. Similar steps would be used to teach prefixes.

Minilessons Using Suffixes. Suffixes (and inflectional endings) tend to have abstract meanings. Therefore, instruction should focus on removing the suffix and identifying the base word. The following lessons are recommended:

- ***Lesson 1:*** Teach the concept of suffixes (and inflectional endings).
- ***Lesson 2:*** Teach *-s/es, -ed,* and *-ing* with no spelling changes. Show students the suffixed word, and have them identify the suffix and define the base word (examples: *boxes, talking, lasted*).
- ***Lessons 3–5:*** Focus on three major spelling changes that occur using suffixes:
  Consonant doubling: *begged, thinner, funny*
  Change from *y* to *i: flies, worried, reliable*
  Deleted silent *e: saved, rider, believable*
  Follow the same pattern as suggested for lesson 2, but discuss the spelling change that has occurred. The suffixes used should be drawn from the list suggested in the table on p. 512.
- ***Lesson 6:*** Suffixes that change the part of speech: *-ly, -er, -ion, -able, -al, -y,* and *-ness.* Again, follow the same pattern used with the other lessons. More than one lesson might be needed for this category of suffixes.

The exact grade levels for teaching prefixes and suffixes really depend on students' needs. However, it is recommended that all instruction should be completed by the end of grade 5.

White et al. (1989) report favorable results with students who were taught lessons similar to those just described. They stress that "the goal of prefix and suffix instruction is *use* of word-part clues to derive the meaning of unfamiliar words" (p. 307). They believe that even in a literature-centered classroom, a "reasonable" amount of direct teaching helps students learn to use an independent strategy for inferring word meanings.

The Dictionary and Thesaurus as Aids to Decoding and Independence

Two final areas of knowledge students must have to use the strategy for independently inferring word meanings and achieving independence in vocabulary learning are using the dictionary and using the thesaurus (Graves, 1987). The dictionary is an aid for reading, writing, and spelling; the thesaurus is more valuable for writing.

Using a Dictionary. The dictionary is an invaluable tool for determining both the pronunciations and meanings of words. It is especially useful when students have tried all other skills and still have not determined the meaning or pronunciation of an unknown word. Unfortunately, students are often turned off by the way they are exposed to the dictionary. Therefore, keep the following "don'ts" in mind:

- ***Don't*** give students lists of isolated words to look up and define. Words out of context have no meaning, and students will not know which definition to select. Furthermore, this type of activity becomes boring and is not good instruction.
- ***Don't*** use the dictionary as a means of punishment. Too many teachers turn to the dictionary to "punish" students by having them copy pages. Who would ever want to see a dictionary again after that?
- ***Don't*** require that every word on each week's spelling list be looked up in the dictionary and defined. This becomes a deadly, useless activity.
- ***Don't*** teach phonetic respelling, except in relation to determining the pronunciations of words in the dictionary.

These don'ts for teaching use of the dictionary can be balanced with some very important and positive do's:

- ***Do*** let students know that you, the teacher, often turn to the dictionary to check the spellings, pronunciations, and meanings of words.
- ***Do*** teach students how to use a dictionary.
- ***Do*** show students how to make use of a dictionary in their reading and writing.
- ***Do*** show students how to use a dictionary in all content areas.

Dictionary use must be taught in a manner that will leave students with positive attitudes. The teaching should begin in kindergarten and proceed through the primary grades, until students know and understand the components of the dictionary and can use them effectively. The sequence in Table 6.3 should guide the use of the dictionary, which should be developed through meaningful experiences, not isolated skill lessons.

Once students have learned the basics of using the dictionary, it can become a part of their strategy for independently inferring word meanings.

Using a Thesaurus. A thesaurus such as *Roget's Thesaurus* (1965) is a dictionary of synonyms and antonyms and is very useful for helping readers and writers locate synonyms and antonyms, as well as subtle shades of meaning for words. Teachers can introduce elementary-grade students to a thesaurus appropriate to their level. The media specialist in your school can tell you what's available in your building.

It may be easier to learn to use a thesaurus than a dictionary. Once students know how to alphabetize and have learned the concepts of synonyms and

TABLE 6.3	Sequence for Teaching Use of the Dictionary

1. Use picture dictionaries to introduce the concept of the dictionary in kindergarten and first grade. Have students learn to locate words in the dictionaries, and teach them to make picture dictionaries of their own.

2. As soon as students have some knowledge of the alphabet, teach them how words are arranged in the dictionary. Give them practice in locating words.

3. Show students how words in the first half of the alphabet fall in the first half of the dictionary and words in the second half fall in the second half. Point out that this knowledge can help students save time by eliminating the need to sift through lots of extra pages.

4. Introduce the concept of phonetic respelling in relation to the pronunciation key, and show students how this key can help them figure out pronunciations.

5. Teach students to locate the meanings of words by using guide words; point out that the dictionary lists more than one meaning for many words.

6. Finish teaching students how to locate words alphabetically, showing them how words are alphabetized not just through the first letter but also through the second, third, fourth, and subsequent letters.

7. Have students learn to select the correct dictionary definitions for multiple-meaning words that are presented in written context.

8. Teach the special symbols used in dictionaries, such as *n* for noun, *v* for verb, and *sing.* for singular.

9. Show students all the other types of information they can find in the dictionary, including lists of synonyms, an atlas, and geographic listings.

10. Provide students with experiences using many different dictionaries and glossaries.

antonyms, the rest is quite easy. They must be taught how the thesaurus is organized, how to locate a word, and how to read the synonym or antonym entries. Show students how writers use the thesaurus to locate words they want to change in their writing to avoid repetition.

After students have learned to use the thesaurus, encourage them to use it as a means of improving their writing. One very effective way to do this is through minilessons during the writing workshop, in which you demonstrate the use of the thesaurus in a group-written story.

The strategies for developing vocabulary just discussed help students become independent vocabulary learners and constructors of meaning. All of these strategies require continual integration of new knowledge with old knowledge. Of course, no one strategy alone can meet the needs of all students and all learning situations, and *no one strategy or combination of strategies is as powerful for developing vocabulary as are wide reading and extensive writing.* Nevertheless, when used *judiciously* in combination with wide reading and extensive writing, these strategies should give students the experiences they need to develop strong vocabularies and improve their meaning construction.

☑ **NCTE/IRA Standards: 3, 4, 5, 6.9, 11, 12**

Standards-Based
Literacy
Lesson

Ananse's Feast

Ananse's Feast is an Ashanti tale, retold by Tololwa M. Mollel and illustrated by Andrew Glass (Clarion Books, 1997). It fits into a fourth-grade unit on literature genre.

Before Reading the Plan

1. Recall with a peer what you know about activating prior knowledge, vocabulary development, and modes of reading. These concepts are your prior knowledge for reading and evaluating this literacy lesson.
2. Read the text and study the art of Ananse's Feast on the following pages.
3. Read the Teacher Preparation section which explains the decision-making process used in planning this lesson.

While Reading the Plan

1. Notice how prior knowledge is activated and how vocabulary is developed. Also note mode(s) of reading.
2. Think about changes you might make in the lesson, and be ready to discuss your ideas.

🦋 Teacher Preparation

This plan was developed for a fourth-grade class of twenty-eight students. The class includes some ELLs, some students who attend special classes for learning problems, some children who come from affluent families, and some others who are on free lunch. In other words, it is a typical class with a range of backgrounds. The entire class will read *Ananse's Feast* as part of a larger unit of study in which they read other traditional tales independently. The following outlines the steps used to plan the lesson and gives a rationale for each.

Unit Activities Prior to Reading the Book Ananse's Feast

1. The class has been studying various genres, including folk tales. Students are using a feature analysis to understand and compare and contrast the different genres.
2. The media specialist has provided many books and computer-supported media for independent use during the unit. Students have been encouraged to bring books from home for the duration of the unit. Students whose families are from other cultures have shared folk tales they know. Some families have come to the class to tell such tales.

Specific Outcomes Developed in This Lesson

1. Vocabulary: use context to determine meaning
2. Constructing meaning: predicting and drawing conclusions
3. Literature: recognizing characteristics of the folk tale genre
4. Attitudes and habits: increased knowledge about genre; increased knowledge of and interest in reading for pleasure; increased awareness of the contribution of art to text

continued

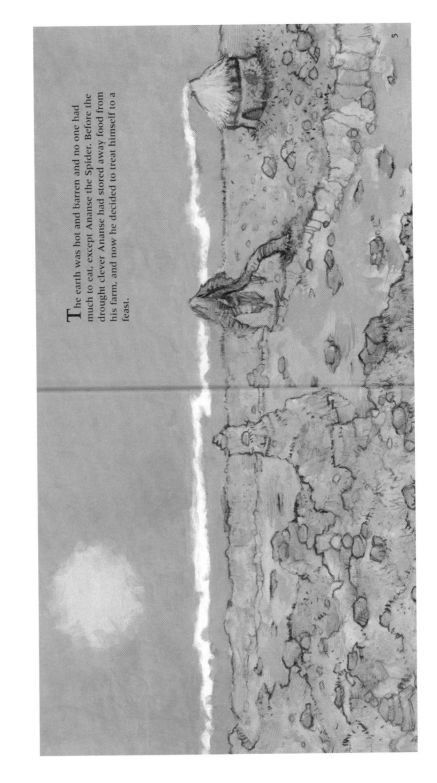

The earth was hot and barren and no one had much to eat, except Ananse the Spider. Before the drought clever Ananse had stored away food from his farm, and now he decided to treat himself to a feast.

Standards-Based
Literacy
Lesson

continued

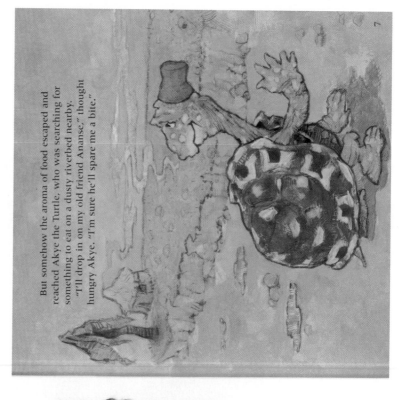

But somehow the aroma of food escaped and reached Akye the Turtle, who was searching for something to eat on a dusty riverbed nearby.

"I'll drop in on my old friend Ananse," thought hungry Akye. "I'm sure he'll spare me a bite."

Ananse shut his door and windows and sealed all the cracks in the walls of his old hut.

"I don't want the delicious smell of my cooking to bring hungry visitors," he muttered.

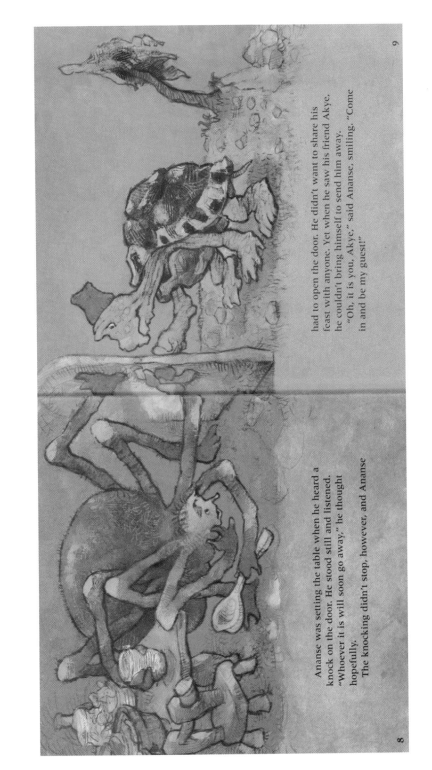

had to open the door. He didn't want to share his feast with anyone. Yet when he saw his friend Akye, he couldn't bring himself to send him away.

"Oh, it is you, Akye," said Ananse, smiling. "Come in and be my guest!"

9

Ananse was setting the table when he heard a knock on the door. He stood still and listened.

"Whoever it is will soon go away," he thought hopefully.

The knocking didn't stop, however, and Ananse

8

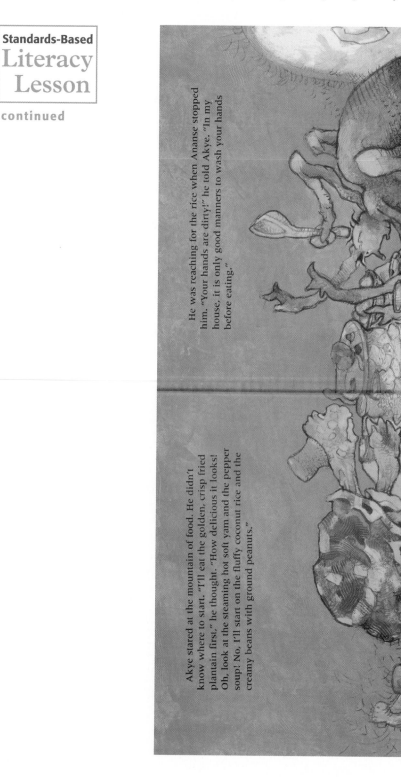

He was reaching for the rice when Ananse stopped him. "Your hands are dirty!" he told Akye. "In my house, it is only good manners to wash your hands before eating."

Akye stared at the mountain of food. He didn't know where to start. "I'll eat the golden, crisp fried plantain first," he thought. "How delicious it looks! Oh, look at the steaming hot soft yam and the pepper soup! No, I'll start on the fluffy coconut rice and the creamy beans with ground peanuts."

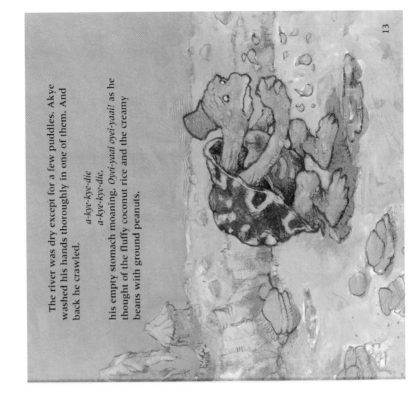

The river was dry except for a few puddles. Akye washed his hands thoroughly in one of them. And back he crawled.

a-kye-kye-die
a-kye-kye-die,

his empty stomach moaning. *Oyei-yaai oyei-yaail* as he thought of the fluffy coconut rice and the creamy beans with ground peanuts.

13

Akye looked at his hands, dusty and dirty from his manner of walking on all fours. "Can I have some water to wash them?" he asked.

"I'm sorry. I've used up all the water," replied Ananse. "You must go and wash your hands at the river."

12

Standards-Based
Literacy
Lesson

continued

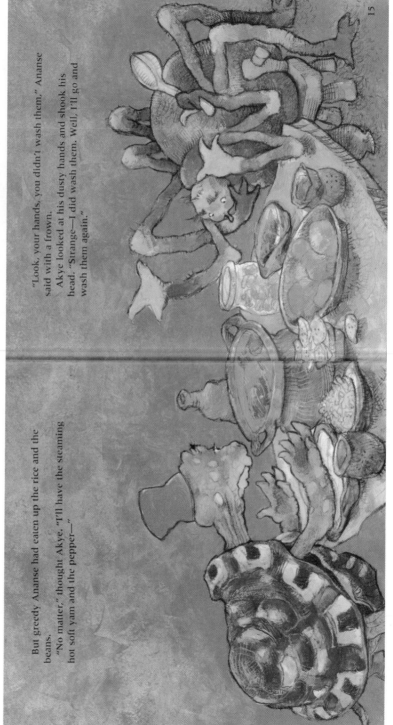

"Look, your hands, you didn't wash them," Ananse said with a frown.

Akye looked at his dusty hands and shook his head. "Strange—I did wash them. Well, I'll go and wash them again."

But greedy Ananse had eaten up the rice and the beans.

"No matter," thought Akye, "I'll have the steaming hot soft yam and the pepper—"

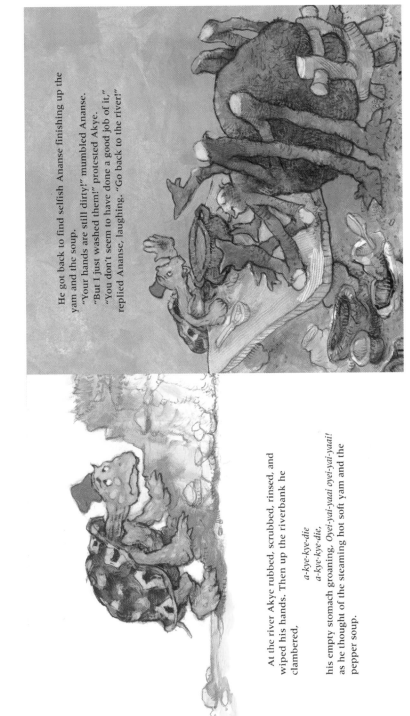

He got back to find selfish Ananse finishing up the yam and the soup.

"Your hands are still dirty!" mumbled Ananse.

"But I just washed them!" protested Akye.

"You don't seem to have done a good job of it," replied Ananse, laughing. "Go back to the river!"

At the river Akye rubbed, scrubbed, rinsed, and wiped his hands. Then up the riverbank he clambered,

a-kye-kye-die
a-kye-kye-die,

his empty stomach groaning, *Oyei-yai-yaai oyei-yai-yaai!* as he thought of the steaming hot soft yam and the pepper soup.

16

19

Akye suddenly realized how Ananse had tricked him. He only smiled, however, and said to well-fed Ananse, "Thank you for inviting me to the feast. I hope one day I can repay you."

By the time Akye returned from the river, cunning Ananse had eaten all the food and was wearing a big satisfied grin.

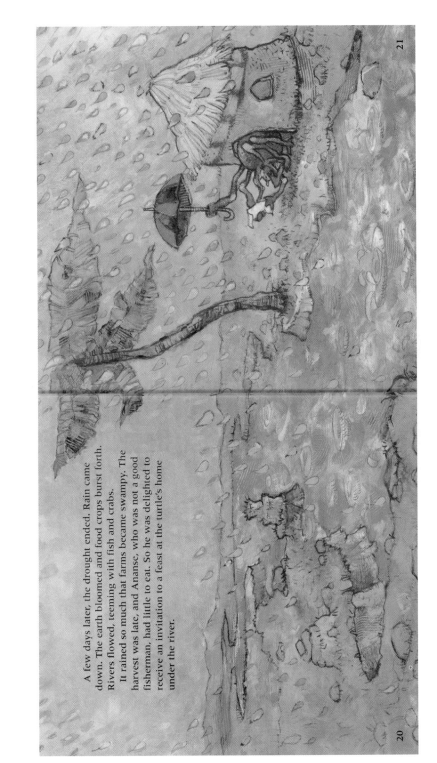

A few days later, the drought ended. Rain came down. The earth bloomed and food crops burst forth. Rivers flowed, teeming with fish and crabs. It rained so much that farms became swampy. The harvest was late, and Ananse, who was not a good fisherman, had little to eat. So he was delighted to receive an invitation to a feast at the turtle's home under the river.

20 21

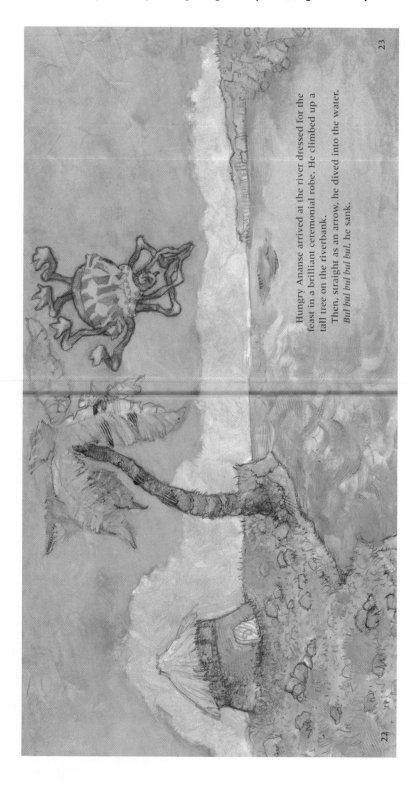

Hungry Ananse arrived at the river dressed for the feast in a brilliant ceremonial robe. He climbed up a tall tree on the riverbank.

Then, straight as an arrow, he dived into the water. *Bul bul bul bul bul,* he sank.

Standards-Based
Literacy
Lesson

continued

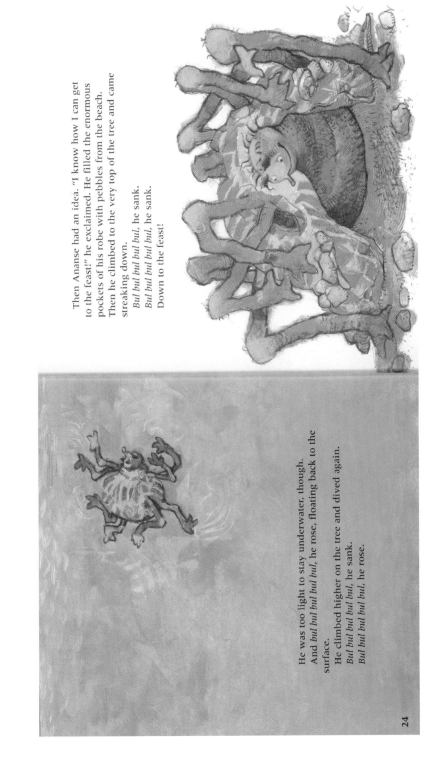

Then Ananse had an idea. "I know how I can get to the feast!" he exclaimed. He filled the enormous pockets of his robe with pebbles from the beach. Then he climbed to the very top of the tree and came streaking down.
Bul bul bul bul bul, he sank.
Bul bul bul bul bul, he sank.
Down to the feast!

He was too light to stay underwater, though.
And *bul bul bul bul bul,* he rose, floating back to the surface.
He climbed higher on the tree and dived again.
Bul bul bul bul bul, he sank.
Bul bul bul bul bul, he rose.

24

Standards-Based Literacy Lesson

continued

Akye was seated at a table laden with plump mounds of juicy, tender crabmeat, dressed in a brilliant ceremonial robe of his own. With his heavy shell, he had no trouble staying down.

The turtle noticed the bulging weight of pebbles in Ananse's pockets and touched the spider's robe admiringly.

"What a beautiful robe!" he said, and smiled. "But I suggest you take it off before we eat."

"What!" cried Ananse.

"In my house," Akye said sweetly, "it is only good manners to take off your robe before eating." And he began to slip out of his own robe.

Ananse couldn't let Akye think he was an ill-mannered guest. Reluctantly, he took off his robe. And although he tried hard to cling to the table . . .

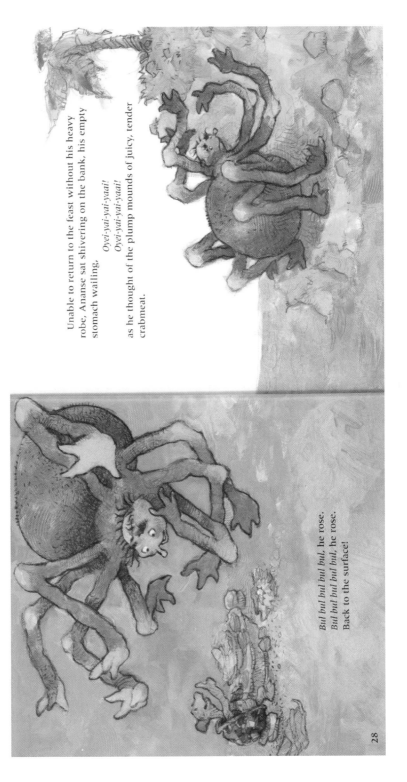

Unable to return to the feast without his heavy robe, Ananse sat shivering on the bank, his empty stomach wailing,

Oyei-yai-yai-yaai!
Oyei-yai-yai-yaai!

as he thought of the plump mounds of juicy, tender crabmeat.

Bul bul bul bul bul, he rose.
Bul bul bul bul bul, he rose.
Back to the surface!

28

Standards-Based
Literacy
Lesson

continued

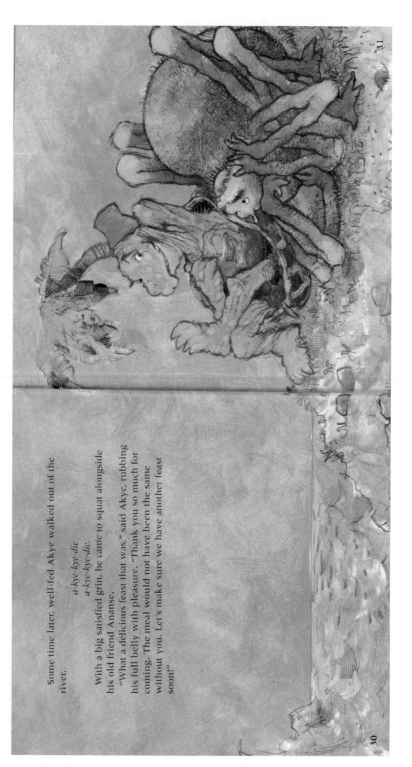

Some time later, well-fed Akye walked out of the river,

a-kye-kye-die
a-kye-kye-die.

With a big satisfied grin, he came to squat alongside his old friend Ananse.

"What a delicious feast that was," said Akye, rubbing his full belly with pleasure. "Thank you so much for coming. The meal would not have been the same without you. Let's make sure we have another feast soon!"

Standards-Based
Literacy
Lesson

continued

About This Lesson

1. Prior knowledge (including some vocabulary) will be activated by reviewing the ongoing semantic feature analysis about genre.
2. As a whole class, we will use the preview-and-predict strategy for the book, discussing the title and the art.
3. Two words—*barren* and *drought*—occur on the first page and are critical to understanding the story. These will be taught using the preview-in-context strategy. Although several other words may be unfamiliar to students, students should be able to use independent strategies to infer meaning from context.
4. Students will choose words for the self-collection strategy as they read.
5. Students will choose which mode they prefer for reading: cooperative or independent. They will also be encouraged to reread the book in preparation for reading it aloud to students in a lower grade.

🦋 Introducing Ananse's Feast

Activity	*Procedures and Comments*
Activate prior knowledge and vocabulary; feature analysis	Display ongoing semantic feature analysis chart that compares various genres and reviews what students know so far about the characteristics of folk tales. *Note: Students are reading this book as part of a unit on genre, so the appropriate prior knowledge to activate for this story is as much related to the genre as it is to the story itself.*
Present the book; preview and predict	1. Distribute books to students. Read the title aloud, and then allow a few minutes for students to leaf through the book and look at the art. 2. Lead students to make predictions about the story based on the art, the title, and what they know about folk tales. Record the predictions for later discussion
Vocabulary strategy: preview in context	Have students follow as you read aloud the first page of the story, which contains the key words *barren* and *drought*. Use the steps of the preview-in-context strategy (page 265) to help students determine the meaning of these two key words. Note: *Students should consider the art as part of the context for these two words.*

🦋 Reading and Responding to *Ananse's Feast*

Activity	Procedures and Comments (continued)
Revise predictions	Have students read the second page of the story to themselves and think about whether they want to add to or change earlier predictions.
	Note: *This activity reinforces for students that with additional information about a text, one's predictions about "what's going to happen" will change. Predictions should therefore be continuously revised as one reads.*
Vocabulary; self-collection strategy	Remind students about the strategy, which they already have been taught.
	Note: *This strategy leads to a deeper study of words following reading.*
Read the story	1. Review modes of reading from which students may choose.
	2. Allow students to choose their preferred mode.
	3. Have students read the rest of the story.
	Note: *Partner or independent reading are likely choices for most students. Of course, if there is a need in your class, you could do a guided reading with some or all of the students.*
Return to predictions	Revisit predictions made prior to reading. Discuss.
Genre study	1. Add to the chart with characteristics of folk tales. Discuss how *Ananse's Feast* conformed to the characteristics.
	2. Some students may want to compare Ananse's Feast to other folk tales in terms of theme or moral (for example: Aesop's fable about the ant and the grasshopper).
Vocabulary; self-collection strategy	Complete the self-collection strategy steps (page 268).
	Note: *When revisiting vocabulary in a selection, you have opportunities to reinforce whatever other strategies students have been learning. For example, if you had been teaching about inflected endings or suffixes, you might direct attention to examples of these in the story.*

🦋 Extending *Ananse's Feast*

1. Students may add vocabulary words to their individual word banks.
2. Students may "rehearse" reading *Ananse's Feast* aloud for a "reading buddy" program with a lower grade.
3. Students may compare the structure of this folk tale with that of other folk tales they have read.
4. Students may write an adaptation of this story using another setting and other characters.

Standards-Based
Literacy
Lesson

continued

After Reading the Plan

1. Review and discuss the plan with your peers. Focus on how prior knowledge was activated and vocabulary development was supported. Discuss how these two aspects of reading are linked.
2. Plan a different lesson for *Ananse's Feast* using one or more other strategies for teaching vocabulary.

Summary

Standards continue to be important at the upper elementary and middle school levels. The main focus of students in terms of decoding is the application and expansion of the basic skills and strategies they have learned. Students develop two reading vocabularies: recognition and meaning. This chapter focused on meaning vocabulary and what we know about how it grows and how it is learned.

Effective vocabulary development includes helping students become aware of words, wide reading and extensive writing, and the use of strategies. *The ultimate goal of all vocabulary development is for students to become independent word learners.*

This chapter presented suggestions and guidelines for supporting effective vocabulary growth as well as expanding students' decoding skills and strategies.. It suggested several strategies for direct teaching of vocabulary. The chapter emphasizes, however, that students learn vocabulary primarily through wide reading and extensive writing.

For Additional Reading

Adams, T. L. (2003). Reading mathematics: More than words can say. *The Reading Teacher, 56*(8), 786–795.

Beck, I. L., McKeown, M. G., & Kucan, L. (2002). *Bringing words to life: Robust vocabulary instruction*. New York: Guilford Press.

Hammerberg, D. D. (2004). Comprehension instruction for socioculturally diverse classrooms: A review of what we know. *The Reading Teacher, 57*(7), 648–658.

Heimlich, J. E., & Pittelman, S. D. (1986). *Semantic mapping: Classroom applications*. Newark, DE: International Reading Association.

Jongsma, K. (2003). Beyond beginning learners. *The Reading Teacher, 56*(6), 550–553.

Nagy, W. E. (1988). *Teaching vocabulary to improve reading comprehension*. Newark, DE/Urbana, IL: IRA/NCTE.

Nilsen, A. P., & Nilsen, D. L. J. (2003). A new spin on teaching vocabulary: A source-based approach. *The Reading Teacher, 56*(5), 436–439.

Pittelman, S. D., Heimlich, J. E., Berglund, R. L., & French, M. P. (1991). *Semantic feature analysis: Classroom applications*. Newark, DE: International Reading Association.

Towell, J. (1998). Fun with vocabulary. *The Reading Teacher, 51*(4), 356–358.

For Exploration: Electronic Products and Resources

Use the Internet as a tool to keep up with the latest research in effective vocabulary development. The ERIC Clearinghouse on Reading, English, and Communication offers up-to-date information, as do journals and publications of such organizations as IRA, NCTE, and NECC.

The following Web sites and software will help you provide students with effective vocabulary learning opportunities:

Web Sites

The Alphabet Superhighway

The Alphabet Superhighway, under sponsorship of the U.S. Department of Education's READ*WRITE*NOW! Initiative, helps secondary and upper elementary students create, locate, and communicate information through active learning, guided discovery, mentoring, competitions, and other on-line activities.
http://www.ash.udel.edu/ash/index.html

The Clearinghouse on Reading, English, and Communication

Prepared by the ERIC Clearinghouse on Reading, English, and Communication and Indiana University, this site discusses the importance vocabulary plays in reading comprehension.
http://reading.indiana.edu/

Puzzle Depot

Puzzle Depot challenges your brain with free puzzles, Shockwave and Flash games, crosswords, logic games, IQ tests, trivia games, and contests for prizes.
http://www.puzzledepot.com/

Quia

This site allows teachers to create their own activities, puzzles, games, or quizzes on-line or access hundreds of activities created by other educators in all content areas.
http://www.quia.com/

Software

Carmen Sandiego Word Detective by Borderbund/The Learning Company and *Word Munchers Deluxe* are software programs used to enhance and extend vocabulary development.
http://www.learningco.com/Category.asp?CID=208

Responding and the Construction of Meaning

✓ **STANDARDS FOCUS**

NCTE/IRA Standards: 1, 2, 3, 4, 5, 6, 7, 8, 9, 10, 11, 12
Standards for Reading Professionals: 1, 2, 3, 4, 5

"Educators Speak   pp. 323, 327

Technology Helps Children Respond to Literature and
Connect to the World
                    —*Cynthia Sleeth, Camden, New Jersey*

A Variety of Literature Connects with Diverse Students
                    —*Jan Richard, Muncie, Indiana*"

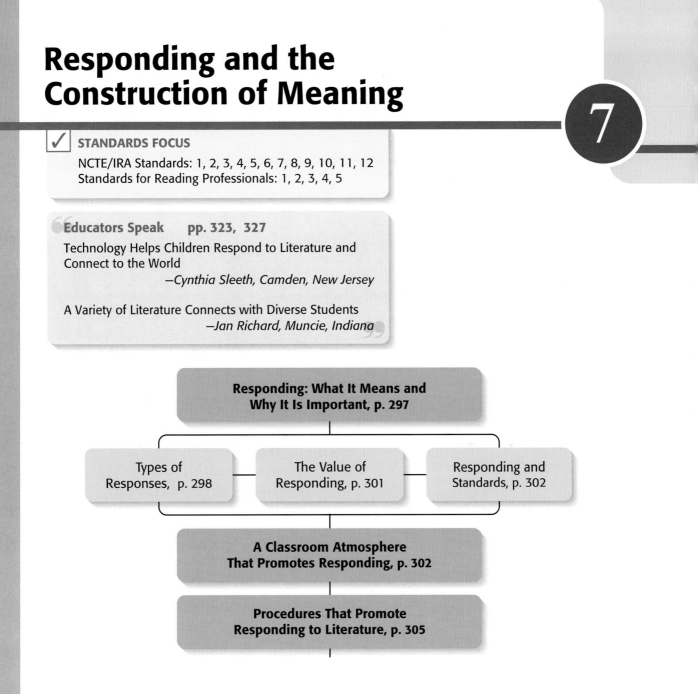

**Responding: What It Means and
Why It Is Important, p. 297**

Types of
Responses, p. 298

The Value of
Responding, p. 301

Responding and
Standards, p. 302

**A Classroom Atmosphere
That Promotes Responding, p. 302**

**Procedures That Promote
Responding to Literature, p. 305**

Journals, p. 305 — Response Charts, p. 318 — Literature Discussion, p. 324 — Readers Theater, p. 326

Summary, p. 330

Terms
You Need to Know

- analysis
- creative response
- dialogue journals
- diaries
- double-entry journals
- generalization
- journals
- learning logs
- literature discussion group (or circle)
- personal response
- readers theater
- responding
- response charts
- response journals (reading journals, literature logs)
- retelling
- summary

*L*et's begin by looking in on a third-grade classroom, where many different activities are taking place. Melissa and several other students are sitting at their desks reading Mississippi Bridge *(Taylor, 1990)*. Melissa leans over to one of her classmates and points out an illustration. They chat for a few minutes and then return to their reading.

Other students work with the book James and the Giant Peach *(Dahl, 1961)*. Some students are reading the book, some are making notes in their journals, and one very excited young man, Mark, is working on a project. I stop to talk to him.

"This looks like an interesting project," I say. "Tell me about it."

Mark shows me the cover of his book. "Have you ever read it?" he asks.

"Yes, I have."

"Did you like it?"

"Yes! Did you like it?"

"I sure did! I loved when the peach started to roll away and the things that happened. I'm making a movie box about this book with my favorite parts."

In another area of the room, Mrs. Eggars, the teacher, and a group of students sit around a table discussing How Many Days to America? *(Bunting, 1988)*. Joe says it would be really tough to leave everything you had and go off to a new country. Maria says, "Yes, but it would be better; they might have more things, and they wouldn't be afraid of the soldiers. I'd go."

Mrs. Eggars adds, "You know, I don't know how I would feel. I've never had to leave my home like the people in our story. Do you know of anyone who has ever had this kind of experience?"

Lisa says, "Our neighbors came from Vietnam."

The discussion continues in this manner.

Notice what we saw in this classroom:

- While Melissa and her classmates were reading a book, it was very natural for them to stop and talk about some point in the story. This type of activity shows that students are taking control of and monitoring their own reading.

- Other students were writing in journals about their books, and one student was working on a movie box, a series of pictures drawn on a roll of paper and shown as a movie by turning the roll through an opening in a box.

- Some students and the teacher were part of a discussion group. Each member participated in the discussion, no right or wrong answers were expected, and the teacher was an active participant.

- The teacher's role in this class was very important. Mrs. Eggars had planned the experiences that allowed and encouraged children to read, respond, and monitor their own learning. At the same time she participated in groups, modeling for students and prompting them as needed.

As all of the students in this class and their teacher show, active responding is an important element in learning to construct meaning and become literate (Hansen, 1987).

🦋 Responding: What It Means and Why It Is Important

Responding is what one does as a result of and/or as a part of reading, writing, or listening to any kind of text, fiction, poetry, drama, or nonfiction. The children in the third-grade classroom took different actions during and after reading. You too do it all the time. You respond to a textbook chapter you are reading by discussing it with a peer (it was easy or too difficult), or you respond to a newspaper article on hunger and homeless people by finding out how to make food donations to a local mission. Responding is part of the natural process of constructing meaning.

When you respond to a piece of literature or any other kind of writing, you use prior knowledge to construct meaning. Therefore, each person's construction is individual and personal, the result of the transaction between the reader and the text (Rosenblatt, 1938, 1976, 1991). Recall from your own college experience when you were asked to read a short story or poem and write your interpretation of it. When your paper came back, perhaps you saw you received a C because your interpretation did not agree with that of your instructor. What we know about the construction of meaning leads us to conclude that many acceptable interpretations and responses are possible from reading a single piece of literature. Although there may be a generally accepted response, personal response varies greatly from student to student. Even within the generally accepted responses, different interpretations often occur. Therefore, as the teacher, you must be prepared to *expect, respect,* and *accept* a variety of responses from students (Martinez & Roser, 1991). These responses will help you decide what types of additional support students need.

For more discussion of using responses as a part of assessment, see Chapter 11.

Responding is also valuable to you as a teacher because it can serve as part of your assessment. Many school districts now have standards that call for students to respond in different formats—learning logs, projects, and so forth.

Types of Responses

Responses to literature fall into two basic categories: personal and creative.

Personal responses are usually oral or written. Students may retell, generalize, and tell how they felt about what they read, their favorite part or character, or how what they read relates to their lives. For example, a fifth-grade student finished reading *The Lion, the Witch, and the Wardrobe* (Lewis, 1950) and wrote the personal response shown in Figure 7.1 in her dialogue journal. This student responded personally by relating the book to her own life and her parents, though her teacher will want to encourage deeper thinking. Some personal responses are at a much simpler level, especially when students first begin responding. The second grader's response shown in Figure 7.2 consisted of nothing more than identifying his favorite story, *Skip to My Lou* (Westcott, 1989). Obviously this student needs much more support in responding. There will be more later in the chapter about how teachers support students' responses.

Creative responses are often expressed through such means as art, music, drama, and dance. Students use what they have read in some creative way; of course, a creative response is personal also. The response shown in Figure 7.3 is a two-sided poster that a student made after reading *Miss Nelson Is Missing* (Allard & Marshall, 1977).

Personal responses may be prompted by the teacher, or they may be spontaneous on the part of the students. Personal responses are good lead-ins for discussion. Creative responses are important but sometimes overdone. It is easy to fall into the trap of spending too much time on a particular piece of literature by doing too many creative activities. Keep in mind that *it is not the number of activities that makes better readers; it is the amount of reading.*

Applebee (1978) suggests another way to look at responses: he describes four types of responses, each reflecting a different level of thought processes:

- *Retelling:* This is a simple recall of title, beginning and ending situations, and some dialogue, with no relative importance given to any of the events.

- *Summary:* Events are retold in order of importance. Summaries are usually shorter than retellings.

- *Analysis:* The response to the story is personal and subjective. For example, a student responding to *Annabelle Swift, Kindergartner* (Schwartz, 1988) might say, "This story is like what happened to me in kindergarten," and then relate a similar experience.

- *Generalization:* This addresses the theme or meaning of the story. For example, a generalization of *Annabelle Swift, Kindergartner* (Schwartz, 1988) might focus on the idea that you should trust yourself and not depend on the advice of others.

FIGURE 7.1

Personal Response to *The Lion, the Witch, and the Wardrobe* (Lewis, 1950)

10-19

Dear Mrs. Fugler,

I think The Lion, The Witch, and The Wardrobe. Was a very good book, and that you should redd it some day in the class. It was a 186 pages long and has 11 chapters. Lucy in this story is kind of like me because I tell my parents but they don't believe me and I have to bother them and bother them just like Lucy did. Then they go and see for thier selfs and Then they believe her or Lucy.

Sincerely

Nichole B.

Dear Nichole,

I enjoy that book myself. Are you going to read the rest of the series? yes I am

You did a fine job of relating Lucy to yourself. You are ready to choose your next book.

Sincerely,
Mrs Fugler

FIGURE 7.2

Personal Response to *Skip to My Lou* (Westcott, 1989)

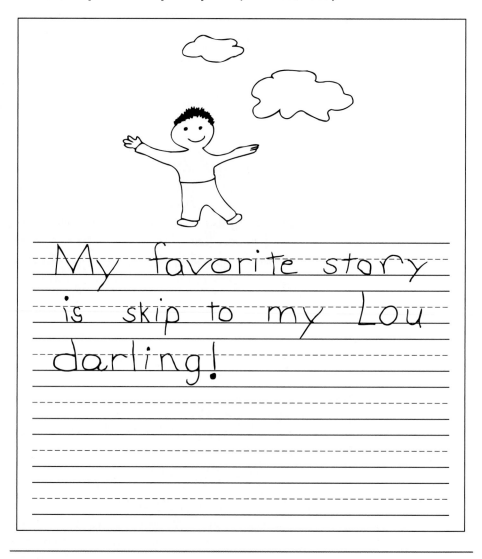

Even younger children can often make limited generalizations or analyze a story to some degree (Many, 1991). Fourth graders can actively construct meaning by analyzing and evaluating literature (Kelly & Farnan, 1991).

Studies indicate that encouraging personal responses is important in helping students learn to construct meaning (Cullinan, Harwood, & Galda, 1983; Eeds, 1989; Galda, 1982, 1983; Gambrell, 1986; Hickman, 1983; Morrow, 1985; Purves, 1972). As Kelly (1990) says, "Allowing students to respond to what they read or

FIGURE 7.3

Creative Response to *Miss Nelson Is Missing* (Allard & Marshall, 1977)

heard from a read-aloud provided the framework for what Piaget [in Gallagher & Reid, 1983] referred to as the active involvement in learning through the construction of meaning" (p. 470). Harste, Short, and Burke (1988) maintain that "readers deepen and extend their interpretations of literature when they respond to that literature in a variety of ways" (p. 305). As responses take place and are encouraged over time, students develop more complex responses that help them become more adept at constructing meaning.

See "For Exploration: Electronic Products and Resources" at the end of the chapter for other ideas of ways to share literature with students outside the classroom.

English Language Learners (ELLs) can respond in their primary language, or draw pictures and label them, which keeps them involved in the classroom (Freeman & Freeman, 2001). Even if teachers can't read the response, it will be clear that the student did respond. Sometimes another student, an aide, or a parent can read these responses and react to them or help ELLs reframe them in English.

Students may enjoy posting their responses to literature on a Web site such as amazon.com. Here they can also read what others have said about books.

The Value of Responding

When all children are given opportunities to function in a response-centered classroom, they develop a sense of ownership, pride, and respect for learning (Hansen, 1987). Because all students respond to the same piece of literature, they know their responses will be valued and accepted as much as anyone else's. In addition, when gifted students and at-risk students respond to the same piece of literature together, each responds in a manner consistent with his or her functioning level. Students learn that the teacher values their responses, and they learn to value the responses of their peers. This type of respect leads to a sense of community and ownership. Responding also helps students learn to monitor their own reading and writing. By being continually encouraged to think about and react to what they are reading and writing, students develop their metacognitive processes, which are important in constructing meaning (Palincsar & Brown, 1986; Paris et al., 1991). Since responses to literature are personal, the goal of response activities is to get students to construct meaning by interacting with the text. It is through this interaction, or transaction, that students become better comprehenders.

Responses also help students learn skills and strategies. Look back at the poster in Figure 7.3. This student obviously knows how to locate important information and character traits. She developed the use of these skills partly through reading and responding.

Responding and Standards

When students respond to what they read, they are engaged in activity that matches many standards, including those of the IRA/NCTE. For example, Standard 11 states: "Students participate as knowledgeable, reflective, creative, and critical members of a variety of literacy communities." Clearly, any response to literature meets this standard. No matter where you teach, you will be planning instruction to meet these or similar state or local standards. In fact, if you turn to the standards on the inside cover of this book, it will be clear that a written, oral, or other creative response to reading will meet several of the standards: responding helps students increase their range of understanding, requires them to adjust their use of language, use strategies and different writing processes, apply knowledge of language structure and conventions, perhaps use their first language to develop competency in English, and use spoken, written, and visual language to accomplish their own purposes.

🦋 A Classroom Atmosphere That Promotes Responding

If you want students to respond to literature, you must begin by creating a classroom environment that supports and promotes responding. Of course, you must create a literate environment and include extensive opportunities for students to read and write. But the response-centered classroom has many other characteristics as well.

As the teacher in this classroom, you must believe that all students have reactions and feelings that are important and valid, and students must have this belief about one another and about you. This sense of community may begin with the physical arrangement of the room, but it also includes how you treat students. If they learn that you always expect "right" answers or reward only thinking that you agree with, they will treat one another in that manner and strive to give only expected responses. But if they learn that you accept many possible answers and interpretations of what they have read, they will become more tolerant and accepting of one another's ideas.

This classroom attitude evolves partly out of the way you ask and respond to students' questions. Traditionally, the teacher's role has been to ask a series of questions to determine whether students have comprehended what they have read. For example, if students have just finished reading *The True Story of the 3 Little Pigs* (Scieszka, 1989), the teacher "checks" their comprehension by asking them a series of questions such as these: *Who told this story? What caused the wolf to go to the house of the first little pig? What happened at the house of the second little pig? What made the wolf angry at the third little pig's house? How did you feel about the wolf's story?*

Notice that only the last question begins to move students toward thinking more openly and relating what they have learned to their own experiences. Contrast these questions with the following:

1. What was different about this story and the one you already know about the three pigs?
2. Why do you suppose the wolf would choose to tell his story?
3. If you had been in the wolf's place, how would you have approached this situation?

These questions seek varied responses and say to students that it is entirely appropriate for each person to have a different response. A critical difference with this second group of questions is in the way you respond to the students. If a student answers question 2 by telling you that the wolf probably told this story because he just wanted to tell another story, and you say or imply that the answer is wrong, that student and others who heard your response will begin to get the message that you are looking for a certain answer, despite what you say. But if you say, "That is certainly a possibility; let's hear some other thoughts," students will get a totally different message from you.

There is indeed a time and a place to ask "mostly-right-answer" questions such as those in the first group; one time might be when students need support in understanding a story during teacher-guided reading. However, when you want to prompt children's responses to reading, you should ask more open-ended, suppositional questions and then show that you accept and value a variety of responses. Table 7.1 gives some examples of questions that suit this purpose. The questions in group I specifically relate to the text being read; the questions in group II encourage deeper thinking and more comparisons. Both groups of questions support divergent thinking.

Opportunities for students to respond to literature will come primarily in two ways: through self-selected books and materials and through those that you assign. Students may be reading self-selected literature as a part of independent reading, or you may have reached a point where you encourage self-selected reading for instructional purposes.

Many times you will want the entire class to read the same piece of literature. Obviously, students of differing abilities will approach the literature differently: some will read it independently, some cooperatively, and some supported by you through directed reading or read-alouds. In all instances, students will respond to the literature according to their own abilities. The literature you have students read

TABLE 7.1   **Sample Open-Ended Questions That Promote Responses to Literature**

Group I

1. Where and when does the story take place? How do you know? If the story took place somewhere else or in a different time, how would it be changed?
2. What incident, problem, conflict, or situation does the author use to get the story started?
3. What does the author do to create suspense and make you want to read on to find out what happens?
4. Trace the main events of the story. Could you change their order or leave any of them out? Why or why not?
5. Think of a different ending to the story. How would the rest of the story have to be changed to fit the new ending?
6. Did the story end the way you expected it to? What clues did the author offer to prepare you to expect this ending? Did you recognize these clues as important to the story as you were first reading or hearing it?
7. Who is the main character of the story? What kind of person is the character? How did you know?
8. Are any characters changed during the story? If they are, how are they different? What changed them? Did it seem believable?
9. Some characters play small but important roles in a story. Name such a character. Why is this character necessary for the story?
10. Who is the teller of the story? How would the story change if someone else in the book or an outside narrator told the story?
11. Does the story as a whole create a certain mood or feeling? What is the mood? How is it created?
12. Did you have strong feelings as you read the story? What did the author do to make you feel strongly?
13. What are the main ideas behind the story? What makes you think of them as you read the story?
14. Is this story like any other story you have read or watched?
15. Think about the characters in the story. Are any of them the same type of character you have met in other stories?

Group II

1. What idea or ideas does this story make you think about? How does the author get you to think about this?
2. Do any particular feelings come across in this story? Does the story actually make you feel in a certain way, or does it make you think about what it's like to feel that way? How does the author do this?
3. Is there one character that you know more about than any of the others? Who is this character, and what kind of person is he or she? How does the author reveal the character to you?
4. Are there other characters important to the story? Who are they? Why are they important?
5. Is there anything that seems to make this particular author's work unique? If so, what?
6. Did you notice any particular patterns in the form of this book? If you are reading this book in more than one sitting, are there natural points at which to break off your reading? If so, what are these?
7. Were there clues that the author built into the story that helped you to anticipate the outcome? If so, what were they? Did you think these clues were important when you read them?
8. Does the story language seem natural for the intent of the story and for the various speakers?
9. Every writer creates a make-believe world and peoples it with characters. Even where the world is far different from your own, how does the author make the story seem possible or probable?
10. What questions would you ask if the author were here? Which would be the most important question? How might the author answer it?

Source: Group I: Reprinted by permission of the author and publisher from Sloan, Glenna Davis, *The Child as Critic: Teaching Literature in Elementary and Middle Schools,* 2d ed., pp. 104–106. (New York: Teachers College Press, 1984.©1984 by Teachers College, Columbia University. All rights reserved.) Group II: From *Child and Story* by Kay Vandergrift.©1980 Neal-Schuman Publishers. Reprinted with permission of the publisher. Both cited by Harste et al. (1988).

See Chapter 2 for a detailed discussion of the literacy lesson.

as an entire class will usually be the materials used for your literacy lessons, which are designed to promote responding. (Recall that the parts of that lesson are introducing, reading and responding, and extending.)

Procedures That Promote Responding to Literature

There are many ways to encourage and support students as they respond to literature, and each procedure has a special function. This section discusses four procedures: journals, response charts, literature discussion groups, and readers theater.

Journals

Journals are any place where students record personal reflections about their reading and writing. They can range from a simple student-made booklet with a cover and pages to a spiral notebook or binder with loose-leaf pages to a floppy or compact disk.

See Chapter 10 for more about writing workshop.

Students who are involved in a writing workshop using process writing develop fluency and confidence in their writing, and using journals extends, reinforces, and supports these skills. Journals help tie together reading and writing, and give students opportunities to construct their own personal meanings (Atwell, 1987; Harste et al., 1988; Parsons, 1990; Tierney et al., 1990; Weaver, 1990a).

Basically, journals can be divided into five categories: diaries, response journals, dialogue journals, double-entry journals, and learning logs. Except diaries, all of these journal types can be diagnostic, in that they add to your assessment information about a student. Although these forms are similar in many ways, there are significant differences:

- *Diaries* are private records of personal observations or random jottings, or a daily record of thoughts and feelings. These are usually not shared, and students do not usually use them for responding to a piece of literature.

- *Response journals* are used by students to keep a record of their personal reactions to, questions about and reflections on what they read, view, write, or listen to. Response journals are sometimes called *reading journals* or *literature logs*. They might include lists of words students want to learn, goals for reading (such as number of pages to be completed), predictions made before and during reading, notes or comments made during reading, and reactions, thoughts, or feelings recorded after reading. If you just want students to keep track of their independent reading for themselves, you may not read these journals, but if you want them to respond to literature they have read or to pieces they have written, you probably will read them. Figure 7.4 shows a sample page from a fourth grader's response journal.

- *Dialogue journals* have the same basic purpose as response journals, except that the teacher (and sometimes peers) reads and responds in writing to the student's responses. "The major characteristic that distinguishes Dialogue Journals from other forms is the importance given to communications between the student and the teacher" (Tierney et al., 1990, p. 97). The comments from others help the student construct meaning more effectively. Figure 7.5 presents a sample page from a dialogue journal. Notice how the teacher's responses help the student think and construct meaning. This kind of journal lends itself to email. Students might share literature responses with friends many miles away.

- *Double-entry journals* have pages that are divided into two parts. On the left side of the page, students make notes, list predictions, and draw diagrams before and during reading. On the right side, they write a response to their reading. If the double-entry journal is also being treated as a dialogue journal, the teacher replies on the right-hand side of the page. These journals have been recommended for use with all students, including at-risk learners (Coley & Hoffman, 1990). Figure 7.6 shows a double-entry journal completed by a seventh grader reading *The Summer of the Swans* (Byars, 1970).

- *Learning logs* are daily records of what students have learned (Harste et al., 1988; Thompson, 1990). Figure 7.7 shows a sample entry from a third grader's learning log; this is simply a daily account of what this student has learned, with little response to the book. Sometimes, however, the learning log focuses on the learning that has taken place in a particular content area, such as math, science, or social studies. Learning logs may be treated as response journals with no teacher response or as dialogue journals between the teacher and students.

Deciding Which Journal Type to Use

As you can see, many similarities exist among various types of journals. Table 7.2 on page 311 summarizes their features. You must decide which types you want to use, and you may find you want to use a combination. The important thing is to know why you are having students keep a journal. Is it for:

- prompting students to reflect on their personal thoughts and feelings?
- encouraging students to keep a personal record of independent reading?
- encouraging students to respond to literature or their writing?
- carrying on a dialogue with students to help them learn to construct meaning?
- having students summarize what they have learned?

Once you have determined your purpose for using journals, you can decide on the type or combination of types you want to try. As you begin to make decisions, keep in mind that students do not have to write in their journals every day or after

FIGURE 7.4

Page from a Fourth Grader's Response Journal

The Witch on Forth Street

Tuesday, April 9

I felt ok about it but there is no sitch thing ~~about~~ as a witch. My favorite part was when ~~the~~ Cathy run home. I would not change anything.

Vednesday April 10

I felt OK about the chapter. It was ok I guess. My favorite part was when Vincent lied to his Mother. I would chang nothing.

Thursday, April 11

This Chapter I feel ok about. My favorite part is when they say click clop clap clop its a good Part so I would not change it.

every piece of literature they read. Imposing such stringent requirements makes journal writing a laborious task and defeats its purpose. At first, you may have to nudge some students to write in their journals; however, as they become comfortable with their journals, most will write in them more readily.

FIGURE 7.5

Page from a Dialogue Journal

<u>Wait Till Helen Comes</u>
Mary Downing Hahn
Date I started: February 5
Jeth February 6
I would really hate moving away from my home town &
live in the country where there aren't no other
kids to be friends with and to have to be nice to
such a little snot like Mary and be nice to her even
when she isn't nice to you and be nice to her dad to
when he isn't even your real dad

2-6   Heather,
            Glad you are reading this book.
         Sometimes when things change in
         a family, it might be best to
          move to someplace new. Why do
         you think Mary is being so
           mean?
                Miss Reid

February 9
I don't think living in an old time church with
a graveyard would be bad but I mite get real
scared like. If it stormed thundered and lightning'd
I would <u>not</u> like it NO WAY!!!

2-9   I don't like being in scary places
         when it storms either. Is Mary
         being any nicer?
               Miss Reid

Double-Entry Journal of a Seventh Grader

> May 8
> The Summer of the Swans
>
> by Betsy Byars
>
> _Predictions_
>
> | | |
> |---|---|
> | Sara is going to have a good summer because swans are beautifull. | Sara is really bored. She is not having a good summer. It is hard to be a teenager. Summers are tough. Sara loves Charlie even if he is a pain. |
> | Sara and Charlie are going to do something good together. | Sara has been sort of nice to Charlie. She is still feeling sorry for her self. I think she is really going to grow up this summer. Last summer I was a lot like Sara. |

Getting Started Using Journals

Once you decide which type of journal you will use, you are ready to introduce the idea to your class. Journals can be used with students at any grade level, though beginning learners are not expected to write as much as or use their journals in the same ways older students do. You should adapt the generalized procedures and suggestions given here to your students. There are no absolute rules to follow.

FIGURE 7.7

Sample Entry from a Learning Log, Third Grade

> Jan. 28
>
> The Titanic
>
> I learned that the Titanic was a great ship. It is going on the first trip. A lots of people are on the ship. The ship hits a big iceberg. It starts to fill up with water. It is not supose to sink. People do not want to leave the ship. Music is playing. The ship sinks. Many people die. The safe ship was not safe. It was sad.

Begin by making a journal of your own with some entries in it. Share your journal with your students, and discuss how all of you will keep journals in which you will write about what you have read. If you plan to read and respond to your students' journals, you should give them the opportunity to read and respond to yours too. It is important that you model this process for students as well as experience what they are going through.

Explain the idea of journal writing to your class. Tell students that the purpose of journal writing is to encourage them to think about what they are reading and to

| TABLE 7.2 | Types of Journals | | |

Journal Type	Description	Features
Diary	Private records of personal observations and thoughts	Not read by anyone unless student requests
Response journal (literature log or reading journal)	Reactions, questions, and reflections about what has been read	Sometimes a personal record and sometimes read by the teacher
Dialogue journal	A conversation between student and teacher about what has been read	Read by the teacher and sometimes peers; comments written by the reader
Double-entry journal	A split page on which students jot down ideas before and during reading on one side and give reactions after reading on the other side	May or may not be read by the teacher or peers
Learning log	A listing of what has been learned	May be treated as a dialogue journal or as a response journal

share their thoughts. If you are going to respond to students' journals, point out that this is a way for you to talk to each of them and for them to talk to you.

Talk with students about what types of entries they might make in their journals. Tell students they may write about what they have read, draw about it, make notes indicating they have shared their book in some way with another person, or perhaps decide on some other idea of their own. The main thing is that they respond in some way to their reading. Stress that there is no right or wrong way to respond. Obviously, responses will vary in quality, but you will help students improve through your responses to their writing. Encourage students to suggest how they might respond to a piece of literature, such as by telling about a character, writing about what they would have done in a particular situation, constructing a diorama, or relating events to their own lives.

Have students work in cooperative groups to write some journal entries. Cooperative groups support students as they begin journal writing without necessitating the use of models or samples. We have found that when we give samples of journal writing, students tend to copy the samples and be hampered by them. However, collaborative writing lets students see that they can create their own types of responses. Encourage students to share their responses with the class.

Talk with students about the format of their journals and how often they should write in them. Give students a simple format (or several formats) for recording such information as the date of entry, book title, author, and copyright date. Then have them write whatever they want to say. Be sure the format or guidelines are not too rigid, or you may inhibit their responding. Help your students evaluate and choose from among several formats and make modifications, if needed.

See Chapter 10 for information about writing workshop.

If journal entries will be read by others, students should strive to express their ideas so others can understand. Do not over emphasize legibility, spelling, or grammar at first. During the writing workshop students will be learning about the common courtesy of writing and spelling to communicate with others. Since some journal entries are simply personal notes, words, or predictions, accuracy is less important than meaning. Moreover, if you tell students their journal entries will not be evaluated for mechanics and spelling, you will begin to free them from some of the hang-ups that might discourage writing.

Atwell (1987) tells how she uses a letter to introduce journal writing to her middle school students. A copy of a similar letter used by a third-grade teacher appears in Figure 7.8. You could adapt this idea for use at any grade level.

Use a response chart or some other device to prompt and support students who need it. Response charts are discussed in detail later in this chapter. These charts are designed to help students think of how to respond to their reading.

Plan with students a system for using and storing journals. Choose a place for storing the journals alphabetically, such as in boxes, a file drawer, or a crate. Students can then find them easily. If journals are stored on floppy or compact disks, students may keep them in their desks or store them in a box next to the computers.

For more detailed discussions about journal use, see the "For Additional Reading" section at the conclusion of this chapter.

During the initial stages of journal writing, evaluate with students how the procedure is progressing. Whenever students try something new or different, there are likely to be some details that need to be worked out. Therefore, it is a good idea to take time periodically to talk about how things are going and identify ways to improve them.

What to Expect When Students Begin to Use Journals

Some students will embrace the use of journals from the start. Others may resist or have difficulties of one kind or another. With time and continued teacher support, all students can successfully use journals as one kind of response to literature.

"I don't know what to do." This is a likely reaction from students who are insecure about their own literacy and are having difficulty constructing meaning. Most will become more comfortable with the process as they gain experience. Students may also react this way if they have had many past experiences in which only "right" answers were expected. Writing journal responses may be totally new for students. In a sense they are redefining reading for themselves, because they are learning that a text can have multiple interpretations. For students who exhibit these behaviors, make some suggestions for possible responses and use a response chart, discussed later in this chapter.

Concerns about accuracy in spelling and usage. Some students may be uncertain about the language or may have been in environments that stressed correctness. Keep reassuring them that you are not concerned about correctness in their journals; you are concerned only about their thinking and their reactions.

FIGURE 7.8

Letter for Introducing Journals to Third Graders

Michael D. Robinson   Third Grade Teacher   ☺

Dear Girls and Boys,   August

This year you will be using your Reading Journal to write me letters about the books you are reading. I will write letters back to you as I read your letters. This will be one of the ways we talk about your books. I will also tell you about the books I am reading.

As you write each letter, tell me about your book — how you feel about it, what you like and don't like, what it makes you think about, your favorite parts, etc.... Draw pictures if you want to. I may even draw some pictures for you!

These letters will help you and me decide how you are doing with your reading and writing. We will discuss them during conferences. Here are some things for you to remember:
- date all your letters
- be sure to give the title and author
- write at least two letters each week
- tape this letter in the front of your journal

I'm excited about getting your letters. We'll learn a lot about each other.

Happy Reading,
Mr. Robinson

Retelling but not responding. Still other students may simply retell what they have read rather than responding personally. This is normal behavior. Students will progress beyond retelling as they gain more experience in responding, and your responses in their journals should consist of questions that focus their attention beyond this point. For example, you might write, "How would you have reacted in this situation?" or "What lesson do you think we can learn from this book?"

Some teachers encourage students to retell or summarize as one way to respond to literature. This can be an effective way to help children construct meaning (Gambrell, Pfeiffer, & Wilson, 1985; Marshall, 1983; Morrow, 1989), and such responses are also easy for teachers to evaluate.

Retellings and evaluation of responses are discussed more fully in Chapter 11.

Getting in a rut. Some students immediately become comfortable with a particular mode of response and latch onto it, using it again and again. Your responses are important in moving these students forward. Asking a question such as, "Have you ever thought about the characters [or other aspects] in the stories you are reading?" will help them think of alternatives.

Anxiety about teacher opinion. Finally, if you are using dialogue journals, some students may be anxious about what you will write in their journals and what you will think of their ideas. In these instances, you need to respond with very positive, upbeat, nonjudgmental comments that will allay these fears.

Journals are an excellent tool to use with all students. Barone (1990) notes that even young children begin responding by focusing on explicit story elements but soon become more interpretive, which indicates that they are working through the text they are reading, focusing on more than literal comprehension, and understanding the story more completely.

Responding to Students' Journals

In a response-centered classroom, both the students and the teacher are responsible for responding (Hansen, 1987). The students respond to their reading and writing and to one another's journals, including the teacher's. The teacher, in turn, responds to the students' journals, especially when dialogue journals are being used.

Teachers who want to use journals often raise two major questions: (1) "When do I find time to read all the journals?" and (2) "What exactly do I write in response to students' journal entries?" Both questions deserve serious consideration.

Finding Time to Read Journals. You do not have to read every journal entry students make. A response journal is often an individual record for the student's own use and thus requires no reading or responding by the teacher. Even when students are using journals that require you to respond, you do not have to do it every day for every entry. Dialogue journals require the most consistent form of response by the teacher because this is a major means of "talking" with students and helping them learn.

Finding the time to read journals is not nearly as difficult as it may seem at first.

Journals replace many of the papers that have been previously assigned to try to engage students in learning, and they provide a much more meaningful learning task. One fourth-grade teacher said, "I read some of my students' journals during conference period if there is no one ready to talk with me. If there are any journals that I need to see on any day and haven't, I read them right after school. I rarely carry any of them home."

You may read journals at various times during the day. Some teachers use part of silent reading time to read students' journals or any other time when students are working independently. Others like to read journals just before or right after school. However you decide to proceed, your plan must fit your teaching style and needs. There is no one best way or best time to read journals.

How to Write Responses. When you write responses in students' journals, keep in mind that you want to encourage students, guide them, refocus their responses, and make helpful suggestions. *Encouragement* is your number one goal. You want to encourage students to continue to read and think about what they are reading, as well as to feel good about themselves and what they are writing in their journals. Some examples of encouraging types of responses appear below. Notice that each of these responses provides a different type of encouragement in different situations. Although you will do more than encourage with your comments, *encouragement is essential.*

Dear Jeri,

You are doing a very good job telling about the characters in *Now One Foot, Now the Other*. Which character do you think is most important in this story? Why? I'm looking forward to your next entry.

Mr. C

Source: Now One Foot, Now the Other (de Paola, 1980).

> Dear Sam,
>   The way you are retelling this story, I can tell that you are enjoying it !! Have you ever had an adventure like April's? If you have, why don't you compare your adventure to hers. Keep going! I can't wait to see what you think later in this book.
>   Mr. C

Source: The Egypt Game (Snyder, 1976).

Sometimes as you are reading a student's journal, you will find that more *guidance* is needed in helping the student see important points or the big message the author is trying to deliver. For example, Nichole (see Figure 7.1) did not address the big ideas in *The Lion, the Witch, and the Wardrobe* (Lewis, 1950) and would benefit from guidance. Guidance may be often needed when the entire class is reading the same book. For example, suppose your third graders are all reading *Fly Away Home* (Bunting, 1991) and you notice that some students are not understanding why it is important for the father and little boy not to be noticed in the airport. (This story is about a homeless father and son who make their home in a large airport, moving from terminal to terminal to keep from getting caught.) One student wrote the following:

> The boy in this story did not talk to people. He was not a friend.

The teacher might respond as follows:

> *I thought the little boy really wanted to be friends. He was friends with Mrs. Medina and her family. He just couldn't be friends with everyone in the airport. Look back through the book and see if you can find places that show why he can't be friends with everyone.*

At other times, students will just need to be *refocused* in their journals and in their reading. If a student always responds by drawing a picture and labeling it "My Favorite Part," you might ask the student to try a different response. For example:

> *Your pictures of favorite parts are great. For your next entry, draw three pictures that show the three main events in the next chapter. Write a sentence or two about each picture.*

This type of response shows how instruction and the student's growth work together. It helps the student use drawing but begins to move her or him toward looking at important events in the story. Refocusing might also be needed when students get so caught up in minute story details that they miss the real message or story line.

At other times, your responses may need to include various other kinds of *suggestions*—suggestions for other books to read, responses to try, or things to consider or think about as reading continues. Your response in the journals and the students' responses to you are part of the running dialogue that lets you know how they are growing and gives you another way to guide them individually. Thus, the journal is both a teaching tool and a diagnostic tool.

See Chapter 11 for a discussion of using students' responses for assessment.

When students read and respond to one another's journals, they learn from one another. These are sometimes called "buddy journals." It is best to delay using this type of journal until students have used dialogue journals with you, are comfortable with the procedure, and trust has been built between you. When you are ready, model appropriate responses, showing that the focus should not be on the mechanics of writing or on whether an idea is right or wrong, but rather reacting to each other's ideas and feelings.

Precautions When Using Journals

You need to take several precautions when using journals:

- *Beware of overusing journals.* Sometimes teachers get so excited about journals that they use them in every subject area. Students become bored, and the journals lose their effectiveness.

- *Don't require all students to write in their journals every day.* To get everyone to write, teachers often require a daily entry. This turns students off to journals. Allow students to use journals as a choice. Some teachers require a minimum number of entries each week, especially in middle school.

- *Make sure you know your reason for having students use journals.* Be confident about why you are using journals before you begin. Avoid using journals just for the sake of using them.

- *Remember that journals are instructional tools.* Journals should replace other, less meaningful types of activities that students might do. They should not become just more busy work that is added on to what students already need to complete.

These precautions and the guidelines in this chapter should help you use journals effectively.

Response Charts

If students need support in learning how to respond, you can use **response charts,** which give suggestions of ways to respond to a piece of literature. Figure 7.9 presents a response chart from a sixth-grade classroom. The teacher used it to get students back into journal writing at the beginning of the new school year. You and your students may develop a response chart together before or after reading.

Response charts should be useful on several occasions. First, they accustom students to the concept of responding. By giving students suggestions, you will prime their thinking and help them learn how to select their own modes of response. Beginning learners or those experiencing difficulty in learning often need this type of support. Such charts also provide scaffolding for ELLs, who may have trouble with open-ended responses such as journals.

Response charts are appropriate when you observe that students do not clearly understand what they have read or are missing the point an author is trying to make.

FIGURE 7.9

Sample Response Chart from a Sixth-Grade Classroom

RESPONSE SUGGESTIONS

Before Reading

- List the title and author of the book in your journal. Give the date you started the book.

During Reading

- Note words of interest in your journal.
- Think about the story you are reading. Does it make sense? Write any questions you have in your journal.

After Reading (select one or more)

- Write a short summary of the story.
- Select your favorite character and describe his or her role in the story.
- Meet with a friend to talk about the story.
- *Other*—You decide what you would like to do.

You can make this judgment by reading students' written responses or listening to or observing their oral or other creative responses. For example, suppose a group of fifth graders just read *The Scarebird* (Fleischman, 1987), and several students have decided to give a skit based on the book. If they portray Lonesome John as crazy instead of just lonely, you can tell they have missed the point and that they need support in identifying the story's problems. Therefore, you might model how you would identify the problem in this story. With the next few stories students read, you might suggest one or two ways for them to respond that would focus their attention more directly on identifying story problems, such as constructing a group story map or writing a paragraph describing the story problem.

See Chapter 4 for more about this reading strategy.

Constructing Response Charts

Response charts are not necessary for every piece of literature students read. *Ultimately, you want students to be able to decide on their own modes of response.* However, even the best readers in a class may need some ideas from a response chart from time to time. One way to meet the individual needs of your students is to present different types of response activities but allow choices. Therefore, you need a variety of ideas about how students might respond to literature. In all cases, the activities on a response chart should be things students might naturally choose to do after reading a book; in other words, they should be authentic activities.

When constructing response charts, you need to consider two factors: the type of text being read and the needs of your students. Occasionally, the same response activity might work for both narrative and expository texts, but in most instances it will not. Students' needs will range from missing the basic ideas, to an inability to be inferential and evaluative in their responses. In the first case, a structured response such as a story map might be helpful; in the second case, students might think about and be ready to discuss why, for instance, the main character behaved as he or she did.

All response charts should contain one option that says, "Other—You decide how you want to respond." When students effectively use the "other" option, it's a good sign that they no longer need response charts. Limit the number of options. A new response chart might have five options, whereas one you are adding to regularly might get only three new response options at one time.

Tables 7.3 and 7.4 list response options that should be helpful in constructing your own response charts for narrative and expository texts. They were developed from a variety of sources, including the works of Spritzer (1988) and Parsons (1990) and the ideas other teachers and we have found to be effective. As you work with your students, you will develop other options that are appropriate for them. Two response options, discussion and readers theater, are explained in more detail later in this chapter.

Sometimes the response chart may include questions that cue students to respond in different ways. Parsons (1990) suggests that some students really need these aids to get them started and recommends the following questions for narrative texts:

- What surprised you about the section you read today? How does this change affect what might happen next in the story?

- What startling, unusual, or effective words, phrases, expressions, or images did you come across in your reading today that you would like to have explained or clarified? Which ones would you like to use in your own writing?

- How much do you personally agree or disagree with the way various characters think and act and the kinds of beliefs and values they hold? Where do you differ, and why?

- What issues in this story are similar to real-life issues that you've thought about or had some kind of experience with? How has the story clarified or confused or changed your views on any of these issues?

For expository texts, cuing questions also need to be open-ended. Some suggested questions for expository texts are as follows:

- After reading this far in this text, what do you think you will learn about next?

- How would you feel if you were the scientist who made the discovery you just read about? Why?

- How do you feel the information in this text will be helpful in your life?

- How does the information you have just learned compare to what you already know about this topic?

You will find that you will develop your own bank of questions to use on response charts as you work with your students.

TABLE 7.3 **Response Options for Narrative Texts**

Response Option	Description
Discussion	Talk about the story with others who have also read it (use questions from the response chart to structure your discussion).
Story mapping	Make a story map.
Rewriting	Rewrite a part of the story illustrating how you would have solved the problem.
Retelling	Retell the story to a friend or small group of friends.
Illustrating	Illustrate your favorite part or important scenes from the story. Write a sentence or two about each illustration.
Sharing	Tell a friend or classmate about the story you have read. Or read aloud your story to a friend, a classmate, or someone in a grade lower than yours.
Puppetry	Use puppets to share your story with other classmates or students in another class.
Posters	Make a poster to "sell" classmates on reading this book. Remember to make it exciting so they will want to "buy" it.
Other books by the author	Select another book by this author. Read and compare the two stories.
Book talk	Give a short (3–5 minute) book talk focusing on what you feel is most exciting about your book.
Dress-up	Dress like a character from your book and act out a favorite scene for your class.
Play/readers theater	Work with other students who have read the book to present a play or make a readers theater presentation.
Topical study	Use the topic of your story as the basis for an informational study. For example, a child who is reading *Nine-in-One Grr! Grr!* (Xiong & Spagnoli, 1989) might do a study about the Hmong people of Laos.
Mobile	Make a mobile of important characters or events in the story.
Movie	Work with others who have read the book to make a movie using a video camera. Have a movie party to share your work with others.

TABLE 7.4 **Response Options for Expository Texts**

Response Option	Description
Discussion	Talk about what you have read with others who have also read it. Use questions from the response chart to structure your discussion.
Graphic presentation	Share the important ideas you have learned through a graphic device, such as a chart, time line, diagram, or graphic organizer.

Response Option	Description
Speech	Give a persuasive talk using the information you have gained about the topic of your book.
Display	Create a display related to the book you read.
Newspaper article	Write a newspaper article expressing your point of view about the book.
Book	Use the information from the book you read to make a book of your own on the topic. Include text, charts, illustrations, and diagrams if appropriate.
Debate	Have a debate with others who have read the book. Each group debating must take a different point of view.
Bibliography	Read other books on the same topic, and compile an annotated bibliography to share with others.
Written report	Write a report about your book focusing on what you learned and how it might be helpful in the world.
Map	Make a map to show important information you have learned. Focus on products, cities, recreation areas, and so forth.
Experiment	Use what you have learned to conduct an experiment. Write your results.
Newsreel	Use a video camera to make a newsreel using the information you and others have gained from their books. Write a script including facts and opinions.

Technology Helps Children Respond to Literature and Connect to the World

"Kids engrossed in learning is the rule rather than the exception in this nearly 100-year-old red brick elementary school that covers a city block inside one of America's poorest cities. Outside, litter lines the chain link fences of the once elegant row houses, and police sirens are as frequent as birdsongs. Despite the differences between this community and mainstream America, our kids have one significant thing in common with kids in other districts, and that is simply that they *want* to learn.

Picture a group of children watching a herd of elephants thunder across a savanna. They can almost smell the dust they kick up as they head for safer ground. Children watch with wide eyes as adult elephants surround their babies to keep them safe from predators. No, these children are not on safari; they are at computers in the media center fascinated by the video clip in an online encyclopedia.

This particular second-grade class had read an elephant story during their classroom literacy period and wrote about it in their response journals. What a great opportunity for learning when the kids are excited about a topic! After collaborating with the classroom teacher, the kids and I were off and running. Collaboration is a wonderful way to continually integrate my program with the classroom teachers. Though I use different media and different formats, I can address my media literacy objectives while I enhance classroom content simultaneously.

Our first step was to use a graphic organizer to plot what we knew and what we didn't know, so we created a KWL chart. Then we brainstormed how to find information and what materials we could use. Each group's challenge was to use one print source and one electronic source. By second grade, children are learning how to find materials, how to navigate software programs, and are beginning to perform simple Internet searches. I gave them a list of software programs, bookmarked Web sites (previewed in advance), and electronic encyclopedias, and taught them how to search our automated on-line catalogue of current library items.

Assistance was provided to each group as needed, but independent work was heartily encouraged. Once data were collected, their final charge was to make a creative presentation of their findings. Past projects include written reports, a digital photo diary with captions, a taped oral report, dioramas, dramatic skits, and murals, and soon we'll be adding the camcorder, scanners, and PowerPoint presentations.

As an information specialist, I teach children from preschool to grade 4 how to acquire and evaluate various information resources, using print, nonprint, and electronic information materials. One of my major goals for my students (besides becoming lifelong readers) is that they will become independent locators, evaluators, and users of the wealth of information available today. I believe this will not only empower them, but it will improve their critical thinking skills. No doubt this in turn may enhance their self-concepts as they spread their wings and successfully achieve their goals in ways they may never have believed possible."

Cynthia Sleeth, Media Specialist
Alfred E. Cramer Elementary School
Camden, New Jersey

Literature Discussion

Another procedure for promoting responses to literature is sometimes called the literature circle (Harste et al., 1988), literature groups (Calkins, 1994; Weaver, 1994), or **literature discussion group (or circle).** Regardless of the name, the purpose is the same: to get students to read and respond to literature. Remember that the term *literature* here refers to any text read: stories, poems, plays, biographies, historical fiction, memoir, nonfiction. Having students discuss what they have read is essential to developing their ability to construct meaning.

Children who have read the same book get together to discuss it and react to it. Initially, the teacher may start the discussion, but as students learn to function in the literature group, they often take over this role. Sometimes a teacher may participate as an equal member of a group, not the discussion leader.

See Chapter 10 for more about organizing.

The procedures for using literature discussion groups have been described in detail by Harste et al. (1988). The guidelines given here are based on their ideas and our own experiences in working with children and teachers.

Guidelines for Using Literature Discussion Groups

Selecting Literature. There are three options: one book read by the whole class, multiple books chosen by students, or individual self-selection. If several students have read or are reading the same book or selection as part of their independent reading, these students may form a literature discussion group of their own.

Organizing Discussion Groups. If everyone in the class is reading the same book, establish how many groups you will need to form in order to have three members in each; then have students quickly divide themselves into groups. Allowing students to select the discussion group they want to join gives them some control over their own learning and also helps to accommodate their individual needs. Many times, students will sign up to be with their friends; there is nothing wrong with this. If behavior problems arise, you may have to adjust the groups, but this is usually not necessary.

If you are having the class select their reading from several different books, you can give a bit of information about each book as a teaser to spark interest and to help students make their selections. Then list the titles on a chart or the chalkboard, and have students sign up for the book they want to read. If more than four or five students want to read the same book, form more than one group for that book.

The entire class need not be in literature groups at the same time. Those not involved may be doing independent reading or writing or other reading and writing activities.

Starting Discussion Groups. Students begin by reading. If they are reading a short book or selection, they should read the entire book before coming to the group. If they are reading a longer book, one with several chapters, they can meet at the conclusion of each chapter and at the end of the book. As they meet to discuss each chapter, the groups may decide on reading goals to be completed before the next meeting and should record these goals in their journals.

FIGURE 7.10

Literature Discussion Chart

LITERATURE DISCUSSIONS

1. Begin by telling the title and author of your book.
2. Talk about what you read.
   - What was your favorite part? Why?
   - How does this book relate to your life?
   - If you felt strongly about what happened to a character, what techniques did the author use to lead you to feel that way?
   - How important is the setting at this point?
   - What surprised you about the events in the story since last time the group discussed the story? Now what do you think will happen?
3. Make a list of things to discuss at your next meeting.

If you are working with beginning readers or students having problems reading, you can read aloud the book to that group. So that students do not feel any stigma in being part of the read-aloud group, you can announce before students sign up for their groups that a certain book will be read aloud and then invite all students to be part of this group. Most will want to be in the listening group from time to time. You can also provide a tape of the book in the listening center.

Promoting Discussions. Each literature discussion group meeting will usually last from 5 to 10 minutes, depending on the book or selection being discussed and the students' experience in this procedure. Since the primary focus of the discussion is to bring the students and the literature together and to allow students to construct their own meanings in an authentic way, the discussion must be open-ended.

Many teachers find that using a discussion chart such as the one in Figure 7.10 helps get the groups started and keeps the discussion moving. Present the chart to students and explain it. As students become more comfortable, you will find they will start their own discussions, using the chart as a prompt. You may need to change the chart from time to time, and you can use some of the open-ended questions for cuing presented earlier in this chapter. After students have learned to work in groups, discontinue the use of charts.

As each group carries out its discussion, move from group to group to monitor what is taking place. You may want to remind students to refer to posted questions on a response chart. In many cases, you may want to become a member of the group and add to or stimulate the discussion with questions. For example, suppose a group is discussing *Regina's Big Mistake* (Moss, 1990) and you notice that the discussion seems to be lagging. You might join the group by saying, "You know, when I was in school, I often felt just like Regina. I was afraid of making mistakes. What problems like that have you had in school?" In this way, you become part of the group by modeling and prompting other things to think about.

In the initial stages of using literature discussion groups, you will need to model and demonstrate good questioning and discussion behaviors. You might model for the entire class using a small group. Then discuss with the class what happened and any problems they might see.

Concluding Literature Discussion Groups. When students have completed a book, they can then decide whether they want to share it with the entire class or respond to it in some other way. The literature discussions may be sufficient response for most students. *It is neither necessary nor advisable for students to always complete additional activities. Only when they are really excited about a book should they be encouraged to respond further.*

Tips for Using Discussion Groups

There is no one correct way to use discussion groups; they are a flexible tool and should be used accordingly. At the beginning, proceed slowly and carefully. Teachers have found two ways to move themselves and their classes into literature discussion groups successfully.

One teacher starts her class by inviting students to help select a book for the entire class. She then introduces and explains the concept of literature discussion groups. After the groups are established, the class reads the book (or the first chapter in a longer book) and the teacher presents a literature discussion chart such as the one in Figure 7.10. She poses one open-ended question to get all the groups started. As they work, she moves from group to group to see what is taking place, joining groups as needed. She repeats this pattern several times using different books until she is comfortable that her students understand literature discussion and are working in the group effectively. Then she expands to two or more books, letting the children choose which books they will read.

A second procedure is to get one small group started, following the same basic procedure as that just described. When that group is working smoothly, you can add a second and then a third until all students are comfortable.

Teachers may group students with the same first language for purposes of discussion. The students discuss the book in their first language and then, in English, report key ideas to the class or the teacher (Freeman & Freeman, 2001).

Regardless of the pattern you select, you will want to move slowly. When students have not had the experiences of such open discussions and have been accustomed to giving the teacher the "correct answer," they are often reluctant to talk. You may need to model open discussions several times before students are able to accept the idea that there are no absolute or correct answers.

For further reading, see Roser and Martinez (1995), listed in the "For Additional Reading" section.

Readers Theater

The **readers theater** is a form of response in which children turn a story into a play. Sloyer (1982) describes readers theater this way:

> *Readers Theatre is an interpretive reading activity for all children in the classroom. Readers bring characters to life through their voices and gestures. Listeners are capti-*

Educators Speak

A Variety of Literature Connects with Diverse Students

"As a primary school teacher I feel my most important job is to teach my students the love of reading. Every opportunity I have, I incorporate children's literature into my lessons.

Author studies are the most enjoyable part of my curriculum. Starting with the first day of school, the children "meet" Kevin Kenkis through *Wemberly Worried*. For several authors' studies, I have many stuffed characters or projects or puppets that add to their enjoyment. For example, by the end of the Henkes study, the class feels they know Lily of *Lily's Purple Plastic Purse*.

The Arthur series by Marc Brown is another big hit. As a culminating activity, I have the children write their own Arthur or D.W. adventure. When we have a story about a mouse in our basal reader, I declare one day Leo Lionni Day, and we read several of his stories with correlating art projects. *Frederick* and *Fish Is Fish* are their favorites.

Throughout the year, Jack Prelutsky poetry is often used as learning through humor. Several of his poems are about food, so I plug these into our Health chapter on that subject. Traesher's Black Lagoon series is fun when I replace the characters' names with my students' names. Tomi DePaola is another author I use year round. It is interesting to see that the children learn to recognize his illustrations even when he is not the author.

The most encompassing study we do is midyear on Jan Brett. I have almost two dozen of her books, and she provides such wonderful materials and such a great Web site that the children are convinced she is a personal friend of mine. Hedgie the Hedgehog, a character in most of her books, becomes our class pet. He, his backpack, and his journal spend weeks going home with my students, and they love sharing his writing with the class.

The school librarian says she can always tell whose books we're reading this week. When the book fairs come to our school, the first books the children grab are the authors they know. I see these as great signs that my tactics are working. I also use lots of literature in my social studies and science units. Mem Fox books are terrific for learning about Australia. A seasonal display is a monthly occurrence, and the children are delighted when they find a book by an author they "know." Jerry Polatta's alphabet books are a wonderful way to practice handwriting skills rather than mundane drill.

With every author we study, the children write them letters. The responses are wonderful and reinforce their enthusiasm to read more.

The Laura Numeroff books like *If You Give a Mouse a Cookie* are great to use if you want your children to write a cumulative story.

Patricia Pollaco, for two reasons, is saved for the end of the year. First, her stories require a higher level of thinking, which the children are then better prepared for. Second, our school requires all students to write a personal narrative for our Young Authors program. Pollaco stories are the perfect modeling tool. *My Rotten Red-Haired Older Brother* and *Betty's Doll* are good examples.

When my students learn that Patricia has a learning disability and is now a famous author, it gives all of them more self-confidence no matter what their ability level.

After many years of teaching, I always have students return to visit. They often tell me that they learned to love books in my classroom. I guess that says it all."

Jan Richard, Second-Grade Teacher
Mitchell Elementary School
Muncie, Indiana

First graders using readers theater with minimal costumes. ©Elizabeth Crews/The Image Works

vated by the vitalized stories and complete the activity by imagining the details of a scene or action. . . . Readers Theatre becomes an integrated language event centering upon oral interpretation of literature. The children adapt and present the material of their choice. A story, a poem, a scene from a play, even a song lyric, provide the ingredients for the script. As a thinking, reading, writing, speaking, and listening experience, Readers Theatre makes a unique contribution to our language arts curriculum. (p. 3)

This form of response allows all children to take part in the creative interpretation of a story. Even second-language or at-risk learners can succeed in this activity (Werthemer, 1974). Readers theater is also effective in helping students improve fluency (Rasinski, 2003).

The following procedures for using readers theater have been developed from numerous sources and from our own experiences in working with children and teachers (Coger & White, 1982; Harste et al., 1988; Sloyer, 1982).

For a detailed discussion of fluency, see Chapter 4.

Select the Literature. As you begin using the readers theater, help students select stories with lots of dialogue, strong story lines, and suspense, humor, or surprise. Discuss with students the characteristics of a good piece to use.

FIGURE 7.11

Partial Readers Theater Script for *Tye May and the Magic Brush* (Bang, 1981) Developed by Second Graders and Their Teacher

TYE MAY AND THE MAGIC BRUSH

NARRATOR: Many years ago a cruel and greedy emperor ruled over China. His people were very poor. One of the poorest was Tye May. Her mother and father were dead and she lived alone. Every day she gathered firewood and cut reeds to sell in the marketplace. One day Tye May passed the school and saw the teacher painting. She knew right then what she wanted to do.

TYE MAY: "Please, sir, I would like to learn how to paint, but I have no money to buy a brush. Would you lend me one?"

TEACHER: (Angry) "Beggar girls don't paint. Get out of here!"

NARRATOR: But Tye May did not give up. She had an iron will. She drew pictures in the dirt when she collected wood. Her pictures looked real but she still didn't have a brush. One night when she was very tired she fell into a deep sleep.

WOMAN: "This is a magic brush. Use it carefully."

TYE MAY: "Thank you! Thank you!"

NARRATOR: The woman was gone and Tye May woke up.

Read or Reread the Literature. After reading, students should discuss the story, focusing on the characters, setting, problem, action, and outcome. Many teachers have students develop a story map. This will help students know what needs to be included in the readers theater script and what is not essential.

Develop a Script. A good way to do this is through shared writing. Use a chart or an overhead projector, and develop the script with students. This is also a good place to refer students to the story map. Talk about the types of things that can be left out, such as the word *said* and lengthy descriptions that are not essential to the story. Generate a list of story characters, and help students see how to identify the parts that must be read by a narrator. Figure 7.11 shows a partial script developed by some second graders and their teacher. Eventually, children will be able to do this on their own.

While it is possible to purchase readers theater scripts for many pieces of literature (write to Readers Theatre Script Service, P.O. Box 178333, San Diego, CA 92117), one of the major values of using this activity comes from developing the script. Therefore, even if you decide to purchase some scripts, you should also have students develop some of their own to give them the experience of translating a story into a script. In either case, you will need multiple copies of the script.

Discuss Props. Only a few simple props are to be used in a readers theater presentation. These might include chairs, a stool, a yardstick for a sword, paper faces, hats, and so forth. There is no scenery. Talk with students to identify the props to use.

Prepare and Rehearse for the Presentation. Select students to be the characters in the presentation. If you are working with the whole class, you might want to divide the class into groups so that everyone can participate in this first production; each group could give its own performance of the same program. Discuss with students how and where to stand and make hand, body, or facial gestures to convey parts of the story to their audience. Give students time to rehearse their program.

Present the Program. When students have had ample time to rehearse, have the groups perform for the class. After all performances are completed, discuss with the students what was successful and what could be improved in future productions. Focus on all aspects, from selecting the literature to giving the program.

There is no one right way to use the readers theater in your class. Feel free to experiment, following your own ideas and those of your students.

🦋 Summary

Responding is an activity that occurs as a reaction to or as part of reading or listening. This chapter focused on the importance of responding to literature in the process of constructing meaning. Students can do this in a number of verbal and nonverbal ways. The atmosphere of the classroom sets the tone that promotes and supports students' responding activities. Journals, response charts, literature discussion groups, and readers theater are all procedures that promote responding to literature. Organizing and managing a response-centered literacy classroom is an important task for the teacher.

For Additional Reading

Atwell, N. (1987). *In the middle.* Portsmouth, NH: Heinemann.

Daniels, H. (2001). *Literature circles* (2nd ed.). Portland, ME: Stenhouse.

Daniels, H. (2001). *Looking into literature circles.* Portland, ME: Stenhouse. [Videotape.]

Evans, K. S. (2001). *Literature discussion groups in the intermediate grades.* Newark, DE: International Reading Association.

Gambrell, L. B., & Almasi, J. F. (Eds.). (1996). *Lively discussions!* Newark, DE: International Reading Association.

Hoyt, L. (1998). *Revisit, reflect, retell: Strategies for improving reading comprehension.* Portsmouth, NH: Heinemann.

Long, T. W., & Gove, M. K. (2003/2004). How engagement strategies and literature circles promote critical response in a fourth-grade, urban classroom. *The Reading Teacher, 57*(4), 350–361.

McMahon, S. I., Raphael, T. E., Goatley, V. J., & Pardo, L. S. (1997). *The book club connection.* Newark, DE: International Reading Association and New York: Teachers College Press.

Parsons, L. (2001). *Response journals revisited.* Portland, ME: Stenhouse.

Roser, N. L., & Martinez, M. G. (Eds.) (1995). *Book talk and beyond: Children and teachers respond to literature.* Newark, DE: International Reading Association.

Szymusiak, K., & Sibberson, F. (2001). *Beyond leveled books: Supporting transitional readers in grades 2–5.* Portland, ME: Stenhouse.

Wiseman, A. J., (2003). Collaboration, initiation, and rejection: The social construction of stories in a kindergarten class. *The Reading Teacher, 56*(8), 802–810.

For Exploration: Electronic Products and Resources

Explore multimedia and hypermedia that support children in responding to literature. Check the Web site addresses of companies and organizations listed at the end of other chapters in this book. The following may also be helpful.

International Society for Technology in Education
www.iste.org

International Reading Association
The International Reading Association is a professional membership organization dedicated to promoting high levels of literacy for all by improving the quality of reading instruction, disseminating research and information about reading, and encouraging the lifetime reading habit. The Web site provides resources and links to a diverse array of topics and issues in reading.
www.reading.org

National Council of Teachers of English
The National Council of Teachers of English is devoted to improving the teaching and learning of English and the language arts at all levels of education. Its Web site provides a forum for the profession, an array of opportunities for teachers to con-

tinue their professional growth throughout their careers, and a framework for cooperation to deal with issues that affect the teaching of English.
www.ncte.org

Web Sites

Aaron Shepard's RT Page
A page devoted to readers theater. Includes advice on creating scripts from children's literature and a number of ready-to-use scripts to download. Also offers contact information and a means of sharing scripts.
http://www.aaronshep.com/rt

Book Raps
A book rap is a book discussion conducted by email. Individuals or groups of students from across the country or around the world can discuss the scheduled books. Teachers or teacher librarians can nominate a book for discussion by becoming a book rap coordinator. Current titles for discussion are listed on the book rap calendar. Some book raps may include special events such as author involvement, illustrators online, access to content area experts, and live chat sessions. Subject areas include English, study of society and environment, English as a Second Language, and science.
http://rite.ed.qut.edu.au/oz-teachernet/projects/book-rap/

LiteratureCircles.Com
This is a Web resource for educators who are using or interested in student-led book discussion groups. The goal is to support conversation and idea sharing among people who are exploring this important "best practice" strategy. Features include discussions, book recommendations, classroom management ideas, links to related sites and organizations, and news of relevant publications and events.
http://www.literaturecircles.com/

Literature Circles Resource Center
Hosted by Seattle University and Katherine L. Schlick Noe, the purpose of this site is to provide in-depth information and resources on literature groups, including book lists, guidelines, and resources for literature groups.
http://fac-staf.seattleu.edu/kschlnoe/LitCircles/

Writing and the Construction of Meaning

8

✓ **STANDARDS FOCUS**

NCTE/IRA Standards: 4, 5, 6, 7, 8, 9, 10, 11, 12
Standards for Reading Professionals: 1, 2, 3, 4

Educators Speak   p. 356

A Mobile Lab and Individual Laptops Engage
At-Risk Students in the Writing Process
          —Caroline Goddard, Stafford, Virginia

Terms

You Need to Know

- conventional writing phase
- clustering
- domain
- drafting
- invented spelling phase
- mode of writing
- picture writing
- planning/ previewing
- process writing
- proofreading/ editing
- publishing
- random letter phase
- revising
- scribble writing
- story frames
- traits

*R*ecently a third-grade teacher was asked, "What do you think it means to develop reading and writing together?" His answer was very clear:

Children often read books that are related to the topics they are using in writing. At the same time, they often write about what they are reading. For example, a child in my last class was reading the personal narrative Little House in the Big Woods *[Wilder, 1932]; it was very natural for her to extend personal narrative into her writing. Another boy was writing a story about dinosaurs. His writing experience became the catalyst for him to read other books on dinosaurs. So you see, I can't just think of reading or writing. I think of a literacy experience or event. By giving my children support in the event they are experiencing, I am able to help them become better comprehenders; it doesn't really matter whether it is a reading focus or a writing focus. They use both of these things together.*

In this chapter, we take a more detailed look at the relationships between writing and reading and how these processes develop together.

🦋 Why Writing and Reading Together?

Educators have supported integrating the language arts for many years (Durkin, 1989; Loban, 1963; Moffett & Wagner, 1983), and research has helped us understand how and why these processes develop together (Tierney & Shanahan, 1991). Several researchers have helped us to formulate a clearer (although not final) answer to the question, "Why writing and reading together?"(Dahl & Farnan, 1998; Pearson & Tierney, 1984; Shanahan, 1990; Tierney & Leys, 1984; Tierney & Shanahan, 1991). There are at least five major reasons for teaching writing and reading together:

- Both writing and reading are constructive processes.
- Reading and writing share similar processes and kinds of knowledge.
- Writing and reading, when taught together, improve achievement.
- Reading and writing together foster communication.
- Combining reading and writing develops critical thinking.

Let's discuss each of these reasons in more detail.

Both Writing and Reading Are Constructive Processes. The fact that reading and writing are both constructive processes is obvious from Pearson and Tierney's (1984) description of readers as composers: thoughtful readers plan reading around a given purpose. With this purpose in mind, readers think about the text and begin to activate background relating to the topic. Writers go through a very similar process. They have some purpose for writing and think about what they know or need to know before beginning to write.

Next, readers begin to read and construct meaning in the light of their purposes and background. The cues in the text help them compose these meanings. In the same way, writers begin to write and construct meaning; their task is to compose meaning so it can be conveyed to a reader. As they write, they think about the topic or plot and develop it; they may have a general idea when they start to write, but they really develop it only as they think more about it in the process of writing.

As the reading process continues, readers reread and change meaning as necessary. Again, writers do the same: they think about what they have written, reread it, and rewrite to make it clearer.

Finally, readers reach a point where they are confident that the meaning they have composed, or constructed, is the best possibility for that given point in time. Writers do the same in their final drafts.

Pearson and Tierney (1984) refer to these four phases as the *planner, composer, editor,* and *monitor* stages. Table 8.1 summarizes the similarities between the reader and the writer as composers (or constructors) of meaning. Of course, readers and writers do not proceed through these stages one after another; they go back and forth between them as they perform the overall process (Dahl & Farnan, 1998; Graves, 1984; Murray, 1985; Pearson & Tierney, 1984).

Proficient readers and writers may use the two processes simultaneously. Think about your own experiences in writing. As you write your ideas, you reread them to

TABLE 8.1 Readers and Writers as Composers of Meaning

Processes	Readers	Writers
Planner	Have purpose for reading	Have purpose for writing
	Generate background	Generate background
Composer	Read and compose meaning	Write and compose meaning
Editor	Reread, reflect, and revise meaning	Reread, reflect, and revise
Monitor	Finalize meaning	Finalize copy

see if they make sense. Often you turn to books or other sources to get more information to include in your writing or to clarify your meaning. The processes of proficient reading and writing not only function in similar ways but also tend to be used together.

Teaching students to write helps them construct meaning by making them more aware of how authors organize their ideas. As they learn to write and organize their own ideas, they will have a greater appreciation and understanding of how other authors do the same.

Writing and Reading Involve Similar Kinds of Knowledge and Processes. There are other reasons reading and writing should be taught together; they naturally develop together (Baghban, 1984; Bissex, 1980; Calkins, 1983; Sulzby & Teale, 1991), and they share many of the same processes and types of knowledge (Tierney & Shanahan, 1991). Researchers have consistently found reading and writing to be highly related (Applebee, 1977; Loban, 1963; Shanahan, 1988; Shanahan & Lomax, 1988), and they have been able to identify some specific similarities, such as the use of similar cognitive processes (Birnbaum, 1982; Langer, 1986; Martin, 1987).

Writing and Reading Improve Achievement. One area that researchers have studied is the effect of teaching reading and writing together on overall achievement. The classic U.S. Office of Education study of first-grade reading concluded that programs that incorporate writing are generally more effective in improving reading than those that do not (Bond & Dykstra, 1967). This conclusion continues to be supported. Research on the effects of teaching writing and reading together concludes that "studies have shown that writing led to improved reading achievement, reading led to better writing performance, and combined instruction in both led to improvements in both reading and writing" (Tierney & Shanahan, 1991, p. 258). Caution must be exercised, however. We cannot say that simply providing instruction in one area will automatically lead to improvements in another area; it depends on how the instruction is provided. All we know is that reading and writing together have benefits that neither taught alone will convey. Also, by teaching writing and reading together, we are able to help students recognize and understand the connections between the two processes.

Writing and Reading Promote Communication. Reading and writing are processes that help us more effectively understand and communicate with one another.

Through this communication, we are able to improve our world, prosper, and enjoy life. Since both communication and learning are social processes, developing reading and writing together has many social benefits.

Writing and Reading Together Develop Critical Thinking. An underlying element of all literacy learning and learning in general is thinking. In combined writing and reading instruction, learners engage in a greater variety of experiences that lead to better reasoning and higher-level thinking than is achieved with either process alone (McGinley, 1988). Since thinking is a critical part of meaning construction, classrooms that actively foster meaning construction through reading and writing will produce better thinkers (Tierney & Shanahan, 1991).

For more detailed discussion of the research on writing and reading, see the "For Additional Reading" section at the end of the chapter.

Let's return to the question posed at the beginning of this section: *Why writing and reading together?* Although reading and writing are both constructive processes that share common knowledge, they are not absolutely the same. Nevertheless, teaching reading and writing together fosters a broad perspective of literacy as a social process; it results in better achievement in both activities and leads to better thinking. Tierney and Shanahan (1991) conclude, "We believe strongly that in our society, at this point in history, reading and writing, to be understood and appreciated fully, should be viewed together, learned together, and used together" (p. 275).

Many classrooms still focus on reading and writing as separate entities, but research supports a view of reading and writing as a single entity called *literacy*. In the remainder of this chapter, we focus on how to build the reading-writing connection.

Standards and Writing

When you read through the IRA/NCTE standards presented in this book, you will note that many of them deal with literacy as a comprehensive process that includes not just reading but oral and written language. There is no question that the literacy processes must be integrated in order for students to become members of the literacy community.

Your state or school may have specific standards that students must meet in order to be considered competent writers. Many states now require students to demonstrate writing ability, which is judged by the use of rubrics. While you must help your students meet these particular standards, don't lose sight of the larger picture: writing as a component of literacy.

Ways to Think About Writing

In Chapter 2, we discussed two types of texts—narrative and expository—and their relationship to meaning construction. Other ways to think about writing are domains, modes, and traits.

Domains

Writing can be seen in terms of broad categories, called **domains,** that somewhat parallel the types of texts students read. The four basic domains for writing are sensory/descriptive, imaginative/narrative, practical/informative, and analytical/expository (McHugh, 1987). Each domain represents a specific purpose for writing. Because different languages may use different styles or patterns for various types of writing, teachers may need to help ELLs understand the patterns used in English.

Being aware of each domain and its purpose helps students clearly develop their own purposes for writing. Knowledge about domains also helps you plan a variety of literacy experiences. Within each domain, many possible student projects may represent the functions and uses of literacy as identified by Heath (1983). Table 8.2 summarizes the four domains of writing. As you will see, many projects may cut across several domains.

Modes

Modes of writing were introduced in Chapter 2.

Another way to think about writing is in terms of **modes of writing.** The five modes are *independent writing,* *collaborative writing* (partners or a small group work together on a single writing product), *guided writing* (parallels guided reading), *shared writing* (group with the teacher; this parallels shared reading), and *write aloud* (teacher writes and verbalizes thinking aloud; students read and listen).

Figure 8.1 shows an example of a collaborative story written by a group of fourth graders. Any of the domains may be addressed in any mode, and the products or projects produced within one domain may also be developed in another domain. Table 8.3 identifies sample products that might be developed in each; notice how some products appear in several domains and modes.

TABLE 8.2 **Domains of Writing**

- *Sensory/descriptive domain:* The sensory/descriptive domain focuses on describing something in such rich and clear detail that the reader or listener can almost see or feel it. Description also incorporates the feelings of the writer.
- *Imaginative/narrative domain:* The imaginative/narrative domain focuses on telling a real or imaginary story. In incorporating some aspects of the descriptive domain, the writer learns to use the elements of a story, including setting, problem, action, and outcome or resolution.
- *Practical/informative domain:* The practical/informative domain presents basic information clearly. The author provides the information without analyzing it.
- *Analytical/expository domain:* In the analytical/expository domain, the writer's primary purpose is to explain, analyze, and persuade. This most abstract form of writing uses elements of all of the other forms. The difference between a report written in this domain and one written in the practical/informative domain is that this report focuses more on *why.*

FIGURE 8.1

Collaborative Story by a Group of Fourth Graders

By Ryan
and Terry
Larry and Stacy Juarez

Once upon a time there were the martians. The first martian said, "Let's explore that planet. Of course, that planet was earth. When they landed, they saw a dog and a man. Suddenly..... the dog started to bark. He got very mad. And then the man saw the martians he was scared and he ran. The martians were scared, too... then Suddenly..., They both ran every which way and bumped into each other and fell to the ground. The martians was about to get up and run but... The dog caught the martions One had a lazer gun and shot the dog in the nose and then... The martions one got a gun. And shot a cat and The cat ran in the Hows.

| TABLE 8.3 | Domains and Modes of Writing with Sample Products or Projects |

| Mode | Domain | | | |
	Sensory/ Descriptive	Imaginative/ Narrative	Practical/ Informative	Analytical/ Expository
Independent writing	Diary Journal Letters Class notes Poems	Letters Short stories Poems	Lists Reports Letters Directions Class notes Invitations	Reports Letters to the editor Reviews Poems
Collaborative writing	Diary Journal Letters Poems	Letters Short stories Poems	Lists Reports Letters Directions Class notes Invitations	Reports Letters to the editor Reviews Poems
Guided writing	Any of the above	Any of the above	Any of the above	Any of the above
Shared writing	Diary Journal Letters Poems	Letters Short stories Poems	Lists Reports Letters Directions Class notes Invitations	Reports Letters to the editor Reviews Poems
Write Aloud	Any of the above	Any of the above	Any of the above	Any of the above

Traits

See Northwest Regional Educational Laboratory in "For Exploration: Electronic Resources and Products" for information about these traits.

Still another way of thinking about writing is based on identified **traits** or characteristics of all good writing, regardless of the age of the writer. The Six-Trait Analytical Assessment model from the Northwest Regional Educational Laboratory (NWREL) gives teachers a way to link instruction and assessment and makes evident that knowing what good writing looks like is essential for becoming a good writer. The NWREL model has spawned as many as fifty versions of the six-trait model. The six traits identified for grades 3 and up are *ideas, organization, voice, word choice, sentence fluency,* and *conventions.* There is a separate continuum of development to help teachers with writers in grades K-2. Complete information, which is continually evolving, is available at the NWREL Web site.

🦋 Activities That Connect Reading and Writing

Throughout your literacy program, you must continually help students see the connections between reading and writing, and think about how each carries over to the other. The following suggestions are a few ways to help students begin to make this explicit connection (Shanahan, 1988).

Reading Specific Types of Writing

Students need to use their writing as a springboard to reading, just as they use their reading as a springboard to writing. If you have a student who has written (or is writing) a mystery, encourage her or him to read some other mysteries, such as *Encyclopedia Brown: Boy Detective* (Sobol, 1963) or *The Mysterious Disappearance of Leon (I Mean Noel)* (Raskin, 1971), to see how these authors developed their ideas.

Reading Student-Written Materials

As students begin to publish, they can read and enjoy one another's books. Student-written books should be displayed in both the classroom and the school library and be used as a part of the reading material for the literacy program. In many schools, student-written books are among those most frequently selected and checked out.

Developing a collection of student-written books is a simple procedure. Begin the school year by telling students that there will be a classroom library of their books and that throughout the year selected books will be placed in the school library. You and your students should develop criteria for selecting books—for example:

1. Well written
2. Favorite topic or story
3. Topic others would most likely enjoy
4. Book student would like others to read

The student-written book collection for the library can become a schoolwide project. At the conclusion of each school year, students may donate a certain number of their books to the library, and copies should then be made so that authors can also have a copy.

As student-written books are added to the school library, special announcements should be made so that everyone in the school can see them. This can be done through a school newspaper or a bulletin board display similar to that in Figure 8.2.

A special time may be designated for students to read the books their peers have written. For example, teachers can designate an hour every other week for this purpose and increase the time to an hour or longer each week as more books are available. Students should use this time to read the books and talk about them in small groups or as a whole class. Be sure to focus on talking about the books, not evaluating them. In some classrooms, guidelines require making only positive comments about a classmate's book.

Having a time in the literacy program for students to read books written by their peers spotlights both reading and writing. It helps show students that these processes are related and also gives them an incentive to read and write.

Summaries

Another way to help students make the connection between reading and writing is to have them write a summary of a text they have just read (Hill, 1991). This is a skill that must be taught. The following steps for summarizing expository texts are based on research by Brown and Day (1983):

FIGURE 8.2

Bulletin Board Publicizing Student Books in the School Library

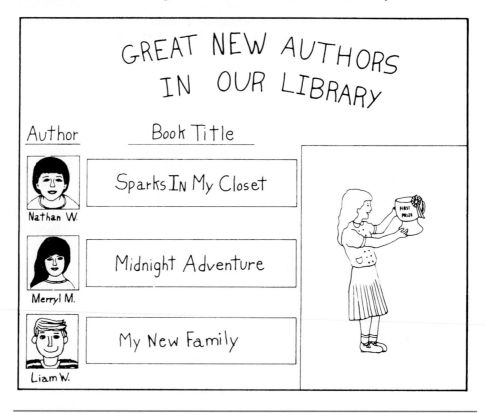

1. Determine the topic of the paragraph or text.
2. Identify unnecessary information or trivia, and delete this information; it should not be included in the summary.
3. Look for information that is repeated; it should be included in the summary only once.
4. Note places where ideas or terms can be grouped together. For example, if the paragraph or text being summarized discusses travel by plane, ship, train, and car, all of these modes can be referred to as "transportation."
5. Identify a main-idea sentence for each paragraph, if possible. If no main-idea sentence exists, formulate one of your own.
6. Formulate your final summary, rechecking to be sure you have followed each guideline. Keep your summary short.

You should model writing a summary for students using procedures similar to those suggested for teaching the writing process, presented later in this chapter. Writing summaries after reading can be handled in creative ways—for example:

* Pretend to be newspaper reporters or TV newscasters who must present a summary of what they have read. First, write the summary; then distribute it to other students in newspaper form, or give the summary as a part of a TV news report.

* Maintain a log or journal that reports a summary of your readings. Write the log entries after reading your favorite selections. (Students can also be instructed to write log entries for particular selections you assign.)

See Chapters 2 and 3 for more about story maps.

Summaries may also be written for narrative texts, in which case the same type of guidelines should be followed, focusing on the parts of a story map instead of main ideas.

Story Frames

A **story frame** is a basic outline for a story that is designed to help readers organize their ideas about what they have read. It consists of a series of spaces hooked together by transition words; each story frame usually follows a single line of thought or aspect of a selection. Story frames focus on story elements and are a good way to build the connection between reading and writing (Fowler, 1982). See Figure 8.3 for examples of story frames.

After students read a selection, you can use the story frame as an oral discussion starter. You should encourage students to fill in the slots in the frame, basing their responses on their reading; encourage them to express the ideas in their own words. When students have become familiar with the concept, you can use story frames in written activities following reading. Although story frames can be written for specific selections, some of the basic patterns can be used repeatedly.

See Chapter 10 for ways to create a climate that promotes and supports writing in your classroom and ways to organize and manage time and materials and keep track of student writing.

Activities such as those just described are necessary but not sufficient for maintaining a reading and writing program.

The next section of this chapter explains how to teach students to use the writing process, followed by a sample lesson using the shared writing routine. We then present information about the conventions of writing, such as spelling, grammar, and usage, and provide sample lessons of each.

Process Writing: A Way to Construct Meaning

Process writing (Calkins, 1994; Graves, 1983, 1991; Hillocks, 1987a, 1987b) is an approach to teaching writing that allows students to take charge of their own writing and learning; it applies to both narrative and expository writing. It has five steps: selecting the topic (sometimes called *planning* or *previewing*), drafting (sometimes called *composing*), revising, proofreading (sometimes called *editing*), and publishing.

FIGURE 8.3

Sample Story Frames

Character Frame

This story is about _____.

_____ is an important character.

_____ tried to _____.

The story ends when _____

_____.

Setting Frame

This story takes place _____

_____. I can tell this because the

author uses such words as _____

_____ to tell

where this story happens.

Plot Frame

This story begins when _____

_____. Next,

_____.

Then _____

_____. The story ends when

_____

_____.

Character Comparison Frame

_____ and _____ are

two characters in our story. _____ is

_____, whereas _____ is

_____. For instance, _____

tries to _____ and

_____ learns a lesson when _____

_____.

A good way to help students become accustomed to using these steps is to display them on a classroom poster such as the one shown in Figure 8.4. We will discuss each of these steps in full.

As you introduce process writing, use write aloud, shared writing, and guided writing to model, guide, and support each step until students take charge of their own

FIGURE 8.4

Poster for Process Writing

FIGURE 8.5

Picture-Writing Phase

writing. Gradually the need for modeling will diminish; however, you will always be a partner in learning with the students, interacting with them through individual and group conferences, discussing their writing ideas, having them share their own writing, and providing minilesson support as needed. Through this continuing scaffolded support, students will grow into writers and come to think of themselves as authors, a process that further develops their ability to construct meaning.

Process writing should begin in kindergarten, where students will be at various developmental phases in their writing. Some will be at the **picture-writing** phase, where they will simply draw a picture for their stories, as the student in Figure 8.5 has done. Other students will be at the **scribble-writing** phase, as shown in Figure 8.6. As students progress, they will move into the **random letter phase** depicted in Figure 8.7 and then into the **invented spelling phase** shown in Figure 8.8, in which they begin to associate some letters and sounds. Finally, they will reach the **conventional writing phase,** in which they will spell most words correctly. It is normal for students in any grade to be at varying points in these stages. Beginning or less experienced writers are more likely to be at the picture, scribble, or invented spelling phases, and more experienced writers are usually closer to the conventional writing phase. In other words, it is normal to see some degree of invented spelling all the way through the elementary grades. Students' invented spelling will reflect their first language; for example, whereas English speakers usually begin with the use of consonants, Spanish-speaking children typically start with vowels (Freeman & Freeman, 1997). Teachers should be aware of these differences.

For more discussion of spelling, see the "For Additional Reading" section at the conclusion of this chapter.

FIGURE 8.6

Scribble-Writing Phase

The following discussion focuses on one way to introduce process writing. As students become comfortable using the steps, teacher modeling can gradually be dropped. Adjust your suggestions to fit the grade level you teach. To begin, have a brief discussion about writing with students. Then show them a chart such as the one presented earlier in Figure 8.4 and talk briefly about each step in process writing, using the name of the step.

FIGURE 8.7

Random Letter Phase

FIGURE 8.8

Invented Spelling Phase

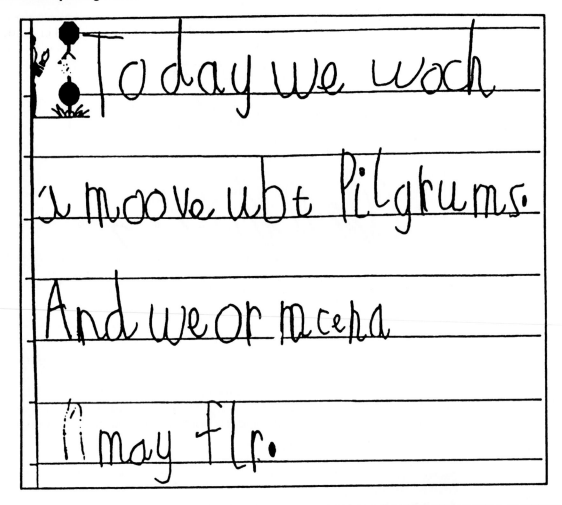

Selecting the Topic

As students learn the process of writing, they should begin to *select their own topics* (**planning/previewing**). The teacher's role in this process is that of guide and facilitator. The following steps will help students learn the process of generating and selecting topics:

1. Give each student a blank sheet of paper, and ask the students to list anything they might like to write about. You may identify the particular domain or product you want them to produce; for example, "Think of some topics you could write a story about" would be appropriate if the focus is on the imaginative/

narrative domain. As students are making their lists, model by making your own list, telling students what you are doing. After finishing your list, move around the room to spot any students who are having trouble. Stop and ask these students such questions as, "What have you read that you would like to write about?" or "What topics are you thinking of?" Don't be critical or condescending; students must feel free to think for themselves and generate their own ideas.

After a few minutes, stop the class and share your list of possible topics, commenting on your reasons for choosing them. Next, ask for volunteers to share their lists, encouraging students to comment on their own and one another's topics. Model positive comments with such remarks as, "Those are all exciting topics"; "I'd like to read a story about that"; "You have so many topics that you are going to have to really think about which one you want to write on."

Be certain your comments are supportive and encouraging regardless of the length of a student's list. After several students have shared their lists, help them see that it doesn't matter whether their lists are long or short; all they need is one idea to begin writing.

2. Have students review their lists to decide whether they want to add any topics. You can model the process with your own list, perhaps by adding a topic similar to one a student has selected. This lets students know that it is all right for them to get ideas from others.

3. Have students review their lists and select a topic for their first piece of writing. Suggest that they consider the following points as they make their decisions: (a) Which topic is the most interesting to you? (b) Which topic do you feel you know the most about? and (c) Which topic do you think others might enjoy reading the most? Have students circle their choices. Then share your choice with the group and have volunteers do the same.

By following these steps, you will help students select their first topic for writing. It doesn't really matter what the topics are as long as the choices are the students' and the students want to write about them.

Students should keep their lists of possible topics in their writing folders and should be encouraged to add to them when they think of new ideas. Of course, they should be assured that they will not necessarily write on every topic on their lists. Their ideas will change; therefore, the lists can change.

Here are some other ways to have students select topics for writing:

See Chapter 3 for an explanation of brainstorming to activate prior knowledge.

- **Partners:** Have each student work with a partner to brainstorm and develop lists of possible topics. This is a particularly good strategy to use for the student who appears to have few ideas or doesn't want to write.

For more on clustering, see the "For Additional Reading" section at the end of the chapter.

- **Clustering:** "**Clustering** is a nonlinear brainstorming process akin to free association" (Rico, 1983, p. 28). Working alone, with partners, or with the teacher, students start with a topic or idea that forms the core, or nucleus, for the cluster. They then add all of the things they can think of that are related to it and select the specific topic from the cluster they wish to write about or use the ideas to develop their writing. Figure 8.9 presents a cluster on animals

FIGURE 8.9

Cluster on Animals Developed by Second Graders

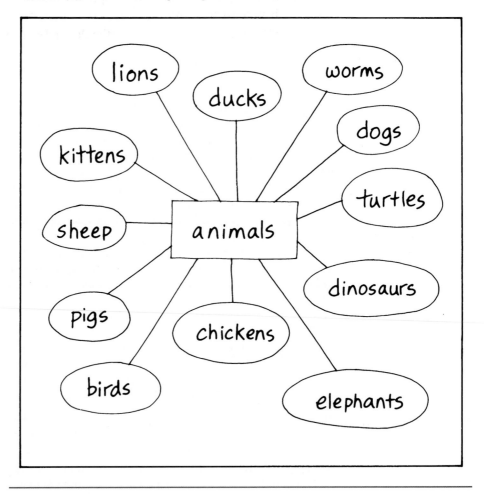

developed by a second-grade teacher and his class to get ideas for writing. Teachers report that clustering is a successful technique to use with all students, including at-risk and second-language learners (Carr, 1987; Martinez, 1987; Pierce, 1987).

- *Looking for ideas away from school:* Encourage students to look for and jot down writing ideas on the way home from school, at home, or in places they visit.
- *Photography ideas:* Let students use cameras to take pictures of possible topics. If possible, have them take pictures away from school as well. You can also encourage them to bring to class photographs from home that could be topics for their writing.

- **TV topics:** Encourage students to look for interesting topics as they watch their favorite TV shows.
- **The Internet:** Students may find a topic while browsing the Internet that prompts them to write about it.
- **Reading:** Books or other reading may stimulate a desire to write about a topic.

Selecting topics for writing is not always easy. Some of the problems students encounter and suggestions for overcoming these problems include the following:

- **No ideas:** Some students will insist they have no ideas to use for writing. One way to help these students is to get them to talk about things they do away from school. As they talk, suggest that each of these activities could be a topic for writing. Another tactic is to ask the students to think about places they would like to go, or something special they would like to do, pointing out that these too can be ideas for writing. You might serve as the students' "secretary," writing their ideas as they give them.
- **Too many ideas:** Some students will have so many ideas that they won't know which one to select for writing. In these cases, you can help students focus by discussing the ideas with them. If discussion doesn't get the student any nearer to making a selection, select one of the topics for the student. One teacher who had tried other strategies to no avail finally said to a student, "Close your eyes and point to a topic. Since you like them all, write about the one you point to." That was enough encouragement to get the child started.
- **Don't like to write:** This problem is tougher to deal with than having too many ideas, and there are no easy solutions. Some students simply don't like to write and don't want to write, for a number of reasons. (And some teachers don't like to write and don't want to teach writing.) These students need to be encouraged to write and helped to see some of the fun of writing, as well as the very practical need for everyone to be able to write clearly. You can begin by serving as the student's secretary, recording not only the topics but also the first draft of the writing. Another tactic is to allow the student to dictate topics onto a tape recorder or enter them in a computer and then write the first draft on the computer. Shared and collaborative writing are also good ways to get students started.

Selecting the topic for writing is a critical part of the writing process. Although there are times when students must write on assigned topics, they must be allowed to choose their own topics when they are learning "how" to write. Even in classes such as social studies, in which students are required to write reports, students are more likely to end up with a good product if they have some choice of topic.

Drafting

Once students have selected their topics, the teacher must show students how to write. **Drafting** has two stages, planning and composing, both of which should be modeled as students are learning to use process writing.

Students work with their teacher at the computer to write a first draft. ©Bob Daemmrich/The Image Works

Planning

Good writers think about what they are going to write and organize their ideas. To do this, they consider the purpose for their writing and their audience. You should model this process using your own topic and the following steps:

1. Tell the class a little bit about your topic and what you want to write about it. Mention your audience and purpose for writing, and allow students to ask questions. Next, on the chalkboard, overhead projector, or large sheets of paper, jot down some of the ideas you have about the topic. Group ideas that go together, but don't be concerned about getting all of them organized at this point. Tell students that you now have a general plan of what you want to include in your writing and you know how you want to begin. Figure 8.10 shows the notes one teacher made while planning to write about her family's camping trip. If you are modeling expository writing, graphic organizers can help.

2. Have students work in pairs, telling each other about their topics. Afterward, have each student jot down some ideas or words about his or her topic on a

FIGURE 8.10

Teacher's Notes for Planning Writing

where we camp
    in the mountains
    at the campgrounds
    in national parks

what we take
    sleeping bags
    tents
    stove
    plastic jugs
    lanterns
    matches

what we do
    walk trails
    sing around fire
    go on nature hikes
    fish

sheet of paper. Volunteers should share their ideas with the class, and talk about what they want to include in their writing. Help students understand that this is a beginning plan for their writing and that it will probably change as they actually write.

As students mature in their writing abilities, you can introduce outlining and include it in modeling when focusing on expository writing. Students will find outlining a useful planning tool for such activities as report writing. They may also use clustering (discussed earlier in this chapter) or semantic mapping to help them organize their ideas.

Semantic mapping is discussed in Chapter 3.

The more students mature in their writing, the less they will need to go through the planning phase as a group. However, students should be given enough teacher modeling and support to see how planning is done and how it can help them in their own writing. The more students write, the more automatically they will carry out the process of writing.

Planning for narrative writing may be less structured, but the process holds for story writing as well as for expository writing. In both, students need guidelines and modeling to help them move from having an idea to sitting down to write.

Composing

The second phase in the drafting stage is the actual composing. Students should be told to write on lined paper (unlined for beginners), using every other line to leave room for revisions. This practice helps them develop a positive attitude toward revision; it lets them know that changes are not only acceptable but are a sign of good writing.

You must model this activity as well, because it is important that the students see the teacher write. Although the teacher and students can write independently and share their results later, this works best with older, more mature writers; it is less satisfactory for beginning writers, since it does not let students see all of the process of writing. For most students, the following procedure will be effective:

1. Using the chalkboard, overhead projector, or large sheets of paper, begin to develop the topic you selected, discussing what you are doing as you go. You may also have technology in your classroom that allows you to compose on the computer and project your work onto a screen. Note the mechanics of starting a sentence and paragraph, and show students how to organize ideas into sentences and paragraphs, asking them to suggest words or make changes in your writing. As you write, cross out some words to show students how to make changes without erasing, which often becomes a big problem for them. Don't be afraid to tell students that you don't know what to say next and that you need some help. Figure 8.11 shows a sample of a teacher's draft for modeling the family camping trip story.

2. After the initial teacher modeling, have students start their own writing using their planning notes. While students are writing, move about the room offering guidance, assistance, and encouragement to those who need it. If some students are not writing, offer to be their secretary for the beginning few sentences of their drafts.

   If the writing is going smoothly, continue to move about the room offering assistance and support. A few minutes of talking about the topic or a few prompts from the teacher are often enough to keep students writing. Give students as much time to write as the schedule will allow and as much time as they can use productively. If you see that the writing time is producing little or nothing, it is probably best to resume modeling or to stop the writing at this time.

   ELLs who are literate in their first language may benefit from doing brainstorming and initial drafting in their first language. This allows them to get ideas down quickly and serves as a basis for what they will later write in English.

FIGURE 8.11

Teacher's Draft for Modeling Writing

> Our family likes to go camping. We usually go to a campground
>
> nearby ~~camp~~, but sometimes we go to the mountains or a national park.
>
> Getting ready to go camping is a big job. We have to take our tents, sleeping bags, and things needed for cooking. Plastic jugs are always needed to store water.

These students do not simply translate what they have written in their first language; instead, they use the draft as a source of ideas for their English writing.

3. If you find it necessary to resume modeling, return to your story and continue to write, explaining as you go. Continue to encourage students to help you. As you model your writing, you can note different elements of good writing. However, during the initial introduction of writing, do not overemphasize isolated mechanics.

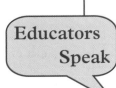

Educators
Speak

A Mobile Lab and Individual Laptops Engage At-Risk Students in the Writing Process

The topic of writing can bring many sighs and expressions of dread to first graders. Even at such a young age, writing is a daunting task and one not enjoyed by all. Many first graders will say they don't have anything to write about or they have completed their piece in one attempt. So you can only imagine what it is like to try and take these students through the writing process.

I have a class of at-risk readers this year. This class was developed so that these students would receive more instruction at their level, with the aid of a reading specialist and a smaller class size. My first graders struggle with all areas of their literacy development. They do not like to write because it is difficult for them. One of the best ways to engage my students in the writing process is through the use of computers.

Writer's workshop began during the first week of school, and this was a real challenge for my students. I was able to make them a part of the writing process with dictated stories. This year my school purchased a mobile (computer) lab, and I am very fortunate to have a set of I-books, so each child is able to have a laptop during writing time. During September I was able to type the stories for the students and they would have a story they had "written." The students would then be able to listen to me read their story, and we could talk about the story elements seen and those missing. We then printed it out and they could illustrate them. As the year progressed, the students wanted ownership over their own laptop and began to take risks and write their own stories. They were encouraged to use their invented spelling, and later we corrected it during the editing process. They can save their story and add to it or change it as they feel is needed. Since each child is able to have his or her own laptop, as they develop their literacy skills, they can move on at their pace. With the use of this technology, there is the possibility of all students working to their potential.

Now that the year is half over, I have a class full of writers with many stories to their credit. The stories look professional, and the students love to share each one they write. I also have the advantage of three other adults in the room to aid in the use of the laptops as well as a smaller class size. I think that all of these components—small class size, more adults, and individual laptops—have helped to create a proficient class of authors.

Caroline Goddard, First Grade Teacher
Parkridge Elementary School
Stafford, Virginia

Composing is the phase of drafting in which students develop their topics. Usually they will have received enough direction up to this point that they can proceed with their own writing without additional instruction. Students should have uninterrupted writing time to develop their ideas. Modeling occurs for individuals as the teacher moves about the room offering assistance.

While composing, students should concentrate on expressing their ideas freely and creatively, using whatever words are in their vocabularies; they should not be hampered by worrying about spelling. During composing, encourage students to spell words the way they think they sound (invented spellings), reassuring them that spelling problems will be taken care of during revision. For students who are overly concerned about spelling words correctly or are unable to use invented spelling, provide the correct spellings by writing the words in question on a sheet of paper or the chalkboard, or tell them to pretend they are alone on an island with no one to ask. Other techniques include having one student serve as a spelling helper or having a list of troublesome words on the board or a chart. *But nothing works as well to develop a sense of spelling as having students try to spell words the way they think they sound and then make corrections during revision and proofreading.*

The amount of time allowed for the composing phase depends on the students, their writing abilities, the nature of the piece being written, and the length of time allocated to writing in the classroom. Usually the composing phase will extend over several days or writing periods. Students can store their writing in their writing folders and return to it at the next writing period or when they have some extra time during the day. If students are composing on the computer, they can save their drafts to disk and store them until the next writing period. The writing, especially in the beginning stages, should be done at school in order to provide supervision and assistance.

Throughout the composing phase, you should continue to be available to help students with their writing. If students get stuck, encourage them to ask you or a peer for suggestions. For example, if a student can't think of a good word to describe his or her old dog, you might give several suggestions and let the student select one of them, or even suggest just using any word for the time being and planning to find the exactly right word when revising. Asking questions and offering suggestions as the students are writing is an extension of modeling and also serves as a quick conference.

Revising

Revising, the third stage in the writing process, is the step in which the students begin to look at their work to examine content—ideas, choice of words, and so forth. Revision may involve modeling by the teacher, conferences between student and teacher or student and student, and individual student work. It is not a natural step for students to employ (Graves, 1984). Most beginning writers, especially kindergartners and first graders, are not ready for much revision; they think everything they have written is wonderful! Gradually, however, teachers must help students learn to appreciate the importance of revision by systematically working through this stage with them.

You can model revision by using your own writing on an overhead or computer projection as an example. You and your students should first discuss what to look for when revising content:

* Have I expressed my ideas clearly so that my audience will understand what I am saying?
* Are there other ideas that I should add to my writing?

- Are there other words that I can use to make my writing more exciting and interesting?
- Are there better ways I can express my ideas?

The questions generated can be posted for students to think about as they work on their revisions. The items considered in content revision will vary according to the students' level and degree of sophistication.

After you and your students have developed guidelines for revision, show them how to go about revising their writing. Use the write-aloud process to show how you would revise your piece. Check each of the points listed on the revision checklist and discuss problem areas with them, making changes with their help. Have them try better ways to express their ideas. Throughout the revision step, you should stress the importance of clear expression because others will read the writing. Figure 8.12 shows a copy of the teacher's story about the family camping trip after the teacher and students revised the content.

See Chapter 10 for a discussion of writing conferences.

Students are now ready to begin to work on their own revisions. At this point, they should begin to have revision conferences with one another and with you. During these conferences, students talk about their writing and look for places where they might make changes, with you and/or other students taking on the role of an editor who asks questions and points out areas for possible improvement. Many students will already know what some of these areas are. The teacher and peers should not become the "fixers" of students' writing; rather, they should help students note places where more work is needed, discuss ideas with students, and have the writers make the changes. Be sure students know that they do not have to make a change they don't agree with; writing belongs to the author.

Proofreading

The fourth step in process writing is **proofreading,** or **editing,** which should take place after students have made all the content changes they believe are necessary. In proofreading, students get their writing in order for the final copy, checking spelling, writing mechanics, and sentence structure. The teacher and students should work together to develop a list of things to look for in proofreading, and the list should be posted in the room so that students can refer to it as they work. In addition to spelling, the list should reflect the writing mechanics that were modeled throughout the writing. Figure 8.13 shows a proofreading checklist developed by a fifth-grade class and their teacher. This generic checklist can be used by the author (writer) or the editor (such as a peer or the teacher) for any domain of writing. As you become more comfortable with process writing, you will want to develop more specific checklists for each domain, varying the items according to the level and sophistication of the students. If students are proofreading a computer document, teach them to use and respond to spelling and grammar checks. They must realize that they are the final decision maker about whether a word is correct, that a computer cannot recognize homonyms as incorrect, and that such elements as paragraphing are beyond the capabilities of a computer to analyze.

Teacher's Story Used for Modeling Revision

Our family likes to go camping. They all have fun.
^We usually go to a nearby campground, but sometimes we go to the mountains or a national park. ^ The campground is my favorite ~~spot.~~

Getting ready to go camping is a big job. We have to take our tents, sleeping bags and equipment ~~things~~ needed for cooking.

Plastic jugs are always needed to store water.

Publishing

The final stage of the writing process is **publishing,** which has two steps: (1) making a final copy of the writing and (2) putting the writing in a form to be shared with others. Although most students will make a final copy of their writing, if they are not making progress with a piece of writing, they may elect to drop it. This may occur at any point in the writing process. Indeed, not all writing should be published. The

---

FIGURE 8.13

Proofreading Checklist Developed by a Fifth-Grade Class

	Author	*Editor*
1. Sentences and questions begin with capital letters.	☐	☐
2. Sentences and questions have the correct end marks.	☐	☐
3. Paragraphs are indented.	☐	☐
4. Possible misspellings have been circled and checked.	☐	☐

Author _____

Editor _____

---

student, together with the teacher, should make this decision after considering both the quality of the writing and how the student feels about it. In a conference, you might ask the student such questions as, "How do you think others will feel about this piece of writing?" and, "Do you think it is a good idea to publish this one?"

Sometimes it is appropriate for the teacher to say, "I don't think this is one of your best pieces of writing. Maybe you should just stop working on this piece or make a final copy for your file and start work on something new." If a student feels strongly that the piece should be published, it is probably best to proceed, but you must always weigh the consequences of having a student publish an inappropriate piece.

Publishing is important for all students, not just a special few. This phase of the writing process authenticates the reason for writing, and gives students pride and enjoyment in their own work. The more students publish their writing, the more they will develop a sense of themselves as authors and grow in the writing process. One precaution: a few students will not want to create final copies or publish. You must support and guide these students until they experience the satisfaction of seeing their work published, because publishing will motivate them to write more.

See Chapter 11 for information about portfolios.

When the decision is to make a final copy only, that copy can be put in the student's writing folder. Even writing that is not published may be used for later review and placed in the literacy portfolio.

Producing Final Copy

After students have completed their revisions and held their initial publishing conference with you, they are ready to make a final copy of their writing. In making their final copy, they should be encouraged to be as neat and accurate as possible. One way to get students to produce a good final copy is to use a computer with a word-processing program, since even very young children succeed with this approach.

You and your students should work together to develop a list of guidelines to follow in making final copies, and the list should be kept where students can refer to it easily. Points such as the following can be included, but each list must reflect the needs, abilities, and level of the students:

Final Copy Guidelines

- Be neat.
- Indent each new paragraph.
- Keep margins at the top, bottom, and sides of the paper straight.
- Check punctuation.
- Check spelling.
- Reread your final copy to be sure it is correct.

The manner in which the final copy is prepared will depend on whether it is to be published or simply filed.

Ideas for Publishing

Publishing is a very important part of the writing process (Calkins, 1994; Graves, 1983). Students need this aspect of the writing process to help them develop a sense of the importance of their writing, an understanding of why one must learn to write, and a sense of their audience.

One way for students to publish their writing is in book form. Individual students can produce their own books, or several students can collaborate on a book. The excitement and pleasure on the faces of students after producing their first book are almost indescribable! Publishing also brings closure to the students' writing experience.

Books can be produced in many forms: construction paper covers over paper, folder books made from manila folders and paper, shape books cut to show the topic (for example, a snowman shape for a winter topic), or hardcover books made from cardboard and cloth.

Students can move from simple types of books to more complex forms as they become more practiced. They should be encouraged to include a cover page that presents their names, the illustrator's name, and the date. At the end of the book, they should place a page titled, "About the Author," on which they describe themselves and other books they have written. Also, when books are to be shared with other classmates, it is a good idea to include a sheet in the back where students can indicate they have read the book and comment on how they felt about it.

There are many other ways for students to share their writing without producing a book. Some of the following ideas broaden the concept of publishing to any form of sharing:

- *Bulletin boards:* Use a bulletin board with a catchy title and an attractive background for students to display final copies that have not been made into a book. The title might be "Great Writing from Great Kids," "Writing We Are Proud Of," "Great Writers Are Blossoming," "Award Winners," and so on. Sometimes you can attach a clothesline to the bulletin board on which students can hang their writing out for others to read.

- *Author's chair:* A special chair may be labeled "Author's Chair" (Graves & Hansen, 1983). The student who has a piece of writing to share sits in the chair and reads it to the group, and a discussion of the writing follows. Usually the piece that is shared is the final copy.

- *Class or school newspaper:* A class or school newspaper is an excellent way to create authentic reasons for students to write. Because of the nature of a newspaper, students can get experiences with many domains of writing and numerous products—articles, stories, letters to the editor, and so forth. The newspaper can have a staff, and students can publish it using a computer.

- *Magazines of student-written works:* Students may choose to submit their writing to a magazine that publishes student-written works.

- *Writing circles:* In a writing circle, students get together to share and discuss their writing. Also referred to as RAGs, or Read Around Groups (Olson, 1987), the writing circle consists of five or six students who sit together to read and talk about (not critique) their writing. Several writing circles may be in operation at the same time. (They may also be used for selecting and discussing a topic, revising, and proofreading. To ensure that students know the real purpose of the circle, it might be better to use the title "Writing Circle" for sharing and "RAGs" when the circle is used for other purposes.)

- *Online postings:* Students may post writing for others to read. Some schools or classrooms have their own Web sites that parents can access.

- *Floppy disk or CD:* Student writing may be published by copying the final work to floppy disk or CD, which other students can read on the class computer. Collections of class stories can be copied to disks for students to take home.

The concept of the literature group or circle was introduced in Chapter 6.

See later in this chapter and "For Exploration: Electronic Resources and Produces" at the end of this chapter for other ideas about online postings.

It does not matter how children publish and share their writing as long as they *do* it, since it is through sharing that they develop their sense of authorship and show how they have constructed meaning by conveying their ideas to others. At any grade level, sharing is an essential part of constructing meaning through writing.

Sample Lesson Using the Shared Writing Routine

The following lesson is a sample of using the shared writing mode to teach both the mechanics of writing and the writing process.

PURPOSE	The Shared Writing Routine is used to model both the mechanics and the process of writing.
WHEN TO USE	This routine is used in the Learning to Write block of the literacy program.
DESCRIPTION/ PROCEDURES	In the Shared Writing Routine, children dictate a text, and the teacher adds his or her own ideas. By using modeling and writing together, you will systematically teach children how to write. Use the following procedures:

1. *Select a Topic*

   - Decide on the type of writing you want students to do—story, information, and so forth.

   - Tell students about the type of writing and define it.

     Example:

     "Boys and girls, we're going to learn to write a story today. Remember, stories have problems and there is a beginning, a middle, and an end."

   - Select a topic for the writing. Have children brainstorm with you and make a list of suggestions.

     Example:

     "What might we write about in our story?
       —a boy who gets lost
       —my new puppy's problem
       —our zoo adventure
     Raise your hand if you agree that the boy who gets lost will be our topic."

2. *Write Together*

   - After the topic has been selected, discuss how the type of writing might begin. Ask students to give ideas; you should feel free to add your own ideas to the writing. As students give ideas, begin to write them using the overhead, large chart paper, or the chalkboard.

     Example:

     A little boy named Roger got lost. He was walking in the woods. He meeted a talking bear. He met a talking tree.

   - When students give an incorrect usage, add a correct example soon after. Note the *meeted/met* example in the story. Continue the writing until you complete the piece.

3. *Revise*

   - On the same day or another day, use the piece you have written together to model ways to improve it. Ask students for ideas as well as giving your own.

   - As students give ideas and you add ideas, write them on the original piece so that everyone can see it. Sometimes you will want to share your thinking as to why you did something. This is modeling or thinking aloud for students.

Example:

> A little boy named Roger got lost. He was
> walking in the woods. He ~~meeted~~ met a talking
> bear. The bear was big. His teeth were
> long. The boy met a talking tree. The bear
> and the tree helped him find his way home.

- Say, "I see one way we need to edit our story: we should change *meeted* to *met—He met a talking bear.* To make our story interesting, we should tell some more about the bear."

- The process continues until the story is revised. Many times you will add content or ideas to the story, not just focus on usage elements.

DISCUSSION/ COMMENTS   The Shared Writing Routine is an excellent way to teach children how to write. In the process, you can also incorporate writing conventions such as spelling and grammar, which are discussed in the next section of this chapter. Following the shared writing, children should write the same type of piece on their own or with a partner.

🦋 Writing Conventions

We discussed the importance of writing in helping children learn to spell in Chapter 5. Writing is also important in helping students learn the various conventions of English.

Formal grammar teaching as a way to promote meaning construction through writing is not a useful activity for students. As Hillocks and Smith (1991) state, "Why does grammar retain such glamour when research over the past 90 years reveals not only that students are hostile toward it, but that the study of grammar has no impact on writing quality?" (p. 602). They also state that "the grammar sections of a textbook should be treated as a reference tool that might provide some insights into conventions of mechanics and usage" (p. 602).

The basic premise that children learn to read and write by reading and writing while receiving instruction as needed also applies to grammar, usage, and spelling. Repeated opportunities to write, which include revising and proofreading, help children learn the conventions of writing and also help them construct meaning through reading. Minilessons held during conferences or in small groups are good ways to support students in learning mechanics, usage, and spelling, and these lessons can be built around a demonstrated need in students' writing. Figure 8.14 shows the steps for using students' writing as a basis for minilessons. This model is based on the work of Wilde (1990, 1996), Gentry (1997), and Gentry and Gillet (1993).

Figure 8.15 presents a sample spelling lesson, and Figure 8.16 shows a sample grammar lesson.

FIGURE 8.14

Six Steps to Meaningful Teaching of Grammar and Spelling Based on Writing

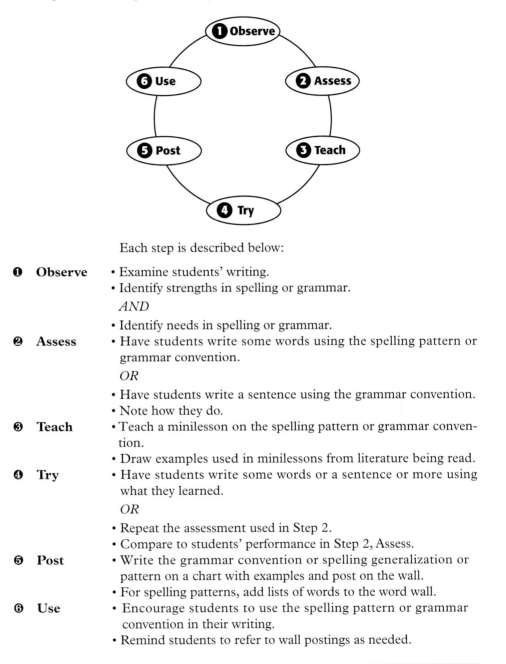

Each step is described below:

❶	**Observe**	• Examine students' writing.
		• Identify strengths in spelling or grammar.
		AND
		• Identify needs in spelling or grammar.
❷	**Assess**	• Have students write some words using the spelling pattern or grammar convention.
		OR
		• Have students write a sentence using the grammar convention.
		• Note how they do.
❸	**Teach**	• Teach a minilesson on the spelling pattern or grammar convention.
		• Draw examples used in minilessons from literature being read.
❹	**Try**	• Have students write some words or a sentence or more using what they learned.
		OR
		• Repeat the assessment used in Step 2.
		• Compare to students' performance in Step 2, Assess.
❺	**Post**	• Write the grammar convention or spelling generalization or pattern on a chart with examples and post on the wall.
		• For spelling patterns, add lists of words to the word wall.
❻	**Use**	• Encourage students to use the spelling pattern or grammar convention in their writing.
		• Remind students to refer to wall postings as needed.

FIGURE 8.15

Sample Spelling Lesson

❶ Observe • Several students have written sentences in their stories like the following:

The dog had muddy feet. He jumped on the chair seet to get the met on the table.

Major Strengths
- Knows beginning consonants *d, m, f, j, s, t*
- Knows high-frequency words *the, had, he, on, to, get*
- Knows the double consonant pattern *dd.*

Needs
- Needs to learn long *e* pattern *ee* and *ea.*
- Needs to learn *ed* ending.

> ✪   Start by teaching a lesson on *ee, ea* words.

❷ Assess • Ask students to write four words on their papers before you teach a minilesson—*beat* (My team will beat your team.), *keep, seat, tree.*

Examples of Students' Second Answers		
1	**2**	**3**
beat	*beat*	*beet*
keep	*ceep*	*keep*
seat	*seat*	*seet*
tree	*tree*	*tree*

❸ Teach • Write the following list* of words on the board:

    see   eat

    three   meat

    sleep   bead

  * (*Note:* Words should be taken from literature students are reading.)

• Have students underline what is the same in each column.

    <u>see</u>   <u>ea</u>t

    thr<u>ee</u>   m<u>ea</u>t

    sl<u>ee</u>p   b<u>ea</u>d

(continued)

Sample Spelling Lesson (continued)

- Read aloud each list (or have the list read aloud).
- Ask what vowel sound you hear in each column of words (long *e*).
- Point out that long *e* may be spelled *ee* or *ea*.

❹ **Try** • Repeat the assessment used in Step 2.

Examples of Students' Second Answers		
1	**2**	**3**
beat	beat	beet
keep	ceep	keep
seat	seat	seet
tree	tree	tree

- Student 1 has the knowledge to spell words using *ea* and *ee*.
- Student 2 understands the *ea/ee* patterns but needs to work on the *k*.
- Student 3 understands the *ee* pattern but needs more work with *ea*.

❺ **Post** • Make a chart.

> Spelling
>
> The long *e* may be spelled *ee* or *ea* in words.
>
> Examples: meat
>   keep

- Add to the word wall.

> Long e
>
> ea   ee
> sea   see
> meat   tree
> seal   sleep
> meal   keep

- Continue to add other words over time.

❻ **Use** • Remind students to check the posting on the chart and the word wall to check their spelling as they write.
- Observe students' writing to see if they are using the *ee, ea* spelling patterns correctly.

FIGURE 8.16

Sample Grammar Lesson

❶ **Observe** • Several students have written sentences like the following:

Student 1

My dad drives a dodge ram truck. His name Harry. The truck is red.

Student 2

We went to california on a Vacation. We had fun and saw

the golden gate bridge.

Student 3

I live in kentucky near Barkley lake. I like to
fish and catch perch.

Major Strengths
   – Capitalizes beginning of sentences.
   – Uses correct end punctuation.
   – Uses nouns.

Needs
   – Does not know difference between common and proper nouns.
   – Does not capitalize nouns correctly.

✪   Teach a lesson on common and proper nouns.

❷ **Assess** • Dictate the following sentences to students:

Mr. Brown likes ice cream. His favorite brand is Blue
Bunny which really is nonfat yogurt.

(continued)

Sample Grammar Lesson (continued)

┌───┐
│ **Examples of Students' Answers**   │
├───┤
│ **1** Mr. Beaver likes ice cream.   │
│   His favorite brand is Blue   │
│   Bunny which really is nonfat yogurt.   │
├───┤
│ **2** Mr. Brown likes ice cream. His favorite brand is │
│   Blue Bunny which really is not fat Yogurt. │
├───┤
│ **3** Mr. Brown likes ice cream. His favorite brand is │
│   Blue Bunny which really is Yogurt.   │
└───┘

❸ **Teach** • Write the following on the board:

> ● A <u>noun</u> is the name of a person, place, or thing.
>
> ● A <u>common noun</u> names any person, place, or thing.
>
> ● A <u>proper noun</u> is a particular person, place, or thing. Capitalize proper nouns.

• Have students open a book that the whole class is reading. Locate examples of common and proper nouns. Make a list of them.

Common Nouns	Proper Nouns
airplane	Boeing 747
ship	the Queen Elizabeth
submarine	Bob Marshall
mountain	Mt. Hood
book	<u>Bridge to Terabithia</u>

• Ask students what they notice about the two groups and how they are capitalized. (Point out if not given.)
• Note that little words like *to* in *Bridge to Terabithia* are not capitalized.

❹ **Try** • Repeat the assessment used in Step 2.

(continued)

Sample Grammar Lesson (continued)

Examples of Students' Answers
1 Mr. Beaver likes ice cream. His favorite brand is Blue Bunny which really is nonfat yogurt.
2 Mr. Brown likes ice cream. His favorite brand is Blue Bunny which really is not fat Yogurt.
3 Mr. Brown likes ice cream. His favorite brand is Blue Bunny which really is Yogurt.

- All students have learned to differentiate between common and proper nouns. Students 2 and 3 need to focus on the word *nonfat*.

❺ **Post** • Make a chart for the wall about common and proper nouns. Add to the list over time.

Nouns
Names of persons, places, or things

dog, baby, house, automobile, airplane, Maple Tree, The White House, table, zoo, The Brookfield Zoo.	

Common Nouns	**Proper Nouns**
Names of any person, place, or thing	Name of particular persons, places, or things. Capitalize proper nouns except for little words in the middle.
dog baby house automobile airplane table zoo	Maple Tree The White House The Brookfield Zoo

❻ **Use** • Remind students to check the posting and use what they have learned in their writing.
- Observe students to see if they are using common and proper nouns appropriately in their writing.

🦋 Using Technology to Support Writing and Reading

Technology is increasingly common in classrooms. Three important types of technology that especially support writing and reading are word-processing and writing programs, the Internet, and software literacy programs.

Word-Processing Tools and Writing Programs

Research has shown that the use of word processing leads students at all levels to write longer pieces and to revise more (Dahl & Farnan, 1998). The teacher still plays a critical role in the process by serving as a monitor and a coach for students. Following is a list of some of the more popular software programs for word processing:

Amazing Writing Machine, Broderbund
The Children's Writing & Publishing Center, The Learning Company
Great Beginnings, Teacher Support Software
Kid Pix Studio, Broderbund
Kid Words 2, Davidson & Associates
Kid's Media Magic, Humanities Software
Magic Media Slate, Sunburst
Media Weaver, Humanities Software
Microsoft Works, Microsoft
The Scholastic Process Writer, Scholastic
Storybook Weaver, MECC
Student Writing Center, The Learning Center
Write Away! Sunburst

The Internet

Web sites on the Internet are another important way to enhance the writing program. Even though Web sites come and go, Dahl and Farnan (1998) identify four related to writing that they feel would be interesting for both teachers and students:

http://www.writingproject.org/

This is the home page for the National Writing Project. It helps teachers stay abreast of research and new ideas on writing.

http://www.kidauthors.com/

KidAuthors is a creative place for students to share stories and poems with people around the world and to read stories and poems written by students around the world.

http://www.readwritethink.org/materials/stapleless/index.html

Stapleless Book is an interactive site that asks students to follow prompts to produce their own books. Students can work with bulleted lists, headlines, and text; they can leave space to add pictures after printing. Everything prints out on one piece of paper. Follow the instructions to fold and cut.

http://www.kidpub.com/kidpub/

This site, known as KidPub, is a place where young writers can read stories written by children from all over the world. They can also submit their own work for publication.

Software Literacy Programs

Software programs that support effective literacy learning are available for classroom use. For example, one series, *The Little Planet Literacy Series* (1996), a research-based program, develops writing, listening, viewing, reading, and thinking together. Lessons can be done by the whole class, cooperative learning groups, or individual students. *Little Planet* programs are well supported technically and theoretically and include a CD component with background on its research base and use, and a Web site at **www.littleplanet.com.**

Summary

This chapter stressed that writing and reading should be taught together because both are constructive processes, share similar types of knowledge and processes, improve achievement in both areas, foster communication, and together produce outcomes that are not achievable by either alone. Writing can be classified by domains, modes, or traits. Various activities that connect reading and writing were discussed.

Process writing was developed as a major procedure for helping students learn to construct meaning through writing. A sample writing lesson using the Shared Writing Routine was presented. The chapter discussed ways to teach spelling and grammar based on needs demonstrated in student writing.

This chapter has presented only a basic overview of how writing and reading work together to help students construct meaning. You will want to read more extensively from some of the sources mentioned in "For Additional Reading," as well as other sources.

For Additional Reading

Booth, D. (2001). *Reading and writing in the middle years*. Portland, ME: Stenhouse Publishers.

Calkins, L. M. (1994). *The art of teaching writing*, 2nd ed. Portsmouth, NH: Heinemann.

Dahl, K. L., Barto, A., Bonfils, A., Carasello, M., Christopher, J., Davis, R., Erkkila, N., Glander, S., Jacobs, B., Kendra, V., Koski, L., Majeski, D., McConnell, E., Petrie, P., Siegel, D., Slaby, B., Waldbauer, J., & Williams, J. (2003/2004). Connecting developmental word study with classroom writing: Children's descriptions of spelling strategies. *The Reading Teacher. 57*(4), 310–319. Durr, D. (2003). Struggling readers get hooked on writing. *The Reading Teacher, 56*(6), 518–525.

Dorn, L. J., & Soffos, C. (2001). *Scaffolding young writers: A writers' workshop approach*. Portland, ME: Stenhouse Publishers.

Gentry, J. R. (1987). *Spel . . . is a four-letter word.* Portsmouth, NH: Heinemann.

Gentry, J. R., & Gillet, J. W. (1993). *Teaching kids to spell.* Portsmouth, NH: Heinemann.

Graves, D. H. (1983). *Writing: Teachers and children at work.* Exeter, NH: Heinemann.

Harwayne, S. (2001). *Writing through childhood: Rethinking process and product.* Portsmouth, NH: Heinemann.

Helman, L.A.(2004). Building on the sound system of Spanish: Insights from the alphabetic spellings of English-language learners. *The Reading Teacher, 57*(5), 452–460.

Henk, W.A., Marinak, B.A., Moore, J.C., & Mallette, M.H. (2003/2004). The Writing Observation Framework: A guide for refining and validating writing instruction. *The Reading Teacher, 57*(4), 322–333.

Kern, D., Andre, S., Schilke, R., Barton, J., & McGuire, M.C. (2003). Less is more: Preparing students for state writing assessments. *The Reading Teacher, 56*(8), 816–826.

Scala, M. C. (2001). *Working together: Reading and writing in inclusive classrooms.* Newark, DE: International Reading Association.

Strickland, D. S., Ganske, K., & Monroe, J. K. (2001). *Supporting struggling readers and writers.* Portland, ME: Stenhouse Publishers.

🖳 For Exploration: Electronic Resources and Products

The following Web sites and electronic resources should be helpful as you work to teach reading and writing together:

Web Sites

http://www.kidsonlinemagazine.com/
Kidsonline Magazine is a Web site that encourages children to write by allowing them to send in their work to be published on the site. Check out "Writing Tips" and "Teacher's Corner."

http://www.magicoul.com/
Magicoul's Nook is a Web site dedicated to presenting the best of middle school writing. Here, writers in grades 5 through 8 can publish their work. Short fiction, poetry, opinion, real-life happenings—anything goes.

http://www.nwrel.org
The Northwest Regional Educational Laboratory Web site provides complete information about the initial and continuing development and revising of the 6 + 1 traits of writing. At this site, you can read about the history of the model, read descriptions of each of the traits, see the continuum for beginning writers, and learn about scoring for writers in grades 3 and up. You can also find out about resources and training opportunities.

http://www.realebooks.com

This Web site provides a printing template for publishing books on the Internet. It correlates with the book *Real e Publishing, Really Publishing!* by Mark Condon and Michael McGuffee (2001), Heinemann, Portsmouth, NH. This book and its correlated Web site provide many sound suggestions for helping students of all ages create digital books.

Software

Imagination Express
by Edmark
http://www.edmark.com

Kid Pix, The Print Shop Deluxe, Storybook Weaver, and The Student Writing Center
by The Learning Company
http://www.learningco.com/Category.asp?CID=208

Kid's Media Magic and **Write On! Plus, Integrated Language Arts for Grades K–12**
by Humanities Software, Inc.
http://www.humanitiessoftware.com

Microsoft PowerPoint and Microsoft Word
http://www.microsoft.com

Write:OutLoud and **Co:Writer 4000** [talking word processors]
by Don Johnston
http://www.donjohnston.com

Helping Struggling Readers

✓ **STANDARDS FOCUS**

NCTE/IRA Standards: 1, 2, 3, 4, 5, 6, 7, 8, 9, 10, 11, 12
Standards for Reading Professionals: 1, 2, 3, 4, 5

"Educators Speak   p. 395

Helping Struggling Readers
—*Leslie Ericson-Alti, Rio Rancho, New Mexico*"

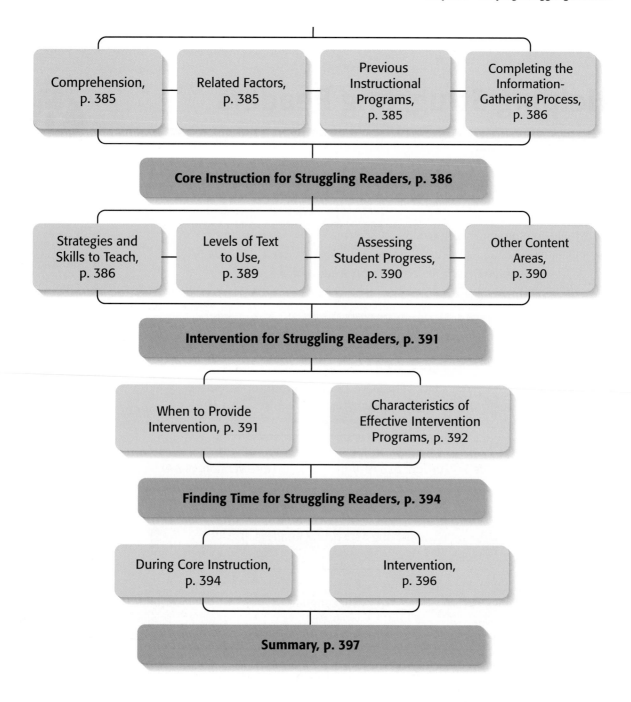

Terms
You Need to Know

- acceleration
- adequate yearly progress
- frustration
- graphic organizers
- independent
- instructional
- intervention
- jump-start
- more than adequate yearly progress
- reading intervention program
- reciprocal teaching
- remediation/ remedial reading
- scaffolded
- struggling reader

*F*ranklin School is a K–6 elementary school with 728 students who come from a full range of economic levels. Most students ride a bus to school. There are seventeen different languages represented in the school. Today we are visiting Mr. Lazio in his first-grade classroom and Ms. Crystal in her sixth-grade class.

Mr. Lazio has just completed reading instruction for the morning. All twenty-one boys and girls in his class participated in the instructional activities of the day. Mr. Lazio directs students to a variety of centers in the room, where they are to work on a number of different activities involving independent reading and writing, doing projects, or practicing needed skills.. He reviews with them the directions chart posted at the front of the room and discusses with students what they should do if they encounter any problems.

Mr. Lazio then calls a small group of seven students to the reading table, where he conducts a 30-minute reading lesson using two short books. Each student begins by silently rereading a book that he or she completed in a previous lesson. As the students read for 5 minutes, Mr. Lazio listens to one student read and coaches him as needed. This activity is followed by some phonemic awareness and phonics instruction using three consonants and two short vowels. This activity lasts for about 10 minutes.

Next, Mr. Lazio introduces the new book for the day; we notice immediately that the text has many words with the letter sounds that were just taught to the group. Students first read the book silently. Then Mr. Lazio asks different students to take turns reading sentences aloud. As the students read orally, Mr. Lazio jots down notes about how accurately each student reads. The lesson concludes with the group dictating a sentence about the book they have just read. Mr. Lazio records it on a chart.

As we leave the room, Mr. Lazio explains that the group we saw consisted of his seven most struggling readers. He notes that he gives them 30 minutes additional reading instruction four days a week.

Next we go to Ms. Crystal's room. As we arrive, six students are leaving the room for reading class. Ms. Crystal tells us that she has just finished her day's reading lessons and these students are going to Miss McMurray, the reading teacher, for additional reading instruction. Ms. Crystal suggests that we go with these students to see what they do in this extra reading time.

Miss McMurray conducts a lesson using a teaching strategy known as reciprocal teaching (see Chapter 4). We can tell that the group started the book on the previous day. They begin by summarizing their previous day's reading using a graphic organizer Students work together with partners as Miss McMurray has them complete a cooperative preview of the section of the book the group is going to read today; they pose a question that they think will be answered in the text. Next, students read the text silently and then take turns with Miss McMurray modeling the four strategies of reciprocal teaching: question, summarize, clarify, and predict. The students conclude the lesson by writing about what they read and then discussing the process as well as their understanding of what they read.

As the students walk back to their class, we stay to talk with Miss McMurray. She explains that these are some of Ms. Crystal's lowest readers. She noted that their reading has improved several levels over the last six months.

In the two classes we visited, we encountered **struggling readers:** students who were having difficulty learning to read. Think about what happened in each classroom:

* The struggling readers in both classrooms received the same core reading instruction that the entire class received.

* Mr. Lazio conducted the additional instruction that his group received in the classroom while other students did enrichment work at centers.

* Ms. Crystal's group went to the reading teacher for their additional reading instruction, but they did not miss any of the core reading instruction provided in the classroom.

* Mr. Lazio's group of struggling readers had additional instruction that focused on elements of fluency, phonemic awareness, and phonics. They read short texts that allowed them to apply immediately what they had been taught.

* Miss McMurray used reciprocal teaching, a strategy that works effectively to help older struggling readers accelerate their reading (Palincsar & Brown, 1986; Oczkus, 2003).

Both classrooms reflect effective ways to help struggling readers. In this chapter, we discuss all of the techniques seen in Mr. Lazio's, Ms. Crystal's, and Miss McMurray's classrooms, plus others to help struggling readers. First let's explore who our struggling readers are.

🦋 Who Are Struggling Readers?

A struggling reader is any student who is having difficulty learning to read. The student may have difficulty with oral language, phonemic awareness, phonics, vocabulary, comprehension, motivation, or some other factor that prevents adequate yearly progress. A student who is struggling with reading may exhibit difficulties in one or all of these areas. No two struggling readers are exactly the same.

Some struggling readers have their situations complicated by other issues, such as health problems, visual problems, auditory problems, environmental issues, or background issues. For students whose reading problems are complex, the reading specialist, psychologist, school nurse, or other specialist should be contacted for help in working out a plan of action for the child. To determine whether a student has a complex reading problem requiring the services of one or more specialists, begin by doing a thorough diagnosis as described in this chapter and developing a treatment plan. Follow the diagnosis by trial teaching and ongoing assessment to determine whether the treatment plan is working. If at the end of four to six weeks you see that the student's reading is not improving, seek the services of a reading specialist or other learning specialist. If your district does not have a reading specialist, contact a local college or university to find out what services are available in your area.

No reading problem is simple. However, most reading problems can be helped through good instruction. For many years, the usual approach to struggling readers was to provide **remediation** or **remedial reading.** *Remediation* is the process of correcting a deficiency. Essentially teachers waited until the child had an established problem and then tried to correct it. This approach has not been successful or effective (Allington & Walmsley, 1995; Snow, Burns, & Griffin, 1998) in helping struggling readers overcome their problems, primarily because this instruction tends to focus on students' weaknesses in skill areas and not enough on actual reading.

A more accepted approach now is **intervention.** By definition, intervention is the act of coming into or between so as to hinder or alter an action. A **reading intervention program** is one that either prevents or stops failure by providing additional instructional time. With reading intervention, we don't wait for a problem to occur; instead, we recognize that a student is beginning to struggle with reading and provide the necessary instruction to help him or her catch up.

See Chapter 2 for more discussion of adequate yearly progress.

All schools today are striving to help students achieve **adequate yearly progress,** generally defined as a month of growth for a month of instruction. Struggling readers who are reading two, three, four, or more years below level will never catch up with just adequate yearly progress. These students must make **more than adequate yearly progress** in order to catch up and ultimately read on grade level. Therefore, helping struggling readers requires **acceleration** of their reading, increasing the rate of growth so they will have more than a month's growth for a month of instruction.

🦋 The Comprehensive Literacy Program, Standards, and Struggling Readers

For a detailed discussion of the Comprehensive Literacy Program, see Chapter 2.

The best way to deal with reading problems is to prevent them from occurring by providing good instruction. This is what this text and our model for a comprehensive literacy program are all about. Our model for a comprehensive literacy program consists of two main parts: core instruction and intervention.

Core Instruction

Core instruction has six blocks: Daily Independent Reading, Daily Independent Writing, Reading: Learning Skills and Strategies, Reading: Application of Skills and Strategies, Writing: Learning to Write, and Writing: Developmentally Appropriate Writing. These six blocks are provided for all students—those who are developing literacy skills as we would expect as well as those who are struggling. The standards for your school or state guide the content of your program for all students. All students, those who are struggling and those who are not, follow the same standards.

Intervention

Intervention, the second part or seventh block of the comprehensive literacy program, is designed to help struggling readers make more than adequate yearly progress. Intervention can be thought of as having two levels. The first level consists of activities that can be delivered on a day-to-day basis to help struggling readers be successful within the core instruction. For example, if a struggling reader lacks background for a particular selection, you might provide a **jump-start** for the selection by doing a very structured, guided preview with this student and others needing this support before introducing the selection to the whole group. Jump-start activities give struggling readers a head start with a learning task before they actually begin it with other students.

See Chapter 5 for more discussion on previews and picture walks.

The second level of intervention is the acceleration type, which is designed to raise students' reading levels at a rate that is faster than would be expected and thus lead to more than adequate yearly progress. The extra reading instruction that Mr. Lazio and Miss McMurray provided shows acceleration in action. Acceleration intervention is characterized by a number of critical features:

- Instruction is very structured and fast paced.
- It is delivered in addition to the core instruction.

For a discussion of authentic texts, see Chapter 2.

- Texts used for instruction are sequenced in difficulty, moving from simple to more complex. Beginning texts may be created and more decodable. As soon as possible, students move to reading authentic texts.
- The teacher provides **scaffolded** instruction by providing lots of teacher modeling in the beginning, moving to student modeling and then to independence.
- The instruction is delivered as a one-on-one tutorial program or as a small group of five to seven students.

See Chapter 11 for a discussion of assessment.

- Ongoing assessment is a part of the instruction. This lets you continuously know whether what you are trying for each student is really working.
- Acceleration intervention is taught by a certified teacher.

Both the core instruction and intervention are developed using the same standards as are used to guide instruction for all other students. Struggling readers need both good core instruction and acceleration intervention to make more than adequate yearly progress.

🦋 Identifying Struggling Readers

Your first task as a classroom teacher is to evaluate each student's reading and determine which students are struggling and what instruction each one needs. To do this, you will need to make the following decisions:

1. Determine how each student is reading.
2. Decide which students are struggling and need more than the regular core instruction.
3. Plan the core instruction and intervention for the struggling readers in accordance with your program and available resources.
4. Carry out the instruction, continually evaluating and revising in the light of student performance.

Figure 9.1 presents a reading evaluation checklist that will guide the decision-making process that you need to follow in order to identify the struggling readers and plan their instruction. Look over the checklist, noting the areas to be evaluated. Some of the information that you need may be available from the students' cumulative records. In some cases, you will need to do some assessment and gathering of information of your own. Always begin by checking the records to see what information is already available.

In the following sections, we discuss each of the areas on the checklist presented in Figure 9.1. The remainder of the chapter then focuses on planning and carrying out core instruction and intervention with struggling readers.

Reading Levels

First, you need to determine each student's reading levels: **independent, instructional,** or **frustration.** You can do this by using an informal reading inventory (IRI) or a running record with leveled texts. You can also do this by having students read different leveled texts, and noting both their decoding skills and comprehension. This information will help you decide which level of text you need for starting instruction, and know what level the student can read independently. It will also help you plan all aspects of your instruction including fluency practice. If you are working with a nonreader, move on to the next area of concern, oral language.

For more information on determining reading levels, see Chapter 11 and "For Additional Reading."

Oral Language

Oral language is the foundation for learning to read. You need to determine what type of oral vocabulary each student has, whether the student can express himself accurately and effectively, and how well the student listens. Observation in the classroom is the most efficient way to gather some of this information. Give each student an opportunity to talk by telling about himself or herself; note the vocabulary used and how the student uses language. You will not have a quantitative score. Rather, you will have your general observations about how the student uses vocabulary and language. This assessment will help you determine what the student's background, vocabulary, and general oral language are like. You will be able to tell which students need more oral language development.

To determine the student's level of listening, use a series of graded (leveled) passages. Read aloud the passages and then ask questions orally. The highest grade level where the student can answer 75 percent of the questions correctly is considered this student's listening level. By comparing this score to the student's reading level, you can tell how much growth this student is likely to make. Look at Example 9.1:

Example 9.1

> Gilberto: Grade 2–Instructional Reading Level–1
> Listening Level–4
> Santiago: Grade 2–Instructional Reading Level–1
> Listening Level–1

FIGURE 9.1

Reading Evaluation Checklist

Name _____ Date _____

Grade _____ Teacher _____

Area Being Evaluated	Findings/Comments
1. Reading Levels	Independent _____ Instructional _____ Frustration _____
2. Oral Language	Listening Level _____ General ability to use language: _____ _____ _____
3. Decoding	Phonemic Awareness: _____ _____ Phonics: _____ _____ Fluency: _____ _____
4. Comprehension	Background/Prior Knowledge: _____ _____ _____ Strategies: _____ _____

(continued)

Reading Evaluation Checklist (continued)

Area Being Evaluated	Findings/Comments
5. Related Factors	What other factors seem to be affecting this student's reading? _____ _____
6. Previous Program	What type of instruction has been provided for this student before? _____ _____

Instructional Plans

Core Instruction

Reading Level: _____

Materials: _____

_____

Skills: _____

_____

Intervention

_____

_____

Comments:

_____

_____

_____

A teacher administers an Informal Reading Inventory.

© Michael Zide

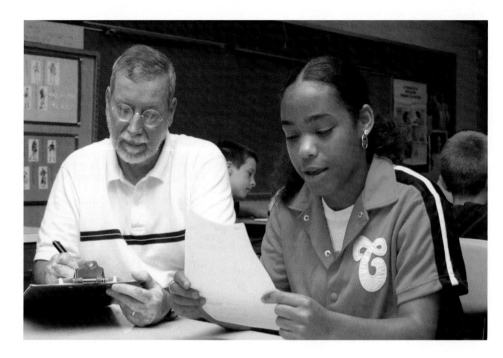

For more information about the content of phonemic awareness, phonics, and structural analysis, refer to the Handbook Resource at the back of this text.

For more information about assessing a student's decoding needs, including phonemic awareness, phonics, fluency, and comprehension, see Chapter 11 in this text and Cooper and Kiger (2005) listed in "For Additional Reading" at the end of this chapter.

Gilberto's listening level is three grade levels higher than his reading level: clearly, he has the oral language base that should be sufficient for his reading to improve once she is given the appropriate instruction. Santiago's reading and listening levels are the same: he needs a strong oral language program as a part of his reading instruction.

You can give the listening test to a group of students or the entire class. To do this, convert the questions that accompany the passages you are going to use to multiple-choice items. Then read aloud two passages below the students' actual grade placement and at least two levels above the students' grade placement. Use the same scoring criteria as discussed above.

Decoding

In this area, you need to gather information about how the student uses phonemic awareness, phonics (including use of structural elements), and fluency. When you listen to each student read orally, note the student's miscues and analyze them to determine the student's ability to use phonics and structural analysis. For phonemic awareness, you can use informal observations (Cooper & Kiger, 2005) or a test like the Yopp-Singer Test of Phoneme Segmentation (Yopp, 1995). For fluency assessment, you will need to take a one-minute fluency check (Hasbrouck & Tindal, 1992).

Comprehension

In the area of comprehension, you need to know the student's general level of comprehension as well as his or her ability to use the important comprehension strategies discussed in Chapter 4—visualizing, monitoring, inferencing, identifying important information, generating and answering questions, summarizing, and synthesizing. The specific strategies you assess will depend on the student's level of functioning. For example, for students at the beginning reading level, assess only a few of the strategies, such as identifying important information, inferencing (including predicting), and summarizing. The student's general level of comprehension can best be determined from the informal reading inventory when you are determining the reading levels and/or by using the process of retelling as discussed in Chapter 11. The use of strategies can best be determined by having the student read text appropriate to his or her level and then model the use of each strategy.

Related Factors

Among the many factors that can affect how students learn to read are home environment, vision, hearing, general health, interest, and attitude. If a student has a problem or issue in one of these areas that may be affecting his or her learning to read, you need to be aware of it. In many instances, you may not be able to do anything about it in the classroom and may need to seek outside help. Always begin by checking the student's cumulative record to get as much information as possible. Then do the following as needed:

- Interview the student. Try to identify the student's feelings about learning to read and anything that may be causing him or her problems.

- Meet with the student's parents or guardian to discuss the student's reading. Get their perceptions of how the student is performing. Discuss the student's general health.

- If you have a school nurse, request a vision and hearing screening. If no school nurse is available, explore options that are available within the community.

See Chapter 11 for information on interest inventories.

- Have the student complete an interest inventory or attitude survey, or both. This information will let you know what really interests the student. This will help you in selecting materials to use for instruction and let you know how to direct the student in selecting materials to be read independently.

Gathering this information will help you more fully understand the student's reading. Knowing about many of these factors will make it easier for you to plan instruction for the student and help you know how to relate to him or her.

Previous Instructional Programs

If possible, you need to find out what type of instruction the student has had in the past. What has seemed to help? What has not worked? Has the student been involved in any intervention programs? Were these programs helpful? Knowing this information will help you decide how to approach this student in the classroom as well as make decisions about what other instruction and interventions you might try.

Completing the Information-Gathering Process

Once you have completed gathering as much information as possible in each of these six areas, use the checklist in Figure 9.1 to summarize what you have learned. You will know which students are struggling in learning to read. You will know their reading levels; have a picture of their oral language development; and know how they are doing in terms of phonemic awareness, phonics, fluency, overall comprehension, and using comprehension strategies. You should have a better understanding about any extenuating circumstances that may be influencing the student's learning to read. You may have some information about what types of instruction have been tried for this student and what worked and did not work.

With this type of information available, you should now be able to proceed with planning the core instruction for struggling readers. You should also be able to decide what additional intervention is needed and plan how to provide intervention depending on what is available in your school. Figure 9.2 shows what a completed checklist might look like.

🦋 Core Instruction for Struggling Readers

All the principles and guidelines for effective literacy instruction that are presented throughout this text also apply to struggling readers. All struggling readers, including students in special education, need high-quality classroom instruction. The intervention instruction that they might receive, whether provided by the classroom teacher or by another teacher, is *in addition to* the core instruction they receive in the classroom. (How to find time for intervention is discussed later in this chapter.)

Planning core instruction for struggling readers requires careful thought and continuous monitoring on your part as the teacher. However, it is very rewarding for both you and your students when you see the results in terms of your students' success. As you plan core instruction for struggling readers, there are four important factors to consider: strategies and skills to teach, level of texts to use, assessing student progress, and other content areas.

Strategies and Skills to Teach

You need two sets of strategies and skills in order to teach struggling readers:

1. The strategies and skills you determined from your diagnosis that the student is lacking.
2. The grade-level strategies and skills that you are required to teach.

FIGURE 9.2

Completed Reading Evaluation Checklist

Name _Lisa R._____ Date _9-8_____

Grade __4___ Teacher __C. Spaulding_____

Area Being Evaluated	Findings/Comments
1. Reading Levels	Independent _1___ Instructional _2-3_ Frustration _4__
2. Oral Language	Listening Level _6___ General ability to use language: _seems shy but has good oral language in social situations. Has lots of knowledge to share in groups._
3. Decoding	Phonemic Awareness: _Passed all tests on district PA Test_ Phonics: _Knows all basic phonic skills; unable to apply to longer words._ Fluency: _97 words per minunte. Below expected progress._
4. Comprehension	Background/Prior Knowledge: _Seems to have good background knowledge; often does not share._ Strategies: _Makes good predictions; does not monitor, summarize, or synthesize._

(continued)

Completed Reading Evaluation Checklist (continued)

Area Being Evaluated	Findings/Comments
5. Related Factors	What other factors seem to be affecting this student's reading? _Wears glasses, but has no other problems._
6. Previous Program	What type of instruction has been provided for this student before? _Has been in special reading class for 2 years._

Instructional Plans

Core Instruction

Reading Level: _3_

Materials: _Use grade level basal anthology & leveled books at 3rd grade level_

Skills: _Decoding longer words strategy; monitoring, summarizing, & synthesizing_

Intervention

Talk with parents and special reading teacher about available options.

Comments:

Needs to have self-confidence developed. Work on fluency as part of reading program. Ask parents to consider a private tutor.

See Chapter 10 for information on flexible grouping.

See Chapters 2, 3, 4, 5, and 6 for detailed information on skill teaching.

The strategies and skills that you have determined the student is lacking, either because they were not taught or the student did not learn them, are taught during intervention, which we will discuss later in this chapter.

Some of the grade level skills may be taught to the whole class including the struggling readers. However, most of the time, the struggling readers will work with you in a separate small group because you will need to adjust your instruction to their needs. Adjust your skill instruction in a variety of ways to meet the individual needs of the struggling readers:

- Provide more modeling of the strategy or skill being taught.
- Break the skill or strategy instruction into shorter segments or more component parts.
- Give students more guided practice before allowing them to do independent practice.
- Provide more reteaching of strategies and skills as well as practice.
- Allow more time for reading of text that offers students the opportunity to apply the strategies and skills.

Adjusting instruction for struggling readers requires continuous monitoring on your part as the teacher. As you teach or reteach the skills and strategies, check continuously to see that students are applying them in texts they can read.

Level of Texts to Use

For more information on modes of reading, see Chapter 2.

You will need two levels of text to use for each student: the grade-level text and a text that is appropriate for each student's reading level. When struggling readers are reading from the grade-level text, they should work in a small group under your direction. In this small group, you will vary the modes of reading to accommodate the individual needs of your students. You will need to provide more structured guided reading, sometimes even guiding the reading line by line. Many times you may alternate between using the Teacher Read Aloud mode and the students reading a short section independently. On other occasions, you will use the Shared Reading mode. By changing the mode of reading, you are able to scaffold support, moving from heavy teacher support to student independence. It is important for students to read at least some of the text successfully, though they may not read the entire text. This is how you make students successful with the grade-level text. This also allows struggling readers to see themselves as being successful with the grade-level text. When there is a whole-class discussion of the grade-level text, struggling readers who have been given guidance can be successful in participating with the remainder of the class.

The second text needed for each student is one that is appropriate to the student's instructional reading level. Students will work in a group with other students who are at a similar level. Using this text, students will apply the grade-level skills they learned but using text that they can easily read successfully. Usually the mode of reading is silent guided reading, where students read a section to check their predictions or answer questions that they share with you during follow-up discussion. As soon as you are sure students can successfully read one level of text with a mode that provides strong support, move the mode to more independent reading. When students can successfully read that text independently, advance them to the next higher level of text. With all readers, and especially struggling readers, the goal is to advance their levels as quickly as possible. This is necessary in order for them to make more than adequate yearly progress. Without this accelerated progress, struggling readers will remain forever behind.

Assessing Student Progress

For more information on oral reading checks and fluency progress checks, see Chapter 11 of this text and books listed in "For Additional Reading."

For information on AIMSweb or DIBELS go to their respective Web sites: **http://www.aimsweb. com** *and* **http://dibels. uoregon.edu/.**

Continual assessment of progress for struggling readers is critical. You need to monitor their growth in knowledge of strategies and skills and their application of these strategies and skills as they read increasingly difficult texts.

You can determine student growth in strategy and skill knowledge by noting how they are performing in each area on daily work. Another important way to do this is through periodic oral reading samples and fluency progress checks. For struggling readers, fluency progress checks should be made every two to three weeks.

You can also use a published assessment system such as AIMSweb or DIBELS (Dynamic Indicators of Basic Early Literacy Skills). Both are systems for monitoring student progress in literacy.

Application of strategies and skills in increasingly difficult texts can be determined as students work in texts appropriate to their reading level and through the use of informal reading inventories and running records. Each student's level of progress should be reevaluated at least three or four times during the school year, and more often if you deem it appropriate.

Other Content Areas

See Chapter 4 for information on teaching strategies.

Another major concern about working with struggling readers is how to help them in other subject areas such as science and social studies. Readers in general often have difficulty adjusting the use of their reading strategies to informational texts, and struggling readers in particular have this problem. Therefore, as we have noted throughout this text, it is important to teach all students how to use their reading strategies in narrative and expository texts.

Since struggling readers are unable to read the text adequately, how are they to learn? First, remember that not all learning in science, social studies, or other content areas occurs through reading. Many hands-on activities can and should take place to make learning more effective. Therefore, always consider using as many of the following types of activities as possible in order to make learning more effective for struggling readers:

- **Focus on pictures and illustrations.** When texts contain pictures and illustrations that convey some of the content, guide students in looking at them to gain information. This can be done in small groups of mixed ability levels. ELLs and other students can also benefit from this type of activity.

- **Experiments.** Make use of experiments in science where struggling readers can draw conclusions from the results they see. Help students read directions by printing them on charts or cards, broken down into simple steps.
- **Role playing.** Set up role-playing situations where students act out certain events. Follow each role-playing scene with discussions where conclusions are drawn and group summaries are written.
- **Video, audio, and CD-ROM.** Use a variety of media to support learning. Videos, audiotapes, and CD-ROMs can help struggling readers attain the content you want them to learn.

As you select activities for content-area teaching, keep struggling readers in mind. Choose activities that will help them access content through means other than reading.

For information on guided reading, see Chapter 2.

To help struggling readers improve their reading of content material, use what you have learned about the guided reading mode to assist them. Make the guided reading very structured by breaking the text into small chunks of paragraphs or even sentences. Before beginning the guided reading, introduce the key vocabulary for each section. Use a picture walk or structured preview to introduce key concept words.

See Chapters 3, 5, and 6 for information on prior knowledge, vocabulary, and introducing text.

You may also locate reading material on the subject that may be easier for struggling readers. Such material may cover the important concepts of the topic but include less extraneous information and fewer details.

🦋 Intervention for Struggling Readers

Intervention is additional instruction that prevents or stops reading failure. Research has clearly demonstrated that some students will never achieve complete success in reading without instructional support that is given in addition to the core instruction provided in the classroom (Snow, Burns, & Griffin, 1998). We have discussed how to adjust core instruction for struggling readers. Here we discuss when to provide intervention and give the characteristics of effective intervention programs, along with descriptions of some existing programs.

When to Provide Intervention

Intervention may be provided in a number of ways:

- **In the classroom as a small group taught by you or another teacher who comes into the room.** If you provide the intervention in addition to the core instruction, the challenge you face is finding the time to do it. If another teacher comes into the room to conduct a small intervention group, the question becomes, "What does the student miss?" The best answer we can give is that the student should never miss the core instruction in reading and language arts or math. (We discuss the time issue in more detail later in this chapter.)
- **As a pullout program.** Struggling readers leave the classroom for instruction provided by another teacher, usually a reading specialist. The students who

attend these programs should never miss the core reading or language arts instruction or math. Pullout programs are easier than in-class programs for you as the classroom teacher to manage.

- **Extended-day programs.** Extended-day programs take place before or after the time for the regular school day. The advantage of this type of intervention program is that students do not miss any of the regular instructional day. You have to consider whether students are too tired or too involved in other activities to attend an instructional program before or after school.

- **Summer school.** The primary issue that must be considered here is whether the period of time is long enough to make a significant difference in the student's learning.

Characteristics of Effective Intervention Programs

Considerable research has been conducted on various types of intervention programs (Hiebert & Taylor, 1994; Pikulski, 1994; Snow, Burns, & Griffin, 1998). Successful programs share the following characteristics:

- **Small groups or individual instruction.** The most successful programs are either individual or small groups of five to seven students.

- **Structured, fast-paced lessons.** A lesson plan that is very structured and fast paced is followed. The same pattern of instruction is followed every day. Usually the lessons are 30 to 40 minutes in length, and are taught daily.

- **Skills systematically taught in the context of reading.** Skills are taught prior to reading texts, where the students immediately apply them. Sometimes skills and strategies are modeled within the actual context of reading.

- **Texts leveled and sequenced in difficulty.** The texts that students read are leveled and sequenced in difficulty, moving from simple to complex. This is part of the scaffolding process, which moves from heavy teacher support to student independence.

- **Lessons taught by a certified teacher.** The intervention lessons are taught by a certified teacher, not a paraprofessional. Paraprofessionals, aides, or volunteers can be used for other activities, such as listening to a student read or for individual or small-group discussions.

Many schools develop their own intervention programs based on these characteristics. Some intervention plans have been published. A few of these follow with brief descriptions and references for further reading: Although the research on the effectiveness of these programs is inconclusive at this time, they are widely used, and there is much anecdotal evidence in support of their success. It is important that you select the intervention program that meets the students' needs and continually collect data on its effectiveness:

Early Intervention in Reading (EIR): A small-group intervention model for first-grade children. The research from this model served as the basis for the published program *Early Success* (Taylor, Pikulski, & Cooper, 2003). *Early Success* is designed for first- and second-grade children.

A fourth-grade teacher conducts an intervention group.
© Michael Newman/ PhotoEdit

Taylor, B. M., Frye, B. J., Short, R., & Shearer, B. (1992). Classroom teachers prevent reading failure among low-achieving first-grade students. *The Reading Teacher, 45,* 592–597.

Reading Recovery: A one-on-one tutorial program for first-grade children. This model was developed in New Zealand and brought to the United States through Ohio State University.

Clay, M. M. (1985). *The early detection of reading difficulties* (3rd ed.). Portsmouth, NH: Heinemann.

Pinnell, G. S., Fried, M. D., & Estice, R. M. (1990). Reading recovery: Learning how to make a difference. *The Reading Teacher, 43,* 282–295.

Facilitating Reading for Optimum Growth (FROG): A small-group intervention program for first- and second-grade children.

Allington, R. L., & Walmsley, S. A. (Eds.). (1995). *No quick fix: Rethinking literacy programs in America's elementary schools.* New York: Teachers College Press.

Right Start: A small-group intervention program for first-grade children.

Hiebert, E. H., Colt, J. M., Catto, S. L., & Gury, E. C. (1992). Reading and writing of first-grade students in a restructured Chapter I program. *American Educational Research Journal, 29,* 545–572.

Project SUCCESS/Soar to Success: A small-group intervention program using reciprocal teaching, scaffolding, and graphic organizers to help struggling readers in grades 3–6 accelerate their reading.

Cooper, J. D., Boschken, I., McWilliams, J., & Pistochini, L. (1998). *Soar to Success: The intermediate intervention program, Levels 3–6.* Boston: Houghton Mifflin.

Cooper, J. D., Boschken, I., McWilliams, J., & Pistochini, L. (2000). A study of the effectiveness of an intervention program designed to accelerate reading for struggling readers in the upper grades. In T. Shanahan & F. V. Rodriguez-Brown (Eds.), *49th Yearbook of the National Reading Conference* (pp. 477–486). Chicago: National Reading Conference.

🦋 Finding Time for Struggling Readers

There are two major questions that every classroom teacher must address: "How do I find time to work with my struggling readers during core instruction?" and "How and when do I provide intervention?"

During Core Instruction

Sometimes you may have only one struggling reader who needs special instruction. Other times you may have two, three, or more students, each at a different level. There is no easy solution to this dilemma. Finding enough time to meet the needs of every student during core instruction is never easy but can be done provided you keep several key points in mind:

See Chapter 10 for information on routines.

- Carefully plan each day, keeping in mind that effective management requires a schedule where you use routines and have a system to your day.

- It is not necessary to meet with all groups every day. At times it is better to meet with some groups three times a week and give them longer periods of time to work independently. But for struggling readers, it is often better to meet more frequently for shorter periods of time.

- Always have a sufficient number of constructive, independent activities for students to turn to when they finish their assigned work and you are working with an individual or another group.

- Establish patterns and routines of working for your students. Rehearse these, and review them periodically.

- Have in mind times during your day when you can meet with an individual or small group for short periods of instruction. This might be right before or after lunch, in the morning while students are arriving, or between special classes.

With these points in mind, you will be able to find time to provide your struggling readers core instruction that has been adjusted to meet their individual needs.

Helping Struggling Readers

"The school district where I work is committed to the development of programs that ensure that every student is a successful reader by the end of third grade. Each school within the district is required to submit a strategic plan that details how that goal will be met. By using a variety of assessments and careful analysis of the test results, teachers can confidently identify students who are experiencing difficulties in core subject areas. Over the past five years, the district has allocated monies to train staff and implement several intervention programs. These programs provide a safety net for our lowest-performing students and are meant to supplement classroom literacy practices, not replace them.

As one of two reading specialists on our school campus, my instructional time is divided between two programs: Reading Recovery and Literacy. Reading Recovery is an internationally known program developed by New Zealand educator and psychologist Marie Clay. Students who struggle with reading and writing in first grade are likely to continue to struggle in subsequent grades. Intensive one-to-one instruction is needed to accelerate their progress to meet the average of their grade-level peers.

Reading Recovery involves daily individual 30-minute lessons with a highly trained teacher. My training last year was quite involved, encompassing theory and practical application of how to work with the lowest-performing students. Additional training is ongoing this year through continuing contact hours.

Each Reading Recovery lesson includes the following components:

- Rereading two or more familiar books
- Rereading a book introduced the day before and taking a running record.
- Analysis of the running records directs the focus for the next day's lesson.
- Letter identification and/or word making and breaking
- Composing and writing a sentence
- Cutting up that sentence to rearrange and reread
- New book introduction

At the end of a full course of lessons, most Reading Recovery students have internalized effective reading strategies and no longer need substantial assistance to continue to make progress within the regular classroom setting. Those who do are considered for additional assessments and other instructional options.

The other half of my teaching day is spent as a literacy teacher. The primary-aged Literacy Program is a pullout program designed to help first- and second-grade students not reading on grade level. Students are placed in the program based on teacher recommendations and assessment test scores. Groups are leveled to accommodate students' specific needs. Each group meets four to five times per week for an average of 30 to 45 minutes.

Daily lessons include:

- Sight word review.
- Familiar reading.
- Taking a running record once a week on each student. Information gained is used to determine a student's current reading level and address specific needs.

(continued)

- Guided reading instruction focusing on developing independent reading strategies.
- Interactive and independent writing activities.
- Skills practice to strengthen students' decoding skills.

Data collected on current and former Reading Recovery and Literacy students show that the majority have benefited from their involvement in the programs and gone on to succeed in the classroom.

Leslie Ericson-Alti, Reading Recovery and Literacy Teacher
Rio Rancho Public Schools
Rio Rancho, New Mexico

Intervention

The first issue to address for readers requiring intervention is where to provide it: in the classroom or out of the classroom. You have read about the different ways intervention may be provided.

If you have no outside assistance of any type, you must work out a plan that will allow you to provide the intervention to a small group within the classroom. You can do this by having a special block of 30 to 40 minutes that you call something like "Special Time." During this period, you work with your intervention group; students who do not need intervention do a variety of constructive activities that provide them enrichment, give them practice in an area of special need, or allow them time to complete work or do a special project. Conducting an intervention group within the classroom is not easy but is possible with careful planning and establishment of routines.

If your struggling readers participate in a pullout program, you must be sure that they are not penalized by being required to make up work they miss. In order for pullout programs to work in a school, coordination with other classroom teachers and special teachers is necessary. You should find some of the following suggestions helpful:

- **Meet with your grade-level colleagues.** Meet and talk with other teachers about when they have core instruction. Try to arrange times so that everyone in a given grade level is having it at about the same time of day. This will make it possible for students from a given grade level who need intervention to be pulled from several classrooms at the same time.

- **Involve the principal in planning.** Talk with the principal about the importance of having special classes such as art, music, and computer lab at times other than when students are pulled out for intervention.

- **Plan classroom activities to be missed carefully.** Think about the activities that will take place in the classroom while students are going out to intervention. Arrange for activities to take place that intervention students can miss. For example, if you have a time when students do special projects or independent work, schedule intervention at this time.

- **Make sure that intervention students do not miss creative, fun activities.** It is important that intervention students get to participate in creative or fun types of activities. Therefore, try not to have struggling readers always miss these activities.

- **Consider how and when you teach science, social studies, health, and other subjects.** Struggling readers should not miss content-area instruction. However, if their reading level is so low that they cannot participate successfully in content-area instruction, consider having them miss a subject area for a given period of time in order to provide them intervention. Alternate the subject areas missed. At middle school and junior high levels, intervention can be substituted for a class or study hall.

Obviously, there is no one right answer about how to find time to teach struggling readers. Every school has different circumstances and factors to consider. We do know that it is possible to work out plans that make it possible to provide struggling readers their core instruction and the intervention they need in order to make more than adequate yearly progress.

🦋 Summary

Struggling readers are any students who are experiencing difficulty in learning to read. The approach to helping these students make more than adequate yearly progress has moved from remediation to intervention, which means providing a program of additional instructional time that is designed to prevent or stop reading failure. Struggling readers should be given both core instruction and intervention that meets the same standards as other students within their grade level are required to meet.

To plan effective instruction for struggling readers, you need to make decisions about what they need by finding out about their reading levels, oral language, decoding, comprehension, related factors, and previous instructional programs. On the basis of this information, you plan core instruction and intervention.

The core instruction must be adjusted in terms of the strategies and skills taught, and the levels of text used. Throughout this process, progress must be carefully monitored and accommodations made to help struggling readers continue to learn successfully in other content areas.

Intervention instruction must be provided by a certified teacher and can be provided as an in-class, pullout, extended-day, or summer school program. Based on current research findings, the intervention program may be individual or small group with the following characteristics: structured, fast-paced lessons; skills systematically taught within the context of reading; and texts sequenced in difficulty. There are numerous developed and published programs available. There are many ways schools can find time to provide both core instruction and intervention within any school day. This is not easy but is possible.

For Additional Reading

Allington, R. L. (2001). *What really matters for struggling readers: Research-based programs.* New York: Longman.

Cooper, J. D., & Kiger, N. D. (2005). *Literacy assessment: Helping teachers plan instruction* (2nd ed.). Boston: Houghton Mifflin.

Ganske, K., Monroe, J. K., & Strickland, D. S. (2003). Questions teachers ask about struggling readers and writers. *The Reading Teacher, 57* (2), 118–128.

Pikulski, J. J. (1994). Preventing reading failure: A review of five effective programs. *The Reading Teacher, 48*(1), 30–39.

Valencia, S. W., & Buly, M. R. (2004). Behind test scores: What struggling readers really need. *The Reading Teacher, 57*(6), 520–531.

For Exploration: Electronic Products and Resources

CIERA's Building Comprehension in Struggling Readers
Useful resources and guidance from the Center for the Improvement of Early Reading Achievement (CIERA); a national center for research on early reading, representing a consortium of educators.
http://www.ciera.org/library/presos/2001/birdyshaw/01LAcompr/01lacdby.pdf

Gail Lovely's Strategies for Struggling Readers
A comprehensive clearinghouse of links to resources for educators dealing with struggling readers.
http://www.gaillovely.com/struggling%20readers%20resources.htm

The International Reading Association's Focus on Struggling Readers and Writers
Resources, position statements, journal articles, and professional development links for educators who are working with struggling readers and writers.
http://www.reading.org/focus/struggling.html

Reading Rockets
A wealth of strategies, lessons, and activities designed to help young children learn to read. The site's resources assist parents, teachers, and other educators in working with struggling readers who require additional help in reading and comprehension skills development.
http://www.readingrockets.org/

University of Texas Center for Reading and Language Arts
These professional development guides, videos, CD-ROMs, and booklets cover various topics related to effective, research-based reading instruction for struggling readers.
http://www.texasreading.org/utcrla/products/default.asp

What Does It Mean to Be a Struggling Reader? (Wisconsin LEARNS)
http://wilearns.state.wi.us/apps/default.asp?cid=21

Developing a Management System for a Comprehensive Literacy Classroom

10

✓ **STANDARDS FOCUS**

NCTE/IRA Standards: 3, 5, 6, 7, 8, 10, 11, 12
Standards for Reading Professionals: 1, 2, 4, 5

"Educators Speak   pp. 427, 453

Sixth-Grade Literacy Block Enhanced with Computers
            —*Jill Baker, Citrus Heights, California*

Parallel Block Scheduling Helps Students with
Diverse Needs
            —*Kelly L. Andrus, Fredricksburg, Virginia*"

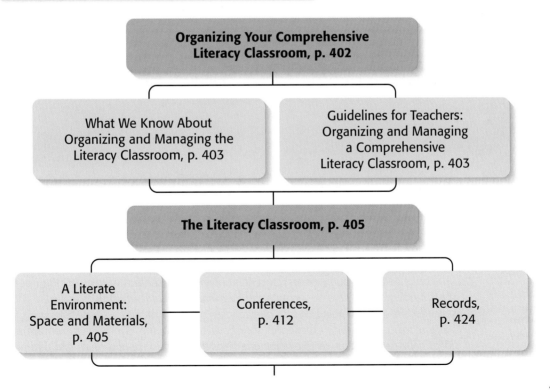

Organizing Your Comprehensive Literacy Classroom, p. 402

What We Know About Organizing and Managing the Literacy Classroom, p. 403

Guidelines for Teachers: Organizing and Managing a Comprehensive Literacy Classroom, p. 403

The Literacy Classroom, p. 405

A Literate Environment: Space and Materials, p. 405

Conferences, p. 412

Records, p. 424

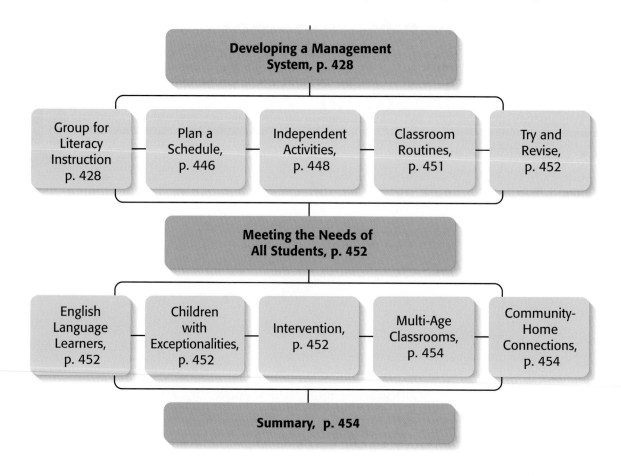

Developing a Management System, p. 428

Group for Literacy Instruction p. 428

Plan a Schedule, p. 446

Independent Activities, p. 448

Classroom Routines, p. 451

Try and Revise, p. 452

Meeting the Needs of All Students, p. 452

English Language Learners, p. 452

Children with Exceptionalities, p. 452

Intervention, p. 452

Multi-Age Classrooms, p. 454

Community-Home Connections, p. 454

Summary, p. 454

Y ou have learned a great deal about literacy and how children construct meaning. Now your challenge is to take all of your knowledge and begin to plan, organize, and manage your classroom to provide your students with balanced literacy experiences. A short visit to Mrs. Dopheide's second-grade class on Monday morning will show you how she accomplishes this task.

As we enter the room, the last student is sharing what she has written over the weekend; she is reading aloud to the class a note she has written to her friend who has moved to another state. Each Monday morning, Mrs. Dopheide takes about 15 minutes to invite boys and girls to share reading and writing experiences they have had at home. She tells us that this activity builds good relationships with the home and helps the children see how much they use reading and writing in their lives.

"Boys and girls, we need to talk for a few minutes about what we will be doing this week," Mrs. Dopheide begins. Then she points to a chart entitled "Our Weekly Plans" [Figure 10.1] and

Terms
You Need to Know

- conferences
- peer conferences
- reading workshop
- writing workshop

FIGURE 10.1

Weekly Class Plan

> # Our Weekly Plans
>
> <u>Theme</u> –   Learning About Families
>
> <u>Everyday</u> –   * Reading Club
>   * Writing Club
>
> <u>Special Jobs for the Week</u>
>
>   – Begin <u>Too Many Tamales</u>
>
>   – Writing Workshop – our
>   personal narratives
>
>   – Listing items and costs
>   for Family Fair
>
> <u>Things to Add</u>

continues, "We are all going to read a wonderful new book, Too Many Tamales *[Soto, 1993]*, which goes with our Family theme. Of course, we will have our Writing Workshop to continue work on our personal narratives that we are writing for our Families book. We have to get started on planning for our family fair. Can you think of any other things we need to do this week?"

"What about conference time? I need to talk with you about my new book," says Larry.

"Yeah, me too," adds Rosie.

"Aren't we having Reading Workshop this week?" asks Sonja.

"Yes, we are," replies Mrs. Dopheide.
"What new books do you have for us?" asks Eric.
"It's a surprise; you'll have to wait until Wednesday when we start our Reading Workshop."
"Oh, come on," groans nearly everyone.
Mrs. Dopheide adds children's suggestions to the chart and then says, "Let's begin our morning with Writing Club." She then shows the children the day's schedule and begins the Writing Club, the class time for independent writing.

From this brief visit to Mrs. Dopheide's class, you can see that she organizes and manages a comprehensive literacy classroom in many different ways:

- She makes strong connections between the classroom and her students' homes. By inviting those who wish to do so to share their reading and writing experiences from the weekend, she demonstrates the importance of literacy at home and brings students' homes into the classroom community of learners.

- Children are an integral part of the process of planning. By sharing her plans with the class and asking for their suggestions, Mrs. Dopheide makes everyone feel part of the learning process.

- Mrs. Dopheide uses several organizational frameworks and concepts to organize her class: Reading Club (independent reading), Writing Club (independent writing), **Writing Workshop, Reading Workshop,** books for the whole class, **conferences,** and others. A comprehensive literacy classroom requires a variety of organizational structures.

Throughout this chapter you will learn about many frameworks, organizational techniques, and procedures that will help you organize and manage a comprehensive literacy classroom. All of the ideas suggested here are based on our knowledge of *how children and young adults develop literacy.*

🦋 Organizing Your Comprehensive Literacy Classroom

Recall the reading and writing instruction you had when you were in elementary school. Did you have reading groups? Did you spend much time writing, or did anyone even teach you how to write? Were you in the same reading group all the time? Was English or language arts instruction generally taught from an English textbook, with units on various parts of speech or writing conventions such as punctuation, with little time for actual writing? Chances are you recall some or all of these experiences from your own education. In addition to all we have learned about literacy learning, we have learned a great deal about organizing the classroom for literacy instruction.

What We Know About Organizing and Managing the Literacy Classroom

For years, most elementary teachers divided their classes into three reading groups (Barr & Dreeben, 1991). Sometimes classes were tracked; that is, all students at one ability level were assigned to one teacher for all or part of the day. Both of these patterns of instruction were generally referred to as *ability grouping* or *tracking* (Cunningham & Allington, 1994). After this concept of organizing for instruction came under considerable criticism (Allington, 1983; Dawson, 1987; Harp, 1989; Hiebert, 1983; Slavin, 1986; Sorensen & Hallinan, 1986), research showed that these types of ability groupings do not lead to success or prevent failure for students (Allington & Walmsley, 1995). Therefore, some other types of organizational structures are needed.

For detailed descriptions of intervention programs, see Chapter 9 and Hiebert and Taylor (1994) in the "For Additional Reading" section at the end of this chapter.

One of the most important findings from research on reading and writing is *who* can learn to do it. For many years, teachers often thought that students who were having difficulty learning were "slow" or even unable to learn to read and write. These students—considered remedial or at risk—generally included English Language Learners (ELLs). Many different types of programs were provided for these students, but none of them worked effectively (Allington & Walmsley, 1995; Cunningham & Allington, 1994). More recently, however, some effective programs such as Reading Recovery (Clay, 1985; DeFord, Lyons, & Pinnell, 1991) and small-group intervention plans (Hiebert & Taylor, 1994) have demonstrated that nearly *all* children can learn to read and write.

A related issue is the pace of instruction. Evidence indicates (DeFord et al., 1991; Allington & Walmsley, 1995) that students who are having difficulty learning need instruction that is paced *faster* to help them catch up. In fact, we believe that *all* students need instruction that is appropriately fast paced. When instruction is paced too slowly, many students lose interest and fail to learn.

Students who are having difficulty learning often need extra support to help them catch up. This can be delivered through strong early intervention programs such as Reading Recovery and small-group intervention models. However, the key to having successful literacy programs for *all* students is to create classroom instruction that is oriented toward success for all students.

We need to know how to organize classrooms that prevent failure and promote success! To accomplish this, we need to use the concepts about literacy learning developed in this text and in other sources and organize classrooms based on what we know about how children and young adults learn.

Guidelines for Teachers: Organizing and Managing a Comprehensive Literacy Classroom

Regardless of the grade level you teach, you will find it easier to organize and manage a literacy-centered classroom that promotes success if you consider the following eleven guidelines:

Guidelines for these literacy blocks were provided in Chapter 2.

1. *Provide an exciting classroom environment that supports many literacy activities.*
2. *Provide daily times for independent reading and writing.*

Chapter 11 gives suggestions for determining students' interests and strengths.

3. *Base your organization on students' interests and literacy strengths.* Find out what students can do and what their interests are. For example, if you have many students who are very good oral readers but poor constructors of meaning, have them do readers theater and other types of activities involving oral reading.

4. *Make students part of the decision-making process.* This involves having students set goals for themselves and help to set goals for the class. Within the literacy activities of the classroom, students should be given choices as to what they read, how they read, and how they respond and share. Similarly, they should be given choices as to what they write, how they write, and how they publish and share. By giving students choices, you are better able to accommodate individual needs and encourage students to take ownership of their own learning. Teachers may guide students to make thoughtful choices.

See Chapter 11 for a discussion of the use of portfolios.

5. *Provide blocks of time for direct or explicit instruction as needed.* A well-designed, comprehensive literacy program includes both direct and indirect instruction. Use small groups for directly teaching skills and strategies.

6. *Provide blocks of time when all students can be successful at reading and writing.* Provide some times when everyone in the class has the opportunity to experience or read the same text and do the same type of writing. This helps to build self-esteem and lets all students in the class know they can do some of the same tasks others can do.

7. *Provide blocks of times when all students have the opportunity to receive instruction with books that are leveled to be at their instructional reading levels.* Students need to have times when they read from books appropriate to their reading levels. This allows students to get instructional support with books they can read.

8. *Provide blocks of time when students receive instructional support as they write on products and topics of their own choosing.* During this time, you can provide specific instructional support in writing.

9. *Keep in contact with students' homes.* Have activities that encourage home-school cooperation (Boyer, 1995). These might include home read-aloud programs and writing.

10. *Keep the pace of instruction appropriately fast for all students.* Instruction needs to be delivered at a pace that holds students' attention. Avoid asking students to do too many activities with one book. The number of activities does not make the difference in how well students read and write; the amount of actual reading and writing they do is what matters.

11. *Be flexible.* Try many different organizational techniques and procedures. Don't latch on to one procedure and use it all the time, or you will risk losing sight of students' needs. Remember that a variety of patterns will be needed to accommodate students' needs.

No set of guidelines can make classroom organization and management foolproof. However, keeping these eleven points in mind can help you make good decisions and develop a success-oriented classroom that runs smoothly.

🦋 The Literacy Classroom

Effective organization and management are dependent on careful, ongoing planning (Morrow, 2003). As you begin to plan your classroom, consider these factors: a literate environment (space and materials), conferences, and recordkeeping.

A Literate Environment: Space and Materials

A teacher begins to build motivation by creating a literate classroom environment rich in language and print. Such an environment stimulates learning and promotes the concept of the class as a community of people who are learning together. It is basic to every classroom at every grade level and provides part of the motivation needed to encourage all learners to want to construct meaning.

The literate environment should include a variety of areas or centers, each with a specific focus. The contents, organization, and arrangement of these areas will vary from classroom to classroom and from grade level to grade level. *It is most important to place these special areas where they are readily accessible to the children.* The center of the room is a good location, but space is at a premium in many classrooms, and this will not be possible. Therefore, you need to think about how to arrange these special areas to make the best use of the available space. Limited space need not be a deterrent to creating a literate environment.

The areas or centers in the classroom should include the following:

- a library area,
- a writing and publishing area,
- a listening, speaking, and viewing area,
- a sharing area,
- a creative arts area,
- a group meeting area, and
- a display area.

Classrooms vary in the amount of space available for the students and instructional activities, and teachers vary in the ways they want their classrooms organized and arranged. But the main goal is the same for everyone: to make sure the room arrangement promotes and supports the community of literacy learners and contributes to an exciting, literacy-centered atmosphere. Use the following steps to organize your classroom space:

1. Take an inventory of what you have available: desks, tables, bulletin boards, bookcases, storage areas, electrical outlets, a water source, chalkboards, and other equipment such as computers, tape players, or an overhead screen. Think about which of these are fixed in place and which are movable.

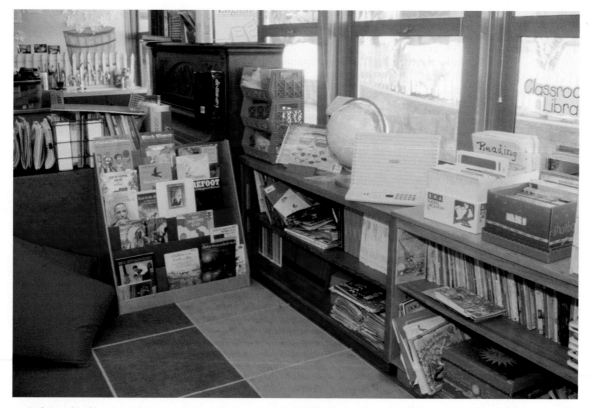

A sixth-grade classroom has special work areas even with limited space. © Felicia Martinez/Photo Edit

2. Think about what you want in your classroom: centers or areas, small- and large-group instructional areas, bulletin boards students can use, storage areas for student work, a place for teacher materials, and space to store extra materials. Take some time just to sit and look around your room, and consider how you want to arrange it.

3. Draw a quick sketch of the layout to get you started. Here are some tips to keep in mind as you make your plans:

   - Pushing desks together promotes conversation and interaction, an important goal of a literacy-centered classroom.
   - Some students need space away from other students, where they can work alone. Use movable bookshelves to section off the room.
   - Art and science areas need access to water.
   - The teacher's desk or work table is often best placed off to the side, where the teacher can also hold conferences with students.
   - Areas where students are likely to be talking together are best placed away from an instructional area where you will be meeting with small groups.
   - Centers or areas requiring electrical equipment or computers need to be placed near outlets.

4. Once you have a plan in mind, begin to arrange the room. If you have time before students arrive, live with the arrangement for a few days as you do other things.

5. After students arrive, try out the arrangement for several days. If you discover certain areas aren't working, change them.

Library Area

The major purpose of the library area is to promote and support independent reading. It should include many books of varying levels and interests, books on tapes, books on CD-ROMs, magazines, newspapers, brochures, and posters, all organized and displayed attractively. To promote the concept of the children as both readers and writers, this area should also include books that have been "published" by the students themselves.

Your library area should include books by past and current award winners appropriate to your grade. For example, in a fifth or sixth grade, you might include *So You Want to Be President?* by Judith St. George (2000), illustrated by David Small, which won the Caldecott Medal for 2001; and *A Year Down Yonder* by Richard Peck (2000), which won the 2001 Newbery Medal. Change or add to the collection of books in the library area frequently. Books may be borrowed from the school library, local library, or bookmobile; brought in by the children; or donated by parents or community groups.

The library area should have some appropriate seating, such as a rocker, beanbag chairs, a bathtub with pillows, or tables and chairs. There should also be a bulletin board where you might display book jackets or children might display an advertisement for their favorite book. For example, a child who has just finished reading *El Chino* (Say, 1990), a book about the first Chinese bullfighter, might want to make a poster to advertise and "sell" the book to other children.

If your school has a central library staffed with a librarian, media specialist, or some other type of support person, you can work with this person as you create your classroom library area. It is important to view the school library as an extension of the classroom library, since both it and the librarian are valuable resources for your program. For example, the librarian can help you select books and plan units, and the school library should become a place where students can come and go freely to select books and other resources.

When you are working with emergent, or beginning, readers, it is useful to have lots of little, easy-to-read books. Many teachers organize these books in baskets, boxes, or barrels that are color-coded for difficulty. For example, the easiest "Basket of Books" might be yellow, with each book having a yellow dot; red might be average; and green might be more challenging. This coding helps students select books, but students can move from one color to the next color when they feel ready. The books in the baskets can be trade books or may come from the many collections of books for emergent readers published by such companies as Houghton Mifflin, Rigby, and the Wright Group.

As students become more mature readers, teach them how to select books for themselves. One way is the *thumbs-up test.* You open a book and read a page aloud or to yourself. For each word you come to that you don't know, put a finger down. If you finish the page and your thumb is still up—meaning that there are no more than four fingers down, and therefore no more than four unfamiliar words—the book is probably right for you. Of course, if a student really wants to read a book with more than five unfamiliar words on a page, encourage and then support the effort. Strong interest goes a long way in overcoming word recognition difficulty.

The library area materials require a simple checkout system: a card with the book title and a place for students to write their names will work. Letting different students take turns being the librarian helps develop responsibility and provides an opportunity for students to learn more about "real-world" literacy.

If you have older ELLs, you must provide books for them. Some picture books with limited text may be appropriate so long as the pictures are not obviously meant for younger children. Other books might include those with side-by-side text in English and another language.

Instructional Materials

You will need class sets of books, sets of decodable texts for the beginning literacy program, multiple copies of single titles, and a variety of single titles. If you are using a published reading or language arts program, you may have an anthology that you will use primarily as your class set of books. However, an anthology alone is not enough. You also need sets of trade books covering a wide range of interests and difficulty levels.

Class sets or multiple copies of trade books may be stored in a central location within the school to facilitate wider use. Rolling carts make it easier to move sets of books in and out of classrooms. Teachers at each grade level usually agree that certain pieces of literature are core at that grade level. For example, fourth-grade teachers might agree that *Big Boy* (Mollel, 1995) would be a core piece for their grade. Choosing core books helps to prevent students from reading the same books over and over again.

Writing and Publishing Area

Every classroom needs a writing and publishing area or center, where you promote writing and display some of the children's writing. Furnish it with:

- Tables and chairs
- Paper (unlined for beginners)
- Pencils, pens, markers, crayons
- Scissors
- Tape and glue
- Construction paper and cardboard
- Wallpaper sample books
- Yarn, brads, and staplers
- A computer (or typewriter)
- A place to display writing
- A storage area for writing folders or computer disks

For a detailed discussion of the use of word processing in writing and other topics about educational technology, see Grabe and Grabe (2001) in the "For Additional Reading" section at the end of the chapter.

You can learn about new software from magazines such as *Electronic Learning* (902 Sylvan Avenue, Englewood Cliffs, NJ 07632) and *Learning and Leading with Technology* (formerly *The Computing Teacher,* International Society for Technology in Education, 1787 Agate Street, Eugene, OR 97403).

The writing area should also have a place where each child can store writing ideas and products. This might be an individual file folder or some type of box or bin for each child. If children are writing on a computer, provide a storage place for individual disks.

To help children publish their books, you should include in this area materials for making book jackets, such as wallpaper samples, cardboard, construction paper, yarn, and brads.

The writing center can be the place where students write, meet for conferences with peers or the teacher, or do the final work on a piece of writing they wish to publish. By having this area or center in your classroom, you give significance to writing.

All students need a place, such as a folder, to store such items as a list of possible topics for writing (see Figure 10.2 for a sample form), pieces of writing in progress, and a list of pieces of completed writing (see Figure 10.3 for a sample form). Students may also choose to keep a list of words from their own writing that cause them spelling problems; many teachers encourage students to do this.

FIGURE 10.2

Form for Recording Writing Topics

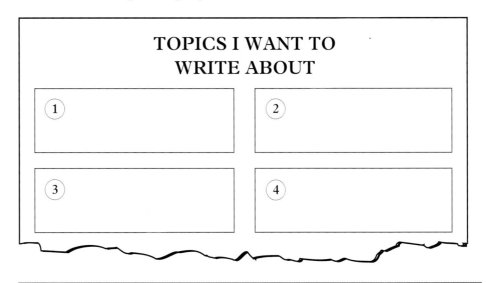

FIGURE 10.3

Form for Recording Completed Writing Projects

WRITING RECORD

Name _____

P=Published

Date Started	Type of Writing	Title of Piece	Date Completed or Dropped

Some teachers also encourage students to keep a record of their conferences with classmates, or peers. Such a record helps students prepare for their conferences with the teacher. Figure 10.4 shows a sample form that can be used for this purpose.

The writing folder is basically the student's working folder. The student brings it to conferences with the teacher, but it is primarily for the student's use. Both the writing folder and the reading journal are places where students keep their work.

FIGURE 10.4

Peer Conference Record

PEER CONFERENCE RECORD

DATE	CONFERENCE WITH	WRITING PIECE	SUGGESTIONS

Another record students might keep in their writing folder is a list of goals established with the teacher during a conference. These may range from general goals such as, "Complete my story," or, "Try a different ending" to goals that are very specific, such as, "Make more use of descriptive words," or, "Pay attention to capital letters and periods." After goals are set, the student and the teacher discuss the progress made and establish new goals. Figure 10.5 shows a goal sheet from a sixth grader's writing folder.

When you begin to use writing folders with your students, keep them simple. Many students have difficulty keeping records and need help in learning their importance (Graves, 1991). Don't have students put in so many pieces that the folders lose their real purpose: as *a place to keep writing in progress.*

Listening, Speaking, and Viewing Area

This area should contain a listening post with headphones, a tape recorder, and/or a compact disc player. There should be tapes of books and stories to which students can listen, as well as blank tapes for students to record their own stories. For viewing, the area needs personal filmstrip viewers. Many schools have video players and recorders, making it possible to use educational videos, as well as computers with CD-ROM drives that allow students to practice literacy skills with electronic books and a wide variety of instructional technology.

Sharing Area

An important part of learning to construct meaning is sharing what you have read or written and approximating authentic reading and writing experiences (Holdaway, 1979), and children need a special place for this activity. This area should include

---

FIGURE 10.5

Goal Sheet from a Sixth Grader's Writing Folder

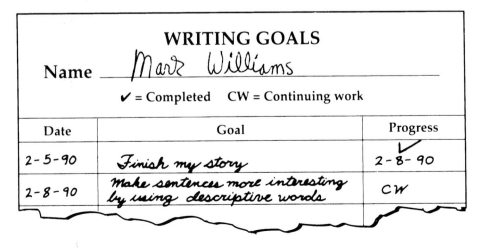

See Chapter 8 for a description of the author's chair.

tables and chairs or other comfortable seating, and some places for students to display some of the products they have developed. The author's chair might be kept in this area or in part of the library or writing area.

Creative Arts Area

Drama, art, and music are important to children as they respond to their reading and writing and share it with others. Therefore, there should be some area that includes puppets and items students can use for costumes and props for giving plays, retelling stories, or giving readers theater performances.

A portion of this area might have materials for painting, drawing, paper sculpture, or other art activities. If space is available, develop a separate area for art. Make available some simple musical instruments, such as recorders, autoharps, or xylophones. Using music with pieces of literature such as *Ben's Trumpet* (Isadora, 1979) or *Song and Dance Man* (Ackerman, 1988) is appropriate at many different grade levels (Lamme, 1990). A teacher does not have to be musically inclined to help children carry out many of these activities.

Group Meeting Area

You will need an area where you can meet with small groups for discussion and instruction. This area might contain a chalkboard, an overhead projector, and other materials you will need for teaching, such as books and charts.

Display Area

Displays of items related to topics of study, art pieces, photographs, and posters all help to motivate students and expand their backgrounds. The display area should be changed frequently and include material brought in by students. For example, a class that is reading or listening to *Where the Red Fern Grows* (Rawls, 1961) might create a display of photographs of pets that have meant a great deal to the children, just as Old Dan and Little Ann were important to Billy.

A literate environment is both motivating and a vital part of developing oral language, expanding prior knowledge, and creating an atmosphere that promotes opportunities for authentic reading and writing experiences that children share with all members of the classroom community. Figure 10.6 presents a checklist for evaluating the literate environment in your classroom.

Conferences

Conferences in literacy-centered classrooms may take place between students or between the teacher and students. During a reading conference, the focus is on a book or other reading material, and during a writing conference, the focus is on a piece of student writing. Conferences play an important role in all aspects of literacy learning (Calkins, 1994; Graves, 1983, 1991). Graves (1991) maintains that "the conference—the listening stance—is the heart of good teaching" (p. 89).

FIGURE 10.6

A Checklist for Evaluating the Classroom Literate Environment

1. Do I have the following areas or combinations
of areas in my classroom?

	Yes	No	Needs Work
• Library area			
• Writing and publishing area			
• Listening, speaking, and viewing area			
• Sharing area			
• Creative arts area			
• Group meeting area			
• Display area			

2. Do I change or improve areas within reasonable time frames?
3. Do students utilize certain areas more than others?

   Which ones? _____

   _____

4. Areas that I need to add:

   _____

   _____

5. Areas that I need to improve or change:

   _____

   _____

Conferences may be formal, planned events or informal ones that take place any number of times during the day—in the hallway, in the lunchroom, on the playground, or during any part of the daily classroom routine. Some educators refer to informal conferences as *miniconferences* or *on-the-spot conferences* (Tompkins & Hoskisson, 1991). These conferences are really nothing more than times when you stop to chat and listen carefully to students. Good teachers do this all the time.

During such informal miniconferences, you might ask children such questions as, "What are you reading?" "How do you like this book?" or, "What writing piece are you working on now?" For example, Mrs. Laird, a fourth-grade teacher, stopped by the desk of one student:

Mrs. Laird: What have you been reading lately?

   Mark: I'm still reading the same book I got last week.

Mrs. Laird: How do you like it?

   Mark: I don't.

Mrs. Laird: Why don't you stop reading this book and select another one?

   Mark: I don't know.

Mrs. Laird: Don't you like dinosaurs?

Mark: Yes!

Mrs. Laird: I saw a great dinosaur book in the reading center this morning. You'll love it! It's called *Tyrannosaurus Was a Beast* [Prelutsky, 1988]. Try that one.

In this brief discussion, Mrs. Laird determined that this student was bogged down with a book he didn't like and then directed him to a book in an area of his interest. Although informal conferences may last only a minute or two, they yield valuable information about how students are doing and enable the teacher to provide on-the-spot support.

After this brief encounter, Mrs. Laird wrote a note about this miniconference on the student's page in her notebook. (Some teachers record such notes on a computer.) Sometimes she relies on memory and makes notes later. However, it is not always necessary to make notes about a miniconference. This conversation just happened to be one during which the teacher gathered some valuable information about the student that she felt needed to be recorded. Some teachers carry sticky notes that they write on and date; later they stick them on the students' pages in their notebook.

Purposes of Formal Teacher-Student Conferences

Formal literacy conferences may have several purposes. First, they may be held for *sharing and discussing a book.* The teacher and the student talk about a book the student is reading or has completed, and the student may read aloud favorite parts. The teacher might share thoughts or feelings about the book, or make suggestions for other books for the student to read. If the students are keeping journals, responses might be shared and discussed, or questions about the book or words of concern to the student might be reviewed.

Second, conferences may be used for the teacher and student to *discuss some aspect of the student's writing* and for the teacher to *ask probing or guiding questions* that will help the student formulate ideas. This is a time for modeling and coaching to help students develop their writing.

Third, the literacy conference may be used to *provide a minilesson on a particular strategy or skill* that seems to be causing the student difficulty—perhaps a problem with phonics or an aspect of punctuation or comprehension. During this conference, the teacher uses the minilesson concept and models the particular strategy or skill needed.

Finally, literacy conferences may be held to *assess student progress.* By having students share their responses to a piece of literature, the teacher can tell how well they comprehend or construct meaning. Oral reading gives clues to the students' decoding abilities, and written responses in journals provide evidence about spelling, grammar and usage, and comprehension.

One conference might have several purposes. For example, students might be sharing a book at the same time the teacher is assessing progress. In fact, a single conference should serve as many purposes as possible. The following suggestions should be helpful in planning conferences:

* ***When you begin to use conferences, explain their purpose and procedures to students.*** Role-play several conferences to establish routines and guidelines for behavior.

- *Keep conferences short and focused.* If students don't need a conference, don't have one. Their time is better spent reading or writing.
- *Maintain a positive, interactive environment.* Use probing questions and statements that encourage students to think about and talk about their writing.
- *From time to time, have group conferences during which you talk with several students about their writing.* This is an especially useful procedure if students are doing similar types of writing or appear to have similar needs for support.
- *In writing conferences with ELLs (as with all other writers), it is important to start by discussing the content of the piece.* Don't focus on the mechanics first, even though the writing may show many second-language errors. When you do talk about the mechanical aspects of writing, limit the focus to only one or two types of errors so as not to overwhelm ELLs.
- *Keep a simple record sheet for each student.* Figure 10.7 shows a sheet you can use for writing. This will tell you what students are doing and what their needs are.

FIGURE 10.7

Record Sheet for Keeping Track of Students' Writing

Name _____ Grade _____

Date	Writing Piece	Suggestions	Minilesson Needs	Goals/Comments

Scheduling Conferences

Literacy conferences seldom last more than 5 to 10 minutes. It is best to keep conferences as short as possible and focused on your purpose.

Students should sign up for their conferences on a sign-up sheet or a section of the chalkboard at least once per week. (Sometimes you will initiate a request to see a student.) Figure 10.8 shows a conference sign-up chart that a second-grade teacher uses. Notice that no one requested a conference on Friday, so the teacher had extra time to meet with students she had not seen recently. A good rule of thumb is to hold conferences with students at least once a week for first, second, and third grades and once every other week for fourth grade and above. However, students' needs, not an arbitrary schedule, should be the major determining factor in establishing the frequency of conferences.

Each teacher must work out the best time during the daily schedule to hold conferences. Some prefer to schedule a few each day, and others schedule on designated days, such as Monday, Wednesday, and Friday.

FIGURE 10.8

Conference Sign-up Chart

	READING CONFERENCES	
	Student Requested	**Teacher Requested**
Monday	Leo Susan Lisa Joan Jeff	
Wednesday	Terri Frank Joey Sid	Tim Mike
Friday		Sara Mary Anne Bill

FIGURE 10.9

Chart Showing Students What to Do While the Teacher Is in Conference

THINGS TO DO DURING
CONFERENCES

• Read your book or selection
• Write in your journal
• Work on your writing project
• Meet with a Literature Circle
• OTHER- You decide on something
      worthwhile to do
• Work in the Listening Center
• Prepare for your conference

Preparing for Conferences

To ensure successful conferences, you must be certain that both you and the students are prepared and understand how and why conferences take place. The best way to do this is to role-play and model a conference period so that students see what happens and know how it occurs.

When teachers begin to use conferences, they are often concerned about what the rest of the class does while one or two children are in conference. A chart such as the one shown in Figure 10.9 lists options that other students have during the conference period. Once students become comfortable with conference times, a chart is usually not needed.

Students also have to prepare themselves for the conference. Figure 10.10 shows a conference chart that many teachers find helpful in directing students in this process. After a week or so of conferencing, *you and the class* should evaluate how the conferences are going and make adjustments as needed.

Finally, you too must prepare for the conferences. A loose-leaf notebook with a section for each student is helpful. On the first page, write the student's name, age,

FIGURE 10.10

Chart for Helping Students Prepare for a Conference

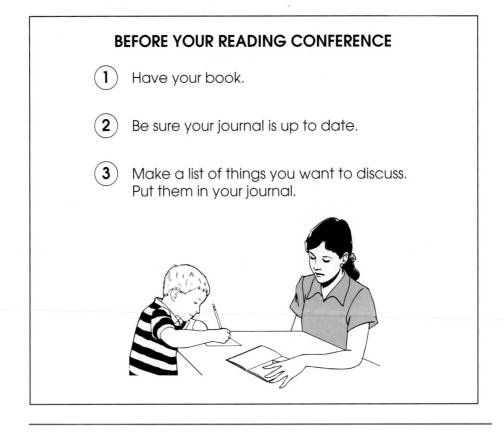

BEFORE YOUR READING CONFERENCE

1 Have your book.

2 Be sure your journal is up to date.

3 Make a list of things you want to discuss.
   Put them in your journal.

and grade, and also list the student's interests and any pertinent information about his or her reading and writing strengths. One of these pages might look like Figure 10.11. Following the opening page, you will need several blank pages on which to record your observations and comments from the conference, and any goals you and the student agree on to be accomplished before the next conference. Keep the page simple, such as that shown in Figure 10.12.

Have some ideas about questions or statements you might use to prompt students to discuss the book they are reading (you might consult the lists of open-ended questions presented in Table 7.1). In addition, Veatch (1978) suggests that individual conferences should explore four areas with students: personal involvement of the child with the book, ability to read and understand, sheer mechanical reading ability, and oral reading. According to Veatch, hundreds of questions can be asked in each of these areas. Here are some of her samples:

FIGURE 10.11

Partial Teacher's Notebook Page for Each Student

Name *Lisa Smith*   Age *8*   Grade *3*

Interests: *horses, roller skating, making clay figures*

Reading Strengths	Writing Strengths
– *Rereads when things aren't clear* – *always previews her book*	– *Loves to write* – *Uses descriptive words*

OTHER OBSERVATIONS

1. Area of personal involvement

   Teacher: *Why did you choose this story? Do you know anyone else in this class who would like it also?*

   Why do you think you are more interested in this kind of story than others in this class are?

   Would you like to be this character? Why?

2. Area of critical reading or general comprehension

   Teacher: *What kind of a story is this? Real?*

   or

   Could this story have happened? Why? Or why not?

   Tell me the story rapidly.

   If this character did so and so, would you think he would get in trouble?

   At the time this story was supposed to have happened, what was going on in our country that was very important?

FIGURE 10.12

Sample Conference Page from Notebook

Date	Comments	Goals for Next Conference
9/7	Terri had finished reading _Jam_. She loved the story and said her uncle was like Mr. Castle. She thought it was OK for dads to stay home. No problems with vocabulary or comprehension. Excellent oral reading. Needs to select more challenging book.	1. Select a more challenging book. 2. Use different responses in journal other than drawing.

3. Area of mechanical skills

   Teacher: _What words did you have trouble with?_

   or

   Here are two words that look very much alike. Tell me how you know the difference.

   or

   Let me point to several words in your story. Tell me what they are and what they mean.

4. Area of oral reading

   Teacher: _Which part of the book have you chosen to read aloud to me?_
   Make your voice go up and down.
   Make your voice spooky, or scary, or sad, or mean, or whatever the story calls for. (Veatch, 1978, p. 69)

The questions you ask during a writing conference should help students reflect on their writing (think about it critically), expand their writing, and select ways to improve their writing. The following questions are from Millett (1986, pp. 27–29):

Reflecting Questions

- What part is most interesting to you?
- What feeling do you want your reader to have?
- Is this the idea that you wanted me to get?

Expanding Questions

- That's interesting—would you like your reader to know about that?
- Can you tell more about . . . ?
- Is that important to add?

Selecting Questions

Phrase questions that relate to focus and order:

- Which part is most important?
- Where could this new idea go?
- Which parts talk about the same thing?
- How might you put these parts together?

Ask questions about beginnings and endings:

- Which of three or four titles did your partner like best? Why?
- Can you turn your topic sentence beginning into a more interesting lead?
- Do you end with the most important thing you want your readers to know or feel?
- Does your ending repeat what you said in the beginning, or does it say the same thing in a different way? Which kind of ending is better for this piece? Why?

Ask questions about sentences:

- How many of your sentences begin the same way?
- How else could you start two or three of these sentences?
- Could you break this long sentence into shorter ones?
- How might you combine two or three short sentences?

Ask questions about wording and phrasing:

- Which sentences do the best job of showing, not just telling?
- Where else could you use words that show instead of tell?

Many of the ideas discussed in Chapter 11 on assessment can easily be incorporated into conference sessions.

Conducting Conferences

During literacy conferences, you will talk with students about books they have read independently or the pieces they are writing or have written. Conferences may also be about books you have assigned for the whole class to read, but these are usually dealt with through literature groups or whole-class discussions.

The conference time with each student should be a relaxed, pleasant experience. You can let the conference evolve naturally, but it may also be a good idea to have a plan in mind. Here is one possible sequence for a reading conference:

1. What would you like to focus on today?
2. Tell me about your book.
3. What have you written in your journal that you would like to share?
4. Read aloud the part that you liked best.
5. Let's talk about what you think our goals should be for next time.

You also need a plan for writing conferences. If the student asked for the conference, begin by having the student tell what he or she wants to discuss and proceed from there. A simple basic plan that works well for many teachers is as follows (Calkins, 1994; Graves, 1983; Millett, 1986):

1. *Opening:* The student reads his or her draft. You listen or read along as the student reads.
2. *Discussion:* Talk about the content and sequence of ideas, unless the student has some other specific purpose. Ask questions that prompt the student to talk about the piece of writing.
3. *Closing:* Help the student focus attention on one thing to do to improve the writing. This will help the student realize quick success.

Every conference will be different, but having a plan such as one of these in mind is helpful in the beginning. As you and your students have more experiences with conferences, you will devise a plan that works best for you.

You can have a reading conference even if you have not read the book yourself. Just tell students if you don't know the book they are reading; they will enjoy sharing something new with you. It is easier to talk about a book if you have read it, but you can talk about any book by using very general questions:

- Tell me about your book.
- Who are the characters?
- Where does it take place?
- What happened?
- How did the story end?

You will notice that this line of questioning follows the story map concept discussed earlier in this text. You can also develop very general questions for expository texts:

- What is the topic of your book?
- What are the big ideas the author tells you?
- Find me a place to read aloud that supports one of the author's big ideas.

Sometimes you will find it helpful to have conferences with two students at the same time. This is always possible when you have assigned a book for the entire class to read or when students have read the same book or are reading books that are closely related. With two students, you can encourage higher-level thinking by comparing and contrasting books.

Peer Conferences

Peer conferences are another good way for students to have a conversation with someone about their writing or reading (Dahl, 1988). Students need to know what is expected of them and what they should do during the conference. Peer conferences are often held in preparation for a teacher conference.

Peer conferences work well with ELLs because teachers can pair students who have the same first language. The students confer in their first language and then prepare for their teacher conference, which will be in English.

An effective way to get peer conferences started is to develop with the class a set of guidelines to follow, such as those for writing from a third-grade class shown in Figure 10.13. Similar guidelines can be developed for reading. Adjust the guidelines for your grade level. Teacher conferences may serve as models for peer conferences. It is also a good idea to role-play peer conferences and talk with students about how to improve them.

FIGURE 10.13

Peer Conference Guidelines from a Third-Grade Class

Our Peer Conference Guidelines
- Remember that your friend's writing is his/her own work. Don't try to rewrite it.
- Let the writer read the piece of writing aloud.
- Talk about the things you like.
- Ask questions about things you don't understand.
- Make one or two suggestions for improving the writing.
- If you are proofreading, also read it silently.

Evaluating Conferences

As you work with conferences, you and your students should take time to evaluate them. Together you should talk about them, using questions like these:

1. How are our conferences working?
2. What is especially good about our conferences?
3. What problems do we have?
4. What can we do to improve our conferences?

If your students are new to conferences, you will probably need to evaluate them several times early in the year until they are running smoothly.

You must also evaluate your own skill in conducting conferences. The more experience you have, the better you will be at this activity. Here is a list of questions to ask yourself:

1. How are my conferences going overall?
2. Are they too long or too brief?
3. Am I asking questions that prompt children to think?
4. Is the conference truly a discussion, or am I testing?
5. Am I getting helpful information about my students' abilities to use reading and writing?
6. Are the other students in the class engaged in productive activities while I am conferencing?

A good way to evaluate yourself is to tape-record one or two conferences and listen to them. This will help you see how you can improve and will suggest many more questions than those raised here. Conference procedures may change from year to year, because new circumstances arise with each new class.

Records

An important part of keeping your classroom running smoothly is keeping sufficient records of what is happening and what individual students are doing. Teachers must develop ways to do this that suit their own circumstances. Consider several options as you decide on the types of records you want to keep.

Teacher Notebook or Portfolio

The teacher notebook or portfolio is an excellent way to organize a lot of information in one location. You use a large three-ring binder with dividers. Here are some possible sections for your teacher notebook or portfolio:

- *Theme plans:* This section contains a simple outline plan for the theme you are covering. It may also include themes that have been completed or that you are planning.
- *Schedules and lesson plans:* Daily or weekly schedules and lesson plans are kept here. Your lesson plans may take on many different forms. Some teachers like to keep lesson plans separate from this notebook, whereas others like to include as much information as possible in one place.

- ***Book lists:*** Lists of books you want to use or obtain for your class are compiled here. These may be books you want for a particular theme, want to order through the librarian, or want to purchase with funds you have available. A simple list with title, author, publisher, and ISBN number will give you the information you need to obtain the book when the time comes. Lists can also be located in professional journals and on various Web sites.

- ***Student information:*** This section contains a separate tab for each student and includes copies of forms such as those shown in Figures 10.14 and 10.15 to record pertinent observations and conference information. A page such as the one in Figure 10.16 is for parent conferences.

Other Ways to Keep Records

Not all teachers like the teacher notebook or portfolio concept. Some teachers prefer to keep separate folders or spiral notebooks for each student. The same types of information described above would be kept here. Other teachers use 5-by-8-inch

---

FIGURE 10.14

Student Data Sheet for Teacher Notebook

Name _____Birthdate _____Age _____

Address _____Telephone_____

Parent(s)/Guardian _____

Reading Data

Writing Data

Listening, Speaking, and Viewing Data

FIGURE 10.15

Sheet for Recording Observations and Student Conference Results

Name _____			Grade _____
Date	Observation	Date	Observation

FIGURE 10.16

Sheet for Recording Observations and Parent Conference Results

Name _____				Grade _____
Date	Parent Comments	Teacher Comments	Student Comments	Actions

Portfolios are discussed in Chapter 11.

cards to make notes of observations and conferences. Some rely more heavily on the student portfolio concept. You may decide to keep records on a computer, devising your own method of recording information to build a cumulative record of each student's literacy growth as well as plans, schedules, and book lists.

The important point is that there is more than one way to keep records. You should choose the method that best helps you monitor and adjust your classroom organization.

Educators Speak

Sixth-Grade Literacy Block Enhanced with Computers

"Meeting the individual needs of thirty-four sixth-grade students can prove to be a daunting task for anyone. One thing that I have established in my classroom to help with this task is a 45-minute block of time each day when every student is reading at his or her level. It is during this time that I am able to work in a small group with my most critical students.

Technology is extremely beneficial during this time. I present my students with extensive research projects. These projects often relate to our social studies curriculum. The students delve deeper into a certain aspect of an ancient civilization that we are in the midst of studying. They are able to use the computers to conduct in-depth research, practice their word processing skills, and turn their research into slide show presentations to share with the rest of the class.

The use of computers allows them access to a wealth of information that otherwise would not be available. They are developing critical thinking skills by being able to locate the necessary information. In order to pull out the important, relevant facts they need, they must sift through the extraneous information. The reading strategies of summarizing, clarifying, and questioning that have been ingrained in these students now must be used at a much higher level. The students enjoy these challenges, and it is a great way for them to extend their learning through the use of technology.

At first glance, word processing skills may not seem to tie into literacy at all. However, if students are quick and accurate with their typing skills, it is going to help them in many different aspects of their education as they progress through the grades. The less they have to concentrate on where the keys are, the more attention they can pay to the content of what they are writing. Allowing students access to the computers during this research time gives them hands-on application and practice they need to become proficient in these skills.

After the students have completed their research and typed a paper, they then make a presentation in the form of a slide show on the computer. This allows them to share what they have learned with the rest of the class. For this, they need to again gauge the importance of the information they have found and whittle it down to the main details. They also must think about the sequencing of events and how this will affect their presentations.

In essence, having students complete these projects independently while I am working with a small group allows them to apply several different reading and writing strategies that they have been taught thus far in elementary school. It also allows them to improve on a variety of technology skills that are a necessity in today's world."

Jill Baker, Sixth-Grade Teacher
Grand Oaks Elementary School
Citrus Heights, California

Developing a Management System

In this section, we show you the five steps for developing a management system for your classroom:

1. Group for literacy instruction
2. Plan a schedule,
3. Identify types of independent activities,
4. Teach students routines of the classroom, and
5. Try and revise.

Each of these steps is elaborated below. Figure 10.17 presents a flow chart to help you visualize how your planning will proceed.

Step 1: Group for Literacy Instruction

During much of the day, students will be grouped in various ways for various purposes. First, we discuss the concept of flexible grouping and give examples of such groups. Then we present five frameworks for grouping for literacy instruction: three for reading and two for writing. The three frameworks for reading are core books/anthologies, leveled (developmentally appropriate) books, and Reading Workshop. The two frameworks for writing are teacher-modeled writing and Writing Workshop.

An important teaching and organizational strategy is using *flexible groups*. As the name implies, these are groupings that exist temporarily for a particular purpose and change frequently. Flexible groups may consist of two, three, or more students working together to accomplish a specific purpose. Flexible groups may change every day or may last for several days. The size of a group depends on the purpose. For example, literature discussion groups are usually most successful when they contain three to five students. This number allows for interaction but is small enough to ensure that everyone gets to participate. The rule of thumb is to keep the group small enough to accomplish the intended purpose:

Chapter 7 provides information on literature discussion groups.

- Use *interest groups* any time you want students with similar interests to work together to discuss something, complete a project, or have a lesson. For example, if several students have very strong interests in science, you could pull them together to teach them how to perform a particular experiment, or they might complete a project together.

- *Strengths and needs groups* build on students' strengths or help them learn something they need. For example, after students have read and discussed the book *Pelicans* (Patent, 1992), you might bring together those who had trouble identifying the main ideas. This would also be a minilesson group and would receive direct instruction on main ideas. At other times, you might have a support-in-advance activity (described more fully later in this chapter), which builds background knowledge by mixing students who have some background with those who have little background in a topic.

FIGURE 10.17

A Management System Flow Chart

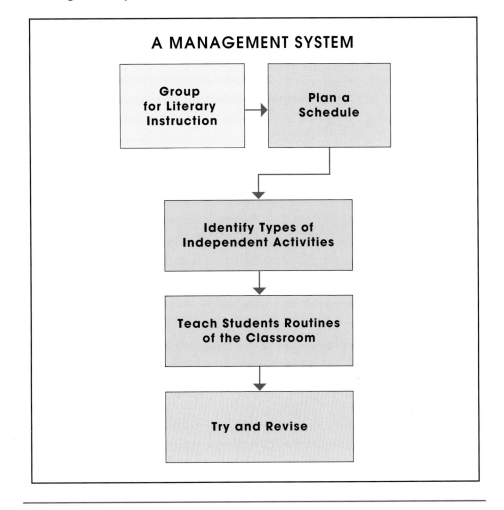

A MANAGEMENT SYSTEM

- *Minilesson groups* are for teaching lessons that certain students need. Many times these groups will be used for direct instruction on a specific skill or strategy. However, minilessons are not always based on need. Some are taught simply because there is something you want a group or the class to learn. For example, you may teach a minilesson at the beginning of the year to the whole class on how to select books that are appropriate for their reading levels. Some minilessons may be taught several times throughout the year. For example, you may need to teach a minilesson on adjectives every time some students are writing a description.

- *Discussion groups* often follow the reading of parts of books or complete books. These groups may be formed by students who elect to work together, by the teacher, or by a combination of the two. Discussion groups may also be used for writing; students meet to share their writing and to get peer reactions. In one sixth-grade class, discussion groups were being held for students to read aloud and talk about mysteries they had written.

- *Project groups* may be formed for long- or short-term projects related to any aspect of the curriculum. For example, a first-grade class may be making a mural about seasons that they develop throughout the year; different groups are responsible for different seasons. Often project groups are composed of students with differing abilities and needs.

- *Modeling groups* may be used any time students need more modeling of reading, writing, or other skills or strategies. This modeling may involve students, the teacher, or another adult as a model. For example, fourth graders who need extra support in reading might prepare a book to read aloud to a group of first graders. The first graders get good models, and the fourth graders build their confidence and skill in reading.

The important thing to keep in mind about these various types of groups is that they are *flexible;* they are always changing based on students' strengths, needs, interests, and various purposes for learning. Flexible grouping is one of the most useful tools you have for creating and maintaining a successful literacy classroom.

Reading Frameworks for Instruction

Three frameworks for reading will help you plan instruction: using core books/anthologies, using leveled (developmentally appropriate) books, and using Reading Workshop.

Using Core Books/Anthologies

This framework for organizing the classroom is often referred to as *whole-class instruction,* but a better name is *core book/anthology with flexible groups,* because the only aspect of it that is really whole class is the fact that everyone has experience reading the same text. Figure 10.18 shows how it operates.

Description. Everyone in the class will read the same piece of text. This could be the grade-level anthology or a trade book (the core book) such as *Head for the Hills!* (Walker, 1993), which is the story of the Johnstown, Pennsylvania, flood. *Each student needs a copy of the book being read.*

Prior knowledge is discussed in Chapter 3.

Begin by activating prior knowledge and developing background and vocabulary for the piece of literature. Some students may have only limited prior knowledge for the book. For them, you need to provide a preview or develop key concepts to give them a stronger base for what the whole class will read. This concept is known as *support in advance* or *jump-starting.* Support in advance may be provided by the classroom teacher or a support teacher such as a Title I teacher. When the whole class begins the book, a

FIGURE 10.18

Core Book/Anthology with Flexible Groups

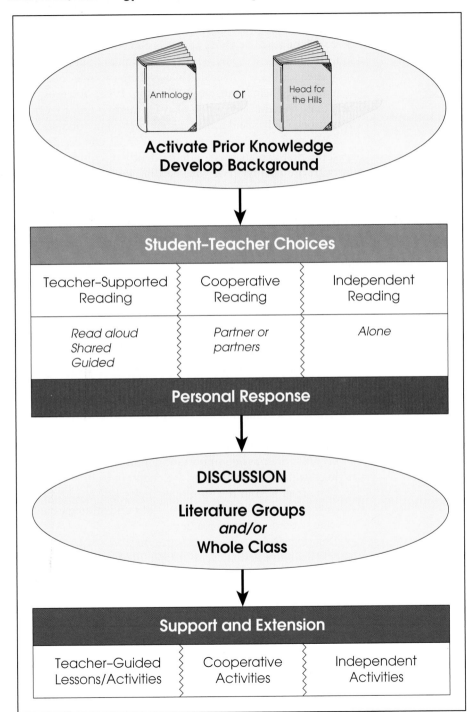

different prior-knowledge activity is used; the students who were given support in advance are now able to function more successfully with the whole class.

After prior knowledge has been activated and developed, students are ready to read. You accommodate individual differences among students by using different modes of reading. Either you or the students, or everyone together, decide how the piece will be read. By giving students choices in how they will read, you accommodate individual needs. Keep in mind, however, that when less able readers are given choices, they often select the choice that allows them to "hide" because they don't want to reveal that they need help (Johnston & Allington, 1991). You must be alert to this situation and help these students believe it is okay for them to get support. You may do this by having very strong readers and those needing help come together with you.

You may give the students two or three choices, for example: "Today you may read the first two chapters independently or come to the table and I will guide you through the chapters." If you see that students are not making good choices, you guide them to better decisions. It is not necessary to always offer students three choices, and sometimes you may decide how the whole class will read the book. A critical element in making this pattern of instruction work is varying the modes of reading to accommodate individual needs. Kindergarten and first-grade teachers are likely to conduct most of their initial readings as teacher-supported reading. After students have read the piece of literature, they should make a personal response to what they have read, often by writing.

Personal response is followed by discussion, another form of response. Discussion does not mean students simply answer the teacher's questions. Research has demonstrated the importance of students' discussing what they have read as a way to construct meaning (Sweet, 1993). For discussion, you should use the literature discussion group concept, giving students the option to decide with whom they will meet to discuss what they have read. The literature discussion groups may be followed by whole-class discussion to pull together the ideas of various groups. During the discussion groups, you should pay close attention to how students respond. This information will help you plan the support and extension activities that students need. For example, if during response you notice that some students reading *Head for the Hills!* are missing important details, you might provide a minilesson on identifying significant details using the chapters students have read.

The final step in the core book/anthology framework is providing support and extension. This is where you teach skills and strategies and do other types of activities that extend students' reading.

Support and extension activities may consist of teacher-guided lessons or activities, cooperative activities, or independent activities. It is not necessary to do all of these; you select what you believe is needed to thoroughly develop the students' abilities to construct meaning. For example, after reading the first two chapters in *Head for the Hills!* you may teach a needed skill lesson and defer other activities for when the book is completed. In addition to minilessons, support and extension activities may include more creative responses, vocabulary activities such as making word maps or word webs, writing, art, and so forth. You have probably already recognized how you have used all parts of the literacy lesson concept you have been learning throughout this text.

Modes of reading are discussed in Chapter 2.

For more information on observing students during responses, see Chapter 11.

An important question to address is how much time this framework requires. Obviously, the answer depends on the text being read and the students themselves. However, the following guidelines should help you:

- Prior knowledge should be activated quickly. If support in advance is given, it is likely to be completed on a day prior to beginning the literature with the whole class. Therefore, the whole-class prior-knowledge activity should last no longer than 10 to 15 minutes. After students start reading, you may discover they need more prior-knowledge support; therefore, you provide it at the time needed. *Remember, students want to read!* Don't wear out the book with too much prior-knowledge work.

- The amount of time allotted to reading each day will vary with the book and the grade level. It may range from 15 to 30 minutes.

- Discussion groups should be kept short to keep students focused and on task. In kindergarten and first grade, these discussions may last only a matter of seconds. Beyond these levels, 5 to 10 minutes is usually long enough.

- The amount of time for support and extension activities depends on the nature of the activities. Minilessons may last only 5 to 10 minutes, whereas other types of activities may last longer.

Be sure to keep the pace of instruction *appropriately fast*. The pace depends on students' strengths and needs. It is important to keep students reading and not spend too long on one book by doing too many activities. A chapter or two in a book such as *Head for the Hills!* should take one or two blocks of class time. More will be said about time in the section on scheduling.

Benefits of the Core Book/Anthology Framework. This framework offers many benefits. First, it puts everyone in the class on a level playing field. All students are confident that they are able to read the same types of books everyone else in the class can read; this reduces the stigma that has been attached to ability grouping.

Second, it provides a way to teach key skills and strategies. Students then apply these when they read leveled, or developmentally appropriate, books.

Third, this framework promotes and supports discussion involving *all* students. This is very important in helping students construct meaning.

A final benefit is flexibility; this framework is not linear. You may start by activating prior knowledge, having students read, and then having them discuss. You may reserve the support and extension for later. The next day you may continue the book with just reading because no further activation of prior knowledge is needed. Another way to use this framework is to teach the skill or strategy before the selection is read; reading then provides immediate practice and application in the selection.

Problems to Avoid. Although this is a strong framework for promoting success, it can have problems and pitfalls if the plan is misused. First, in the comprehensive literacy program, this plan *must be balanced* with the leveled (developmentally appropriate) books framework described in the next section. *All students must be given instruction with books that are appropriate for their reading levels.*

Second, although all students are reading the same book, the plan can fail if all students are treated exactly the same. In other words, you must vary the modes of

See Chapter 2 on leveling, or determining the developmental appropriateness of books.

reading, the discussion groups, and the support and extension activities. You can't just have the whole class read the book independently, answer questions, and complete one activity.

Choice for students is critical. You must allow some student choice to truly accommodate individual needs.

Avoid the pitfall of having everyone in the class read the same book but dividing the class into several reading groups by ability level. This does *not* achieve the goal of a success-centered classroom, because the focus is only on students' ability. The one-book framework should allow *all* students to experience success together using the same text at the same time.

Using Leveled/Developmentally Appropriate Books

The leveled/developmentally appropriate book framework is based on the idea that all students need to read books that are appropriate for their reading ability. Figure 10.19 shows how this framework operates.

Description. You begin by selecting several books that cover a range of reading levels. In the example described here, we are looking at books that would be used in a first-grade classroom. You may use two or more books; usually four is about the most teachers want to use at one time. The easiest book shown in Figure 10.19 is *Sheep in a Jeep* (Shaw, 1986), and the most difficult is *Clean Your Room, Harvey Moon* (Cummings, 1991). The other two books, *The Wonderful Pigs of Jillian Jiggs* (Gilman, 1988) and *Mommy Doesn't Know My Name* (Williams, 1990), fall in between. If you are using only two books, one of them must be the right level for your students whose needs are greatest. When using this framework, you need enough copies of each book so that each student can have one.

You designate one of the books the *teacher book*. This means that students who read this book will work with you for part of the book or throughout the whole book. The teacher book gives students who need teacher support a place to go. The teacher book is not necessarily the easiest book; sometimes it is a very challenging book for which any student would need teacher support.

Sometimes you will assign students to the book you want them to read, and at other times you should allow student choice. If students are going to select their own book, begin by introducing each book to the class. Read aloud just a portion to activate prior knowledge and to give students a sense of the book. Then tell students which book is to be the teacher book. Give students a few minutes to look at the books, select the one they want to read, and decide how they will read it. Remind them to use "thumbs up" to select the book that is right for them.

If you are working with older students and longer books, you might display the books for several days, allowing students to look them over and sign up for the book they want to read. Students should make a second choice in case too many sign up for the same book.

After students make their selection, they read the book in the mode they have decided to use. Since the books in this example are short, they will easily be completed in about 20 minutes or so. After students complete their reading, they do their personal responses and then have a literature discussion group with others who have read the same book. To prompt the discussion, you can use a generic response

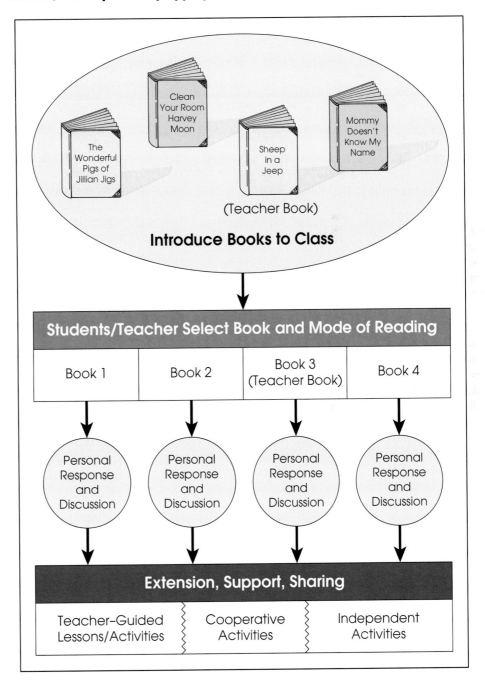

FIGURE 10.19

Leveled/Developmentally Appropriate Books Model

FIGURE 10.20

Generic Response Chart for Prompting Leveled/Developmentally Appropriate Book Discussions

> **Discussion**
> 1. Retell what you read.
> 2. Tell your favorite part or character.

chart such as the one in Figure 10.20. As students discuss their books, you move from group to group to participate in or monitor the discussions.

Finally, you provide one or more activities that all students can do to extend and support the books and allow students to share. For example, with the four books suggested in Figure 10.19, each group of students might complete a story map as a way to share their books with one another; this would also help them focus on constructing meaning. The extension and support may also include minilessons or other types of activities as described in the previous framework for support and extension.

The amount of time required to complete this framework using these four books is approximately 60 to 80 minutes for a first-grade class. When you use this framework with four books in first grade, the same books may be used over three or four days. Often students reread the same book several times. As long as they continue to enjoy rereading a book, their reading ability is probably growing. However, if they get stuck on one book and fail to move on, you can remove the book or add new ones to the group and entice them to try a new one.

The leveled-book framework is effective at all grade levels. For upper grades, you might use three chapter books, such as *The Summer of the Swans* (Byars, 1970), *Number the Stars* (Lowry, 1989), and *The Kid in the Red Jacket* (Park, 1987). When using this framework with chapter books, the books may last a week or longer. Discussion does not necessarily take place at the end of each chapter, and the title used as the teacher book rotates from book to book to allow teacher interaction for each book.

Benefits of the Leveled/Developmentally Appropriate Books Framework. The major benefit of the leveled-books framework is that it allows all students to have instructional support with books that are appropriate to their reading ability. While reading these books, students can apply the skills and strategies they learned while reading the core book or anthology. By incorporating the element of student choice with a range of teacher-selected books, you more effectively accommodate students' individual needs.

Problems to Avoid. Teachers report that the biggest problem with this framework is management: it is often difficult to have so many books going at one time. We suggest that you use the core book/anthology framework first. When that is working effectively, slowly begin using the leveled-books framework, beginning with just two books.

Third graders in a reading tent with self-selected books. © Bob Daemmrich/The Image Works

Another problem may be the teacher's reluctance to allow students to choose what they read some of the time. Teachers worry that students will select a book that is not appropriate to their level of reading. If you see this happening, confer with individual students, and guide them to make better selections.

Finally, you and your school will need to build collections of books with multiple copies at a wide range of levels. Centralized book collections facilitate the developmentally appropriate books process.

Using a Reading Workshop Framework

The Reading Workshop is a third framework you can use to organize and manage the literacy-centered classroom. Atwell (1987) discusses the Reading Workshop as a way to approach reading in her middle school classes. The workshop is a time when the entire class is engaged in reading, responding, and sharing books with the teacher and with peers. Although it provides time for the teacher to help students improve their construction of meaning, the heart of the Reading Workshop is time for reading. Reutzel and Cooter (1991) have adapted the Reading Workshop as proposed by Atwell for use in elementary grades 2 through 5.

Description. The Reading Workshop consists of five main components: teacher sharing time, minilessons, state-of-the-class conference, self-selected reading and responding, and student sharing time. These are outlined in Figure 10.21, along with suggested times.

Teacher Sharing Time. The teacher uses this initial sharing time to motivate or excite students about literature. For example, you might use a short story such as *Hemi's Pet* (de Hamel, 1985) to introduce students to a series of books on pets or one of Jack Prelutsky's poems from *Tyrannosaurus Was a Beast* (Prelutsky, 1988) to excite children about the study of dinosaurs. This sharing takes from 5 to 10 minutes and serves to warm up the class. Holdaway (1979) describes this process for

---

FIGURE 10.21

Reading Workshop Plan

- **Teacher Sharing Time** (5–10 minutes)
  A time when the teacher shares some literature to spark students' interests and motivate them for independent reading.

- **Minilessons** (5–10 minutes)
  A teacher-directed lesson focusing on prereading activities that activate and develop prior knowledge for a particular piece of literature or a skill or strategy needed.

- **State-of-Class Conference** (3–5 minutes)
  Each student tells the teacher and the rest of the class what he or she is doing that day. The teacher records on the state-of-the class chart. This lets the teacher determine needs for conferences, etc.

- **Reading and Responding** (40–60 minutes)
  Alternative A
    During this time, students engage in several possible activities:
      - Self-selected reading (10–20 minutes)
      - Literature groups (20–30 minutes)
      - Conferences with the teacher (20 minutes)
  Alternative B
    A variation of this plan requiring 60 minutes is often used.
      - Whole-class reading and responding (10–20 minutes)
      - Self-selected reading and responding (10–20 minutes)
      - Literature groups (10–20 minutes)
      - Conferences with the teacher, held during teacher-assigned reading or only on selected days (10 minutes)

- **Student Sharing Time** (5–10 minutes)
  Students share what they are doing or have done. This may be done in sharing circles or as a whole class. The teacher may comment about activities or commend students who participated in conferences.

kindergarten and first grade. Older students also profit from teacher sharing time. Many teachers allow students to share a poem they have read or written or to tell a story. You can use this sharing time to lead into a minilesson.

Minilesson. A minilesson on a strategy or a skill is designed to meet a need based on students' responses to reading or to provide prereading support such as background or vocabulary for a particular piece of literature. This lesson, using direct instruction, incorporates the skill or strategy within the context of a piece of literature students have already read or listened to. It may be done with the whole class or a small group.

Minilessons may be drawn from teachers' resource books or developed by the teacher. However, skills from a published curriculum guide or teacher's manual should be taught only if a real need exists.

State-of-the-Class Conference. During this brief period (5 minutes), you will take stock of what students are doing or planning to do during the remainder of the day's workshop. Reutzel and Cooter (1991) suggest using a chart similar to that shown in Figure 10.22 to keep track of what each student is doing. Initially, many teachers keep this chart on a clipboard and simply ask each student what he or she is doing on that day. They complete the chart using the code at the bottom. As you and the students become more comfortable with the Reading Workshop, the students can assume responsibility for completing the chart themselves, and a large version can be posted each week. In Figure 10.22, the teacher has partially completed the chart. By having students announce what they will be doing, you encourage them to commit themselves to a particular task.

The information from this assessment keeps you in touch with what students are doing and lets you know which students may need a conference or other teacher support. For example, if you notice that a student has been reading the same book for several days with no response activity, you know you may need a special meeting with the student to find out what progress has been made and to set new goals or change existing ones.

Reading and Responding. This is the heart of the Reading Workshop, the time when students read and respond to books. There are two alternatives for using this time. Alternative A has three basic types of activities: self-selected reading, literature responses, and individual reading conferences. Usually this portion of the workshop lasts from about 40 to 60 minutes, depending on the age level of your students:

- *Self-selected reading* usually lasts from 10 to 20 minutes, depending on the grade level. During this time, the students read independently or with a partner, and you read for some portion of the time to serve as a model. However, you should also circulate to hold individual miniconferences, keep students motivated and encouraged, and do on-the-spot, incidental teaching. Throughout this time, students may make entries in their journals.

- *Literature responses* can involve a number of activities, such as writing in journals or meeting with a literature group. During this time, you continue to circulate and confer with individuals, or you meet with a literature group to participate in the discussion or serve as a recorder. Some students may continue their silent reading, while others meet in literature groups, work in journals, or do some other response activity. If students have not chosen to meet with a literature

Reading State-of-the-Class Chart

STATE-OF-THE-CLASS

Name	M	Tu	W	Th	F
Ann	SSR	J			
Beth	LG-D	SSR			
Bill	SSR	LG-D			
Carl	J	SSR			
Cathy	LG-DNR	SSR			
Darin	R	SSR			
David	SSR	SSR			

CODE   SSR - Self-Selected Reading   LG - Literature Group Meeting
        J   - Journal   D   - Discussing
        R   - Response Activity   G   - Setting Goals
        RK - Record Keeping   DNR - Determining New
                                               Response

group, they should always be encouraged to respond in some other way, such as by sharing with a friend or completing a project about the book they have read.

- *Individual reading conferences* with students who are not in literature groups make up the last 10 minutes of the period. During these conferences, other students may complete a literature group or continue with self-selected reading. Usually two or three conferences are held each day.

If you want the whole class or a selected group of students to read the same book, you will use alternative B, in which you assign a book and provide the appropriate activities for a literacy lesson. You also include time for self-selected reading, and you adjust the code for the state-of-the-class chart to RT—Reading Time, SS—Self-Selected, and AR—Assigned Reading (see Figure 10.22). You can adjust the times for the other activities according to students' needs.

If you decide to move into the Reading Workshop gradually, you can schedule two days for the workshop and use the remaining days for other reading activities. Then you can expand the Reading Workshop to your full program.

You may be in a school that uses a literature anthology. If so, you can use the anthology for students to select what they want to read or combine the reading workshop framework with the core-book/anthology framework discussed earlier. Lessons suggested in the teacher's resources that accompany an anthology may be used selectively for minilessons. Basically, this pattern is alternative B suggested in Figure 10.21. You will have to adjust the code for your state-of-the-class chart to go with this combined approach.

Student Sharing Time. During the last 5 to 10 minutes of the Reading Workshop, students share books they have read and report their progress on literature projects or other response activities. Sharing time "advertises" the excitement of literacy learning and helps to promote the class as a community of readers. During this time, students may ask one another for ideas to improve what they are doing. Some teachers often divide the class into small sharing groups (three to five students) for greater student involvement. The teacher then circulates among the groups, commenting or just listening. Longer sharing times may be scheduled when certain literature groups have a special activity or project to share, such as a readers theater performance or a puppet play.

Benefits of the Reading Workshop. The Reading Workshop provides one effective framework for systematically developing the reading block in your comprehensive literacy classroom. If you use alternative B as outlined in Figure 10.21, you are also able to incorporate both core-book/anthology supported reading and leveled/developmentally appropriate reading.

Problems to Avoid. If you choose to use the Reading Workshop as a totally self-selected reading block (alternative A), you may risk overlooking the need for more instruction and in-depth discussion that comes when all students experience the same book or self-select from a controlled set of books. This problem can be easily avoided by going to alternative B for the Reading Workshop. Starting the Reading Workshop without appropriate student preparation may also cause problems. Atwell (1987) suggests that you develop and clarify rules of the workshop with students before you begin and during its initial use.

Writing Frameworks

A classroom that promotes and supports writing must have identified times for this activity. Our model of a comprehensive literacy program provides three such blocks of time. On the basis of his research, Graves (1991) recommends that children write 35 to 40 minutes per day for a minimum of four days a week. If you really believe children and young adults learn to read and write by reading and writing, there is no way to accept anything less than a plan that calls for *writing every day*.

The time provided for writing means the time for students to actually write, beyond the time for minilessons and other modeling or demonstrations of writing. The Writing Workshop plan discussed later in this chapter is a highly effective way to build in times for both student writing and needed instruction. Once you become comfortable with both Reading and Writing Workshops, you can integrate them into a literacy workshop. Such a plan would be similar to the concept of integrated language arts that many teachers have tried to achieve in their classrooms (Templeton, 1991).

Two writing frameworks will help you plan instruction: teacher-modeled writing and Writing Workshop.

Teacher-Modeled Writing

See Chapter 8 for a discussion of modes of writing as well as domains.

The teacher-modeled writing framework is an effective way to model writing using the shared writing mode discussed earlier in this text.

Description. This framework begins by having the whole class (or a large group) work with the teacher to develop a common piece (the Writing: Learning to Write block). The teacher or students may actually write the text. At another time, the teacher conducts a minilesson using the group-written piece to revise and improve the particular type of writing. The teacher elicits ideas from the students and models various elements to help students see how to write in the domain or product being modeled. Depending on their needs, students move to either supported writing (Writing: Developmentally Appropriate Writing block) or independent writing; students who first do supported writing will later move on to independent writing.

Benefits of Teacher-Modeled Writing. This framework provides a sound way for you to model writing for your students. By having students move from shared to guided, collaborative and cooperative, and independent writing, you scaffold instruction and gradually release responsibility to students. Modeling writing is especially important for ELLs, in that such scaffolded instruction makes the input comprehensible.

In addition, this framework can be easily combined with the Writing Workshop, the next framework discussed. By combining the two frameworks, you achieve a balance of modeled writing and developmentally appropriate writing.

Problems to Avoid. The biggest problem in using the teacher-modeled writing framework is moving students too quickly or too slowly through the various stages of writing. Providing either too little or too much modeling can cause problems for students. Once students know how to write in the particular domain or for the particular product, the way they develop and become mature writers is by *writing*. Even when students move to independent writing, you need to keep in mind that through conferencing, you continue to model for students and support them in their growth as writers.

Writing Workshop Framework

The Writing Workshop, which is similar to the Reading Workshop, has been recommended by numerous researchers and writing specialists (Atwell, 1987; Calkins, 1994; Hansen, 1987). It is a flexible plan that places students and teacher in a partnership for learning.

Description. The Writing Workshop consists of four basic parts: minilessons, state-of-the-class conferences, writing and conferring, and group sharing. Each part flows into the next to make up the block of time allocated for writing. The ideas and suggestions given here are based on the work of Atwell (1987), Calkins (1994), and Hansen (1987) and our own experiences in working with children and teachers.

Minilessons. The minilesson is done with the whole class and usually lasts from 5 to 10 minutes. The content of the minilesson is determined by student needs as evidenced during a previous Writing Workshop. The guidelines presented earlier also apply here.

Since the minilesson content is based in part on student needs, the topics covered may range from how to select a topic to how to write a business letter. Following is a list of possible topics for minilessons:

- Procedures for the Writing Workshop
- Writing an opening paragraph
- Punctuating items in a series
- Selecting words to show fear, suspense, bravery, or other characteristics
- Selecting topics
- Writing a friendly letter
- Examples of humor from a piece of literature
- Correct use of paragraph form
- Outlining for a report
- Writing description
- Punctuating dialogue

There are many more possible topics for minilessons. On some days, no minilesson is needed; this time may be used for more sharing or writing.

State-of-the-Class Conference. The state-of-the-class conference, a very brief activity, helps to ensure that you know exactly what all students are doing during each Writing Workshop. Atwell (1987) uses a clipboard and chart similar to the one in Figure 10.23 to keep track of students each day.

After you have completed the minilesson, take 5 minutes to ask students to identify what they will be doing during the day's workshop. Use codes such as those shown in Figure 10.23 to record each student's reply. By examining your chart, you can tell who might need some extra conference time or just a quick visit from you during writing. As you become more comfortable with this procedure, you might choose to make a large state-of-the-class chart and have students complete it each day as the Writing Workshop begins.

The state-of-the-class conference builds in a comfort factor for you: it lets you know what students are doing and gives you a way to know what is happening over the week. Teachers who use the Writing Workshop indicate repeatedly that this portion of the workshop gives them the control they feel they need but still encourages student independence.

Writing and Conferring. The writing and conferring block is the core of the Writing Workshop and usually lasts from 30 to 40 minutes, depending on the grade level. During this block of time, students are writing; you may be writing yourself or holding conferences with students.

FIGURE 10.23

Partial Writing State-of-the-Class Chart

State of Class Chart					
Names	M	T	W	Th	F
Lisa	①	ⓒ	②	RV	PR
Ted	①	①	ⓒ	②	②
Larry	②	ⓒ	RV	PR	P
Susan	ⓒ	P	⑤①	①	ⓒ
Mike	②	PR	P	⑤	①

Code
① – First Draft
② – Second Draft
ⓒ – Conference
RV – Revising
PR – Proofing
P – Publishing
⑤ – Shaving

Since students will be at various stages in developing their writing piece, you will need to do a variety of things, depending on their needs. Some of the time you will be working on some writing of your own, thus modeling adult writing and expressing that you value this activity. At other times you will be circulating through the class, talking with individual students, reading portions of their writing, prompting and encouraging them, and offering whatever support they need. These brief encounters may be viewed as miniconferences or just times to talk with, guide, and support students. During this time, you will gain valuable information that will help you plan minilessons and assess students' progress. You will want to carry note cards, a pad, or sticky notes so that you can make notes for future use in planning or for insertion into your notebook page for each student.

During this time, students may be holding a peer conference, working on revision, editing, planning a new piece, or just getting topics for writing. You might stop to visit, but remember that these are *peer* conferences. You will have a time to meet with students later.

During writing and conferring, you will also hold formal group and individual conferences with students. Using a sign-up chart or an area of the chalkboard, students should sign up in advance of conference time to meet with you, either at the beginning of each day's Writing Workshop or the day before you announce you will hold conferences. You need to be flexible about this.

Group Sharing. Group sharing is just like an individual or peer conference, except that the whole group reacts to a piece of writing. This portion of the Writing Workshop usually lasts 5 minutes or longer, depending on your schedule and what needs to take place. During this time, you might incorporate the concept of the author's chair.

Group sharing is not just a show-and-tell time; it is a time for students to talk about their writing with peers and get some additional reactions, as well as a time to celebrate their successes by sharing finished products. All of this sharing promotes the classroom as a community of writers, a place where writers discover how well they have constructed meaning. For example, if a student gives a report on dinosaurs, other students might ask questions about things they don't understand or think are incorrect, or even suggest another book on dinosaurs that the author should read before finishing the piece.

Some teachers divide the class into two or three sharing groups so that more individuals can share at one time. Don't skip sharing time or cut it short: it provides enormous benefits:

- It provides students with authentic reasons for writing and gives them the audience writers need.
- It brings closure to the construction of meaning by having both readers and writers discover whether they have successfully accomplished their purpose.
- It helps students grow in both their writing and reading by getting feedback from peers and having to respond to that feedback.
- It is another point in the development of literacy where reading and writing are integrated into one process within the community of learners.

Benefits of the Writing Workshop. The Writing Workshop is a flexible, manageable framework that allows you to meet individual needs. It is possible to combine it with the teacher-modeled writing framework to provide balanced writing instruction. The teacher-modeled writing piece can be inserted into the minilesson slot of the Writing Workshop, thereby giving you a way to model writing while at the same time having students write independently. You might do one shared piece each week or follow a regular cycle, using the remaining time to have students do guided, collaborative or cooperative, or independent writing.

Problems to Avoid. It takes time to move effectively into the Writing Workshop framework. Therefore, you need to develop a systematic plan for its use and try it out gradually. It is especially important to share the framework with students, discussing each section. As you work with students in the Writing Workshop, periodically evaluate how its components are working. Teachers at various grade levels have found the following procedures very helpful in starting the Writing Workshop:

1. *Familiarize yourself with the Writing Workshop plan.* Think about how you will use it in your classroom.
2. *Think through procedures you will use.* The state-of-the-class chart, conference scheduling, and simple recordkeeping for your conferences are enough to get started. Gradually add other procedures you have learned from this text and other sources.
3. *Talk with your students about the workshop.* Make a chart showing the parts of the plan, and use it as a guide for you and your students.
4. *Designate a day to begin.* This may take place at the beginning of the year or at any point during the year. Students may have pieces of writing in progress, or you may want everyone to start with a new piece of writing. Teachers find both approaches successful.
5. *Use your first few minilessons to establish basic routines.* After the first day, you will begin to know what types of support your students need with procedures and routines. (There really aren't many to be concerned about.)
6. *Evaluate what is happening with your students.* Talk about the Writing Workshop. Ask students for suggestions to make it better.
7. *Trust your judgment.* You are a professional and know how to make decisions. If something feels right, do it; if it feels wrong, don't do it. However, give new ideas time to work; don't just drop something after one attempt.

Now that you are familiar with the five frameworks for organizing and managing a success-centered literacy classroom, we will focus on how to plan daily routines and schedules using these frameworks, along with time for independent reading and writing.

Step 2: Plan a Schedule

Regardless of the type of program you have in your school, you must have a daily plan that will help you manage the instruction and activities of your classroom. There is *no one right schedule* that works for all teachers. However, having a system for thinking about your schedule makes planning easier and more efficient for you. Researchers have found that blocking leads to improved student achievement and more effective and efficient use of student and teacher time (Cunningham, Hall, & Defee, 1998).

A Blocked Plan for Scheduling

See page 27 to review the Model for a Comprehensive Literacy Program.

We presented a model for a comprehensive literacy program in Chapter 2, and have consistently referred to this model throughout this text. This model balances the essential components of a literacy program in seven blocks; six of these are necessary for all students, and an additional intervention block may be necessary for some students. Each block is given varying amounts of time, depending on what needs to be done.

Thinking about your literacy program schedule in blocks does the following:

- It gives you a way to organize and plan systematic daily instruction.
- It helps you avoid skipping things because you know that each block is generally included every day.

- It allows you to effectively plan for and use any support staff you may have (aides, reading specialists, resource teachers, and volunteers).
- It helps students participate more fully in their literacy program because they know what is to come and what to expect each day.

Amount of Time Required. A daily blocked plan will work from kindergarten through grade 8. Although research does not specify the exact amounts of time that should be devoted to literacy instruction in general or to each block, we suggest that the times presented in Table 10.1 are the minimum times that you need at each grade level to have an effective literacy program. As you will see when you read the sample schedules, the blocks may be separated by breaks, other subjects, or lunch. When combined, they add up to the recommended total amount of time. How do the suggested times stack up against what you know about the amount of time teachers usually have for literacy instruction? If you find yourself saying, "I [or teachers I know] usually have more time," *great.* If you find yourself saying, "No way. I [or teachers I know] don't have this much time," you need to rethink and discuss the amount of time available for literacy instruction. Remember, it *takes time* to provide quality literacy instruction that prevents student failure.

Sample Schedules Incorporating Framework

As you plan your daily schedule, you will want to incorporate the various frameworks we have discussed as needed. A look at some sample schedules from several teachers will help you see how to incorporate the frameworks into your blocked schedule and get in all the necessary components of a comprehensive literacy program. Figures 10.24, 10.25, 10.26, and 10.27 present sample schedules from four teachers. Read and study all the schedules with the following points or questions in mind:

- Does each teacher plan for all blocks? How do they vary the way it is done?
- How do these teachers' time allotments compare to the times given in Table 10.1?
- How does each teacher start the day? What is the teacher's purpose with this type of activity?

TABLE 10.1 **Minimum Amounts of Time for a Daily Blocked Literacy Schedule**

Grade Levels	Minimum Times
Kindergarten	3 hours[a]
Grades 1–2	2–3 hours
Grades 3–5	1 1/2–2 hours
Grades 6–8	1–2 hours

[a]Most half-day kindergartens don't have this much time.

FIGURE 10.24

Ms. Barnett's Kindergarten Schedule

8:30	Arrival and Sign-in independent Writing
8:45	Warm-up/Daily News/Morning Message
9:00	Reading: Learning Skills and Strategies
9:15	Reading: Application of Skills and Strategies
9:30	Independent Reading
9:40	Center Time (math, science, social studies)
10:00	Break/Recess/Specials art, music, computer lab)

10:30	Writing (blocks alternate as needed)
	    Writing: Learning to Write
	    Writing: Developmentally Appropriate Writing

11:10	Sharing
11:30	Dismiss

Step 3: Identify Types of Independent Activities

When you have planned for grouping your students and worked out your schedules, your first thought may be, "But what do the other students do while I'm working with a small group?" The answer to that question lies with the concept of *independent activities*. As the name suggests, these are activities students can engage in without supervision. Students may work alone, with a partner, or in a small group. Some of these activities, such as independent reading or writing, may be part of your blocked schedule; for example, during the block of time allotted to independent reading, you may be teaching a minilesson to a small group.

The following are a few such independent activities. As the year progresses, you and your students will be able to add to this list:

- Independent reading
- Independent writing
- Response to a book
- Vocabulary game
- Computer work
- Audiotapes

Mr. Lopez's First-Grade Schedule

8:45	Opening exercise/Morning Message
9:00	Reading blocks
	Independent Reading
	Reading: Application of Skills and Strategies
	Specially written texts/Leveled texts
	Reading: Learning Skills and Strategies
	Core Book/anthology
	Instruction in decoding skills
	Construction of meaning
10:15	Break
10:30	Writing blocks
	Independent Writing
	Writing: Learning to Write
	Writing: Developmentally Appropriate Writing
11:15	Morning share and lunch
11:45	Math
12:20	Specials (art/music/PE)
1:10	Teacher read-aloud
1:25	Science/social studies/health
1:50	Projects/response activities
2:20	Clean up/closing activities
2:30	Dismiss

- Map activities
- Projects
- Learning centers

You may want to limit which independent activities you want students to engage in at certain times. Activities written on individual strips of tag board to post on a bulletin board or affix with magnets will make it easy to mix and match and add and delete activities. Some teachers keep a comprehensive list posted, but clip a clothespin next to those from which students can choose on a given day.

Ms. Sanders's Fifth-Grade Schedule

8:30	Arrival/journal writing
8:45	Writing blocks
	Daily Independent Writing
	Writing: Learning to Write/Developmentally Appropriate Writing
9:30	Reading blocks
	Reading: Learning Skills and Strategies (core book/anthology)
	Reading: Application of Skills and Strategies (leveled books)
10:30	Break
10:45	Specials (art, music, PE, computer lab)
11:30	Lunch
12:00	Independent Reading block
12:30	Math
1:45	Social studies/science
2:30	Clean up and end of day activities
2:40	Teacher read-aloud
3:00	Dismiss

Mr. Burgess's Eighth-Grade Schedule (60-minute period)

Writing Workshop—M-T-W (Writing/Language—Word Work)
Reading Workshop—Th-F (Reading—Word Work)

Upon arrival	• State-of-class check
5 minutes	• Group sharing
10 minutes	• Minilesson
30 minutes	• Read/Write/Confer
10 minutes	• Partner/Class share
5 minutes	• Goal setting/Close

Step 4: Teach Students Routines of the Classroom

In order to manage your classroom effectively, you must develop routines with your students. There are three critical steps in the process of developing management routines:

1. ***Develop a daily schedule.*** We have discussed this in detail in a previous section. Review any parts of that section now if you need to do so.
2. ***Identify independent activities for students to do.*** We have already suggested what these activities might include. Students need to know what to do when they have completed any of their work and are not working with you. The list of possible activities should be posted where students can easily refer to them, and they should be changed frequently. Teach students how to engage in these activities without disturbing each other or the group that is working with you.
3. ***Develop and discuss routines with students.*** To help students feel comfortable working in groups and working independently, you need to develop routines within the classroom. The following steps have been used effectively by many teachers:
   * Develop with students a set of classroom guidelines for general behavior. Post these where they can be easily seen (see Figure 10.28).
   * Appoint one or two students as monitors each week. Students can go to these persons with questions if you are busy with a group.
   * Present and post your daily schedule for students to see. Discuss what will be happening throughout each day.
   * Role-play the schedule and procedures with students. Create situations where problems are likely to arise (e.g., need to go to the restroom, student doesn't know a word). Discuss and evaluate the role playing. This may need to be done several times at the beginning of the year. Allow room for new guidelines to be added.

FIGURE 10.28

Classroom Behavior Chart

During work times we will . . .

* Work quietly

* Go to our weekly monitors for help if Miss Janes is busy.

* Select an independent activity to do when my work is finished

Step 5: Try and Revise

Try your plans, and revise them as needed. After using your schedule and routines for a few days, discuss with students how things are going. Ask for suggestions for improving or changing the schedule or any routines. Talk about how monitors are being used.

Although a management plan is essential, no plan should be written in stone. In fact, the beauty of the plan is that it can and should be modified. What might have seemed essential at the beginning of the school year may not be necessary as classroom routines become second nature and students have grown in their ability to work independently.

Meeting the Needs of All Students

The four classrooms and schedules just reviewed show you a variety of ways teachers plan a schedule. There are, however, five special considerations you must also address in scheduling: ELLs, children with exceptionalities, intervention, multi-age classrooms, and community-home connections.

English Language Learners

All four of the teachers reviewed earlier have students who are ELLs. Although these students often require more patience and extra support, they participate in the same literacy learning experiences that other students do. Routines are especially important for ELLs, because a routine makes the classroom day predictable. Once such learners know the routines, they can focus more fully on learning activities. The ideas presented throughout this text work effectively with ELLs.

Children with Exceptionalities

Our four teachers all have children who are classified as exceptional. Some have been included in the regular classroom from special education, some are gifted and talented, and others have learning disabilities. In all cases, the teachers used flexible grouping along with the various frameworks and a variety of teaching strategies to meet the needs of all students.

Intervention

See Chapter 9 for information about working with struggling readers and programs designed to meet this need.

Intervention is additional instruction (usually in reading) that prevents or stops reading failure. Research has clearly demonstrated that some students will never achieve complete success in reading without instructional support that is given *in addition to the balanced classroom program* that everyone receives (Snow, Burns, & Griffin, 1998).

Parallel Block Scheduling Helps Students with Diverse Needs

"The range of instructional needs in my first-grade class is incredibly diverse. The students come from varied backgrounds. At the beginning of the year, I have students who do not have the concept of a word, as well as students reading on a second-grade level. The way I meet these needs is by using small, homogeneous groups. This year, parallel block scheduling was introduced in grades 1 and 2. Each grade level consists of five teachers, but only four homerooms. The fifth teacher is a content specialist in either science or social studies. My homeroom is divided so that reading and math groups have low student-to-teacher ratios. This helps my instruction to be more effective. The other half of the class goes to the science or social studies extension room. After approximately 50 minutes, the groups rotate.

My reading block consists of guided reading and word study. Through assessment of students, I am able to target my instruction to their specific instructional needs. Small groups meet with me during my reading block by using a procedure known as circle, center, seat rotation. This allows all students to work on reading activities at their targeted, instructional level. This involves a weekly schedule for word study instruction that is consistent throughout the year. My word study schedule includes activities for each day of the week—for example:

Monday: Introduce new words, cut out and sort words, and keep in our word study notebooks.
Tuesday: Sort words and draw and label or write a sentence for one word from each category.
Wednesday: Word hunt for words that follow the same patterns in books we are reading.
Thursday: Buddy speed sort and games.
Friday: Spell check

Students meet with me during circle time, where I conduct guided reading with instructional text, as well as word study. I am able to monitor progress by using observation, spell checks, as well as running records. These assessments allow for flexible grouping. For example, Jenny was not being successful on specific word features, and I transitioned her to another group, where she was able to experience success and progress. While this small group of students is working with me, the remainder of the class is divided into seat and center time. Students at their seats work on word study and writing activities. Students at centers work on activities related to literacy. My guided reading and word study schedule allows me to manage groups of students with diverse educational needs in my classroom, and all students make progress when their individual, instructional needs are met. It sure has made a difference in my classroom!"

Kelly L. Andrus, First-Grade Teacher
Parkside Elementary School
Fredricksburg, Virginia

Multi-Age Classrooms

Some schools incorporate the multi-age concept, whereby several ages are placed in the same class (Chapman, 1995). These classes are sometimes called "families." Within each family, students usually study a common theme. Within this theme, the teacher can use the same five frameworks described in this chapter to organize and manage instruction.

For more information on multi-age classrooms, see Chapman (1995), listed in the "For Additional Reading" section.

Frameworks such as the leveled and developmentally appropriate books approach, Reading Workshop, and Writing Workshop are very effective in organizing the multi-age classroom. If you review the schedules of the first three teachers presented in the previous section, you can easily see that they could also be used for a multi-age class. The biggest mistake often made in multi-age classes is treating each age as a separate group. This is contrary to the theory and research behind the multi-age concept.

Community-Home Connections

Our four teachers maintain close ties with students' homes and communities. They do this by drawing on community resources, having students share at home books they have read and pieces they have written in school, and maintaining constant communications with families through conferences and newsletters. Teachers can use paraprofessionals and bilingual parents to help develop good connections with the homes of ELLs. Having a continuous connection with the home is critical to the effective literacy classroom.

❧ Summary

This chapter presented guidelines to help teachers organize and manage their classrooms while meeting the needs of all students. These guidelines are based on what we know about how children learn. We discussed creating a literate environment by using certain spaces and materials. We also presented information about conferences and recordkeeping.

The section on developing a management system presented a flow chart with five steps leading to a successful management system. The first step to consider is grouping for literacy instruction. This section included information about creating flexible groups and grouping students in different ways for different purposes. It also described three frameworks for reading grouping (using core books/anthologies, leveled/developmentally appropriate books, and Reading Workshop) and two frameworks for writing (teacher-modeled writing and Writing Workshop). The second step is scheduling to incorporate the blocks of the model for a comprehensive literacy program; several sample schedules were presented. The final three steps were: having a number of independent activities available, teaching and practicing classroom routines, and trying one's plan and revising as needed. The last section briefly addressed topics related to meeting the needs of all children. These included English Language Learners, children with exceptionalities, intervention programs, multi-age classrooms, and community-home connections.

For Additional Reading

Allington, R. (2001). *What really matters for struggling readers: Designing research based programs.* Reading, MA: Addison-Wesley-Longman.

Chapman, M. L. (1995). Designing literacy learning experiences in a multi-age classroom. *Language Arts, 72*(8), 416–428.

Cooper, J. D., Boschken, I., McWilliams, J., & Pistochini, L. (2000). A study of the effectiveness of an intervention program designed to accelerate reading for struggling readers in the upper grades. In T. Shanahan & F. V. Rodriguez-Brown (Eds.), *49th Yearbook of the National Reading Conference* (pp. 477–486). Chicago: National Reading Conference.

Cunningham, P., & Allington, R. L. (1994). *Classrooms that work: They can all read and write.* New York: HarperCollins.

Gaskins, I. (1998). There's more to teaching at-risk and delayed readers than good reading instruction. *The Reading Teacher, 51*(7), 534–547.

Grabe, M., & Grabe, C. (2001). *Integrated technology for meaningful learning* (2nd ed.). Boston: Houghton Mifflin.

Hiebert, E., & Taylor, B. (Eds.) (1994). *Getting reading right from the start: Effective early literacy instruction.* Needham Heights, MA: Allyn and Bacon.

Lipson, M. Y., Mosenthal, J. H., Mekkelsen, J., & Russ, B. (2004). Building knowledge and fashioning success one school at a time. *The Reading Teacher, 57*(6), 534–542.

Morrow, L. M. (2003). *Organizing and managing the language arts block.* New York: Guilford Press.

National Council of Teachers of English. (2001). *Language Arts* (entire issue focuses on organizing for literacy instruction), Vol. 79, No. 2. Champaign-Urbana, IL: National Council of Teachers of English.

Pikulski, J. (1994). Preventing reading failure: A review of five effective programs. *The Reading Teacher, 48*(1), 30–39.

Solvie, P. A. (2004). The digital whiteboard: A tool in early literacy instruction. *The Reading Teacher, 57*(5), 484–487.

🖥 For Exploration: Electronic Products and Resources

Center for Applied Special Technology (CAST)

CAST is a nonprofit organization whose mission is to expand opportunities for individuals with disabilities through the development of innovative uses of technology. This site has publications, sample software programs, and interactive teaching strategies that demonstrate the universal curriculum concept for students of all learning abilities and disabilities.

http://www.cast.org

Comprehensive Literacy

A clearinghouse of information on comprehensive literacy, balanced literacy programs, U.S. literacy initiatives, and global literacy initiatives. Compiled by the Literacy Web at the University of Connecticut.

http://www.literacy.uconn.edu/complit.htm

Council for Exceptional Children

This is the site for the largest international organization dedicated only to special education. It includes information about the organization, its special interest groups, and its publications. It also discusses professional standards and accreditation, training and events, public policy, and legislative information.

http://www.cec.sped.org

Inclusion Literature

This article from the *ALAN Review* covers children's and adolescent literature that is written by parents and teachers and is related to inclusion issues such as self-esteem and individuality.

http://scholar.lib.vt.edu/ejournals/ALAN/spring98/andrews.html

LD Online

This site is a guide to learning disabilities for parents, teachers, and children. Included are highlights of new information in the field of learning disabilities, the basics about learning disabilities, material from leading organizations and professionals, a comprehensive listing of resources and events, and personal essays, artwork, and stories by adults and children with learning disabilities.

http://ldonline.org/index.html

Learning to Read/Reading to Learn Campaign

This informative Web site is sponsored by the National Center to Improve the Tools of Educators, based at the University of Oregon. It contains research results that shed light on the literacy skills and understandings that children must acquire to learn to read.

http://idea.uoregon.edu/~ncite/programs/read.html

National Institute on Child Health and Human Development: Publications

This Web site provides a list of publications available from the National Institute on Child Health and Human Development.

http://www.nichd.nih.gov/

National Institute on Early Childhood Development and Education

This comprehensive site focuses on research and resources for families, educators, communities, and policymakers in an effort to assist all children, regardless of societal, economic, family, linguistic, and/or disability conditions.

http://www.ed.gov/offices/OERI/ECI/

Assessment and Evaluation in the Comprehensive Literacy Classroom

11

✓ **STANDARDS FOCUS**

NCTE/IRA Standards: None. This chapter addresses assessing these standards.
Standards for Reading Professionals: 1, 3, 5

Educators Speak   p. 465

Helping Teachers Understand Assessment
—*Michael D. Robinson, Miami, Florida*

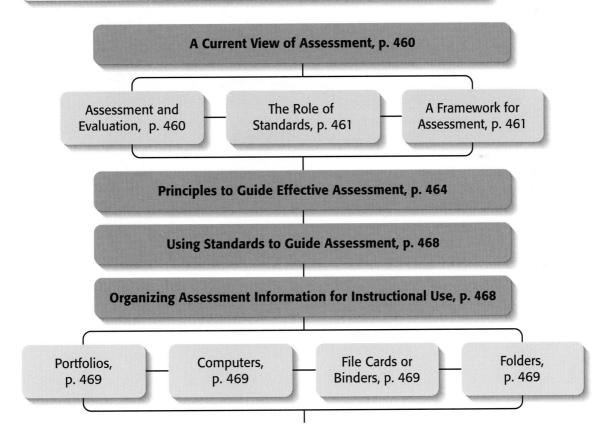

A Current View of Assessment, p. 460

Assessment and Evaluation, p. 460

The Role of Standards, p. 461

A Framework for Assessment, p. 461

Principles to Guide Effective Assessment, p. 464

Using Standards to Guide Assessment, p. 468

Organizing Assessment Information for Instructional Use, p. 468

Portfolios, p. 469

Computers, p. 469

File Cards or Binders, p. 469

Folders, p. 469

Terms
You Need to Know

- authentic assessment
- benchmarks (standards)
- checklist
- fluency check
- formal assessment
- grade score/grade equivalent
- informal assessment
- informal reading inventory (IRI)
- interest inventory
- miscue
- miscue analysis
- observation (kid watching)
- percentile
- performance assessment
- process interview
- reflection
- retellings
- rubric
- running record
- standard score
- standardized test

*M*r. Ryan is a second-grade teacher who is very concerned about the growth his students are showing in learning to construct meaning. A look at some of the activities that take place in his classroom will give us a sense of how Mr. Ryan assesses students' progress in literacy.

As we enter Mr. Ryan's second-grade classroom, we see that the class is divided into four small literature discussion groups, each group discussing the same book, Ira Says Goodbye (Waber, 1988). Three discussion points are listed on the chalkboard:

1. Why Reggie acted as he did
2. Your favorite part
3. How you would feel

Mr. Ryan is seated with one of the groups, listening. At one point he joins in by saying, "When my best friend moved away, I wouldn't talk to anyone about it. How would you act if you had been in Ira's place, Lisette?"

Mr. Ryan carries a clipboard and a pad of sticky notes. As he moves from one group to the other, he jots down observations on the sticky note and sticks them on sheets on the clipboard.

After the literature groups are completed, the class begins self-selected, independent reading time. When it is over, some students go to a box marked "Reading and Writing Portfolios" and record the book they just read.

At the end of the day, Mr. Ryan looks over the notes he has placed on the clipboard throughout the day. He has a notebook with a section for each student, and he places some of the sticky notes on students' pages, reading and discarding others. Then he quickly looks through the portfolios to see how much independent reading students have done and whether they have added any other pieces of writing to their portfolios.

From his notes and his examination of the portfolios, Mr. Ryan sees that all students except one are doing a lot of independent reading, so he makes a note to have a conference with her as soon as possible. After seeing that several students did not seem to understand the story Ira Says Goodbye, he lists their names so he can form a group in which he will teach the skill of noting details using a story map and the text students have read.

Think about this classroom in terms of assessment, and list all the places where you thought assessment was taking place. Then compare your list to the following discussion.

Some observers may see no evidence of assessment in Mr. Ryan's classroom: what you "see" depends on your perspective on assessment and literacy learning. However, Mr. Ryan obviously believes that children learn to read and write by reading and writing, and assessment is an integral part of his instructional activities. Look at all the places where this is evident:

- Mr. Ryan participated in the literature groups, so he was able to observe students' responses to *Ira Says Goodbye*.

- Mr. Ryan made notes as he observed various aspects of students' reading. Later he reviewed those notes and placed some of them in his notebook for use in planning future instructional activities.

- Students participated in their own assessment by recording books in their reading and writing portfolios that they had completed during independent reading time. Independent reading is an important part of literacy learning and assessment.

- At the end of the day, Mr. Ryan reviewed his notes and reviewed students' portfolios to assess their progress and plan future activities.

- Mr. Ryan assessed students against their previous performances, comparing performances on current work to those on work already in their portfolios.

- Mr. Ryan used his observations to determine skills that should be taught.

Although this was only a small part of the overall assessment plan in Mr. Ryan's room, we begin to get a picture of how he views and approaches assessment. In this chapter, we examine some basic ideas about how to develop assessments that are in line with the overall concept of the comprehensive literacy program stressed throughout this text. We will focus on the classroom, giving only minor attention to the overall school literacy program. *The material in this chapter should be viewed as a basic framework for thinking about assessment in the comprehensive literacy classroom.*

🦋 A Current View of Assessment

Practices in literacy assessment should reflect what we know about literacy learning. Mr. Ryan's perspective on assessment matches his view of literacy learning. While other kinds of assessment might be required by his school system or state, he finds that daily interactions with students and careful attention to what they are doing as they read and write provide the most valid information for making instructional decisions.

Assessment and Evaluation

Although the terms *assessment* and *evaluation* are often used interchangeably within the field of education and especially within the field of literacy, they really represent different aspects of related processes (Bertrand, 1991). *Assessment* is the process of gathering information about something (getting students to respond), and *evaluation* is the process of judging that information (judging students' responses) to determine how well individuals are achieving or have achieved what they or someone else expects them to achieve. For example, asking a student to retell a story is *assessment;* you are asking that student to respond. Then, when you judge the accuracy of the retelling and give it a score or a grade, or make an instructional decision based on it, you are *evaluating* the response.

In the comprehensive literacy classroom, procedures for assessment and evaluation are not as clearly delineated as they were in classrooms where teachers often gave students a test and expected students to achieve a certain score. If they achieved that score, it was assumed they knew whatever the test was supposed to measure. If they did not, teachers simply retaught what the test was claimed to measure and then retested the students. However, teachers often saw students who could pass the skills tests, but could not read or write, and vice versa; what was being assessed and evaluated clearly did not reflect the full processes of reading and writing.

Assessment and evaluation must go together in the comprehensive literacy classroom: one has no value without the other. A beginning step in planning for assessment in your classroom is to think about why you are assessing students.

The Role of Standards

We have addressed standards throughout this text at the opening of each chapter and within each chapter. Later in this chapter, we will talk about using standards to guide assessment. Standards state what students are expected to know or be able to do; often they specify achievement at various grade levels. These standards may be local, but they are often established at the state level. You, as a classroom teacher, must assess how well your students meet such standards. Some states spell out exactly what information each teacher must gather, what instrument should be used to gather the information, and how it is to be recorded. Each teacher must document that the required assessment is being carried out with each student. Your local school administrators will ensure that they carry out the required testing and meet the state standards, though there may be local adaptations. Each school system disseminates assessment information to individual schools and individual teachers. These are assessments about which you will have no choice. Assessments may include standardized tests as well as informal tests.

Teachers need to assess students—of that there can be no doubt. Teachers need to know how their students are doing; students also need to know how they are doing; and parents and the community need to know how students are doing. Ideally, such assessment would be a perfect match with what has been taught, would be free of cultural bias, and would lead directly to instructional decisions. It may seem that imposing standards-based assessment on classroom teachers would preclude this sort of ideal assessment, but it does not. All the techniques provided in this chapter will help you assess how well your students are meeting standards, as well as help you make instructional decisions.

A Framework for Assessment

As you begin to think about assessment in your classroom, you will need to understand a number of concepts and terms. Table 11.1 presents a selected list of these terms and their definitions. Most of them are discussed in more detail throughout this chapter. You may want to review these terms before reading further.

Assessment may be considered in terms of two broad categories: informal and formal. *Informal assessment* uses observations and other nonstandardized procedures; *formal assessment* uses standardized procedures or procedures carried out

TABLE 11.1 **Assessment Terminology**

Term	Description
Authentic assessment	Assessment activities that reflect literacy in the community, the workplace, and the instructional activities of the classroom. *Example:* Students write a letter to the editor about an environmental problem; the letter may be used to assess and evaluate students' writing abilities and skills. (See also *performance assessment.*)
Benchmarks (standards)	Statements of expectations of what students are to learn, usually given grade by grade or age by age. *Example:* First graders will orally read age-/grade-appropriate text with 90% accuracy.
Checklist	A form that lists targeted behaviors as indicators of achievement, knowledge, or skill. *Example:* An oral language checklist that a kindergarten teacher might use.
Formal assessment	A test or task using procedures that are carried out under controlled conditions. *Example:* A state-level competency test.
Grade score/ grade equivalent	A score transformed from a raw score on a standard test that is the equivalent earned by an average student in the norming group; these scores are not recommended for use because they may be misleading. *Example:* A grade 3 student scores 7.1 on a reading comprehension test but was never tested on passages at the grade 7 level.
Informal assessment	Observations or other nonstandardized procedures. *Example:* A teacher-made checklist.
Informal reading inventory (IRI)	A series of graded passages used to determine students' levels of reading and strengths and needs in decoding and comprehension. (See also *miscue* and *running record.*) *Example:* Most published reading series have passages that correlate with their materials.
Miscue	An oral reading response that differs from the text; may be analyzed to assess a student's reading development. (See also *informal reading inventory* and *running record.*) *Example:* A student reads the following sentence with the miscues noted:

               pony
The horse/ galloped so
          (1)
fast that the man was thrown
               ark   night
through the air/ at lightning/
        (2)   (3)
 sky
speed/.
 (4)

| TABLE 11.1 | **Assessment Terminology** (continued) |

Term	Description
	Miscue 1 does not change meaning; miscues 2, 3, and 4 do change meaning and should be analyzed further.
Percentile	A score on a scale of 100 showing the percentage of a distribution that is equal to or below it. *Example:* A score at the 70th percentile is equal to or better than 70 percent of the scores of others on whom the test was normed.
Performance assessment	A task that requires the student to demonstrate his or her level of knowledge and skill by making a response such as that required in instruction or the real world. (See also *authentic assessment.*) *Example:* A student is asked to construct a model of a catapult. The task requires the student to demonstrate such abilities as reading, following directions, and so forth.
Reflection	The process by which students and/or the teacher look back at what they have learned, discussing how it has helped them, where they might use it, and what they might concentrate on next. *Example:* After students have read a text with emphasis on certain strategies, they discuss with the teacher and peers how the strategies helped them construct meaning.
Rubric	A set of guidelines or acceptable responses for the completion of a task. *Example:* A rubric for assessing the writing quality of a story would include being able to identify the story elements (setting, character[s], problem, action, outcome) and a 4-point scale in which 4 is high, 3 is average, 2 is low, 1 is inadequate, and 0 indicates insufficient material.
Running record	A written record of a student's oral reading in which a blank sheet of paper rather than a copy of the actual text is used in coding. *Example:* A first-grade teacher has a student read aloud a previously read book, noting the correct and incorrect words.
Standard score	A score that tells how far an individual is from the average score (mean) on a test in terms of the standard deviation. Standard scores are most commonly used on standardized tests. *Example:* A student scores 60 on a test; the standard deviation is 5, and the average (mean) score is 55. This student is one standard deviation above average.
Standardized test	A test given under specified conditions allowing comparisons to be made; a set of norms or average scores are given to allow comparisons. *Examples: Metropolitan Achievement Tests; Iowa Test of Basic Skills*

under controlled conditions (Harris & Hodges, 1995). Examples of informal assessments are the use of checklists, observations, and performance assessments or tasks. Informal assessments are clearly and easily made a part of instruction. Formal assessments include such tests as state tests, standardized achievement tests, or tests accompanying a published program. These formal types of assessment are not embedded in instruction, but they *must reflect the instruction* to be of value in assessing students' literacy development. The standardized achievement test is most useful in evaluating overall program growth as opposed to evaluating individual student progress or determining instructional needs.

Over the years, criticisms have been leveled at standardized tests. Although written a number of years ago (Tyler & White in Farr and Carey, 1986, p. 11), the following are still legitimate concerns:

- Tests do not reflect the full range of student cultural backgrounds and thus lead to decisions that are often unfair to minority students.
- Standardized tests have only limited value for holding teachers, schools, and school systems accountable for the quality of education.
- Tests impose a limiting effect on classroom teaching.
- Tests are too narrow in scope to provide fair evaluation of new approaches to teaching.

Current assessment is beginning to reflect current knowledge about literacy learning and effective literacy instruction. Efforts are being made to address the following:

- making sure assessment focuses on the standards being covered,
- not just testing isolated skills,
- using full-length authentic texts to construct meaning,
- accounting for prior knowledge,
- including samples of student work, and
- incorporating student self-assessment.

It is critical that we demonstrate to our communities that our programs are successfully helping students develop literacy, especially as we try new instructional techniques. Failure to do this will result in a return to practices that we have learned are not as valuable to students as we once thought.

🦋 Principles to Guide Effective Assessment

As you begin to plan for informal and formal assessment in your classroom, you should consider the following eight principles. Numerous researchers and educators have developed guidelines for comprehensive literacy assessment (Farr & Tone, 1994; Harp, 1991; Valencia, 1990a, 1990b; Valencia, Hiebert, & Afflerbach, 1994). These eight principles are based in part on their ideas and our personal interpretations of this research while working with teachers. These ideas and principles are not new, but they are as valid today as ever.

Helping Teachers Understand Assessment

"Dealing with teachers and assessment is probably the most challenging part of my job. It seems all teachers want all information about all students in less than twenty minutes. My charge is to be sure teachers are using the information they have about student performance to make informed educational decisions about placement in materials for guided reading and other interventions.

Miami-Dade County Public Schools (M-DCPS) divides assessment into three categories: Screening/Diagnostic, Progress Monitoring, and Outcome. I work with all elementary teachers to help them understand each category of assessment and how it relates to instructional procedures. Emphasis is given to baseline data (collected from the previous year's outcome measures) as a starting point. Students who fall below standard or are judged as being at "high risk" of failure are tracked for immediate, intensive intervention based on these data as well as a diagnostic measure given so that instruction can be targeted. A true challenge is to get teachers to use the progress monitoring instruments as teaching tools. Too often these measures are given with little or no effect on classroom instruction. This challenge may come from an idea that teachers are so overwhelmed by the breadth of assessments that they simply see the objective as getting the assessment completed and the data to the "powers that be" rather than seeing these assessments as valuable parts of the instructional-assessment cycle.

Management of the huge amounts of data has been made much easier because of M-DCPS commitment to data-driven decision making. It has been the district's charge to provide classroom teachers, reading leaders, and administrators with electronic templates that manage both individual student data and whole-class data. These templates allow all stakeholders to view data in a way that promotes analysis and analytical discussion. My job is helping teachers look at these vast amounts of data and look for trends in their classrooms and students who need more support through intervention.

Helping teachers see trends involves looking at whole-class data. We work collaboratively and ask, "What does this mean? How should this information be affecting instruction?" If teachers are unable to make connections, I work individually to help them see the holes that exist in achievement and hope they make the connection that a lack of instruction usually leads to a drop in achievement. Looking at these holes and then looking at what needs to happen in the classroom that is now missing is the key to helping teachers use this data effectively.

Teachers are just beginning to see the power of informed teaching. For too long, they have allowed publishers and district personnel to dictate what and when they teach, even though they are the ones who have access to the information that can make their teaching highly effective. It is my hope that my work with teachers makes all this information useful so teachers will see that it is not done just for the state or district but rather for the benefit of teachers and ultimately their students."

Michael D. Robinson, Curriculum Support Specialist
Miami-Dade County Public School
Division of Language Arts/Reading
Miami, Florida

1. ***Assessment should be an ongoing process.*** Literacy assessment is not a test given at the end of a unit or a block of study, separate from the ongoing daily activities of instruction. Instead, assessment should take place every time a child reads, writes, speaks, listens, or views something. When assessment is considered an ongoing part of instruction, it becomes natural and expected.

2. ***Effective assessment is an integral part of instruction.*** The best forms of assessment are the routine daily activities of instruction, which tell us exactly how students are performing. By comparing the work of individual students over time, we can determine patterns of growth. When a student writes a story about her trip to visit friends, you can assess her ability to organize ideas, express herself, and use the various conventions of language. Overall, you get a picture of how effectively she constructs meaning through writing. Throughout our years of teaching and working with teachers, many teachers have said, "There was no reason to give that test. I already knew what my kids could do from their daily activities." In other words, we must learn to trust our judgments as we make them from evidence gathered during instruction.

3. ***Assessment must be authentic, reflecting "real" reading and writing.*** For years, we have asked teachers in workshops and classes, "If you want to know how well children read and write, what do you need to have them do?" They have always replied in unison, "Have them read and write." The tasks of assessment in a balanced literacy classroom must reflect and honor the "wholeness" of language (Harp, 1991). It is possible for learners to be very effective readers and writers and not do well on a test covering an isolated piece of the process. For example, when a student reads the wonderful Roald Dahl book *Esio Trot* (1990) and writes a response to it, it is possible to authentically assess his or her ability to construct meaning.

4. ***Assessment should be a collaborative, reflective process.*** It should not be viewed as something the teacher does to the students. We know learning is a collaborative process; we learn alongside and with our students and our peers (Collins, Brown, & Newman, 1987). If this is true for learning, it is also true for assessment. As students collaborate with their teacher on assessment, they reflect and ask themselves, "How have I done?" "What can I do to improve?" "How can I use what I have learned?" Thus, students should help you assess and evaluate their own progress in literacy. One of us learned this the hard way many years ago from a fifth-grade student named Paul. Paul was an excellent student. He could read and critically discuss anything put in his hands. However, I often asked Paul to read aloud because he wasn't a good oral reader. I then decided he needed to be placed in a lower-level book group, but he still couldn't read aloud. Finally, I asked Paul what he thought his problem was. He was not only very intelligent but also very outspoken. He said, "I don't have a problem. When are you going to learn that I don't like to read out loud?" Needless to say, I learned pretty fast! It turned out that Paul could construct meaning better than any other fifth grader I had that year.

Collaboration means students sometimes help select *what* they want evaluated. This becomes a joint effort in which teacher and students work and think together, and it should also involve parents and other caregivers (Dillon, 1990).

When students, teacher, and parents collaborate on evaluation, the responsibility is shared, as it should be.

5. ***Effective assessment is multidimensional.*** Quality assessment should use several different tasks, such as samples of writing, student retellings, records of independent reading, self-evaluations, and checklists. In making these choices, you need to trust your own intuition based on your knowledge and observations about students. More formal types of assessments have proclaimed their validity and reliability using various statistical procedures. Although many of the techniques being suggested today are more informal, we must still know that they are trustworthy (Valencia, 1990a), and one way to determine this is to use multiple tasks to get a consistent pattern of performance. Cambourne and Turbill (1990) argue that data generated from multiple sources using teacher observations and judgments are just as trustworthy and "scientific" as those generated by what have been called "measurement-based" approaches to assessment.

6. ***Assessment should be developmentally and culturally appropriate.*** We know children develop literacy and their ability to construct meaning by "trying out" their reading and writing and making approximations. Therefore, tests or procedures that require absolute mastery at a given level or complete mastery of a given set of words before moving to a new book are *completely contrary* to how we know children learn. We must select assessment tasks that respect children's developmental levels of learning.

   At the same time, we must consider the cultural diversity of our classrooms. Children from different cultures have not only different language bases but also different patterns and styles of learning (Au, 1993; Garcia, 1994). We must take these into consideration as we plan assessment procedures.

7. ***Effective assessment identifies students' strengths.*** Children learn to construct meaning by doing what they already know how to do and by getting support in gaining new strategies and techniques. Effective assessment therefore must help us identify what students do well. For many years, we have given students tests to find out what they do *not* know; then we have proceeded to plan lessons totally around these weaknesses. This is contrary to how students acquire language and contrary to how they learn to construct meaning.

8. ***Assessment must be based on what we know about how students learn to read and write.*** This entire text has focused on how students learn to read and write and construct meaning. Clearly, we know assessment has not kept pace with our knowledge about reading and writing. We know the two processes are similar but different. We also know they develop together and produce benefits that are attainable by neither one alone (Tierney & Shanahan, 1991). And we know that reading and writing are both constructive processes. As we plan assessment tasks, we must keep this knowledge in mind, incorporating new knowledge as it becomes available.

We should always remember that we are a part of our students' learning processes. We are working *with* them, not *on* them. In the remainder of this chapter, we focus on ideas and techniques for applying these eight principles to the balanced literacy classroom.

🦋 Using Standards to Guide Assessment

Assessment must be based on goals. What do we want students to do? How will we know if they are learning to do it? This rather simple view of assessment has not changed over the years. What has changed is that many states and most local school systems now have standards or benchmarks that dictate exactly what we want students to do, as well as how we will know if they are learning to do it. Each teacher must become familiar with these local and state literacy standards and use them to guide assessment.

For a detailed look at how to use standards and benchmarks to plan instruction, see Cooper and Kiger (2005) listed in the "For Additional Reading" section at the end of the chapter.

It is likely that most activity in your classroom can be linked to one or more literacy standards. In fact, since reading and writing occur every day in every classroom, assessment should be an integral part of instruction in which the routine daily activities of reading and writing also serve as the assessment activities. Although this ongoing, daily assessment may not be sufficient to demonstrate that your students have reached the mandated standards, the standards can guide your daily assessment decisions. Ongoing, daily assessment helps us determine whether students are making adequate yearly progress.

🦋 Organizing Assessment Information for Instructional Use

The primary reason for assessing what students have done is to help you plan the instructional activities and experiences you will need to provide to help students continue to improve their literacy development. Instruction is assessment; in other words, every instructional activity is an assessment activity. By looking at how students perform during instruction, you are able to get a sense of what they are learning and using in terms of reading, writing, speaking, listening, thinking, and viewing. Many times your observations during instruction become your best assessment tools.

Three guiding principles will help you use assessment information for instructional purposes:

1. *Organize.* For the information you gather to be helpful to you in planning instruction, it must be organized in a way that is useful to you. It doesn't matter how you organize it. It only matters that you *do organize it.*
2. *Review.* You must review the information on a regular basis—daily or weekly. This means that you are constantly looking at how students are performing and deciding what needs to happen next. This is what Cooper and Kiger (2005) call assessment-based literacy instruction.
3. *Update.* Updating information is really a part of the reviewing process. As you are continuously reviewing how students are performing, you should also add new information and revise information you have. We often think we will remember what students have done, but it is easy to forget, especially when dealing with large numbers of students.

We present four alternatives for organizing assessment information: portfolios, computers, file cards or binders, and folders. The next section discusses several assessment techniques. You should select the organizational procedure and techniques that will work best for you.

Portfolios

Portfolios are collections of an individual student's work gathered over time, with the primary purpose of presenting a picture of each student's performance and progress. Many schools now use the portfolio concept for organizing all of their assessment data.

For more information on portfolios, see "For Additional Reading."

Many schools have a master version of the portfolio that is passed each year from teacher to teacher. Individual teachers keep more specific daily instructional information in one of the other forms described in the following sections.

Computers

With the increasing use of computers come new ways to organize information for quick retrieval and use. Individual teachers and entire school systems are making more use of the computer as a way to organize and store assessment data. You will want to learn about the options available in your school or district. You may also devise your own ways to organize information for your own instructional use.

File Cards or Binders

Many teachers like to use 5-by-8-inch file cards or binders to keep records of students' performance. The type of information is structured by a checklist of some type (see the section on assessment techniques). Each student is assigned a file card or a section in the notebook. The teacher can then refer to it easily on a daily basis.

Folders

Teachers have used folders of work for years to keep track of how each student is performing. This is much like using a portfolio. Like the portfolio, this technique must have an organizational structure to be effective. This is usually done using some type of checklist.

🦋 Assessment Techniques

Assessment as discussed in this chapter is a dynamic and interactive process that is an integral part of instruction. Instruction and assessment blend into one ongoing activity. You can use many different techniques as part of this process. Some blend naturally into instruction; others give you a somewhat more formal way to assess student progress.

Since the overall goal of literacy learning is meaning construction, the techniques suggested in this section look at either the process as a whole or an important aspect of the process. Most of them can be easily used on the basis of the information given here; appropriate references are given for those that require more detailed study. As you study and review these techniques, you should be thinking about those that will be most advantageous to you in your classroom and those you need to learn more about. *You do not need to use them all.*

Observation

In comprehensive literacy classrooms, assessment and evaluation are based on a combination of formal and informal techniques, and many of these are highly dependent on observing students as they read and write. **Observation,** or "kid watching" (Goodman, 1986), as it is frequently described, is the process of observing students as they perform authentic literacy tasks or looking at the results of those tasks.

You learn to be an observer of children by first realizing that observation is a powerful and reliable part of your assessment and evaluation process. Observations must be based on what you know about how children learn to read and write. Therefore, you need to understand what responses are expected and typical, and what responses might indicate a need for more or different support. For example, the first grader who writes a sentence about his *dg* is not misspelling the word *dog;* rather, he is making an approximation that shows he is learning the spelling pattern in the word *dog.* This student would benefit from more shared reading experiences with natural, repetitive language and words following the type of spelling pattern found in the word *dog,* as well as many opportunities to continue writing his own stories.

As a teacher, you must develop the habit of always looking, thinking, and asking, "What does this mean?" Opportunities to observe students are unlimited and include the following:

- Listening to a student read aloud
- Watching students give a play
- Reading and noting how a student has written a response to a story
- Analyzing a student's written report
- Listening to and studying what students say as they give oral reports
- Listening to conversation between two students waiting in line for lunch

Nearly every classroom activity can be used for some form of observation of literacy learning, and all of these observations can become the data on a checklist or a note placed in a literacy portfolio.

When you observe, you must keep in mind that good assessment is multidimensional. Therefore, one observation is not sufficient: you must look at several observations over time, watching for patterns of performance. From these patterns, you can assess and evaluate students' ability to construct meaning.

Many techniques can be combined with observation, or used in addition to observation to help you become an effective observer. As you gain more experience with observation, you will become more and more comfortable. You will soon realize that instruction and assessment are really one ongoing process. Figure 11.1 shows some sample observation notes made by Mrs. Ehrman in her third-grade class. She used sticky notes and put the student's initials and the date on each. These notes could then be easily transferred to the student's portfolio.

Checklists

Checklists are excellent tools for guiding observation of various aspects of students' ability to construct meaning. They may be developed in general areas related to meaning construction, such as reading, writing, speaking, listening, and viewing, or for specific aspects of literacy learning, such as concepts of print or story retelling.

Each checklist should contain the qualities or traits you are looking for and some procedure for recording what you observe. Some may be designed to record growth over time. Other checklists simply help you look for the presence or absence of the traits.

General checklists, such as that shown in Figure 11.2, may be used and placed in the literacy portfolio. This kind of checklist has four places to record observations during the school year. It can be completed by the teacher, the student, or both.

You will often want to develop your own checklists for the particular thing(s) you want to observe. There are many sources of checklists, including curriculum guides, textbooks, and journal articles. You can take an existing checklist and adapt it to fit your needs. Some checklists can be developed for group observations and others for individual observations.

Records of Independent Reading and Writing

An important factor to consider in assessing students' meaning construction is the amount of self-selected, independent reading and writing they do. These records may be kept in journals or learning logs, where students record their independent reading or do their writing. However, it is often useful to have a form that summarizes this information to place in the student's literacy portfolio. Figures 11.3 and 11.4 present forms you can use to record independent reading. A similar form can be devised for summarizing the progress of writing projects.

Retellings

Retellings are powerful tools; they are one of the most authentic techniques you can use for both instructional and assessment purposes. Although retellings integrate instruction and assessment, here we focus on their use as assessment tools.

"Retellings are postreading or postlistening recalls in which readers or listeners tell what they remember either orally or in writing" (Morrow, 1989, p. 40). By studying the students' retellings, you can gain insights into their thinking, organization,

Observation Notes from Mrs. Ehrman's Third-Grade Class

10/14   M. R.

Asks for help when a word is not known; does not try his own strategies.

10/14   M. L. C.

Self corrects many temporary spellings during revision.

10/14   I. S.

Could use a mini-lesson on quotations; experimented with them in writing.

10/14   R. B.

Referred to glossary for word meanings and spellings during reading and writing. Much improved.

10/14   B. T.

Is having trouble selecting appropriate books; needs guidance.

10/14   R. M.

Retelling showed much improvement in story comp. Needs more exp. text.

FIGURE 11.2

Checklist for Meaning Construction

Construction of Meaning

Name _____

Date	1	2	3	4
Retells stories and text accurately				
Gives responses to stories and text that show understanding				
Conveys meaning through written stories and reports				
Conveys meaning through spoken language				
Comments:				

CODE:
+ = very effectively
√ = effectively
− = needs improvement
NO = Not Observed

Figure adapted from L.M. Morrow, "Using Story Retelling to Develop Comprehension," D. Muth et al., *Children's Comprehension of Text*. Copyright © 1989 International Reading Association. Used with permission.

FIGURE 11.3

Independent Reading Record

Name _____

Date Completed	Title and Author	Comments

and general understanding of what they have read or listened to. For instance, you can learn how they identify important information, make inferences, and summarize information. This is one of the most effective techniques for holistically assessing the process of meaning construction.

Retellings can be used with both narrative and expository texts. By comparing students' retellings over time, you can determine their progress in learning to construct meaning. In addition, each retelling can be used diagnostically to help you develop support activities.

Morrow (1989) has given complete guidelines for using retellings as assessment tools. The following guidelines are based on her suggestions as well as on our own experiences in working with children and teachers.

Guidelines for Using Retellings for Assessment

Selecting the Text. Select the story or informational text (expository text) that students are to read, or have students make the selection. If you are comparing students' retellings over time, use the same type of texts each time; for example, compare narrative with narrative and expository with expository. As texts are selected, examine them to be sure their conceptual difficulty is not drastically different. In other words, don't compare retellings from a simple text such as *Cranberries* (Jaspersohn, 1991) with a more complex text such as *Franklin Delano Roosevelt* (Freedman, 1990).

Preparing the Text. Read the text yourself. With stories, identify the setting (place and time if important), characters, problem, action (events leading to outcome), and outcome or resolution. For informational texts, identify the topic, purpose, and main ideas. List this information on a sheet of paper.

FIGURE 11.4

Independent Reading Record

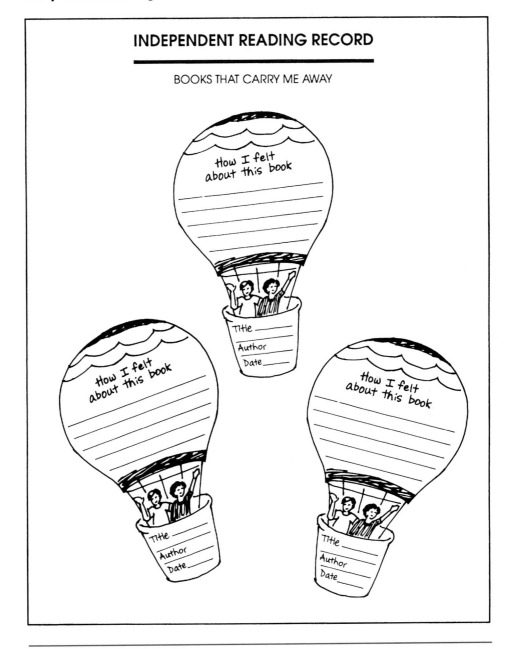

Reading and Retelling the Text. Have the student read the text silently. (If you are using this as a listening experience, read the text to the students.) This should be treated as a routine instructional activity. Immediately following the reading, ask the student to retell the story or text. Do not prompt initial retellings, except for generic prompts such as, "Tell me more," or, "Keep going; you're doing a nice job."

As students give their retellings, check off the ideas given on the paper you prepared earlier. After they have completed their unprompted retellings, you may then prompt them with questions about specific parts of the story or text that they did not include in their unprompted retellings.

Summarizing and Evaluating the Retelling. Figures 11.5 and 11.6 present sheets you can use for summarizing each student's retelling. Each retelling has a possible score of 10, and the guidelines for scoring each retelling are basically the same. One point is given for correct responses, and exceptions to this rule are given on the summary sheets. In scoring retellings, use your own judgment and your observations.

After scoring each retelling, you can examine it to determine whether the student understands the story or text, has ideas well organized, or has used various strategies. You will then want to discuss and review the retelling with the student. This information can help you develop instructional experiences. As Morrow (1989) notes, retellings can develop essentially the same skills and processes they assess.

Responses to Literature

Responses to literature were discussed in Chapter 7.

The way a student responds to literature may help indicate how the student has constructed meaning. For example, the student who continuously says or writes, "I liked it," "It was funny," or, "The best part was _____," may not be processing or understanding what was read, or perhaps has not learned to respond to literature and needs more support and prompting from the teacher. The student who gave the following response to *Where the Red Fern Grows* (Rawls, 1974) demonstrated in her journal that she had constructed appropriate meaning from this book:

> Billy's love for his dogs is like my love for my cat Prince. I had to work hard to get Prince. I love him so much. Billy learned how important love was. I did to. Everybody needs somebody to love.

FIGURE 11.5

Retelling Summary Sheet for Narrative Text

Story Retelling Summary Sheet

Name _____ Date _____

Title _____

Student selected _____ Teacher selected _____

	Scores	
	Unprompted	*Prompted*
Setting:		
Begins with introduction (1 pt.)	_____	_____
Gives time and place (1 pt.)	_____	_____
Characters:		
Names main character (1 pt.)	_____	_____
Identifies other characters (1 pt.)	_____	_____

     Gives names _____
     Gives number _____
     Actual number _____
     Number given _____

Problem:		
Identifies primary story problem (1 pt.)	_____	_____
Action:		
Recalls major events (1 pt.)	_____	_____
Outcome:		
Identifies how problem was solved (1 pt.)	_____	_____
Gives story ending (1 pt.)	_____	_____
Sequence:		
Retells story in order (2 pts. = correct; 1 pt. = partial, 0 = no evidence of sequence)	_____	_____
TOTAL SCORE (10 pts. possible)	_____	_____

Observations/comments:

Analysis:

Source: Adapted from L. M. Morrow, Using story retelling to develop comprehension, in K. D. Muth, ed., *Children's comprehension of text: Research into practice,* pp. 37–58. Copyright © 1989 International Reading Association. Used with permission.

FIGURE 11.6

Retelling Summary Sheet for Informational Text

Informational Text Retelling Summary Sheet

Name _____ Date _____

Title _____

Student selected _____ Teacher selected _____

	Scores	
	Unprompted	*Prompted*

Introduction:
   Identifies topic (1 pt.) _____   _____

   Gives some purpose or focus (1 pt.) _____   _____

Main Ideas:
   Number given _____
   Actual number _____
   (6 pts. = all correct; 4 pts. = 2/3 correct;
   2 pts. = 1/3 correct; 0 pts. = none correct)

Shows logical understanding of how ideas are
related; explains ideas   _____   _____
   (2 pts. = relates all ideas; 1 pt. = relates
   some ideas; 0 pts. = shows no relationship of ideas)

                           TOTAL SCORE   _____   _____
                           (10 pts. possible)

Observations/comments:

Analysis:

_____

As you encourage students to respond to literature, you will need to develop some criteria for evaluating those responses. The following questions should be helpful:

1. Does the response show that the student knows the story line (narrative) or main ideas (expository) of the text?
2. Did the student simply retell the text or relate it to his or her own experiences?
3. Does the response show that the student is thinking clearly and logically?
4. Does the response show that the student is using any skills or strategies?

How would you evaluate the response given to *Where the Red Fern Grows* using these questions?

Teachers can encourage English Language Learners (ELLs) to respond in their first language. Aides, parents, or other bilingual students can read the response. Such first-language responses can be added to the students' portfolios (Freeman & Freeman, 2001).

Many teachers use a simple form, such as the one in Figure 11.7, to evaluate students' responses to literature. They then attach the evaluations to the response and place it in the portfolio. Teachers also use this evaluation for grading purposes.

Student Self-Evaluations

Student self-evaluations have been recommended as a vital part of assessing and evaluating meaning construction (Flood & Lapp, 1989; Tierney, Carter, & Desai, 1991). You can promote these evaluations very easily by asking students to write in their journals about the progress they are making in reading and writing. Self-evaluation can be prompted by such questions as the following:

- How do you feel you are doing in reading/writing?
- What are your strengths in reading/writing?
- What do you enjoy the most about reading/writing?
- What do you feel you need to do to improve your reading/writing?

FIGURE 11.7

Form for Evaluating Responses to Literature

Constructing Meaning Evaluation

Name _____ Date _____

Title _____

Circle one:

+	√	0
Shows thorough understanding	Shows some understanding	Needs support in developing understanding

Comments:

FIGURE 11.8

Form for Self-Evaluation of Reading

Self-Evaluation of Reading

Name_____ Date_____

Book read_____

Mark the scale below:

|----------------------|----------------------|----------------------|

I feel that   I don't
I thoroughly   feel that
understood   I understood
this book.   this book.

Why I marked the scale as I did:

_____

_____

_____

_____

_____

Another way to get students to evaluate their construction of meaning is by giving them a form such as the one in Figure 11.8 to evaluate their understanding of what they read. The form can be completed periodically and placed in the literacy portfolio. Similar types of self-evaluation forms may also be completed for writing.

Self-evaluation is important in helping students learn to monitor their own reading and writing. The actual process of self-evaluation needs to be taught to students as they use it. For example, they can use a checklist such as the one in Figure 11.9 to evaluate how they have used various strategies as they read a text. As a part of the teaching, you would model the process for students. This type of checklist can be shortened to include only those strategies students have learned.

Process Interviews

Learning more about students' metacognitive development, or how they "think about their reading," is important in helping them learn to construct meaning. To assess students' thinking about their reading, Paratore and Indrisano (1987) developed a procedure known as the **process interview,** sometimes called a *reading interview.* It consists of the following questions:

1. *How do you choose something to read?*
2. *How do you get ready to read?*
3. *When you come to a word you can't read, what do you do?*

FIGURE 11.9

Student Self-Monitoring Checklist

THINKING ABOUT MY READING

HOW DID I DO?

BEFORE READING

- Did I preview the text?

- Did I make predictions?

DURING READING

- Did I STOP AND THINK about what I was reading?

- Did I change my predictions?

AFTER READING

- Did I think back about my predictions?

- Did I summarize in my head?

To improve my reading, I need to: _____

_____

_____

---

4. *When you have a question you can't answer, what do you do?*
5. *What do you do to help remember what you've read?*
6. *How do you check your reading?*
7. *If a young child asked you how to read, what would you tell him or her to do?*
   (Paratore & Indrisano, 1987, p. 782)

After a student orally answers the questions and you record the responses, you analyze them to see what type of support the student needs. For example, a student who answers question 6 even after prompting by saying that she "looks for pictures" does not have a good set of monitoring strategies. It might be helpful to teach this student to use a strategy such as stop and think, focusing on rereading, reading ahead, and other techniques for monitoring reading.

A process interview for writing may be done using questions that follow a pattern similar to those used for reading. Since this is an informal procedure, questions for either the reading or writing interview can be rephrased or changed to ensure that students understand them. Interviews of this type can be conducted with students of all ages as long as the questions are worded appropriately.

Teacher-Selected Reading Samples

One of the most important criteria for assessing and evaluating students' progress is that the materials used be books and texts that students read every day. Select a book, a chapter of a book, or a short story or other text you want students to read, and introduce the material as you would in a literacy lesson. Have students read the text silently, and then ask them to complete a task appropriate to their grade level that will let you see how effectively they have constructed meaning. These tasks could include:

- Completing a story map
- Listing the most important or main ideas in the text
- Writing a summary (this is a very sophisticated process and should be reserved for the upper elementary and middle school levels)
- Answering questions that focus on the story elements
- Answering questions that draw out the main ideas of the text

All tasks except the summary can be scored by determining the percentage of items correct. The summary has to be scored more holistically by giving it a rating such as the following:

A teacher takes a fluency check.
© Michael Zide

1 = All major ideas included
2 = Most major ideas included
3 = Many major ideas missing

Samples of reading can be taken over time, and compared to each other to determine student progress.

Fluency Checks and Application of Decoding Skills

See Chapter 2 for a complete discussion of fluency.

Many teachers find it helpful to use teacher-selected or student-selected samples for oral reading. After students practice their passages, they read them aloud into a tape recorder or to the teacher. The teacher takes several passages over time and compares them to show student development in decoding; effective constructors of meaning know how to decode words automatically. The **fluency check** technique differs from miscue analysis (discussed later in this chapter), because in miscue analysis, students do not prepare their passages. This procedure allows a teacher to compare a student's "best" performances over time.

You can analyze these taped passages by looking at the patterns of students' responses to determine their ability to decode words. Many teachers find it useful to make the tape recordings a part of the students' portfolios. In this way, students can compare their passages to determine their own growth in decoding; the tapes can also be used during parent conferences to help parents determine the progress their children are making. Figure 11.10 shows a passage a second grader read from *Fix-It* (McPhail, 1984). The teacher's markings and notes show what the student read and how the teacher judged the student's decoding abilities.

Literature Groups

See Chapter 7 for a discussion of using literature groups as a response.

The literature group presents a good opportunity to observe students' ability to construct meaning and react personally in an authentic literacy experience. Wood's (1988) procedure for assessing and evaluating comprehension during a group discussion involves looking at nine behaviors related to meaning construction as students discuss what they have read: making predictions, participating in discussion, answering questions on a variety of levels, determining word meaning through context, reading smoothly and fluently, retelling selections in own words, comprehending after silent reading, reading between the lines, and having a broad background knowledge. A grid is used to record students' responses using a simple code: Often = +, Sometimes = S, Seldom = –, and Not Observed = N.

We have found that teachers are able to use the literature group to assess and evaluate meaning construction. However, like Paradis et al. (1991), we have also found that teachers need to develop (or adapt from some other source) their own specific procedures and indicators. The following general guidelines should help you accomplish this purpose.

FIGURE 11.10

Second-Grader's Marked Oral Passage

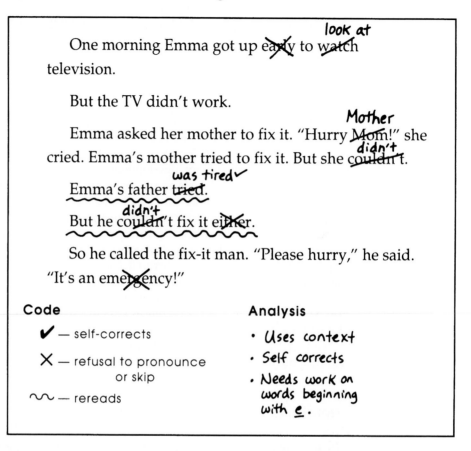

Guidelines for Developing Procedures for Observing Literature Groups

Select indicators for meaning construction. Use the information in this text and other sources to help you decide what indicators you should look for to tell you that your students are effectively constructing meaning. In the beginning, keep the number small, remembering the importance of strategies such as predicting, confirming or changing predictions, inferencing, and summarizing. Following are examples of indicators you might use:

General Indicators

- Participates in discussion
- Listens to responses of others
- Builds own response on ideas of others

Indicators for Narrative Texts

- Identifies important parts of story (setting, characters, and so forth)
- Identifies favorite parts or characters
- Relates story to own experiences
- Compares to other stories

Indicators for Expository Texts

- Identifies topic
- Identifies main ideas
- Sees relationships in text
- Shows signs of using knowledge gained
- Can relate information to own life

Develop a procedure for recording information. You can use a simple grid such as the one in Figure 11.11 with a code similar to the one developed by Wood (1988), discussed earlier. This grid contains a space for comments or observations.

Designate a time for observation. It is not necessary to observe every literature group for assessment purposes; use selected ones. You may either participate in the discussion or sit off to the side to observe. Teachers who become accustomed to this procedure report that they find themselves always observing even when they are just participating in the groups. This activity becomes a natural part of teaching.

Review the data for yourself and with students. After you have completed your observation, study the data you have collected to see what your students' strengths are. Think about ways to use these strengths and also provide ongoing support. For example, if you observe that several students are very good at predicting but have difficulty summarizing, have them make predictions using story map prediction. Then use their story map predictions to lead into the summarizing story strategy. Take time to review and discuss your observations with students, asking them for their perceptions and reactions.

Interest Inventories

Another valuable assessment and evaluation technique is the **interest inventory.** The information obtained may be useful to you in a number of ways:

- Choosing book collections from the library to bring into the classroom
- Ordering books
- Planning thematic unit topics
- Creating study groups
- Conferring with individual students or groups of students

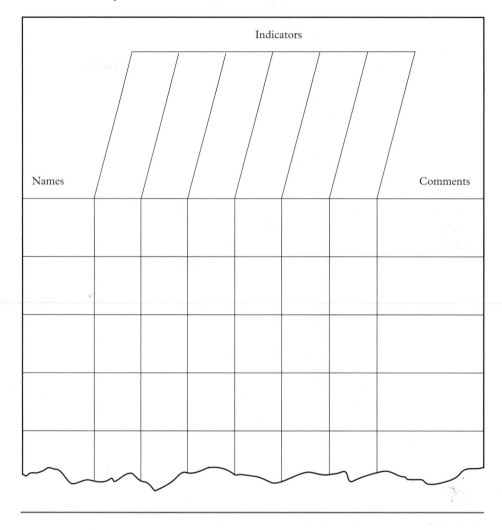

FIGURE 11.11

Grid for Observing Construction of Meaning During a Literature Discussion Group

There are many different forms of interest inventories, but they generally consist of a number of statements that students respond to orally (during conferences or interviews) or in writing. Often these are incomplete statements that students are asked to complete; Figure 11.12 contains examples.

Scoring Writing Using Rubrics

Holistic scoring is a widely used procedure to assess and evaluate a student's ability to construct meaning through writing. It involves looking at a piece of writing in its

FIGURE 11.12

Completion Statements for an Interest Inventory

Directions: Use these statements to develop an interest inventory. Add your own ideas.

Read the statements aloud and ask the student to complete them orally or have students read and complete them in writing.

1. I enjoy _____.

2. My favorite subject in school is _____.

3. When I read, I like to read _____.

4. My favorite thing in the world is _____.

5. I like to spend time _____.

6. My hobbies are _____.

7. I like to write about _____.

8. When I finish school, I want to be _____.

9. My favorite television shows are _____.

10. I would like to learn more about _____.

11. I would like to spend more time in school _____.

entirety and assigning it a score, using a set of guidelines called a **rubric** (Cockrum & Castillo, 1991). This process is generally used on instructional writing tasks rather than on self-initiated writing or written responses to literature. Holistic scoring assumes that all aspects of writing are related and must be viewed in their entirety.

When using the holistic procedure, the teacher reads the piece of writing and assigns it a score from 0 to 4. Although a detailed discussion of holistic scoring is beyond the scope of this text, the following scale (or rubric) from Millett (1986) may give you a sense of how this procedure is used:

0   *Papers in this category cannot be scored for one reason or another. Papers that are blank, that respond to an assignment different from the one given, that merely comment on the assignment ("This topic is silly"), that only copy or rephrase the assignment, or that are illegible would all be included in this category.*

1   *Papers in this category attempt to deal with the assignment, but they fail to do so adequately. These papers are too general, abrupt, or refer to the assignment only indirectly.*

2   *Papers in this category respond to the task set up in the assignment, but they do so in a way that is sketchy, inconsistent, and incomplete. There are gaps or other problems in the organization. Vocabulary may be too general and the paper*

See Chapter 8 about the 6 +1 TRAIT™ model linking writing instruction and assessment; the model provides rubrics that correspond to each trait. See the NWREL Web site for further information.

lacking in the detail necessary to convey the purpose clearly and exactly. The reader has a basic idea of what the writer is trying to say but has to make many inferences.

3 *Papers in this category fulfill the requirements of the assignment although the reader might encounter a little confusion from time to time. The paper is generally well organized so that the reader does not need to make a lot of inferences. These papers include sufficient details so that the reader understands the writer's message.*

4 *Papers that merit this highest score are well organized, complete, and explicit. These papers include all of the strengths of the 3 category, but they are more clearly and consistently presented. The reader grasps the writer's message easily without having to make inferences. The writer uses a varied and exact vocabulary that enhances as well as clarifies the message.* (pp. 51–52)

Miscue Analysis

Miscue analysis is a procedure that lets the teacher "get a window on the reading process" (Goodman, 1965). A **miscue** is an oral response that is different from the text being read. For example, if the text reads, "Billy rode his horse around the ranch," and a child reads, "Billy rode his pony around the ranch," this miscue shows that the child has constructed the appropriate meaning for this sentence, even though she didn't say the exact words. Sometimes miscues are referred to as *unexpected responses* or *errors*.

Many years ago, Goodman (1965) concluded from his research that by studying a student's miscues from an oral reading sample, the teacher could determine the cues and strategies the student was using or not using in constructing meaning. This procedure attempts to look at the process of reading holistically.

On the basis of Goodman's research, the reading miscue inventory (Goodman & Burke, 1972) was developed. Although this analysis is normally reserved for students who are having difficulty constructing meaning, the classroom reading miscue assessment (CRMA), a simplified version of miscue analysis (Rhodes & Shanklin, 1990), can be used with all students in a classroom. The CRMA takes from 10 to 15 minutes per student. Rhodes and Shanklin (1990) indicate that it "helps teachers gather important instructional information by providing a framework for observing students' oral reading and their ability to construct meaning" (p. 254). All of the variations of miscue analysis require additional study on your part as a teacher.

See "For Additional Reading" for where to learn more about miscue analysis.

Informal Reading Inventories

The **informal reading inventory (IRI)** consists of a series of samples of text organized in increasing difficulty; students individually read the texts orally or silently. By studying their oral reading patterns and their responses to comprehension questions, the teacher can get a picture of how they analyze words in context, how they construct meaning, and what their approximate levels of reading are. IRIs usually consist of four types:

1. *Teacher constructed*, using materials from which students will be reading
2. *Publisher constructed* to match series of texts to be used for reading instruction

3. *Generic IRIs*, using samples of a variety of types of texts
4. *Group IRIs* that have been adapted from the individual IRI concept; these are usually teacher made

For a fuller explanation of the procedures for using IRIs, see Cooper and Kiger (2005), listed in the "For Additional Reading" section.

In the past, a major advantage of IRIs was that students' reading was used as the basis for seeing how well they could read. Their ability to analyze words was determined by looking at how they actually carried out this process in context. Since then, applying some of the concepts of miscue analysis to the analysis of oral reading improved the process. As you learn to use this widely used procedure, keep the following questions in mind:

1. Does the reading of samples or portions of text give you the same picture of students' ability to construct meaning that the reading of complete texts does?
2. Is it really possible to identify precise levels of text and determine students' reading levels using these texts?
3. In general, are the procedures used to administer, score, and interpret the IRI consistent with what we know about how children develop literacy?

These questions should help you to be a more critical (evaluative) user of the IRI. The value of IRIs is enhanced when miscue analysis is used to analyze oral reading or when the running record (see the next section) concept is applied to the IRI.

Running Records

Another procedure for analyzing a student's reading is the **running record** (Clay, 1985), which is similar to miscue analysis. In this procedure, students read complete texts or samples of text. By looking at the students' responses, you are able to see their strengths and weaknesses in using various reading strategies and cueing systems. Running records are an important part of the assessment and evaluation used in the Reading Recovery Program in New Zealand and the United States (Clay, 1985; Pinnell, Fried, & Estice, 1990). They are also very useful for any classroom with beginning literacy learners.

See Chapter 5 on beginning literacy.

The following guidelines should be helpful in learning to take a running record. Teachers in kindergarten through third grade should find this technique useful in determining students' progress as they develop what Clay (1982) calls a "self-extending system," or independence in using reading strategies (though these procedures may also be used at upper levels with students developing beginning reading strategies). The guidelines are as follows:

1. Choose or have the child choose a book (or selection) she or he has read previously. For longer books, use a sample containing at least one hundred words.
2. Have the child read aloud the text. As the child reads, make a check mark on a blank sheet of paper for each word called correctly. (See Figure 11.13, which shows a sample running record taken by a first-grade teacher using the book *My Five Senses* [Miller, 1994].)
3. If the child makes miscues, mark as follows:

   * *Misreads word:* Write the word with the error above it (see Figure 11.13 [p. 2]).
   * *Omits word:* Write the word and circle it (p. 4).

FIGURE 11.13

Running Record Summary Sheet

Lisa S.   11-21-99

My Five Senses

p. 2   ✓ ✓ ✓ ✓ ✓ nose^noise SC
p. 3   ✓ ✓ ✓ ✓ ✓ ✓
p. 4   ✓ ✓ ✓ ✓ ✓   (myself)
p. 5   ✓ shadow^shoe
p. 6   ✓ ✓
p. 7   ✓ ✓ ✓
p. 8   ✓ ✓ ✓ ✓ ✓ ✓
p. 9   ✓ ✓
p. 10 ✓
p. 11 ✓ ✓
p. 12 ✓ ✓ ✓ ✓ ✓ ✓
p. 13 ✓ ocean^sea
p. 14 ✓
p. 15 ✓ ✓ ✓
p. 16 ✓ ✓ ✓ ✓ ✓ ✓ ✓
p. 17 ✓ ✓ ✓
p. 18 ✓ ✓
p. 19 ✓ whispered ✓
p. 20 ✓ ✓ ✓ ✓ ✓ ✓ ✓
p. 21 ✓
p. 22 ✓
p. 23 ✓ ✓ ✓
p. 24 ✓ ✓ ✓ ✓ ✓ ✓ ✓

$$\frac{81}{85} \times 100 = \underline{95}\%$$

Good progress; good use of strategies

- *Self-corrects:* Write the word with SC above it (p. 2).
- *Teacher tells word:* Write the word with *T* above it (p. 19).

4. To score, use the following formula:

For a detailed discussion of running records, see Clay (1985), listed in the "For Additional Reading" section.

$$\frac{\text{Total Words Read Correctly}^\star}{\text{Number of Words in Book/Sample}} \times 100 = \underline{\hspace{2cm}}\%$$

$\star$Self-corrections are correct

5. Ninety percent accuracy or higher is considered good progress.

6. Look at the student's miscues to determine strategies used and those not used.

Performance Assessments

Performance assessments are tasks that require students to demonstrate their literacy knowledge and skills by making real-world responses. Research has shown that such tasks are effective instructional tools (Khattri, Kane, & Reeve, 1995). Performance assessments include such devices as reports, posters, construction projects, and plays, all of which require students to demonstrate what they have learned. There are several important guidelines to consider as you develop performance assessments:

- Identify the specific strategies, skills, and knowledge you want students to learn.
- Be sure the performance task selected actually requires the use of the strategies, skills, and knowledge identified.
- Develop a rubric for evaluating the task.

Assessment Procedures Accompanying Published Materials

For many years, the publishers of basal readers have produced different types of tests to accompany their materials. Many publishers are moving more and more toward authentic literature and real books as resources for literacy development and are including in their packages a variety of suggestions and procedures for more authentic assessment and evaluation. If you are using one of these published resources, you should keep in mind what you have learned about effective literacy learning and assessment and select only those procedures that fit your needs and the needs of your students.

🦋 Making Decisions from Assessment Data

Table 11.2 summarizes the assessment techniques discussed in the previous section; it can serve as a reference guide for your use. Each technique can be used in the comprehensive literacy classroom and reflects what we know about literacy learning and assessment at this time. As mentioned earlier, *no classroom needs all of these techniques all of the time.* You must become a selective user of the various techniques.

TABLE 11.2 **Reference Guide to Assessment Techniques**

Technique	Purpose	Comments
Observation or "kid watching" (p.470)	Watch students' performance in authentic learning situations	An essential procedure for good classroom assessment and evaluation
Checklists (p.471)	Guide observations	May be used to guide observations in many areas related to literacy learning
Records of independent reading and writing (p.471)	Keep track of independent reading and writing	Should be used at all levels; gives insights about students' attitudes and habits
Retellings (p.473)	Assess comprehension	One of the best procedures to assess construction of meaning
Responses to literature (p.473)	Assess comprehension, levels of thinking, and use of strategies	Shows how students use what they have read and integrate ideas into their own experiences
Student self-evaluations (p.479)	Determine students' perceptions of their own reading and writing	Helps students take ownership of learning
Process interviews (p.479)	Gain insight into students' metacognition processes	Individual procedure that should be used selectively
Teacher-selected reading samples (p.481)	Assess meaning construction Assess decoding, if done orally	Informal procedure; may be collected and compared over time
Fluency checks and application of decoding skills (p.483)	Check decoding	Checks application of decoding in context
Literature groups (p.483)	Assess meaning construction	Integrates instruction and assessment
Interest inventories (p.486)	Determine students' interests	Provides a basis for planning learning activities
Scoring writing using rubrics (p.487)	Evaluate meaning construction through writing	Provides a way of judging writing by looking at the entire piece
Miscue analysis (p.488)	Assess decoding and use of strategies	Requires detailed training (see "For Additional Reading")
Informal reading inventories (p.489)	Assess meaning construction and decoding	Requires detailed training (see "For Additional Reading"); use judiciously
Running records (p.489)	Assess use of decoding strategies	Requires detailed training (see "For Additional Reading")
Performance assessments (p.490)	Assess application of all strategies, skills, and knowledge	Makes assessment an integral part of instruction
Assessment procedures accompanying published materials (p.490)	Varies according to publisher	Should be used selectively

Consider the following points as you decide which techniques to use:

- *How children develop literacy:* This is paramount to everything we have discussed in this text. Any assessment technique used should be in line with what we know about how children learn and develop literacy.

- *Principles for effective assessment:* Continuously refer to these principles and ask yourself whether the techniques you are using are consistent with them.

- *Trust your judgment:* If you know or believe a technique is inappropriate, question it; maybe you shouldn't use it. Consider an alternative. However, give a technique several trials before discarding it.

- *Start small:* Select one or two techniques to use, and try them out. Add others if necessary.

- *Evaluate techniques:* As you use various assessment techniques, evaluate them. Are they assessing what you want to assess? *If they don't inform instruction and help you and your students improve literacy learning, they shouldn't be used.* Talk with your colleagues to come up with alternative techniques.

As you gather assessment information from students' literacy activities, you should use it to make decisions about instruction for and with your students. The following scenarios illustrate how assessment and evaluation help with instructional decisions:

- As you observe a group of six students reading a little version of a big book, you notice that four of them have not developed fluency with the text. Therefore, you decide to reread the big book, using sentence strips and word cards to reconstruct the book in the pocket chart. You will also have children add words to the word wall.

- During Writing Workshop, many students are still having trouble writing persuasive paragraphs. Therefore, you decide that tomorrow you will conduct a minilesson on persuasive writing using the shared writing technique. This will be followed by collaborative or cooperative writing to provide continued scaffolding for those who need it.

- After having seven students retell a story they have read, you note that all of them have good understanding of story elements and concepts. Therefore, you decide they are ready for more challenging chapter books.

The use of assessment and evaluation data as described in the preceding examples shows how assessment and instruction truly go hand in hand.

🦋 What to Do About Grading

One issue continues to frustrate many teachers: grading. Nearly all schools continue to give grades, which may or may not be a good match for the assessment plan they have implemented.

Under the old concept of assessment, teachers could easily take numerical grades from worksheets, workbooks, and tests; place them in a grade book; total them; and average them for a grade. They could then show the students, parents, and administrators their "proof" for the grades given without feeling they had to judge or evaluate what the students had actually done. This was a very comfortable position, but it did not really reflect what the students were doing. Now, many schools are rethinking and evaluating the report card system.

If letter grades must be given in a comprehensive literacy classroom, evaluation must be viewed as being more subjective. Therefore, there are a number of factors to consider.

First, written descriptions (or rubrics) for each letter grade should be developed that vary by grade level and school and are based on the overall school objectives. The descriptions could include some of the benchmarks or standards discussed earlier. For example, an A at grade 3 might read as follows: "A = Reads many self-selected books with understanding. Is able to compare books and draw conclusions. Shows a thorough understanding of what has been read." These letter descriptions would guide the assessment.

Second, a rating scale might be used to evaluate written and oral responses to literature. For example, "A = Response indicates *thorough* understanding of what was read; B = Response shows some understanding of what was read"; and so forth.

Third, students should participate in their own grading. After discussing your grading criteria with them, you might ask them to determine their own grades and place their grades in their portfolios with written justification.

You will find that establishing your own criteria will make the job of grading far less difficult than most people make it out to be. Use the principles for assessment discussed earlier in this chapter. These principles, along with your criteria for grading, should help to make this difficult task easier.

🦋 Summary

This chapter presented information related to standards-based assessment and evaluation in the comprehensive or balanced literacy classroom. Eight principles for effective assessment were suggested:

1. Assessment should be an ongoing process.
2. Effective assessment is an integral part of instruction.
3. Assessment must be authentic, reflecting "real" reading and writing.
4. Assessment should be a collaborative, reflective process.
5. Effective assessment is multidimensional.
6. Assessment should be developmentally and culturally appropriate.
7. Effective assessment identifies students' strengths.
8. Assessment must be based on what we know about how students learn to read and write.

A way was suggested to use standards to guide assessment, followed by four ways to organize assessment information so that it is useful in making instructional decisions. The chapter then presented a variety of assessment techniques that are consistent with these principles: observation, checklists, records of independent reading and writing, retellings, responses to literature, student self-evaluations, process interviews, teacher-selected reading samples, fluency checks, application of decoding skills, literature groups, interest inventories, scoring of writing using rubrics, miscue analysis, informal reading inventories, running records, performance assessments, and assessment procedures accompanying published materials. The need to use these techniques selectively and as a basis for making instructional decisions was stressed. The chapter concluded with a brief discussion of grading.

For Additional Reading

Barrentine, S. J. (Ed.). (1999). *Reading assessment: Principles and practices for elementary teachers.* Newark, DE: International Reading Association.

Clay, M. M. (1985). *The early detection of reading difficulties* (3rd ed.). Auckland, New Zealand: Heinemann.

Cobb, C. (2003/2004). Effective instruction begins with purposeful assessments. *The Reading Teacher, 57*(4), 386–388.

Cooper, J. D., & Kiger, N. D. (2005). *Literacy assessment: Helping teachers plan instruction* (2nd ed.). Boston: Houghton Mifflin.

Dewitz, P., & Dewitz, P. K. (2003). They can read the words, but they can't understand: Refining comprehension assessment. *The Reading Teacher, 56*(5), 422–435.

Dickinson, D. K., McCabe, A., & Sprague, K. (2003). Teacher Rating of Oral Language and Literacy (TROLL): Individualizing early literacy instruction with a standards-based rating tool. *The Reading Teacher, 56*(6), 554–563.

Flippo, R. F. (2003). *Assessing readers.* Portsmouth, NH: Heinemann.

Forbes, S., Poparad, M. A., & McBride, M. (2004). To err is human; to self-correct is to learn. *The Reading Teacher, 57*(6), 566–572.

Goodman, Y., Watson, D., & Burke, C. (1987). *Reading miscue inventory: Alternative procedures.* New York: Richard C. Owen.

Jimenez, R. T. (2004). More equitable literacy assessments for Latino students. *The Reading Teacher, 57*(6), 576–578.

Johnson, M. S., Kress, R. A., & Pikulski, J. J. (1987). *Informal reading inventories* (2nd ed.). Newark, DE: International Reading Association.

Johnston, P. (2003). Assessment conversations. *The Reading Teacher, 57*(1), 90–92.

McCabe, P. P. (2003). Enhancing self-efficacy for high-stakes reading tests. *The Reading Teacher, 57*(1), 12–20.

Popham, W. J. (2001). *The truth about testing.* Alexandria, VA: Association for Supervision and Curriculum.

Tierney, R. J., Carter, M. A., & Desai, L. E. (1991). *Portfolio assessment in the reading-writing classroom.* Norwood, MA: Christopher-Gordon.

Valencia, S. W., & Buly, M. R. (2004). Behind test scores: What struggling readers really need. *The Reading Teacher*, *57*(6), 520–531.

Valencia, S. W., Hiebert, E. H., & Afflerbach, P. P. (Eds.). (1994). *Authentic reading assessment: Practices and possibilities.* Newark, DE: International Reading Association.

🖳 For Exploration: Electronic Products and Resources

FairTest: National Center for Fair and Open Testing

The National Center for Fair and Open Testing (FairTest) is an advocacy organization working to end the abuses, misuses, and flaws of standardized testing and to ensure that evaluation of students and workers is fair, open, and educationally sound. The site provides survey information on state-by-state assessment practices for K–12, university, and employment tests. It also provides links to publications, articles, and fact sheets on standardized and alternative assessment.
http://www.fairtest.org

Ideas and Rubrics

Developed by the Chicago Public Schools, this site provides a comprehensive discussion of rubrics.
http://intranet.cps.k12.il.us/Assessments/Ideas_and_Rubrics/ideas_and_rubrics.html

National Assessment of Educational Progress

The National Assessment of Educational Progress (NAEP) is mandated by Congress to provide objective data about the levels of knowledge, skills, and student performance at national, regional, and, on a trial basis, state levels. This site provides access to information and data about government-mandated, nationwide assessments at the national, regional, and state levels.
http://nces.ed.gov/nationsreportcard/

National Center for Research on Evaluation, Standards, and Student Testing (CRESST)

The National Center for Research on Evaluation, Standards, and Student Testing (CRESST) conducts research on important topics related to K–12 educational testing. This site provides publications, research reports, parents' guides, sample assessments, and a searchable database of alternative assessments in practice.
http://cresst96.cse.ucla.edu/index.htm

The ReadWrite Site

This fabulous site is host to the reading estimator, assessment calculator, and book browser.
http://www.readwritesite.com

Toolkit98: Alternative Assessment

Developers of *Toolkit98* describe the contents as "materials that are like the hammers, saws, and screwdrivers of a carpenter's toolkit." As the name implies, a toolkit contains a number of items that can be used to construct a multitude of authentic instruments to assess student achievement. This site contains chapters that provide background or foundation information on alternative assessments, and training activities designed to model effective teaching strategies.

http://www.nwrel.org/eval/toolkit98/index.html

Epilogue: A Gift for Every Child

Education is plagued by local, state, and national groups, and by politicians and special interest groups. Mandates, standards, and tests beset teachers from all sides. We are asked to prove children are growing at the desired rate. We are warned not to leave anyone behind. We are threatened with "bad" grades and possible withdrawn funding if we fail. We are told to put reading first.

But none of that is the point.

The point is that literacy is a gift that every child deserves. Literacy is the key that unlocks the door to full participation in life. We don't need legislation or slogans to make us do the right thing. We are teachers. We know literacy matters. We'd be doing it anyhow.

We two cannot imagine a world without literate citizens. We have worked hard to help you give the gift of literacy to the children whose lives you touch.

J. David Cooper
Nancy D. Kiger

Word Skills:
Phonics and Structural
Analysis for Teachers

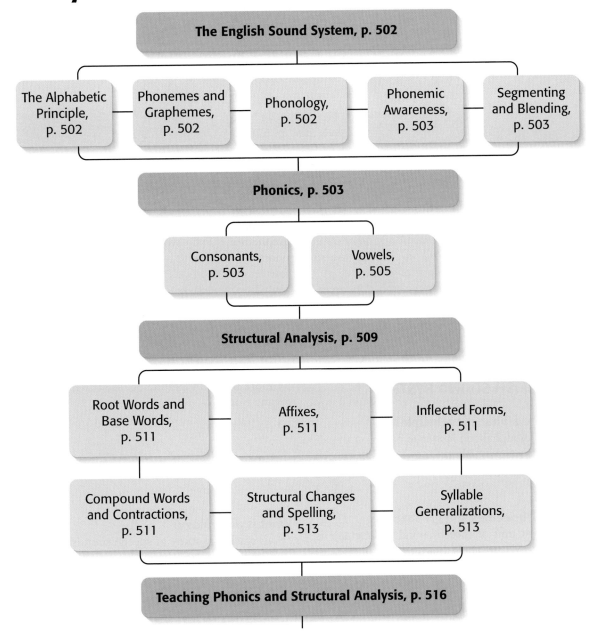

The English Sound System, p. 502

The Alphabetic Principle, p. 502

Phonemes and Graphemes, p. 502

Phonology, p. 502

Phonemic Awareness, p. 503

Segmenting and Blending, p. 503

Phonics, p. 503

Consonants, p. 503

Vowels, p. 505

Structural Analysis, p. 509

Root Words and Base Words, p. 511

Affixes, p. 511

Inflected Forms, p. 511

Compound Words and Contractions, p. 511

Structural Changes and Spelling, p. 513

Syllable Generalizations, p. 513

Teaching Phonics and Structural Analysis, p. 516

This handbook resource is designed to help you develop a basic knowledge about phonics and structural analysis. *It is not intended in any way to provide complete coverage of all the technical aspects of the structure of language and/or phonology.*

    Read pages 502–517 using the embedded questions to guide your reading. After reading, complete the practice exercise on pages 517–520. Check your answers.

THE ENGLISH SOUND SYSTEM

What is the alphabetic principle?

English is an alphabetic language based on the alphabetic principle. This means that each speech sound of the language is represented by a graphic symbol.

What are phonemes and graphemes?

The smallest unit of speech sound in language is the *phoneme*. The symbols that represent phonemes are referred to as graphemes. The word *cat* has three phonemes—/c/ /ă/ /t/—represented by three graphemes. The word *deep* also has three phonemes—/d/ /ē/ /p/—even though the word has four letters—*d-e-e-p*. The middle phoneme is represented by two letters—*ee*.

    Although English is an alphabetic language, it does not have one-to-one phoneme-grapheme correspondence. In other words, not all phonemes are represented by the same grapheme every time. For example, the /f/ phoneme can be represented by more than one grapheme, as shown in the following words:

/f/	*phone*
	fork
	puff
	rough

What is phonology?

Phonology is the study of speech sounds. *Phonological awareness* is the knowledge that words have

---

*This section is adapted from J. D. Cooper, E. W. Warncke, & D. Shipman. (1988). *The What and How of Reading Instruction,* 2nd ed. Copyright © 1988. Reprinted by permission of Pearson Education Inc., Upper Saddle River, NJ.

separate parts. There are three ways to look at the parts of words:

syllables: *look* (one syllable)

onsets and rimes: *look*

/l/ = onset

/o͝ok/ = rime

or

brick

/br/ = onset

/ick/ = rime

phonemes: /l/ /o͝o/ /k/

What is phonemic awareness?

One part of phonological awareness is *phonemic awareness,* which is the awareness that spoken words are made up of speech sounds or phonemes. Think of the word for each of the following pictures and think of the number of phonemes the word has:

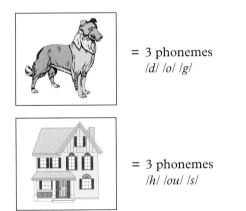

= 3 phonemes

/d/ /o/ /g/

= 3 phonemes

/h/ /ou/ /s/

What are segmenting and blending?

There are two major processes involved in phonemic awareness: segmenting and blending. *Segmenting* is the process of hearing a spoken word and being able to identify its phonemes; for example, *boat* has three phonemes—/b/ /ō/ /t/. *Blending* is the process of hearing the phonemes and being able to put them together (blend) to tell what the word is; for example, /s/ /ō/ /k/ is *sock*. Phonemic awareness is a prerequisite to learning phonics. Children are able to perform

segmenting and blending tasks without being able to name the letters.

PHONICS

What is phonics?

Phonics is the study of the relationships between the speech sounds (phonemes) and the letters (graphemes) that represent them. Phonics is sometimes called *decoding.* It is the sounding out of unknown words. The amount of phonics instruction that individual learners need varies greatly.

Phonics produces *only* pronunciation, or an approximate pronunciation, of the unknown word. The pronounced word must be in the reader's oral language, to check both the accuracy of the decoding process and the meaning of the word in its contextual usage. For example,

Pitta are almost extinct because of acid rain.

Although readers may be able to say "pitta," they may not understand the above sentence. No real reading has taken place unless the author's meaning has been conveyed to the reader, even if the decoding was perfect! The reader may infer that "pitta" is plural because of the word *are* and a living thing because *extinct* is a term used with creatures. Therefore, some meaning has been conveyed. It is just not complete. (By the way, pitta are brightly colored birds found in southern Asian and Australian forests.)

Consonants

What is a consonant?

There are two basic categories of sounds in English: consonants and vowels. A *consonant* is a speech sound (phoneme) in which the flow of breath is constricted or stopped by the tongue, teeth, lips, or some combination of these. The letters (graphemes) representing such speech sounds are also called consonants. Most single consonants are regular in sound in that they represent only one sound no matter where they appear in a word.

boy	*tab*	*rabid* (*b*s all sound alike)
dog	*had*	*radar* (*d*s all sound alike)

What sounds are expected for *c* and *g*?

There are several notable exceptions to consistent single consonant sounds. Consonants *c* and *g* have hard and soft sounds. The grapheme *c* is expected to have its hard sound /*k*/ when it is followed by the vowels *a, o, u,* or by another consonant. The hard sound of *c* is the sound usually associated with the letter *k*.

    cat   *cot*   *cut*   *class*   *alcove*

The soft sound of *c* is the sound heard in *city*. The soft sound of *c* occurs when the *c* is followed by *e, i,* or *y*.

    cell   *cider*   *cycle*

The hard and soft *g* generalization is not as consistent as the hard and soft *c* generalization. The grapheme *g* is expected to have its hard sound when it is followed by the vowels *a, o, u,* or another consonant. The hard sound of *g* is the guttural sound that is heard in the following words:

    gate   *got*   *gum*   *glad*   *rag*

The soft sound of *g*—/*j*/—is expected when it is followed by the vowels *e, i,* or *y*. The soft sound of *g* is the sound usually associated with the letter *j*, as in the following words:

    gentle   *giant*   *gym*

What sounds are associated with *s*?

The letter *s* has four different sounds. There is no generalization covering when the reader should expect each sound. The sounds represented by *s* are illustrated by:

see—/*s*/
sure—/*sh*/
has—/*z*/
treasure—/*zh*/

What are some other exceptions to consistent consonant sounds?

The following exceptions to consistent single consonant sounds are far less common than those noted above. They are presented here to illustrate that there are other exceptions and as a caution to teachers to think carefully before requiring learners to decode phonetically unpredictable words.

Grapheme	Phoneme	Word
f	/*v*/	o*f*
x	/*ks*/	e*x*it
x	/*z*/	*x*ylophone
qu	/*k*/	anti*que*
qu	/*kw*/	*qu*iz

What are consonant clusters, and what else may they be called?

Consonants may also appear in *clusters* in words; that is, more than one consonant may come together before a vowel or between vowels in a word. Some materials for reading instruction refer to all groups of consonants as consonant clusters. Other materials divide them into two categories: consonant digraphs and blends.

What are digraphs?

Consonant Digraphs. A consonant digraph is two consecutive consonants (in a word or syllable) that represent one speech sound. In other words, two graphemes represent just one phoneme. The word *digraph* means (di) two (graph) letters. In fact, the word *digraph* contains a digraph, *ph*. There are essentially three kinds of digraphs:

1. **New sound.** Some consonant digraphs represent a new sound that is unlike the sound of either of the single consonants or any other consonants. This type of consonant digraph may have more than one sound.

Digraph	Word	Phoneme
sh	*sh*ut	/*sh*/
th	*th*is	(voiced *th*)
	*th*in	(unvoiced *th*)
wh	*wh*en	/*hw*/
	*wh*o	/*h*/
ch	whi*ch*	/*ch*/
	*ch*asm	/*k*/
	*ch*ef	/*sh*/

2. Either sound. Some consonant digraphs represent the sound of one of the single consonants contained in the digraph.

Digraph	Word	Phoneme
ck	ki*ck*	/*k*/
kn	*kn*ot	/*n*/
wr	*wr*ite	/*r*/
gn	*gn*at	/*n*/
pn	*pn*eumatic	/*n*/
gh	*gh*ost	/*g*/

3. Another sound. Some consonant digraphs represent the sound of another grapheme.

Digraph	Word	Phoneme
gh	lau*gh*	/*f*/
ph	*ph*one	/*f*/

Other consonant clusters often referred to as digraphs include *nk* as in ba*nk;* *ng* as in si*ng;* and double consonants as in mi*tt*en, su*mm*er, and ru*dd*er.

What are consonant blends?

Consonant Blends. A consonant blend is two or three consonant sounds clustered together in a word or syllable, where all consonant sounds are heard. The phonemes merge in speech sounds. The reader produces a speech sound for each consonant seen. The word *blend* contains two blends: *bl* and *nd.* There are three major categories of blends:

1. Blends beginning with the letter *s:*

str	*str*ong	sc	*sc*ab	sn	*sn*ail
spl	*spl*ash	sk	ri*sk*	sp	wa*sp*
scr	*scr*eam	sl	*sl*ow	st	la*st*
spr	*spr*ing	sm	*sm*og	sw	*sw*an

2. Blends concluding with the letter *r:*

br	*br*oth	fr	*fr*esh	tr	*tr*out
cr	*cr*owd	gr	*gr*ass	spr	*spr*ay
dr	*dr*aft	pr	*pr*ove	str	*str*aw

3. Blends concluding with the letter *l:*

bl	*bl*ue	gl	*gl*ass	cl	*cl*ose
pl	*pl*ace	fl	*fl*ip	sl	*sl*ave

The *lp* in he*lp*, the *tw* in *tw*in, the *dw* in *dw*arf, and the *nd* in sa*nd* are all examples of other consonant blends. Remember, whenever each consonant in a cluster can be heard, the cluster is called a blend.

Why are consonant sounds important?
Consonant sounds are more consistent than vowel sounds. There is less deviation in the sounds of consonants, whether they are single or in clusters. Therefore, a few consonants, along with a vowel, are usually taught first so children can begin to build words.

Vowels

What is a vowel? What are the categories of vowel sounds?
A vowel is a speech sound in which the flow of breath is relatively unobstructed. The letters representing such sounds are also called vowels. The letters *a, e, i, o,* and *u* always function as vowels. The letter *y* is sometimes a consonant (as in *y*ell) and sometimes a vowel (as in b*y* and ma*y*). The letter *w* functions as a vowel in combination with another vowel (as in la*w*). The categories of vowel sounds are short vowels, long vowels, vowel digraphs, diph-

thongs, the schwa sound, exceptions to expected vowel sounds, and *y* and *w* functioning as vowels.

What are short vowels?

Short Vowel Sounds. Short vowel sounds are sometimes referred to as unglided. The five short vowel sounds are represented in the following words:

/ăt/   /ĕd/   /ĭt/   /ŏx/   /ŭp/

The breve (brĕv), or curved line over a vowel (ă), is the diacritical marking used to indicate the short vowel sound in phonetic respellings. Sometimes dictionaries make no mark for the short vowel sound.

Two other vowel sounds also referred to as short vowel sounds are the /aw/ sound as represented by the *a* in c*a*ll, the *ou* in c*ou*gh, the *au* in c*au*ght, and the *aw* in l*aw;* and the short *oo* sound /o͝o/ as in l*oo*k and g*oo*d.

What are long vowels?

Long Vowel Sounds. Long vowels are those in which the name of the letter is heard. These sounds are sometimes referred to as the glided sounds. There are five long vowel sounds in English, as represented in the following:

Word	Pronunciation
ate	/āt/
eat	/ēt/
ice	/īs/
open	/ō·pən/
use	/ūz/ v.
	/ūs/ n.

The macron /mā′-kron/, a straight line over the vowel (ā), is the diacritical mark used to indicate the long vowel sound in phonetic spellings. Another vowel of this type is the long *oo* sound /o͞o/, as heard in r*oo*m and c*oo*l.

What are vowel digraphs?

Vowel Digraphs. Vowel digraphs, like consonant digraphs, occur when two adjacent vowels in a syllable represent one speech sound; that is, two vowel letters evoke only one phoneme and are therefore considered one grapheme. The most frequently occurring vowel digraphs are:

Vowel Digraph	Word	Vowel Phoneme
ee	s*ee*d	/ē/
oa	g*oa*t	/ō/
ea	s*ea*t	/ē/
ai	p*ai*n	/ā/
ay	d*ay*	/ā/

The most usual sound of these vowel digraphs is the long sound of the first vowel. However, there are exceptions—for example:

Vowel Digraph	Word	Vowel Phoneme
ea	br*ea*k	/ā/
ea	br*ea*d	/ĕ/
ie	p*ie*ce	/ē/
oa	br*oa*d	/aw/

What are diphthongs?

Diphthongs. Diphthongs, like consonant blends, consist of two vowels in one syllable where two sounds are heard. In some reading materials, diphthongs are called vowel blends. The most frequently occurring diphthongs are:

Diphthong	Example Word
oi	*oi*l
oy	*oy*ster
ou	h*ou*se
ow	n*ow*

What vowel combinations can be either diphthong or digraph?

Two vowel combinations function sometimes as digraphs and sometimes as diphthongs: *ou* and *ow*. The *ou* in *out* is a diphthong; in *brought*, it is a vowel digraph. The *ow* in *now* is a diphthong; in *show*, it is a vowel digraph. When teaching the phonemes to be associated with these graphemes, it is necessary to teach that each has two distinct sounds.

ou

Digraph	Diphthong
c*ou*gh /aw//	c*ou*ch /ou/
thr*ou*gh /o͞o/	
t*ou*gh /ŭ/	

ow

Digraph	Diphthong
sn*ow* /ō/	c*ow* /ou/

What is a schwa?

Schwa. The schwa sound of a vowel is known as the softened or indeterminate sound. It sounds like a short *u* and frequently occurs in the unstressed or unaccented syllable of a word. It may be spelled with any vowel or combination of vowels. The diacritical mark representing the schwa sound is often an upside down and backward *e* (ə).

Vowel	Example of Schwa Sound	
a	above	/ə·buv′/
e	craven	/krā′·vən/
i	beautiful	/byoo′·tə·fəl/
o	committee	/kə·mit′·ē/
u	cherub	/chĕr·əb/

The schwa sound may be represented sometimes by two vowels as shown with the *io* in the word port*io*n /pôr′·shən/.

What are the exceptions to expected vowel sounds?

Exceptions to Expected Vowel Sounds. Short vowel sounds are the most common vowel sounds in words. The short vowel is expected in a closed syllable, a syllable (or word) ending with one or more consonants. For example, *cat* and *at* are closed syllables; they end with a consonant. There are four standard exceptions to the expected short vowel sounds in a closed syllable.

1. When a vowel is followed by *r*, the vowel sound is not short; rather, it is called an *r*-controlled vowel.

ar	c*ar*	er	h*er*	ir	f*ir*
or	f*or*	ur	f*ur*		

Notice that the *er, ir,* and *ur* all sound the same. The *ar* sounds like the letter name *r*, and the *or* sounds like the word *or*.

2. When the vowel *a* is followed by *l*, it usually represents the /aw/ phoneme.

s*al*t (sôlt)
t*al*k (tôk)
b*al*l (bôl)

3. When the vowel grapheme *o* is followed by *lt* or *ld*, it has the long *o* phoneme.

b*o*lt   g*o*ld

4. When the vowel grapheme *i* is followed by *gh*, *ld*, or *nd*, it usually has the long *i* phoneme (exception wĭnd).

n*igh*t   s*igh*   w*ild*   m*ind*

When do *y* or *w* serve as vowels?

Y as a Vowel. The letter *y* functions as a vowel when it represents either the short or long sounds of the letter *i* or is part of a digraph or diphthong. The short *i* sound of *y* is expected in a closed syllable.

g*y*m   g*y*p   s*y*mbol

The long *i* sound of *y* is expected when it occurs alone in an open syllable, that is, one ending with a vowel, in this case *y*.

m*y*   dynamic   p*y*thon

When *y* is preceded by the vowels *a* or *e*, it functions as the second vowel of a vowel digraph.

d*ay*   th*ey*   k*ey*

When *y* is in the final position in words of two or more syllables, it usually represents the long *e* sound.

part*y*   assembl*y*

Note: In some dialects, this final *y* sound is the short *i*. Some dictionaries mark its pronunciation both ways.

There are two infrequent patterns in which *y* also represents a vowel: when *y* is preceded by *u* or followed by *e*.

g*uy*   b*ye*

W as a Vowel. The letter *w* functions as a vowel only when it is in combination with another vowel: as part of a digraph when preceded by *a*, *e*, or *o*; as part of a diphthong when preceded by *o* (sometimes).

W as Part of a Digraph

p*aw*

bl*ow*

gr*ew*

W as Part of a Diphthong

cl*ow*n

What generalizations govern vowel sounds?

Vowel Sound Generalizations. There are no hard and fast rules for the expected vowel sounds, only generalizations. The generalizations are quite interrelated. Only those generalizations determined to be the most consistent and applicable are presented in this text (Bailey, 1967; Clymer, 1963/1996; Emans, 1967).

- **The most common vowel sound generalization relates to the short vowel sound.** This sound is expected in a closed syllable, one ending with a consonant. This kind of syllable is sometimes referred to as the CVC pattern (C = Consonant, V = Vowel, C = Consonant). The consonants may be single or in clusters, and it is not mandatory to have a consonant in the initial position of such a syllable or short word. The following words follow the CVC pattern:

  rag (CVC)
  slot (CCVC)
  wish (CVCC)
  at (VC)

  The CVC generalization is useful in pronouncing one-syllable words as well as the individual syllables of polysyllabic words. The following words all contain closed syllables with a short vowel sound:

hamlet	/hăm·lĭt/
fancy	/făn′·sē/
section	/sĕk′·shən/

- **There are three generalizations for when to expect long vowel sounds.** The first is the sound expected in an open syllable, one that ends in a vowel. It is sometimes referred to as the CV pattern (C = Consonant, V = Vowel). There may or may not be a consonant before the vowel. The following words and syllables within words follow the CV pattern:

m*e*	/mē/
*o*pen	/ō·pən/
h*o*tel	/hō·tĕl′/
m*u*sic	/myoo′·zĭk/

The CV generalization is useful in pronouncing one-syllable words as well as individual syllables of polysyllabic words. The following words contain open syllables with long vowel sounds:

m*u*sic	/myo͞o′·zĭk/
prem*o*lar	/prē·mō′·lər/
r*o*mance	/rō·măns′/
T*i*tanic	/tī·tan′·ĭk/
m*e*ter	/mē′·tər/

- **A long vowel sound is also expected with certain vowel digraphs.** When the vowel digraphs *ee, oa, ea, ai,* and *ay* are in the CVVC pattern, the first vowel often represents its long sound, and the second vowel is not sounded. The following words follow the CVVC pattern:

b*oa*t	s*ay*	str*ai*n	*ea*t	s*ee*
c*oa*st	del*ay*	p*ai*nt	tr*ea*t	sl*ee*p

- **A long vowel sound is also expected in the CVCe (the *e* is usually shown in lower case) pattern.** This is sometimes referred to as the final *e* pattern. The final *e* serves to indicate that the preceding vowel should probably represent the long sound. It occurs most frequently in one-syllable words. The following words follow the CVCe pattern:

ate	make	rebate	stroke	fine

Summary

What is the key to a reader using phonics effectively?

It is important to remember that when a reader uses phonics, it will have value only if the word to be decoded is in the reader's oral language. Once phonic generalizations have been applied to an unknown word, the reader has to test it against his or her oral vocabulary to determine whether the decoding process has resulted in a recognizable English word. In effect, the reader pronounces a sound(s) and asks: Is this a word I know? The reader also needs to use context clues to decide whether the decoded word makes sense in the sentence.

Phonics is one of several word recognition skills students need in order to learn to read. Phonics is not the goal of reading instruction. It serves as a means to an end: the construction of meaning. Some learners may have difficulty learning phonics; in this case, other word recognition skills such as context should be taught.

STRUCTURAL ANALYSIS

What is structural analysis?

Structural analysis is a word recognition skill in which knowledge of the meaningful parts of words aids in the identification of an unknown written word. A reader may use structural analysis as an aid to either the pronunciation of an unknown word or to understanding the meaning of an unknown word. Structural analysis may be considered both a word recognition and a comprehension skill. A mature reader may use structural analysis for both purposes simultaneously.

Structural analysis requires the reader to look at meaningful units or parts of words in order to decode a word or to decide what a word means. The following diagram shows the relationships among the parts of structural analysis that will be discussed in this section.

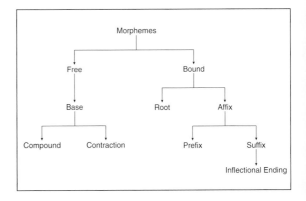

What are morphemes?

The meaningful structural parts of words are called *morphemes*. A morpheme is the smallest unit of meaning in a word. Any unit of meaning in a word is a morpheme.

> *Cat* is a single morpheme.
>
> *Cats* is two morphemes.

The *s* added to the word *cat* means more than one cat, so it is a second meaning unit added to the meaning unit *cat*.

What are the two types of morphemes?

There are two types of morphemes: bound morphemes and free morphemes. A bound morpheme must be attached to another morpheme in order to carry meaning. A free morpheme can stand alone, as a word, in the English language. The *s* in *cats* has no meaning unless it is attached to a word; it is a bound morpheme. The word *cat* can stand alone; it is a free morpheme. The following words illustrate bound and free morphemes.

> *Unhappy* has two morphemes. (*un* is bound; *happy* is free)
>
> *Redoing* has three morphemes. (*re* and *ing* are bound; *do* is free)
>
> *Disagreeable* has three morphemes. (*dis* and *able* are bound; *agree* is free)
>
> *Desk* has one morpheme. (it is free)

Root Words and Base Words

What are root words and base words?

Every word has a major meaning-bearing morpheme. This morpheme may be either a bound or a free morpheme, and is either a root word or a base word. Root words come from or are derived from another language and will not stand alone in English; they are bound morphemes. Base words are English words and will stand alone; they are free morphemes. Following are examples of root words/derived words:

Root Words/Derived Words

con*tain*	de*tain*	re*tain*
re*fer*	con*fer*	de*fer*
con*cede*	re*cede*	

Notice that *tain*, *fer*, and *cede* are the major meaning-bearing parts of these words, but are not English words. An English word is formed only when other bound morphemes are added to these roots. Each of the above words contains two bound morphemes. Following are examples of base words:

Base Words

girl	*girls*
comfort	un*comfor*table
mark	re*marking*

Notice that the base word remains a free morpheme even when one or more affixes have been added to it.

Affixes

What are affixes?

An affix is any morpheme attached to the main meaning-bearing part of a word. Affixes are prefixes, suffixes, and inflectional endings and are bound morphemes. An affix may either precede or follow the root or base word, or both. Base and root words may have more than one affix. Root words must have at least one affix.

What is a prefix?

A *prefix* is a bound morpheme added to the beginning of a word. Prefixes add to and change the meaning of the base or root word.

Prefix	Meaning	Example
dis	not	disable
	remove, to make not	disappear
	undo, reverse	disassemble
ex	out	exhale
	beyond	expand
re	back	revert
	again	remake

What is a suffix?

A *suffix* is a bound morpheme added to the end of a word. Suffixes add to and change the meaning of the base or root word.

Suffix	Meaning	Example
er	one who has to do with	laborer
	resident of	southerner
	performs an action	worker
ness	condition of being	fullness
less	without	powerless
	beyond the range of	sightless

Words formed by the addition of prefixes or suffixes to base or root words are known as *derived words,* or derivatives. A different meaning has been derived, or obtained, from the meaning of the original root or base word.

Inflected Forms

What are inflectional endings?

Inflectional endings are a special set of suffixes. They, like other suffixes, are added to the end of a root or base word. Inflectional endings change the number, case, or gender when added to nouns; tense when added to verbs; and form when added to adjectives and adverbs.

Group

n.	Number: cats	more than one
n.	Case: child's	shows ownership
n.	Gender: hostess	changes to female
v.	Tense: helped	past tense
adv/adj	Form: taller	compares two things

The most common inflectional endings are:

Nouns

- **Number** *s* and *es* when affixed to nouns to indicate plurality, as in *toys* and *dresses.*
- **Case** *'s* when attached to nouns to indicate possession, as in "John's ball is red."
- **Number and case** *s'* to indicate plurality and possession, as in "It is the girls' recess time."
- **Gender** *ess* when attached to nouns to indicate change of gender, as from *steward* to *stewardess.*

Verbs

- **Tense** *ed* and *ing* when attached to verbs to indicate, respectively, past tense and present participle, as in *walked* and *walking* and *s* to verbs to indicate agreement with third-person singular nouns, as in "Mary works."

Adjectives/Adverbs

- **Form** *er* and *est* when affixed to adjectives or adverbs to indicate, respectively, comparative and superlative forms, as in *faster* and *fastest.*

When new words are formed by the addition of inflectional endings, they are called inflected forms of the words. The *er* in *taller* is an inflectional ending because it changes the form of the word, but *er* in *helper* is not an inflectional ending because it does not change the tense, case, number, form, or gender of the word. (The *er* in *helper* is a suffix; it changes the verb *help* into a noun—one who helps.)

It is possible for a word to be both derived and inflected. Any word that has had a prefix or suffix added to it is a derived form of that word. The addition of an inflectional ending produces the inflected form.

> *Independent* is a derived form of *depend.* (prefix *in* + *depend* + suffix *ent*)
>
> *Unhappier* is both derived and inflected. (prefix *un* [not] + *happy* [base word] + inflected ending *er* [comparative])

Compound Words and Contractions

What are compound words and contractions?

Two other types of words are formed by the combination of meaningful structural units, or morphemes: compound words and contractions. *Compound words* are a combination of two free morphemes. The meaning of the new word must

PREFIXES AND SUFFIXES THAT MERIT INSTRUCTION

PREFIXES

[a]*un-*	Meaning "not":
dis-	*unhappy*
[a]*in-, im-*	*disrespectful*
[a]*non*	*inactive*
ir-	*impossible*
	nonresistant
	irresponsible
re-	Meaning "back" or "again":
	revisit
[a]*un-*	Meaning "do the opposite of":
dis-	*untie*
	disassemble
in-, im-	Meaning "in" or "into":
	indoors
en-, em-	Meaning "into" or "within":
	entangle
over-	Meaning "too much":
	overdose
mis-	Meaning "wrong":
	misspell

SUFFIXES

	Plural:
-s, -es	*girls*
	Tense:
	jumps
-ed	Tense:
	jumped
-ing	Tense:
	jumping
-ly	Meaning "like":
	sisterly
-er, -or	Meaning "one who performs a specialized action: *swimmer;* Used to form comparative degree with adjectives: *darker*
-tion	Meaning "action":
-ion	*absorption*
-ation	
-ition	
-able	Meaning "susceptible," "capable" "worth":
-ible	*debatable*
-al, -ial	Meaning "of" or relating to:
	parental
-y	Meaning "consisting of" or "inclined toward":
	sleepy
-ness	Meaning "state," "quality," "condition," or "degree":
	brightness

[a] Accounts for nearly 50 percent of all prefixed words (Graves, 1987).
Source: Based on White, Sowell, and Yanagihara (1989).

retain elements of both meanings and pronunciation of the two previous morphemes in order to be classified as a compound word. *Dollhouse, racetrack,* and *bathroom* are compound words; *office, target,* and *together* are not compound words.

Contractions are formed by combining two free morphemes into a shortened form by the omission of one or more letters and the insertion of an apostrophe where those letters were omitted.

> *are* + *not* form the contraction *aren't*
>
> *they* + *are* form the contraction *they're*
>
> *he* + *will* form the contraction *he'll*

Without the use of context clues, confusion may arise with the use of *'s* with singular nouns. The word *boy's* could be the contracted form of *boy* + *is* or it may be a change of case and the possessive form of boy.

> John's sister can't say what John's going to do.

In this sentence, the first *John's* is possessive, while the second one is the contracted form of *John is.*

Structural Changes and Spelling

What are the important structural changes in a word that influence spelling?

Structural analysis can be helpful, but sometimes beginning readers find the addition of a structural part to a known word confusing. The word may look so different that they are unable to recognize the derived word. This is especially true when a spelling change occurs in the base word.

The following generalizations should be taught to aid in the reader's recognition of base words and derived words as well as to aid in the spelling of such words.

1. When a word ends with *e,* the *e* is dropped before adding an inflectional ending that begins with a vowel.

   > *bake* + *ing* becomes *baking*
   >
   > *hope* + *ed* becomes *hoped.*

2. When a word ends with a single vowel followed by a single consonant, that consonant is doubled before adding *ing* or *ed.*

   > *hop* + *ed* becomes *hopped*
   >
   > *begin* + *ing* becomes *beginning*

3. When a word ends with *f* or *fe* (with a silent *e*), the *f* is usually changed to *v* before the ending is added.

   > *calf* + *es* becomes *calves*
   >
   > *wife* + *es* becomes *wives*

4. When a word ends in *y* preceded by a consonant, the *y* is usually changed to *i* before endings are added, unless the ending begins with *i.*

   > *dry* + *ed* becomes *dried*
   >
   > *party* + es becomes *parties*
   >
   > *sorry* + *est* becomes *sorriest*
   >
   > *cry* + *ing* becomes *crying*

5. When a word ends with *y* preceded by a vowel, no change is made in the base word before adding endings.

   > *boy* + *s* becomes *boys*
   >
   > *stay* + *ed* or *ing* becomes *stayed* or *staying*

6. When the base word ends with *s, ss, ch, sh,* or *x,* the inflectional ending *es* is added rather than *s;* when the word ends in *f/fe,* change to *v* and add *es;* when the word ends in *y,* change to *i* and add *es.*

   > *focus* becomes *focuses*
   >
   > *mess* becomes *messes*
   >
   > *lunch* becomes *lunches*
   >
   > *dish* becomes *dishes*
   >
   > *box* becomes *boxes*
   >
   > *half* becomes *halves*
   >
   > *cry* becomes *cries*

Syllable Generalizations

What is a syllable, and how does knowledge of syllables aid in word pronunciation?

A syllable is an oral language unit in which a vowel sound is heard. There are as many syllables in a word as there are vowel sounds. In word recognition, we don't worry about conventions of "correct" division of words; rather, we divide in order to deal with pronunciation of one syllable at a time. A syllable may or may not contain a consonant sound.

a, my, ate, dog, boat (these are monosyllabic words)
dis-con-tin-ue, re-lat-ed (these are polysyllabic words)

Knowledge governing vowel sounds (discussed earlier) applies whether to a one-syllable word or a polysyllabic word.

The primary reason for teaching or learning how to divide words into syllables for reading or decoding purposes is to give the reader clues to the possible pronunciation of vowel sounds in unknown words.

What are the generalizations concerning syllable division?

Generalizations for syllabic division of words give the reader possibilities to chunk an unfamiliar word so that he or she may decode it by applying phonic and structural analysis. (Syllabication is *not* used for dividing words in writing. The dictionary should be used for this purpose. Therefore, students must be taught to read phonetic respellings.) If the decoded word is in the reader's oral language, this serves as the reader's check on the accuracy of the generalizations that have been applied. Structural elements of the word are dealt with first; then phonic generalizations are applied as needed.

What are 3 structural generalizations for dividing words into syllables?

The first three generalizations for syllables deal with the structural parts of unknown words; that is, bases, roots, and affixes. Whenever readers are being taught to divide words into syllables, they should first look for meaningful chunks of the unknown word.

1. Almost all affixes form separate syllables. In the word *rewrite*, *re* is a separate syllable; in the word *useless, less* is a separate syllable. Exceptions to

this include the inflectional endings *'s, s,* and *ed* except when *ed* is preceded by *d* or *t.*

books is one syllable
Sue's is one syllable
chained is one syllable
wanted is two syllables
loaded is two syllables

2. The two words of a compound word form separate syllables, even if there are additional syllables in one or both of the words used to form the compound word.

Word	Morphemes	Syllables
cowboy	*cow + boy*	2 syllables
lumberjack	*lumber + jack*	2 + 1 = 3 syllables
policewoman	*police + woman*	2 + 2 = 4 syllables

3. The contracted form of two words sometimes produces just one syllable because it is a vowel that has been deleted to form the contraction. Sometimes it produces two syllables:

can't is one syllable
they'll is one syllable
couldn't is two syllables
wasn't is two syllables

The next five syllabication generalizations help readers apply phonic generalizations by dividing long words into syllables (chunking).

1. When two consonants occur between two vowels, the syllabic division is usually *between the two consonants.* (Do not divide consonant digraphs and blends; they are treated as single consonants.) This pattern is known as the -VCCV-pattern. There may or may not be other consonants preceding or following this pattern.

bargain	bar-gain
circus	cir-cus
enter	en-ter
entertain	en-ter-tain

2. In the -VCCV- pattern, divide before or after the blend or digraph. (There is an exception: double consonants. Many experts treat double consonants as digraphs.)

letter   lett-er
graphic graph-ic
doctrine doc-trine

3. When one consonant occurs between two vowels, the syllabic division may put the consonant with either the first or second vowel. This is known as the -VCV- pattern. There may or may not be other consonants preceding or following this pattern.
   a. When the consonant goes with the first vowel, the first syllable is closed, and the first vowel sound is expected to be short (VC-V).

      riv-er ex-it liz-ard

   b. When the consonant goes with the second vowel, the first syllable is open and the first vowel is expected to be long (V-CV).

      ma-jor ho-tel ba-con

First, try the consonant with the first vowel, and check against oral language. If this seems incorrect, try the consonant with the second vowel.

There are a few words in our language with the -VCV- pattern that actually appear to divide both ways. These words are called *homographs* because they are spelled the same. However, they are two different words with different pronunciations and meanings. The contextual usage of the words and the reader's oral language are the only checks on the correct pronunciation. The words don't actually divide differently; the accent is placed differently.

record (rē-cord′ rĕ′-cord) Be sure to record record low temperatures.

present (pr ē-sent′ pr ĕ′-sent)
Will you present the present to our guest?

4. When a word ends in *le* preceded by a single consonant, the final syllable usually consists of the consonant plus the *le*.

cradle cra-dle (krā-dəl)
trifle   tri-fle   (tr ī-fəl)

If two consonants precede the *le*, usually divide after the second consonant to prevent splitting blends and digraphs.

rattle   ratt-le
ankle   ank-le

5. The vowel sound in an unstressed or unaccented syllable is often the schwa sound. Any vowel may have the schwa sound, which sounds like the short *u*.

com-mit′-tee (kə•m ĭt′•ē)
a-gain   (ə•gĕn′)
dem′-*on*-strate (dem′•ən•strāt)

Summary

The division (or chunking) of unfamiliar words is guided by generalizations or possibilities, not by rules. These generalizations must be used in conjunction with each other and with phonics. Because many words in the English language are not phonetically regular, sometimes it is necessary to check the pronunciation of a word in the dictionary. Before requiring students to sound out words, teachers must be sure that the words follow accepted generalizations for their pronunciations. The following steps summarize how to apply generalizations for dividing words into syllables or chunks:

1. Separate affixes.
2. Follow generalizations to divide base or root words.
3. Apply phonic generalizations.
4. Try alternates if the first attempt doesn't result in an acceptable word for the context.

TEACHING PHONICS AND STRUCTURAL ANALYSIS

Is it important to teach phonics and structural analysis in a systematic way?

Yes. While some children may seem to acquire phonic and structural analysis skills either on their own or through incidental teaching, most do not. A systematic system ensures that no skills are overlooked and works best for most children.

Can I teach phonics and structural analysis as needed while children are reading meaningful text?

This kind of instruction, sometimes referred to as incidental instruction, may work for some children some of the time. It will not work for all children. Therefore, we recommend a systematic system of instruction.

Should all children be taught in the same way? That is, given that I should teach systematically, should I use the same system for all children?

Begin with the assumption that the chosen system will be successful for all children, but observe very carefully as you teach and as children begin to apply newly taught skills to reading meaningful text. If what you are doing is not bringing success for some children, be prepared to change the pace of instruction or look for a different system for those children.

Should children who are already reading fluently without having had phonics instruction be required to do such lessons anyhow?

Sometimes a child learns to decode words without formal instruction, apparently having learned intuitively. Remember that phonics analysis is a means to an end. Use your judgment about the need for such a child to participate in phonics lessons. Most such children have no need for the lessons.

Can I use the phonics component of my school's adopted published reading or language arts program?

Yes. In fact, following the phonics component of the published reading program you are using makes good sense. Absent this, a stand-alone published program may also be useful to you.

Sequence for Teaching Using a Published Program

Should I follow the sequence of phonics instruction in our published basal reading program or change the sequence?

Follow the sequence as given in the published program. It has been developed to fit well with what children are asked to read in their pupil books.

What if my school purchases and recommends using a stand-alone phonics program in addition to the basal program?

We recommend sticking to the sequence suggested by the basal reading program publisher because it logically works with material children will be reading. You can use lessons on particular skills from the stand-alone program to supplement the basal lessons when needed.

When should I supplement the published program?

If, after teaching the published program lessons, you find some or all children have not grasped the skill or are not able to apply the skill, you may need to reteach. Repeating the very same lesson may not be effective. Instead, locate (or create) another lesson for teaching the same skill. You should also adjust the pace of the lesson, the number of examples provided, and the amount of repetition to fit the needs of the children. This requires you to assess continually as you teach, being alert to signs that a child has become lost or failed to get what you are teaching.

Should I ever omit or change the sequence or content of the published program?

While we recommend systematic teaching, which means omitting nothing and not changing a well-developed sequence, there may be times when it is appropriate to do either or both. For example, if you have observed that your students are already using a skill, there is no need to spend time having them go through a lesson on that skill. If they will be reading something that lends itself to a lesson on a particular skill that is not next in the sequence, adjust the sequence to meet the needs of the students. If the children are engaged in writing and it seems sensible to you to teach a phonics lesson on the spot, then do so. Such as-needed incidental lessons should not, however, take the place of adherence to the systematic sequence of lessons.

Sequence for Teaching Phonics and Structural Analysis Without a Published Program

If our school doesn't have a structured series of phonics and structural analysis lessons within a reading program or as a stand-alone program, does the sequence I use matter?

Yes. There is a logical sequence for teaching phonics that forms the basis for most published programs. The sequence that makes sense is based on utility; that is, in what order can we expect children to find phonics elements easiest to learn and most helpful as they become literate? We teach phonics and structural elements in a sequence that helps children learn most easily, building on what is known as new elements are taught, and giving many opportunities to apply skills as they are learned.

What is an appropriate sequence for teaching phonic and structural analysis elements?

If you have state or local standards, the sequence you follow should reflect the one suggested in those standards. If the standards do not provide a sequence, we suggest that you look at the sequence for a published program. The following general guidelines should be helpful in developing an appropriate sequence for teaching phonics and structural analysis skills:

1. Teach and develop phonemic awareness skills.

2. Teach one short vowel and a few consonants that will make a word or words—for example, short *a* and the consonants *s*, *t*, and *m*. These letters can be used to make words.

3. Teach a few high-frequency words.

4. Continue teaching consonants and vowels until all have been taught.

5. Continue adding high-frequency words.

6. Teach other phonic elements, such as blends/clusters and digraphs.

7. Teach students a strategy that will assist them in applying the decoding skills being taught.

8. Teach structural elements such as endings, prefixes, and suffixes.

9. Continue teaching all phonic and structural elements until students are able to apply their knowledge independently while reading.

PRACTICE EXERCISE

Directions

This series of exercises is designed to help you practice and check the knowledge you gained from this resource. Complete each exercise; then check your answers with those on pages 520–521.

Part I

Write the answer on the line for each question.

1. How many sounds do your hear in 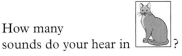 ? _____

2. Write the word for these sounds:
/h/ /ou/ /s/. _____

3. Identify the onset and rime in the following words:

	onset	rime
street	_____	_____
day	_____	_____
race	_____	_____

Part II

Classify the italicized letters in the following words as (a) diphthong, (b) vowel digraph, (c) consonant digraph, or (d) consonant blend. Write the correct letter in the blank to the left of each word.

_____	**1.** *bl*ack	_____	**11.** *gn*aw
_____	**2.** *oy*ster	_____	**12.** p*ai*l
_____	**3.** *sh*ine	_____	**13.** br*ou*ght
_____	**4.** t*oi*l	_____	**14.** wre*ck*
_____	**5.** *br*ight	_____	**15.** t*ow*
_____	**6.** d*w*indle	_____	**16.** thi*ng*
_____	**7.** *pn*eumatic	_____	**17.** cra*ft*
_____	**8.** g*oa*t	_____	**18.** *n*eed
_____	**9.** *ea*se	_____	**19.** *str*ing
_____	**10.** h*ow*	_____	**20.** l*ay*

Part III

From among the four words in each list, select the one that *does not* conform to the phonics generalization that the other three do. Write the letter of the exception on the line to the left. Then write the generalization to which the other words conform on the next line. If all words conform, choose "e," no exception.
Example:

__c__	a. bait	b. sail	c. said	d. bail	e. no exception

CVVC generalization – ai digraph

___ 1.	a. rate	b. line	c. mete	d. seem	e. no exception
___ 2.	a. gin	b. gift	c. gym	d. gem	e. no exception
___ 3.	a. cup	b. pin	c. slur	d. get	e. no exception
___ 4.	a. eat	b. seat	c. coat	d. seem	e. no exception
___ 5.	a. be	b. no	c. music	d. me	e. no exception
___ 6.	a. fir	b. fur	c. order	d. me	e. no exception

Part IV

From column B, select the synonym, example, or definition that best fits the term in column A. Then write the letter of the synonym, example, or definition on the line to the left.

Column A   **Column B**

_____ **1.** grapheme   a. *can't*

_____ **2.** morpheme   b. blended vowel sound

_____ **3.** derived word   c. *inhospitable*

_____ **4.** phoneme   d. letter

_____ **5.** digraph   e. clues provided by sentence meaning

_____ **6.** compound   f. speech sound

_____ **7.** phonics   g. merging consecutive consonant sounds, each retaining its
                                      own identity

_____ **8.** basic sight word   h. meaningful structural unit

_____ **9.** affixes   i. *meaner*

_____ **10.** base word   j. two letters representing one phoneme

_____ **11.** possessive   k. *tablecloth*

_____ **12.** diphthong   l. *women's*

_____ **13.** contraction   m. study of phoneme-grapheme relationships

_____ **14.** inflected word   n. *an*

_____ **15.** phonemic awareness o. major meaning-bearing unit

                                   p. prefixes, suffixes, inflectional endings

                                   q. awareness of sounds in spoken words

Part V

Divide each of the following nonsense words in syllables, and mark the vowels with diacritical marks. Be ready to state your reasons for syllabication and for vowel sounds. Where two possibilities for division exist, give both.

1. ekon   **6.** drackle

2. roashing   **7.** mastle

3. whochment   **8.** kromsul

4. sluppelgug   **9.** bleting

5. presilnapishment

HANDBOOK RESOURCE

Part VI

Choose the best answer among the stated possibilities.

1. The study of the phoneme/grapheme relationship in English is called
   a. phonetics.
   b. phonics.
   c. linguistics.
   d. both a and b

2. The word pronounced by the use of phonics must be in the reader's oral language in order to
   a. check the accuracy of the pronunciation.
   b. check the accuracy of phonics rules.
   c. check the contextual meaning of a word.
   d. All of the above.

3. The sounds of *c* and *g* may be identified as
   a. hard and soft.
   b. short and long.
   c. hiss and guttural.
   d. None of the above.

4. Which of the following words contains a digraph?
   a. blind
   b. must
   c. kick
   d. gram

5. Which of the following words contains a consonant blend?
   a. wash
   b. letter
   c. ship
   d. stripe

6. The sounds of *s* may be
   a. c, st, sh, s
   b. s, sh, z, zh
   c. k, c, z, s
   d. gz, ks, s, c

7. In which of the following groups of words are all three exceptions to vowel generalizations?
   a. sir, cat, bake
   b. colt, see, out
   c. car, find, old
   d. vie, sigh, my

8. Which of the following words is probably correctly divided into syllables?
   a. mis-thez-ment
   b. bomn-y
   c. ci-mtor
   d. ba-tmle

9. Which of the following words contains a schwa?
   a. again
   b. cart
   c. book
   d. below

See Answer Key to check your answers.

ANSWER KEY

Part I

1. three
2. house
3. *str   eet*
   d   ay
   r   ace

Part II

1. d	**8.** b	**15.** b
2. a	**9.** b	**16.** c
3. c	**10.** a	**17.** d
4. a	**11.** c	**18.** b
5. d	**12.** b	**19.** d
6. d	**13.** b	**20.** b
7. c	**14.** c	

Part III

1. d—final *e* or CVCe generalization
2. b—soft *g* generalization or
   e—CVC generalization
3. c—CVC generalization
4. e—CVVC generalization
5. e—if only first syllable of music is considered;
   c—if second syllable is—open syllable generalization
6. d—r-controlled vowel sound

Part IV

1. d
2. h
3. c
4. f
5. j
6. k
7. m
8. n
9. p
10. o
11. l
12. b
13. a
14. i or l
15. q

Part V

1. ē•kŏn, ĕk•ən
2. rōash• ĭng
3. whŏch•mənt
4. slŭp•pĕl•gŭg, slŭpp•əl•gəg
5. prē•sĭl•năp• ĭsh•mĕnt, prē•sĭl•nā•pĭsh•mənt
6. drăck•əl
7. măs•təl, măst•le
8. krŏm•sŭl
9. blĕt•ing

Part VI

1. b
2. a
3. a
4. c
5. d
6. b
7. c
8. a
9. a

Glossary

acceleration More than the expected rate of growth.

adequate yearly progress The expected amount of growth a student should make in reading during one school year. A term used in various government-supported educational programs. Currently defined for each state by its state education agency.

analogy In decoding, using letter-sound relationships in known words to figure out the probable pronunciation of unfamiliar words.

analysis As a form of response, telling how a story event relates to a personal event.

anticipation guide A series of statements with which students agree or disagree prior to reading and to which they return after reading; used to activate prior knowledge and help students establish a purpose for reading.

application Part of the follow-up to a minilesson in which students use a strategy in a totally new reading experience; this step supports the ability to transfer strategy use.

authentic assessment Assessment activities that reflect literacy in the community, the workplace, and the classroom.

authentic literature Narrative and expository text in its original form. Often referred to as real or trade book literature.

automaticity Fluent processing of information that occurs with little effort. Doing something automatically.

background knowledge (also background information, prior knowledge) What students already know, through learning and experience, about a topic or about a kind of text.

basal series A set of texts and other materials produced by a given publisher for teaching literacy. Usually these series are for grades K–6 or K–8. They are often referred to as basal readers or basal programs and are usually called by the publisher's name.

base words Meaningful linguistic units that can stand alone and contain no smaller meaningful parts; also called free morphemes.

benchmarks Behaviors exhibited by students at certain stages of development. Sometimes used interchangeably with the term **standards.**

checklist A form that lists targeted behaviors as indicators of achievement, knowledge, or skill.

clustering A way of brainstorming on paper; a topic is positioned centrally and concepts and ideas related to that topic are clustered around the center, or core.

comprehension The part of reading that involves constructing meaning by interacting with text. Comprehension is one part of the reading process.

comprehensive literacy instruction A combination of teacher-directed instruction and student-centered activities.

concept development Activating and/or developing student knowledge or background of ideas, understandings, or issues in material to be read.

concepts of print Features of printed text; usually divided into four categories: *books, sentences, words,* and *letters.*

conference A meeting between teacher and student or between students; teacher-student conferences may be held in order to share and discuss a book, discuss an aspect of writing, provide a mini-lesson, assess progress, or a combination of these purposes. A conference may be scheduled and structured or informal and unstructured.

context   In literacy, the setting in which a certain word occurs and which contributes to the inference of meaning; context can be a phrase, a sentence, a paragraph, a chapter, or an entire body of work.

conventional writing phase   The time when students will spell most words correctly, or conventionally.

core instruction   The part of the comprehensive literacy program that all students need.

corrective feedback   The process of helping a student overcome a mistake or error by asking leading questions or guiding him or her to achieve a correct response.

created text   Any text especially written to be decodable or to control high-frequency words, concepts, skills, strategies, and overall difficulties.

creative response   An individual or group response to literature that involves such things as art, music, or drama.

cross-curricular   Involving more than one content area.

cueing systems   Sources of information that help in the identification of a word; these include phonics, structural elements of words, meaning, and language clues.

decodable text   A published or created text that is suitable for the application of previously taught phonics skills.

decoding   The process of translating written language into verbal speech sounds. Decoding is one part of reading.

dialogue journals   Response journals in which another person (teacher or peer) reads and responds in writing to the student writing.

diaries   Private journals, not usually about something read; not intended to be read by others.

differentiated instruction   Instruction that is designed to accommodate a student's strengths, needs, and stage of development.

direct teaching   Planning explicit lessons to teach specific words, information, concepts, or skills.

diversity   In education, having classrooms with students of various backgrounds, languages, needs, and conditions.

domain   A category of writing based on the purpose or type of writing.

double-entry journals   Journals in which a page is divided in half vertically: on the left side students record predictions, take notes, and draw before and during reading; on the right side students write a response after reading. Can also be used as a dialogue journal with the teacher responding on the right side.

drafting   The second part of process writing, with two parts: (1) planning what to write and how to write it, and (2) composing, or writing.

explicit instruction   Direct, teacher-led instruction. Involves teacher modeling, student practice with teacher guidance and feedback, and student application in a new situation. Term is used interchangeably with *direct instruction* or **direct teaching.**

explicit modeling   Directly showing and talking about what is to be learned.

expository text   Text that presents information and is organized in whatever way best suits the type of information being presented and the purpose for presenting it.

fluency   In reading, the ability to read words of connected text smoothly and without significant word recognition problems. A fluency record is taken by keeping track of words read aloud correctly and those not read correctly. See **running record.**

fluency check   Record of student reading aloud a prepared passage to show development in decoding.

formal assessment   A test or task using procedures that are carried out under controlled conditions.

generalization A response that shows the student has grasped the theme or meaning of a story.

generating and answering questions Thinking of questions while reading that require integration of new information and then reading to answer those questions.

grade score/grade equivalent A score derived from a raw score on a standardized test that is the equivalent earned by an average student in the norming group.

grapheme A written or printed symbol representing a phoneme; for example *cat* has three phonemes /c/, /a/, /t/ and three graphemes; *goat* has three phonemes and three graphemes /g/, /o/, /t/. The /o/ is represented by two graphemes, *oa*.

graphic organizer Any visual representation that organizes information, such as a story map or semantic map; can be used when activating prior knowledge before reading or when reviewing or summarizing information after reading.

guided listening lesson A structure for planning a listening lesson around a text that has been read aloud to teach a particular strategy or skill. A guided listening lesson has three parts: introduce the text, listen and respond to the text, and extend the text.

guided practice The part of a minilesson in which students continue to use a strategy with teacher guidance, but without modeling.

hierarchical array Graphic display showing the relationship of concepts, often branching to show which concepts are part of some other concept.

high-frequency words The most commonly occurring words in the English language.

implicit modeling Modeling that is not directly stated.

inferencing Judging, concluding, or reasoning from given information.

inflectional endings Word parts that can be added to the endings of base or root words and that change the number, gender, tense, or form of the word; sometimes included in the term *suffixes*.

informal assessment Observations or other nonstandardized procedures.

informal reading inventory (IRI) A series of graded passages used to determine a student's reading level as well as strengths and needs in decoding and comprehension.

interest inventory A series of statements to which students respond orally or in writing; meant to reveal a student's interests and/or attitudes.

intervention An instructional program that prevents or stops failure by providing additional instructional time beyond the core instruction.

invented spelling phase In spelling development, the period when the child is associating letters and sounds but not yet using entirely conventional spelling.

journals Places where students record personal reflections, including those about their reading and writing.

jump-start Giving struggling readers a head start with a learning task before they actually begin the task with other students.

K-W-L A strategy for accessing prior knowledge and setting purposes for reading a given text, usually expository, and then recording what has been learned after reading; K = what I know, W = what I want to know, and L = what I have learned or still need to learn.

learning logs Daily records of what a student has learned; does not include a response. Logs can be focused on a particular area of learning.

linear array A kind of hierarchical array that shows a straight-line relationship of certain concepts, such as from highest to lowest, or coldest to hottest.

literacy Ability to listen, speak, read, write, and think. Viewing is a part of literacy that uses many of the skills and strategies involved in the other aspects of literacy.

literacy lesson A structure for planning a teacher-directed reading and writing lesson around a given piece of text. A literacy lesson has three parts: introducing the text, reading and responding to the text, and extending the text.

literature discussion group (or circle) An activity in which children who have read the same book discuss that book; can also be focused on a single author or theme. A teacher may be part of the group or circle initially in order to guide students; the goal is a group discussion without teacher guidance.

mapping A kind of graphic organizer; students show important information and the relationships among pieces of information by using a series of boxes, ovals, or lines.

metacognition Knowledge and control of one's own thinking and learning. In reading, metacognition refers to the reader being aware of when reading makes sense and adjusting his or her reading when comprehension fails.

minilesson or focus lesson A concise teacher-directed lesson that is designed to teach a specific strategy, skill, concept, or process.

miscue An oral reading response that differs in some way from the text.

miscue analysis Analyzing a student's reading miscues in order to infer which strategies a student is or is not using.

modeling The process of showing or demonstrating how to use or do something.

modes of reading Different ways in which a text can be read, moving from teacher-directed reading to student independent reading. Usually there are five modes of reading: independent reading, cooperative reading, guided reading, shared reading, and read aloud.

modes of writing Different ways that writing can take place, moving from teacher-directed writing to student independence. Usually there are five modes of writing: independent writing, collaborative/cooperative writing, guided writing, shared writing, and write aloud.

monitoring/clarifying A developmental process; while reading, knowing when meaning is lost and having a plan to overcome the problem.

more than adequate yearly progress More than a year's growth in a year's time.

narrative text Text that tells a story; it is usually organized in a sequential pattern and consists of story elements. See **story map.**

observation (kid watching) Looking at student performance of literacy tasks in order to note achievement and draw inferences on which to base instruction.

peer conference Conference between two students having to do with reading or writing.

percentile A score on a scale of 100 indicating the percentage of scores that occur at or below a given raw score; derived from those on whom the test was normed.

performance assessment A task that requires the student to demonstrate literacy knowledge or skill through "real-world" response; a form of authentic assessment.

personal response An oral or written response to something heard or read; it could involve, for example, retelling, generalizing, sharing favorite elements, or telling how a piece of literature relates to one's feelings or one's life.

phoneme The smallest unit of sound in speech; for example, the word *dog* has three phonemes and the word *goat* has three phonemes.

phonemic awareness The knowledge that words are composed of sounds (phonemes).

phonics The use of one's knowledge of the relationship between the letters and the sounds the letters represent to help in determining the pronunciation of a word.

picture walk A strategy to activate prior knowledge and develop concepts and vocabulary before reading; the teacher guides students through a text's pictures, illustrations, or graphics by asking questions to get students to respond.

picture writing A stage in writing development; the child draws a picture to tell a story.

planning/previewing Another term for "selecting the topic," this is the first step in process writing; during this step students decide what they want to write about.

predictable text A text with some type of repeated pattern that allows students to anticipate what is likely to come on subsequent pages.

prediction In reading, telling what one thinks will happen in a story or what information will be presented before actually reading the text.

prefixes Units of meaning that can be added to the beginning of base words or root words to change their meanings; these are bound morphemes and cannot stand alone.

preview and predict A strategy for accessing prior knowledge by previewing the text to be read and making predictions about it.

prior knowledge See **background knowledge.**

process interview In literacy, a series of questions designed to elicit how a student thinks about reading or writing; used to plan future teacher support.

process writing An approach to teaching writing that involves five steps: planning, drafting, revising, proofreading, and publishing.

project A task undertaken to achieve a certain goal; can be used before reading as students activate prior knowledge and after reading to display what has been learned.

proofreading/editing Terms often used interchangeably for the fourth part of process writing; students examine mechanics such as spelling, punctuation, grammar, and paragraphing and make corrections.

publishing The final stage in process writing, involving two steps; students make a final copy and put their writing in a form for sharing with others.

quick writing A strategy for activating prior knowledge by writing for three to five minutes about a topic or idea.

random letter phase In spelling development, the period when the child uses letters in writing that have little or no relationship to the sounds in words.

readers theater A response in which students turn a story into a play by writing the script and then reading (or performing) the play.

reading workshop A framework to organize and manage reading in a literacy classroom; includes teacher sharing, minilessons, a state-of-the-class conference, self-selected reading and responding, and student sharing time.

reciprocal teaching An interactive process in which the teacher and students alternate modeling the use of strategies.

reflection Part of the follow-up to a minilesson in which students recall and talk about their use of strategies. Reflection is also part of assessment; students and teachers discuss what has been learned, how the learning has helped, where it can be used, and what to concentrate on next.

remediation The process of correcting a deficiency.

resources In thematic units, the books, computer software, publications, pictures, videos, films, and so forth to support the study.

responding In literacy, what one does as a result of and/or as a part of reading, writing, or listening.

response charts A way to present response options to students from which they can choose.

response journals/reading journals/literature logs Record of students' personal reactions to, questions about, and reflections on something read, seen, listened to, or written.

retelling Recall of something read, usually in the order in which it was presented, including key story elements, main ideas, or important details. See **summary.** As a method of assessment, retelling refers to using a student's unprompted recall of text to infer the student's construction of meaning.

revising The third part of process writing, during which students examine their work in terms of such things as ideas, organization, word choice, flow, and voice and make changes to improve each of these.

role playing Taking parts and acting out a situation; can be used to activate prior knowledge before or after reading to retell or summarize.

root words Words, often from another language, from which other words are derived; roots are bound morphemes in that they cannot stand alone as a **base word** in English; sometimes *root* and *base* are used interchangeably.

routine A pattern of instruction or classroom activity that is used over and over again.

rubric A set of guidelines or acceptable responses for a given task.

running record A written record of a student's oral reading, usually recorded on a blank sheet of paper.

scaffolding The process of providing strong teacher support at the beginning of new learnings and gradually taking it away to allow the student to achieve independence.

schema theory (pl. schemata) Theory that individuals develop a cognitive structure of knowledge in the mind to which new information and experiences are added as they occur.

scribble writing A stage in spelling development; the child makes scribble marks on paper that are clearly attempts at writing and not a picture.

semantic feature analysis Looking at related words (concepts) in terms of similarities, contrasts, or shared characteristics.

semantic mapping A visual, or graphic, representation of a concept; when used before reading, it is a strategy for activating prior knowledge and developing vocabulary and concepts.

stages of literacy development Various points in time in the development of the overall literacy process. There are five stages: early emergent literacy, emergent literacy, beginning reading and writing, almost fluent reading and writing, and fluent reading and writing.

standard score A score that indicates how far an individual is from the average score (mean) on a test in terms of the standard deviation.

standardized test A test given under specified conditions that allow comparisons to be made; norms or average scores are given to allow comparisons.

standards Statements that express a degree or level of performance that is expected from students at certain times.

stop and think A monitoring strategy; also known as a "fix-up" strategy.

story frame A basic outline for a story with key information omitted; the student fills in the empty slots. A frame may focus on a particular story element or on the whole story.

story map A graphic display of story elements (setting, character, problem, action or events, and solution); can be used to help students activate prior knowledge about narrative text structure before reading and to summarize a story after reading.

strategy A plan to accomplish a particular goal.

structural analysis Using meaningful parts of words such as prefixes, suffixes, inflectional endings, roots, and bases to identify words.

structured preview Guided preview of text that may include a graphic display of information; used to activate prior knowledge before reading.

struggling reader Any student who is having difficulty learning to read.

student modeling The part of a minilesson in which students take over the modeling process with the guidance of the teacher.

study guide A written guide that substitutes for teacher guidance by supporting students who need help in constructing meaning as they read text.

study techniques Techniques taught to students to help them study, think about, and remember information; common techniques are underlining, note taking, outlining, and using mapping or graphic organizers.

suffixes Units of meaning that can be added to the ending of base or root words to change the meaning or the function; these are bound morphemes.

summarizing Pulling together the essential elements or main ideas of expository text; also, recapping the story elements of a narrative.

summary Based on something read, an oral or written statement of key story elements, theme or main ideas. See **retelling.**

synthesizing Integrating new information into existing knowledge as one reads; this leads to a new perspective.

talk-aloud A kind of explicit modeling in which the teacher presents a series of steps and guides students through the process.

text structure   The organization of informational text.

text walk   Similar to a picture walk; refers to a procedure for activating prior knowledge in narrative and expository text that has few pictures, illustrations, or other graphic examples.

thematic unit   A framework for planning and organizing learning experiences around common bodies of knowledge, thinking, or concepts; cuts across curricular lines.

theme   The major focus of a unit that crosses curricular areas; usually a concept or understanding and may involve more than one topic.

think-aloud   A kind of explicit modeling in which the teacher shares his or her own thinking processes when performing a task.

traits   Characteristics; e.g., the NWREL Six-Trait Analytical Assessment model links writing assessment with writing instruction.

visualizing   Forming mental pictures while reading to connect the questions and knowledge in one's head with what one is reading.

vocabulary   Words known by an individual; *recognition vocabulary* refers to words an individual can pronounce and understand when he or she encounters them in print; *meaning vocabulary* refers to words one knows the meaning of whether or not one can yet recognize them in print.

webbing   A technique for planning a thematic unit; ideas are grouped, connected, and elaborated in a weblike graphic organizer.

word bank (word file, word book)   One's personal collection of words learned or words one would like to learn.

word wall   A cumulative display of words related to a particular topic, to an interest, or to a structural or phonetic feature.

writing workshop   A framework to organize and manage writing in a literacy classroom; includes minilessons, a state-of-the-class conference, writing and conferring, and group sharing.

Literature

Ackerman, K. (1988). *Song and dance man*. New York: Alfred A. Knopf.

Adler, D. A. (1986). *Martin Luther King, Jr.: Free at last*. New York: Holiday House.

Alexander, M. (1970). *Bobo's dream*. Boston: Houghton Mifflin.

Allard, H., & Marshall, J. (1977). *Miss Nelson is missing!* Boston: Houghton Mifflin.

Allard, H., & Marshall, J. (1978). *The Stupids have a ball*. Boston: Houghton Mifflin.

Apfel, N. H. (1991). *Voyager to the planets*. New York: Clarion.

Aylesworth, J. (1992). *Old black fly*. New York: Holt.

Bang, M. G. (1981). *Tye May and the magic brush*. New York: Greenwillow Books.

Baylor, B. (1976). *Hawk, I'm your brother*. New York: Charles Scribner's Sons.

Baylor, B. (1982). *The best town in the world*. New York: Charles Scribner's Sons.

Behrens, J. (1978). *Fiesta!* Chicago: Childrens Press.

Bunting, E. (1988). *How many days to America?* New York: Clarion.

Bunting, E. (1991). *Fly away home*. New York: Clarion.

Bunting, E. (2002). *Girls A to Z*. Honesdale, PA: Boyds Mills Press.

Burningham, J. (1970). *Mr. Gumpy's outing*. London: Henry Holt.

Byars, B. (1970). *The summer of the swans*. New York: Viking Penguin.

Carle, E. (1971). *Do you want to be my friend?* New York: HarperCollins.

Carle, E. (2002). *Slowly, slowly, slowly, "said the sloth."* New York: Philomel Books.

Carroll, L. (1960). *The annotated Alice/by Lewis Carroll: illustrated by John Tenniel; with an introduction and notes by Martin Gardner*. New York: Random House.

Cummings, P. (1991). *Clean your room, Harvey Moon!* New York: Bradbury Press.

Dahl, R. (1961). *James and the giant peach*. New York: Viking Penguin.

Dahl, R. (1988). *Matilda*. London: Jonathon Cape.

Dahl, R. (1990). *Esio trot*. New York: Viking.

de Hamel, J. (1985). *Hemi's pet*. Auckland: Reed Methuen.

de Paola, T. (1978). *The popcorn book*. New York: Holiday House.

de Paola, T. (1980). *Now one foot, now the other*. New York: G. P. Putnam.

de Paola, T. (1989). *The art lesson*. New York: G. P. Putnam.

Falwell, C. (1993). *Feast for 10*. Boston: Houghton Mifflin.

Falwell, (1998). *Word wizard,* New York: Clarion.

Fleischman, S. (1987). *The scarebird*. New York: Greenwillow Books.

Flournoy, V. (1985). *The patchwork quilt*. New York: Dial Books for Young Readers.

Forbes, E. (1971). *Johnny Tremain*. New York: Dell.

Fox, D., & Marks, C. (1987). *Go in and out the window: An illustrated songbook for young people*. New York: Henry Holt.

Fox, M. (1985). *Wilfrid Gordon McDonald Partridge*. New York: Kane/Miller.

Frazier, D. (2000). *Miss Alainious*. Orlando, FL: Harcourt.

Freedman, R. (1987). *Lincoln: A photobiography*. New York: Clarion.

Freedman, R. (1990). *Franklin Delano Roosevelt*. New York: Clarion.

Gerth, M. (2000). *Ten little ladybugs*. Los Angeles: Intervisual Books.

Gibbons, G. (1989). *Monarch butterfly*. New York: Holiday House.

Giff, P. R. (1980). *Today was a terrible day*. New York: Viking.

Giff, P. R. (1988). *Ronald Morgan goes to bat*. New York: Viking Kestrel.

Gilman, P. (1985). *Jillian Jiggs*. New York: Scholastic.

Gilman, P. (1988). *The wonderful pigs of Jillian Jiggs*. New York: Scholastic.

Graham, F. (illus.). (1987). *Roundabout cozy cottage*. New York: Grosset & Dunlap.

Guilfoile, E. (1957). *Nobody listens to Andrew*. Cleveland: Modern Curriculum Press.

Hahn, M. D. (1986). *Wait til Helen comes*. New York: Clarion.

Hamilton, V. (1990). *Cousins*. New York: Philomel.

Hodges, M. (1976). *Knight prisoner: The tale of Sir Thomas Malory and his King Arthur*. New York: Farrar, Straus and Giroux.

Howard, E. F. (1991). *Aunt Flossie's hats (and crab cakes later)*. New York: Clarion.

Huck, C. (1989). *Princess Furball*. New York: Greenwillow Books.

Hutchins, P. (2002). *We're going on a picnic*. New York: HarperCollins.

Isadora, R. (1979). *Ben's trumpet*. New York: Greenwillow Books.

Jaspersohn, W. (1991). *Cranberries*. Boston: Houghton Mifflin.

Lamott, A. (1994). *Bird by bird*. New York: Doubleday and Company, Inc.

Levitt, P. M., Burger, D. A., & Guralnick, E. S. (1985). *The weighty word book*. Longmont, CO: Bookmakers Guild.

Lewis, C. S. (1950). *The lion, the witch, and the wardrobe*. New York: Macmillan.

Lobel, A. (2000). *One lighthouse, one moon*. New York: Greenwillow.

Lowry, L. (1979). *Anastasia Krupnik*. Boston: Houghton Mifflin.

Lowry, L. (1989). *Number the stars*. Boston: Houghton Mifflin.

Macaulay, D. (1977). *Castle*. Boston: Houston Mifflin.

Maestro, B., & Maestro, G. (1989). *Taxi: A book of city words*. New York: Clarion.

Maestro, B., & Maestro, G. (1990). *Delivery van: Words for town and country*. New York: Clarion.

Markun, P. M. (1993). *The little painter of Sabana Grande*. New York: Bradbury Press.

Marshall, J. (1988). *Goldilocks and the three bears*. New York: Dial Books for Young Readers.

Martin, B., Jr. (1967). *Brown bear, brown bear*. New York: Henry Holt and Co.

Martin, J. (1998). *Snowflake Bentley*. Boston: Houghton Mifflin.

Marzollo, J. (1990). *Pretend you're a cat*. New York: Dial Books for Young Readers.

Masurel, C. (1997). *No, No, Titus!* New York: North-South Books.

McCloskey, R. (1948). *Blueberries for Sal*. New York: Viking.

McPhail, D. (1984). *Fix-it*. New York: Dutton Children's Books, a Division of Penguin.

Miller, M. (1994). *My five senses*. New York: Simon & Schuster.

Mohr, N. (1979). *Felita*. New York: Dial Books for Young Readers.

Mollel, T. M. (1995). *Big boy*. New York: Clarion.

Mollel, T. M. (1997). *Ananse's feast: An Ashanti tale*. New York: Clarion.

Mora, P. (1997). *Tomás and the library lady*. New York: Alfred A. Knopf, a Division of Random House.

Moss, M. (1990). *Regina's big mistake*. Boston: Houghton Mifflin.

Murphy, J. (1990). *The boys' war*. New York: Clarion.

Myers, W. D. (1990). *The mouse rap*. New York: Harper & Row.

O'Neill, M. (1966). *Words, words, words*. New York: Doubleday & Company, Inc.

Park, B. (1987). *The kid in the red jacket*. New York: Random House.

Patent, D. H. (1992). *Pelicans*. New York: Clarion.

Paterson, K. (1977). *Bridge to Terabithia*. New York: HarperTrophy.

Peck, R. (2000). *A year down yonder*. New York: Dial Books for Young Readers.

Peek, M. (1985). *Mary wore her red dress and Henry wore his green sneakers*. New York: Clarion.

Perl, L. (1987). *Mummies, tombs, and treasure*. New York: Clarion.

Prelutsky, J. (1984). "Never mince words with a shark." In J. Prelutsky, *The new kid on the block* (p. 89). New York: Greenwillow Books.

Prelutsky, J. (1988). *Tyrannosaurus was a beast.* New York: Greenwillow Books.

Prelutsky, J. (2000). *It's raining pigs and noodles.* New York: Greenwillow.

Prelutsky, J. (2002). *The frog wore red suspenders.* New York: Greenwillow.

Raffi. (1980). *The Raffi singable songbook.* New York: Crown.

Raskin, E. (1971). *The mysterious disappearance of Leon (I mean Noel).* New York: E. P. Dutton.

Rawls, W. (1961). *Where the red fern grows.* New York: Doubleday.

Robison, B. H. (1978). *Lurkers of the deep: Life within the ocean depths.* New York: David McKay.

Sachar, L. (1989). *Wayside School is falling down.* New York: Lothrop, Lee & Shepard.

Sancha, S. (1983). *Luttrell Village: Country life in the Middle Ages.* New York: HarperCollins.

Say, A. (1990). *El Chino.* Boston: Houghton Mifflin.

Schwartz, A. (1988). *Annabelle Swift, kindergartner.* New York: Orchard Books.

Scieszka, J. (1989). *The true story of the 3 little pigs.* New York: Viking Kestrel.

Sendak, M. (1962). *Chicken soup with rice.* New York: Scholastic Inc.

Seuss, D. (1963a). *Dr. Seuss's ABC.* New York: Random House.

Seuss, D. (1963b). *Hop on Pop.* New York: Random House.

Seuss, D. (1974). *There's a wocket in my pocket.* New York: Random House.

Shaw, N. (1986). *Sheep in a jeep.* Boston: Houghton Mifflin.

Small, D. (1985). *Imogene's antlers.* New York: Crown.

Snyder, Z. K. (1976). *The Egypt game.* New York: Atheneum.

Sobol, D. J. (1963). *Encyclopedia Brown: Boy detective.* New York: Lodestar Books.

Soto, G. (1993). *Too many tamales.* New York: G. P. Putnam's Sons.

Sperling, S. K. (1985). *Murfles and wink-a-peeps: Funny old words for kids.* New York: Clarkson N. Potter.

St. George, J. (2000). *So you want to be president?* New York: Philomel.

Steptoe, J. (1987). *Mufaro's beautiful daughters: An African tale.* New York: Scholastic Inc.

Taback, S. (2002). *This is the house that Jack built.* New York: Putnam.

Taylor, M. D. (1990). *Mississippi bridge.* New York: Dial Books for Young Readers.

Twain, M. (1987). *A Connecticut Yankee in King Arthur's court.* New York: Morrow.

Van Allsburg, C. (1984). *The mysteries of Harris Burdick.* Boston: Houghton Mifflin.

Van Allsburg, C. (1985). *The polar express.* Boston: Houghton Mifflin.

Viorst, J. (1981). *If I were in charge of the world.* New York: Atheneum.

Waber, B. (1988). *Ira says goodbye.* Boston: Houghton Mifflin.

Walker, P. R. (1993). *Head for the hills!* New York: Random House.

Weeks, S. (1998). *Mrs. McNosh hangs up the wash.* New York: HarperCollins.

Weisner, D. (1999). *Sector 7.* New York: Clarion Books.

Westcott, N. B. (1988). *The lady with the alligator purse.* Boston: Little, Brown.

Westcott, N. B. (1989). *Skip to my Lou.* Boston: Little, Brown.

Wiesner, D. (1991). *Tuesday.* New York: Clarion.

Wilder, L. I. (1932). *Little house in the big woods.* New York: Harper.

Williams, S. (1990). *Mommy doesn't know my name.* Boston: Houghton Mifflin.

Williams, V. B. (1997). *Lucky song.* New York: Greenwillow Books.

Wright, S. (1988). *Age of chivalry.* New York: Watts.

Xiong, B. (told by), & Spagnoli, C. (adapted by). (1989). *Nine-in-one. Grr! Grr!* San Francisco: Children's Book Press.

Yep, L. (1989). *The rainbow people.* New York: Harper & Row.

Yolen, J. (1998). *Raising Yoder's barn.* Boston: Little, Brown.

References

Adams, M. J. (1990). *Beginning to read: Thinking and learning about print*. Cambridge, MA: The MIT Press.

Adams, M., & Bertram, B. (1980). *Background knowledge and reading comprehension* (Reading Ed. Rep. No. 13). Urbana: University of Illinois Press, Center for the Study of Reading. (ERIC Document Reproduction Service ED 181 431)

AIMSweb. (n.d.). Evidence-based progress monitoring and improvement system. http://www.aimsweb.com

Alexander, P. A., & Jetton, T. L. (2000). Learning from text: A multidimensional and developmental perspective. In M. L. Kamil, P. B. Mosenthal, P. D. Pearson, & R. Barr (Eds.), *Handbook of reading research* (Vol. 3, pp. 285–310). Mahwah, NJ: Lawrence Erlbaum Associates.

Allen, R. V. (1976). *Language experiences in communication*. Boston: Houghton Mifflin.

Allington, R. L. (1977). If they don't read much, how they ever gonna get good? *Journal of Reading, 21,* 57–61.

Allington, R. L. (1983). The reading instruction provided readers of differing reading abilities. *Elementary School Journal, 83,* 548–559.

Allington, R. L. (1997). Overselling phonics. *Reading Today,* August/September, pp. 15–16.

Allington, R. L. (2004). Setting the record straight. *Educational Leadership,* 61(6), 22–25.

Allington, R. L., & Walmsley, S. A. (Eds.). (1995). *No quick fix: Rethinking literacy programs in America's elementary schools*. New York: Teachers College Press.

Alvermann, D. E., Dillon, D. R., & O'Brien, D. G. (1987). *Using discussion to promote reading comprehension*. Newark, DE: International Reading Association.

Alvermann, D. E., & Hynd, C. R. (1987, December). *Overcoming misconceptions in science: An on-line study of prior knowledge activation*. Paper presented at the meeting of the National Reading Conference, St. Petersburg, FL.

Alvermann, D. E., & Moore, D. W. (1991). Secondary school reading. In R. Barr, M. L. Kamil, P. B. Mosenthal, & P. D. Pearson (Eds.), *Handbook of reading research* (Vol. 2, pp. 951–983). New York: Longman.

Alvermann, D. E., Smith, L. C., & Readence, J. E. (1985). Prior knowledge activation and the comprehension of compatible and incompatible text. *Reading Research Quarterly, 20,* 420–436.

Anders, P., & Bos, C. (1986). Semantic feature analysis: An interactive strategy for vocabulary development and text comprehension. *Journal of Reading, 29,* 610–616.

Anderson, R. C., & Freebody, P. (1981). Vocabulary knowledge. In J. T. Guthrie (Ed.), *Comprehension and teaching: Research reviews*. Newark: International Reading Association.

Anderson, R. C., Hiebert, E. H., Scott, J. A., & Wilkinson, I. A. G. (1985). *Becoming a nation of readers: The report of the Commission on Reading*. Washington, DC: The National Institute of Education.

Anderson, R. C., & Pearson, P. D. (1984). A schema-theoretic view of basic processes in reading comprehension. In P. D. Pearson (Ed.), *Handbook of reading research* (pp. 255–291). New York: Longman.

Anderson, R. C., Reynolds, R. E., Schallert, D. L., & Goetz, E. T. (1977). Frameworks for comprehending discourse. *American Educational Research Journal, 14,* 367–381.

Anderson, T. H., & Armbruster, B. B. (1984a). Content area textbooks. In R. C. Anderson, J. Osborn, & R. J. Tierney (Eds.), *Learning to read in American schools* (pp. 193–226). Hillsdale, NJ: Lawrence Erlbaum Associates.

Anderson, T. H., & Armbruster, B. B. (1984b). Studying. In P. D. Pearson (Ed.), *Handbook of reading research* (pp. 657–679). New York: Longman.

Applebee, A. N. (1977). Writing and reading. *Journal of Reading, 20,* 534–537.

Applebee, A. N. (1978). *The child's concept of story: Ages two to seventeen.* Chicago: University of Chicago Press.

Armbruster, B. (1991, May 5). *Content area reading instruction.* A presentation given at the Conference on Reading Research, CORR, Las Vegas, NV.

Armbruster, B. B., Anderson, T. H., & Osterlag, J. (1989). Teaching text structure to improve reading and writing. *The Reading Teacher, 43,* 130–137.

Armbruster, B. B., Lehr, F., and Osborne, J. (2001). *Put reading first.* Washington, D.C.: The Partnership for Reading.

Armbruster, B. B., & Osborn, J. (2001). *Put reading first: The research building blocks for teaching children to read (K–3).* Ann Arbor: Center for the Improvement of Early Reading Achievement, University of Michigan.

Armento, B. J., Nash, G. B., Salter, C. L., & Wixson, K. (1991). *America will be.* Boston: Houghton Mifflin.

Association for Supervision and Curriculum Development. (1995). *Educating everybody's children: Diverse teaching strategies for diverse learners.* Alexandria, VA: Author.

Atwell, N. (1987). *In the middle.* Portsmouth, NH: Heinemann.

Au, K. H. (1991). Speech delivered at the Notre Dame Reading Conference, South Bend, IN, June 25, 1991, sponsored by Houghton Mifflin Company, Boston.

Au, K. H. (1993). *Literacy instruction in multicultural settings.* Orlando: Harcourt, Brace, Jovanovich.

Au, K. H., Carroll, J. H., & Scheu, J. A. (1997). *Balanced literacy instruction: A teacher's resource book.* Norwood, MA: Christopher-Gordon Publishers.

Au, K. H., Scheu, J., & Kawakami, A. J. (1990). Assessment of students' ownership of literacy. *The Reading Teacher, 44,* 154–156.

Au, K. H., Scheu, J. A., Kawakami, A. J., & Herman, P. A. (1990). Assessment and accountability in a whole literacy curriculum. *The Reading Teacher, 43,* 574–578.

Baghban, M. (1984). *Our daughter learns to read and write: A case study from birth to three.* Newark, DE: International Reading Association.

Bailey, M. H. (1967). The utility of phonic generalizations in grades one through six. *The Reading Teacher, 20,* 413–418.

Baker, L., & Brown, A. L. (1984a). Cognitive monitoring in reading. In J. Flood (Ed.), *Understanding reading comprehension* (pp. 21–44). Newark, DE: International Reading Association.

Baker, L., & Brown, A. L. (1984b). Metacognitive skills in reading. In P. D. Pearson (Ed.), *Handbook of reading research* (pp. 353–394). New York: Longman.

Ball, E. W., & Blachman, B. A. (1991). Does phoneme segmentation training make a difference in early word recognition and developmental spelling? *Reading Research Quarterly, 26,* 49–66.

Bandura, A. (1986). *Psychological modeling: Conflicting theories.* Chicago: Aldine-Atherton.

Barone, D. (1990). The written responses of young children: Beyond comprehension to story understanding. *The New Advocate, 3,* 49–56.

Barr, R., & Dreeben, R. (1991). Grouping students for reading instruction. In R. Barr, M. L. Kamil, P. Mosenthal, & P. D. Pearson (Eds.), *Handbook of reading research* (Vol. 2, pp. 885–910). New York: Longman.

Barr, R., Kamil, M. L., Mosenthal, P., & Pearson, P. D. (1991). *Handbook of reading research* (Vol. 2). New York: Longman.

Barrera, R. B. (1983). Bilingual reading in the primary grades: Some questionable views and practices. In T. H. Escobedo (Ed.), *Early childhood bilingual education* (pp. 164–184). New York: Teachers College Press.

Bartlett, F. C. (1932). *Remembering.* Cambridge: Cambridge University Press.

Baumann, J. F. (1984). The effectiveness of a direct instruction paradigm for teaching main idea comprehension. *Reading Research Quarterly, 20*(1), 93–115.

Baumann, J. F. (1986). *Teaching main idea comprehension.* Newark, DE: International Reading Association.

Baumann, J. F., & Schmitt, M. C. (1986). The what, why, how, and when of comprehension instruction. *The Reading Teacher, 39,* 640–647.

Bean, T. W., & Steenwyk, F. L. (1984). The effect of three forms of summarization instruction on sixth graders' summary writing and comprehension. *Journal of Reading Behavior, 16,* 297–306.

Beck, I., & McKeown, M. (1981). Developing questions that promote comprehension: The story map. *Language Arts, 58,* 913–918.

Beck, I., & McKeown, M. (1991). Conditions of vocabulary acquisition. In R. Barr, M. L. Kamil, P. Mosenthal, & P. D. Pearson (Eds.), *Handbook of reading research* (Vol. 2, pp. 789–814). New York: Longman.

Beck, I. L. (1984). Developing comprehension: The impact of the directed reading lesson. In R. C. Anderson, J. Osborn, & R. J. Tierney (Eds.), *Learning to read in American schools: Basal readers and content texts* (pp. 3–20). Hillsdale, NJ: Lawrence Erlbaum Associates.

Beck, I. L., McCaslin, M., & McKeown, M. (1980). *The rationale and design of a program to teach vocabulary to fourth-grade students.* Pittsburgh: University of Pittsburgh, Learning Research and Development Center.

Beck, I. L., McKeown, M. G., McCaslin, E. S., & Burkes, A. M. (1979). *Instructional dimension that may affect reading comprehension: Examples from two commercial reading programs.* Pittsburgh: University of Pittsburgh, Learning Research and Development Center.

Beck, I. L., McKeown, M. G., & Kucan, L. (2002). *Bringing words to life: Robust vocabulary instruction.* New York: Guilford Press.

Beck, I. L., McKeown, M. G., & Omanson, R. C. (1987). The effects and uses of diverse vocabulary instructional techniques. In M. G. McKeown & M. E. Curtis (Eds.), *The nature of vocabulary acquisition.* Hillsdale, NJ: Lawrence Erlbaum Associates.

Beck, I. L., McKeown, M. G., Worthy, J., Sandora, C. A., & Kucan, L. (1996). Question the author: A year-long classroom implementation to engage students with text. *Elementary School Journal, 96,* 385–414.

Beck, I. L., Omanson, R. C., & McKeown, M. G. (1982). An instructional redesign of reading lessons: Effects on comprehension. *Reading Research Quarterly, 17*(4), 462–481.

Beck, I. L., Perfetti, C. A., & McKeown, M. G. (1982). Effects of long-term vocabulary instruction on lexical access and reading comprehension. *Journal of Educational Psychology, 74,* 506–521.

Beldin, H. O. (1970). Informal reading testing: Historical review and review of the research. In W. K. Durr (Ed.), *Reading difficulties: Diagnosis, correction, and remediation* (pp. 67–84). Newark, DE: International Reading Association.

Bertrand, J. E. (1991). Student assessment and evaluation. In B. Harp (Ed.), *Assessment and evaluation in whole language programs* (pp. 17–33). Norwood, MA: Christopher-Gordon Publishers.

Birnbaum, J. C. (1982). The reading and composing behavior of selected fourth- and seventh-grade students. *Research in the Teaching of English, 16,* 241–260.

Bissex, G. L. (1980). *Gnys at wrk: A child learns to read and write.* Cambridge, MA: Harvard University Press.

Blachowicz, C. L. Z. (1986). Making connections: Alternatives to the vocabulary notebook. *Journal of Reading, 29,* 643–649.

Blachowicz, C. L. Z., & Fisher, P. (2000). Vocabulary instruction. In M. L. Kamil, P. B. Mosenthal, P. D. Pearson, & R. Barr (Eds.), *Handbook of reading research* (Vol. 3, pp. 503–523). Mahwah, NJ: Lawrence Erlbaum Associates.

Bloomfield, L., & Barnhart, C. (1961). *Let's read: A linguistic approach.* Detroit: Wayne State University Press.

Bond, G. L., & Dykstra, R. (1967). The cooperative research program in first-grade reading instruction. *Reading Research Quarterly, 2*(entire issue).

Boyer, E. L. (1995). *The basic school*. Princeton, NJ: The Carnegie Foundation for the Advancement of Teaching.

Bridge, C., Winograd, P. N., & Haley, D. (1983). Using predictable materials vs. preprimers to teach beginning sight words. *The Reading Teacher, 36*(9), 884–891.

Bromley, K. D. (1989). Buddy journals make the reading writing connection. *The Reading Teacher, 43*, 122–129.

Brown, A. L. (1980). Metacognitive development and reading. In R. J. Spiro, B. C. Bruce, & W. F. Brewer (Eds.), *Theoretical issues in reading comprehension* (pp. 453–481). Hillsdale, NJ: Lawrence Erlbaum Associates.

Brown, A. L., & Day, J. D. (1983). Macrorules for summarizing texts: The development of expertise. *Journal of Verbal Learning and Verbal Behavior, 22*(1), 1–14.

Brown, J. S., Collins, A., & Duguid, P. (1989). Situated cognition and the culture of learning. *Educational Researcher, 18*, 32–42.

Brown, K. J. (2000). What kind of text—For whom and when? Textual scaffolding for beginning readers. *The Reading Teacher, 53* (No. 4), 292–307.

Burns, P. C., Roe, B. D., & Ross, E. P. (1988). *Teaching reading in today's elementary schools* (4th ed.). Boston: Houghton Mifflin.

Cain, K. (1996). Story knowledge and comprehension skills. In C. Cornoldi & J. Oakhill (Eds.), *Reading comprehension difficulties: Processes and interventions* (pp. 167–192). Mahwah, NJ: Lawrence Erlbaum Associates.

Calfee, R. C., & Drum, P. A. (1986). Research on teaching reading. In M. C. Wittrock (Eds.), *Handbook of research on teaching* (3rd ed., pp. 804–849). New York: Macmillan.

Calkins, L. M. (1983). *Lessons from a child on the teaching and learning of writing*. Exeter, NH: Heinemann.

Calkins, L. M. (1994). *The art of teaching writing* (new ed.). Portsmouth, NH: Heinemann.

Cambourne, B., & Turbill, J. (1990). Assessment in whole language classrooms: Theory into practice. *The Elementary School Journal, 90*, 337–349.

Carnine, L., Carnine, D., & Gersten, R. (1984). Analysis of oral reading errors made by economically disadvantaged students taught with a synthetic phonics approach. *Reading Research Quarterly, 19*, 343–356.

Carr, E., & Wixson, K. K. (1986). Guidelines for evaluating vocabulary instruction. *Journal of Reading, 29*, 588–595.

Carr, M. (1987). Clustering with nonreaders/writers. In C. B. Olson (Ed.), *Practical ideas for teaching writing as a process* (pp. 20–21). Sacramento, CA: California State Department of Education.

Cassidy, J., & Cassidy, D. (2001). What's hot, what's not for 2001. *Reading Today, 18*(3), 1.

Cazden, C. (1972). *Child language and education*. New York: Holt, Rinehart and Winston.

Center for the Study of Reading. (n.d.) *Suggestions for the classroom: Teachers and independent reading*. Urbana: University of Illinois Press, Center for the Study of Reading.

Chall, J. S. (1967). *Learning to read: The great debate*. New York: McGraw-Hill.

Chall, J. S. (1983). *Learning to read: The great debate* (rev. ed.). New York: McGraw-Hill.

Chall, J. S. (1987). Two vocabularies for reading: Recognition and meaning. In M. G. McKeown & M. E. Curtis (Eds.), *The nature of vocabulary acquisition* (pp. 7–17). Hillsdale, NJ: Lawrence Erlbaum Associates.

Chall, J. S. (2000). *The academic achievement challenge*. New York: The Guilford Press.

Chall, J. S., & Conrad, S. S. (1990). Textbooks and challenge: The influence of educational research. In D. L. Elliott & A. Woodward (Eds.), *Textbooks and schooling in the United States* (pp. 42–55). Chicago: The National Society for the Study of Education.

Chapman, M. L. (1995). Designing literacy learning experiences in a multiage classroom. *Language Arts, 72*(8), 416–428.

Chard, D., & Osborne, J. (n.d.). *Guidelines for examining phonics and word recognition instruction in early reading programs*. Austin, TX: Texas Center for Reading and Language Arts. (photocopy)

Chard, D. J., & Osborne, J. (1999). Phonics and word recognition instruction in early reading programs: Guidelines for accessibility. *Learning Disabilities Research and Practice, 14*(2), 107–117.

Chomsky, N. (1965). *Aspects of the theory of syntax.* Cambridge, MA: MIT Press.

Clark, C. M. (1984). Teacher planning and reading comprehension. In G. G. Duffy, L. K. Roehler, & J. Mason (Eds.), *Comprehension instruction: Perspectives and suggestions* (pp. 58–70). New York: Longman.

Clark, M. M. (1976). *Young fluent readers.* London: Heinemann.

Clay, M. M. (1979). *Reading: The patterning of complex behavior* (2nd ed.). Auckland, New Zealand: Heinemann.

Clay, M. M. (1982). *Observing young readers: Selected papers.* Exeter, NH: Heinemann.

Clay, M. M. (1985). *The early detection of reading difficulties* (3rd ed.). Portsmouth, NH: Heinemann.

Clay, M. M. (1991). *Becoming literate: The construction of inner control.* Portsmouth, NH: Heinemann.

Clymer, T. (1968). What is "Reading"? Some current concepts. In H. M. Robinson (Ed.), *Innovation and change in reading instruction, Sixty-seventh Yearbook of the National Society for the Study of Education.* Chicago: University of Chicago Press.

Cockrum, W. A., & Castillo, M. (1991). Whole language assessment and evaluation strategies. In B. Harp (Ed.), *Assessment and evaluation in whole language programs* (pp. 73–86). Norwood, MA: Christopher-Gordon Publishers.

Coger, L. E., & White, M. R. (1982). *Readers theatre handbook: A dramatic approach to literature.* Glenview, IL: Scott, Foresman.

Coley, J. D., & Hoffman, D. M. (1990). Overcoming learned helplessness in at-risk readers. *Journal of Reading, 33,* 497–502.

Collins, A., Brown, J. S., & Newman, S. E. (1987). *Cognitive apprenticeship: Teaching the craft of*

reading, writing and mathematics. Technical Report No. 403. Urbana: University of Illinois Press, Center for the Study of Reading.

Cook-Gumprez, J. (Ed.). (1986). *The social construction of literacy.* Cambridge: Cambridge University Press.

Cooper, J. D. (1986). *Improving reading comprehension.* Boston: Houghton Mifflin.

Cooper, J. D., Boschken, I., McWilliams, J., & Pistochini, L. A study of the effectiveness of an intervention program designed to accelerate reading for struggling readers in upper grades. In T. Shanahan & F. V. Rodriguez-Brown (Eds.), *Forty-ninth Yearbook of the National Reading Council* (pp. 477–486). Chicago: National Reading Conference.

Cooper, J. D., Boschken, I., McWilliams, J., & Pistochinni, L. (2001). *Soar to Success, 3–8.* Boston: Houghton Mifflin.

Cooper, J. D., & Kiger, N. D. (2001). *Literacy assessment: Helping teachers plan instruction.* Boston: Houghton Mifflin.

Cooper, J. D., & Kiger, N. D. (2005). *Literacy assessment: Helping teachers plan instruction* (2nd ed.). Boston: Houghton Mifflin.

Cooper, J. D., Warncke, E., Shipman, D., & Ramstad, P. A. (1979). *The what and how of reading instruction.* Columbus: Charles E. Merrill.

Cullinan, B., Harwood, K., & Galda, L. (1983). The reader and the story: Comprehension and response. *Journal of Research and Development in Education, 16,* 29–38.

Cummins, J. (1981). The role of primary language development in promoting educational success for language minority students. *Schooling and language minority students: A theoretical framework* (pp. 3–49). Los Angeles: Los Angeles Evaluation, Dissemination and Assessment Center, California State University.

Cunningham, J. W., Cunningham, P. M., & Arthur, S. U. (1981). *Middle and secondary school reading.* New York: Longman.

Cunningham, P., & Allington, R. L. (1994). *Classrooms that work: They can all read and write.* New York: HarperCollins.

Cunningham, P. A., Hall, D. P., & Defee, M. (1998). Nonability grouped, multilevel instruction: Eight years later. *The Reading Teacher,* 5(18), 652–664.

Cunningham, P. M. (1995). *Phonics they use.* New York: HarperCollins.

Cunningham, P. M., & Cunningham, J. W. (1992). Making words: Enhancing the invented spelling-decoding connection. *The Reading Teacher,* 46(2), 106–115.

Dahl, K. L. (1988). Peer conferences as social contexts for learning about revision. In J. E. Readence & R. S. Baldwin (Eds.), *Dialogues in literacy research* (pp. 307–315), Thirty-seventh Yearbook of the National Reading Conference. Chicago: The National Reading Conference.

Dahl, K. L., & Farnan, N. (1998). *Children's writing: Perspectives from research.* Newark, DE; International Reading Association; and Chicago, IL: National Reading Conference.

Davey, B., & McBride, S. (1986). Effects of question generating training on reading comprehension. *Journal of Educational Psychology,* 78(4), 256–262.

Davis, F. (1971). Psychometric research in reading comprehension. In F. Davis (Ed.), *Literature of research in reading with emphasis on models.* Brunswick, NJ: Rutgers University Press.

Dawson, M. M. (1987). Beyond ability grouping: A review of ability grouping and its alternatives. *School Reading Review,* 16, 348–369.

DeFord, D. E., Lyons, C. A., & Pinnell, G. S. (1991). *Bridges to literacy: Learning from reading recovery.* Portsmouth, NH: Heinemann.

Denner, P. R., & Rickards, J. P. (1987). A developmental comparison of the effects of provided and generated questions on text recall. *Contemporary Educational Psychology,* 12, 135–146.

Dillon, D. (1990). Editorial. *Language Arts,* 67, 237–239.

Dillon, J. T. (1984). Research on questioning and discussion. *Educational Leadership,* 42, 50–56.

Dolch, E. W. (1936). A basic sight vocabulary. *Elementary School Journal,* 36, 456–460.

Dole, J. A., Duffy, G. G., Roehler, L. R., & Pearson, P. D. (1991). Moving from the old to the new: Research on reading comprehension instruction. *Review of Educational Research,* 61, 239–264.

Dole, J. A., & Smith, E. L. (1989). Prior knowledge and learning from science text: An instructional study. In the *Thirty-eighth Yearbook of the National Reading Conference, Cognitive and Social Perspectives for Literacy Research and Instruction* (pp. 345–352). Chicago: The National Reading Conference.

Dressel, J. H. (1990). The effects of listening to and discussing different qualities of children's literature on the narrative writing of fifth graders. *Research in the Teaching of English,* 24, 397–414.

Driver, R., & Erickson, G. (1983). Theories in action: Some theoretical and empirical issues in the study of students' conceptual frameworks in science. *Studies in Science Education,* 10, 37–60.

Duffy, G. G. (1993). Rethinking strategy instruction: Four teachers' development and their low achievers' understandings. *Elementary School Journal,* 93(3), 231–247.

Duffy, G. G., et al. (1987). Putting the teacher in control: Basal reading textbooks and instructional decision making. *Elementary School Journal,* 87(3), 357–366.

Durkin, D. (1966). *Children who read early.* New York: Teachers College Press.

Durkin, D. (1978). What classroom observations reveal about reading comprehension instruction. *Reading Research Quarterly,* 14(4), 481–533.

Durkin, D. (1981). Reading comprehension instruction in five basal reader series. *Reading Research Quarterly,* 16(4), 515–544.

Durkin, D. (1989). *Curriculum reform: Teaching reading in kindergarten* (Tech. Rep. No. 465). Urbana: University of Illinois Press, Center for the Study of Reading.

Durkin, D. (1990). Dolores Durkin speaks on instruction. *The Reading Teacher,* 43, 472–476.

Editors of the American Heritage Dictionary (1986). *Word mysteries and histories.* Boston: Houghton Mifflin.

Education Commission of the States. (2001). *Building on progress: How ready are states to implement President Bush's education plan?* Denver, CO: Author.

Eeds, M. (1989). Grand conversations: An exploration of meaning construction in study groups. *Research in the Teaching of English, 23,* 4–29.

Ehri, L. (1991). The development of the ability to read words. In R. Barr, M. Kamil, P. Mosenthal, & P. D. Pearson (Eds.), *Handbook of Reading Research* (Vol. 2, pp. 383–417). New York: Longman.

Ehri, L. (1997). Learning to read and learning to spell are one and the same, almost. In C. Perfetti, L. Rieben, & M. Fayol (Eds.), *Learning to spell: Research, theory, and practice across languages* (pp. 237–269). Mahwah, NJ: Lawrence Erlbaum Associates.

Ehri, L. C., & Robbins, C. (1992). Beginners need some decoding skill to read words by analogy. *Reading Research Quarterly, 27,* 13–26.

Eldredge, J. L. (1995). *Teaching decoding in holistic classrooms.* Englewood Cliffs, NJ: Merrill, An Imprint of Prentice Hall.

Elley, W. (1998). *Raising literacy levels in third world countries: A method that works.* Culver City: Language Education Associates.

Elliott, D. L. (1990). Textbooks and the curriculum in the postwar era: 1950–1980. In D. L. Elliott & A. Woodward (Eds.), *Textbooks and schooling in the United States* (pp. 42–55). Chicago: The National Society for the Study of Education.

Elliott, D. L., & Woodward, A. (1990). Textbooks, curriculum and school improvement. In D. L. Elliott & A. Woodward (Eds.), *Textbooks and schooling in the United States* (pp. 222–232). Chicago: The National Society for the Study of Education.

Emans, R. (1967). The usefulness of phonic generalizations above the primary grade. *The Reading Teacher, 20,* 419–425.

Farr, R., & Carey, R. F. (1986). *Reading: What can be measured?* (2nd ed.). Newark, DE: International Reading Association.

Farr, R., & Tone, B. (1994). *Portfolio and performance assessment: Helping students evaluate their progress as readers and writers.* Orlando: Harcourt Brace College Publishers.

Feitelson, D., Kita, B., & Goldstein, Z. (1986). Effects of listening to stories on first graders' comprehension and use of language. *Research in the Teaching of English, 20,* 339–356.

Fielding, L. G., Anderson, R. C., & Pearson, P. D. (1990). How discussion questions influence children's story understanding (Tech. Report No. 490). Urbana: University of Illinois Press, Center for the Study of Reading.

Flesch, R. (1955). *Why Johnny can't read.* New York: Harper & Row.

Flood, J., & Lapp, D. (1988). Conceptual mapping strategies for information texts. *The Reading Teacher, 41,* pp. 780–783.

Flood, J., & Lapp, D. (1989). Reporting reading progress: A comparison portfolio for parents. *Reading Teacher, 42*(7), 508–514.

Flood, J., & Lapp, D. (1991). Reading comprehension instruction. In J. Flood, J. M. Jensen, D. Lapp, & J. R. Squire (Eds.), *Handbook on the teaching of the English language arts* (pp. 732–742). New York: Macmillan Publishing Co.

Fountas, I. C., & Pinnell, G. S. (1996). *Guided reading: Good first teaching for all children.* Portsmouth, NH: Heinemann.

Fountas, I. C., & Pinnell, G. S. (2001). *Guiding readers and writers grades 3–6.* Portsmouth, NH: Heinemann.

Fowler, G. L. (1982). Developing comprehension skills in primary grades through the use of story frames. *The Reading Teacher, 36*(2)176–179.

Fredericks, A., Meinbach, A., & Rothlein, L. (1993). *Thematic units.* New York: HarperCollins.

Freedle, R. P. (1979). *New directions in discourse processing.* Hillsdale, NJ: Lawrence Erlbaum Associates.

Freeman, D. E., & Freeman, Y. S. (2000). *Teaching reading in multilingual classrooms.* Portsmouth, NH: Heineman.

Freeman, D. E., & Freeman, Y. S. (2001). *Between worlds: Access to second language acquisition.* Portsmouth, NH: Heinemann.

Freeman, Y. S., & Freeman, D. E. (1997). *Teaching reading and writing in Spanish in the bilingual classroom.* Portsmouth, NH: Heinemann.

Freppon, P., & Dahl, K. L. (1998). Theory and research into practice: Balanced instruction: Insights and considerations. *Reading Research Quarterly, 33*(2), 240–251.

Fries, C. (1962). *Linguistics and reading.* New York: Holt, Rinehart and Winston.

Galda, L. (1982). Assuming the spectator stance: An examination of the responses of three young readers. *Research in the Teaching of English, 16,* 1–20.

Galda, L. (1983). Research in response to literature. *Journal of Research and Development in Education, 16,* 1–7.

Gallagher, J. M., & Reid, D. K. (1983). *The learning theory of Piaget and Inhelder.* Austin, TX: Pro-Ed.

Gambrell, L., Pfeiffer, W., & Wilson, R. (1985). The effects of retelling upon reading comprehension and recall of text information. *Journal of Educational Research, 78,* pp. 216–220.

Gambrell, T. (1986). Growth in response to literature. *English Quarterly, 19,* 130–141.

Garan, E. M. (2001). Beyond the smoke and mirrors: A critique of the National Reading Panel report on phonics. *Phi Delta Kappan, 82*(7), 500–506.

Garcia, G. E. (1994). Assessing the literacy development of second language students: A focus on authentic assessment. In K. Spangenberg-Urbschat & R. Pritchard (Eds.), *Kids come in all languages: Reading instruction for ESL students* (pp. 180–205). Newark, DE: International Reading Association.

Garcia, G. E. (2000). Bilingual children's reading. In M. L. Kamil, P. B. Mosenthal, P. D. Pearson, & R. Barr (Eds.), *Handbook of reading research,* (Vol. 3, pp. 813–834). Mahwah, NJ: Lawrence Erlbaum Associates.

Gaskins, I. W., Downer, M. A., Anderson, R. C., Cunningham, P. M., Gaskings, R. W., Schommer, M., & The Teachers of Benchmark School. (1988). A metacognitive approach to phonics: Using what you know to decode what you don't know. *Remedial and Special Education, 9,* 36–41.

Gentry, J. R. (1977). *My kid can't spell.* Portsmouth, NH: Heinemann.

Gentry, J. R., & Gillet, J. W. (1993). *Teaching kids to spell.* Portsmouth, NH: Heinemann.

Gipe, J. P. (1978–79). Investigating techniques for teaching word meanings. *Reading Research Quarterly, 14,* 624–644.

Goldenberg, C. (1991). Learning to read in New Zealand: The balance of skills and meaning. *Language Arts, 68,* 555–562.

Goodman, K. (1986). *What's whole in whole language.* Portsmouth, NH: Heinemann.

Goodman, K., & Goodman, Y. (1991). Consumer beware! Selecting materials for whole language readers. In K. S. Goodman, L. B. Bird, & Y. M. Goodman (Eds.), *The whole language catalog* (p. 119). American School Publishers.

Goodman, K. S. (1965). A linguistic study of cues and miscues in reading. *Elementary English, 42,* 639–643.

Goodman, Y., & Burke, C. (1972). *Reading miscue inventory manual: Procedures for diagnosis and evaluation.* New York: Richard C. Owen.

Good, R. H., & Kaminski, R. A. (Eds.). (2002). *Dynamic indicators of basic early literacy skills* (6th ed.). Eugene, OR: Institute for the Development of Educational Achievement.

Grabe M., & Grabe, C. (2001). *Integrated technology for meaningful learning* (2nd ed.). Boston: Houghton Mifflin.

Graves, D. (1989). When children respond to fiction. *Language Arts, 66,* 777–783.

Graves, D., & Hansen, J. (1983). The author's chair. *Language Arts, 60,* 176–182.

Graves, D. H. (1983). *Writing: Teachers and children at work.* Exeter, NH: Heinemann Educational Books.

Graves, D. H. (1984). *A researcher learns to write.* Exeter, NH: Heinemann.

Graves, D. H. (1991). *Build a literate classroom.* Portsmouth, NH: Heinemann.

Graves, M. F. (1986). Vocabulary learning and instruction. *Review of Research in Education, 13,* 91–128.

Graves, M. F. (1987). The roles of instruction in fostering vocabulary development. In M. G.

McKeown & M. E. Curtis (Eds.), *The nature of vocabulary acquisition* (pp. 165–184). New York: Lawrence Erlbaum Associates.

Graves, M. F., & Cooke, C. L. (1980). Effects of previewing difficult short stories for high school students. *Research on Reading in Secondary Schools, 6,* 28–54.

Graves, M. F., Cooke, C. L., & LaBerge, H. J. (1983). Effects of previewing difficult and short stories on low-ability junior high school students' comprehension, recall and attitude. *Reading Research Quarterly, 18,* 262–276.

Haggard, M. R. (1982). The vocabulary self-collection strategy: An active approach to word learning. *Journal of Reading, 27,* 203–207.

Haggard, M. R. (1986). The vocabulary self-collection strategy: Using student interest and world knowledge to enhance vocabulary growth. *Journal of Reading, 29,* 634–642.

Halliday, M. A. K. (1975). *Learning how to mean.* New York: Elsevier North-Holland.

Hansen, J. (1981). The effects of inference training and practice on young children's reading comprehension. *Reading Research Quarterly, 16,* 391–417.

Hansen, J. (1987). *When writers read.* Portsmouth, NH: Heinemann.

Harp, B. (1989). What do we know about ability grouping? *The Reading Teacher, 42,* 430–431.

Harp, B. (1991). Principles of assessment in whole language classrooms. In B. Harp (Ed.), *Assessment and evaluation in whole language programs* (pp. 35–50). Norwood, MA: Christopher-Gordon Publishers.

Harris, T. L., & Hodges, R. E. (Eds.). (1995). *The literacy dictionary.* Newark, DE: International Reading Association.

Harste, J. C., Short, K. G., & Burke, C. (1988). Literature circles. In *Creating classrooms for authors* (pp. 293–304). Portsmouth, NH: Heinemann.

Harvey, S., & Goudvis, A. (2000). *Strategies that work.* York, MN: Stenhouse Publishers.

Hasbrouck, J. E., & Tindal, G. (1992, Spring). Curriculum-based oral reading fluency norms for students in grades 2 through 5. *Teaching Exceptional Children,* 41–44.

Heath, S. B. (1983). *Ways with words.* Cambridge: Cambridge University Press.

Heimlich, J. E., & Pittelman, S. D. (1986). *Semantic mapping: Classroom applications.* Newark, DE: International Reading Association.

Herber, H. L. (1984). Subject matter texts—Reading to learn: Response to a paper by Thomas H. Anderson and Bonnie B. Armbruster. In R. C. Anderson, J. Osborne, & R. J. Tierney (Eds.), *Learning to read in American schools: Basal readers and content texts* (pp. 227–234). Hillsdale, NJ: Lawrence Erlbaum Associates.

Hickman, J. (1983). Everything considered: Response to literature in an elementary school setting. *Journal of Research and Development in Education, 16,* 8–13.

Hickman, J., & Cullinan, B. E. (1989). A point of view on literature and learning. In J. Hickman & B. E. Cullinan (Eds.), *Children's literature in the classroom: Weaving Charlotte's web* (pp. 3–12). Needham Heights, MA: Christopher-Gordon Publishers.

Hiebert, E. H. (1983). An examination of ability grouping for reading instruction. *Reading Research Quarterly, 28,* 231–255.

Hiebert, E. H., Colt, J. M., Catto, S. L., & Gury, E. C. (1992). Reading and writing of first-grade students in a restructured Chapter I program. *American Educational Research Journal, 29,* 545–572.

Hiebert, E. H., Pearson, P. D., Taylor, B. M., Richardson, V., & Paris, S. G. (1998). *Every child a reader.* Ann Arbor, MI: Center for the Improvement of Early Reading Achievement (CIERA).

Hiebert, E. H., & Taylor, B. M. (1994). *Getting reading right from the start: Effective early literacy interventions.* Boston: Allyn & Bacon.

Hill, M. (1991). Writing summaries promotes thinking and learning across the curriculum—but why are they so difficult to write? *Journal of Reading, 34,* 536–539.

Hillocks, G. (1987a). What works in teaching composition: A meta-analysis of experimental treatment studies. *American Journal of Education, 93,* 133–170.

Hillocks, G. Jr. (1987b). Synthesis of research on teaching writing. *Educational Leadership, 45,* 71–82.

Hillocks, G. Jr., & Smith, M. W. (1991). Grammar and usage. In J. Flood, J. M. Jensen, D. Lapp, & J. R. Squire (Eds.), *Handbook of research on teaching the English language arts* (pp. 591–603). New York: Macmillan Publishing Company.

History–Social Science Curriculum Framework and Criteria Committee. (1988). *History-social science framework.* Sacramento, CA: California State Board of Education.

Holdaway, D. (1979). *The foundations of literacy.* Sydney: Ashton Scholastic, distributed by Heinemann, Portsmouth, NH.

Holmes, B. C., & Roser, N. L. (1987). Five ways to assess readers' prior knowledge. *The Reading Teacher, 40,* 646–649.

Hynd, C. R., & Alvermann, D. E. (1986). Prior knowledge activation in refutation and non-refutation text. In J. A. Niles & R. V. Lalik (Eds.), *The Thirty-fifth Yearbook of the National Reading Conference, Solving problems in literacy: Learners, teachers, and researchers* (pp. 55–60). Rochester, NY: National Reading Conference.

Indiana State Board of Education. (2000). *Indiana's academic standards: English language arts.* Indianapolis: Indiana Department of Education.

International Society for Technology in Education. (1998). *National educational technology standards for students.* Eugene, OR: Author.

Jenkins, J., Stein, M., & Wysocki, K. (1984). Learning vocabulary through reading. *American Education Research Journal, 21,* 767–788.

Jenkins, J. R., & Pany, D. (1981). Instructional variables in reading comprehension. In J. T. Guthrie (Ed.), *Comprehension and teaching: Research reviews.* Newark, DE: International Reading Association.

Johnson, D. D., & Pearson, P. D. (1984). *Teaching reading vocabulary* (2nd ed.). New York: Holt, Rinehart and Winston.

Johnston, P. (1981). *Prior knowledge and reading comprehension test bias.* Unpublished doctoral dissertation, Urbana: University of Illinois Press.

Johnston, P., & Allington, R. (1991). Remediation. In R. Barr, M. L. Kamil, P. Mosenthal, & P. D. Pearson (Eds.), *Handbook of reading research* (Vol. 2, pp. 984–1012). New York: Longman.

Juel, C. (1991). Beginning reading. In R. Barr, M. L. Kamil, P. Mosenthal, & P. D. Pearson (Eds.), *Handbook of reading research* (Vol. 2, pp. 759–788). New York: Longman.

Juel, C., Griffith, P. L., & Gough, P. B. (1986). Acquisition of literacy: A longitudinal study of children in first and second grade. *Journal of Educational Psychology, 78,* 243–255.

Juel, C., & Minden-Cupp, C. (2000). Learning to read words: Linguistic units and instructional strategies. *Reading Research Quarterly, 35,* pp. 458–492.

Juel, C., & Roper/Schneider, D. (1985). The influence of basal readers on first grade reading. *Reading Research Quarterly, 20,* 134–152.

Just, M. A., & Carpenter, P. A. (1987). *The psychology of reading and language comprehension.* Boston: Allyn & Bacon.

Kail, R. V., Chi, M. T. H., Ingram, A. L., & Danner, F. W. (1977). Constructive aspects of children's reading comprehension. *Child Development, 48,* 684–688.

Kaplan, R. (1966). Cultural thought patterns in intercultural education. *Language Learning, 16,* 1–20.

Keene, E. O., & Zimmermann, S. (1997). *Mosaic of thought.* Portsmouth, NH: Heinemann.

Kelly, P. R. (1990). Guiding young students' response to literature. *The Reading Teacher, 43,* 464–470.

Kelly, P. R., & Farnan, N. (1991). Promoting critical thinking through response logs: A reader response approach with fourth graders. In S. McCormick & J. Zutell (Eds.), *The Fortieth Yearbook of the National Reading Conference, Learner factors/teacher factors: Issues in literacy research and instruction* (pp. 277–284). Chicago: National Reading Conference.

Khattri, N., Kane, M. B., & Reeve, A. L. (1995). How performance assessments affect teaching and learning. *Educational Leadership, 53*(3), 80–83.

Krashen, S. (1982). *Principles and practice in second language acquisition.* New York: Pergamon Press.

Krashen, S. (2004). False claims about literacy development. *Educational Leadership, 61*(6), 18–21.

LaBerge, D., & Samuels, S. J. (1976). Toward a theory of automatic information processing in reading. In H. Singer and R. Ruddell (Eds.), *Theoretical models and processes of reading* (pp. 548–579). Newark, DE: International Reading Association.

Lamme, L. L. (1990). Exploring the world of music through picture books. *The Reading Teacher, 44,* 294–300.

Langer, J. A. (1986). Reading, writing and understanding: An analysis of the construction of meaning. *Written Communication, 3,* 219–267.

Learning First Alliance. (2000). *Every child reading: A professional development guide.* Alexandria, VA: Association for Supervision and Curriculum Development.

Lenneberg, E. (1967). *Biological foundations of language.* New York: John Wiley.

Lesgold, A. M., & Curtis, M. E. (1981). Learning to read words efficiently. In A. M. Lesgold & C. A. Perfetti (Eds.), *Interactive processes in reading.* Hillsdale, NJ: Lawrence Erlbaum Associates.

Lipson, M. Y. (1982). Learning new information from text. The role of prior knowledge and reading ability. *Journal of Reading Behavior, 14,* 243–261.

Lipson, M. Y. (1983). The influence of religious affiliation on children's memory for text information. *Reading Research Quarterly, 18,* 448–457.

Lipson, M. Y. (1984). Some unexpected issues in prior knowledge and comprehension. *The Reading Teacher, 37,* 760–764.

Lipson, M. Y., & Wixson, K. K. (1986). Reading disability research: An interactionist perspective. *Review of Educational Research, 56,* 111–136.

Loban, W. D. (1963). *The language of elementary school children.* Champaign, IL: National Council of Teachers of English.

Lorge, I., & Chall, J. S. (1963). Estimating the size of vocabularies of children and adults: An analysis of methodological issues. *Journal of Experimental Education, 32,* 147–157.

Lyon, G. R., & Chhabra, V. (2004). The science of reading research. *Educational Leadership, 61*(6), 12–17.

Mandler, J. M. (1984). *Stories, scripts and scenes: Aspects of schema theory.* Hillsdale, NJ: Lawrence Erlbaum Associates.

Many, J. E. (1991). The effects of stance and age level on children's literary responses. *Journal of Reading Behavior, 23,* 61–85.

Maria, K. (1988, December). *Helping fifth graders learn with science text.* Paper presented at the meeting of the National Reading Conference, Tucson, AZ.

Maria, K. (1990). *Reading comprehension instruction: Strategies and issues.* Parkton, MD: York Press.

Marino, J. L., Gould, S. M., & Haas, L. W. (1985). The effect of writing as a prereading activity on delayed recall of narrative text. *Elementary School Journal, 86,* 199–205.

Marshall, N. (1983). Using story grammar to assess reading comprehension. *The Reading Teacher, 36,* 616–620.

Martin, S. (1987, December). *The meaning-making strategies reported by provident readers and writers.* Paper presented at the National Reading Conference, St. Petersburg, FL.

Martinez, E. B. (1987). It works! In C. B. Olson (Ed.), *Practical ideas for teaching writing as a process* (p. 23). Sacramento, CA: California State Department of Education.

Martinez, M. G., & Roser, N. L. (1991). Children's responses to literature. In J. Flood, J. M. Jensen, D. Lapp, & J. R. Squire (Eds.), *Handbook of research on teaching the English language arts* (pp. 643–654). New York: Macmillan Publishing Co.

Mason, J. M., & Au, K. H. (1990). *Reading instruction for today* (2nd ed.). Glenview, IL: Scott, Foresman and Company.

McCormick, S. (1977). Should you read aloud to your children? *Language Arts, 54,* 139–143.

McGinley, W. (1988). *The role of reading and writing in the acquisition of knowledge: A study of college students' reading and writing engagements in the development of a persuasive argument.* Unpublished doctoral thesis, University of Illinois, Urbana.

McHugh, N. (1987). Teaching the domains of writing. In C. B. Olson (Ed.), *Practical ideas for teaching writing as a process* (pp. 81–87). Sacramento, CA: California State Department of Education.

McKenzie, M. (1985). Shared writing. In *Language matters*. London: Inner London Educational Authority.

McKeown, M. G., Beck, I. L., Omanson, R. C., & Pople, M. T. (1985). Some effects of the nature and frequency of vocabulary instruction on the knowledge and use of words. *Reading Research Quarterly, 20*(5), 522–535.

McKeown, M. G., & Curtis, M. E. (1987). *The nature of vocabulary acquisition.* Hillsdale, NJ: Lawrence Erlbaum Associates.

McNeil, D. (1970). *The acquisition of language: The study of developmental psycholinguistics.* New York: Harper & Row Publishers.

Meichenbaum, D. (1985). Teaching thinking: A cognitive behavioral perspective. In S. Chapman, J. Segal, & R. Glaser (Eds.), *Thinking and learning skills: Current research and open questions* (Vol. 2, pp. 407–426). Hillsdale, NJ: Lawrence Erlbaum Associates.

Menyuk, P. (1984). Language development and reading. In J. Flood (Ed.), *Understanding comprehension* (pp. 101–121). Newark, DE: International Reading Association.

Meyer, B. J. F. (1975). *The organization of prose and its effects on memory.* Amsterdam: The Hague North-Holland Press.

Meyer, B. J. F., & Freedle, R. O. (1984). Effects of discourse type on recall. *American Educational Research Journal, 21,* 121–143.

Mezynski, K. (1983). Issues concerning the acquisition of knowledge: Effects of vocabulary training on reading comprehension. *Review of Educational Research, 53,* 253–279.

Millett, N. C. (1986). *Teaching the writing process: A guide for teachers and supervisors.* Boston: Houghton Mifflin.

Moffett, J., & Wagner, B. J. (1983). *Student-centered language arts and reading, K-13* (3rd ed.). Boston: Houghton Mifflin.

Moore, D. W., Readence, J. E., & Rickelman, R. J. (1989). *Prereading activities for content area reading and learning* (2nd ed.). Newark, DE: International Reading Association.

Morrow, L. (1985). Retelling stories: A strategy for improving children's comprehension, concept of story structure, and oral language complexity. *Elementary School Journal, 85,* 647–661.

Morrow, Leslie Mandel (2003). Organizing and Managing the Language Arts Block: A Professional Development Guide. New York: Guilford Press.

Morrow, L. M. (1989a). *Literacy development in the early years. Helping children read and write.* Englewood Cliffs, NJ: Prentice Hall.

Morrow, L. M. (1989b). Using story retelling to develop comprehension. In K. D. Muth (Ed.), *Children's comprehension of text: Research into practice* (pp. 37–58). Newark, DE: International Reading Association.

Moss, B. (1991). Children's nonfiction trade books: A complement to content area texts. *The Reading Teacher, 45,* 26–32.

Murray, D. M. (1985). *A writer teaches writing* (2nd ed.) Boston: Houghton Mifflin.

Nagy, W. E. (1988). *Teaching vocabulary to improve reading comprehension.* Newark, DE/Urbana, IL: IRA/NCTE.

Nagy, W. E., & Anderson, R. C. (1984). How many words are there in printed school English? *Reading Research Quarterly, 19,* 304–330.

Nagy, W. E., & Herman, P. A. (1987). Breadth and depth of vocabulary knowledge: Implications for acquisition and instruction. In M. G. McKeown & M. E. Curtis (Eds.), *The nature of vocabulary acquisition* (pp. 19–35). Hillsdale, NJ: Lawrence Erlbaum Associates.

National Council of Teachers of English (NCTE) & International Reading Association (IRA). (1996). *Standards for the English language arts.* Urbana, IL/Newark, DE: NCTE/IRA.

National Reading Panel. (2000a). *Teaching children to read: An evidence-based assessment of the scientific research literature on reading and its implications for reading instruction.* Washington, DC: National Institute of Child Health and Human Development.

National Reading Panel. (2000b). *Report of the National Reading Panel—Teaching children to read: An evidence-based assessment of the scientific research literature on reading and its implications for reading instruction, reports of the subgroups.* Washington, DC: National Institute of Child Health and Human Development.

Neuman, S. (1988). Enhancing children's comprehension through previewing. In J. E. Readence & R. J. Baldwin (Eds.), *The Thirty-seventh Yearbook of the National Reading Conference, Dialogues in literacy research* (pp. 219–224). Chicago: National Reading Conference.

Norton, D. E. (1982). Using a webbing process to develop children's literature units. *Language Arts, 59,* 348–356.

Norton, D. E. (1999). *Through the eyes of a child—An introduction to children's literature* (5th ed.). Englewood Cliffs, NJ: Prentice Hall.

Noyce, R. M., & Christie, J. F. (1989). *Integrating reading and writing instruction in grades K–8.* Boston: Allyn & Bacon.

Oczkus, L. D. (2003). *Reciprocal teaching at work.* Newark, DE: International Reading Association.

Ogle, D. M. (1986). K-W-L: A teaching model that develops active reading of expository text. *The Reading Teacher, 39*(6), 564–570.

Olson, C. B. (1987). *Practical ideas for teaching writing as a process.* Sacramento, CA: California State Department of Education.

Otto, W., et al. (1977). *The Wisconsin design for reading skill development—Comprehension.* Minneapolis, MN: NCS Educational Systems.

Pace, A. J., Marshall, N., Horowitz, R., Lipson, M. Y., & Lucido, P. (1989). When prior knowledge doesn't facilitate text comprehension: An examination of some of the issues. In *The Thirty-eighth Yearbook of the National Reading Conference, Cognitive and social perspectives for literacy research and instruction* (pp. 213–224). Chicago: The National Reading Conference.

Palincsar, A. S., & Brown, A. L. (1986). Interactive teaching to promote independent learning from text. *The Reading Teacher, 39*(8), 771–777.

Pappas, C. C., Kiefer, B. Z., & Levstik, L. S. (1990). *An integrated language perspective in the elementary school: Theory into action.* New York: Longman.

Paradis, E. E., Chatton, B., Boswell, A., Smith, M., & Yovich, S. (1991). Accountability: Assessing comprehension during literature discussion. *The Reading Teacher, 45,* 8–17.

Paratore, J. R., & Indrisano, R. (1987). Intervention assessment of reading comprehension. *The Reading Teacher, 40,* 778–783.

Paris, S. G., Cross, D. R., & Lipson, M. Y. (1984). Informed strategies for learning: A program to improve children's reading awareness and comprehension. *Journal of Educational Psychology, 76,* 1239–1252.

Paris, S. G., Lipson, M. Y., & Wixson, K. K. (1983). Becoming a strategic reader. *Contemporary Educational Psychology, 8,* 293–316.

Paris, S. G., Wasik, B. A., & Turner, J. C. (1991). The development of strategic readers. In R. Barr, M. L. Kamil, P. Mosenthal, & P. D. Pearson (Eds.), *Handbook of reading research* (Vol. 2, pp. 609–640). New York: Longman.

Parsons, L. (1990). *Response journals.* Portsmouth, NH: Heinemann.

Pearson, P. D. (1985). Changing the face of reading comprehension instruction. *The Reading Teacher, 38,* 724–738.

Pearson, P. D., & Dole, J. A. (1987). Explicit comprehension instruction: A review of research and a new conceptualization of instruction. *The Elementary School Journal, 88*(2), 151–165.

Pearson, P. D., Roehler, L. R., Dole, J. A., & Duffy, G. G. (1990). *Developing expertise in reading comprehension: What should be taught? How should it be taught?* (Tech. Rep. No. 512). Urbana: University of Illinois Press, Center for the Study of Reading.

Pearson, P. D., Roehler, L. R., Dole, J. A., & Duffy, G. G. (1992). Developing expertise in reading comprehension. In S. J. Samuels & A. E.

Forstrup (Eds.), *What research has to say about reading instruction* (pp. 145–199). Newark, DE: International Reading Association.

Pearson, P. D., & Tierney, R. J. (1984). On becoming a thoughtful reader: Learning to read like a writer. In A. C. Purves & O. Niles (Eds.), *Eighty-third Yearbook of the National Society of the Study of Education, Becoming readers in a complex society* (pp. 144–173). Chicago: The University of Chicago Press.

Pehrsson, R. S., & Robinson, H. A. (1985). *The semantic organizer approach to writing and reading instruction.* Rockville, MD: Aspen Systems Corporation.

Peregoy, S. F., & Boyle, O. W. (1997). *Reading, writing and learning in ESL* (2nd ed.). New York: Longman.

Perfetti, C. (1985). *Reading ability.* New York: Oxford University Press.

Perrone, V. (1991). Toward more powerful assessment. In V. Perrone (Ed.), *Expanding student assessment* (pp. 164–166). Alexandria, VA: Association for Supervision and Curriculum Development.

Piaget, J., & Inhelder, B. (1969). *The psychology of the child.* New York: Basic Books.

Pierce, K. (1987). Clustering in first grade. In C. B. Olson (Ed.), *Practical ideas for teaching writing as a process* (pp. 22–23). Sacramento, CA: California State Department of Education.

Pikulski, J. J. (1990a). Informal reading inventories. *The Reading Teacher, 43,* 514–516.

Pikulski, J. J. (1990b). The role of tests in a literacy assessment program. *The Reading Teacher, 43,* 686–688.

Pikulski, J. J. (1994). Preventing reading failure: A review of five effective programs. *The Reading Teacher, 48*(1), 30–39.

Pinnell, G. S., & Fountas, G. S. (1998). *Word matters.* Portsmouth, NH: Heinemann.

Pinnell, G. S., Fried, M. D., & Estice, R. M. (1990). Reading recovery: Learning how to make a difference. *The Reading Teacher, 43,* 282–295.

Pittelman, S. D., Heimlich, J. E., Berglund, R. L., & French, M. P. (1991). *Semantic feature analysis: Classroom applications.* Newark, DE: International Reading Association.

Pressley, M. (1998). *Reading instruction that works: The case for balanced teaching.* New York: The Guilford Press.

Pressley, M. (2000). What should comprehension instruction be the instruction of? In M. L. Kamil, P. B. Mosenthal, P. D. Pearson, & R. Barr (Eds.), *Handbook of reading research,* (Vol. 3, pp. 545–562). Mahwah, NJ: Lawrence Erlbaum Associates.

Pressley, M., Burkell, J., Cariglia-Bull, T., Lysynchuck, L., McGoldrick, J. A., Schneider, B., Snyder, B. L., Symons, S., & Woloshyn, V. E. (1990). *Cognitive strategy instruction that really improves children's academic performance.* Cambridge, MA: Brookline Books.

Pressley, M., & Harris, K. R. (1990). What we really know about strategy instruction. *Educational Leadership, 48,* 31–34.

Pressley, M., Johnson, C. J., Symons, S., McGoldrick, J. S., & Kurita, J. A. (1989). Strategies that improve children's memory and comprehension of text. *The Elementary School Journal, 90,* 3–32.

Purves, A. C. (1972). *How porcupines make love: Notes on a response-centered curriculum.* New York: Wiley.

Raphael, T. E., & Englert, C. S. (1990). Writing and reading: Partners in constructing meaning. *The Reading Teacher, 43,* 388–400.

Rasinski, T. V. (2003). *The fluent reader.* New York: Scholastic.

Readence, J. E., Bean, T. W., & Baldwin, R. S. (1981, 1985, 1989). *Content area reading: An integrated approach.* Dubuque, IA: Kendall/Hunt.

Reutzel, D. R., & Cooter, R. B., Jr. (1991). Organizing for effective instruction: The reading workshop. *The Reading Teacher, 44,* 548–554.

Rhodes, L. K., & Shanklin, N. L. (1990). Miscue analysis in the classroom. *The Reading Teacher, 44,* 252–254.

Rico, G. L. (1983). *Writing the natural way.* Los Angeles: J. P. Tracher, Inc. Distributed by Houghton Mifflin Company, Boston.

Rigg, P., & Allen, V. G. (1989). *When they don't all speak English.* Urbana, IL: National Council of Teachers of English.

Roehler, L. R., & Duffy, G. G. (1991). Teacher's instructional actions. In R. Barr, M. L. Kamil, P. Mosenthal, & P. D. Pearson (Eds.), *Handbook of reading research* (Vol. 2, pp. 861–883). New York: Longman.

Roget, P. (1965). St. Martin's edition of the original *Roget's thesaurus of English words and phrases*. New York: St. Martin's Press.

Rosenblatt, L. (1938/1976). *Literature as exploration*. New York: Modern Language Association.

Rosenblatt, L. (1978). *The reader, the text and the poem*. Carbondale: Southern Illinois University Press.

Rosenblatt, L. M. (1991). Literary theory. In J. Flood, J. M. Jensen, D. Lapp., & J. R. Squire (Eds.), *Handbook of research on teaching the English language arts* (pp. 57–62). New York: Macmillan Publishing Co.

Rosenshine, B. V. (1980). Skill hierarchies in reading comprehension. In R. J. Spiro et al. (Eds.), *Theoretical issues in reading comprehension* (pp. 535–554). Hillsdale, NJ: Lawrence Erlbaum Associates.

Rosenshine, B. V., & Meister, C. (1994). Reciprocal teaching: A review of research. *Review of Educational Research, 64*(4), 479–530.

Routman, R. (1991). *Invitations*. Portsmouth, NH: Heinemann.

Ruddell, R. B. (1963). The effect of the similarity of oral and written patterns of language structure on reading comprehension. *Elementary English, 42*, 403–410.

Rumelhart, D. E. (1980). Schemata: The building blocks of cognition. In R. J. Spiro et al. (Eds.), *Theoretical issues in reading comprehension* (pp. 33–58). Hillsdale, NJ: Lawrence Erlbaum Associates.

Rupley, W. H., Wilson, V. L., & Nichols, W. D. (1998). Exploration of the developmental components contributing to elementary school children's reading comprehension. *Scientific Studies in Reading, 2*(2), 143–158.

Sanders, M. (1987). Literacy as "passionate attention." *Language Arts, 64*, 619–633.

Sawyer, W. (1987). Literature and literacy: A review of research. *Language Arts, 64*(1), 33–39.

Schatz, E. K., & Baldwin, R. S. (1986). Context clues are unreliable predictors of word meanings. *Reading Research Quarterly, 21*, 439–453.

Schwartz, R. (1988). Learning to learn vocabulary in content area textbooks. *Journal of Reading, 32*, 108–118.

Schwartz, R. M., & Raphael, T. E. (1985). Concept of definition: A key to improving students' vocabulary. *The Reading Teacher, 39*, 198–203.

Seashore, R. H. (1947). How many words do children know? *The Packet, 2*, 3–17.

Shake, M., & Allington, R. (1985). Where do teachers' questions come from? *The Reading Teacher, 38*, 434–438.

Shanahan, T. (1988). The reading writing relationship: Seven instructional principles. *The Reading Teacher, 41*, 636–647.

Shanahan, T. (1990). Reading and writing together: What does it really mean? In T. Shanahan (Ed.), *Reading and writing together* (pp. 1–18). Norwood, MA: Christopher-Gordon Publishers.

Shanahan, T., & Lomax, R. (1988). A developmental comparison of three theoretical models of the reading-writing relationship. *Research in Teaching English, 22*, 196–212.

Short, E. J., & Ryan, E. B. (1984). Metacognitive differences between skilled and less skilled readers: Remediating deficits through story grammar and attribution training. *Journal of Educational Psychology, 76*, 225–235.

Simons, H., & Ammon, P. (1989). Child knowledge and primerese text: Mismatches and miscues. *Research in the Teaching of English, 23*(4), 380–398.

Singer, H., & Donlan, D. (1982). Active comprehension: Problem-solving schema with question generation for comprehension of complex short stories. *Reading Research Quarterly, 17*, 166–186.

Slavin, R. E. (1986). *Ability grouping and student achievement in elementary schools: A best evidence synthesis* (Report No. 1). Baltimore, MD: The Johns Hopkins University, Center for Research on Elementary and Middle Schools.

Slavin, R. E. (1990). *Cooperative learning: Theory, research and practice*. Englewood, NJ: Prentice Hall.

Sloyer, S. (1982). *Readers' theatre: Story dramatization in the classroom*. Urbana, IL: National Council of Teachers of English.

Smith, F. (1988). *Understanding reading* (4th ed.). New York: Holt, Rinehart and Winston.

Smith, N. B. (1965). *American reading instruction*. Newark, DE: International Reading Association.

Snow, C., Burns, M. S., & Griffin, P. (Eds.) (1998). *Preventing reading difficulties in young children*. Washington, DC: National Academy Press.

Sorensen, A., & Hallinan, M. (1986). Effects of ability grouping on growth in academic achievement. *American Educational Research Journal, 23*, 519–542.

Spiro, R. J. (1979). *Etiology of comprehension style*. Urbana: University of Illinois Press, Center for the Study of Reading.

Spritzer, D. R. (1988). Integrating the language arts in the elementary classroom using fairy tales, fables, and traditional literature. *Oregon English, 11*, 23–26.

Stahl, S. A. (1983). Differential word knowledge and reading comprehension. *Journal of Reading Behavior, 15*, 33–50.

Stahl, S. A., & Fairbanks, M. M. (1986). The effects of vocabulary instruction: A model-based meta-analysis. *Review of Educational Research, 56*(1), 72–110.

Stahl, S. A., & Vancil, S. J. (1986). Discussion is what makes semantic maps work in vocabulary instruction. *The Reading Teacher, 39*, 62–67.

Stanovich, K. E. (1980). Toward an interactive-compensatory model of individual differences in the development of reading fluency. *Reading Research Quarterly, 16*, 32–71.

Stanovich, K. E. (1986). Matthew effects in reading: Some consequences of individual differences in the acquisition of reading. *Reading Research Quarterly, 21*, 360–407.

Stauffer, R. G. (1969). *Teaching reading as a thinking process*. New York: Harper & Row.

Sternberg, R. J. (1987). Most vocabulary is learned from context. In M. G. McKeown & M. E. Curtis (Eds.), *The nature of vocabulary acquisition* (pp. 89–105). Hillsdale, NJ: Lawrence Erlbaum Associates.

Stevens, K. C. (1982). Can we improve reading by teaching background information? *Journal of Reading, 25*, 326–329.

Stieglitz, E. L., & Stieglitz, U. S. (1981). SAVOR the word to reinforce vocabulary in the content areas. *Journal of Reading, 25*, 46–51.

Strickland, D. (1994). Reinventing our literacy programs: Books, basics, and balance. *The Reading Teacher, 48*(4), 294–306.

Strickland, D. S. (1977). Prompting language and concept development. In B. Cullinan (Ed.), *Literature and young children*. Urbana, IL: National Council of Teachers of English.

Strickland, D. S., & Taylor, D. (1989). Family storybook reading: Implications for children, families, and curriculum. In D. S. Strickland & L. M. Morrow (Eds.), *Emerging literacy: Young children learn to read and write* (pp. 27–34). Newark, DL: International Reading Association.

Sulzby, E. (1989). Assessment of writing and of children's language while writing. In L. Morrow & J. Smith (Eds.), *The role of assessment and measurement in early literacy instruction* (pp. 83–109). Englewood Cliffs, NJ: Prentice Hall.

Sulzby, E., & Teale, W. (1991). Emergent literacy. In R. Barr, M. L. Kamil, P. Mosenthal, & P. D. Pearson (Eds.), *Handbook of reading research* (Vol. 2, pp. 727–757). New York: Longman.

Sweet, A. P. (1993). *State of the art: Transforming ideas for teaching and learning to read*. Washington, DC: U.S. Department of Education, Office of Research.

Taba, H. (1967). *Teacher's handbook for elementary school social studies*. Reading, MA: Addison-Wesley.

Taylor, B., Pikulski, J. J., & Cooper, J. D. (2003). *Reading intervention for early success, levels 1 and 2*. Boston: Houghton Mifflin.

Taylor, B. M., Frye, B. J., & Maruyama, G. M. (1990). Time spent reading and reading growth. *American Educational Research Journal, 27*(2), 351–362.

Taylor, B. M., Frye, B. J., Short, R., & Shearer, B. (1992). Classroom teachers prevent reading failure among low-achieving first-grade students. *Reading Teacher, 45*, 592–597.

Taylor, D., & Dorsey-Gaines, C. (1988). *Growing up literate*. Portsmouth, NH: Heinemann.

Taylor, D., & Strickland, D. S. (1986). *Family storybook reading*. Portsmouth, NH: Heinemann.

Teale, W. H., & Sulzby, E. (1986). *Emergent literacy: Writing and reading*. Norwood, NJ: Ablex Publishing Corporation.

Templeton, S. (1991). *Teaching the integrated language arts*. Boston: Houghton Mifflin.

Thomas, R. L. (1989). Knowing poetry: Choosing poetry for children. In J. Hichman & B. E. Cullinan (Eds.), *Children's literature in the classroom: Weaving Charlotte's web* (pp. 161–172). Needham Heights, MA: Christopher-Gordon Publishers.

Thompson, A. (1990). Thinking and writing with learning logs. In N. Atwell (Ed.), *Coming to know: Writing to learn in the intermediate grades* (pp. 35–51). Portsmouth, NH: Heinemann.

Tiedt, I. M. (2000). *Teaching with picture books in the middle school*. Newark, DE: International Reading Association.

Tierney, R. J., Carter, M. A., & Desai, L. E. (1991). *Portfolio assessment in the reading-writing classroom*. Norwood, MA: Christopher-Gordon Publishers.

Tierney, R. J., & Cunningham, J. W. (1984). Research on teaching reading comprehension. In P. D. Pearson (Ed.), *Handbook of reading research* (pp. 609–655). New York: Longman.

Tierney, R. J., & Leys, M. (1984). *What is the value of connecting reading and writing?* Reading Education Report No. 55. Urbana: University of Illinois Press.

Tierney, R. J., Readence, J. E., & Dishner, E. K. (1990). *Reading strategies and practices: A compendium* (3rd ed.). Boston: Allyn & Bacon.

Tierney, R. J., & Shanahan, T. (1991). Research on the reading-writing relationship: Interactions, transactions, and outcomes. In R. Barr, M. L. Kamil, P. Mosenthal, & P. D. Pearson (Eds.), *Handbook of reading research* (Vol. 2, pp. 246–280). White Plains, NY: Longman.

Tompkins, G. E., & Hoskisson, K. (1991). *Language arts: Content and teaching strategies*. New York: Merrill, an imprint of Macmillan Publishing Company.

Trelease, J. (1989). *The new read-aloud handbook*. New York: Penguin Books.

Tyson, H., & Woodward, A. (1989). Why students aren't learning very much from textbooks. *Educational Leadership, 47,* 14–17.

Valencia, S. (1990a). Alternative assessment: Separating the wheat from the chaff. *The Reading Teacher, 44,* 60–61.

Valencia, S. (1990b). A portfolio approach to classroom reading assessment: The whys, whats and hows. *The Reading Teacher, 43,* 338–340.

Valencia, S., Hiebert, E. H., & Afflerbach, P. P. (Eds.). (1994). *Authentic reading assessment: Practices and possibilities*. Newark, DE: International Reading Association.

Veatch, J. (1966/1978). *Reading in the elementary school* (2nd ed.). New York: John Wiley.

Venezky, R. L. (1995). Literacy. In T. L. Harris & R. E. Hodges (Eds.), *The literacy dictionary* (p. 142). Newark, DE: International Reading Association.

Vygotsky, L. S. (1978). *Mind in society*. Cambridge, MA: Harvard University Press.

Walmsley, S. A. (1994). *Children exploring the world: Theme teaching in elementary school*. Portsmouth, NH: Heinemann.

Ward, G. (1988). *I've got a project on . . .* Australia: Primary English Teaching Association, distributed by Heinemann, Portsmouth, NH.

Weaver, C. (1990a). *Understanding whole language*, Portsmouth, NH: Heinemann.

Weaver, C. (1990b, March 28). Weighing claims of "phonics first" advocates. *Education Week*, p. 32.

Weaver, C. (1994). *Understanding whole language: From principles to practice* (2nd ed.). Portsmouth, NH: Heinemann.

Weaver, C. A., & Kintsch, W. (1991). Expository text. In R. Barr, M. L. Kamil, P. Mosenthal, & P. D. Pearson (Eds.), *Handbook of reading research* (Vol. 2, pp. 230–245). New York: Longman.

Weber, R. (1991). Language diversity and reading in American society. In R. Barr, M. L. Kamil, P. Mosenthal, & P. D. Pearson (Eds.), *Handbook of reading research* (pp. 97–119). New York: Longman.

Weisberg, R. K., & Balajthy, E. (1985, December). *Effects of semantic mapping training on disabled readers' summarizing and recognition of expository text structure.* Paper presented at the National Reading Conference, San Diego, CA.

Weiss, A. S., Mangrum, C. T., & Liabre, M. M. (1986). Differential effects of differing vocabulary presentations. *Reading Research and Instruction, 25,* 265–276.

Wells, G. (1986). *The meaning makers: Children learning language and using language to learn.* Portsmouth, NH: Heinemann.

Wells, G. (1990). Creating the conditions to encourage literate thinking. *Educational Leadership, 47*(6), 13–17.

Werthemer, A. (1974). Story dramatization in the reading center. *English Journal, 64,* 85–87.

White, T. G., Sowell, J., & Yanagihara, A. (1989). Teaching elementary students to use word-part clues. *The Reading Teacher, 42,* 302–308.

Wilde, S. (1990). A proposal for a new spelling curriculum. *Elementary School Journal, 90,* 275–289.

Wilde, S. (1996, November). The minilesson and assessment: From writing to spelling and back again. *Primary Voices K–6, 4*(4), 16–18.

Wilkinson, L. C., & Silliman, E. R. (2000). Classroom language and literacy learning. In M. L. Kamil, P. B. Mosenthal, P. D. Pearson, & R. Barr (Eds.), *Handbook of reading research,* (Vol. 3, pp. 337–360). Mahwah, NJ: Lawrence Erlbaum Associates.

Winograd, P. N., & Bridge, C. A. (1986). The comprehension of important information in written prose. In J. B. Baumann (Ed.), *Teaching main idea comprehension* (pp. 18–48). Newark, DE: International Reading Association.

Wixson, K. K. (1986). Vocabulary instruction and children's comprehension of basal stories. *Reading Research Quarterly, 21,* 317–329.

Wood, K. D. (1988). Techniques for assessing students' potential for learning. *The Reading Teacher, 41,* 440–447.

Wood, K. D., Lapp, D., & Flood, J. (1992). *Guiding readers through text: A review of study guides.* Newark, DE: International Reading Association.

Yaden, D. (1988). Understanding stories through repeated read-alouds: How many does it take? *The Reading Teacher, 41,* 556–560.

Yaden, D. B., Jr., Rowe, D. W., & MacGillivray, L. (2000). Emergent literacy: A matter (polyphony) of perspectives. In M. L. Kamil, P. B. Mosenthal, P. D. Pearson, & R. Barr (Eds.), *Handbook of reading research* (Vol. 3, pp. 425–454). Mahwah, NJ: Lawrence Erlbaum Associates.

Yopp, H. K. (1995). A test for assessing phonemic awareness in young children. *The Reading Teacher, 49,* 20–22.

Author/Source Index

Subject Index